Emotions

Are emotions becoming more conspicuous in contemporary life? Are the social sciences undergoing an 'affective turn'? This reader gathers influential and contemporary work in the study of emotion and affective life from across the range of the social sciences. Drawing on both theoretical and empirical research, the collection offers a sense of the diversity of perspectives that have emerged over the last thirty years from a variety of intellectual traditions. Its wide span and trans-disciplinary character is designed to capture the increasing significance of the study of affect and emotion for the social sciences, and to give a sense of how this is played out in the context of specific areas of interest. The volume is divided into four main parts:

- Universals and particulars of affect
- Embodying affect
- Political economies of affect
- Affect, power and justice

Each main part comprises three sections dedicated to substantive themes, including emotions, history and civilization; emotions and culture; emotions, selfhood and identity; emotions, space and place; emotions and health; emotions in work and organizations; emotions and the media; emotions and politics; emotions and law, with a final section dedicated to themes of compassion, hate and terror. Each of the twelve sections begins with an editorial introduction that contextualizes the readings and highlights points of comparison across the volume. Cross-national in content, the collection provides an introduction to the key debates, concepts and modes of approach that have been developed by social scientists for the study of emotion and affective life.

Monica Greco is a Senior Lecturer in the Department of Sociology at Goldsmiths, University of London. She is the author of *Illness as a Work of Thought: A Foucauldian perspective on psychosomatics* (Routledge 1998) and co-editor of *The Body: A reader* (with M. Fraser, Routledge 2005).

Paul Stenner is Professor of Psychosocial Studies at the University of Brighton. He has lectured in Psychology at East London, Bath and University College, London. Following his Doctoral thesis on jealousy entitled *Feeling deconstructed?* (Reading 1992) he has published widely on the emotions and psychosocial theory.

D1465351

Routledge Student Readers

Series Editor: Chris Jenks, Professor of Sociology, Goldsmiths College, University of London.

Already in this Series:

Emotions

A social science reader

Edited by Monica Greco and Paul Stenner

Routledge
Taylor & Francis Group

LONDON AND NEW YORK

First published 2008
by Routledge
2 Park Square, Milton Park, Abingdon, Oxon OX14 4RN

Simultaneously published in the USA and Canada
by Routledge
711 Third Avenue, New York, NY 10017, USA

Routledge is an imprint of the Taylor & Francis Group, an informa business

© 2008 Greco and Stenner for selection and editorial matter; individual chapters,
the contributors

Typeset in Perpetua and Bell Gothic by
RefineCatch Ltd, Bungay, Suffolk

British Library Cataloguing in Publication Data
A catalogue record for this book is available from the British Library

Library of Congress Cataloging in Publication Data
Greco, Monica, 1966–
Emotions : a social science reader / Monica Greco, Paul Henry Stenner.
    p. cm. – (Routledge student readers)
  Includes bibliographical references and index.
  ISBN 978–0–415–42564–3 (pbk.) – ISBN 978–0–415–42563–6 (hardback)
  1. Emotions.   I. Stenner, Paul Henry, 1966–.   II. Title.
BF531.G73 2008
152.4–dc22

                                                            2008016530

ISBN10: 0–415–42563–8 (hbk)
ISBN10: 0–415–42564–6 (pbk)

ISBN13: 978–0–415–42563–6 (hbk)
ISBN13: 978–0–415–42564–3 (pbk)

There is nothing in the real world which is merely an inert fact. Every reality is there for feeling: it promotes feeling; and it is felt.

A. N. Whitehead, *Process and Reality*

Contents

Notes on Contributors

Ben ANDERSON is a Lecturer in Human Geography at the University of Durham. He is the author of several articles on affect and emotion, materiality and technology, and non-representational theory. He is currently preparing a monograph on theories of affect and emotion, provisionally entitled *Spaces of Affect and Emotion*.

Minna ASLAMA is the Program Officer for the Necessary Knowledge for a Democratic Sphere Program at the SSRC. She holds a Ph.D. from the University of Helsinki and is the author of several articles for Finnish and international publications on topics ranging from European media polities to national identity and reality television.

James R. AVERILL is Professor of Psychology at the University of Massachusetts, Amherst. He works in the fields of personality theory, stress and emotion, creativity, aesthetics, history and systems of psychology. He was amongst the pioneers of a social constructionist approach to the emotions and his books include *Anger and Aggression: An Essay On Emotion* (Springer-Verlag, 1982), *Rules of Hope* (Springer-Verlag, 1990), *Voyages of the Heart: Living an Emotionally Creative Life* (The Free Press, 1992).

Jack BARBALET is Professor of Sociology at the University of Leicester and Director of the Centre for Classical and Critical Sociology. He is the author of *Emotions, Social Theory and Social Structure: A Macrosociological Approach* (Cambridge University Press, 1998) and editor of *Emotions and Sociology* (Blackwell, 2002).

Lauren BERLANT is George M. Pullman Professor in the Department of English at the University of Chicago. Her work concentrates on the legal and normative production of personhood in the U.S. nineteenth, twentieth and twenty-first centuries. She has recently finished a trilogy of books on US sentimentality: *The*

Anatomy of National Fantasy (Chicago, 1991), *The Queen of America Goes to Washington City: Essays on Sex and Citizenship* (Duke, 1997), and *The Female Complaint: the Unfinished Business of Sentimentality in American Culture* (forthcoming 2008).

Judith BUTLER is Maxine Elliot Professor in the Departments of Rhetoric and Comparative Literature at the University of California, Berkeley. She is a post-structuralist philosopher with a background in Hegel, and she has made significant contributions to feminist and queer theory and to political and ethical philosophy. Her books include *Gender Trouble: Feminism and the Subversion of Identity* (Routledge, 1990), *Bodies that Matter: On the Discursive Limitations of 'Sex'* (Routledge, 1993), *Excitable Speech: A Politics of the Performative* (Routledge, 1997) and *The Psychic Life of Power: Theories of Subjection* (Stanford University Press, 1997).

Colin CAMPBELL is professor of sociology at the University of York. He has written on the sociology of religion, the sociology of consumption and sociological theory. His books include *Toward A Sociology of Irreligion* (Macmillan, 1971), *The Myth of Social Action* (Cambridge University Press, 1996) and *The Shopping Experience* (Sage, 1997).

Randall COLLINS is the Dorothy Swaine Thomas Professor in Sociology at the University of Pennsylvania. In 2004 he was awarded an American Sociological Association Lifetime Contributions Award for his work on the emotions. His books include *Four Sociological Traditions* (Oxford University Press, 1994), *The Sociology of Philosophies: A Global Theory of Intellectual Change* (Harvard University Press, 1998) and *Interaction Ritual Chains* (Princeton University Press, 2005).

W. Ray CROZIER is a Professor in the School of Social Work and Psychosocial Sciences at the University of East Anglia. He is the author of numerous articles on shyness, and co-editor (with L. E. Alden) of *The Essential Handbook of Social Anxiety for Clinicians* (Wiley, 2005).

Abram DE SWAAN is Emeritus Professor of Social Science at the University of Amsterdam, where he held the chair of sociology between 1973 and 2001. Since 2004 he has been the director of the European Academy of Yuste (Spain). His books include *In Care of the State; Health Care, Education and Welfare in Europe and the USA in the Modern Era* (Oxford University Press, 1988); *The Management of Normality; Critical Essays in Health and Welfare* (Routledge, 1990); *Human Societies* (Polity, 2001) and *Words of the World: The Global Language System* (Polity, 2003).

Natalie DIGIACOMO is Vice President, Development/Outreach Programs of The Humane Society of the United States, Washington, DC.

Thomas DIXON is a Lecturer in the Department of History at Queen Mary's, University of London. He is the author of *From Passions to Emotions: The Creation of a Secular Psychological Category* (Cambridge University Press, 2003).

Norbert ELIAS (1897–1990) was a German-Jewish sociologist. He coined the expressions 'process sociology' and 'figurational sociology' to describe his approach, which now influences work by many other scholars. His main work, *The Civilizing Process*, was first published in German in 1939 (latest English edition 1994) but remained largely unknown and unread among the German and English speaking publics for nearly thirty years, due to Elias' precarious academic existence as a refugee from Nazi Germany. His other works include: *The Established and the Outsiders* (1965), *What is Sociology?* (1978), *The Court Society* (1983), *The Loneliness of the Dying* (1985), *Involvement and Detachment* (1987), *The Symbol Theory* (1991), *The Society of Individuals* (1991) and *Time: An Essay* (1992).

Jon ELSTER is the Robert K. Merton Professor of Social Sciences with appointments in Political Science and Philosophy at Columbia University and *professeur attaché* at the Collège de France. He was awarded the Jean Nicod Prize in 1997. His books include *Nuts and Bolts for the Social Sciences* (Cambridge, UK, 1989); *Strong Feelings: Emotion, Addiction, and Human Behavior* The Jean Nicod Lectures. (MIT press, 1997); *Alchemies of the Mind: Rationality and the Emotions* (Cambridge, 1999); *Ulysses Unbound: Studies in Rationality, Precommitment, and Constraints* (Cambridge, 2002); *Closing the Books: Transitional Justice in Historical Perspective* (Cambridge, 2004) and *Explaining Social Behavior: More Nuts and Bolts for the Social Sciences* (Cambridge, 2007).

Marguerite FEITLOWITZ is Professor of Literature at Bennington College. She has published three volumes of literary translations from French and Spanish and she is an author of fiction, poetry, essays and art criticism. Her work has been published widely in the Americas, Europe, and Israel.

Stephen FINEMAN is Professor in Organisational Behaviour at the School of Management of the University of Bath. His work explores the implications of viewing organizations as emotional arenas. Recent books include *The Emotional Organization: Passions and Power* (Blackwell, 2007), *Organizing and Organizations* (Sage, 2005), and *Understanding Emotion at Work* (Sage, 2003).

Agneta H. FISCHER is a Professor in the Department of Social Psychology at the University of Amsterdam. She is the author of numerous articles on gender differences in emotionality and other aspects of the relation between emotion and culture. She is the editor of *Emotion and Gender: Social Psychological Perspectives* (Cambridge University Press, 2000) and co-editor (with A. Manstead and N. Frijda) of *Feelings and Emotions: The Amsterdam Symposium* (Cambridge University Press, 2004).

Anne-Marie FORTIER is a Senior Lecturer in the Department of Sociology at Lancaster University. She is the author of *Migrant Belongings: Memory, Space, Identity* (Berg, 2000).

Peter E. S. FREUND is Professor of Sociology at Montclair State University in New Jersey. He is the author of numerous articles linking the sociology of the body to that of the emotions and of health and illness. His books include *The Civilized Body: Social Domination, Control and Health* (1982) and *Health, Illness and the Social Body: A Critical Sociology* (2002).

Arie FREIBERG is Foundation Chair of Criminology at the University of Melbourne. He has held positions with the Australian Institute of Criminology and the Commonwealth Director of Public Prosecutions and was President of the Australian and New Zealand Society of Criminology Inc between 1996 and 1998.

He is an expert on criminal sentencing and confiscation of the proceeds of crime. He has authored major works in both of these fields and has published over seventy monographs and articles.

Erving GOFFMAN (1922–1982) was an American sociologist, best known for his contributions to the study of symbolic interaction through a dramaturgical perspective. He held posts at the University of Chicago, the University of California (Berkeley) and the University of Pennsylvania. He was also 73rd President of the American Sociological Association. His books include *The Presentation of Self in Everyday Life* (University of Edinburgh Social Science Research Centre, 1959); *Asylums* (Doubleday, 1961); *Stigma: Notes on the Management of Spoilt Identity* (Prentice-Hall, 1963); *Relations in Public: Microstudies of the Public Order* (Basic Books, 1971) and *Frame Analysis: An Essay on the Organization of Experience* (Harper & Row, 1974).

Deborah GOULD is Assistant Professor in the Department of Sociology, University of Pittsburgh. She is interested in emotions in relation to social movements, queer studies, and social and political theory and has written several papers on HIV related activism.

Michael E. HARKIN is Professor of Anthropology at the University of Wyoming. He is the author of *The Heiltsuks: Dialogues of Culture and History on the Northwest Coast* (University of Nebraska Press, 1997).

Elaine HATFIELD is Professor of Psychology at the University of Hawaii. She has made significant and influential contributions to the social psychology of emotion, including her book *Psychology of Emotion* (Harcourt, Brace, Jovanovich, 1992) and she is co-author (with Richard Rapson) of *Love, Sex, and Intimacy: Their Psychology, Biology, and History* (HarperCollins, 1993) *Emotional contagion* (Cambridge University Press, 1994) and *Love and Sex: Cross-cultural Perspectives* (Allyn & Bacon, 1996/2005).

Arlie Russell HOCHSCHiLD is Professor of Sociology at the University of California (Berkeley). In 2001 she was awarded an American Sociological Association Lifetime Contributions Award for her work on the emotions. She is the author of *The Managed Heart: The Commercialization of Human Feeling* (University of California Press, 1983) and numerous articles on the sociology of emotion. Her more recent books include *The Time Bind: When Home Becomes Work and Work Becomes Home* (Metropolitan/Holt 1997); *Global Woman: Nannies, Maids and Sex-Workers in the New Economy* (co-edited with B. Ehrenreich, Metropolitan Books, 2002); *The Commercial Spirit of Intimate Life and Other Essays* (University of California Press, 2003).

Birgitta HÖIJER is Professor of Media and Communication at the University of Örebro in Sweden. She is the author of several articles on the the media and meaning creation in the audience.

Jeroen JANSZ is a Senior Associate Professor in the Department of Communication Science at the University of Amsterdam and researcher in the Amsterdam School of Communications Research (ASCoR). He has written extensively on video games and their emotional appeal and on the history and theory of psychology.

Susanne KARSTEDT is Professor of Criminology in the School of Criminology, Education, Sociology and Social Work at Keele University. She is the author of several articles and has co-edited (with K. Bussman) *Social Dynamics of Crime and Control: New Theories for a World in Transition* (Hart, 2000) and (with G. D. LaFree) *Democracy, Crime and Justice (the ANNALS of the American Academy of Political and Social Science Series)* (Sage, 2006).

Rani KAWALE is an independent researcher working on questions of sexuality and space.

Michael KEMPA is a socio-legal theorist and a Lecturer in the Department of Criminology at the University of Melbourne. He is the author of several articles on policing and other governance processes.

Theodore D. KEMPER is Professor of Sociology at St. John's University, New York. In 2003 he was awarded an American Sociological Association Lifetime Contributions Award for his work on the emotions. His books include *A Social Interactional Theory of Emotions* (Wiley, 1978), *Research Agendas in the Sociology of Emotion* (State University of New York Press, 1990) and *Social Structure and Testosterone: Explorations of the Socio-bio-social Chain* (Rutgers University Press, 1990).

Sherryl KLEINMAN is Professor of Sociology at the University of North Carolina at Chapel Hill. She works on the sociology of emotions and memoirs and is interested in class, race and gender and in methodology. Her books include *Feminist Fieldwork Analysis* (Sage, 2007), *Opposing Ambitions: Gender and Identity in an Alternative Organization*, (University of Chicago Press, 1996) and *Emotions and Fieldwork* (Sage, 1993).

Bettina LANGE is University Lecturer in Law and Regulation and a Fellow of Wolfson College at Oxford University. She is the author of *Implementing EU Pollution Control: Law and Integration* (Cambridge University Press, 2008).

Kathy LASTER is Associate Professor in the School of Law at La Trobe University, Melbourne. She specializes on legal culture and multiculturalism, legal education and gender. Her books include *The Drama of the Courtroom: A Filmography* (Federation Press, 2000), *Domestic Violence: Global Responses* (A B Academic, 2000) and *Law as Culture* (Federation Press, 1997).

Daniel LEFKOWITZ is Associate Professor in the Department of Anthropology at the University of Virginia and Chair of MESA (Middle East Studies Association). He is the author of *Words and Stones: Language and the Israeli/Palestinian Conflict* (Oxford University Press, 2004).

Johan LINDQUIST is Assistant Professor of Social Anthropology at the University of Stockholm. He is the author of *The Anxieties of Mobility: Emotional Economies at the Edge of the Global City* (University of Hawaii Press, 2008) and co-editor (with T. Boellstorff) of a special issue of *Ethnos* entitled *Bodies of Emotion: Rethinking Culture and Emotion Through Southeast Asia* (2004).

Niklas LUHMANN (1927–1998) was a German sociologist, administration expert and systems theorist. He held posts at the universities of Münster and Frankfurt before becoming a Professor of Sociology at the University of Bielefeld in 1969, where he remained until his retirement in 1993. His *magnum opus, Die Gesellschaft der Gesellschaft* (The Society of Society) appeared in 1997. English translations of his books include *Social Systems* (Stanford University Press, 1996) and *Love as Passion: The Codification of Intimacy* (Stanford University Press, 1998).

Catherine LUTZ is a Watson Institute Professor (research) and holds a joint appointment with the Department of Anthropology at Brown University. She is the author of *Unnatural Emotions: Everyday Sentiments on a Micronesian Atoll and their Challenge to Western Theory* (Chicago, 1988) and numerous articles on the anthropology of emotion. Her most recent books include *Local Democracy under Siege: Activism, Public Interests, and Private Politics* (New York University Press, 2007) and *Homefront: A Military City and the American 20th Century* (Beacon Press, 2001, winner of the Leeds Prize and the Victor Turner Prize).

Danny MILLER is Professor of Material Culture in the Department of Anthropology at University College, London. He has written extensively on material culture, mass consumption, value and new media and relationships. His recent books include *The Cell Phone: An Anthropology of Communication* (Berg, 2006), *The Dialectics of Shopping* (University of Chicago Press, 2001), *Car Cultures* (Berg, 2001), *The Internet: An Ethnographic Approach* (Berg, 2000).

Kiran MIRCHANDANI is an Associate Professor in the Department of Adult Education and Counselling Psychology, University of Toronto. Her research and teaching focuses on home-based work, telework, contingent work, entrepreneurship, transnational service work and self-employment and she is coordinator of the Democratizing Workplace Learning Working Group at the CSEW.

Charles MORGAN collaborated with James Averill in the writing of the article included in this volume, which was based on his Master's Dissertation.

Pat O'MALLEY is a Professor in the Departments of Sociology and Anthropology and of Law at Carleton University, Ottawa. He has published widely in the field of risk and security, and has been a member of various government bodies working in related areas of criminal justice, drug policy and crime prevention. His books include *Risk, Uncertainty and Government* (Cavendish Press, 2004), *Crime and the Risk Society* (Dartmouth, 1988), *Crime Prevention in Australia* (Federation Press, 1997) and *Law Capitalism and Democracy: A Sociology of Australian Legal Order* (George Allen and Unwin, 1983).

Yael NAVARO-YASHIN Lectures in the Department of Social Anthropology at the University of Cambridge. Her work explores affect, subjectivity, and psychical/psychological mechanisms in the domains of politics, the public sphere, bureaucracy, and law. She is author of *Faces of the State: Secularism and Public Life in Turkey* (Princeton University Press, 2002), and has recently co-edited (with Jane Cowan) a special issue of *Anthropological Theory* entitled 'Phantasmatic Realities, Passionate States: Special Issue in Memory of Begona Aretxaga,' 7 (1), 2007.

Mervi PANTTI is a research fellow in the Amsterdam School of Communications Research (ASCoR), University of Amsterdam and in the Department of Communication, University of Helsinki. She has published books and articles on the national cinema, popular television and emotions in news journalism.

Dick POUNTAIN is a technical author and a director of Dennis Publishing. He is the author (with David Robins) of *Cool Rules: Anatomy of an Attitude* (Reaktion Books, 2000).

Laurie J. PRICE is Professor of Sociocultural and Applied Anthropology at the California State University (Hayward). She has conducted research on Ecuador dealing with illness management, cultural identity, geographies of power and participatory planning.

Alan RADLEY is Professor of Social Psychology in the Department of Social Sciences at Loughborough University. His is the author of numerous articles on the social psychological aspects of health and illness, and on the aesthetics of illness representation. He is the author of *Prospects of Heart Surgery* (Springer, 1988); *The Body and Social Psychology* (Springer, 1991); *Making Sense of Illness* (Sage, 1994), and has edited the volume *Worlds of Illness* (Routledge, 1993).

Richard L. RAPSON is Professor of History at the University of Hawaii and was Founder and Director of New College. He has written numerous books on American history and culture and is co-author (with Elaine Hatfield) of *Love, Sex, and Intimacy: Their Psychology, Biology, and History* (HarperCollins, 1993) *Emotional contagion* (Cambridge University Press, 1994) and *Love and Sex: Cross-cultural Perspectives* (Allyn & Bacon, 1996/2005).

William M. REDDY is the William T. Laprade Professor of History and Professor of Cultural Abnthropology at Duke University. He is the author of *The Navigation of Feeling: A Framework for the History of Emotions* (Cambridge University Press, 2001); *The Invisible Code: Honor and Sentiment in Post-revolutionary France, 1815–1848* (University of California Press, 1997), and of several articles on the historiography and ethnography of emotion. He is currently writing a history of romantic love.

Charlie L. REEVE is Associate Professor in the Department of Psychology at the University of North Carolina at Charlotte. He has published numerous scientific articles, particularly on psychometrics.

Barry RICHARDS is Professor of Public Communication and Head of Research at the Media School at the University of Bournemouth. He is author of *Disciplines of Delight: The Psychoanalysis of Popular Culture* (Free Association Books, 1994), Images of Freud (Palgrave Macmillan, 1990), *The Dynamics of Advertising* (Harwood Academic Press, 2000) and *Emotional Governance: Politics, Media and Terror* (Palgrave Macmillan, 2007).

David ROBINS (1945–2007) was an underground journalist, sociologist and charity worker and author, amongst other books, of *Tarnished Visions: Crime and Conflict in the Inner City* (Oxford University Press, 1992).

Steven G. ROGELBERG is Professor of Organizational Science and Professor of Psychology at the University of North Carolina at Charlotte. He is also Director of

Organizational Science, Director of Industrial and Organizational Psychology, and is the founder/director of the Organizational Science Consulting and Research Unit. His research interests include team effectiveness, health and employee well-being, meetings at work, organizational research methods, and organizational development. He served as Editor-in-Chief of the two-volume *Encyclopedia of Industrial and Organizational Psychology* (Sage, 2006) and the *Handbook of Research Methods in Industrial and Organizational Psychology* (Blackwell, 2002, 2004).

Nikolas ROSE is the James Martin White Professor of Sociology, and the Director of the BIOS Centre for the Study of Bioscience, Biomedicine, Biotechnology and Society at the London School of Economics and Political Science. His books include *The Psychological Complex: Psychology, Politics and Society in England, 1869–1939* (Routledge, 1984); *Governing the Soul: The Shaping of the Private Self* (Routledge, 1989); *Inventing Our Selves: Psychology, Power and Personhood* (Cambridge University Press, 1996); *Powers of Freedom: Reframing Political Thought* (Cambridge University Press, 1999), and *The Politics of Life Itself: Biomedicine, Power, and Subjectivity in the Twenty-First Century* (Princeton University Press, 2006).

Clifford SHEARING is Professor of Criminology and Director of the Institute of Criminology at the University of Cape Town. His books include *Imagining Security* (with Jennifer Wood; Willan, 2007) and *Governing Security: Explorations in Policing and Justice* (with Les Johnston; Routledge, 2003).

Mimi SHELLER is a Visiting Associate Professor in the Department of Sociology and Anthropology at Swarthmore and a Visiting Senior Research Fellow in the Faculty of Arts and Sciences at the University of Lancaster. Her books include *Consuming the Caribbean: From Awawaks to Zombies* (Routledge, 2003), *Democracy After Slavery: Black Publics and Peasant Radicalism in Haiti and Jamaica* (Macmillan, 2000), *Tourism Mobilities, Places to Play* (Routledge, 2004) and *Mobile Technologies of the City* (Routledge, 2006).

Susan SHOTT was based at the University of Chicago. Her 1979 article 'Emotion and social life: a symbolic interactionist analysis' is widely recognised as an early and influential contribution in the sociology of emotions.

Allen C. SMITH, III co-authored 'Managing emotions in medical school' whilst at the University of North Carolina at Chapel Hill.

Greg M. SMITH is Associate Professor of Communication at Georgia State University, Atlanta. He has written extensively on mediated communication and emotions and is author of *Beautiful TV: The Art and Argument of Ally McBeal* (University of Texas Press, 2007), *Film Structure and the Emotion System* (Cambridge University Press, 2003), *On a Silver Platter: CD-ROMs and the Promises of a New Technology* (New York University Press, 1999) and *Passionate Views: Film, Cognition, and Emotion* (Johns Hopkins University Press, 1999).

Christiane SPITZMÜLLER is Assistant Professor in the Department of Psychology at the University of Houston. She has published scientific articles in the fields of occupational psychology and organizational behaviour.

Deborah C. STEARNS is Adjunct Professor in the Department of Psychology at

Georgetown University. She earned her Ph.D. from the University of Pennsylvania and her research interests include person perception and intimate relationships with a particular focus on power, gender, sexuality and sexual orientation.

Peter N. STEARNS is Professor of History at George Mason University. His books include *Emotions and Social Change: Towards a New Psychohistory* (with C. Z. Stearns; Holmes and Meier, 1989); *American Cool: Constructing a Twentieth-century Emotional Style* (NYU Press, 1994); *An Emotional History of the United States* (co-edited with Jan Lewis, NYU Press, 1998); *Anxious Parents: A History of Modern Childrearing in America* (NYU Press, 2003); *American Fear: The Causes and Consequences of High Anxiety* (Routledge, 2006) and *Anger: The Struggle for Emotional Control in America's History* (with C. Z. Stearns; University of Chicago Press, 1986).

Nathan SZNAIDER is Professor of Sociology in the School of Behavioural Sciences at the Academic College of Tel-Aviv-Yaffo. He is currently working on a monograph on memory and human rights, and his books include *The Holocaust and Memory in the Global Age* (Temple University Press, 2005), *The Compassionate Temperament: Care and Cruelty in Modern Society* (Rowman & Littlefield, Bolder, Co. 2000), and *Über das Mitleid im Kapitalismus* (Edition München, 2000).

Nigel THRIFT is the Vice-Chancellor and a Professor at the University of Warwick. He is also a Visiting Professor of Geography at Oxford University, and an Emeritus Professor of Geography at Bristol University. He is a Fellow of the British Academy and an Academician of the Academy of Social Sciences. His books include *Spatial Formations* (Sage, 1996); *Money/Space: Geographies of Monetary Transformations* (with A. Leyshon; Routledge, 1997); *Cities: Reimagining the Urban* (with A. Amin; Polity, 2002); *Automobilities* (with M. Featherstone and J. Urry; Sage, 2005) and *Non-Representational Theory: Space, Politics, Affect* (Routledge, 2007).

Silvan S. TOMKINS (1911–1991) was one of the most influential theorists on emotion and emotional expression of the twentieth century. After completing a doctorate in philosophy and working on personality assessment at the Harvard Psychological Clinic under the tutelage of Henry Murray and Robert White, he took up a post at the Psychology Department at Princeton University in 1947. His *Magnum Opus* was the four volume work *Affect, Imagery, Consciousness*. The first two volumes were published in 1962 and 1963 and the last two were sent to the publishers during the final year of his life. In 1965 Tomkins helped to establish the Center for Cognition and Affect at the Graduate Center of the City University of New York and from 1968 until his retirement he worked at Livingston College, Rutgers University.

Imogen TYLER is a Lecturer in the Sociology Department at Lancaster University. Her research focuses on the intersections of gender, race and class research in the formation of social and cultural identities and has a particular interest in social marginality and 'border identities'. She is currently working on a monograph on social abjection.

James M. WILCE is Professor of Anthropology at Northern Arizona University. He is the author of *Eloquence in Trouble: The Poetics and Politics of Complaint in Rural Bangladesh* (Oxford University Press, 1998) and of *Crying Shame: Metaculture,*

Modernity, and the Exaggerated Death of Lament (Blackwell, in press). He has edited *Social and Cultural Lives of Immune Systems* (Routledge, 2003).

Elizabeth A. WILSON is an Australian Research Fellow in the School of English, Media and Performing Arts at the University of New South Wales, Sydney. She has a Ph.D. (USyd) in Psychology and is author of a book on neuroscience entitled *Psychosomatic: Feminism and the Neurological Body* (Duke University Press, 2004).

Preface

The process of producing a Reader of this kind is challenging, inherently frustrating in some ways, and yet also tremendously instructive. We have learned much along the way, and accumulated many debts that we want to acknowledge here. We are grateful, first and foremost, to the authors who have given their permissions for us to reprint extracts from their previously published articles or books. The comments of the anonymous reviewers at the early stages of the process were extremely helpful, and we are grateful for them. We wish to thank the several friends and colleagues who responded with advice and suggestions: although we did not always use them, they got us thinking. In particular, our thanks go to Andrew Barry, Georgina Born, Steve Brown, Ros Gill, Katherine Johnson, Sonia Livingstone, Peter Lunt, Kate Nash, and Andy Pratt. At Routledge, we wish to thank Gerhard Boomgarden who so warmly welcomed the idea of this project, and Ann Carter who undertook the arduous task of sourcing permissions.

Our most important thanks go to our two children, Ezra and Anna. They are too young to realize what exactly has been competing with them for our time and attention – yet they have shown a remarkable deal of understanding and patience (most of the time), while never ceasing to reward us with their laughter and love. This book is for them and for their generation.

Monica Greco – Goldsmiths, University of London
Paul Stenner – University of Brighton
2008

Acknowledgements

The publishers would like to thank the following for their permission to reprint their material:

American Economic Association for permission to reprint Jon Elster, *Emotions and Economic Theory*, in *Journal of Economic Literature* (1998), volume 36 (1), pp. 63–68.

American Sociological Association for permission to reprint Allen C. Smith and Sherryl Kleinman, *Managing Emotions in Medical School*, in *Social Psychology Quarterly* (1989), volume 52 (1), pp. 5–69.

Blackwell Publishing for permission to reprint Norbert Elias, *On Changes in Agressiveness*, pp. 157–166, 475–478; W. Ray Crozier, *Self-Consciousness in Shame*, in *Journal for the Theory of Social Behaviour*, volume 28 (3), pp. 0–21; Agneta H. Fischer and Jeroen Jansz, *Reconciling Emotions with Western Personhood*, in *Journal for the Theory of Social Behaviour*, volume 25 (1), pp. 0–21; Nigel Thrift, *Intensities of Feeling*, volume 86B (1), pp. 64–68; Peter E. S. Freund, *The Expressive Body* (1990), volume 12 (4), pp. 452–477; Charlie L. Reeve, Steven G. Rogelberg, Christiane Spitzmüller and Natalie DiGiacomo, *The Caring-Killing Paradox*, in *Journal of Applied Social Psychology*, volume 35 (1), pp. 119–135; Daniel Lefkowitz, *Investing in Emotion*, in *Journal of Linguistic Anthropology*, volume 13 (1), pp. 71–97; Bettina Lange, *The Emotional Dimension in Legal Regulation*, in *Journal of Law and Society* (2002), volume 29 (1), pp. 197–225.

Cambridge University Press for permission to reprint Thomas Dixon, *From Passions to Emotions* (2003), pp. 1–3, 4, 21–24; Catherine Lutz, *Engendered Emotion: Gender, power and the rhetoric of emotional control in American discourse*, in Lutz and Abu-Lughod, *Language and the Politics of Emotion* (1990); Jack Barbalet, *Emotion in Social Life and Social Theory*, in *Social Theory and Social Structure* (1998), pp. 8–9,

11–13; Silvan S. Tomkins, *Revisions in Script Theory*, in Tomkins and Demos, *Exploring Affect* (1995); Elizabeth A. Wilson, *The Work of Antidepressants*, in *BioSocieties* (2006), volume 1 (1), pp. 125–131; Nikolas Rose, *Disorders Without Borders*, in *BioSocieties* (2006), volume 1 (4), pp. 465–484; extracts from Greg M. Smith, *Film Structure and the Emotion System* (2003), pp.41–51; Elaine Hatfield and Richard L. Rapson, *Emotional Contagion*, in Tiedens and Leach, *The Social Life of Emotions* (2004), pp. 129–143.

Colin Campbell for permission to reprint extracts from Colin Campbell, *The Romantic Ethic and the Spirit of Modern Consumerism* (1987) pp. 1–2; 202–206.

Duke University Press for permission to reprint Michael E. Harkin, *Feeling and Thinking in Memory and Forgetting*, in *Ethnohistory* (2003), volume 50 (2), pp. 261–284.

Elsevier Ltd for permission to reprint Kathy Laster and Pat O'Malley, *Sensitive New-Age Laws*, in *International Journal of the Sociology of Law* (1996), volume 24 (1).

Oxford University Press for permission to reprint extracts from Marguerite Feitlowitz, *A Lexicon of Terror* (1999), pp. 48–49, 50–60.

Polity Press Ltd for permission to reprint extracts from Daniel Miller, *A Theory of Shopping* (1998) pp. 15–21.

Reaktion Books Ltd for permission to reprint extracts from Dick Pountain and David Robins, *Cool Rules* (2000), pp. 19–32.

Rowman & Littlefield for permission to reprint extracts from Nathan Sznaider, *The Compassionate Temperament* (2001).

Sage Publications Ltd for permission to reprint Mimi Sheller, *Automotive Emotions*, in *Theory, Culture and Society* (2004), volume 21 (4/5), pp. 221–242; Alan Radley, *Portrayals of Suffering* in *Body and Society* (2002), volume 8 (3), pp. 1–23; Kiran Mirchandani, *Challenging Racial Silences in Studies of Emotion Work* in *Organizational Studies* (2003), volume 24 (5), pp. 721–742; Stephen Fineman, *Getting the Measure of Emotion – and the Cautionary Tale of Emotional Intelligence*, in *Human Relations* (2004), volume 57 (6), pp. 719–740; Birgitta Höijer, *The Audience and Media Reporting of Human Suffering*, in *Media, Culture and Society* (2004), volume 26 (4), pp. 513–531; Minna Aslama and Mervi Pantti, *Talking Alone*, in *European Journal of Cultural Studies* (2006), volume 9 (2), pp. 167–184; Susanne Karstedt, *Emotions and Criminal Justice*, in *Theoretical Criminology* (2002), volume 6 (3), pp. 299–317; Arie Freiberg, *Affective Versus Effective Justice*, in *Punishment and Society* (2001), volume 3 (2), pp. 265–278; Yael Navaro-Yashin, *Make-Believe Papers, Legal Forms and the Counterfeit*, in *Anthropological Theory* (2007), volume 7 (1), pp. 79–98.

Stanford University Press for permission to reprint Niklas Luhmann, translated by John Bednarz, Jr, *Individuality of Psychic Systems*, in *Social Systems*, © 1996 by the Board of Trustees of the Leland Stanford Jr. University for the translation; 1984 by Suhrkamp Verlag for the original German edition.

Taylor & Francis Journals for permission to reprint Johan Lindquist, *Negotiating Shame in the Indonesian Borderlands*, in *Ethnos* (2004), volume 69 (4), pp. 487–508; Rani Kawale, *Inequalities of the Heart*, in *Social and Cultural Geography* (2004), volume 5 (4), pp. 565–577; Ben Anderson, *Domestic Geographies of Affect*, in *Social and Cultural Geography* (2005), volume 6 (5), pp. 645–659; Anne-Marie Fortier, *Pride Politics and Multiculturalist Citizenship*, in *Ethnic and Racial Studies* (2005), volume 28 (3), pp. 559–578; Imogen Tyler, *Chav Mum, Chav Scum*, in *Feminist Media Studies* (2008), volume 8 (1); Barry Richards, *The Emotional Deficit in Political Communication*, in *Political Communication* (2004), volume 21, pp. 339–352.

The University of Chicago Press for permission to reprint William M. Reddy, *Against Constructionism*, in *Current Anthropology* (1997); Arlie Russell Hochschild, *Emotion Work, Feeling Rules and Social Structure*, in *American Journal of Sociology* (1979); Erving Goffman, *Embarrassment and Social Organization*, in *American Journal of Sociology* (1956); Susan Shott, *Emotion and Social Life*, in *American Journal of Sociology* (1979); Deborah Gould, *Rock the Boat, Don't Rock the Boat, Baby*, in Goodwin, Jasper and Polletta, *Passionate Politics* (2001).

Verso for permission to reprint extracts from Judith Butler, Precarious Life (2006), pp. 19, 20–23, 23–25.

The publishers have made every effort to contact authors and copyright holders of works reprinted in *Emotions*. This has not been made possible in every case however, and we would welcome correspondence from individuals or companies we have been unable to trace.

Introduction: emotion and social science

LONG A KEY interest amongst psychologists and biologists, the study of emotions has become increasingly important to the work of social scientists in the course of the last three decades. The sociology and anthropology of emotions, for instance, are now well established sub-disciplines with their own textbooks, courses and research networks. Beyond sociology and anthropology however, concern with emotion, passion, feeling, mood and sentiment – let us for convenience call it 'affective life' – has come to provide a shared focal point for an emerging community of scholars and students based in a wide range of disciplines including history, geography, cultural studies, politics, economics, legal studies and criminology, media studies, gender studies, management studies; the list could go on. *The Emotions: A Social Science Reader* has been designed to give students, scholars and the general reader a birds-eye view of some of this research activity. The task of addressing such a vast and complex area of work may appear overambitious, and the result of our efforts is certainly destined to remain provisional. Nevertheless, we considered it important to offer a collection framed in terms of 'social science' broadly defined rather than, as is more often the case, in terms of an individual discipline or research tradition. It is important for the simple reason that most of us researchers, scholars and students are so preoccupied with the overwhelming number of developments in our own discipline or sub-discipline, that it has become almost unthinkable to 'see the wood for the trees' and to strive for a more general perspective. The recent proliferation of publications on emotions across the field, though in itself a positive development, has compounded this problem. In many cases, there is a noticeable tendency to celebrate the conceptual novelty (still) associated with the study of affect and emotion, at the expense of rigorous reflection on continuities and differences with previous research. The inclusive notion of social science adopted in this volume is informed by the idea that academic disciplines are historical creatures in a constant process of change; some changes – in the type of questions asked, or in the manner of asking them – are discipline-specific, while others transcend disciplinary boundaries. Our aim has been to capture the more general significance of the study of affect and emotion for the social sciences, as well as to give a sense of how this is played out in the context of specific sub-fields. We have thus deliberately tried to give a sense of the diversity of perspectives that have emerged over the years from a variety of intellectual traditions. As a whole, the collection is intended to provide an introduction to the key debates, concepts and modes of approach that have been developed by social scientists for the study of emotion and affective life.

It is in the nature of a Reader to present but a selection of all the authors or texts that might have been included, and this volume is no exception. Having stressed that variety and inclusiveness have been key criteria for us in putting together this collection, it is equally important to stress that our selections cannot claim to be representative of all that has been accomplished in social science research on the emotions. We have gathered together texts that, in our view, could productively be made to speak to each other in the interest of facilitating their understanding and discussion; we have almost exclusively drawn from traditions of qualitative, rather than quantitative research. We expect that readers will appreciate our editorial choices differently, at least to some degree, depending on their own disciplinary and intellectual location. Nevertheless, we hope they will find that the collection as a whole reflects much of the diversity constituting the field, and that it works in stimulating learning and debate. As editors, we have considered it important to ease access to the material by providing a substantive introduction at the beginning of this volume, as well as shorter introductions to each of the sections within it. The general introductory overview is designed to give a sense of the background, both intellectual and social, against which the study of emotion and affect in social science has emerged and evolved in recent years. By contextualizing the material in this way, our intent has been to make some of the fundamental continuities and differences inherent in the field more clearly intelligible to readers. The final section of the introduction outlines the structure of the Reader and a number of other features of the volume.

THE AFFECTIVE SOCIETY

If interest in emotions and affect has burgeoned in social science, this is not due simply to intellectual reasons, internal to the disciplines in question. A concern with 'the emotional' is indeed apparent in all aspects of social life and, at one level, the turn to affect and emotions in social science reflects and responds to this broader societal development. For a number of years now, social scientists have observed that emotions have become conspicuous and increasingly important in the forms of interaction and communication that are typical of late – or post-modern societies (see, Lasch 1978; Wouters 1986; Williams 2001). We now live, it is claimed, in an 'affective society' (Watson 1999, Squire 2001). This diagnosis has been made not only in relation to society as a whole, but also in relation to the specific institutions, sectors or sub-systems that make it up. Let us unpack this last point first. According to classical historical sociology, a key characteristic of modern societies is the fact of being structured into functionally distinct sectors or sub-systems (as opposed to being predominantly structured into clan-based segments or into a fixed hierarchy of types of people, as in feudal Europe). The law, economics, medicine, education, politics, science, art and so on are examples of such functionally specialized spheres of social activity. In relation to each of these, it is now remarkably easy to find specialists commenting on an 'affective turn' within their area of interest.

In the criminal justice system, to give a first example, emotions have become conspicuous in connection with what Bottoms has called 'populist punitiveness' (1995; see also Pratt 2000, Garland 2001) and, in a more positive vein, with emerging practices of 'restorative justice' that bring victims of crime fact-to-face with perpetrators (Van Stokkom 2002; Masters and Smith 1998; Braithwaite, 1993). For some this is an unwelcome shift from the 'jurisdiction of law' to the 'jurisdiction of emotion' (Garapon, 1996), whilst it is embraced by others as a positive corrective to an overly dry and rational system (Freiberg 2001, Solomon 1995). Others still prefer to take the position of neutral observers (Lange 2002). On the one hand, emotionalization is sometimes critically associated with the role of the mass media and with spectacular events such as the OJ Simpson trial. On the other hand, it may also be championed in the interest of taking emotions and 'sensibilities' (e.g. 'emotional harm') seriously in the making, applying and enforcing of laws.

Theorists of the media, to give a second example, have similarly noted the rise of a new culture of intimacy associated particularly with the emergence of 'factual television' and its sub-genres – talk shows (both traditional and 'tabloid') docu-soaps and docu-drama, and reality TV (Dovey 2000; Bignell 2000a and 2000b; Coles 2000; Holmes and Jermyn 2004; Hill 2005). First person media and factual television are characterized by subjective, autobiographical and confessional modes of expression, with narratives involving the intimate revelation of real life experiences of deviance, crime, illness or accident. Some see this squarely as a form of exploitation of sometimes tragic circumstances, turning audiences into voyeuristic consumers of second-hand, or 'vicarious' emotions (Meštrović 1997). Others have argued that these shows offer the opportunity of representation to marginalized groups, in what has been described as a 'counter public sphere' (Shattuc 1997; see also Gamson 1998). Others yet have stressed how tabloid shows such as *Jerry Springer* constitute an 'emotional public sphere'. Rather than simply undermining the possibility for rational debate, this emotional public sphere offers a forum for the airing of moral dilemmas in the absence of traditional community frameworks (Lunt and Stenner 2005). A shift towards emotionally saturated modes of expression is also evident in the context of news reporting (Altheide 2002), and has been associated to a 'hybridization' of television genres whereby the traditional distinction between information and entertainment has been eroded (Brants 1998; Dovey 2000; Coles 2000). This hybridization, in turn, is sometimes held responsible for a general climate of 'compassion fatigue' (Moeller 1999; Tester 2001).

The fields of business and management offer a third example. These have seen a great proliferation of academic publications and manuals on the importance of addressing emotions in the workplace. Topics range from how to recognize and handle 'toxic' emotions (e.g. Frost 2004, 2007; Jordan et al. 2006) to the relevance of emotional intelligence in decision making and leadership (Jordan et al. 2007; Kerr *et al.* 2006; Humphrey 2002; Cherniss and Goleman 2001; Goleman, Boyatzis and McKee 2002; Goleman 1998). A clear symptom of the new conspicuousness of emotions in the workplace is the inauguration, in 2005, of the *International Journal of Work, Organization and Emotion*, alongside a steady stream of journal special issues in the field. A similar conspicuousness of emotion is evident in the economy more generally, where the emphasis on consumption is closely related to the fore-grounding of aesthetic and hedonistic concerns. The study of the role of emotion in marketing has been expanding over the last 25 years (Erevelles and Granfield 1998), while the commercialization of emotions has become a topic in journals of general sociology (Martin et al. 2003). Companies now explicitly adopt strategies of 'emotional branding' (Gobé 2001).

The political sphere, to mention a fourth example, has allegedly abandoned its former seriousness and severity and become the kind of setting where people expect to see, and experience, emotional engagement. Prominent politicians now routinely sport caring and smiling facial expressions, where once it was compulsory to look stern and disciplined. 'Feel good' policies are 'spun' along with images crafted for their emotional appeal (such as senior ministers wearing baseball caps or carrying low strung electric guitars) and it is commonplace for serious world events to be mediated via accounts of personal joys and sorrows. Policies, we are told, are increasingly tailored around predictions of mass 'fears' and mass 'hopes' (Shearing and Kempa 2004; Furedi 2005; Braithwaite 2004). Liberal politics is said to depend upon 'emotional intelligence' (Shalin 2004) and the new international security paradigm upon 'emotionology' rather than 'ideology' (Pupavac 2004, 2006).

Many more accounts of the emotionalization of different sectors of social life could be provided. Observers of the education system, for example, write of 'the emotional turn in education' (Tamboukou 2003: 209). Education has allegedly become more 'child centred', stressing dialogue and emotional engagement over didactic and rational instruction; there is increasing discussion of the 'pleasures' and other affective dimensions of pedagogy (Boler 1999; McWilliam 1999; Schutz and Lanehart 2002; Bendelow and Mayall 2002; Price 2002). Observers of the health system claim that it has become 'patient centred', stressing choice, wellbeing, quality of life and 'happiness' over 'doctor knows best' paternalism (Layard 2005; Williams 1998). Theorists of social policy and welfare have stressed the increased relevance of 'love and hate' (Froggett 2002) and of 'feeling and fear of feeling' (Cooper and Lousada 2005) to the policy process. Even natural science appears to have made moves to shed its 'Dr Strangelove' image of cold martial rationality in favour of a science in the loving image of a feeling Venus (Serres 2000: 107–109; Malin 2001; Eastman and Keeton 2004; Stenner 2004).

To these observations of specialized spheres we must add the various diagnoses of society in general. For some (e.g. Richards 2004), this general 'affective turn' is associated with a more 'human' and 'civilized' form of social order. For this reason it is embraced and valued positively. For others, the same trends are associated with negative values such as a culture of selfish hedonism (e.g. Furedi 2004). Mestrovic (1997) goes as far as to argue that emotions have become fetishized as consumable items in the context of a media-led 'authenticity industry'. As such, they have been subjected to processes of McDonaldization and Disneyfication that have ultimately corrupted their power to move us. He thus writes of a 'postemotional' society in which emotions are ubiquitous yet so shallow as to be effectively meaningless.

The suggestion of an 'emotionalized' contemporary society and a corresponding turn amongst its social sciences stands in rather stark contrast to a more familiar picture that is painted of 'Enlightenment modernity' and of modern scientific knowledge. When classical sociologists began offering their descriptions of modern society they tended, if anything, to describe modernity as a move away from the alleged emotionality of so called traditional societies. Weber, for instance, wrote of the spread of bureaucratic and calculative forms of rationality associated with the rise of capitalism. A little later, Elias wrote of the gradual encroachment of a 'civilizing process' entailing ever increasing forms of affective restraint and disciplined self-control. Parsons, to briefly mention a third, wrote of a trend towards 'affective neutrality' as society differentiates itself into functional sub-systems. He argued for example that money, as a symbolically generalized medium of communication, can remove the need for the more complex and emotionally fraught circumstances of barter: one merely pays the agreed price. On the few occasions when emotion was directly addressed by early social scientists, it was typically associated with the primitive, the embodied, the female. Le Bon (1895) and Sighele (1898), for example, were concerned with the irrationality and infective emotionality of crowd (mob) behavior (see Stainton Rogers et al. 1995).

In addition to the content of these classical accounts, it can also be noted that the *manner* in which these social scientists wrote and conducted their research was framed in the characteristically detached form of objective and rational science. If the transition to modernity was grasped as a move from nature to society and from emotion to reason (as expressed in the famous *Gemeinschaft/Gesellschaft* distinction, for example), it was also grasped in this way via forms of thinking and research which themselves valorized detached reason over the affective.

MOVING DISCIPLINES

We have suggested that the turn towards affect and emotion in social science may be regarded, on one level, as the expression of a broader societal turn in the same direction. To the extent that we may speak of an *affective turn* now taking place in social science, however, this does not simply mean that social science disciplines have come to take the emotions on board as an object of study, each in its own distinctive way. While this is certainly the case, what is at stake in this 'turn' is not only the incorporation of a novel subject matter into an existing disciplinary framework. Rather, the phrase indicates that an engagement with affective life has the potential to transform the ways in which social science disciplines conceive their own way of knowing and their objects of research. Where this has happened, we might say that the social sciences themselves are being *moved* or *affected*.

When we speak of social science disciplines, it is important to remember that these are far from constituting homogenous and coherent wholes. Some social scientists embrace a new paradigm, for instance, while others dismiss it as a shallow fad and still others reach for a compromise position (even the use of the term 'paradigm' is problematic here, precisely due to the absence of a general consensus). Several distinct ways of construing and enacting a discipline can – and mostly do – exist during any one time period, and it is important not to lose sight of this variability. In addressing the *affective turn*, we are dealing with a transdisciplinary shift comparable to the *textual turn* that transformed a great portion of social scientific practice during the last quarter of the twentieth century. Although the two shifts occurred at different times and involve some important theoretical differences, strong elements of continuity between them become apparent when they are considered in a broader historical context.

When cultural anthropology, critical social psychology and interpretive sociology went through their respective *textual turns*, they did not simply take on a new subject matter (narrative, for instance). Rather, those who were part of this intellectual movement began to *see* the full gamut of their inherited subject matter *as* a complex weave of socially constructed cultural 'texts' implicated in relations of power. What had previously been treated as objectively measurable variables or factually observable processes (such as, 'attitudes', 'personality traits', 'class', 'gender' and even Balinese cock fights) came to be newly construed as 'discursive formations', 'interpretive repertoires', 'local and contingent scripts' and other 'modes of textuality'. Again, it is important to recognize that the textual turn was by no means total or uncontested (particularly in those disciplines closer to the natural sciences, such as psychology). Nevertheless, this new way of seeing was, for those who embraced it, part of a wholesale rethinking of the very nature and mission of the social sciences. It was a shift in self-definition away from a so-called 'positivism' associated with the natural sciences, and towards different ways of constructing knowledge as accountable and valid. Intellectually, the sources of this transformation included philosophical movements such as existential hermeneutics and phenomenology, ordinary language philosophy and semiotics, pragmatism and post-structuralism, as well as the work of symbolic interactionist and dramaturgical sociologists, and feminists offering critiques of masculinist forms of power (Curt 1994; Gorton 2007). These forms of thought and practice challenged, among other things, the scientific superiority of 'detached reason' and 'objective observation' over the 'emotional' and the 'subjective'.

Historically, the resurgence of empirical and theoretical interest in the emotions among social scientists is thus closely associated with the textual turn. It was first in that context that affective life became the site of an intellectual battleground of sorts. Emotions became the object of a tug-of-war in which social scientists influenced by the textual turn struggled to drag them across the line separating the psychobiological from the socio-cultural. Prior to this struggle, affective life had fallen squarely within a territory claimed by the natural sciences. For the most part, social scientists who wished to tackle the emotions had been obliged to deal with more peripheral issues, such as the social shaping of the *expression* of emotions. The implicit understanding was that emotions, at root, were psychobiological, 'natural' objects. It is worth dwelling on this last point in just a little more detail, for it helps us to appreciate the magnitude of the challenge social scientists faced (and posed) when they proposed emotions as viable objects of research for their own disciplines.

From a positive science of emotion to social constructionism

Emotions have long been a core topic of scientific psychology. When William James articulated his definition in the famous article 'What is emotion?' (1884), he was drawing upon more than half a century of physiological and medical research on the topic. James proposed that emotions are but the awareness of the bodily changes that accompany the perception of an exciting fact (for example, the raised heartbeat that accompanies the encounter with a threatening animal). Around the same time, the Danish physician and psychologist Carl Lange proposed that vaso-motor changes themselves *are* the emotion. In the standard histories of psychology, the James–Lange theory of emotion (thus named despite the fact that James and Lange had developed their accounts independently) is superseded in the 1920s by Walter Cannon's theory, in which emotions are identified with thalamic processes (later elaborated as the 'limbic system'). While the two theories are significantly different, the move from the James–Lange theory to Cannon's is a move from a physiological account grounded in the functioning of the autonomic nervous system – or the 'viscera' to use the terminology of James' day – to another physiological account, grounded in sub-cortical brain processes.

Naturally, the science of emotion did not end with the work of Walter Cannon (see Cornelius 1996, for an overview). However, with a few exceptions, it did continue in the same direction, deepening the conception of emotions as psychobiological phenomena. This trend has been boosted in recent years by the development of tech-nologies such as functional magnetic resonance imaging (FMRI) that can provide 'real-time' representations of brain processes in action and that have facilitated the development of new fields such as affective neuroscience. Panksepp (1998), for instance, argues on the basis of neuroanatomical evidence for the existence of a number of distinct emotional systems – including systems for *seeking* (interest, curi-osity, excitement), *rage, fear*, and *panic* (distress) – that are effectively homologous in all mammals. These are associated with very localized neural circuits that mature shortly after birth and whose stimulation in experimental animals yields coherent affective displays. In the same vein, Hyman (1998) asserts that emotions 'really are circuits in our brain that allow us to survive'.

Perhaps the standard approach amongst contemporary experimental psycholo-gists is to define emotions as *response systems* or *response syndromes* (Parkinson 1995). The idea here is that what we call emotions involve multiple components or factors, coordinated or organized into a temporarily unified and coherent response. There appears to be reasonably good agreement about what these multiple factors or components might be, and they are either biological or psychological. Cornelius (1996), for instance, mentions four factors: expressive reactions (such as facial expressions); physiological reactions (such as increased heart-rate); behavior (such as withdrawal from danger) and cognition (such as persistent trains of thought). What we call distress or joy would thus be a temporary coordination of these factors into a generally recognizable form. Scherer (1984, 2005), to give a second example, defines emotion as a sequence of state changes in five organismic sub-systems. Four of these correspond to the components offered by Cornelius: the motor system (which deals with expressive reactions); the autonomic system (arousal); the motivational system (action tendencies); and the cognitive system (appraisal). To these, Scherer adds a fifth: the monitor system, which he argues supplies the conscious feeling of emotion. Scherer argues that usually these sub-systems function relatively independently. But in response to important events that trigger emotions, they converge into interdependence, giving rise to familiar emotions like fear, anger and shame.

Emotions have thus been territorialized by the psychobiological sciences which take them to be 'natural kinds' amenable to analysis in terms of measurable factors and variables, and hence to objective scientific observation and intervention: emotions can, in principle, be described, predicted and controlled. It is this conception that came to be challenged by social scientists in the context of the textual turn. In the 1970s and 80s, influential figures such as James Averill, Theodore Sarbin, Arlie Russell Hochschild and Rom Harré published landmark texts articulating broadly 'constructivist' or 'social constructionist' accounts of emotion (Averill 1974, 1980; Harré 1986; Hochschild 1979; Sarbin 1986). A key issue here, as we have suggested, was to lay claim to the emotions as a properly social and cultural subject matter *as opposed to* a subject matter belonging firmly within the biopsychological sciences. Rather than viewing emotions as organic systems hard-wired through evolution, these authors began to stress some of the very different ways in which emotions are played out interactionally amongst people from different cultural backgrounds, and the variety of ways in which they have been made sense of in different historical periods. A key feature of the social constructionist accounts of emotion is their 'non-representational' epistemology which holds that discourse does not merely describe reality but is a constitutive part of that reality. With respect to affective life, this means that *emotion talk* is considered to be constitutive of emotional experience rather than simply reflective of it (Harré 1986; Harré and Parrott 1996). For this reason, the empirical study of emotion talk became a focal point for social constructionist approaches to emotion, demonstrating that great variation exists concerning how people talk and think about the *location*, the *genesis* and the *management* of emotional episodes (see Heelas 1986, for a review).

It should be noted that the door to social constructionist accounts had been partially opened by the famous experimental work of Schachter and Singer (1962) and by the broadly cognitive accounts of emotion articulated by figures such as Arnold (1960). These stressed that emotions are essentially permeated and indeed constituted by cognition, including high level thought processes. The Schachter and Singer studies, for example, provided some mixed support for the idea that subjects injected with adrenalin can interpret the resulting feelings of arousal as a range of different emotional experiences, depending upon the causal attributions they make (e.g. as anger in one experimentally engineered set of circumstances and euphoria in another). The resulting 'two factor' theory – the two factors being *arousal* and *cognition* – directly challenged the hegemony of previous biological accounts and chimed with some of the insights emerging from the work of figures such as Goffman. In this theory, organic factors were relegated to the minor role of supplying undifferentiated arousal whilst the cognitive system had the more subtle job of lending specific emotional meaning to this arousal. It was a short step from here to argue – as did Averill and his social constructionist colleagues – that the content of the meaning at play is largely 'second-hand' and social. In other words, cognitive processes such as thinking could be framed within the broader communicative and interactional practices of a given culture. Ergo, if emotions were irreducibly cognitive, then they were also irreducibly social.

In the context of the textual turn emotions came to be considered as *discursive, dialogical* phenomena, structured and influenced by the historical and cultural contingencies of communicational interactions. Positivist accounts were criticized for being scientist and reductionist and for stripping emotions away from the social context in which they acquire their force and meaning. There was a call for qualitative and phenomenological methodologies capable of reflexively grasping the subjective dimension of emotion through its modes of narration, and these were often contrasted with the quantitative methods associated with positivism (Denzin 1984; Stenner 1993; Stenner and Stainton Rogers 1998). Given these origins within an intellectual tug-of-war between the two extremes of (social) constructionism and positivism, it is not surprising that arguments raged about the degree to which this thesis concerning the fundamentally social nature of emotions could be sensibly maintained. Some sociologists, such as Kemper (1978), sided with the positivists and advanced theories of emotion aiming at general predictions. Anthropologists and historians joined the fray, some providing ammunition in support of cultural and historical relativism, and some arguing for universals.

From the textual to the affective turn in social science

While the textual turn gained ascendancy in the 1970s and has been around ever since, references to the *affective turn* are a lot more recent and very much presented as the cutting-edge *way forward* (e.g. Massumi 2002; Sedgwick 2003; Clough 2007; see Hemmings 2005; and Agnew 2007 for critiques relative to the fields of feminist cultural studies and historiography respectively). What is the relationship between the textual and the affective turn? Genealogically speaking, the textual turn may be described as one of the conditions of possibility for the more recent affective turn. The affective turn follows on from the textual turn, in the context of a theoretico-political landscape dominated by different concerns – some of which stem from the intellectual legacy of the textual turn itself. A key concern, for example, is that of avoiding the theoretical *impasse* of relativism that is associated with the methodological bracketing out of all pre- or extra-discursive reality. At one level, the affective turn is thus a turn against the privileging of text and discourse as the key theoretical touchstones, drawing attention instead to the 'pitfalls of writing the body out of theory', and to the 'residue or excess that is not socially produced, and that constitutes the very fabric of our being' (Hemmings 2005: 550, 549). This agenda also (cor-)responds to a renewed dominance and cultural presence of biology, including the ascendancy of neuroscientific, biochemical, genetic and evolutionary accounts of affect and emotions within both psychology and psychiatry (Le Doux 1998; Panksepp 1998; Greenfield 2000; Damasio 2003).

Despite a reconnection with issues of materiality and embodiment, what is involved in the *affective turn* is by no means a return to the naïve representationalism associated with positivism. On the contrary, invoking affect is closely related, in many accounts, to the call for a post-deconstructive rethinking of ontology (Thrift 2008). The move from 'text' to 'affect' thus parallels a shift in emphasis from *epistemological* questions as to the nature, sources and limits of knowledge, to *ontological* questions as to the nature of (pre-discursive) realities. In foregrounding these ontological questions, the relationship between the natural and the social sciences is no longer construed simply in terms of opposition and critique. Social scientists – in the wake of the ascendancy of sub-disciplines that take natural science and the work of scientists as their object – have come to recognize the need to be more discerning of the variety and multiplicity that characterizes the natural sciences themselves, not all aspects of which can by any means be lumped together under the label of 'positivism'. On this basis, social scientific theories of affect may well draw on post-positivist forms of biology and psychology, as well as on forms of process philosophy that take their constructivism well beyond the limitations of *social* constructionism. These influences include cybernetic and second-order systems theories, forms of psychoanalytic theory, and Silvan Tomkin's work on the psychology of affect. On the side of philosophy, they include the work of Henri Bergson, Alfred North Whitehead and Gilles Deleuze.

Having outlined some of the clear differences between the textual and the affective turn in social theory, we hope this outline also shows that there is a strong element of continuity between them. The critique of the social and discursive limits of the textual turn represents a *deepening* of constructivism and not its abandonment (Stenner 2008). The constructivist notions of power, performativity and activity which gave value to the concept of *discourse* in the textual turn have been extended beyond the socio-cultural domain to include pre-conscious and pre-discursive forms of existence, and the concept of 'affect' has become a marker of this extension. If the textual turn involved a tug-of-war between positivists and social constructionists, then the affective turn turns against what is perceived as a linguistic imperialism that threatens to throw the babies of 'the body' and its 'affects' out with the bathwater of naïvely scientistic 'representational theory'.

Affect and emotion

In this volume so far we have been using the terms 'affect' and 'emotion' as if they were interchangeable. It is worth mentioning that this would be considered deeply problematic by many proponents of the affective turn. A brief anecdote might serve to illustrate this point. At a conference on Psychosocial Studies recently held at a College of the University of London (Birkbeck 2007), Barry Richards stressed what he saw as the fundamental importance of distinguishing affect from emotion, suggesting that emotion is a more superficial and conscious affair, whilst affect refers to the deep and often unconscious organismic processes discussed by psychoanalysts. Consistent with the shift we outlined above, Richards was at pains to distinguish his own 'psychosocial' approach from social constructionist accounts that treat 'emotions' as social categories amenable to explicit communication and to conscious reflection (see also Hollway and Jefferson 2000; Rustin 2002; Froggett and

Richards 2002). A re-engagement with psychoanalytical theory – within which the concept of affect has a long pedigree – is thus one clear pathway into the affective turn (Redding 1999; Matthis 2000; Green 1977). But it is not the only pathway. Interestingly enough, comparable moves were made by a number of delegates at a conference held at another London College (Goldsmiths 2007) just two days earlier. This time the traditions invoked in connection with a turn to affect were philosophical rather than psychoanalytical, stemming from Deleuzian post-structuralism and Whiteheadian metaphysics. The concept of affect *as opposed to* emotion was at play in both conferences, but the theoretical resources informing it were quite distinct. It was notable, however, that in both settings the term 'affect' was being associated with all things sophisticated and good and the term 'emotion' with all things superficial and bad.

A similar tendency can be detected more generally. Thrift (2004), for instance, works hard to separate his preferred concept of affect from the 'nice', 'cuddly' and even 'touchy feely' issues he appears to associate with the words 'emotion' and 'feeling' (cf. Thien, 2005 for a critique). Likewise, McCormack contrasts the limitations of 'emotion' with the 'creative potential of affect'. Emotion is associated with the individual person and with a certain fixity within regimes of discursive meaning, whilst affect is associated with an 'unqualified intensity' that is 'never reducible to the personal quality of emotion' (2003: 500). Both Thrift and McCormack draw on Brian Massumi's elaboration of Deleuzian philosophy (see Massumi 1996; also Wissinger 2007 and Clough 2007).

We believe that insisting on this terminological distinction is not inherently helpful, and may actually obscure more than it clarifies at a conceptual level. If Sedgwick (2003) and her followers prefer 'affect', for instance, then this is probably because it was the term employed by Silvan Tomkins in his magnum opus *Affect, Imagery, Consciousness*. But Tomkins himself used 'affect' to talk about experiences and expressions such as shame, anger, fear, excitement, joy and distress that are quite compatible with the word 'emotion'. Tomkins was not terribly concerned to draw a radical distinction between 'affect' and 'emotion', and often used the terms interchangeably, although he did consider the *conscious* experience of affects to be decisive to their *biological* function as drive amplifiers. Likewise, if Deleuze and his followers prefer to use 'affect', then this is probably because of Spinoza's use of the Latin word *affectus* in his *Ethics*. Spinoza himself used the term as a generic for such specifics as joy, fear, jealousy, shame. Spinoza did not outline – *pace* Massumi – a 'difference in nature between affect and emotion' (Massumi 1996: 222).

It seems to us that drawing an overly sharp (and value laden) distinction between affect and emotion serves, paradoxically, to perpetuate the illusion that such words refer unproblematically to states of the world, thus bypassing the need to think carefully about the conceptual issues at stake. The issue at stake in Deleuzian philosophy, for example, is a shift towards modes of thought and practice that concern the potential and the virtual as much as the actual and the real. Affect is thus a decisive concept for grasping transformations, potentialities, 'unpredictable connections between bodies and forces' (Tamboukou, 2003: 217), and 'shifts in the energetic capabilities of a body' (Conradson, 2007: 104). This shift – which concerns how we address reality more generally – can be masked by a preoccupation with words.

If indeed the concern of the affective turn is to argue for a move beyond a narrowly 'discursive' conceptualization of emotion, then it might be more sensible to argue, along with people such as Katz (1999), that there is more to emotion than *talk about emotion* and more to emotion than can be captured in its conscious experience (see also Stenner 2005b). This strategy serves to highlight that what is at stake is the contestation of a concept and not the mere application of a linguistic label.

In short, our approach to these terminological questions is to stress that terminology serves first of all as a marker of difference for groups of intellectuals, keen to distinguish their own approach from that of specific others. As we have stressed, however, shared terminology need not imply a shared theoretical position. One only has to move from Goldsmiths to Birkbeck College to find the term 'affect' being used in very different ways, albeit to accomplish a comparable criticism and deepening of the textual turn. It is instructive in this context to reflect on the fact that the term 'emotion' is actually a rather recent addition to the English lexicon. As Dixon discusses (see extract in section one of this volume), the term 'emotion' came into common currency amongst speakers of English as late as the nineteenth century. Before that, people were more likely to talk of affections, passions, sentiments and the like. Passions and affections, especially since Augustine and Aquinas, were terms that were very much part of a theological semantic web. They resonated with other terms such as the soul (whether animal, vegetative or intellective) and the will, and they operated within a normative moral framework at whose pinnacle stood a transcendent deity. The term 'emotion' entered into circulation as part of a medico-scientific discourse associated with the early development of scientific psychology. In calling affective life 'emotion', these novel scientific discourses also transformed the ways in which people thought about their affective life. Specifically, the emotions came to be thought of as quasi-mechanical *biological* processes. The association of 'emotion' with physiology has been boosted in recent years by Damasio's (1999; 2003) distinction between 'emotions' and 'feelings', where the former are construed as objectively observable organic processes whilst 'feelings' are the subjective experience of emotions. It is thus somewhat ironic that Massumi, McCormack, Thrift and others associate the word 'affect' with issues of materiality and corporeality, and 'emotion' with subjective experience, since the very term 'emotion' marks a historical rupture whereby the affections of the soul lost their place to the emotions of the viscera.

DISCIPLINING AFFECTS

Despite the rich diversity that characterizes approaches to affect and emotion in the social sciences, there is a clear common denominator in this research. In a nutshell, this lies in the foregrounding of the link between affective life and relations of power. Specifically in the context of the textual and affective turns, this foregrounding becomes reflexive in character. The textual turn and the affective turn, as we have seen, share a non-representational epistemology – the notion that discourse and knowledge are not simply about reality, but constitute an active part of it. Theories of emotion do not simply hover above their subject matter. Rather they intervene in the affective life they scrutinize, a little like a geologist's map of a coal seam might enable the extraction of the coal and hence the transformation of the landscape. At a methodological level, non-representational epistemology translates into a commitment to reflexivity *vis-à-vis* the normative implications of knowledge about emotion. How does knowledge about emotion enter into the power configurations of our time? How does it contribute to the ways in which individuals and collectivities can both *affect* and *be affected*?

In linking emotions to the political dimension of power and governance, the social sciences may be said to re-establish a profound continuity with debates that predate the historical attempt to define and explain emotion scientifically. Prior to the inauguration of 'emotion' as a scientific category, passions, sentiments and affects had been at the centre of practically all the great moral, ethical and religious discourses on what constitutes a good life. Consider for example the connection between ethics and passions in Aristotle, or the doctrine of the seven cardinal sins in Christian morality. The effort to define the proper nature and place of the affects became bound up with struggles of a specifically political character in seventeenth-century Europe. This was part of a broader philosophical reflection on the role and function of nascent secular governments, as distinct from systems of ethical and moral governance (Koselleck 1988). For Spinoza and Hobbes, both witnesses of the political earthquakes engendered by the wars of religion, a reframing of affective life in terms of natural philosophy was part of the search for new, secular answers to political questions. This is especially clear in Hobbes' *Leviathan*, where the discussion of passions, appetites and desires in Part I grounds his proposals for the Commonwealth made in Part II. But this sequence – whereby the discussion of emotions comes 'before' the discussion of political, legal or economic questions – constitutes a more general pattern, common to many of the classics from the late 17th through to the mid 18th century. Locke's *Essay Concerning Human Understanding* (1689) appears the year before his *Two Treatises of Government*. Volume 2 of Hume's *Treatise of Human Nature*, entitled *On the Passions* (1739), is swiftly followed by the essays on political economy, morals and ethics. Smith's *Theory of the Moral Sentiments* (1759) provided the ground for the *Wealth of Nations* (1776). With Rousseau, the analysis of affective life takes place in his novels. *Julie* (1761) precedes the *Social Contract* by one year, and *Emile* is published in the same year (Stenner 2004; see also Barbalet, extract in section 3, for a discussion of Smith and Ferguson in this light).

The normative dimension of knowledge of affective life is thus made perfectly apparent in the work of these Enlightenment thinkers: different political prescriptions literally follow from different ways of thinking about passions or sentiments and their place in human nature. It was only with the functional specialization that marks the establishment of scientific disciplines in the 19th century, and with the appropriation of the domain of affect (as 'emotion') into the territories of biology and psychology, that the link between concepts of emotion and the dimensions of politics, morals and ethics disappeared from view. Although these disciplines – psychology in particular – were no less embroiled in the normative business of governance and social engineering, they intervened in the name of a supposedly value-neutral distinction between the 'normal' and the 'pathological' (Hacking 1991).

As relative late-comers to the study of emotion, the social sciences have constructed their agendas not in a vacuum, but in relation to a social situation already marked by the success of the natural and clinical sciences of emotion. For this reason, one agenda for social scientists has been to critically document the ways in which the psy-disciplines (and, more recently, neuroscience) have actively contributed to the shaping of affective experience in modern and late-modern times. Earlier in this introduction, for example, we addressed what has been called an 'emotionalization' of all spheres of social life in late modernity. This phenomenon has been attributed, at least in part, to a process of 'proto-professionalization', whereby psychotherapeutic concepts and terminology gradually found their way into the everyday vocabulary of social actors (De Swaan 1990). As Doyle McCarthy has put it, it is only in the specific context of a 'psychological age' – one distinguished by the dissemination of psychological knowledge and therapeutic discourse – that 'emotions acquire a social meaning previously absent: . . . emotions are "worked at" and "worked on", one has an "emotional life" ' (1989: 66). But the impact of the sciences of emotion has not been limited to facilitating a greater scope for the awareness, expression, and management of emotional experience. In so doing, these sciences have also facilitated profound transformations in the ways social relations are conducted, at an interpersonal level and beyond. Social scientists have examined the dissemination of psy-concepts and the social conspicuousness of emotion talk within the context of rationalities of government that increasingly rely on reflexive forms of self-management and self-regulation on the part of individuals (Rose 1996a, 1996b, 1999). At a more general level, this development has been addressed in terms of processes of *individualization* (Beck, 1992) and *reflexive modernization* (Giddens 1992; Beck, Giddens and Lash 1994; see also Castells 2004; and Dean 2007 for a critique).

To employ a dramaturgical metaphor, we may say that the occasions and settings wherein we are called to act in the name of our 'selves', beyond the prerogatives and limits of formal roles, have consistently multiplied in the course of the 20th century. These occasions and settings are now ubiquitous in Western liberal democracies, reaching well beyond the context of intimate or private relationships. As a dramaturgical role, the self is characterized by its informal, personal and confessional style: we act as selves by following a (supposedly) unique and authentic motivational script to which we and we alone have access through introspection. The acknowledgment and/or expression of emotion acts a prime signifier and guarantor of the self as a social actor. Emotions, writes Doyle McCarthy, are 'necessary "props" with which the drama of self establishes its realism' (1989: 66). Social scientists have been at pains to demonstrate, in various ways, how these new touchy-feely forms of interaction management do not imply a greater fairness or equality of social arrangements, contrary to the impression their rhetoric conveys.

Social scientists can thus provide a form of critical reflection on how psychological knowledge of emotions contributes to social processes, how it increasingly mediates relations of power and governance, and with it also the sensibilities and likely affective experiences of participants. But what of the social sciences themselves? How does *their* knowledge of emotion enter into these relations, shaping their development in particular directions? Any critical reflexive assessment of their contribution, particularly given the rapidity with which the field is expanding, is necessarily provisional. Generally speaking, however, we may say that the social sciences offer a measure of distance with regard to commonsense accounts. They allow us to consider any proposition regarding affective experience in the context of broader frameworks and dynamics. For example, if it is the case that the expression of authentic feelings increasingly features as a normative feature of interaction management, social scientists may point to the paradoxical character of the situations this generates. Commenting on the phenomenon of 'political correctness', for example, Schwartz writes: '[t]o have to *try* and act in a politically correct manner is to be politically incorrect. As George Orwell put it in *1984*, "A party member is required to have not only the right opinions, but the right instincts". . . . Love of the Oppressed, not the display of love but love itself, is a criterion for one's moral acceptability' (1993: 210, emphasis added). This comment highlights how the opportunities for the expression of 'authentic' emotion can be logically subverted by their institutionalization, codification, and inevitable standardization, once emotional expression becomes a feature of routine interaction management. What can it mean to act 'true to oneself', in the name of deep personal feelings or beliefs as opposed to mere conventions, when doing so also represents the adequate response to social requirements and expectations?

Acknowledging this paradox does not involve an epistemological commitment to the notion of an authentic self as the source of authentic emotions, or indeed an opposite commitment against it – the paradox can be taken either way. On the one hand, it may support a form of ironic detachment from the notion of authenticity as a theoretical possibility, and a view of identity as something to be reflexively 'invented'. On the other hand, the paradox may be taken to suggest that the dynamics of contemporary governance contribute to forms of affective 'false consciousness' that are problematic, for example on grounds of physical and mental health. The point here is that, in each case, the sociological diagnosis has implications of a normative, and thereby also affective character (cf. Greco 2001).

Engagement with the topic of affect and emotion on the part of social scientists may be said to produce a measure of disenchantment with the emancipatory promise of psychological knowledge. At the same time, this engagement carries an emancipatory potential of its own, to the extent that it has produced awareness of the constraints implicit in supposedly relaxed and 'liberatory' forms of interaction. But we must, of course, be careful not to suppose that the work of social scientists is exempt from contributing to the creation of new constraints, as much as it may free us from old ones. We are not, indeed, to think in terms of a dichotomy opposing power and freedom. We may think instead in terms of a need to address the performative value implicit in the interventions we make at any one time, in any particular context. Producing ironic detachment from the theoretical possibility of authenticity, for example, may well be emancipatory in one context, though not necessarily in another. For the community of social scientists, this reflection on performative value is an important aspect of the significance of the turn to affect. To redescribe the social world as saturated with affect and emotion *is* to redescribe it as saturated with value, or with the possibilities of *affecting* and *being affected* in positive or negative ways.

Using the Reader

We have organized the Reader into four Parts, each comprising three Sections. Part I is entitled *Universals and particulars of affect*. As this title suggests, one of the key features of social-scientific research on emotions is an acknowledged tension between those who emphasize the universally 'human' aspects of emotions and those, conversely, that stress the contingency of emotional experience and expression on variables such as historical time, culture, or social situation. This Part aims to introduce how the disciplines of historiography, anthropology and sociology have each differently contributed to the framing of this debate, and how central the debate itself is to the definition of a broadly social-scientific approach to the emotions. Part II, *Embodying affect*, includes texts that address emotion in relation to the embodied individual self, and in relation to subjective space. Spatial metaphors feature prominently in how the relationship between the self and emotions has been conceptualized in different cultures and historical periods. The experience of space through the body, on the other hand, plays a crucial role in rendering space affectively significant. Last but not least, emotions have been described as the embodiment of culture, and thereby as the 'missing link' between the social and the physical determinants of health and illness. The aim of this Part of the book is to introduce the reader to the literatures that have addressed emotions and selfhood, emotions and space/place, and emotions and health as topics in their own right, whilst pointing to the mutual resonances between these subjects. In Part III, *Political economies of affect*, we have included extracts that address emotions from the angle of political economy, broadly defined. Affect is central to contemporary economic processes, whether in the form of 'emotional labor' in the service industry, of 'emotional intelligence' in the context of organizational management, or of the increasing attention paid to feeling in developing marketing strategies for particular products. The centrality of emotions is equally evident in the media. Here, the increasing prominence of talk shows, docu-soaps and other *reality* genres, and the merging of information and entertainment as *infotainment*, reflects an erosion of the boundaries between the public and the private spheres, and between work and leisure. This Part includes texts relative to emotion in the contexts of work and organizations, economics and consumer culture, and the media industry. In the last Part of the book, entitled *Affect, power and justice*, we have gathered extracts that address the relationship between emotions and issues of social justice on a global and local level. These texts address themes such as the role of emotions in political mobilization and social movements; the influence of mass-mediated emotional communications upon criminal justice and the legal system; the importance of a discourse of compassion to contemporary humanitarian and human rights movements; the role of emotions like 'terror' and 'hate' in contemporary political rhetoric and debate.

   In addition to this general introduction, where we have presented the general background and our rationale for the volume as a whole, we have produced a brief introduction for each of the twelve Sections of the book. These shorter introductions are designed to provide a guide to the specific themes covered by the extracts, and to highlight points of mutual relevance and comparison. There then follows an annotated Guide to Further Reading. In this Guide we have listed a number of important texts that are not otherwise included, following the structure of the Reader itself. Although the Guide is by no means comprehensive or complete, we hope it will support readers in following up themes or questions of particular interest.

References

Agnew, V. (2007) 'History's affective turn: historical reenactment and its work in the present', *Rethinking History*, 11 (3): 299–312.

Altheide. D. L. (2002) *Creating Fear: news and the construction of crisis*. New York: Aldine de Gruyter.

Arnold, M. (1960) *Emotion and Personality*. New York: Columbia University Press.

Averill, J. R. (1974) 'An analysis of psychophysiological symbolism and its influence on theories of emotion', *Journal for the Theory of Social Behavior*, 4, 147–90.

Averill, J. R. (1980) 'A constructivist view of emotion', in R. Plutchik and H. Kellerman (eds) *Theories of Emotion*. New York: Academic Press.

Beck, U. (1992) *Risk Society: towards a new modernity*. London: Sage.

Beck, U., Giddens, A., Lash, S. (eds) (1994) *Reflexive Modernization: politics, tradition and aesthetics in the modern social order*. Cambridge: Polity Press.

Bendelow, G. and Mayall, B. (2002) 'Children's emotional learning in primary schools', *European Journal of Psychotherapy and Counselling*, 5 (3): 291–304.

Bignell, J. (2000a) *Postmodern Media Culture*. Edinburgh: Edinburgh University Press.

Bignell, J. (2000b) 'Docudrama as melodrama: Representing Princess Diana and Margaret Thatcher'. In Carson, B. and Llewellyn-Jones, M. (eds) *Frames and Fictions On Television*. Bristol: Intellect Books.

Boler, M. (1999) *Feeling Power: emotions and education*. London: Routledge.

Bottoms, A. (1995) 'The philosophy and politics of punishment and sentencing', in C. Clark and R. Morgan (eds) *The Politics of Sentencing Reform*. Oxford: Clarendon.

Braithwaite, J. (1993) 'Shame and modernity', *British Journal of Criminology* 33 (1): 1–18.

Braithwaite, V. (2004) 'The hope process and social inclusion', *The ANNALS of the American Academy of Political and Social Science*, 592 (1): 128–51.

Brants, K. (1998) 'Who's afraid of infotainment?', *European Journal of Communication*, 13: 315–35.

Cannon, W. B. (1920) *Bodily Changes In Pain Hunger Fear And Rage*. New York: Appleton and Co.

Castells, M. (2004) *The Network Society: a cross cultural perspective*. Cheltenham: Edward Elgar Publishing Limited.

Cherniss, C. and Goleman, D. (eds) (2001) *The Emotionally Intelligent Workplace*. San Francisco. CA: Jossey-Bass.

Clough, P. and Halley, J. (eds) (2007) *The Affective Turn: theorizing the social*. Durham: Duke University Press.

Clough, P. (2007) 'The affective turn: introduction', in P. Clough and J. Halley (eds) *The Affective Turn: theorizing the social*. Durham N.C.: Duke University Press.

Coles, G. (2000) 'Docusoap: actuality and the serial format', in B. Carson and M. Llewellyn-Jones (eds) *Frames and Fictions on Television: the politics of identity in drama*. Exeter: Intellect.

Conradson, D. (2007) 'Freedom, space and perspective: moving encounters with other ecologies', in J. Davidson, L. Bondi and M. Smith (eds) *Emotional Geographies*. London: Ashgate.

Cooper A. and Lousada J. (2005) *Borderline Welfare: feeling and fear of feeling in modern welfare*. London: Karnac Books.

Cornelius, R. (1996) *The Science of Emotion*. Upper Saddle River, NJ: Prentice-Hall.

Curt, B. (1994) *Textuality and Tectonics: troubling social and psychological science*. Buckingham: Open University Press.

Damasio, A. R. (1999) *The Feeling of What Happens: body and emotion in the making of consciousness*. New York: Harcourt Brace.

Damasio, A. (2003) *Looking for Spinoza: joy, sorrow and the feeling of the brain*. Orlando: Harcourt.

Dean, M. (2007) *Governing Societies: political perspectives on domestic and international rule*. Maidenhead, Open University Press.

Denzin, N. (1984) *On Understanding Emotion*. San Francisco: Jossey-Bass.

de Swaan, A. (1990) *The Management of Normality: critical essays in health & welfare*, London: Routledge.

Dovey, J. (2000) *Freakshow: first person media and factual television*. London: Pluto Press.

Eastman, T. E. and Keeton, H (eds) (2004) *Physics and Whitehead: quantum, process, and experience*. New York: SUNY.

Erevelles, S. Granfield, M. (1998) 'Special issue on the role of affect in marketing', *Journal of Business Research*, 42 (3): 197–99.

Freiberg, A. (2001) 'Affective versus effective justice', *Punishment and Society*, 3 (2): 265–278.

Froggett, L (2002) *Love, Hate and Welfare: psychosocial approaches to policy and practice*. Bristol: Policy Press.

Froggett, L. and Richards, B. (2002) 'Exploring the bio-psycho-social', *European Journal of Psychotherapy, Counselling and Health*, 5 (3): 321–326.

Frost, P. J. (2004) 'Handling toxic emotions: new challenges for leaders and their organization', *Organizational Dynamics*, 33 (2): 111–127.

Frost, P. J. (2007) *Toxic Emotions at Work and What You Can Do About Them*. Harvard: Harvard Business School Press.

Furedi, F. (2004) *Therapy Culture: cultivating vulnerability in an uncertain age*. London: Routledge

Furedi, F. (2005) *Politics of Fear: beyond left and right*. Continuum Press.

Gamson, J. (1998) *Freaks Talk Back. Tabloid shows and sexual non-conformity*. Chicago, IL: University of Chicago Press.

Garapon, A. (1996) 'Justice out of court: the dangers of trial by media', in Nelken, D. (ed.) *Law as Communication*. Aldershot: Dartmouth.

Garland, D (2001) *The Culture of Control*. Oxford: Oxford University Press.

Giddens, A. (1992) *The Transformation of Intimacy: sexuality, love and eroticism in modern societies*, Stanford, CA: Stanford University Press.

Gobe, M. (2001) *Emotional Branding: The New Paradigm for Connecting Brands to People*. New York: Allworth.

Goleman, D. (1998) *Working with Emotional Intelligence*. New York: Bantam Books.

Goleman, D., Boyatzis, R. and McKee, A. (2002) *Primal Leadership: Realizing the Power of Emotional Intelligence*. Boston, MA: Harvard Business School Press.

Gorton, K. (2007) 'Theorizing emotion and affect: feminist engagements', *Feminist Theory*, 8 (3): 333–48.

Greco, M. 2001 'Inconspicuous anomalies: alexithymia and ethical relations to the self', *Health*, 6 (4): 471–92.

Green, A. (1977) 'Conceptions of affect', *International Journal of Psycho-Analysis*, 58: 129–56.

Greenfield, S. A. (2000) *The Private Life of the Brain*. London: The Penguin Press.

Hacking, I. (1991) *The Taming of Chance*. Cambridge: Cambridge University Press.

Harré, R. (ed) (1986) *The Social Construction of Emotions*. Oxford: Basil Blackwell.

Harré, R. and Parrott, W. G. (1996) *The Emotions: social, cultural and biological dimensions*. London: Sage.

Heelas, P. (1986) 'Emotion talk across cultures', in R. Harré, R. (ed) *The Social Construction of Emotions*. Oxford: Basil Blackwell.

Hemmings, C. (2005) 'Invoking affect: cultural theory and the ontological turn', *Cultural Studies,* 19: 548–67.

Hill, A. (2005) *Reality TV: audiences and popular factual entertainment*. London: Routledge.

Hochschild, A. R. (1979) 'Emotion work, feeling rules, and social structure', *American Journal of Sociology,* 85: 551–75.

Holmes, S. and Jermyn, D. (2004) 'Introduction: understanding reality TV', in S. Holmes and D. Jermyn (eds) *Understanding Reality Television*. London: Routledge.

Hollway, W. and Jefferson, T. (2000) *Doing Qualitative Research Differently: free association, narrative and the interview method*. London: Sage.

Humphrey, R. H. (2002) 'The many faces of emotional leadership', *The Leadership Quarterly,* 13 (5): 493–504.

Hyman, S. (1998) 'A new image for fear and emotion', *Nature,* 393 (4): 417–18.

James, W. (1884) 'What is emotion?', *Mind,* 9: 188–205.

Jordan, P.J., Lawrence, S.A., and Troth, A.C. (2006) 'The impact of negative mood on team performance', *Journal of Management and Organization,* 12 (2): 131–45.

Jordan, P.J., Ashkanasy, N. M., and Ascough K. (2007) 'Emotional Intelligence in Organizational Behavior and Industrial-Organizational Psychology', in G. Matthews, M. Zeidner, & R. D. Roberts (eds) *Science of Emotional Intelligence: knowns and unknowns*. Oxford: Oxford University Press.

Kemper, T. D. (1978) *A Social International Theory of Emotions*. New York: John Wiley.

Kerr, R., Garvin, J., Heaton, N. and Boyle, E. (2006) 'Emotional intelligence and leadership effectiveness', *Leadership and Organization Development Journal,* 27(4): 265–79.

Koselleck, R. (1988) *Critique and Crisis*. Oxford: Berg.

Lange, B. (2002) 'The emotional dimension in legal regulation', *Journal of Law and Society,* 29 (1): 197–225.

Lasch, C. (1978) *The Culture of Narcissism*. New York: W. W. Horton.

Layard, R. (2005) *Happiness: lessons from a new science*. New York: Penguin Press.

Le Bon, G. (1895) *Les lois psychologiques de l'évolution des peuples*. Paris: Alcan.

LeDoux, J. (1998) *The Emotional Brain*. Phoenix: London.

Luhmann, N. (1995) *Social Systems*. Stanford California: Stanford University Press.

Lunt, P. and Stenner, P. (2005) 'The Jerry Springer Show as an emotional public sphere', *Media, Culture and Society,* 27 (1): 59–81.

Malin, S. (2001) *Nature Loves to Hide: quantum physics and the nature of reality, a western perspective*. Oxford: Oxford University Press.

Martin, B., Roach Anleu, S. and Zadoroznyj, M. (2003) 'Editors' introduction to the special issue "Commercializing emotions" ', *Journal of Sociology,* 39: 331.

Massumi, B. (1996) 'The autonomy of affect', in P. Patton (ed) *Deleuze: a critical reader*. Oxford: Blackwell.

Massumi, B. (2002) *Parables for the Virtual: movement, affect, sensation*. Durham, N.C.: Duke University Press.

Masters, G. and Smith, D. (1998) 'Portia and Persephone revisited: thinking about feeling in criminal justice', *Theoretical Criminology* 2(1): 5–28.

Matthis, I. (2000) 'Sketch for a metapsychology of affect', *International Journal of Psycho-Analysis*, 81: 215–27.

McCarthy, E. Doyle. (1989) 'Emotions are social things: an essay in the sociology of emotions', in D. D. Franks and E. D. McCarthy. (eds) *The Sociology of Emotions: original essays and research papers*. London: JAI Press.

McWilliam, E. (1999) *Pedagogical Pleasures*. New York: Peter Lang.

Meštrović, S. (1997) *Postemotional Society*. London: Sage.

Moeller, S. D. (1999) *Compassion Fatigue: how the media sell disease, famine, war and death*. London: Routledge.

Nathanson, D (1992) *Shame and Pride*. New York: W. W. Norton.

Panksepp J. (1998) *Affective Neuroscience: the foundations of human and animal emotions*. Oxford: Oxford University Press.

Parkinson, B. (1995) *Ideas and Realities of Emotion*. London: Routledge.

Pratt, J. (2000) 'Emotive and ostentatious punishment: its decline and resurgence in modern society', *Punishment and Society* 2(4): 417–40.

Price, H. (2002) 'The emotional context of classroom learning: a psychoanalytic perspective', *European Journal of Psychotherapy & Counselling*, 5 (3): 305–20.

Pupavac, V. (2004) 'War on the couch: the emotionology of the new international security paradigm', *European Journal of Social Theory*, 7(2), 149–70.

Pupavac, V. (2006) 'Humanitarian politics and the rise of international disaster psychology', in *Handbook of International Disaster Psychology*, first. 1. Westport CT: Praeger Publishers.

Redding, P. (1999) *The Logic of Affect*. Ithaca: Cornell University Press.

Richards, B. (2004) 'The emotional deficit in political communication', *Political Communication*, 21: 339–52.

Rose, N. (1996a) 'Power and subjectivity: critical history and psychology'. In K. J. Gergen and C. F. Graumann (eds) *Historical Dimensions of Psychological History*. Cambridge: Cambridge University Press.

Rose N. (1996b) *Inventing Our Selves: psychology, power and personhood*. New York, Cambridge University Press.

Rose, N. (1999) *Powers of Freedom: reframing political thought*. Cambridge: Cambridge University Press.

Rose N (1999) *Governing the Soul: the shaping of the private self*. Second edition, London, Free Associations Books.

Rustin, M. (2002) 'Introduction: ways of thinking about human emotions', *European Journal of Psychotherapy, Counselling and Health*, 5 (3): 197–203.

Sarbin, T. (1986) 'Emotion and act: roles and rhetoric', in R. Harré (ed) *The Social Construction of Emotions*. Oxford: Basil Blackwell.

Schachter, S. and Singer, J. E. (1962) 'Cognitive, social and physiological determinants of emotional state', *Psychological Review*, 69: 379–99.

Scherer, K. R. (1984) 'Emotion as a multicomponent process: a model and some cross-cultural data', in P. Shaver (ed) *Review of Personality and Social Psychology*, Vol. 5. Beverly Hills, CA: Sage.

Scherer, K. R. (2005) 'What are emotions? And how can they be measured?', *Social Science Information*, 44(4), 693–727.

Schutz, P. A and Lanehart, S. L. (2002) 'Introduction: emotions in education', *Educational Psychologist*, 37(2): 67–8.

Schwartz, H. S. (1993) 'Narcissistic emotion and university administration: an analysis of "Political Correctness,"' in S. Fineman (ed), *Emotion in organizations*. London: Sage.

Sedgwick, E. K. (2003) *Touching Feeling: affect, pedagogy, performativity.* Durham: Duke UP.

Serres, M. (2000) *The Birth of Physics.* Manchester: Clinamen Press.

Shalin, D. N. (2004) 'Liberalism, affect control, and emotionally intelligent democracy', *Journal of Human Rights,* 3: 407–28.

Shattuc, J. M. (1997) *The Talking Cure. TV talk shows and women.* New York: Routledge.

Shearing, C. and Kempa, M. (2004) 'A museum of hope: a story of Robben Island', Annals *of the American Academy of Political and Social Science,* 592: 62–78.

Sighele, S. (1898) *Le Foule Criminelle.* Paris: Alcan.

Solomon, R. C. (1995) *A Passion for Justice: emotions and the origins of the social contract.* Lanham, Maryland: Rowman & Littlefield.

Squire, C. (2001) 'The public life of emotions', *International Journal of Critical Psychology,* 1: 16–27.

Stainton Rogers, R. Stenner, P. Gleeson, K. and Stainton Rogers, W. (1995) *Social Psychology: a critical agenda.* Cambridge: Polity Press.

Stenner, P. (1993) 'Discoursing jealousy', in Burman, E. and Parker, I. (eds) *Discourse Analytic Research: repertoires and readings of texts in action.* London: Routledge.

Stenner, P. (2004) 'Is autopoietic systems theory alexithymic? Luhmann and the sociopsychology of emotions', *Soziale Systeme,* 10 (1): 159–85.

Stenner, P. (2005b) 'An outline of an autopoietic approach to emotion', *Cybernetics and Human Knowing,* 12 (4): 8–22.

Stenner, P. (2008) 'A. N. Whitehead and subjectivity', *Subjectivity,* 22: 90–109.

Stenner, P. and Stainton Rogers, R. (1998) 'Jealousy as a manifold of divergent under-standings: a Q methodological investigation', *The European Journal of Social Psychology,* 28, 71–94.

Tamboukou, M. (2003) 'Interrogating the "emotional turn": making connections with Foucault and Deleuze', *European Journal of Psychotherapy, Counselling and Health,* 6 (3): 209–23.

Tester, K. (2001) *Compassion, Morality and the Media.* Buckingham: Open University Press.

Thrift, N. (2008) *Non-representational Theory: space / politics / affect.* London: Routledge.

Tomkins, S. (1963) *Affective, Imagery, Consciousness. Vol. 1 The positive affects.* London: Tavistock.

Van Stokkom, B. (2002) 'Moral emotions in restorative justice conferences: managing shame, designing empathy', *Theoretical Criminology,* 6(3): 339–60.

Watson, S. (1999) 'Policing the affective society: beyond governmentality in the theory of social control', *Social and Legal Studies,* 8: 227–51.

Williams, S. (2001) *Emotions and Social Theory.* London: Sage.

Williams, S.J. (1998) ' "Capitalising" on emotions? Rethinking the inequalities in health debate', *Sociology,* 32 (1): 132–33.

Wissinger, E. (2007) 'Modelling a way of life: immaterial and affective labour in the fashion modelling industry', *Ephemera,* 7 (1): 250–69.

Wouters, C. (1986) 'Formalization and Informalization: Changing Tension Balances in Civilizing Processes', *Theory, Culture & Society,* 3 (2): 1–18.

PART ONE

Universals and particulars of affect

1. Emotions, history and civilization

THIS IS THE FIRST OF three sections where we have gathered texts that share a concern with questions of universality and difference in the study of emotions. The concern is common across the disciplines of history, anthropology and sociology, as are some of the concepts through which it is articulated (e.g. 'constructionism'). Debates in each discipline, however, are coloured by different emphases and priorities. The texts included in this section address the dimension of temporal continuity and difference through the work of historians and historical sociologists.

Historical research on the emotions can be broadly distinguished in terms of the focus on two very different kinds of object. One strand of research addresses *theories* or ideas about emotion as these have been developed by philosophers, theologians, psychologists and psychiatrists. This strand is exemplified here in our first extract, from Thomas Dixon's *From Passion to Emotions: the creation of a secular psychological category* (2003). Ideas and theories of 'emotion' as such are relatively recent, as the term was not widely in use before the early nineteenth century. While much historical writing underplays the significance of this terminological point, sometimes to the point of ignoring it altogether, it is central to Dixon's analysis. Dixon proposes that the shift from 'passions' to 'emotions' cannot be understood simply as the employment of a new word to describe the same thing. Passions and affections, especially since Augustine and Aquinas, were terms embedded in a theological semantic web. They resonated with other terms such as the soul and the will, and they operated within a normative moral framework at whose pinnacle stood a transcendental deity. 'Emotion', by contrast, has its provenance in the secularized idiom of the increasingly specialized and autonomous practices of science and medicine. As a concept, it is born of a quasi-empirical distinction between external and internal affections of the mind. As internal affections of the mind, emotions are in turn distinguished from thought or intellect. In this manner, emotions are dissociated from the dimensions of morality and ethics, and construed as non-rational feeling states with evident ties to the body. The text by Dixon included here points to the historical specificity of the concept of emotion, and to the methodological dangers implicit in the historiographical task of mediating between this modern concept and its equivalents in the past. Dixon's argument in this work parallels anthropological deconstructions of Western concepts of emotion, such as the studies by Lutz (1986; see also extract in this volume), which seek to highlight the epistemological and normative assumptions these concepts imply, and the methodological pitfalls of ignoring them.

Another strand of historical research on the emotions addresses changes not in theories or concepts of emotion, but in the social *norms* regarding their experience and expression – changes in attitudes, standards, or what sociologist Arlie Hochschild named 'feeling rules' (see section 3 below) and what historians Stearns and Stearns called 'emotionology' (1985). Here the focus can be on the historical trajectory of individual emotions such as anger, jealousy or fear, or it can be on general styles of affect management typical of entire epochs. The work of Norbert Elias is the clearest example of this latter approach and, for better or for worse (see the critique by Rosenwein, 2002), it has been credited with providing something like a paradigm for subsequent historical and historico-sociological research on the emotions. The text included here comprises two short extracts from Elias' *magnum opus, The Civilizing Process*, originally published in 1939. The theory of the civilizing process offers an account of the long-term correlation between changes in personality structure and socio-political changes since the late Middle Ages in Europe. In a nutshell, the theory describes how the increasing complexity of networks of human interdependence, as particularly evident in the emergence of the modern state with its increasing functional differentiation, goes hand in hand with the development of increasing capacities for foresight and calculation on the part of individuals. These capacities for foresight and calculation rely in turn on increasing measures of impulse restraint, of detachment and observation of self from the vantage point of others. Over time, both the quality of affective experience and the forms of its expression are profoundly transformed through this process. In relation to emotions, and contrary to some readings of Elias' theory, it is important to realize that the theory of the civilizing process does not suggest changes in the direction of a wholesale repression of affective life. One key word to describe the direction of the overall process is 'psychologization'; this involves an expansion of the occasions for the experience of emotions like shame and repugnance, for example, as much as it involves restraint over the physical expressions of, say, anger and joy.

The theory of the civilizing process constitutes much more than a historiographical endeavour. It also offers a diagnosis of typically modern forms of self-perception, which in turn provides the basis for a historically reflexive sociology of knowledge. For Elias, an historical movement in the direction of increasing capacity for detachment and affective neutrality was crucial for the development of modern science. This capacity occurred earlier in relation to the observation of natural phenomena, and only later in relation to the reflexive observation of human behaviour and relationships. The theory of the civilizing process should be read, on one level, as an expression of the very dynamics it describes: it is designed to bring a further measure of affective detachment (and thus what Elias called 'reality congruence') to the study of human beings. This is evident, for example, in the relationship between Elias' theory and psychoanalysis. Elias borrowed and adapted many Freudian concepts, such as that of 'repression'; but he was also critical of Freud for assuming that the structure of the mental apparatus as he had described it was universal and relatively ahistorical. Elias considered that Freud, like most of his contemporaries, was trapped (or still too 'involved') in the human self-image typical of modernity, one that regarded the opposition between 'individual' psyches and 'social' constraints as a static epistemological given. The constructionism implicit in Elias' theory thus assumes a fundamental plasticity of emotional experience, while positing the availability of universal psychological mechanisms for the moulding of that experience.

The selections from *The Civilizing Process* that we have included in this volume touch on these multiple aspects and valences of the theory. The first part addresses changes in aggressiveness, underscoring the importance that Elias ascribed to violence and to the relative degree of pacification in a society for the purposes of explaining changes in emotional experience and expression. The second part of the text focuses on the concept of 'psychologization', illustrating the pivotal importance of the European courts as sites for the exponential development of capacities for emotional detachment, observation and self-observation.

Abram De Swaan is one of a group of Dutch sociologists who have applied and developed Elias' insights to the study of more contemporary social phenomena. This extract from an essay entitled 'The politics of agoraphobia' (1990) presents an analytical framework for understanding how social developments 'may have altered the intimate relations between people, so that the difficulties they experience with themselves and with one another may have become translatable into the vocabulary of psychotherapy and suitable for treatment as psychic problems'. The argument developed in the text speaks to a number of interrelated theoretical concerns. The broadest of these is the question of whether the relaxation of codes of behaviour and the 'informalization' of many social relations, especially evident since the 1960s, signifies a reversal in the direction of the 'civilizing process' – a movement towards decreasing self-restraint. The answer is a resounding 'no': informalization involves new and subtler forms of affective self-restraint and self-discipline, and these are associated to the proliferation of a range of psychic problems. De Swaan thus takes issue with the constructionist notion that the emergence of psychic problems in their contemporary form is a consequence of the rise of the profession of psychotherapy. According to the constructionist argument, professional and bureaucratic institutions have provided a vocabulary of troubles through which the lay public construct their definition and experience of everyday difficulties, and thereby also the presentation of their complaints. While this may be true on one level, argues De Swaan, the explanation is reductive and simplistic, for it fails to take into account the context of wider changes in the patterns of mutual interdependence between individuals. De Swaan focuses on a transformation in the management of power relations that is implicit in processes of 'informalization', which he describes as a transition from 'management by command' to 'management by negotiation'. Against this background, a range of psychic problems can be interpreted as ways of 'opting out' of forms of social interaction that are not as liberating as their rhetoric often suggests.

The fourth and final extract in this section is from a chapter by Peter and Deborah Stearns, where the authors discuss issues of causation and timing in the historical study of emotions. In the chapter as a whole, Stearns and Stearns present a number of methodological choices in relation to the problem of causation in historical research. One choice is between taking changes in specific emotions the explanatory focus, or adopting a larger, meta-historical focus of analysis by looking at changes in general frameworks, or 'emotional styles'. A focus on larger frameworks assumes 'that changes in individual emotion follow simply from the larger innovations'. These issues of scale in causation have rarely been considered by historians, they claim, but are in fact methodologically crucial. A second choice involved in the analysis of historical change concerns the balance between 'functionalist' and 'culturalist' explanations. Functionalist explanations of emotional change interpret such change as an adaptation to novel social conditions (such as industrialization and urbanization, in the modern period). Culturalist explanations, on the other hand, examine change in connection with factors such as the nature of dominant discourses (e.g. religious vs scientific, and variations within these), and changes in the media employed by advice-givers and educators. While outlining these methodological and analytical alternatives, the authors stress that they are not mutually exclusive and that causation, in most instances, is 'multifaceted'. Our selection from this chapter focuses on the discussion of causation in relation to changes in specific emotions.

References

Rosenwein, B. H. (2002) 'Worrying about emotions in history', *American Historical Review*, 107 (3): 821–845.

Stearns, P. N. and Stearns, C. Z. (1985) 'Emotionology: clarifying the history of emotions and emotional standards', *The American Historical Review*, 90 (4): 813–836.

Chapter 1

Thomas Dixon

FROM PASSIONS TO EMOTIONS

[. . .]

IN THIS BOOK I INVESTIGATE the creation of 'the emotions' as a psychological category. By seeing how this category was conceived, and by looking at the different psychological categories it replaced during the eighteenth and nineteenth centuries, I aim to provide readers with resources that will help them to step back from the contemporary obviousness of the existence and importance of 'the emotions' and to ask fundamental questions about this category's meaning and value. In other words, I hope my historical account will stimulate philosophical and psychological reflection. Of particular importance to this story is the displacement, in the history of systematic psychological theorising, of more differentiated typologies (which included appetites, passions, affections and sentiments) by a single over-arching category of emotions during the nineteenth century. Perhaps these past typologies will give readers pause for thought, and encourage them to ask whether the emotions, as we think of them today in psychology and philosophy, really form a coherent category.[1] I will suggest that a more differentiated typology would be a useful tool, and would help us to avoid making sweeping claims about all 'emotions' being good or bad things, rational or irrational, virtuous or vicious. . . .

My argument about the historical provenance of modern theories of the emotions is revisionist, especially with respect to Robert Solomon's thesis in his influential book *The Passions: Emotions and the Meaning of Life* (1976, 1993).[2] Solomon's thesis is, in short, that Western thinkers have been prone, right up to the late twentieth century, to take a negative view of the emotions and to think of them as inherently bodily, involuntary and irrational. Solomon blames this negative view of emotions on the influence of rationalist views (in which reason and the emotions are antagonists) that have been dominant among Western philosophers in general and certain Christian theologians in particular.

Solomon's was the first in a spate of books in recent decades that all seek, in one way or another, to rehabilitate the emotions. . . . Many of these writers also echo Solomon's thesis that from antiquity up until the late twentieth century philosophers and psychologists have generally, and misguidedly, thought of reason and the emotions as antagonists. . . . One of my aims in this book is to show how these views on the history of ideas about passions and emotions are themselves, in certain respects, mythical and erroneous.

The historical story I tell here turns Solomon's view on its head. I argue that it was in fact the recent departure from traditional views about the passions (not the influence of those views) that led to the creation of a category of 'emotions' that was conceived in opposition to reason, intellect and will. The category of emotions, conceived as a set of morally disengaged, bodily, non-cognitive and involuntary feelings, is a recent invention. Prior to the creation of the emotions as an over-arching category, more subtlety had been possible on these questions. The 'affections', and the 'moral sentiments', for example, could be understood as both rational and voluntary movements of the soul, while still being subjectively warm and lively psychological states. It is not the case that prior to the 1970s no one had realised that thinking, willing and feeling were (and should be) interwined in one way or another. Almost everybody had realised this. Too many contemporary writers still appeal, nonetheless, to the idea . . . that either a particular individual, or school of thought, or period, or even the entire history of philosophy has been characterised by the view that the emotions . . . are entirely insidious and are to be subjected at all times to almighty reason. Anything more than the briefest of glances at the history of thought establishes that this is a thoroughly untenable idea, even when applied to Stoic or Christian philosophers (those most often accused of passion- or emotion-hatred).[3] [. . .]

It is an immensely striking fact of the history of English-language psychological thought that during the period between c.1800 and c.1850 a wholesale change in established vocabulary occurred such that those engaged in theoretical discussions about phenomena including hope, fear, love, hate, joy, sorrow, anger and the like no longer primarily discussed the passions or affections of the soul, nor the sentiments, but almost invariably referred to 'the emotions'. This transition is as striking as if established conceptual terms such as 'reason' or 'memory' or 'imagination' or 'will' had been quite suddenly replaced by a wholly new category.

The puzzling historical question, then, at the heart of this book (a question that, equally puzzlingly, has rarely been posed before, let alone answered) is: when and why did English-language psychological writers stop using 'passions', 'affections' and 'sentiments' as their primary categories and start referring instead to the 'emotions'? . . .

One important element of my answer to this central historical question is that it was the secularisation of psychology that gave rise to the creation and adoption of the new category of 'emotions' and influenced the way it was originally and has subsequently been conceived. [. . .]

The initial backdrop I provide to this story of gradual, complex and incomplete secularisation, takes the form of an analysis of patristic and scholastic Christian theologies of the soul. Classical Christian theologians, especially St Augustine of Hippo and St Thomas Aquinas, . . . produced models of the human soul in which the passions and appetites, which were movements of the lower animal soul, were distinguished from the affections, which were acts of the higher rational soul. The appetites were hunger, thirst and sexual desire. The disobedience of the lower soul to the higher, and of the body to the soul, experienced in sexual appetite and in the passions was a sign of, and punishment for, the original sin of Adam and Eve. Often, passions were unruly and disturbed the body; they included love, hate, hope, fear and anger. The higher affections of love, sympathy and joy were signs of relatedness to God and held out the possibility of reunion with God. The affections were also signs of the order or direction of the will. A carnal will was affected by worldly objects and, ultimately, by love of self; a holy will's affections were for goodness, truth and, ultimately, God.

It is important to have an understanding of the importance of the will to Christian morality and Christian psychology in order to appreciate the significance of its gradual disappearance in eighteenth- and nineteenth-century works. The destiny of each person was determined by freely taken voluntary decisions – decisions of the individual will. The will was divided by Aquinas into two 'appetites': the higher intellectual appetite (the will proper), whose movements were the affections; and the lower, non-rational sense appetite, whose movements were the appetites and passions. It is particularly important, then, to realise that – contrary to popular opinion – classical Christian views about reason and the passions were equivalent neither to the view that reason and the 'emotions' are inevitably at war, nor to the idea that 'emotions' overpower us against our will. Appetites, passions and affections, on the classical Christian view, were all movements of different parts of the will, and the affections, at least, were potentially informed by reason.

Chapter 3 examines some of the movements away from classical Christian psychology towards more secular and mechanistic views of passions and affections in the eighteenth century, as well as ways that the traditional Christian picture was maintained and developed. Christian thinkers such as Joseph Butler, Jonathan Edwards and Thomas Reid adapted the traditional models in various ways. The tendencies to see passions and affections as 'mechanisms' designed by God, and as 'perceptions', were both symptomatic of psychologies in which the will had become less important. Passions and affections were conceived increasingly as mini-agents in their own right, or as a faculty of their own, rather than as acts or movements of the individual will. This had significant moral and theological implications. The discourse of 'moral sentiments' specifically and the culture of 'sentiment' and 'sentimentalism' more generally, which were fascinating features of this same period, are also referred to in chapter 3. These serve as further examples of the variety of categories and conceptualisations used during this period, which was an age of passions and sentiments as much as it was an 'Age of Reason'.

The initial baptism of the term 'emotions' . . . in its modern sense occurred in the school of Scottish empiricist philosophers and mental scientists from David Hume's *Treatise of Human Nature* (1739–40) onwards. The most important text was Thomas Brown's *Lectures on the Philosophy of the Human Mind* (1820) in which 'emotions' was the term adopted for all those feelings that were neither sensations nor intellectual states. Brown developed a new terminology and classification of mental states, motivated by a desire to break away from traditional faculty psychology, and to create a de-Christianised and scientific alternative. 'Emotions' included a wide variety of states that had previously been differentiated, and many of which had been considered active powers of the soul. The term 'emotions' was baptised in a way that suggested these mental states were passive and non-cognitive. The category was over-inclusive and was embedded in a tradition committed to the application of scientific methodology to the study of the mind. However, the application of scientific method and commitment to Christianity were by no means mutually exclusive: the evangelical theologian Thomas Chalmers adopted and even strengthened the non-cognitive, involuntary and mechanical tenor of Brown's 'feeling' theory of emotions.

. . . Physical science replaced mental science as the dominant methodology in works on emotions by Herbert Spencer, Alexander Bain and Charles Darwin in the 1850s to 1870s. The assumption, still made by Christian philosophers and psychologists at this time, that passions and affections were instances of the soul acting upon or using the body, was replaced with the assumption that emotions were instances of the brain and nerves acting upon other parts of the body. The mind or soul per se was not given an active role. Physiological and evolutionary thinkers were quicker to appropriate the category 'emotions' than thinkers within the Christian tradition, some of whom were still speaking the language of 'will', 'passions' and 'affections' in the 1870s. So use of the term was generally indicative of familiarity and sympathy with Brown's secularised mental science. The relationship between these physicalist thinkers and the moral philosophers and natural theologians whose work they were developing upon, was not always straightforward, however. Darwin's relationship with Scottish moral philosophy and Sir Charles Bell's design theology serves as an illustration of these complex relationships. The theories of emotion and expression produced by this generation of scientific psychologists were shaped both positively and negatively by theological and religious ideas. Some Christian and theistic psychologists (for example, William Lyall or James McCosh) adopted the new category of emotions but opposed the physicalist approach of the new emotions theorists and proposed mentalistic and cognitive alternatives. . . .

More presentist and narrower histories of psychology might begin their account of the history of psychological theories of emotions with William James. In this history, in contrast, James' infamous theory is depicted as the culmination of complex processes of secularisation and innovation in psychological discourse. James' iconic 1884 article 'What is an emotion?' made explicit in a new way the tacit epiphenomenalism of the physiological-evolutionary theory of emotions. His theory of emotions – that they were felt awarenesses of visceral activity – was a flagship theory of the new scientific phychological profession. James inverted the traditional assumption that the outward bodily manifestations of emotions were caused by either the activity of the soul or even – as in the case of the physiological-evolutionary school – by the activity of the brain; the viscera were made primary and the brain and its mind secondary by James. [. . .]

Notes

1   For a very helpful article summarising recent debates about the natural kind status of 'emotion', and arguing that 'emotion' is indeed a natural kind term, see Charland (2002).
2   Solomon (1993).
3   On Stoic and early Christian attitudes to passions, will and reason, see Sorabji (2000).

References

Charland, L. (2002) 'The natural kind status of emotion', *British Journal for the Philosophy of Science*. 53(4): 1–27.
Solomon, R. (2003) *The Passions: Emotions and the Meaning of Life*. Indianapolis: Hackett.
Sorabji, R. (2000) *Emotion and Peace of Mind: From Stoic Agitation to Christian Temptation*. Oxford: Oxford University Press.

Chapter 2

Norbert Elias

ON CHANGES IN AGGRESSIVENESS

[. . .]

THE STANDARD OF AGGRESSIVENESS, ITS tone and intensity, is not at present exactly uniform among the different nations of the West. But these differences, which from close up often appear quite considerable, disappear if the aggressiveness of the "civilized" nations is compared to that of societies at a different stage of affect control. Compared to the battle fury of Abyssinian warriors—admittedly powerless against the technical apparatus of the civilized army—or to the frenzy of the different tribes at the time of the Great Migrations, the aggressiveness of even the most warlike nations of the civilized world appears subdued. Like all other instincts, it is bound, even in directly warlike actions, by the advanced state of the division of functions, and by the resulting greater dependence of individuals on each other and on the technical apparatus. It is confined and tamed by innumerable rules and prohibitions that have become self-constraints. It is as much transformed, "refined," "civilized," as all the other forms of pleasure, and its immediate and uncontrolled violence appears only in dreams or in isolated outbursts that we account for as pathological.

In this area of the affects, the theater of the hostile collisions between men, the same historical transformation has taken place as in all others. No matter at what point the Middle Ages stand in this transformation, it will again suffice here to take the standard of their secular ruling class, the warriors, as a starting point, to illustrate the overall pattern of this development. The release of the affects in battle in the Middle Ages was no longer, perhaps, quite so uninhibited as in the early period of the Great Migrations. But it was open and uninhabited enough compared to the standard of modern times. In the latter, cruelty and joy in the destruction and torment of others, like the proof of physical superiority, are placed under an increasingly strong social control anchored in the state organization. All these forms of pleasure, limited by threats of displeasure, gradually come to express themselves only indirectly, in a "refined" form. And only at times of social upheaval or where social control is looser (e.g., in colonial regions) do they break out more directly, uninhibitedly, less impeded by shame and repugnance.

Life in medieval society tended in the opposite direction. Rapine, battle, hunting of men and animals—all these were vital necessities which, in accordance with the structure of society, were visible to all. And thus, for the mighty and strong, they formed part of the pleasures of life.

"I tell you," says a war hymn attributed to the minstrel Bertran de Born,[1] "that neither eating, drinking, nor sleep has as much savor for me as to hear the cry 'Forwards!' from both sides, and horses without riders shying and whinnying, and the cry 'Help! Help!', and to see the small and the great fall to the grass at the ditches and the dead pierced by the wood of the lances decked with banners."

Even the literary formulation gives an impression of the original savagery of feeling. In another place Bertran de Born sings: "The pleasant season is drawing nigh when our ships shall land, when King Richard shall come, merry and proud as he never was before. Now we shall see gold and silver spent; the newly built stonework will crack to the heart's desire, walls crumble, towers topple and collapse, our enemies taste prison and chains. I love the melee of blue and vermilion shields, the many-colored ensigns and the banners, the tents and rich pavilions spread out on the plain, the breaking lances, the pierced shields, the gleaming helmets that are split, the blows given and received."

War, one of the *chansons de geste* declares, is to descend as the stronger on the enemy, to hack down his vines, uproot his trees, lay waste his land, take his castles by storm, fill in his wells, and kill his people. . . .

A particular pleasure is taken in mutilating prisoners: "By my troth," says the king in the same *chanson*, "I laugh at what you say, I care not a fig for your threats, I shall shame every knight I have taken, cut off his nose or his ears. If he is a sergeant or a merchant he will lose a foot or an arm."[2]

Such things are not only said in song. These epics are an integral part of social life. And they express the feelings of the listeners for whom they are intended far more directly than most of our literature. They may exaggerate in detail. Even in the age of chivalry money already had, on occasions, some power to subdue and transform the affects. Usually only the poor and lowly, for whom no considerable ransom could be expected, were mutilated, and the knights who commanded ransoms were spared. The chronicles which directly document social life bear ample witness to these attitudes.

They were mostly written by clerics. The value judgments they contain are therefore often those of the weaker group threatened by the warrior class. Nevertheless, the picture they transmit to us is quite genuine. "He spends his life," we read of a knight, "in plundering, destroying churches, falling upon pilgrims, oppressing widows and orphans. He takes particular pleasure in mutilating the innocent. In a single monastery, that of the black monks of Sarlat, there are 150 men and women whose hands he has cut off or whose eyes he has put out. And his wife is just as cruel. She helps him with his executions. It even gives her pleasure to torture the poor women. She had their breasts hacked off or their nails torn off so that they were incapable of work."[3]

Such affective outbursts may still occur as exceptional phenomena, as a "pathological" degeneration, in later phases of social development. But here no punitive social power existed. The only threat, the only danger that could instill fear was that of being overpowered in battle by a stronger opponent. Leaving aside a small elite, rapine, pillage, and murder were standard practice in the warrior society of this time, as is noted by Luchaire, the historian of thirteenth-century French society. There is little evidence that things were different in other countries or in the centuries that followed. Outbursts of cruelty did not exclude one from social life. They were not outlawed. The pleasure in killing and torturing others was great, and it was a socially permitted pleasure. To a certain extent, the social structure even pushed its members in this direction, making it seem necessary and practically advantageous to behave in this way.

What, for example, ought to be done with prisoners? There was little money in this society. With regard to prisoners who could pay and who, moreover, were members of one's own class, one exercised some degree of restraint. But the others? To keep them meant to feed them. To return them meant to enhance the wealth and fighting power of the enemy. For subjects (i.e., working, serving, and fighting hands) were a part of the wealth of the ruling class of that time. So prisoners were killed or sent back so mutilated that they were unfitted for war service and work. The same applied to destroying fields, filling in wells, and cutting down trees. In a predominantly agrarian society, in which immobile possessions represented the major part of property, this too served to weaken the enemy. The stronger affectivity of behavior was to a certain degree socially necessary. People behaved in a socially useful way and took pleasure in doing so. And it is entirely in keeping with the lesser degree of social control and constraint of instinctual life that this joy in destruction could sometimes give way, through a sudden identification with the victim, and doubtless also as an expression of the fear and guilt produced by the permanent precariousness of this life; to extremes of pity. The victor of today was defeated tomorrow by some accident, captured, and imperiled. In the midst of this perpetual rising and falling, this alternation of the human hunts of wartime with the animal hunts or tournaments that were the diversions of "peacetime," little could be predicted. The future was relatively uncertain even for those who had fled the "world"; only God and the loyalty of a few people who held together had any permanence. Fear reigned everywhere; one had to be on one's guard all the time. And just as people's fate could change abruptly, so their joy could turn into fear and this fear, in its turn, could give way, equally abruptly, to submission to some new pleasure.

The majority of the secular ruling class of the Middle Ages led the life of leaders of armed bands. This formed the taste and habits of individuals. Reports left to us by that society yield by and large, a picture similar to those of feudal societies in our own times; and they show a comparable standard of behavior. Only a small elite, of which more will be said later, stood out to some extent from this norm.

The warrior of the Middle Ages not only loved battle, he lived in it. He spent his youth preparing for battle. When he came of age he was knighted, and waged war as long as his strength permitted, into old age. His life had no other function. His dwelling place was a watchtower, a fortress, at once a weapon of attack and defense. If by accident, by exception, he lived in peace, he needed at least the illusion of war. He fought in tournaments, and these tournaments often differed little from real battles.[4]

"For the society of that time war was the normal state," says Luchaire of the thirteenth century. And Huizinga says of the fourteenth and fifteenth centuries: "The chronic form which war was wont to take, the continuous disruption of town and country by every kind of dangerous rabble, the permanent threat of harsh and unreliable law enforcement . . . nourished a feeling of universal uncertainty."[5]

In the fifteenth century, as in the ninth or thirteenth, the knight still gives expression to his joy in war, even if it is no longer so open and intact as earlier.

"War is a joyous thing." It is Jean de Bueil who says this. He has fallen into disfavor with the king. And now he dictates to his servant his life story. This is in the year 1465. It is no longer the completely free, independent knight who speaks, the little king in his domain. It is someone who is himself in service: "War is a joyous thing. We love each other so much in war. If we see that our cause is just and our kinsmen fight boldly, tears come to our eyes. A sweet joy rises in our hearts, in the feeling of our honest loyalty to each other; and seeing our friend so bravely exposing his body to danger in order to keep and fulfill the commandment of our Creator, we resolve to go forward and die or live with him and never leave him on account of love. This brings such delight that anyone who has not felt it cannot say how wonderful it is. Do you think that someone who feels this is afraid of death? Not in the least! He is so strengthened, so delighted, that he does not know where he is. Truly he fears nothing in the world!"

This is the joy of battle, certainly, but it is no longer the direct pleasure in the human hunt, in the flashing of swords, in the neighing of steeds, in the fear and death of the enemy—how fine it is to hear them cry "Help, help!" or see them lying with their bodies torn open! Now the pleasure lies in the closeness to one's friends, the enthusiasm for a just cause, and more than earlier we find the joy of battle serving as an intoxicant to overcome fear.

Very simple and powerful feelings speak here. One kills, gives oneself up wholly to the fight, sees one's friend fight. One fights at his side. One forgets where one is. One forgets death itself. It is splendid. What more? [. . .]

It is the structure of society that demands and generates a specific standard of emotional control. "We," says Luchaire, "with our peaceful manners and habits, with the care and protection that the modern state lavishes on the property and person of each individual," can scarcely form an idea of this other society.

> At that time the country had disintegrated into provinces, and the inhabitants of each province formed a kind of little nation that abhorred all the others. The provinces were in turn divided into a multitude of feudal estates whose owners fought each other incessantly. Not only the great lords, the barons, but also the smaller lords of the manor lived in desolate isolation and were uninterruptedly occupied in waging war against their "sovereigns," their equals, or their subjects. In addition, there was constant rivalry between town and town, village and village, valley and valley, and constant wars between neighbors

that seemed to arise from the very multiplicity of these territorial units.[6]

This description helps to see more precisely something which so far has been stated mainly in general terms, namely, the connection between social structure and personality structure. In this society there is no central power strong enough to compel people to restraint. But if in this or that region the power of a central authority grows, if over a larger or smaller area the people are forced to live in peace with each other, the molding of affects and the standards of the economy of instincts are very gradually changed as well. As will be discussed in more detail later, the reserve and "mutual consideration" of people increase, first in normal everyday social life. And the discharge of affects in physical attack is limited to certain temporal and spatial enclaves. Once the monopoly of physical power has passed to central authorities, not every strong man can afford the pleasure of physical attack. This is now reserved to those few legitimized by the central authority (e.g., the police against the criminal), and to larger numbers only in exceptional times of war or revolution, in the socially legitimized struggle against internal or external enemies.

But even these temporal or spatial enclaves within civilized society in which belligerence is allowed freer play—above all, wars between nations—have become more impersonal, and lead less and less to an affective discharge having the immediacy and intensity of the medieval phase. The necessary restraint and transformation of aggression cultivated in the everyday life of civilized society cannot be simply reversed, even in these enclaves. All the same, this could happen more quickly than we might suppose, had not the direct physical combat between a man and his hated adversary given way to a mechanized struggle demanding a strict control of the affects. Even in war in the civilized world, the individual can no longer give free rein to his pleasure, spurred on by the sight of the enemy, but must fight, no matter how he may feel, according to the commands of invisible or only indirectly visible leaders, against a frequently invisible or only indirectly visible enemy. And immense social upheaval and urgency, heightened by carefully concerted propaganda, are needed to reawaken and legitimize in large masses of people the socially outlawed instincts, the joy in killing and destruction that have been repressed from everyday civilized life.

Admittedly, these affects do have, in a "refined," rationalized form, their legitimate and exactly defined place in the everyday life of civilized society. And this is very characteristic of the kind of transformation through which the civilization of the affects takes place. For example, belligerence and aggression find socially permitted expression in sporting contests. And they are expressed especially in "spectating" (e.g., at boxing matches), in the imaginary identification with a small number of combatants to whom moderate and precisely regulated scope is granted for the release of such affects. And this living-out of affects in spectating or even in merely listening (e.g., to a radio commentary) is a particularly characteristic feature of civilized society. It partly determines the development of books and the theater, and decisively influences the role of the cinema in our world. This transformation of what manifested itself originally as an active, often aggressive expression of pleasure, into the passive, more ordered pleasure of spectating (i e., a mere pleasure of the eye) is already initiated in education, in conditioning precepts for young people. [. . .]

The muting of drives: psychologization and rationalization

"Life at court", La Bruyère writes,[7] "is a serious, melancholy game, which requires of us that we arrange our pieces and our batteries, have a plan, follow it, foil that of our adversary, sometimes take risks and play on impulse. And after all our measures and meditations we are in check, sometimes checkmate."

At the court, above all at the great absolutist court, there was formed for the first time a kind of society and human relationships having structural characteristics which from now on, over a long stretch of Western history and through many variations, again and again play a decisive part. In the midst of a large populated area which by and large is free of physical violence, a "good society" is formed. But even if the use of physical violence now recedes from human intercourse, if even duelling is now forbidden, people now exert pressure and force on each other in a wide variety of different ways. Life in this circle is in no way peaceful. Very many people are continuously dependent on each other. Competition for prestige and royal favour is intense. "Affaires", disputes over rank and favour, do not cease. If the sword no longer plays so great a role as the means of decision, it is replaced by intrigue, conflicts in which careers and social success are contested with words. They demand and produce other qualities than did the armed struggles that had to be fought out with weapons in one's hand. Continuous reflection, foresight, and calculation, self-control, precise and articulate regulation of one's own effects, knowledge of the whole terrain, human and non-human, in which one acts, become more and more indispensable preconditions of social success.

Every individual belongs to a "clique", a social circle which supports him when necessary; but the groupings change. He enters alliances, if possible with people ranking high at court. But rank at court can change very quickly; he has rivals; he has open and concealed enemies. And the tactics of his struggles, as of his alliances, demand careful consideration. The degree of aloofness or familiarity with everyone must be carefully measured; each greeting, each conversation has a significance over and above what is actually said or done. They indicate the standing of a person; and they contribute to the formation of court opinion on his standing:

"Let a favourite pay close heed to himself: for if he does not keep me waiting as long as usual in his antechamber; if his face is more open, if he frowns less, if he listens to me more willingly and accompanies me a little further when showing me out, I shall think that he is beginning to fall, and I shall be right."[8]

The court is a kind of stock exchange; as in every "good society", an estimate of the "value" of each individual is continuously being formed. But here his value has its real foundation not in the wealth or even the achievements or ability of the individual, but in the favour he enjoys with the king, the influence he has with other mighty ones, his importance in the play of courtly cliques. All this, favour, influence, importance, this whole complex and dangerous game in which physical force and direct affective outbursts are prohibited and a threat to existence, demands of each participant a constant foresight and an exact knowledge of every other, of his position and value in the network of courtly opinion; it exacts precise attunement of his own behaviour to this value. Every mistake, every careless step depresses the value of its perpetrator in courtly opinion; it may threaten his whole position at court.

"A man who knows the court is master of his gestures, of his eyes and his expression; he is deep, impenetrable. He dissimulates the bad turns he does, smiles at his enemies, suppresses his ill-temper, disguises his passions, disavows his heart, acts against his feelings."[9]

The transformation of the nobility in the direction of "civilized" behaviour is unmistakable. Here, it is not yet in all respects so profound and all-embracing as later in bourgeois society; for it is only towards their peers that the courtier and the court lady need to subject themselves to such constraint, and far less so towards their social inferiors. Quite apart from the fact that the pattern of drive- and affect-control is different in courtly from that in bourgeois society, the awareness that this control is exercised for social reasons is more alive. Opposing inclinations do not yet wholly vanish from waking consciousness; self-constraint has not yet become so completely an apparatus of habits operating almost automatically and including all human relationships. But it is already quite clear how human beings are becoming more complex, and internally split in a quite specific way. Each man, as it were, confronts himself. He "conceals his passions", "disavows his heart", "acts against his feelings". The pleasure or inclination of the moment is restrained in anticipation of the disagreeable consequences of its indulgence; and it is, indeed, the same mechanism as that by which adults—whether parents or other persons—increasingly instil a stable "superego" in children. The momentary drive and affect impulses are, as it were, held back and mastered by the fore-knowledge of the later displeasure, by the fear of a future pain, until this fear finally opposes the forbidden behaviour and inclinations by force of habit, even if no other person is directly present, and the energy of such inclinations is channelled into a harmless direction not threatened by any displeasure.

In keeping with the transformation of society, of interpersonal relationships, the affective make-up of the individual is also reconstructed: as the series of actions and the number of people on whom the individual and his actions constantly depend are increased, the habit of foresight over longer chains grows stronger. And as the behaviour and personality structure of the individual change, so does his manner of considering others. His image of them becomes richer in nuances, freer of spontaneous emotions: it is "psychologized".

Where the structure of social functions allows the individual greater scope for actions under the influence of momentary impulses than is the case at court, it is neither necessary nor possible to consider very deeply the nature of another person's consciousness and affects, or what hidden motives may underlie his behaviour. If at court calculation meshes with calculation, in simpler societies affect directly engages affect. This strength of the immediate affects, however, binds the individual to a smaller number of behavioural options: someone is friend or foe, good or evil; and depending on how one perceives another in terms of these black and white affective patterns, so one behaves. Everything seems directly related to feeling. That the sun shines, or lightning flashes, that someone laughs or knits his brow, all this appeals more directly to the affects of the perceiver. And as it excites him here and now in a friendly or unfriendly way, he takes it as if it were meant this way especially for him. It does not enter his head that all this, a flash of lightning that almost strikes him, a face that offends him, are to be explained by remote connections that have nothing directly to do with himself. People only develop a more long-sighted view of nature and other people to the extent that the advancing division of functions and their daily involvement in long human chains accustom them to such a view and a greater restraint of the affects. Only then is the veil which the passions draw before the eyes slowly lifted, and a new world comes into view— a world whose course is friendly or hostile to the individual person without being intended to be so, a chain of events that need to be contemplated dispassionately over long stretches if their connections are to be disclosed.[10]

Like conduct generally, the perception of things and people also becomes affectively more neutral in the course of the civilizing process. The "world picture" gradually becomes less directly determined by human wishes and fears, and more strongly oriented to what we call "experience" or "the empirical", to sequences with their own immanent regularities. Just as today, in a further spurt in this direction, the course of history and society is gradually emerging from the mists of personal affects and involvement, from the haze of collective longings and fears, and beginning to appear as a relatively autonomous nexus of events, so too with nature and—within smaller confines—with human beings. It is particularly in the circles of court life that what we would today call a "psychological" view of man develops, a more precise observation of others and oneself in terms of longer series of motives and causal connections, because it is here that vigilant self-control and perpetual observation of others are among the elementary prerequisites for the preservation of one's social position. But this is only one example of how what we call the "orientation to experience", the observation of events within a lengthening and broadening nexus of inter-dependence, slowly begins to develop at exactly the point where the structure of society itself compels the individual to restrain his momentary affects and transform his libidinal energies to a higher degree.

Saint-Simon in one place observes someone with whom he is on an uncertain footing. He describes his own behaviour in this situation as follows: "I soon noticed that he was growing colder; I closely followed his conduct towards me to avoid any confusion between what might be accidental in a man burdened with prickly affairs, and what I suspected. My suspicions were confirmed, causing me to withdraw from him entirely without in the slightest appearing to do so."[11]

This courtly art of human observation—unlike what we usually call "psychology" today—is never concerned with the individual in isolation, as if the essential features of his behaviour were independent of his relations to others, and as if he related to others, so to speak, only retrospectively. The approach here is far closer to reality, in that the individual is always seen in his social context, *as a human being in his relations to others, as an individual in a social situation.*

It was pointed out above[12] that the precepts on behaviour of the sixteenth century differ from those of the preceding centuries less in terms of their content than in their tone, their changed affective atmosphere; psychological insights, personal observations, begin to play a larger part. A comparison between the precepts of Erasmus or Della Casa and the corresponding medieval rules shows this clearly. Investigation of the social changes of this time, the transformation of human relationships that took place, provides an explanation. This "psychologization" of rules of conduct, or, more precisely, their greater permeation by observation and experience, is an expression of the accelerated courtization of the upper class and of the closer integration of all parts of society in this period. Signs of a change in this direction are certainly not to be found only in writings recording the standard of "good behaviour" of the time; we find them equally in works devoted to the entertainment of this class. The observation of people that life in the courtly circle demands finds its literary expression in an art of human portraiture. [. . .]

Notes

1   A. Luchaire, *La societé française au temps de Philippe-Auguste* (Paris, 1909), p. 273.
2   Ibid., p. 275.
3   Ibid., p. 272.
4   Ibid., p. 278.
5   I. Huzinga, *Herbst des Mittelalters, Studien über Lebens und Geistesform des 14 und 15 Jahrhunderts in Frankreich und in den Niederlanden* (Munich, 1924), p. 94.
6   Luchaire, *La societé française*, pp. 278f.
7   La Bruyère, *Caractères*, 'De la cow' (Paris, Hachette, 1922), *Oeuvres*, vol. 2, p. 237, No. 64 . . .
8   La Bruyère, op. cit., p. 247, No. 94.
9   Ibid., p. 211, No. 2; cf. Also p. 211, No. 10: "The court is like an edifice of marble; I mean it is composed of men who are very hard, but very polished." Cf. also n. 134.
10 See in this context Norbert Elias, "Problems of Involvement and Detachment", *British Journal of Sociology*, 7 (1956), pp. 226–52. [*Author's note to the translation*]
11 Saint-Simon, *Mémoires* (nouv. éd. Par A. de Boislisle) (Paris, 1910), vol. 22 (1711), p. 63.
12 *The History of Manners*, pp. 56ff, partic.62–3.

Chapter 3

Abram De Swaan

THE POLITICS OF AGORAPHOBIA

[. . .]

EARNINGS OF THEIR OWN AND a new occupational prestige, acquired independently of husbands and fathers, made working women less dependent upon their husbands and thus the balance of dependencies between spouses began to shift somewhat in favour of women. Around 1890, the limitations on public appearance by women were quickly disappearing (for example, in the Netherlands). . . . And yet, at a time when restrictions on the movement of women in west European cities were decreasing, psychiatric publications began to include case descriptions of *Platzschwindel*: agoraphobia. Actions that had been socially prohibited before, remained unfeasible to some even after they had become permissible, out of an unreasoned anxiety – a vague fear that had lost its support in contemporary public discussion and could now only be expressed in psychiatric terms as a problem to be managed and treated by psychiatrists.

[. . .]

These observations do not imply that contemporary agoraphobics directly inherited these anxieties from their great-grandmothers who were prohibited from going where they now fear to tread. But they do convey that nineteenth-century society produced circumstances in which bourgeois families, out of concern for their safety and status, imposed restrictions on the movement of their womenfolk; these preoccupations soon acquired added meanings of respectability, chastity, and dependency, were transformed into collective fantasies about public order, sexuality, and violence in the street and about the family as the 'haven in a heartless world'. Such fantasies disappeared from public discourse but survived in the intimate family circle as available themes to be elaborated into a particular agoraphobic relationship. 'Thus the unconscious of modern women contains many remnants of the conscious misperceptions of her grandmother.' Or, rather, all sorts of ideas that were taken very seriously in one generation are gradually abandoned as subjects of adult discussion in another, but these notions continue to be passed on as jokes, nursery tales, innuendoes, and threats and are added to the cultural heritage of later generations. Just as some poets use the themes of half-forgotten legends and folk tales to compose works of art, other people select themes from this shadowy childhood folklore to construct private fantasies that will guide them the more compulsively the more completely they have repressed them. In other words, there is no collective unconscious, there are the abandoned opinions and *idées reçues* of former generations surviving as inconsequential and unverifiable prattle, elaborated upon in infantile fantasy, repressed in a later stage. That may explain the striking similarity and constancy of so many very private fantasies. Although the nineteenth-century restrictions upon the movement of bourgeois women have relaxed, and her dependency on her husband has become less one-sided, the agoraphobic relationship reproduces such restrictions while denying any other motive except an inexplicable anxiety.

It is now time to return to the general question in this chapter: how global developments of society may have altered the intimate relations between people, so that the difficulties they experience with themselves and one another may have become translatable into the vocabulary of psychotherapy and suitable for treatment as psychic problems. Rather than dealing with the problem directly in its full and formidable proportions, it was alluded to in an example: the restriction and relaxation of rules for the movement of women in public during the nineteenth century and the subsequent emergence of agoraphobia.

The early development of capitalism resulted in a strong limitation on the presence in public of urban bourgeois women, whereas bourgeois men could continue to move wherever they wished and, possibly, could allow themselves greater liberty than before towards women in public and with public women, since their own daughters and wives had disappeared from the streets. In the past hundred years, however, women have begun to move more freely in public and, possibly, bourgeois men have lost some of their privileges in approaching women in public. On balance, bourgeois urban men and women have become more equal, at least in this respect. This partial equalization of intimate relations in the course of the past hundred years, however, is not limited to this one aspect in the balance of dependencies between men and women, but covers almost all relations between the sexes. A degree of equalization has also occurred in the relations between parents and children, or between young and old in general. A similar decrease in social distance is developing between adjacent ranks in organizations, between those who used to be called 'superiors' and 'inferiors', and now often prefer to be viewed as members of a 'team'. But even as social distances between adjacent ranks within organizations decreased, with the growth of these organizations the number of such ranks increased, and with it the overall distance between the lowest echelons of production workers, consumers, clients, and the top echelon of company presidents, chairmen, and so on. This double movement may explain the conflicting reports on 'informalization' and 'alienation', the former going on among adjacent ranks, the latter between the lower and the uppermost strata. Finally, the distance between governments and their subjects has been decreasing, formerly in the long-term process of constitutional democratization and more recently in the dealings of participatory citizens' action groups with local and national authorities. . . .

A second line of long-term development in European countries concerns the increasing control of infantile and bodily impulses. Marx and his followers have described extensively how a relatively independent agrarian population was regimented and disciplined into the strict rhythms and routines of the industrial workforce. Weber has demonstrated the intimate connection between a puritan abstinence and the entrepreneurial style of life in early capitalism. Freud has argued that the discontents of civilization constituted its very essence, because well-ordered society exacts the renunciation of drive satisfaction. The gradual process of state formation and the increasing control of domestic violence implied a more equable, more flexible and long-term management of emotions, as Norbert Elias has suggested in *The Civilizing Process*.

Undoubtedly, the relations between people have become less volatile, impulsive, spontaneous, and violent since the Middle Ages, and people have found themselves compelled to steer their impulses more strictly, through external compulsion first, gradually through a social compulsion to self-compulsion, and finally mainly through self-compulsion. By the end of the nineteenth century, this had resulted in rather strict and limiting patterns of intercourse among the bourgeoisie and in severe and restrictive superego formations in middle-class citizens – very much the type of families and the type of patients Freud was familiar with. Unmistakably, these patterns have changed in the course of the twentieth century. This presents a theoretical problem to historical sociologists concerned with problems of societal change, family life, and character formation: how is this recent shift in manners to be interpreted and how can it be explained in terms of societal transformations? . . .

A first survey of contemporary mores suggests that the margins and the variety of acceptable behaviour have increased markedly since the First World War and even more quickly since the Second World War. Examples of the relaxation of restrictions on the movement of women in public are only one case in point. Many others may be added, especially in the realm of intimate relations: the practice of contraception, abortion, concubinage, promiscuity, divorce, homosexuality, pornography, masturbation . . . a wide gamut of sexual relations with oneself and with others has become mentionable, acceptable in many circles, thinkable for most people. But this observation often leads to the conclusion that the relaxation of restrictions also applies to other spheres of life. Although most people believe that violent behaviour is on the increase everywhere in the world, as a general statement this is unlikely to be true. [. . .]

The social acceptability of violent behaviour has probably not increased. In most countries fraternity initiation rites and bar brawls are quickly disappearing as male rituals. On the other hand, gangs of soccer supporters have become almost as violent as they used to be a before spectator sports became organized and broadcast. Paradoxically, an increased aversion among the public against violent behaviour may result in an increased visibility of such violence both in newspaper reporting of shocking incidents and in official statistics: indignant citizens are more prone to report, police to investigate, and courts to convict in cases that before went unremarked as routine roughness. Increasing sexual tolerance does not extend at all to violent forms of sexual conduct such as rape or flagellation; rather, the contrary is true: mounting indignation should not be interpreted as increasing incidence. People, including young, strong, and volatile people, are still being pressured to surrender the advantages and pleasures of physical strength and not to lay hands on others. Even as violence and torture are continually depicted in novels and on the screen, these scenes are without exception accompanied by messages of disapproval and by the punishment of whoever has abandoned himself to such lustful violence. This simultaneous excitation and its denial, this hypocrisy, used to be a characteristic of sexual pornography until recently; it conveys the severity of the prohibition and at the same time the effort it takes for people to give up these pleasures under the moral condemnation by others and their own conscience. This intertwining of disgrace and lust finally comes to characterize the pleasure itself. . . .

People, then, are not only supposed to contain their violent impulses, but there are other emotions they also must inhibit: all those manners of feeling and conduct with which one puts oneself above others are increasingly becoming unacceptable. Scorn for the defects of others, for their ugliness, disability, or indigence only serves to discredit the scoffer in the eyes of most contemporaries. The self-satisfied awareness and ostentatious display of one's superior social position, be it through wealth, descent, rank, or education, do not necessarily add to the deference one will receive, but may be held against one. Even the awareness that such rankings play a role at all in one's own and other people's thoughts is more and more denied. People pretend to be 'colour-blind', not to notice class differences in speech, dress, and demeanour, not to prescribe behaviour but to arrive at a definition of the problem together with the client, to discuss alternatives with co-workers rather than order their assistants around. Differences in social position are denied in every possible way, yet are betrayed in this very denial at the same time that the denial also contributes to diminishing the social distance. Equally, people are expected not to apply themselves in an effort to outdo others, through ambition and competition, because of a desire for fame, glory, honour, power, or the domination over others. This is not to say that people in fact no longer attempt to rise above others, but that they try to control the expression of these strivings in themselves, and especially in others, and that they attempt to convey the impression that they never sought aggrandizement – it just befell them. Nor is there much reason to suppose that people have relaxed their mutual pressure and self-discipline concerning habits of punctuality, reliability, discretion, cleanliness, hygiene, dietary restrictions, precision, and accuracy, whereas their meticulousness in operating and maintaining all sorts of machinery and in participating in automobile traffic has necessarily increased (the sociologically interesting development is not the incidence of road accidents, but their relative rarity and the imposition of a deadly discipline in traffic). A small minority of Bohemians and academics may have abandoned some of these 'anal virtues' to a degree, and in so doing they have become highly visible to university professors commenting on the spirit of the epoch. But at the same time, and almost unnoticed, many millions have each year joined the rigidly timed and regimented life in schools, factories, large organizations, the world of traffic, and of taxes.

Undeniably, the management of affect is changing, but the widely held assumption that, all things considered, restrictions are loosening does not hold; not when it comes to the control of violence, nor with regard to the control of self-aggrandizement or of laxity. It does not even apply to the management of sexuality. As will become apparent from a second look at the development of sexual relations, these have become subject to different but certainly no less restrictive controls. Returning to the list of sexual manners that opened this section on changing morals, it appears to contain only those sexual activities involving no damage or degradation to others. (In the abortion debate, the issue is precisely whether another 'person' is involved.) Where a relaxation of restrictions occurs, it pertains to sexual relations between parties considered to be equal and responsible for their actions. The desires of the parties involved must receive equal consideration. Acceptance concerns intercourse between consenting adults. Less than before these relations are defined by canons of behaviour; wherever the negotiations between these relatively autonomous parties may lead them has become increasingly irrelevant, but these relations must be negotiated in mutual consideration and shaped by mutual consent, and they may not be imposed by unilateral compulsion or openly serve the self-aggrandizement of one of the parties. Rape, roughness, scorn, and degradation, so common and acceptable for employers to inflict upon servants and factory girls, or customers upon prostitutes only a few generations ago, have become more distasteful to the contemporary public. Self-aggrandizement and violence have become less acceptable and are increasingly subject to social compulsion, social compulsion to self-compulsion, and self-control, in that order. In sexual matters some canons of behaviour have relaxed or disappeared, but people now compel others and themselves to take into consideration more aspects of more people at more moments, to arrange their relations accordingly and to subordinate their emotional management to these considerations. In this process, many intimate relations have become less predictable for they no longer depend as much as before on the commands of social canons and personal conscience, but are shaped in a process of negotiation between relatively equal and autonomous parties. This requires new and different forms of self-control. It requires a degree of insistence and sincerity in voicing one's demands (now called 'assertiveness'), the surrender of means of physical or economic compulsion, and it requires a readiness to consider the desires of others and identify with them, along with a degree of patience and inventiveness to cope with them. At the very least, it requires the display of those qualities, for, in the history of morals, appearances are half the work.

Relations between people are increasingly managed through negotiation rather than through command. This applies to relations between the sexes, between parents and children, often to relations between people in adjacent ranks within organizational hierarchies, and sometimes to relations between local authorities and citizen groups. This makes for a larger variety of possible outcomes, but the process of arranging these relations imposes onerous restrictions upon the people involved. In a sense, this transition from management through command to management through negotiation represents an increase in freedom: freedom being taken to mean the possibility to do what one wishes in so far as it does not interfere with that possibility in others. But that is not very far: such a definition of freedom may fit the room for movement in allotment gardens, but it does not apply to most human relations. Desires and rights are almost always demands and claims upon other people and there exists no space which is not occupied also by the desires and rights of others. That is why this management through negotiation, even if it were to be thought of as freedom, is so rarely experienced as liberating. The shift from management through command to management through negotiation has tied people to one another even more intricately, in more and more subtle ways, in all phases of life, at all moments of the day, with regard to many more activities and desires. It compels each person, in turn, to scrutinize his own longings and to speak up for them and, at the same time, to be ready to abandon them if they clash with the claims of others. Now a couple may negotiate a promiscuous relationship, but they must control jealousy and the fear of desertion, deny anger and rivalry with the partner's partner, and force themselves to play the game according to the rules imposed upon them by their own mutual consent. Clearly, in the course of this process some people have gained a larger margin of movement, and others have lost. Municipal authorities have often lost a considerable amount of discretion to carry on business along lines of administrative efficiency; but neighbourhood groups have gained opportunities. Parents have lost the means to chide, chastise, and command children, but young people can afford greater freedom of movement, expression, and consumption. Organizational superiors find themselves forced to listen to their immediate subalterns, instead of running the department as they see fit, and the lower echelons can sometimes exact their demands. Men can afford less liberties towards women than they used to and women have gained in opportunities for physical and social movement. No wonder that many white, middle-aged males in high academic positions who produce the social criticism of the era show a keen eye for the increasing oppression in society and worry about the decay and decadence that others would call freedom.

The transition from management through command to management through negotiation is the result of various societal developments. The increasing and generalizing dependence of people upon one another and the resulting increase in equality between them is one such development. Another process consists in the consecutive tides of emancipatory movements: campaigns for universal suffrage, organized workers' struggle, movements for women's liberation, and the many ethnic, racial, and regional liberation movements. Each movement learned from a preceding one and each time inequalities that were considered natural until then were abolished, this instilled doubt about the inevitability of other types of discrimination. But a third, quite autonomous process may be detected in the emergence and development of large organizations. As such organizations became ever more complex and shifted from simple clerical and productive tasks to the management of increasingly subtle personal relations, clear, rectilinear lines of command proved inadequate. The officials in such organizations no longer performed well-defined routines but engaged in complicated interactions with colleagues, clients, or customers, using their personalities and judgemental capacities as occupational instruments. They could not be managed without a modicum of consent and they would not consent without their interests and desires being taken into consideration. These organizations have had a twofold effect on contemporary family life. First, management through negotiation was carried over by these organizational middle-class workers, often women, from the sphere of work to the sphere of the family. And it is this organizational, 'professional-managerial' middle class that has emerged and expanded in the course of this century and become the arbiter of contemporary life-styles and opinions. Second, a quickly increasing proportion of the population of modern capitalist (and state capitalist) countries has become the clients of such organizations, as pupils and students in schools, as patients in the health-care system, as claimants and clients of the social services. The modes of emotional and relational management of the organizational middle class have been transferred ('imposed,' says Lasch) to these new clientele. Paramount in the innovation of modes of relational and emotional management is the profession of psychotherapy: the helping profession of the helping professions. To a considerable degree, the transition of management through command to management through negotiation was eased by the external effects of the psychotherapy profession upon widening circles, first of related helping professions, then of clients, and then of the general public of potential clients: the process of proto-professionalization.

The argument has come full circle. People in this age define difficulties with one another in terms of psychic problems that refer to professional psychotherapeutic treatment. But these difficulties have changed as the relations between people have changed within a society undergoing global transformations. Increasing and generalized dependency corresponded to some increase in equality between people. Emancipatory movements helped to abolish many unequal relations. The development of complex arrangements of organizational care resulted within the organization in more egalitarian relations that spread from there to family relations. The psychotherapy profession, especially, provided concepts and stances for this transition from management through command to management through negotiation. All things considered, this development has not resulted in broadening margins of movement and expression for everyone, but it has made relations less predictable, because the outcome is not being structured by commands, but the process of relational and emotional management is being shaped by the requirements of mutual consideration and consent, and of the abstention from violence and self-aggrandizement.

The point has been reached where the limits of the argument must be indicated and the conclusions drawn from it. The relaxation of manners in the twentieth century affects only a limited range of activities. The restraint on violent behaviour has not lessened, the inhibition upon self-aggrandizement has probably increased, and the discipline in the handling of time, money, goods, and the body has grown. What has broadened are the margins of tolerance in sexual matters and in the expression of emotions and desires, especially in intimate circles. But even this relaxation is conditional upon the consideration of the wishes of others and upon their negotiated consent. . . . The burdens of poverty and tyranny may have lessened, but in other respects western society has lost little of its oppressive character, and in many respects discipline has increased. Yet, some limitations are not imposed, but rather incurred in relations managed through negotiation.

There is no guarantee whatsoever that such negotiations lead to dignified or fair arrangements: 'Authenticity replaced morality and sincerity replaced judgement.' Worse, negotiators may even relinquish authenticity or sincerity, and mislead or manipulate one another. More important, management through negotiation paralyses rebellion: the dissidents agree themselves to deal, of their own free will, after ample consultation. Thus, the contract theory of citizenship and of economic man is extended to lovers, parents, and colleagues: one may take them or leave them. And this points to the basic flaw in any view of human relations as the outcome of negotiated consent: such negotiations always occur within a wider social context in which one party generally holds better alternative options than another. Within their marriage a man and women may be equal to each other, but outside it job opportunities or chances for remarriage are very different. Moreover, the scope of negotiations, of what is negotiable, are narrowly prescribed, not by the partners, but in the social context in which they find themselves. Thus, collaborators in an agency may bargain with one another – for example, over the distribution of caseloads – until all of them together are transferred by the board of trustees: then they may negotiate over who is to go first. The shift towards management through negotiation represents a change in the manner in which people control themselves and one another, especially in face-to-face relations. Seen within a larger social context such negotiations appear limited in scope, their outcome biased by the options that each party has in society at large, whereas the very occurrence of such negotiations legitimizes the social order in which such mutual consent is being achieved. Judged within its immediate context, management through negotiation seems to allow a greater variety of arrangements, better suited to the strivings of the partners that bring about the arrangement. But even in this context such a form of relational and emotional management forces people to take one another's demands into consideration and to relinquish some of their own. Some people forgo these options and steer clear of such threatening involvements, or avoid the negotiations and the ensuing engagements. They do not rebel but they reject, not with so many words, but tacitly, implicitly, with a strategy that denies itself, until it is expressed in a vocabulary of psychic problems, as depersonalization, as a pleasure-less promiscuity ('tertiary impotence'), or as phobia. [. . .]

The transition to management through negotiation is onerous and hazardous. Where no command can be heard from within or without, people may adopt fears and compulsions to help them refrain from what they are now allowed to do by others but what they find too difficult, too dangerous, and too lonely.

Chapter 4

Peter N. Stearns and Deborah C. Stearns

HISTORICAL ISSUES IN EMOTIONS RESEARCH

Causation and timing

[. . .]

UNQUESTIONABLY, EXPLAINING CHANGES IN specific emotions or emotional constellations forms the essential starting point in assessing causation, for both analytical issues and evidence are most clear-cut at this level. Changes in particular emotional formulations almost always follow from some causes peculiar to the emotion in question—a point to which we must return in dealing with the inescapability of larger frameworks as well. In addition, the factors involved in many specific emotions changes can be directly traced through explicit references in prescriptive literature or a close chronological juxtaposition—this latter connection slightly less definitive, but plausible nevertheless.

Recent changes in emotional standards or relationships, though sometimes difficult to determine simply because of their recency and the dangers of exaggerating contrasts with the past, provide unusually abundant evidence on causation, because the emotional participants can be directly observed. Arlie Hochschild's research on clashes over gratitude, in families where men and women both work, leaves little doubt as to why new confusions have arisen (Hochschild and Machung 1989). The basic correlation involves the alteration in women's work patterns and resultant tensions over family obligations, which began to take shape in the 1950s but still reverberate. Correlation can be tested by the explicit observation of family dynamics, when men make clear their belief that they are exceeding, in their family contributions, what their fathers did and deserve high praise, while women stress the gap between men's and women's family involvement even as work roles have considerably equalized. It would be hard to pretend that causation in this instance involves many mysteries.

Many changes in emotional standards in the more distant past may be explained with almost the same degree of certainty, because of the connections available in the prescriptive evidence. It is true that important shifts in emotional culture are not accompanied by full awareness of the novelty involved, which means that the sources of altered standards rarely reflect on causation; but they may leave abundant clues nevertheless.

In the first edition of his immensely popular baby book issued in 1945, Dr. Benjamin Spock repeated standard advice about anger, of the sort that had been characteristic of childrearing literature for almost a century. Anger required parental monitoring, for children must learn that some forms of anger are inappropriate and that some targets, particularly in the family, should be out of bounds. But anger itself was a vital motivation for future competitive businessmen or farmers, and parents should also be concerned not to discipline it out of existence. A bit more than a decade later Spock's advice had changed. By the 1960s children's anger should be firmly controlled in all circumstances, for the emotion was both dangerous and valueless. Rather than teaching children how to channel their aggressive energies toward useful goals, parents now should help children minimize anger, talking it out harmlessly and so reducing its place in their emotional makeup. Revealingly, when Spock wrote in his subsequent revisions about the work goals toward which this new anger strategy should be directed, he now referred to managers and salesmen, where smooth personalities and emotional self-control held pride of place (Stearns and Stearns 1986).

Spock did not carefully analyze his change of views concerning anger, and so we are speculating slightly in suggesting that a key reason involved recognition that the emotional requirements of work were undergoing alteration and that childrearing standards must follow suit. The margin of error in this speculation is reduced when a variety of additional evidence points in the same direction: from as early as 1928 Dale Carnegie and a host of work-advice popularizers had been urging anger control on adults in the growing service sector of the economy. By the 1950s studies of actual American parents demonstrated that the families most keen to pick up on the newer kinds of childrearing advice, bent on minimizing interpersonal frictions, came disproportionately from the managerial middle class. Here, then, is an accumulation of evidence, including direct prescriptive references, demonstrating that a major cause of evolving anger standards followed from changes in the structure of the labor force, as earlier entrepreneurial and production emphasis gave way to corporate bureaucracies and service sector jobs.

In the decades around 1800, middle-class people in France (and elsewhere in the Western world) began to manifest new levels of disgust at bodily odors and other smells. The change is fascinating, in that this change involves both emotional reactions and a real shift in the evaluation of the physical senses. Smells of sweat, urine, and defecation, previously tolerated or even (in the case of urine) sometimes welcome, now became nauseating. Urine, used for tooth brushing in seventeenth-century Holland and as a mark of courtship in seventeenth-century Wales, now provided sickening smells in the corridors of urban slums or the clothing of ill-disciplined young children. New sanitary procedures, including indoor plumbing and more rigorous toilet training, followed from these new emotional and visceral reactions, abetted of course by technological innovations (Corbin 1986).

None of the contemporaries who manifested the new levels of disgust explicitly stated why they were becoming, by traditional standards, so fastidious. Evidence is more indirect than in the case of Spock and the anger training of children. But two related causes spring out both from the common targets of the new disgust, and from correlations with wider social change. In the first place, growing urbanization and industrialization created heightened anxieties about physical health. Cities were traditionally less healthy than the countryside, and the return of fearsome plagues, like the cholera epidemic of the 1830s, drove the dangers home quite graphically. In advance of the germ theory, reaction to urban odors both expressed health fears and helped propel behaviors, including flight from the worst, smelliest miasmas, that seemed directly useful in reducing disease risk. Relatedly, incipient industrialization heightened social class divisions. Middle-class people feared the wrath and the strangeness of the urban poor, and at the same time needed justifications for their acceptance of new, visible forms of inequality. The notion that the poor were animal-like, almost a different species, legitimized avoidance and neglect. Fastidiousness was an emotional and sensory backdrop to this social differentiation. (Interestingly, young children, fully as logical a disgust target, were increasingly idealized, though also bathed and perfumed—suggesting again the selectivity of disgust causation and its derivation, not from smells in general, but from the smells associated with new social divides.) The poor smelled bad, as part of their feckless, uncivilized habits more generally. They could be called to order by classes who maintained the proper standards of emotion and hygiene, or damned if they refused to come around. Emotional change was, in sum, socially useful, in responding to the novel and rather frightening social context of industrialization, becoming markers of class standing. Correspondingly, people who propounded and utilized the new standards of disgust explicitly targeted problems of disease and the ill-governance of the poor in expressing and illustrating the standards. The causal link is clear.

Other instances of causation applied to particular emotions depend more purely on chronological correlations, as explicit references are largely absent; and, it must be admitted, correlation may be misleading in that two phenomena may be simultaneous without being integrally connected. But the correlation between reduction of birth rate and new emotional attachment to individual children is widely accepted among historians, who find its traces around 1800 in the middle class of countries like the United States, a bit later for the working class, and recently again in areas undergoing demographic transition such as urban China. The link is clear: large families in a traditional demographic regime permitted real affection for children, but the intensity was constrained by the sheer numbers of children involved, the tendency of children to bond as much with older siblings as with parents, and the frequency of infant mortality which introduced some caution in attachments ventured in early childhood. When the birth rate drops, from six to eight children per couple to four or five or less (as began to occur in a well-studied case among Philadelphia Quakers around 1800) (Wells 1971), many of these constraints diminish. Parents have more time and emotional energy for the individual children they do have. Sibling bonding diminishes in favor of ties directly with parents. And efforts to provide better care for young children cut into traditional resignation about young children's deaths, promoting greater emotional commitment to infants (and ultimately, a reduction in the infant death rate). The only analytical problem, aside from the need for careful statement of the change in emotions itself lest the traditional parent-child ties be oversimplified, involves priority. It is very difficult to determine whether some groups first cut their birth rates for non-emotional reasons—economics, for example—and then discovered their commitment to their smaller broods affected; or whether in some cases at least an emotional redefinition occurred first, promoting a new interest in reducing birth rates in order to be able to lavish more attention, care, and money on the children (Trumbach 1978). Yet the demographic correlation stands with the only complexity, not insignificant to be sure, whether it must be supplemented by other factors, such as cultural redefinition of children and their degree of innocence, to explain why emotional change might precede new demographic behavior, serving as cause then enhanced by effect (Scheper-Hughes 1985).

And a final correlation case: around 1900, attitudes toward children's emotional response to death began to change (Fiore 1992). During most of the nineteenth century, advice to parents (and many actual ceremonies and comments associated with death) had stressed the importance of preventing children's fear of death by associating children with death closely while enveloping death itself in a positive and sentimental aura. Beginning about 1880, and with growing intensity early in the twentieth century, this tone began to change. Anxiety about preventing fear escalated. Children were now seen as potentially manifesting very complex reactions to death that could not be diverted simply by religious and familial assurance. Parents must now carefully manage the presentation of death to children with awareness of traumatic response uppermost in their minds. Nineteenth-century staples, such as the association between death and sweet sleep, were now attacked because of their fear-inducing potential. Grief was acknowledged as a problem among children, to be handled with outright manipulation including concealment of parental feelings.

Psychological studies of the emotional complexities of childhood played a role in this new effort to distance children, emotionally, from death. Popularized research findings made it increasingly difficult for middle-class Americans or West Europeans to believe in childish innocence and emotional ease. But the most striking correlation with the new approach to children's fear and grief involved the huge changes occurring in children's mortality itself, and in the institutional practices surrounding death. Improved nutrition, better sanitation including implementation of measures derived from Pasteur's germ theory, and fuller use of trained medical personnel in cases of difficult births, all combined to drive infant mortality down from over 20 percent of all births in 1800, to under 5 percent by 1920. This massive transition had two impacts on adult treatment of children's emotions surrounding death, the one obvious, the other probably more important. It became increasingly likely that a child would not have to experience death in the nuclear family (Stearns and Haggerty 1991). This change however explains why a new emotional culture was possible, but not why it took the anxious shape it did. At this point, a second correlative facet must be introduced. The revolution in child morality was accompanied by growing parental anxiety about children's health. Watchfulness—against germs, for example—became essential, but also fruitful in that it could produce a death-free childhood. As parents acquired new concerns about children's diseases and a new awareness of their responsibility in providing medical care, their own attitude to children's death potential became more vulnerable. When they assimilated new advice about the need to shelter children, emotionally, from death, they were essentially transposing their own growing fears.

This is an obvious correlation in one sense: a development in child mortality so unprecedented as the transition between 1880 and 1920 would almost certainly reverberate in emotional culture. Yet it is not a correlation that can be directly traced, because none of the sources of new advice about children's fears and grief drew the obvious connections. Despite its tentativeness it suggests again the exciting possibilities, when a specific shift in emotional standards can be isolated, of exploring applicable causation directly.

Particular changes in emotion may, of course, uncover not a primary basic cause but a concatenation of factors. A final example will indicate the possibilities here. Around 1920, American parents began to be treated to a barrage of concern about jealousy between siblings, particularly involving the reactions of a toddler to the arrival of a new baby (Stearns 1989). Nineteenth-century family culture had almost completely ignored sibling tensions, and there was no precedent for the concern about children's jealousy that began to swell from the 1920s onward, as parents began to worry both about jealousy—induced violence and about longer-term personality damage for the jealous child himself.

Why did this new feature of familial emotional culture surface when it did? Three primary causes intertwined, the first directly demonstrable, the other two involving the more speculative kind of correlations already sketched in other connections. Factor 1: a new breed of popularizers began to use psychological research on siblings to generate a much less favorable picture of children's natural emotions than had prevailed in the nineteenth-century middle class (Wishy 1968; Kell and Aldous 1960; Dunn 1985). Experts found a novel basis for establishing their authority with parents by calling attention to a previously-undetected but serious problem, and providing solutions.

Factor 2 (helping to explain why parents listened to the experts): several changes in family life made sibling rivalry more likely than had been the case previously. By the early twentieth century the middle class had an average of two children. Smaller family size meant less bonding among siblings, more contention for direct emotional access to parents (Dunn 1985). At the same time, the presence of other adults in the household—live-in servants and grandparents—declined, in the first case after 1890, in the second after 1920. Finally, increasing efforts to promote children's individuality, by earmarking separate toys and insisting on separate bedrooms, indirectly encouraged new levels of emotional tension amid a sibling cohort, even as the new sibling advice promoted further individuation. The strong likelihood then is that new concern about children's jealousy followed from new levels of this same emotion, deeply troubling to parents who now handled children with less outside assistance.

Factor 3: rounding out essential causation was the fact that by the 1920s adults were becoming more concerned about their own jealous reactions (Lynd and Lynd 1929). Removal of restrictions on socializing between men and women, the rise of dating as an adolescent behavior, and greater emphasis on sexuality all produced a growing number of situations in which jealousy was both likely and counterproductive (Bailey 1988; Modell 1989). Attacks on adult jealousy abounded, but the focus on children's jealousy served as an outlet as well. Logically, by reducing children's jealousy adults might be formed who could handle heterosexual socializing more readily (Clanton 1989). Less consciously, anxiety about children's jealousy helped adults express uncertainties about their own responses that they were embarrassed to state openly. This adult displacement factor resembles, of course, the correlation involved in explaining new concerns about children's reactions to death just a short time before and like this factor cannot at least as yet be directly proved.

Growing knowledge about changes in specific emotions has clearly generated a number of relatively precise points of transition that can be fruitfully analyzed in terms of causation, despite variations in precision of proof. The results frequently uncover direct relationships between other developments and the innovations in emotional standards. Even seemingly as changes in the labor force as they reached into formulations about dealing with children's anger, can be demonstrated with high probability. Other relationships involve correlations whose chronological coincidence combines with plausibility in explaining not only new emotional standards but the intensity of their impact, including unacknowledged adult tensions that spill over into childrearing. While some shifts in emotional standards depend particularly on one primary cause others result from a confluence of several factors, which enriches but also complicates analysis. Amid the several scenarios involved the analytical exploration of causation expands understanding of the change itself, well beyond what simple description of shifting standards can provide.

References

Bailey, B. 1988. *From Front Porch to Back Seat: Courtship in Twentieth-Century America.* Baltimore, MD: The Johns Hopkins University Press.

Clanton, G. (1989). "Jealousy in American Culture, 1945–1985: Reflections from Popular Culture." In *The Sociology of Emotions*, edited by David Franks and E. D. McCarthy. Greenwich, CT: JAI Press.

Corbin, A. 1986. *The Foul and the Fragrant: Odor and the French Social Imagination.* Cambridge, MA: Harvard University Press.

Dunn, J. 1985. *Sisters and Brothers*. Cambridge, MA: Harvard University Press.

Fiore, D. 1992. *Grandma's Through: Children and the Death Experience from the 18th Century to the Present.* Unpublished paper, Carnegie Mellon University.

Hochschild, A. R. and A. Machung. 1989. *The Second Shift: Working Parents and the Revolution at Home.* New York: Viking.

Kell, L. and J. Aldous. 1960. "Trends in Child Care over Three Generations." *Marriage and Family Living* 22: 176–177.

Lynd, R. S. and H. M. Lynd. 1929. *Middletown: A Study in Contemporary American Culture.* New York: Harcourt Brace and Co.

Modell, J. 1989. *Into One's Own: From Youth to Adulthood in the United States, 1920–1975.* Berkeley, CA: University of California Press.

Stearns, P. N. (1989) *Jealousy: The Evolution of an Emotion in American History.* New York and London: New York University Press.

Stearns, C.Z. and Stearns, P.N. (1986) *Anger: The Struggle for Emotional Control in America's History*. Chicago: University of Chicago Press.

Trumbach, R. (1978) *The Rise of the Egalitarian Family: Aristocratic Kinship and Domestic Relations in Eighteenth-Century England*. New York: Academic Press.

Wells, R. V. (1971) 'Family Size and Fertility Control in Eighteenth-Century America: A Study of Quaker Families'. *Population Studies*, 25 (1): 73–82.

Wishy, B. W. (1968) *The Child and the Republic: The Dawn of Modern American Child Nurture*. Philadelphia: University of Pennsylvania Press.

2. Emotions and culture

THE QUESTION OF WHETHER OR in what ways emotions can be said to be universal has been articulated, perhaps most exactingly, in the domain of anthropology. The field of relevant contributions spans several decades, and is enormously rich and varied. As early as 1986, anthropologists Lutz and White published a comprehensive analytical review of cross-cultural research on emotions, which we highly recommend as background reading to this complex problem-area. The review cites just under 200 references and surveys the contribution of ethologists, linguists, cross-cultural psychologists and psychiatrists, besides that of physical, psychoanalytic and cultural anthropologists. For the purposes of this brief introduction, it will suffice to say that Lutz and White identify four different approaches positing cross-cultural universals in emotion, namely: *ethological and evolutionary* approaches, *psychodynamic and psychiatric* perspectives, approaches informed by what they call *commonsense naturalism* and, last but not least, approaches that posit *language universals* (linguistic or cultural codes found across cultures) as evidence of universal aspects of emotional experience. Lutz and White then go on to present varieties of research on emotions as culturally and socially constructed. In contrast to the former set of approaches, these posit that different cultural meaning systems have a *primary* role to play in the shaping (or, sometimes, constituting) of emotional experience itself. The emphasis in this equally vast body of work is therefore on cultural variation, mediated by cognitive categories of *ethnopsychological understanding* (such as that of the culturally constituted 'self'), by the *social structural correlates* of such understandings, and/or by *verbal communication*. Generally speaking, this research tends to define emotion 'more as a socially validated judgment than an internal state', and thus focuses largely on 'the translation of emotion concepts and the social processes surrounding their use' (1986: 408). Lutz and White importantly stress that the relativism embraced by authors in these fields involves different degrees of constructionism, as many of them do posit universals in some aspects of emotions – for example, in the types of situations or social positions associated with them.

An influential collection by the title *The Social Construction of Emotion* appeared in the same year as Lutz and White published their review (1986). This collection, edited by Rom Harré, argued for a methodological agenda giving priority to linguistic studies of emotion, with a view to illustrating cultural variation among emotion systems. Such studies would pay particular attention to how specific linguistic repertoires mediate local moral orders, and to the social functions that particular emotion displays and emotion talk 'perform in the dramaturgically shaped episodes of this or that culture' (Harré 1986: 13). Constructionist programs of research gained ascendancy in the wake of these seminal publications, in the context of what we have referred to as the textual turn in social science. More recently, however, an increasing number of authors have articulated the limitations of cultural constructionism, and the need to develop theoretical and methodological tools capable of eschewing the conceptual dichotomies of affect/cognition, individual/ society, body/mind, matter/discourse. If, in 1986, Lutz and White were able to write that research positing cross-cultural universals was 'usually positivist in epistemological orientation' (408), a feature of the more recent critiques of constructionist relativism is their re-framing of the question of universals in terms that do not rely on positivist assumptions. On the one hand, it is argued that the way forward in the study of 'emotions and culture' lies in admitting the relevance of non-reductive form of psychology, in order to address 'the enormous diversity in the way individuals appropriate symbolic forms related to emotions and emotional experience' (Good 2004: 532; see also Good and Good 2005). On the other hand, it is argued that the 'ideational bias' in cultural accounts of emotions must be corrected through a focus on embodiment and non-mechanistic biology (Lyon 1995; see also Csordas 1994; Wilce 2003). The backdrop to these developments in the study of emotion are new and complex ways of thinking about 'culture', in response to processes of globalization and emergent, de- and reterritorialized cultural forms (Gupta and Ferguson 1992).

The first extract included in this section is by Cathrine Lutz, one of the best-known exponents of the constructionist approach to the study of emotion. In this text, Lutz examines the gendered dimensions of the construct of emotion in some sectors of American culture, through the analysis of interview conversations with both men and women. This piece builds on an earlier article (Lutz 1986) where Lutz proposed that Euroamerican conceptions of emotion, both lay and expert, should themselves be subject to a deconstructive reading, for the purpose of translating between cultural systems. If the cultural specificity of Euroamerican concepts of emotion is not immediately apparent, she argued, this is in good part because of the (Western) positivist assumption that it is possible to identify an 'essence' of emotion, and that such an essence is universal. The meaning system that constitutes the Western category of emotion associates this concept with a number of others (nature, irrationality, subjectivity, femininity, chaos) that share a position of inferiority with respect to their dichotomous counterparts (culture, reason, universality, masculinity, order and control). In this extract, drawn from a chapter published in 1990, Lutz focuses on the function of a 'rhetoric of control' in women's talk about emotion. She argues that this rhetoric can be read as 'a narrative about the double-sided nature – both weak and dangerous – of dominated groups' (1990: 70).

The second extract in this section is from an article by William Reddy, where the author takes issue with the 'strong' constructionism he associates with the work of Lutz, among others. Whilst appreciating the reasons, both theoretical and political, for refusing essentialist conceptions of subjectivity and emotions, Reddy draws attention to some of the paralyzing features of the constructionist focus on 'culture' (or language) at the expense of the individual (or feeling). Reddy proposes the term 'emotives' to characterize emotion statements, stressing that such statements are themselves 'instruments for directly changing, building, hiding, intensifying [the inner experience of] emotions'. 'Emotives' are not representational, because there is always a disjuncture between them and the feelings to which they are 'anchored'. But neither do they simply perform emotion in the sense of constructing it from linguistic and cultural conventions. Rather, 'emotives' perform feeling in the sense of shaping it (or *moving* it) in particular directions. Understanding emotion statements in terms of 'emotives' allows theoretically for the existence of a 'residuum that is not satisfactorily shaped', and this residuum 'provides an initial reservoir or possibilities for change' – the source of the possibility for deviance, resistance, or the generation of alternative idioms. Reddy's approach draws on post-structuralist insights about language and on reformulations of classic psychodynamic concepts, to offer a post-positivist and non-essentialist account of feeling as what is 'universally human'. One critique of Reddy's position is that it is pitched against an extreme version of constructionism that is very rarely, in fact, espoused by researchers of emotion and culture. In its original published form, Reddy's article is followed by responses from Brenneis, Garro, Howell, Hunt, Longman, and Lutz, as well as a reply from the author, to which we refer readers who may want to deepen their understanding of this debate.

The author of our third extract is another ethnohistorian of emotions, Michael Harkin, who also draws on psychodynamic approaches in explicit contrast with discursive ones. Harkin poses the methodological question of 'what role the emotions can possibly play in our interpretations of cultures that were destroyed or radically altered in the aftermath of contact with Euroamericans'. One of the most interesting features of this question is that it addresses simultaneously emotions as an aspect of the culture(s) under study, and emotions as an aspect of the research process. Harkin proposes that ethnopsychological approaches that rely on linguistic documentation – bracketing out any assumptions concerning the nature of the human psyche – are not helpful for the purposes of investigating emotional schemata in cultures and languages that are now extinct. Psychodynamic approaches, on the other hand, assume a degree of similarity in the basic mechanisms through which humans manage traumatic events and emotions. On this basis, an explication of the emotional dimensions of specific ethnohistorical events can be offered, and this is illustrated in this extract through examples from the American Northwest Coast. Harkin argues moreover that, in the classical tradition of anthropology, a professional reluctance to think historically can be read as a psychologically defensive response to the 'searing histories of genocide, culture loss, land appropriations, and immense cruelty perpetrated on indigenous peoples'. Among contemporary ethnohistorians, who no longer think in terms of an 'ethnographic present', the unwillingness to consider the emotional dimensions of the past persists, and can similarly be regarded as an unwillingness to face emotions of extreme distress – not only those of the peoples studied, but also those that the practice of studying them may provoke in the researcher.

The last extract in this section, by Johan Lindquist, is a recent contribution to the vast body of anthropological research on emotions in Southeast Asia. This piece follows in the steps of seminal authors like Geertz and Rosaldo in looking at emotions as a basis for theorizing social action; it departs from their classic studies, however, in focusing on social change and cultural transition. The article examines *malu* – approximately translated as shame or embarrassment – as a key emotional trope for contemporary Indonesian migrants, by looking at the practices of two very different groups of migrant women (factory workers and prostitutes). Unlike other possible translations of 'shame-embarrassment', which remain tied to particular ethnic groups and languages, *malu* has become especially salient as a concept that exists in several Indonesian languages and, in the context of migration, as part of the Indonesian *lingua franca*. As such, *malu* functions as an experiential trope that links the spaces of migration and expresses the (gendered) anxieties that emerge from the tensions between them. At the same time, *malu* describes a relationship between individuals and the cultural framework of the 'nation', beyond any one local community.

References

Csordas, T. J. (ed.) (1994) *Embodiment and Experience: The Existential Grounds of Culture and Self*. Cambridge: Cambridge University Press.

Good, B. J. (2004) 'Rethinking "emotions" in Southeast Asia', *Ethnos*, 69 (4): 529–533.

Good, B. J. and Good, M.-J. DelVecchio (2005) 'On the "subject" of culture: subjectivity and cultural phenomenology in the work of Clifford Geertz', in R. Schweder and B. Good (eds) *Clifford Geertz by his Colleagues*. Chicago: University of Chicago Press.

Gupta, A. and Ferguson, J. (eds) (1997) *Anthropological Locations: Boundaries and Grounds of a Field Science*. Berkeley: University of California Press.

Harré, R. (ed.) (1989) *The Social Construction of Emotion*. Oxford: Blackwell. Lutz, C. and White, G. M. (1986) 'The anthropology of emotions', *Annual Review of Anthropology*, 15: 405–436.

Lutz, C. (1986) 'Emotion, thought, and estrangement: emotion as a cultural category', *Cultural Anthropology*, 1 (3): 287–309.

Lyon, M. L. (1995) 'Missing emotions: the limitations of cultural constructionism in the study of emotion', *Cultural Anthropology*, 10 (2): 244–263.

Wilce, J. M. (ed) (2003) *Social and Cultural Lives of Immune Systems*. London: Routledge.

Chapter 5

Catherine A. Lutz

ENGENDERED EMOTION

Gender, power, and the rhetoric of emotional control in
American discourse

[. . .]

WESTERN DISCOURSE ON EMOTIONS CONSTITUTES
them as paradoxical entities that are both a sign of weakness and a powerful
force. On the one hand, emotion weakens the person who experiences it. It does
this both by serving as a sign of a sort of character defect (e.g., "She couldn't rise
above her emotions") and by being a sign of at least temporary intrapsychic disorganization (e.g., "She was in a fragile state" or "She fell apart"). The person who
has "fallen apart," needless to say, is unable to function effectively or forcefully. On
the other hand, emotions are literally physical forces that push us into vigorous
action. "She was charged up," we say; "Waves of emotion shook his body." Women
are constructed in a similar contradictory fashion as both strong and weak (e.g.,
Jordanova 1980), and I will present evidence [. . .] that when American women and
men talk about emotion, they draw on that similarity to comment on the nature of
gender and power. This feature of the emotional and of the female produces
frequent discussion in the interviews of the problem of controlling one's feelings.
Such discussion is found in both men's and women's discourse, but much more
frequently in the latter. I will show that this talk about control of emotions is
evidence of a widely shared cultural view of the danger of both women and their
emotionality. It is also talk that may mean different things to both the speaker and
the audience when it is uttered by women and by men, and this factor will be used
to help account for differences in the rate of use of this rhetoric of control.
Although both women and men draw on a culturally available model of emotion as
something in need of control, they can be seen as often making some different kinds
of sense and claims from it.

The material I turn to first was collected in four extended interviews on
emotion with fifteen American working- and middle-class women and men. All

white, they ranged in age from the early twenties to the mid-seventies and included a bank teller, factory worker, college teacher, retiree, housing code inspector, and stockbroker. Most were parents. The interviews were usually conducted in people's homes, and the interviewers included myself and a number of graduate students, most of them women. Each person was interviewed by the same individual for all four sessions, and although a small number of questions organized each session, every attempt was made to have the interviews approximate "natural conversation." Nonetheless, it is clearly important to keep in mind the context of the discourse to be analyzed, as it was produced by a group of people who agreed on letter and phone solicitation "to talk about emotion" for an audience of relative strangers who were also academics and mostly females.

Many people mentioned at one or several points in the interviews that they believe women to be more emotional than men. One example of the variety of ways this was phrased is the account one woman gave to explain her observation that some people seem inherently to be "nervous types." She remembered about her childhood that

> the female teachers had a tendency to really holler at the kids a lot, and when I was in class with the male teacher, it seemed like he just let things pass by and it didn't seem to get his goat as fast, and he didn't shout at the same time the female may have in the same instance. . . . I think emotional people get upset faster. I do. And like with men and women, things that are sort of important or bothering me don't bother my husband. . . . I think that's a difference of male and female.

One theme that frequently arises in the interviews is what can be called the "rhetoric of control" (Rosaldo 1977). When people are asked to talk about emotions, one of the most common set of metaphors used is that in which someone or something controls, handles, copes, deals, disciplines, or manages either or both their emotions or the situation seen as creating the emotion. For example:

> I believe an individual can exercise a great deal of *control* over their emotions by maintaining a more positive outlook, by not dwelling on the negative, by trying to push aside an unpleasant feeling. I'm getting angry and like I said, he's over being angry, more or less dropped it and he expects me to also. Well we don't have the same temper, I just can't *handle* it that way.

And in a more poetic turn, one person mused:

> sadness . . . dipping, dipping into that . . . just the out-of-*controlness* of things.

People typically talk about *controlling* emotions, *handling* emotional situations as well as emotional feelings, and *dealing* with people, situations, and emotions.

The notion of control operates very similarly here to the way it does in Western discourses on sexuality (Foucault 1980). Both emotionality and sexuality are domains whose understanding is dominated by a biomedical model; both are seen as universal, natural impulses; both are talked about as existing in "healthy" and "unhealthy" forms; and both have come under the control of a medical or quasi-medical profession (principally psychiatry and psychology). Foucault has argued that popular views of sexuality – as a drive that was repressed during the Victorian era and gradually liberated during the twentieth century – are misleading because they posit a single essence that is manipulated by social convention. Rather, Foucault postulated, multiple sexualities are constantly produced and changed. A popular discourse on the control of emotion runs functionally parallel to a discourse on the control of sexuality; a rhetoric of control requires a psychophysical essence that is manipulated or wrestled with and directs attention away from the socially constructed nature of the idea of emotion (see Abu-Lughod and Lutz, this volume). In addition, the metaphor of control implies something that would otherwise be out of control, something wild and unruly, a threat to order. To speak about controlling emotions is to replicate the view of emotions as natural, dangerous, irrational, and physical.

What is striking is that women talked about the control of emotion more than twice as often as did men as a proportion of the total speech each produced in the interviews. To help account for this difference, we can ask what the rhetoric of control might accomplish for the speaker and what it might say to several audiences. . . . At least three things can be seen to be done via the rhetoric of emotional control: It (1) reproduces an important part of the cultural view of emotion (and then implicitly of women as the more emotional gender) as irrational, weak, and dangerous; (2) minimally elevates the social status of the person who claims the need or ability to self-control emotions; and (3) opposes the view of the feminine self as dangerous when it is reversed, that is, when the speaker denies the need for or possibility of control of emotion. Each of these suggestions can only briefly be examined.

First, this rhetoric can be seen as a reproduction, primarily on the part of women, of the view of themselves as more emotional, of emotion as dangerous, and hence of themselves as in need of control. It does this first by setting up a boundary – that edge over which emotion that is *uncontrolled* can spill. A number of people have noted that threats to a dominant social order are sometimes articulated in a concern with diverse kinds of boundaries (whether physical or social) and their integrity (e.g., Martin 1987; Scheper-Hughes and Lock 1987). One of the most critical boundaries that is constituted in Western psychological discourse is that between the inside and the outside of persons; individualism as ideology is fundamentally based on the magnification of that particular boundary. When emotion is defined, as it also is in the West, as something inside the individual, it provides an important symbolic vehicle by which the problem of the maintenance of social order can be voiced. A discourse that is concerned with the expression, control, or repression of emotions can be seen as a discourse on the crossing back and forth of that boundary between inside and outside, a discourse we can expect to see in more elaborate form in periods and places where social relations appear to be imminently overturned.

This rhetoric of emotional control goes further than defining and then defending boundaries, however, it also suggests a set of roles – one strong and defensive and the other weak but invasive – that are hierarchized and linked with gender roles. Rosaldo (1984) notes of hierarchical societies that they seem to evince greater concern than do more egalitarian ones with how society controls the inner emotional self and, we can add, with how one part of a bifurcated and hierarchically layered self controls another. The body politic, in other words, is sometimes replicated in the social relations of the various homunculi that populate the human mind, a kind of "mental politic." When cognition outreasons and successfully manages emotion, male-female roles are replicated. When women speak of control, they play the roles of both super- and subordinate, of controller and controllee. They identify their emotions and themselves as undisciplined and discipline both through a discourse on control of feeling. The construction of a feminine self, this material might suggest, includes a process by which women come to control themselves and so obviate the necessity for more coercive outside control.

There is the example of one woman in her late thirties; she talked about the hate she felt for her ex-husband, who began an affair while she was pregnant and left her with the infant, an older child, and no paid employment:

> So I think you try hard not to bring it [the feeling] out 'cause you don't want that type of thing at home with the kids, you know. That's very bad, very unhealthy, that's no way to grow up. So I think now, maybe I've just learned to control it and time has changed the feeling of the hate.

The woman here defines herself as someone with a feeling of hate and portrays it as dangerous, primarily in terms of the threat it poses to her own children, a threat she phrases in biomedical terms (i.e., "unhealthy"). She replicates a view that Shields (1987) found prevalent in a survey of twentieth-century English-language child-rearing manuals; this is the danger that mothers' (and not fathers') emotions are thought to present to children. In addition, this woman's description of her feelings essentializes them as states; as such, they remain passive (see Cancian 1987 on the feminization of love) rather than active motivators, a point to which we will return.

In other cases, people do not talk about themselves, but rather remind others (usually women) of the need to control themselves. These instances also serve to replicate the view of women as dangerously emotional. Another woman spoke about a female friend who still grieved for a son who had died two years previously: "You've got to pick up and go on. You've got to try and get those feelings under control." The "you" in this statement is a complex and multivocal sign (Kirkpatrick 1987), and directs the admonition to control simultaneously to the grieving woman, the female interviewer, the speaker herself, no one in particular, and everyone in a potential audience.

A second pragmatic effect of the rhetoric of emotional control is a claim to have the ability to "rise above" one's emotions or to approve of those who do. Women, more than men, may speak of control because they are concerned about counteracting the cultural denigration of themselves through an association with emotion. "I think it's important to control emotions," they say, and implicitly remind a critical audience that they have the cooler stuff it takes to be considered mature and rational. It is important to note that, as academics, I and the graduate students who conducted the interviews may have been perceived as an audience in special need of such reminders. The speakers would have been doing this, however, by dissociating themselves from emotion rather than by questioning the dominant view both of themselves and of emotion.

Although women may have less access to a view of themselves as masterful individuals, a common aspect of the cultural scheme that *is* available paints them as masterfully effective with others on joint tasks, particularly interpersonal or emotional tasks (social science versions of this include Chodorow 1978, Parsons and Bales 1955). This subtly alters the meaning of the rhetoric of control; knowledge of what the feelings are that "need" control and of what control should be like is perceived and described as a social rather than an individual process. For example, one woman says: "If you're tied in with a family, . . . you have to use it for guidance how you control your emotions." This is the same woman whose central life problem during the interview period was coping with her husband's ex-wife and family, who lived across the street from her. The regular, friendly contact between husband and ex-wife has left her very unhappy but also unsure about what to do. The ambiguity over who ought to control or regulate what is evident in her description of an argument she had with her husband over the issue.

> I was mad. I was mad. And I said, "I don't care whether you think I should [inaudible word] or stay in this at all, it's too, and cause I'm going to say it." And I said, "How dare you tell me how I'm supposed to feel," you know. Bob [her husband] would say, you know, "You got to live with it" or "You got to do this" or "How dare you tell me this, I don't have to put up with anything" or "I don't have to feel this way because you tell me I have to feel this way." You know, it was, in that case Robin is his ex-wife, "and you have to just kind of deal with it," you know, "all the problems that she presents in your own way." And it was almost sort of like saying "You're going to have to like it." Well I don't. I don't, you know. And for a year and a half he kept saying, you know, "You're going to have to like it, this is the way it's going to be, you're going to have to do this, you're going to have to have, be, act, this certain way," you know, act everything hunky-dory, and it wasn't, you know, and I was beginning to resent a whole lot of things. I, I, I resented him for telling me I had to feel that way when I, I wasn't real fond of the situation. I didn't like it. When I would tell him that I didn't like it, it was "It's your problem, you deal with it." I didn't like that, that made me really angry because I was saying, "Help me out here, I don't know how to deal with this."

This woman is frustrated with her husband for failing to join her in a collaborative project of "dealing with" her feelings of resentment. Here control is given away to or shared with others. This strategy of control is more complex and subtle than the simple self-imposition described in other parts of the transcripts so far; it aims to control both the emotions of the self *and* the attention and assistance of the other. Note also that she speaks of "resenting" or "not liking" (relatively mild terms of displeasure) the overall situation but is most incensed ("mad, mad, mad") about her husband's assumption that she ought not to feel a certain way. She asserts the right to "feel" unhappy about her predicament but is clearly defining that feeling in the standard contemporary sense of a strictly internal and passive event. Nowhere in the interview does she explicitly state or appear to imply that she wants, intends, or ought to act in concert with those feelings. What is being controlled or dealt with, therefore, has already been defined as a relatively innocuous feeling rather than an action tendency.

Finally, the rhetoric of emotional control can also be employed in both idiosyncratic and "reversed" ways that may intend or have the effect of at least minimally resisting the dominant view of emotionality, and thus of women. A few people, for example, spontaneously spoke about the problem of emotional control, thereby evoking the whole schema we have just been looking at. They went on, however, to define "control" in a way that entailed relatively minimal constraints on emotional communication. One woman, a twenty-eight-year-old bank teller, said: "Let me explain control. It's not that you sit there and you take it [some kind of abuse] and, you know, I think controlling them [emotions] is letting them out in the proper time, in the proper place." Perhaps more radically, some women (as well as one of the gay men with whom I spoke) denied that they had the ability to control some or many of their emotions. One man in his twenties critically described a previous tendency he had to over-intellectualize problems and explained that he worked against that tendency because

> It wasn't that I wanted to cut off my emotions, I just didn't, they would get out of control, and I found that the more I tried to suppress them, the more powerful they would become. It was like this big dam that didn't let a little out at a time, it would just explode all of a sudden, and I'd be totally out of control.

The question remains, however, of the validity of seeing these latter seemingly resistant uses of the rhetoric of emotional control as "oppositional" forms (Williams 1977) within that system. This is certainly a dangerous rhetorical strategy, caught as they (we) are within a hegemonic discourse not of our own making. The opposition to self-control will most likely be absorbed into the logic of the existing system and so come to equal not resistance but simple deficiency or lack (of control). A possibly oppositional intent may have collaborative outcomes to the extent that the denial of self-control is taken by most audiences as a deficit and a confirmation of ideas about women's irrationality.

The culturally constructed emotionality of women is rife with contradiction. The emotional female, like the natural world that is the cultural source of both affect and women, is constructed as both pliant (because weak and a resource for use by civilized man) and ultimately tremendously powerful and uncontrollable (Strathern 1980). Emotionality is the source of women's value, their expertise in lieu of rationality, and yet it is the origin of their unsuitability for broader social tasks and even a potential threat to their children.

There are vivid parallels between this and the cultural meanings surrounding colonialism that Taussig (1984) and Stoler (1985) have described. Looking at early-twentieth-century colonists' views of the local Columbian labor force, Taussig describes their alternation between fear and awe of Indians who were perceived as dangerous and powerful figures, on the one hand, and disgust and denigration of their perceived weakness and lack of civilization, on the other. Taussig describes the process as one in which a "colonial mirror" "reflects back onto the colonists the barbarity of their own social relations" (1984:495). In a (certainly less systematic or universally brutal) way, a "patriarchal mirror" can be conceptualized as helping to produce the view of women as emotional – as dangerously "eruptive" and as in the process of weakly "breaking down." A "paradox of will" seems consistently to attend dominating relationships – whether those of gender, race, or class – as the subordinate other is ideologically painted as weak (so as to need protection or discipline) and yet periodically as threatening to break the ideological boundary in riot or hysteria. Emotion talk, as evident in these transcripts, shows the same contradictions of control, weakness, and strength. Given its definition as nature, at least in the West, emotion discourses may be one of the most likely and powerful devices by which domination proceeds.

[. . .]

In all societies, body disorders – which emotion is considered to be in this society – become crucial indicators of problems with social control and, as such, are more likely to occur or emerge in a discourse concerning social subordinates. Foucault has made the claim that power creates sexuality and its disciplining; similarly, it can be said to create emotionality. The cultural construction of women's emotion can thus be viewed not as the repression or suppression of emotion in men (as many lay-people, therapists, and other commentators argue) but as the creation of emotion in women. Because emotion is constructed as relatively chaotic, irrational, and antisocial, its existence vindicates authority and legitimates the need for control. By association with the female, it vindicates the distinction between and hierarchy of men and women. And the cultural logic connecting women and emotion corresponds to and shores up the walls between the spheres of private, intimate (and emotional) relations in the (ideologically) female domain of the family and public, formal (and rational) relations in the primarily male domain of the marketplace.

Rubin has remarked of sexuality that "There are historical periods in which [it] is more sharply contested and more overtly politicized" (1984:267). Emotionality has the same historical dynamism, with shifting gender relations often appearing to be at the root of both academic and lay struggles over how emotion is to be defined and evaluated. In other words, the contemporary dominant discourse on emotions – and particularly the view that they are irrational and to be controlled – helps construct but does not wholly determine women's discourse; there is an attempt to recast the association of women with emotion in an alternative feminist voice.

Feminist treatments of the question of emotion (e.g., Hochschild 1983; Jagger 1987) have tended to portray emotions not as chaos but as a discourse on problems. Some have contested both the irrationality and the passivity of feelings by arguing that emotions may involve the identification of problems in women's lives and are therefore political. Talk about anger, for example, can be interpreted as an attempt to identify the existence of inappropriate restraint or injustice. Sadness is a discourse on the problem of loss, fear on that of danger. By extension, talk about the control of emotions would be, in this feminist discourse, talk about the suppression of public acknowledgment of problems. The emotional female might then be seen not simply as a mythic construction on the axis of some arbitrary cultural dualism but as an outcome of the fact that women occupy an objectively more problematic position than does the white, upper-class, Northern European, older man who is the cultural exemplar par excellence of cool, emotionless rationality. According to a feminist analysis, whether or not women express their problems (i.e., are emotional) more than men, those women's audiences may hear a message that is an amalgam of the orthodox view and its feminist contestation: "We (those) women are dangerously close to erupting into emotionality/pointing to a problem/ moving toward a social critique."

References

Chodorow, Nancy. 1978. *The Reproduction of Mothering*. Berkeley: University of California Press.

Foucault, Michel. 1980. *The History of Sexuality*, Vol. 1. New York: Vintage.

Hochschild, Arlie. 1983. *The Managed Heart: Commercialization of Human Feeling*. Berkeley: University of California Press.

Jagger, Alison. 1987. Love and Knowledge: Emotion as an Epistemic Resource for Feminists. Ms. in possession of author. Department of Philosophy, University of Cincinnati.

Jordanova, L. J. 1980. Natural Facts: A Historical Perspective on Science and Sexuality. In Carol MacCormack and Marilyn Strathern, eds., *Nature, Culture, and Gender*. Cambridge: Cambridge University Press, pp. 42–69.

Kirkpatrick, John. 1987. Representing the Self as 'You' in American Discourse. Paper presented at the annual meetings of the American Anthropological Association, Chicago.

Martin, Emily. 1987. The Ideology of Reproduction: The Reproduction of Ideology. Paper presented to the Upstate New York Feminist Scholars' Network, September.

Parsons, Talcott, and Robert Bales. 1955. *Family, Socialization, and Interaction Process*. Glencoe, IL: Free Press.

Rosaldo, Michelle Z. 1984. Toward an Anthropology of Self and Feeling. In R. Shweder and R. LeVine, eds., *Culture Theory: Essays on Mind, Self, and Emotion*. Cambridge: Cambridge University Press, pp. 137–57.

Rosaldo, Renato. 1977. The Rhetoric of Control: Ilongots Viewed as Natural Bandits and Wild Indians. In B. Babcock, ed., *The Reversible World: Symbolic Inversion in Art and Society*. Ithaca, NY: Cornell University Press, pp. 240–57.

Rubin, Gayle. 1984. Thinking Sex: Notes for a Radical Theory of the Politics of Sexuality. In Carol S. Vance, ed., *Pleasure and Danger: Exploring Female Sexuality*. Boston: Routledge & Kegan Paul.

Scheper-Hughes, Nancy, and Margaret Lock. 1987. The Mindful Body: A Prolegomenon to Future Work in Medical Anthropology. *Medical Anthropology Quarterly* 1:6–41.

Shields, Stephanie A. 1987. Women, Men and the Dilemma of Emotion. In P. Shaver and C. Hendrick, eds., *Sex and Gender*. Newbury Park, CA: Sage Publications, pp. 229–50.

Stoler, Anne. 1985. Perceptions of Protest: Defining the Dangerous in Colonial Sumatra. *American Ethnologist* 12:642–58.

Strathern, Marilyn. 1980. No Nature, No Culture: The Hagen Case. In Carol MacCormack and Marilyn Strathern, eds., *Nature, Culture, and Gender*. Cambridge: Cambridge University Press, pp. 174–222.

Taussig, Michael. 1984. Culture of Terror – Space of Death. Roger Casement's Putumayo Report and the Explanation of Torture. *Comparative Studies in Society and History* 26:467–97.

Williams, Raymond. 1977. *Marxism and Literature*. Oxford: Oxford University Press.

Chapter 6

William M. Reddy

AGAINST CONSTRUCTIONISM

The historical ethnography of emotions

[. . .]

The persistent dilemmas of relativism

THE ABSOLUTE PLASTICITY OF THE individual is a necessary implication of strong constructionist stances on questions of sexuality, ethnicity, and identity. Michel Foucault . . . argued for a view of power so all-pervasive and so insidious in its operation that there was no refuge where the individual could say, "This is me, this is where the true self lives." Every space was subjected to disciplinary determination, so much so that the very experience of being a subject was, in Foucault's view, an outcome of power's discursive workings. . . . Foucault was not a relativist—he deplored this tyranny of discourse—but, as he occasionally acknowledged, his position was inconsistent, for there was nothing in the name of which he could justify his disapproval. In his last works he had begun to distance himself from this extreme position (Foucault 1985). But it is important to recognize that his earlier notion of power does not involve the sway, the persuasive capacity, the authority, or the coercion exercised by one person over other persons. It is not, in this sense, a notion of power that has any Western pedigree; it has nothing to do with what we normally call "politics." Nor does the type of resistance Foucault occasionally alludes to as a possibility represent anything resembling political action. Foucault is, in this sense, a relativist in all but name. . . .

Another influential model widely used to replace older notions of culture is Pierre Bourdieu's (1977) theory of practice, built around the concept of habitus. . . . The concept helped Bourdieu to understand the gap between what informants say to ethnographers and the actual shape of the actions they take. Explicit principle is never simply "applied" to social life, Bourdieu argues; instead, the complex qualifications and reformulations that intervene are themselves ethnography's (and history's) proper object of study. They are formed by an inarticulate sense of rightness and strategy (habitus) which cannot be communicated verbally. Bourdieu's individual is not plastic, because he endows individuals with a desire to pursue advantage and a strategic sense that drives them constantly to sort out and reformulate situations and action plans. However, this pursuit of advantage must be regarded either as empty, the content being completely determined by cultural context, or else as predefined and therefore universal. In the former case, practice theory remains relativist and apolitical; in the latter, it may fall into the economist's fallacy that advantage and interest are easily defined (in Western terms). This fallacy is present, although "corrected" in various ways, in Bourdieu's (1979) notion of "cultural capital." [. . .]

In the debate over essentialism, feminist theorists have been struggling with a version of the same problem that has confronted anthropologists and cultural historians, and extreme relativism still arises as a conceptual necessity at certain junctures of this debate. "Essentialists" maintain that women are endowed with universal characteristics that distinguish them from men, characteristics in virtue of which they must, in justice, demand for themselves a very different place in society from that accorded them in the contemporary West. Antiessentialists insist that claiming special characteristics for women is perpetuating the same error that apologists for male domination have always made (for reviews of this dilemma, see Alcoff 1988, Riley 1988, Miller 1991, Haraway 1991, Mohanty, Russo, and Torres 1991). Woman's difference has justified her disqualifications, antiessentialists note, and any argument based on difference can be turned against women. Moreover, women need to be freed from any and all expectations as to their "nature." . . . The argument that it is constraining to characterize women *as nurturing* or *as emotional* easily becomes an argument against characterizing women and men in any way. The political goal of liberating men and women from constraining expectations or assumptions can easily get lost in this refusal to characterize them, since, if individuals are entirely empty and wholly plastic, then there is nothing in virtue of which liberation is good.

Emotional constructionism as a form of relativism

These dilemmas have come into focus recently, and in a very compelling and important way, in a number of ethnographies of emotion (Abu-Lughod 1986, Lutz 1988, Grima 1992, see also papers collected in Lutz and Abu-Lughod 1990 and the important earlier work by Rosaldo 1980, 1984). These studies have drawn inspiration from Foucault's notion of discourse, Bourdieu's concept of practice, and feminist critiques of essentialism. In each case the ethnographer, a woman, carried out fieldwork in an unusual way; each was integrated into a local household as a woman and shared in the constraints on movement and interaction locally imposed on women. Because of this integration, Abu-Lughod and Grima, working in Muslim societies, had access to "private" female expression and practice that previous male ethnographers had been barred from or considered unimportant. Lutz, working on a Pacific atoll, found no public-private divide in expressing emotion, contrary to both Western and Muslim notions of privacy and propriety. [. . .]

These outstanding contributions to the growing field of the anthropology of emotion are notable for their adamant refusal to allow for any physiological, psychological, or other universal determinant or influence in emotional life. Many other contributions to this field remain neutral or agnostic about the relation between constructed and discursive emotional expression and actual emotional experience. Fred Myers proposes to "leave open" (1986:105) the relation between culturally constructed emotions and individual psychological dynamics. Simultaneously, he wishes to avoid examining the question whether an actor "really" feels emotions that are culturally appropriate in given circumstances (1986:106–7). . . . Whether such epistemological caution is more appropriate than the strong stand of Grima, Lutz, and Abu-Lughod is not the real point, however. The strong constructionist stand is one that views the individual as fully plastic, and it is one that, as a result, cannot provide grounds for a political critique of any given construction. Grima (1992:163–64) condemns the "oppression" of women in Paxtun society, which is firmly in the grip of a male-centered "gerontocracy"; she explains the firmness of this grip by noting that female identity and survival are entirely wrapped up in relationships to males. However, if, as she asserts, "emotion is culture," then we must accept that those women who *perform* no emotional need to free themselves from this oppression *have* no need to do so. One cannot have it both ways. Unless one specifies the grounds—by saying what in fact universally characterizes the individual (which both the strong constructionists and the agnostics wish to avoid doing)—one cannot have a politics of emotion or a meaningful history of emotion.

There is, moreover, troubling evidence against the strong constructionist point of view from other ethnographies of emotion—evidence suggesting that individual emotional life has a dynamic character and that specific communities strive to shape, contain, and channel (not construct) emotional expression. Brenneis's (1990) work on Fijians of Indian descent and White's (1990a, b) study of A'ara speakers' "disentangling" practices both focus on methods employed to encourage expression of hidden or pent-up negative feelings that threaten community solidarity and peace. . . . Besnier (1995) emphasizes the striking contrast between the effusive emotional style of letters written by Nukulaelae Islanders and their reserved style in person. . . . Both contrasts point to an effort to organize or orchestrate rather than construct emotion. . . . Cognitive anthropologists have found that individuals respond to emotion-charged cultural "schemas," such as romantic love or class consciousness, in highly divergent ways, depending upon context and personality; this diversity points to underlying emotional proclivities that such schemas may or may not engage (Holland 1992, Strauss 1992). . . . Many psychologists assert that there are only a few basic varieties of emotions; they certainly have good evidence that autonomic nervous system reactions and facial expressions come in a few basic varieties across the globe, with an apparent genetic basis (Ekman 1982, Ekman and Davidson 1994; but see the important caveats of Barrett 1993 and the argument of Ortony and Turner 1990). [. . .]

Bridging the space between language (practice) and feeling

Here I wish to propose a solution to this political dilemma, which is at the same time a dilemma about conceptualizing history and cultural difference. I propose to find within the very plasticity of the individual grounds for making universal assertions that can motivate ethnographic and historical analysis that is politically meaningful. Grounding universal claims in emotional life rather than in identity, gender, culture, or discourse sidesteps the thorny questions that have recently formed insurmountable stumbling blocks to any universalism or humanism. To say something about the inherent character of emotions offers a way out, a basis for political judgment that is not a *petitio principii*.

The dilemma of emotional constructionism might be reformulated in the following manner: The Western ethnic view (including that of expert social science) of statements about emotions is that they are descriptive in character or, in J. L. Austin's terms, "constative." The strong constructionist view of Grima, Lutz, and Abu-Lughod might be seen as an insistence that statements about emotions are "performative" in Austin's sense. Just as saying "I do" at a wedding *is* to wed, so to say "I am angry" is, in the constructionist view, to *be* angry. To perform anger, sadness, fear, shame, is to be angry, sad, fearful, ashamed. Grima (1992:7), for example, defines emotion as a combination of behavior and expectations, denying that there is any "inner" residuum on which they are based. Abu-Lughod says that it is better "to examine discourses rather than their putative referents" (1990:28). I would argue that both views are mistaken and that statements about emotions are neither descriptive (constative) nor performative—they neither adequately represent nor construct (perform) emotions. An emotion statement is not, as Austin suggested, a "mere report" (1975:78–79). It is an effort by the speaker to offer an interpretation of something that is observable to no other actor. Such an effort is essential to social life, an inescapable facet of one's identity, one's relationships, one's prospects. As such, it has a direct impact on the feelings in question. If asked the question "Do you feel angry?" a person may genuinely feel *more* angry in answering yes, *less* angry in answering no. A common strategy in psychological studies of emotion and mood is to induce emotions in subjects by having them read statements such as "I am joyful" or "I am sad." Such reading exercises dependably produce effects in the subjects consonant with the mood or emotion invoked, as do exercises in which subjects are instructed to adopt certain facial expressions (see, e.g., Rholes, Riskind, and Lane 1987 and, for a general review of such research, Laird 1987; on inducing affect with facial movements, see Ekman, Levenson, and Friesen 1983). Many other effects are possible, including the opposite: expressing a feeling can easily result in its rapid dissipation. Stable patterns of such statements, repeated over years, have very profound, shaping effects on one's whole emotional makeup.

I propose to call emotion statements such as these, in which the statement's referent changes by virtue of the statement, "emotives." Performative utterances, by the way in which they refer to themselves, actually do things to the world. In the statement "I accept your nomination," the verb "accept," used in this way, refers to or names the statement in which it appears, making the statement an acceptance. The acceptance, as an act of the speaker, changes the world in a way that a descriptive statement cannot, because it makes the speaker into a nominee. An emotive utterance, unlike a performative, is not self-referential. When someone says, "I am angry," the anger is not the utterance—not in the way that, in "I accept," "accept" is the acceptance. An emotive statement seems at first glance to have a real external referent, to be descriptive or constative. On closer inspection, however, one recognizes that the "external referent" that an emotive appears to point at is not passive in the formulation of the emotive, and it emerges from the act of uttering in a changed state. Emotives are influenced directly by and alter what they "refer" to. Thus, emotives are similar to performatives (and differ from constatives) in that emotives do things to the world. Emotives are themselves instruments for directly changing, building, hiding, intensifying emotions. There is an "inner" dimension to emotion, but it is never merely "represented" by statements or actions. It is the necessary (relative) failure of all efforts to represent feeling that makes for (and sets limits on) our plasticity. Many ways of expressing feeling work equally well (poorly); all fail to some degree. It is here, rather than in some putative set of genetically programmed "basic" emotions, that a universal conception of the person, one with political relevance, can be founded.

Emotives and poststructuralism

This concept of emotives builds on poststructuralist insights about language but goes beyond them.

In the first place, the existence of emotions is not dependent upon the accuracy of one or more Western notions of intentionality or of the person, which poststructuralists have widely and very successfully attacked. The existence of emotions is not dependent on the accuracy, either, of Western conceptions of what emotions are. Ethnographic research has repeatedly demonstrated the narrowness and partiality of this family of Western conceptions, a narrowness and partiality closely associated with the notions of intention that poststructuralism rejects. But it has also repeatedly confirmed the existence of lexicons and practices significantly similar to those Westerners associate with emotions (see, e.g., Manson, Shore, and Bloom 1985, Heider 1991). On the basis of this research, emotions cannot be regarded—as they have been in the West—as a residual, somatic, antirational domain of conscious life whose turbulence is a constant threat to the formulation of clear intentions. Instead, I argue, they must be regarded as the very location of the capacity to embrace, revise, or reject cultural or discursive structures of whatever kind.[1]

Emotions are the real world-anchor of signs. To restate this in poststructuralist terms, there is a feeling that goes with every sign; emotion generates *parole* against the backdrop of *langue*. Philosophers and researchers have not been able to find language's anchor in the world when regarding signs or language as referring or pointing to a world and have wrongly concluded that signs and language must therefore float free of any possible world. But the world they belong to is the world in which feelings occur, in which utterances and texts grow directly out of feelings. One does not need a questionable Western-style subject to provide the link between them.

An emotive utterance is not self-referential like a performative but claims by definition to refer to something close to its origin, to its own world-anchor. Why does this kind of reference not fail, just as all other kinds of reference to a "world" that is not already signs fail? The answer is that it does fail. The emotive effect derives from the failure. If the emotive did not fail, it would be a "mere report," an accurate representation. A statement about how one feels is always a failure to one degree or another; like a performative it is neither true nor false. Emotives constitute a kind of pledge that alters, a kind of getting-through of something nonverbal into the verbal domain that could never be called an equivalence or a representation. The very failure of representation is recognized and brings an emotional response itself; this response is part of the emotive effect. This is true whether one's "intention" is to speak the "truth" about one's feelings or not. This problematic link between emotive and emotion, this dilemma, is our activity as a person. One might say that, just as a performative can be happy or unhappy, an emotive brings emotional effects appropriate to its content or effects that differ markedly from its content. If it does bring appropriate effects, then the emotive, in a Western context, might be said to be "sincere"; if it does not, the emotive may be claimed, after the fact, to be hypocrisy, an evasion, a mistake, a projection, or a denial. But all of these characterizations—including the notion of sincerity—are problematic, themselves forms of failed reference. [. . .]

Emotives, repression, and cultural styles

The concept of emotives can draw support from recent reformulations of the notion of repression. The question whether repression really occurs has inspired debate among psychologists for decades. There has been a recent convergence among contending views, however, that offers support for a reformulated view of repression consistent with the concept of emotives being elaborated here. . . .

In a recent review, David S. Holmes (1990) argues that there is no laboratory evidence to support the existence of repression, despite sustained efforts over the past 60 years to find empirical proof of its operation. Holmes notes that psychotherapists viewing videotapes of therapy sessions often disagree as to when repression is occurring or how its operation is effectuated. Holmes concedes willingly that laboratory research has yielded abundant evidence of "selectivity in perception and recall" (p. 97) and readily accepts the existence of "denial," a related process which he defines as a conscious decision to ignore and forget (p. 86). These concessions are substantial. It is only because repression is deemed to be an unconscious mechanism that laboratory studies have failed to turn up conclusive evidence of it. Matthew Erdelyi (1990), however, argues that there is no bar in psychoanalytic theory to viewing repression as resulting from a conscious decision to forget. Memory research—Holmes and Erdelyi agree—has identified an array of mechanisms available for use in conscious suppression of unpleasant thoughts or feelings or memories. Such conscious suppression—any act of conscious "denial," in Holmes's sense—may therefore, in Erdelyi's view, be considered an instance of "repression." (Nor is there, he remarks, any reason that a person cannot, in a second stage, consciously decide to forget having consciously decided to forget something.) "If repression (defensive or otherwise) can be conscious, then suddenly it becomes an obvious and ubiquitous device" (Erdelyi 1990:14). . . .

By some models of consciousness, such as Dennett's (1991) "multiple drafts" model, the distinction between conscious and unconscious is never a sharp one in any case. Any report a person might make about an inner state is, by such a model, only one of a number of incomplete "drafts" that contend for focus. The argument here is that explicit emotive statements such as "I am not angry" are instances of such drafts. Feelings involve, at once, action orientations and the unformulated "thick" thinking that bonds contending drafts together. They are summation states, a background against which focal discursive structures emerge.

To characterize such summation states is extremely difficult; in general actors are compelled to fall back on conventional expectations about appropriate emotions. In addition, there is so much at stake in vital relationships that emotives often have the status of contractual commitments. ("I feel like going to a movie." "He frightens me.") These expectations and commitments do not involve mere "display rules," as Ekman (1980, 1982) and others contend, but neither do they "create" emotions out of whole cloth as the strong constructionists would have it. . . .

The inadequacy of conventional emotives to characterize the complex summation states they "describe" can be covered over, to some extent, by the effects of habitual repetition. Isen and Diamond (1989:144), in a review of research into affect as an automatic process, arrive at a telling conclusion that is worth quoting at length:

> To the extent that affect can have an influence automatically—without attention or intention and seemingly irresistibly—it can be understood as a deeply ingrained, overlearned habit, or as a process of chunking and organizing the situation. . . .
>
> We are reminded of the way in which little boys have often been taught to keep from crying by substituting anger for sadness: "When something bad happens don't get sad, get mad." Thus, people may be able to regulate their feelings, through their focus and through changing what they learn in given situations. . . . In this way, problem emotions, even though they feel automatic and uncontrollable, may be alterable. This does not mean that unwanted affective reactions will be easy to change (old habits die hard), but it does suggest that change may be possible and that the very sense of inevitability may be misleading.

Thus, there is good reason to attribute extensive power to the conventional emotives authorized in a given community to shape members' sense of identity and self-awareness, members' manner of confronting contingencies and routine. But power to shape is a very different matter from the capacity to create from nothing. The nature of the residuum that is not satisfactorily shaped is an all-important question for understanding what is universally human and for understanding the politics of that shaping power. In any given field context, one would expect to find a wide range of deviations, resistances, and alternative idioms that point to possibilities for change through crisis, dissolution, or adaptation and that offer grounds for drawing conclusions about who has power and who does not.

Where emotives have their greatest effects and are subject to their greatest failures is in situations of what I will call intense ambivalence. Cultural or conventional action patterns often come into play both in producing such situations and in helping actors navigate them. It is especially because community conventions recommend the use of emotives to manage intense ambivalence that communities may be said to have emotional styles or tones.

To illustrate, I will draw some examples from Grima's (1992) vivid ethnographic review of Paxtun emotional conventions. Paxtun convention dictates arranged marriages in which bride-prices can be quite significant. A recently wed woman is confined to the home, forced to carry more than her share of the housework, and required to submit to the authority and undergo the mistreatment of her husband's mother and sisters as well as any senior wives present. Marriage is therefore conventionally the first great sadness, or *gham,* in a woman's life. The intensity of a woman's suffering, through this and other *gham* experiences, as she unflinchingly submits to the requirements of her family is her principal source of honor. As a result, the bride, dressed in her best and decked out in jewelry and other adornments, is supposed to adopt a downcast expression, tearful, quiet; she takes no part in the celebrations of the marriage ceremony. Her crestfallen demeanor is said to be "beautiful." But does culture create the *gham* of the bride? Structurally, the transition seems likely to be experienced as both a severe loss (of familiar persons and places, the only ones known since birth) and a drop in status (from daughter to in-marrying bride, lowest in the new household's pecking order). What the emotional conventions of the wedding ceremony do is give shape to the likely emotions of the bride, rather than create them. They do so in a manner that allows for a highly restrained display of opposition. Both the restraint and the display accrue to the bride's credit, because they suggest that she is mastering intense negative feelings in order to remain obedient to her male elders and acquiesce in the marriage. This is a convention for managing intense ambivalence (the desire to obey versus the desire not to marry), aiming at the repressive transformation of rebelliousness into *gham.*

Characteristic of Paxtun women's conventional emotional style is that they cannot express an intense emotion or inclination publicly, except in the form of *gham.* To display infatuation with a single young man is forbidden, but loss of that man resulting from arranged marriage to another transforms the infatuation into a source of suffering. The suffering not only may be expressed but, if expressed in a restrained manner as silent sorrow, is rewarded with admiration and respect. To display intense pride in a son's energies, skills, and accomplishments runs the risk of insulting listeners. But if that son is hurt in an accident, falls ill, or dies, the expression of *gham* may be indulged in—indeed it is required that a mother express extremely intense grief, without restraint, in such situations. The intensity of grief is often displayed by momentary lapses in modesty: rushing out of the house without a veil, seeking help from strange men to get to a hospital, bursting into tears when speaking. [. . .]

When viewed as emotives, expressions of suffering by Paxtun women frequently do lead to extreme *intensification* (but, I would argue, not creation) of grief and sorrow. The whole pattern of restrictions of female behavior—involving low estimation of female capacity, fear of their misbehavior, submission of women to male authority—represents an independent source of sorrow. The death of a son is reason enough to grieve in many societies. But when that son was born in a marriage not desired (which is the *normative* case in this society) and raised through self-discipline, self-abnegation, and submission to family authority and the needs of male honor (these are the *local* ways of talking about women's duty), the woman's extreme ambivalence about her life of personal losses may offer deeper reasons to grieve over the loss of a son. . . . Hence the whole pattern of emotives discussed by Grima speaks of emotions *managed* not created. Grima herself speaks frequently of emotional control rather than construction (e.g., pp. 8–9, 141, 163). Just as convention lays down a host of restrictions on female behavior and choice (which are understood locally as harsh), so convention lays down a style for repressing some feelings and intensifying and publicly expressing others. . . .

The implication here is not that certain feelings such as grief at death are "natural" or universal. Situations of intense ambivalence are likely in most social orders because they arrange for and encourage emotional attachments or hopes that inevitably come into conflict. A young Paxtun woman is encouraged by institutional arrangements that offer both rewards and penalties to develop a deep attachment to her mother. At the same time, marriage is an essential element of the normative life cycle. Thus a wedding is highly likely to generate intense ambivalence in a bride. Intense ambivalence can be a nodal point of instability in a normative emotional style. By allowing women full expression of sorrow (but not other feelings) and by treating sorrow as a source of honor for women, Paxtun convention tries to tip the balance of ambivalence toward grief. This is not culture creating grief but convention promoting certain emotives over others because, over time, these emotives strongly influence individual emotion in a manner that allows for a certain stability and ideological comprehensibility in a community's life.

The variation of individual responses (some fitting expectations well, some going all the way to complete deviance) provides an initial reservoir of possibilities for change, something that can be drawn upon when ideological, economic, or political factors put pressure on the system (as is, indeed, happening in the larger towns of the region Grima studied). Those who feel more frustrated or excluded can more readily adopt new norms that are contending for domination. An important question for comparative analysis would be whether certain emotive styles force greater numbers into emotional deviance than others.

If we conceive of community conventions as stipulating styles of emotional control that exploit the capacity of emotives to shape emotions, then power, politics, and liberation regain their meaning. Emotional control is the real site of the exercise of power: politics is just a process of determining who must repress as illegitimate, who must foreground as valuable, the feelings and desires that come up for them in given contexts and relationships. [. . .]

Note

1   This assertion depends on a broad definition of emotion that cannot be fully explored here but that draws on the views of psychologists such as Laird (1987), Oatley (1992), and Averill (1994), who regard emotions as a form of, or aspects

of, thought or cognition, and of philosophers such as Solomon (1984, 1992), De Sousa (1987), and Greenspan (1988), who argue that emotion represents a form of judgment that cannot be readily distinguished from thought or rationality.

References

ABU-LUGHOD, LILA. 1986. *Veiled sentiments: Honor and poetry in a Bedouin society*. Berkeley: University of California Press.

———. 1990. "Shifting politics in Bedouin love poetry," in *Language and the politics of emotion*. Edited by Catherine A. Lutz and Lila Abu-Lughod, pp. 24–45. Cambridge: Cambridge University Press/Paris: Editions de la Maison des Sciences de l'Homme.

ALCOFF, LINDA. 1988. Cultural feminism versus post-structuralism: The identity crisis in feminist theory. *Signs: Journal of Women in Culture and Society* 13:405–36.

AUSTIN, J. L. 1975. 2d edition. *How to do things with words*. Cambridge: Harvard University Press.

AVERILL, JAMES R. 1994. "I feel, therefore I am—I think," in *The nature of emotions: Fundamental questions*. Edited by Paul Ekman and Richard J. Davidson, pp. 379–38. Oxford: Oxford University Press.

BARRETT, KAREN CAPLOVITZ. 1993. The development of nonverbal communication of emotion: A functionalist perspective. *Journal of Nonverbal Behavior* 17:145–69.

BESNIER, NIKO. 1995. *Literacy, emotion, and authority: Reading and writing on a Polynesian atoll*. Cambridge: Cambridge Universisty Press.

BOURDIEU, PIERRE. 1977. *Outline of a theory of practice*. Translated by Richard Nice. Cambridge: Cambridge University Press.

———. 1979. *La distinction: Critique sociale du jugement*. Paris: Editions de Minuit.

BRENNEIS, DONALD. 1990. "Shared and solitary sentiments: The discourse of friendship, play, and anger in Bhatgaon," in *Language and the politics of emotion*. Edited by Catherine A. Lutz and Lila Abu-Lughod, pp. 113–25. Cambridge: Cambridge University Press/Paris: Editions de la Maison des Sciences de l'Homme.

DENNETT, D. C. 1991. *Consciousness explained*. Boston: Little, Brown.

DE SOUSA, RONALD. 1987. *The rationality of emotion*. Cambridge: MIT Press.

EKMAN, PAUL. 1980. *The face of man: Expressions of universal emotions in a New Guinea village*. New York: Garland STPM Press.

———. Editor. 1982. 2d edition. *Emotion in the human face*. Cambridge: Cambridge University Press.

EKMAN, PAUL, AND RICHARD J. DAVIDSON. Editors. 1994. *The nature of emotion: Fundamental questions*. Oxford: Oxford University Press.

EKMAN, PAUL, ROBERT W. LEVENSON, AND WALLACE V. FRIESEN. 1983. Autonomic nervous system activity distinguishes among emotions. *Science* 221:1208–10.

ERDELYI, MATTHEW H. 1990. "Repression, reconstruction, and defense: History and integration of the psychoanalytic and experimental frameworks," in *Repression and dissociation: Implications for personality theory, psychopathology, and health*. Edited by Jerome L. Singer, pp. 1–31. Chicago: University of Chicago Press.

FOUCAULT, MICHEL. 1985. *The history of sexuality*. Vol. 2. *The use of pleasure*. Translated by Robert Hurley. New York: Pantheon.

GREENSPAN, PATRICIA S. 1988. *Emotions and reasons: An inquiry into emotional justification.* New York: Routledge.

GRIMA, BENEDICTE. 1992. *The performance of emotion among Paxtun women.* Austin: University of Texas Press.

HARAWAY, DONNA J. 1991. *Simians, cyborgs, and women: The reinvention of nature.* New York: Routledge.

HEIDER, KARL G. 1991. *Landscapes of emotion: Mapping three cultures of emotion in Indonesia.* Cambridge: Cambridge University Press.

HOLLAND, DOROTHY C. 1992. "How cultural systems become desire: A case study of American romance," in *Human motives and cultural models.* Edited by Roy D'Andrade and Claudia Strauss, pp. 61–89. Cambridge: Cambridge University Press.

HOLMES, DAVID S. 1990. "The evidence for repression: An examination of sixty years of research," in *Repression and dissociation: Implications for personality theory, psychopathology, and health.* Edited by Jerome L. Singer, pp. 85–102. Chicago: University of Chicago Press.

ISEN, ALICE M., AND GREGORY ANDRADE DIAMOND. 1989. "Affect and automaticity," in *Unintended thought: Limits of awareness, intention, and control.* Edited by J. S. Uleman and John A. Bargh, pp. 124–52. New York: Guilford Press.

LAIRD, JAMES D. 1987. Mood affects memory because feelings are cognitions. *Journal of Social Behavior and Personality* 4: 33–38.

LUTZ, CATHERINE A. 1988. *Unnatural emotion: Everyday sentiments on a Micronesian atoll and their challenge to Western theory.* Chicago: University of Chicago Press.

LUTZ, CATHERINE A., AND LILA ABU-LUGHOD. Editors. 1990. *Language and the politics of emotion.* Cambridge: Cambridge University Press/Paris: Editions de la Maison des Sciences de l'Homme.

MANSON, SPERO M., JAMES H. SHORE, AND JOSEPH D. BLOOM. 1985. "The depressive experience in American Indian communities: A challenge for psychiatric theory and diagnosis," in *Culture and depression: Studies in the anthropology and cross-cultural psychiatry of affect and disorder.* Edited by A. Kleinman and B. Good, pp. 331–68. Berkeley: University of California Press.

MILLER, NANCY K. 1991. *Getting personal: Feminist occasions and other autobiographical acts.* New York: Routledge.

MOHANTY, CHANDRA TALPADE, ANN RUSSO, AND LOURDES TORRES. Editors. 1991. *Third World women and the politics of feminism.* Bloomington: Indiana University Press.

MYERS, FRED R. 1986. *Pintupi country, Pintupi self: Sentiment, place, and politics among Western Desert Aborigines.* Berkeley: University of California Press.

OATLEY, KEITH. 1992. *Best-laid schemes: The psychology of emotions.* Cambridge: Cambridge University Press.

ORTONY, A., AND TERENCE J. TURNER. 1990. What's basic about basic emotions? *Psychological Review* 97:315–31.

RHOLES, W. S., J. H. RISKIND, AND J. W. LANE. 1987. Emotional state and memory biases: Effects of cognitive priming and mood. *Journal of Personality and Social Psychology* 52:91–99.

RILEY, DENISE. 1988. *"Am I that name?" Feminism and the category of "women" in history.* Minneapolis: University of Minnesota Press.

ROSALDO, MICHELLE Z. 1980. *Knowledge and passion: Ilongot notions of self and social life.* Cambridge: Cambridge University Press.

———. 1984. "Toward an anthropology of self and feeling," in *Culture theory: Essays on mind, self, and emotion*. Edited by R. Shweder and R. LeVine, pp. 137–57. Cambridge: Cambridge University Press.

SOLOMON, ROBERT C. 1984. "Getting angry: The Jamesian theory of emotion in anthropology," in *Culture theory: Essays on mind, self, and emotion*. Edited by R. Shweder and R. LeVine, pp. 238–54. Cambridge: Cambridge University Press.

———. 1992. Existentialism, emotions, and the cultural limits of rationality. *Philosophy East and West* 42:597–621.

STRAUSS, CLAUDIA. 1992. "What makes Tony run? Schemas as motives reconsidered," in *Human motives and cultural models*. Edited by Roy D'Andrade and Claudia Strauss, pp. 191–224. Cambridge: Cambridge University Press.

WHITE, GEOFFREY M. 1990a. "Moral discourse and the rhetoric of emotions," in *Language and the politics of emotion*. Edited by Catherine A. Lutz and Lila Abu-Lughod, pp. 46–68. Cambridge: Cambridge University Press/Paris: Editions de la Maison des Sciences de l'Homme.

———. 1990b. "Emotion talk and social inference: Disentangling in Santa Isabel, Solomon Islands," in *Disentangling: Conflict discourse in Pacific societies*. Edited by Karen Ann Watson-Gegeo and Geoffrey M. White, pp. 53–121. Stanford: Stanford University Press.

Chapter 7

Michael E. Harkin

FEELING AND THINKING IN MEMORY AND FORGETTING

Toward an ethnohistory of the emotions

[. . .]

ETHNOHISTORIANS SUCH AS RAYMOND FOGELSON have long been sensitive to the problem of emotion. For Fogelson, ethnohistory has been, at least in part, a type of empathy, in which we can hope to understand our subject only if we exercise our full human faculties and not simply our analytic ones. His presidential address on the ethnohistory of "non-events" made the original observation that some events disappear from consciousness because they are too traumatic to be remembered (Fogelson 1989: 143). . . . We might also take note of Robert Levy's notion of "hypocognition," in which certain emotional experiences may not find expression since they lack an appropriate cognitive structuration in the culture that would allow them to become the subject of discourse. In such cases, "their unarticulated, un-namable, and chaotic qualities" make them disturbing and dangerous and, I would argue, potentially creative forces, in revitalization movements, for example (Levy 1984: 228). These insights represent an important contribution to our methodology. The aptly named "trail of tears" of the Cherokee, which provides Fogelson's key example of a repressed event, gives us a clue as to the importance of emotion in the representation of history. If we naively assume that oral history can give us privileged access to the entire range of a culture's past, we risk producing incomplete ethnohistories, not merely because we may omit certain events but also because we fail to take into account the complex relation that pertains between a contemporary community and its past. That this relationship is an emotional one is certain; how to go about taking these emotions into account is still largely an open question.

. . . Thomas Buckley (1996) has noted how Alfred L. Kroeber avoided the study of California ethnohistory because it was merely the "little history of pitiful events." More generally, anthropology has tended to construct the relation between culture and personality heavily in favor of the former, thus distinguishing itself from psychology, which it (rightly) criticized for excessive methodological individualism. And yet the sort of culture and personality studies produced by Ruth Benedict, Margaret Mead, Geoffrey Gorer, and others in midcentury virtually ignored the individual along with the question of emotions in favor of the broad brushstrokes of configurationism and culture at a distance. Edward Sapir's attempt to introduce a more robust concept of the individual psyche failed to survive his death (Darnell 1986). [. . .]

Emotions and culture dissolution

From a methodological perspective, we must ask ourselves what role the emotions can possibly play in our interpretations of cultures that were destroyed or radically altered in the aftermath of contact with Euroamericans. Lacking detailed ethnographies and linguistic documentation, we have no possible way of knowing what schemata of emotions may have existed in extinct cultures and languages or what the consequences for historical events may have been. As Richard and Nora Dauenhauer (1995) have remarked, the loss of a language is a cultural death, and members of the ethnic group go through predictable Kübler-Rossian stages of reaction. While the universality of the phases of death as outlined by Elisabeth Kübler-Ross is debatable, and their applicability to stages of ethnocide uncertain, we must turn to some psychodynamic model to understand this process.

Now it is perhaps time to listen to the psychoanalytical anthropologists while retaining skepticism about the overarching Freudian project. A great advantage of a psychoanalytic perspective is that it assumes that the basic mechanisms humans employ to deal with trauma are similar cross-culturally. Thus their meanings, while rooted in culturally specific idioms, transcend that context and are available to all who would read them carefully. Ethnopsychologists, on the other hand, often seem to assume that the human psyche is a tabula rasa and capable of almost infinite variation, despite the fact that their own results suggest a fairly modest variation of emotion categories across cultures. That the Heiltsuk schema of híl'álá is quite similar to the Ifaluk *song* or the Flathead anger concept is not surprising, nor is the fact that all three are immediately recognizable to Americans, who possess a somewhat different model of anger (Lutz 1988; O'Nell 1996).

It seems that in extreme circumstances the actions of persons to express grief, while famously irrational, are the most transparent to outside interpretation. The Sioux Ghost Dance of 1892 is a case where grief and distress at the destruction of the buffalo and the loss of land, people, and freedom to live as they had in the past prompted the Sioux to address these traumas ritually (DeMallie 1984: 256–82; Mooney 1965 [1896]). Anthony Wallace (1970), the greatest theoretician of religious responses to cultural disruption, addressed a similar chain of events among the nineteenth century Seneca from a psychoanalytic perspective. His particular contribution was linking stress – seen on the levels of individual, group, and ecosystem – and ritual (Wallace 1956).

Responses to cultural dissolution are holistic, totalizing phenomena. The Handsome Lake movement among the Seneca involved all aspects of Seneca culture and its relation to the physical and social environment and was focused equally on the individual and on cultural practices. Indeed, such movements establish a micro-macrocosm relation more explicitly than most religions and attempt to affect the condition of the universe by localized actions. In these points, Wallace extends and sharpens the ethno-historian's understanding of cultural reactions to extreme stress. The problem with Wallace's model is evident in the name usually attached to such phenomena: "revitalization movements." This places, a priori, entirely too optimistic a reading on events, suggesting a necessary trajectory, even a teleology, in which the culture will emerge "revitalized." Of course, we all know of cases where these have not been successful, and Wallace did too, for he wrote an introduction to a modern edition of James Mooney's *Ghost Dance* (Wallace 1965). However, on this view, we can only see such events as tragically blocked revitalizations.

This ignores the more likely interpretation that such movements were not properly about "revitalization," that they were centered not on the life drive but the death drive, not *eros* but, rather, *thanatos*, in Freudian terms. In the Ghost Dances generally, despite the wide variation in versions, the emphasis on death and the dead, and the self-destructive elements of ritual practice, give us strong clues that it was not something properly termed a "revitalization movement." Nor were they cultural "palliation," to borrow the Dauenhauers' suggestive term. Instead, they were, for the most part, ritual enactments of cultural dissolution and death. In some cases, such as the one I examine below, they took on almost the character of abreactive utterances.

I will look at the Ghost Dance as it appeared in southwestern Oregon in the 1870s, where it was known as the "Warm House" cult (DuBois 1939). It was originally exported from California by Indians from the Sacramento River area. By the 1870s, the situation in northern California and southern Oregon was even worse, from the Indian perspective, than that on the Plains. In California, Indians were being hunted down with the complicity and support of the state government. In the borderlands, in a short span of years, the Modoc had been placed on a multiethnic reservation, defeated in an all-out war, and exiled to Indian Territory (Nash 1955 [1937]). In Oregon, after the federal treaties of 1853 and 1855, which concluded the Rogue River Wars, a disparate assortment of groups from the Plateau were grouped with several coastal groups, including the Coos, Alsea, Siletz, Siuslaw, Tillamook, Lower Umpqua, and Tutuni, at the Grand Ronde and Siletz Reservations on the coast (Beckham 1990: 182–3; Jacobs n.d.). The conditions in these two reservations were harsh; during 1857–8, 205 persons died of disease and starvation at Siletz alone (Beckham 1990: 183). This occurred among a population numbering 554 prior to this (ibid.: 184). Mortality was thus close to 40 percent in this two-year period. Because of age and gender skewing in the 1857 population figures, we can surmise that population had declined significantly prior to that point (ibid.).

An increase in interethnic tension and organic and psychological illness ensued. These further increased as more people and tribes were crowded onto reservations and as allotment and other landgrabs further reduced Indian-held land. Melville Jacobs (n.d.) notes intriguingly that, after 1857, when the Coos were first exiled from their land, people in general, and not only shamans, became interested in dreams and their interpretations. We do not know precisely what these dreams entailed, but it is quite likely that they were similar to those that later became the foundation of the Ghost Dance: dreams of the dead in an idyllic setting, which perfectly expressed the trauma of cultural disintegration, with their combination of wish fulfillment and traumatic reenactment.

In 1873, a Shasta prophet named Bogus Tom brought a version of the Ghost Dance to the multiethnic Siletz and Grand Ronde reservations of western Oregon (Beckham et al. 1984: 96; DuBois 1939; Thompson 1935). It became quite popular and spread rapidly among the native populations both on and off reservations. This dance, called the Earth Lodge by the Shasta and other interior Oregon groups who adopted it, became known as the Warm House dance in western Oregon (Nash 1955 [1937]). It involved several novel features brought from California, such as semisubterranean houses with a central pole and the wearing of feather capes and woodpecker quill headbands (DuBois 1939: 25–27; Beckham et al. 1984: 96). It was originally based on a variation of the Round Dance, in which men and women danced in a circle around a central fire. Like previous versions of the Ghost Dance, this ritual promised the return of dead relatives and the restoration of the pre-contact social and moral order. The moral and spiritual state of the participants was crucial to its success. Participants tried to dream and see visions of the dead; failure resulted not only in the dead not returning, but also in the dancer possibly being transformed into an animal in the bargain (DuBois 1939: 27).

Separation from the Euroamerican world was a central value of all versions of the Ghost Dance in Oregon and California. It was thought that living in the white man's way deprived Indians of spiritual power. Communalism was another normative value. This was said to be in keeping with the values of traditional culture, in which people "were never stingy" (Thompson 1935). Dancers pooled their resources so that those without money or food could continue to dance, sometimes for as long as ten days at a time.

Bogus Tom continued summer visits to Oregon and Washington for four or five years, until the religion began to be suppressed by the authorities. In about 1878 the Warm House dance was taken up by two Siletz Reservation Indians, Coquille Thompson and Chetco Charlie, who spread the word among the coastal groups. Both men were Athabaskan, but Thompson had a Coos mother. They brought the dance to the nonreservation community of Coos, Siuslaw, and Lower Umpqua who lived at the mouth of the Siuslaw River, near Florence, Oregon (Beckham et al. 1984: 99; DuBois 1939; Miller and Seaburg 1990; Thompson 1935). Thompson's Coos connection and, reportedly, the men's oratorical and singing skills made their message popular among this community. Both men married local women and began to proselytize throughout southwestern Oregon.

The Warm House dance took on specifically Oregonian cultural features, such as the idea that the dead could not return to earth because the way was blocked by a great rainbowlike structure (Beckham et al. 1984: 100). This recalls the Coos vision of the afterlife, although normally the dead were striving to reach a second level of heaven rather than return to earth (Frachtenberg 1913; Jacobs 1939). Naturally, the dance was condemned by authorities, but for a time it flourished. So great was its apparent success that it produced variants as it spread to different communities. Persons who built warm houses became the "bosses" and used their authority to introduce new practices.

One such practice was the building up of the fire and the blocking of the smoke hole, creating a miasma of smoke in the house, which made breathing difficult (Thompson 1935). Men were rolled in blankets and then placed upon a fire that had been built up with fir boughs. Both of these practices were designed to facilitate visions on the part of the male dancers (for it was only men who could have them) but failed (ibid.). The lack of visions was frustrating and caused the congregants to get "crazy," as Thompson much later told Melville Jacobs (ibid.). The real "craziness" involved not only the building up of the fire and the smokiness of the lodge but communal sex among men and women in the dark smoky corners of the house. While not central to the ritual, and, indeed, apparently unconnected with the attempt to achieve visions, communal sex became an increasingly large part of the Warm House dance in its waning days. Below is Thompson's description of the denouement of the Warm House religion as recorded by Elizabeth Jacobs:

> At that time men and women were getting crazy. They were copulating with one another (there in the dark smoky warmhouse). Lots of men copulated with the women, even married people copulated with others because nothing could be seen; it had gotten to be dark (in there). That's the way it happened; when they danced it changed to a different way. In the daytime the women were around there naked. That's the way they did. (Hoxie [Stephens, a Galice informant] says only 3 or 4 families, and some bachelor fellows, were in on this at the end. Everybody else kept away.) That's why they finally set the Warm House on fire and it all burned up. (They baptized the people after this.)
> (Thompson 1935; parenthetical comments by Jacobs?)

Obeyesekere (1990: 26–29), in his psychodynamic work on Sri Lankan religious expression, divides rituals into two types, *dromena* and cathartic rites. A *dromenon* (Greek for "thing performed") is a solemn and stately ceremony, in which cultural, religious, and philosophical values are represented in a fairly straightforward manner. Individual psychological problems are not absent, and indeed provide a basic motivation for the ritual enactment, but they are transformed into idealized cultural themes and "brought in line with higher cultural values" (ibid.: 27). That is, the relation to real emotions and dilemmas is rather attenuated. Dromena are "progressive" in that they attempt to resolve psychological problems by projecting them forward into the future and the level of the numinous. Cathartic rites, by contrast, represent these things more directly, although in doing so they transform the cultural themes, often parodically. Thus, the Hindu gods and goddesses portrayed in these rites possess, inter alia, large sexual appetites and organs. These representations are the product of symbolic transformations that Obeyesekere (ibid.: 55) calls "the work of culture." It is like dream work in that it transforms the original forms into distortions, the difference being that dream work disguises unconscious thoughts, while the work of culture reveals them (ibid.: 56). Cathartic rites are thus regressive in that they dwell upon psychological conflicts without attempting to transform or resolve them.

We are now in a better position to address the "craziness" that Thompson observed in the latter days of the Warm House movement. The movement was transformed from a dromenon, which attempted to resolve the conflicts that the western Oregon Indians were experiencing in the post-contact period by transferring them onto another plane, into a cathartic rite, in which these themes were radically and parodically distorted. Reunification with dead parents becomes transformed into physical union with contemporaries. [. . .]

Cathartic rites as a response to colonialism

There can be little doubt that religious movements such as the Warm House dance should be seen as ethnohistorical phenomena, that is, viewed within the matrix of Euroamerican invasion and forced culture change (Walker 1969). Further, it is clear that they are mechanisms for dealing with collective stress and powerful negative emotions, and not always therapeutically. Rather, they offer emotional release from the dreary reality of death, disease, starvation, and acculturation. What is more, they replace the specific qualities of each person's suffering with a collective meaning constructed in ritual. In this sense they allow for a certain forgetting of the specific past of massacres and epidemics, which is replaced with the idealized account (Fogelson 1989). At first, such movements are optimistic and future oriented. They are dromena in Obeyesekere's terminology. However, over time, as their participants are repeatedly discomfited, the focus turns away from future-oriented optimism and moves increasingly in the direction of pure catharsis. At such a point the grotesque qualities of the rite are elaborated and come to prevail. [. . .]

Conclusion: for emotional ethnohistories

As Buckley has noted, Kroeber avoided ethnohistorical research because he could not bear all those tears. The invention of the "ethnographic present" by Kroeber and other anthropologists of the profession's "classic" (i.e., late colonial) phase was perhaps above all a psychological response to the searing histories of genocide, culture loss, land appropriations, and immense cruelty perpetrated on indigenous peoples. Kroeber and others constructed an epistemological space in which such questions have no place; they remain outside the paradigm. [. . .] Ethnographic presents, reified and mechanistic cultures, a detached viewpoint: all are conditioned by our professional avoidance of unpleasant realities. Of course, much has changed in the past generation, but much has not. In particular, the unwillingness of ethnohistorians to consider the emotional dimensions of the past has changed little. This resistance, whether from fear of colleagues' censure for being too subjective or from an unwillingness to face all those tears, continues to deform ethnohistorical research and writing.

In addition to these impediments of ancient pedigree, the rise of post-modernism has instilled a stance of ironic detachment among its second generation of scholars (see Bracken 1997). Colonial histories are seen as absurdist documents. While the postmodernist positions himself or herself as rhetorically on the side of the subaltern, or at least as opposed to the colonial authority, such a stance has little significance for the actual project, which, after all, is seen as merely another textual accretion in an already text-saturated field. The textual approach is not without merit, especially if one considers that such texts were, indeed, what made colonial administration possible. However, such a wheels-within-wheels analysis is unlikely to bring to light the "hidden histories" of colonized and encapsulated communities (see Schneider and Rapp 1995).

I have argued that the professional aversion to such histories was and remains inseparable from an unwillingness to face emotions: our own included. (Among these emotions are undoubtedly a certain professional guilt at our complicity with colonial regimes.) The Kurtzian horror of European colonialism in Africa or American conquest of California, written about by novelists and journalists, has not generally been considered a fit subject for anthropologists or historians (but see Taussig 1987; Fabian 2000). Instead, we have tended to seek the comfortable generalities of social organization or mythology while avoiding the historical specificity. . . . I would argue that this view has things exactly reversed: the universals are to be found in the colonizing society because it is participating in a global process carried out in much the same manner everywhere. It is the indigenous responses to colonial encounter that remain to be explored in all their emotional and historical specificity. It is to that specificity that ethnohistory must now turn.

References

Beckham, Stephen Dow
   1990   History of Western Oregon since 1846. *In* Handbook of North American Indians. Vol. 7, The Northwest Coast. Wayne Suttles, ed. Pp. 180–8. Washington, DC: Smithsonian Institution Press.
Beckham, Stephen Dow, Kathryn Anne Popel, and Rick Minor
   1984   Native American Religious Practices and Uses in Western Oregon. University of Oregon Anthropological Papers, No. 31. Eugene: University of Oregon Press.
Bracken, Christopher
   1997   The Potlatch Papers: A Colonial Case History. Chicago: University of Chicago Press.
Buckley, Thomas
   1996   "The Little History of Pitiful Events": The Epistemological and Moral Contexts of Kroeber's California Ethnology. *In* Volksgeist As Method and Ethic: Essays on Boasian Ethnography and the German Anthropological Tradition. George Stocking, ed. History of Anthropology 8. Pp. 257–97. Madison: University of Wisconsin Press.
Darnell, Regna
   1986   Personality and Culture: The Fate of the Sapirian Alternative. *In* Malinowski, Rivers, Benedict, and Others: Essays on Culture and Personality. George Stocking, ed. History of Anthropology 4. Pp. 156–83. Madison: University of Wisconsin Press.
Dauenhauer, Richard, and Nora Marks Dauenhauer
   1995   Oral Literature Embodied and Disembodied. *In* Aspects of Oral Communication. Uta Quasthoff, ed. Pp. 91–111. Berlin: Walter de Gruyter.

DeMallie, Raymond J.
    1984   The Sixth Grandfather: Black Elk's Teachings Given to John G. Neihardt.
            Lincoln: University of Nebraska Press.

DuBois, Cora
    1939   The 1870 Ghost Dance. Anthropological Records of the University of
            California 3 (1): 1–152.

Fabian, Johannes
    2000   Out of Our Minds: Reason and Madness in the Exploration of Central
            Africa. Berkeley: University of California Press.

Fogelson, Raymond
    1989   The Ethnohistory of Events and Non-Events. Ethnohistory 36:
            133–47.

Frachtenberg, Leo
    1913   Coos Texts. Columbia University Contributions to Anthropology 1. New
            York: Columbia University Press.

Jacobs, Melville
    n.d.   Coos Fieldnotes. Melville Jacobs Collection, Box 99, File 19, Manuscripts
            and University Archives, University of Washington, Seattle.
    1939   Coos Narrative and Ethnologic Texts. University of Washington Publications
            in Anthropology 7 (1): 1–27.

Levy, Robert I.
    1984   Emotion, Knowing, and Culture. In Culture Theory: Essays on Mind, Self,
            and Emotion. Richard A. Shweder and Robert A. Levine, eds. Pp. 214–37.
            Cambridge: Cambridge University Press.

Lutz, Catherine
    1988   Unnatural Emotions: Everyday Sentiments on a Micronesian Atoll and
            Their Challenge to Western Theory. Chicago: University of Chicago
            Press.

Miller, Jay, and William Seaburg
    1990   Athapaskans of Southwestern Oregon. In Handbook of North American
            Indians. Vol. 7, The Northwest Coast. Wayne Suttles, ed. Pp. 580–8.
            Washington, DC: Smithsonian Institution Press.

Mooney, James
    1965 [1896]   The Ghost Dance Religion and the Sioux Outbreak of 1890. Chicago:
            University of Chicago Press.

Nash, Philleo
    1955 [1937]   The Place of Religious Revivalism in the Formation of the Inter-
            cultural Community on Klamath Reservation. In Social Anthropology of
            North American Tribes. Fred Eggan, ed. Pp. 377–444. Chicago: University
            of Chicago Press.

Obeyesekere, Gananath
    1990   The Work of Culture: Symbolic Transformation in Psychoanalysis and
            Anthropology. Chicago: University of Chicago Press.

O'Nell, Theresa
    1996   Disciplined Hearts: History, Identity, and Depression in an American Indian
            Community. Berkeley: University of California Press.

Schneider, Jane, and Rayna Rapp
    1995   Articulating Hidden Histories: Exploring the Influence of Eric R. Wolf.
            Berkeley: University of California Press.

Taussig, Michael
    1987   Shamanism, Colonialism, and the Wild Man: A Study in Terror and Healing. Chicago: University of Chicago Press.

Thompson, Coquille
    1935   Ethnologic Text on Religion: The Ghost Dance Cult, Brought Up from the Sacramento Valley. Malville. Jacobs Collection, Manuscripts and University Archives, University of Washington, Seattle.

Walker, Deward
    1969   New Light on the Prophet Dance Controversy. Ethnohistory 16: 245–55.

Wallace, Anthony F. C.
    1956   Revitalization Movements: Some Theoretical Considerations for Their Comparative Study. American Anthropologist 58: 264–81.
    1965   James Mooney (1861–1921) and the Study of the Ghost-Dance Religion. In The Ghost-Dance Religion and the Sioux Outbreak of 1980. Pp. v–x. Chicago: University of Chicago Press.

Chapter 8

Johan Lindquist

NEGOTIATING SHAME IN THE INDONESIAN BORDERLANDS

A S UNEXPECTED AS IT MIGHT seem, migrant women some-times wear Muslim veils or take ecstasy (the popular term for MDMA or 3,4-methylenedioxy-methamphetamine) in the same places and for the same reasons; reasons that are both comprehensible and explicitly moral. On the Indonesian island of Batam – a place characterized by rapid socio-economic change and dramatic demographic shifts – female migrants use these techniques in order to deal with *malu*, meaning approximately shame, embarrassment, shyness, or restraint and propriety (Goddard 1996:432; Peletz 1996:228). While veiling reinforces moral boundaries associated with *malu*, ecstasy use facilitates the transgression of those same boundaries. Wearing the veil, or *jilbab*, offers an identity that protects against the dangers of social interaction in the context of migration, while ecstasy use allows female prostitutes to engage more easily in morally ambiguous forms of transactions. Both activities, however, can be transformed into legitimate models of personal development (*kemajuan*), which may displace *malu* upon return home; one as a sign of religious insight, the other as a means for creating economic value. Veiling and ecstasy use are therefore both directly connected with the demands of home and the expectations of migration. In this context, it is the experience of *malu*, or of being identified as someone who should be *malu*, which becomes an organizing principle for social action and the management of appearances.

In other words, *malu* becomes the emotional link between the *kampung*, the village or home, and the *rantau*, the space of migration, as the demands of what it means to be a moral person haunt the migrant. This link suggests various forms of exchange that bind the individual to broader historically specific moral and social orders, most notably the Indonesian nation. [. . .]

. . . On Batam, . . . it is not other possible translations of 'shame-embarrassment,' such as the Balinese concept of *lek* – famously translated by Geertz as 'stagefright' – or *isin* that have become key emotional tropes, but rather *malu*, a Malay word that exists in other Indonesian languages, but more importantly in this context, a part of the Indonesian *lingua franca*. This also highlights an important difference between Batam, a place where primarily Indonesian is spoken, and the *kampung*, where it is not. As Siegel (1997:15) has argued, the formation of the Indonesian national language 'offers one the opportunity for a certain excursion if not into a new identity, at least away from an old one.' Referring to the same quote, Spyer (2000:30) argues more strongly that it even 'compels' this shift. In this article, I argue that in the context of the more literal excursion that migration entails, *malu* should be understood in relation to emergent identities connected to the nation.

This does not mean, however, that *malu* is played out in the same ways among the two groups that I am discussing. One of the main differences between female prostitutes and factory workers is education. While the latter are required to have a high school degree, the former usually have far more limited education. Furthermore, while religious engagement may be a legitimate model of *kemajuan* for some women, for others who must support families, only economic success counts. In other words, socioeconomic differences structure life trajectories and lead *malu* to become relevant in various ways in the lives of migrants. [. . .]

Batam has commonly been represented by the Indonesian government as a competitor to Singapore – the new 'Houston' or 'Rotterdam' of Southeast Asia, the 'locomotive' of Indonesian national development. The island has a distinct frontier-town atmosphere: it is a place that has changed too quickly. Golf courses, marinas, and gated communities co-exist with factories, squatter communities, karaoke bars, and brothels, while jungle still covers large parts of the island. Along with the industrial estates that offer facilities for multinational corporations, prostitution has expanded rapidly, serving the large number of mainly Singaporean men who take the 40-minute ferry ride across the Straits of Malacca in search of inexpensive sex and drugs. The economy of the day – based in the factories – and the economy of the night – based on prostitution and drug use – have developed together, both depending primarily on female labor and foreign capital. In this context, national-cultural distinctions between men as breadwinners and women as tied to the domestic sphere are easily disturbed (cf. Blackwood 1995:126).

The day

It is just after 4 p.m. at the Batamindo Industrial Estate, the flagship of economic development on Batam. [. . .]

The sidewalks and the general sense of order in the estate serve to strengthen the feeling that Batamindo, which is managed by a Singaporean corporation, is organized according to different principles than those of the world that exists outside its walls. [. . .]

Batamindo houses about 100 multi-national corporations and over 65,000 workers, and is generally considered to be the most successful development project on Batam. Eighty percent of the workers are women between the ages of 18 and 24, with a high-school degree being a prerequisite for employment. Furthermore, most of the women must sign a contract promising not to marry or become pregnant while working there. Approximately 50 percent of the women in the estate wear the *jilbab*, an extraordinarily high number by Indonesian standards, even after the recent wave of Islamization throughout the country.

Religious activities are strongly supported by the management and the local government on the island, and each factory has its own organizations for Christians and Muslims. The convergence of state and corporate interests can be seen, for instance, in attempts by the Department of Religious Affairs to provide pre-marital counseling for workers. At one point, the head of the local office explained the reasoning:

> By counseling them [the workers], we hope to prevent the possibility of negative behaviors [in particular pre-marital sex and pregnancy out of wedlock] being manifested. If these problems occur, workers' productivity could be reduced.
>
> (*The Jakarta Post*, December 19, 1992).

In contrast, young male migrants view Batamindo as a place where it is easy to find a girlfriend, and on Saturday nights the dormitories are packed with visitors long into the early hours of the morning, despite official rules stating that guests must leave by midnight. In interviews with officials at Batamindo, as well as with nurses in the clinic, issues of sexuality arose constantly. [. . .]

Religion appears as not only the solution to preventing immoral behavior, but also to improving worker productivity. The convergence of economic, nationalist, and religious discourses concerning young women is recognizable from other contexts in the region (e.g. Ong 1987, Chapter 8). . . .

The complicated relationship between management and self-management becomes particularly interesting in relation to veiling. In conversations with workers who wore the veil it was clear that most of them began to do so only *after* they had arrived on Batam. The typical response to my enquiry about this was that they had only just 'become aware' (*baru sadar*). For instance, Widya, from the city of Yogyakarta in Central Java, claimed that she had always wanted to wear a *jilbab* before she came to Batam, but that it was rare there. While in Java it was easy to be branded *fanatik* (cf. Brenner 1998:232), on Batam one gained support not only from roommates but also from the agencies and companies that recruited them.

. . . The interests of the workers, the companies, and the local government appear to converge, as the movement of workers is restricted to the mosque (or the church), the dormitories, and the factory. The development of the industrial estate is matched by the spiritual development of the worker. While this may easily be interpreted as an added instrument in the disciplining of workers, in reality it is more complicated.

Although 'becoming aware' was certainly a key motif among women who wear the *jilbab* at Batamindo, many – away from home for the first time – readily admitted that another major reason for veiling was to avoid male attention and *malu* in the streets. Wearing a *jilbab* protects women from being approached by men, or of being identified as a *lontong*, a prostitute. [. . .]

Some researchers have argued that wearing the veil can be understood as a kind of 'symbolic shelter' that allows women to enter public spaces (e.g. Macleod 1992).

Brenner (1996:674) claims that this is not the case in Java, where there is no clear delineation between 'male' and 'female' spheres. On Batam, however, this distinction is far more problematic, since the island has a reputation through-out Indonesia as a place of prostitution and limited social control, making movement through public space particularly sensitive for women. . . . Visiting government officials argue that female workers have too much free time and may easily be lured by the potentially high earnings that prostitution offers.

This is a boundary, however, that women themselves are often concerned with policing. For instance, female factory workers who frequent discos in the main town of Nagoya make clear attempts to distinguish themselves from prostitutes, both spatially and in terms of dress. Most remain on one side of the disco and are easily distinguished by their uniform of loose T-shirts and jeans. Similarly, many women living in the dormitories avoid squatter housing around the estate, which often are associated with premarital cohabitation and a lack of social control. Veils serve a similar purpose in creating social boundaries and formalizing identities. [. . .]

On Batam the *jilbab* as a sign of religious devotion and chastity was, however, often doubted by other people. Rumors of women who wore a *jilbab* during the day but frequented discos by night were common. My neighbor's girlfriend, who worked at Batamindo and wore a *jilbab*, would frequently spend the night in his room, trying to sneak in late at night while my housemates chuckled from our balcony across the street. One of my neighbors told me that he 'didn't trust *jilbabs* anymore' because he thought most women wore them to hide their unattractive bodies, another man claimed that they were 'merely a formality' (*formalitas saja*), while a nurse at the Batamindo clinic revealed that 'if a woman comes into the clinic and has a problem with something like sex and they are wearing a *jilbab*, I tell them to take it off, that they should be *malu*.'

The potential ironies are evident. While veiling protects women from the threats of pre-marital sex or of being harassed by men – thereby displacing potential sources of *malu* – and is considered a legitimate model for personal development, the veil is not always read as a sign of piety and demands a broader transformation of subjectivity. [. . .]

The night

[. . .] With the emergence of the Growth Triangle in the early 1990s, prostitution rapidly expanded on Batam and neighboring islands, as primarily Singaporean men began to take the short ferry trip across the border. This process reached its peak in 1998 at the height of the Asian economic crisis, as the Indonesian rupiah dropped to as little as one sixth of its previous value in relation to the Singapore dollar. While Indonesian men are mainly found in the half dozen quasi-legal *lokalisasi* – low-charge brothel villages – most prostitution on Batam is based in karaoke bars and discos around the main town of Nagoya, which cater primarily to foreign men.

On a busy night, Ozon is nearly filled to its capacity of 2,000 people by 11 p.m. At the back of the disco, the DJ plays techno versions of Indonesian and western pop songs, but only a few people are on the small dance floor in the middle of the club. In contrast, the high tables and barstools that surround the dance floor are packed with people who can afford to buy drinks. Most of them are conspicuously moving their heads back and forth to the beat of the music – in most cases, such people are 'tripping' on ecstasy, the drug of choice in Indonesian night-clubs during the late 1990s. Behind the DJ, and at the entrance to the toilets, there are young men selling drugs, offering their goods to anyone who looks their way.

Lidya, who is in her mid-twenties and comes from Medan in North Sumatra, works as a freelance prostitute and is searching for a *tamu*, a client – preferably a Singaporean. The ecstasy that she has taken has not quite kicked in, and she is indecisive about whom to approach. Lidya claims that she feels *malu* about approaching clients, and she uses ecstasy to cross the barrier.

> I like taking ecstasy because I am not as scared to approach a client. If I don't take ecstasy, I feel inferior; I feel *malu* towards the clients. Ecstasy makes me feel brave.

Most of the freelance prostitutes who work in Ozon use the drug on a regular basis, many of them nearly every night. Unlike brothel areas, which are 'closed institutions' (Cohen 1993), or prostitutes who have pimps to negotiate transactions with clients, Lidya and other freelance women must to a greater degree perform in order to attract clients. Ani, who comes from Central Java, claims that taking ecstasy 'makes everything easier. If I am at the disco and I don't take it, I feel confused and I can't stand the music. I just keep asking myself why I am here. It is also easier to act and dance in a *seksi* way.' . . .

In Ozon and other discos on Batam, ecstasy is crucial in the formation of a space where appearances may be altered and subjectivities may – at least temporarily – be transformed. . . . In the context of the disco, ecstasy allows women to transgress culturally powerful modes of bodily control and perform as prostitutes. It allows them to forget their *malu*, by 'distancing emotion' (Scheff 1977) and to become the kind of woman whom a client will desire, thereby facilitating economic transactions. In this context, there is a whole repertoire of actions that is learned through practical mimesis and which is facilitated by ecstasy: learning to dance in a manner that is *seksi*, or be flirtatious without appearing overly aggressive, or change attitudes depending on the client. The most successful freelance prostitutes are not necessarily the ones who are considered most beautiful, but rather, those who have mastered this repertoire.

To merely understand ecstasy in relation to this specific use within the context of prostitution, however, would be to underestimate its potential meanings and uses. In the disco ecstasy generates distinctions between clients and prostitutes alike by becoming a sign that one is *gengsi* (hip). Not being *on*, therefore, can also become a source of *malu* in relation to other prostitutes, since it can be seen as a sign that one cannot access the drug, implying that one cannot get a client or afford to buy it.

[. . .] Bloch and Parry (1989) argue that all forms of economic systems must allow for an ideological space in which short-term economic acquisition – which often is morally ambiguous – is accepted in order to reproduce a long-term moral order. In relation to this, consider the following quote from Rosa:

of course I feel *malu* when I think about what I am doing – though it has become easier – but it is nothing compared to the *malu* I would feel if I returned home with nothing. Now, I can feel proud (*bangga*) when I return home. I am sure some people suspect that I work as a prostitute, but no one ever asks.

This *malu*, she tells me, is more powerful than the *malu* that she experiences in being a prostitute. In this context, the complexity of the meanings of *malu* – ranging from propriety to shame – becomes evident in the double-bind of modernity (Bateson 1973). Becoming a person is not only about acting in a particular manner and recognizing one's position within society; other demands have become equally important, namely signs of success from the *rantau*. However, Rosa's movement from the space of home, the *kampung*, to the space of migration, the *rantau*, and back again, facilitates this process. *Malu*, it appears, can be erased and forgotten.

The greatest fear of many prostitutes is – as the quote above suggests – that news of their work will spread back to the *kampung*. The use of Western pseudonyms is one example of how identities are masked, while new ones are forged in relation to a broader world. Returning home always means transforming oneself back into an ideal, moral person, primarily through more conservative forms of dress. Being identified as refined (*halus*) rather than crude (*kasar*) is another sign that one knows *malu*. As Rosa puts it:

> Whenever I return to Java and visit my son and my mother, I have to stop smoking and start wearing a sarong again. I have to restrain myself when I speak and not be as *kasar* as I am on Batam.

For those who have partners or children living on Batam, however, this tension becomes more complicated. For instance, one day when I went over to visit the hall that I described in the beginning of this section, Diana had a black eye. Her boyfriend Umar had hit her when she came home from Ozon *on* and without any money. At the time Diana complained to me that Umar:

> always gets mad if I come back without any money even though it sometimes is difficult to get a client. If he had any sense of responsibility (*bertangungjawab*), I wouldn't have to work like this, but he always says that it is difficult for men to find work on Batam. What I really want is to be a housewife and have children, but if he keeps hitting me I will leave him since I am the only one making any money.

Umar, of course, had a different story. He claimed that the first time he had hit her was when she actually brought a client back to their floor. Everyone was shocked by this, and it made Umar furious.

> It's bad enough that she has to work as a prostitute for us to survive, but she doesn't have to make me even more *malu* by bringing this guy back. Now she also seems more interested in taking drugs than she is in

> making money. All I do is sit here and wait for her all night, and when she returns she is *tripping* and has no money! I wish that I had never come to Batam. I had a good job before in Medan [North Sumatra], but I just wanted too much and now I am stuck here. I would rather die than return home *malu* without any money.

In this particular situation, the distinction between the short-term and the long-term sphere does not necessarily represent the distance between the *kampung* and the *rantau*. On the contrary, the distinction is dependent on what each person identifies as 'home' and, thus, the threshold for where the long-term moral order begins. This is perhaps a distinction that makes life bearable: the commodification of the body, and the spaces where this is allowed, are distinguished from personal relationships and the space of 'home.' In the economy of the night the distinction between 'pleasure' and 'labor' is never clear and constantly a source of conflict and anxiety. The distancing of emotion through the use of ecstasy facilitates economic exchange, but also creates personal tensions and moral dilemmas. [. . .]

The malu of modernity

[. . .] In relation to the spread of *merantau* as a cultural form, it is not surprising that *malu* has emerged as a key emotional trope for migrants on Batam. While *isin*, *lek*, and other related emotional tropes remain bound to a particular ethnic group and language, *malu* travels and becomes the link between the *rantau* and the *kampung*, between the citizen and the nation. As I have noted throughout, particular modernist forms associated with the nation and *kemajuan*; most notably economic success, religious development, and the nuclear family, are at the heart of these anxieties.

One is *malu* to return 'home' without having anything to show for the time one has spent in the *rantau*. For migrants, therefore, the links between *malu* and *merantau* effectively describe the contradictions of life on Batam and in the Growth Triangle. In this context *malu* appears as an emotion that describes the failures to live up to the ideals of the nation. It offers migrants an experiential trope as *Indonesians* in the shadows of the promises of *Indonesian* economic development (cf. Siegel 1997; Boellstorff 2002). [. . .]

Though the performance of prostitution may appear as an inversion of the performance of piety, in fact they are both crystallizations of particular gendered styles. Although there are certainly varying degrees of reflexivity involved in these acts, in all situations the primary problem is not self-identity, but rather avoiding being identified as someone who does not belong (cf. Reddy 1997). It is important, however, to highlight the reflexive nature of this process; Batam is a place that not only produces new kinds of power relations, but also offers new forms of freedom and agency for migrants, many of whom are away from the *kampung* for the first time. In the context of *merantau*, *malu* is an emotion that leads women to engage with, rather than withdraw from, a new kind of world and its contradictions; a process that does not, however, necessarily guarantee success. [. . .]

References

Bateson, Gregory. 1973. *Steps to an Ecology of Mind*. London: Paladin.

Blackwood, Evelyn. 1995. Senior Women, Model Mothers, and Dutiful Wives: Managing Gender Contradictions in a Minangkabau Village. In *Bewitching Women, Pious Men: Gender and Body Politics in Southeast Asia*, edited by Aihwa Ong & Michael G. Peletz. Berkeley: University of California Press.

Bloch, Maurice & Jonathan Parry. 1989. *Money and the Morality of Exchange*. Cambridge: Cambridge University Press.

Boellstorff, Tom. 2002. Ethnolocality. *Asia Pacific Journal of Anthropology*, 3(1):24–48.

Brenner, Suzanne. 1996. Reconstructing Self and Society: Javanese Muslim Women and the Veil. *American Ethnologist*, 23(4):673–697.

—— 1998. *The Domestication of Desire: Women, Wealth, and Modernity in Java*. Princeton, NJ: Princeton University Press.

Cohen, Erik. 1993. Open-ended Prostitution as a Skilful Game of Luck: Opportunity, Risk and Security among Tourist-oriented Prostitutes in a Bangkok *Soi*. In *Tourism in Southeast Asia*, edited by Michael Hitchcock, Victor T. King & Michael J.G. Parnwell. New York: Routledge.

Goddard, Cliff. 1996. The 'Social Emotions' of Malay (Bahasa Melayu). *Ethos*, 24(3): 426–464.

Macleod, Arlene Elowe. 1992. Hegemonic Relations and Gender Resistance: The New Veiling as Accommodating Protest in Cairo. *Signs*, 17(3):533–557.

Ong, Aihwa. 1987. *Spirits of Resistance and Capitalist Discipline: Factory Women in Malaysia*. Albany, NY: State University of New York Press.

Peletz, Michael G. 1996. *Reason and Passion: Representations of Gender in a Malay Society*. Berkeley: University of California Press.

Reddy, William M. 1997. Reply. *Current Anthropology*, 38(3):346–348.

Scheff, Thomas J. 1977. The Distancing of Emotion in Ritual. *Current Anthropology*, 18(3):483–505.

Siegel, James T. 1997. *Fetish, Recognition, Revolution*. Princeton, NJ: Princeton University Press.

Spyer, Patricia. 2000. *The Memory of Trade: Modernity's Entanglements on an Eastern Indonesian Island*. Durham: Duke University Press.

3. Emotions and society

WITH ANTHROPOLOGY, THE DISCIPLINE OF sociology has one of the longest records of research and debate on the extent to which, and the processes whereby, emotions are shaped by socio-cultural factors. While American sociologists pioneered the field, today the American, British and European Sociological Associations all have thematic sections or study groups dedicated to the emotions. The field of relevant publications spans more than three decades; some of the concepts and analytical frameworks developed during the 1970s and 1980s still orient research today, as can be seen throughout this volume. Once regarded as an area of specialist interest, the study of emotions is increasingly considered central to the discipline and to the ways in which the discipline conceives of itself. As Barbalet (2002: 3) puts it, 'once the importance of emotions to social processes becomes clear, the intellectual constitution of sociology, and therefore the history of sociology and those who have contributed to it, have to be rethought.'

Just as there is no singular theoretical or methodological framework that can characterize sociology as a whole, so there is not a singular sociology of emotions but rather many variants, each with its particular inclinations and ways of proceeding. Jonathan Turner and Jan Stets have recently published a book-length review of the field (2005), to which we refer readers who are interested in a detailed discussion of key theoretical and methodological differences. Turner and Stets identify seven theoretical variants in the sociology of emotions: *dramaturgical and cultural*; *ritual*; *symbolic interactionist*; *symbolic interactionist with psychoanalytical elements*; *exchange theorizing*; *structural*; and *evolutionary*. In this section we have tried to provide a balanced selection from these variants, while including also a contribution from a systems-theoretical perspective.

Our first reading is from the first chapter of Jack Barbalet's book *Emotion, Social Theory and Social Structure* (2001) which presents a *macro-sociological*

approach to the emotions. The book has two aims. To examine aspects social structure by applying emotions categories (e.g. what role does resentment play in relations
of social class?), and to re-work sociological theory in the light of a focus upon
emotions. The extract we have chosen focuses on the latter, since this provides a useful
and concise introduction to questions such as: What is sociology's 'business' with the
emotions? How has it tackled them? How did emotions feature in the early origins
of sociology? To what extent are subsequent sociological approaches to emotion
themselves the expression of changes in broader social structural factors?

This latter question is of particular interest with respect to Barbalet's picture
of the changing fortunes of emotions in sociology. Whilst the founders of modern
sociology – including figures such as Adam Smith, Adam Ferguson, Alexis de Tocqueville, Gustave Le Bon, Emile Durkheim, Vilfredo Pareto, Ferdinand Tőnnies and
Georg Simmel – regarded emotions as important sociological variables, Barbalet
suggests that they effectively dropped out of the picture from about 1930 to 1970 as
a *cognitive* emphasis came to dominate sociological theory. In the UK context,
Barbalet relates this shift to changes in mass society such as the effective containment and pacification of the working classes in the post-war period of reconstruction
and the relative rise in numbers of white-collar workers in administrative, clerical and
sales positions which factors together 'enhanced the sense of a less passionate and
increasingly rational social order' (2001: 15). Barbalet goes on to associate the rise
of the social constructionist approach to the increased prominence, from the 1970s
onwards, of new social movements such as the Women's the Environmental and the
Black Movements which served to politicize emotions through the foregrounding of a
politics of identity and a critique of 'naturalistic' accounts of 'knowing one's place'.

The second extract is from Goffman's classic article 'Embarrassment and Social
Organization'. This article was published in 1956 at a time when most of sociology
was committed to rather rational and calculative models of social organization.
Where emotion was considered, it tended to feature as a component of more primitive
forms of social organization or in relation to its 'pathological' expression (e.g. in
times of social crisis). The polarity affectivity / neutrality, for example, was one of
Talcott Parsons' 'pattern variables', and he associated affectivity with pre-modern
society and with the family dynamics of modern social systems (cf. Fish 2004).
Goffman, by contrast, is unembarrassed in his dealings with the emotion of
embarrassment. This is perhaps because his 'dramaturgical' approach was more in
tune with ideas coming from the arts and humanities and with the power struggles
of psychiatric wards. Goffman thus recognized that emotion is, in part at least, a
genuinely *social* category by showing how embarrassment is part and parcel of
socially prescribed behaviour and not some primitive and irrational biopsychological
force 'breaking through' the crust of orderly conduct. From Goffman's dramaturgical
perspective, social action is sustained less by reasoned rule following or hedonistic
self-interest than by a delicate dance of affective encounters whose emotional
qualities are, for the most part, carefully concealed.

The next four extracts are drawn from sociologists who made significant contributions from the second half of the 1970s, when explicit sociological interest in the
emotions was re-kindled. Thus Susan Shott begins her article 'Emotion and Social
Life: a symbolic interactionist analysis' by pointing to the neglect of emotion amongst

contemporary sociologists with the exception of figures such as Goffman. Shott provides a clear example of a *constructionist* account of emotion as a *socialized* phenomenon mediated by symbolically organized 'definitions of the situation' and interactional factors such as 'role taking'. The indebtedness to Schachter and Singer's (1962) social psychological two-factor theory is explicit, as is the influence of cultural anthropology, which also challenged prior thoroughly biological accounts of emotion. Shott's concern is with the agency of social action, and it is argued that social systems and their structures do not determine conduct but rather influence the settings for conduct and the ways these are cognitively interpreted. It is also notable that a decisive role is given to the concept of *social norms* as the key elements in a social framework that shape and modify the actors' emotional experiences and expressions by way of their influence on modes of interpretation or reality construction. These norms are approached in two related ways: either through an emphasis on how normative social reality constructs the actor through socialization, or on how the actor constructs reality by way of their normative subjective definitions.

The extract from Arlie Russell Hochschild's article 'Emotion Work, Feeling Rules, and Social Structure' shares this focus on social norms and on the importance of an order of interaction which mediates between the personality structures of individuals and the social structures of a social system. Elsewhere in the article, Hochschild distinguishes an organismic account of emotion-as-biological with the interactive account associated with Schachter, Goffman and others. Hochschild favours the latter because it offers a more deeply social account according to which social norms and knowledge enter into the definition of emotion via interpretive processes of labeling and attribution. Hochschild's specific contribution is to take Goffman's work further by arguing that actors do not simply manage the outward 'impressions' they give off to others but also their inner feelings. Her 'emotions management' approach is thus based upon the idea of *deep* acting through which people struggle to actually alter their emotions to better fit social norms and expectations. Her concepts of 'emotion work' and 'feeling rules' thus extend the focus on social norms. This move allows Hochschild to connect emotions to broader questions of power and social structure, since feeling rules can be thought of as the 'underside' of *ideology* – the side that deals with emotions. A key difference between working class and middle class socialization practices, for example, might well be the extent to which they prepare children to control and manage their emotions. It is no surprise that we now talk of 'emotional intelligence' as a quality necessary for work in economies dominated by service and consumption rather than industrial production. For Hoschschild, such economies require high levels of emotion work (interesting comparisons with Elias's theory of the civilizing process could be made here, cf. Wouters 1989).

In contrast to Shott and Hochschild, Theodore Kemper offers a self-consciously 'positivistic' interactional theory of emotions. The perspective presented in the extract is part of a broader theory (cf. Kemper 1978) in which it is argued that 'a very large class of emotions results from real, imagined or anticipated outcomes in social relationships' (1978: 43). As this quotation indicates, Kemper is mostly interested in the social *causes* of emotions, which are themselves considered to be psychophysiological phenomena. He argues that two universal structural dimensions of social interaction that he calls 'power' and 'status' can parsimoniously predict the generation of many emotions. Happiness, for example, is caused by a gain in power whilst fear and anxiety result from its loss. Pride, to give another example, is caused by a gain in status whilst shame results from its loss. Whilst social norms and cultural knowledge may well mediate the relationships between structural relations and emotions, Kemper's work suggests that it is possible both to overstate the causal role of such factors and to overstate the 'cognitive' nature of emotions as fundamentally related to local interpretations. He is interested in providing a more complete model of the social environment (which naturally includes the macro aspects of social systems) so that variations in that environment can be correlated with varying emotional experiences.

The extract by Randall Collins illustrates his more general theory of interaction ritual (Collins 1975). Under the influence of Durkheim, Goffman and Darwinian animal ethology, Collins deals as much with the social *effects* of emotions as with the social causes. Emotions are tacitly mediated by interaction rituals and are viewed as a form of 'social energy' which upholds social structures and gels groups into coalitions with 'felt' hierarchies of dominance and solidarity. Collins is thus less concerned with specific namable emotional occasions (e.g. this moment of anger) than with a constantly reproduced underlying emotional dynamic that is sometimes only vaguely sensed. This emotional dynamic influences whether or not people feel they 'belong' in a particular situation, group, institution or social relationship, how 'confident' they feel, and so on. From this perspective, property, for instance, is based upon a sense of entitlement to occupy a particular place or to access a particular thing and something like 'authority' is communicated via subtle cues that are affectively apprehended. Little things like 'talking shop' or 'name dropping' or remarks about tasteless internal decoration serve to reproduce such emotional dynamics and Collins is thus less interested in the *content* of such ritualistic conversations than in their unstated emotional effects, both individual and collective (e.g. how they increase and decrease the confidence of the actors and how they reproduce or challenge existing group boundaries).

The final extract is from the German systems theoretician, Niklas Luhmann. Luhmann offers an historically informed post-positivistic sociology grounded in complexity theory (c.f. Stenner 2004, 2006). He draws upon the biological theory of 'autopoiesis' which examines how living organisms must constantly reproduce themselves from out of their own elements. For autopoiesis to occur, a system must be fully self-referential or operationally *closed* upon itself. In contrast to our other authors, Luhmann thus makes a rather clear distinction between social systems (which are systems of communication) and psychic systems (which are systems of consciousness grounded in unconscious biological systems). Both systems face the task of reproducing themselves on an ongoing and self-referential basis either by continuing to generate communication (in the case of social systems) or consciousness (in the case of psychic systems). For Luhmann, the emotions primarily concern psychic systems and they arise whenever the autopoiesis (continuous self-referential reproduction) of consciousness is in danger. Nevertheless, there is a close relationship of 'structural coupling' between psychic and social systems. The stream of consciousness, for instance, is endangered by interruptions and these can be caused by unpredictable social events. More specifically, Luhmann holds that emotion is the process of adaptation to met or unmet *claims*. A claim is more than a mere expectation, since a disappointed expectation can simply be revised or given up. With a claim, by contrast, we have a sense of *right* and so its disappointment or fulfillment is more of a shock to the psychic system and so generates emotional responses. This structural coupling allows Luhmann to connect emotions to cultural semantics (e.g. socially prevalent ideas and rules about who can lay claim to what) and to relate semantics to shifts in social structure (e.g. the shift from a feudal society to one that is functionally differentiated). In a world where our claims are ostensibly 'individual choices' unlimited by social dictates concerning our predefined 'proper place', they are less likely to be routinely met and hence more likely to engender emotion.

References

Barbalet, J. (ed) (2002) *Emotions and Sociology*. Oxford: Blackwell Publishing.

Collins, R. (1975) *Conflict Sociology: Toward an Exploratory Science*. New York: Academic Press.

Fish, J. S. (2004) 'The neglected element of human emotion in Talcott Parsons's The Structure of Social Action', *Journal of Classical Sociology*, 4 (1):115–134.

Kemper, T. D. (1978) *A Social International Theory of Emotions*. New York: John Wiley.

Schachter, S. and Singer, J. E. (1962) 'Cognitive, social and physiological determinants of emotional state', *Psychological Review*, 69: 379–99.

Stenner, P. (2006) 'An outline of an autopoietic systems approach to emotion', *Cybernetics and Human Knowing*, 12 (4): 8–22.

Stenner, P. (2004) 'Is autopoietic systems theory alexithymic? Luhmann and the socio-psychology of emotions', *Soziale Systeme*, 10 (1): 159–85.

Turner, J. H. and Stets, J. E. (eds) (2005) *The Sociology of Emotions*. Cambridge: Cambridge University Press.

Wouters, C. (1989) 'The sociology of emotions and flight attendants: Hochschild's "Managed Heart" ', *Theory, Culture & Society*. 6: 95–123.

Chapter 9

Jack Barbalet

EMOTION IN SOCIAL LIFE AND SOCIAL THEORY

[. . .]

Emotion and sociology: the odd couple

WHAT IS SOCIOLOGY'S BUSINESS WITH emotion? One answer is that sociology attempts to explain social phenomena, and emotion is a social phenomenon. That emotion has a social nature is not immediately obvious, however. An individual's experience of emotion more readily reveals the personal and intimate side of emotion than its collective or social dimension. Nevertheless, it has been shown by anthropologists, historians, and sociologists, that the patterns of emotional experiences are different in different societies. In this sense emotion can be regarded as an outcome or effect of social processes. As a social product, emotion is in principle amenable to sociological examination and explanation. There is in fact a large and growing literature which shows, from a number of different perspectives, that emotion is a social thing (Kemper 1991; McCarthy 1989).

There is another answer to the question, "What is sociology's business with emotion?" Sociology might be concerned with emotion because emotion is somehow necessary to explain the very fundamentals of social behavior. This idea, that emotion is a social cause, is more likely to be resisted by sociologists than the idea that it is a social effect. As this is the more difficult to accept of the two answers concerning sociology's business with emotion, it is the one that we shall focus on here. The only good reason to offer a sociological explanation of emotion is if emotion is itself significant in the constitution of social relationships, institutions, and processes. [. . .]

ology

ns of sociology have been frequently noted
Adam Smith, for instance, in *The Wealth of*
anticipating comparative historical sociology
Adam Ferguson, in *An Essay on the History of*
e secure as a precursor of modern sociology
social as distinct from the economic con-
l for his account of historic development.
ich is essential for an understanding of each
ation of the intellectual formation of the
re a part, is the importance they attach to
onships and as a foundation for their larger

There is a view that in *The Wealth of Nations* Smith developed a line antithetical to that of his earlier book, *The Theory of Moral Sentiments* ([1759] 1982). It is held that whereas one pursues the thread of economic self-interest, the other expands on sympathy as a basis of moral behavior. This reading of the relationship between Smith's books misinterprets each of them (Macfie and Raphael 1976, pp. 20–5). What must be emphasized here is that the much narrower focus of *The Wealth of Nations*, a detailed working out of the consequences for economic actions and institutions of "self-love," derives from Smith's earlier theory. *Moral Sentiments* accounts for moral judgment and social interaction in terms of particular emotions, and argues that the capacity for a sympathetic echo of these emotions in other actors is a further determinant of social conduct.

The underpinning emotions framework of Ferguson's *Essay on the History of Civil Society* ([1767] 1966) is unavoidable to its readers. The book consists of six parts. The first and by far the longest is "Of the General Characteristics of Human Nature." This forms the methodological and theoretical basis of what follows, and is largely concerned with the emotional dispositions associated with social and political relations and organization.

The explanatory value of emotions categories can also be located in the major sociologists of the nineteenth and early twentieth centuries. Alexis de Tocqueville, Gustave Le Bon, Emile Durkheim, Vilfredo Pareto, Ferdinand Tönnies, and Georg Simmel are some of the more notable. European sociologists who, in a number of different ways, regarded emotions categories as important explanatory variables. During this same period American sociology, in the works of such figures as Albion Small, William Graham Summner, and Lester Frank Ward, as well as Edward Ross and Charles Horton Cooley, found explanatory roles for emotions categories. All of this is mentioned here simply to indicate that during an earlier time it would not have been necessary, as it is now, to show that a sociologically robust understanding of emotion makes good sense.

The absence of Max Weber from the lists of the preceding paragraph is not accidental. A number of commentators with projects similar to my own have recruited Weber to their purpose, arguing that Weber was one sociologist who recognized the explanatory importance of emotion. Weber did have an ideal type conception of "affectual action," certainly; but as Talcott Parsons ([1937] 1968, pp. 647–9), for instance, has noted, this category is primarily residual, and was not positively used in Weber's empirical work. Parsons may exaggerate the absence of emotion in Weber's explanations: it is notionally central to (although wholly undeveloped in) his account of charismatic authority. There are, in fact, many references to emotion in Weber's work. He insists on the necessity of passion in the calling of science. The discussion of the role and practice of the priesthood in *Ancient Judaism* (Weber [1917] 1967) includes much on the generation of emotion and its manipulation. Emotion is also important in Weber's discussion of the Protestant ethic and the spirit of capitalism. A consideration of this latter discussion will be developed in the following chapter. It will be shown that Weber's account of emotion is not only in itself seriously flawed, but is associated with the expulsion of emotion from sociology. It is this theme which will be taken up here.

The expulsion of emotion from sociology

[. . .]

Changing fortunes of mass society

It is an enduring feature of political life that those who exercise power experience their enthusiasms as reasonable, but the enthusiasms of those who challenge them as unreasonable and emotional. Etymologically, "enthusiasm" is a state of supernatural possession or inspiration, and in that sense, as a state of being moved by an external concern, it is inherently non-rational. The nineteenth-century theorists of mass society, for instance, were at least partly stimulated in their accounts of contemporary society by a concern for, if not a fear of, the enthusiasm of the popular masses for anarchist, socialist, and syndicalist ideas and engagements. Social analysts do not necessarily express themselves through a political vocabulary. But the salience of an emotions terminology in the sociology of the nineteenth and early twentieth centuries resonates well with the emotions which the researchers themselves experienced during an historic period of unruly crowds, urban masses, and economic, political, and social transformations.

By the end of the First World War, however, and certainly by the 1920s, in western Europe and America, the general image of a wholly threatening seething social landscape appeared less tenable. The war itself had permitted political states to regulate economies and populations in a way which reinforced the constitutionalism that had been developing throughout Europe during the nineteenth century. At the same time, the industrial heart-land could by now be regarded as largely pacified. In the post-war period of reconstruction, militant workers and marginalized radical elements of labor movements were calmed by full employment (Gallie 1983; Middlemas 1979). With the consolidation of industrial order the working classes ceased to be regarded as a threat to "civilization" in the way that they had previously been.

In addition, economic organizations were by this time increasingly large and impersonal (Bendix 1974, pp. 211–26). An associated development was not only a rise in the number of blue-collar workers but at the same time their relative decline as a proportion of the workforce as a whole. This was through a rise in the numbers of white-collar clerical, administrative, and sales workers which accompanied growth in the size and importance of organizations. These factors together enhanced the sense of a less passionate and an increasingly rational social order.

Out of these and associated developments, a new model of social action gained currency, which seemed more commensurate with the emergent social and civic experience, and which gained prominence in sociological thinking. It is from about this time that emotion ceases to find ready acceptance as an explanatory variable in sociology. In fact, the term and concept cease to hold any real interest for sociologists at all. These changes which we have accounted for in political economies were supported by intellectual developments in allied disciplines. [. . .]

The new rise of emotion

. . . The orthodox refusal to accept the significance of emotion in social processes did find opposition from the late 1970s, when a number of sociological works expressly dealing with emotion in social processes began to appear. The creative burst, from the late 1970s to the mid-1980s, of papers and books on emotion in social processes was of a sufficient critical mass to generate serious discussion and debate and to encourage others to join in. [. . .]

As in all intellectual sea-changes, emergent trends are never confined to a single discipline. So it was with the renewed interest in emotion. Historical starting-dates can only be indicative, even speculative, openings for discussion, never definitive demarcations. The refocus of psychology on to emotion might be dated as early as 1964, if Silvan Tomkins's aggressive "Introduction to Affect Symposium, APA 1964" (Tomkins and Izard 1966, p. vii) can be taken as a guide. Certainly, from the 1970s there was enormous growth in psychological research on emotion (Leventhal and Tomarken 1986). In anthropology also, the early 1970s saw the beginning of new interest in emotion (Briggs 1970; Levy 1973), which continued to gain momentum (Lutz and White 1986). Philosophy was another discipline in which the renewed interest in emotion can be dated from the 1970s (Neu 1977; Solomon 1976), although the process was set in motion rather earlier (Bedford 1957; Kenny 1964; Ryle 1949). [. . .]

The notion that social agents are spontaneously moved by and subject to emotion is central to the position that emotions are universal, objectively ascertainable, and biologically rooted. The idea that social agents may control or manage their emotions is core to the view that emotions are cultural artifacts relative to particular societies, significantly subjective, and phenomenologically grounded. In sociology these different aspects of emotion are differentially emphasized by different approaches. The idea that emotion is responsible for social outcomes has been emphasized by writers such as Thomas Scheff and Theodore Kemper. The other possibility, which seems to dominate certain sociological accounts of emotion at the present time, is that emotion is principally a consequence of cultural and cognitive, as opposed to social-structural and relational, processes. This is the approach which concentrates on the "social construction" of emotion.

Constructionism and culture

New Social Movements, from the 1970s, challenged prevailing political arrangements and undermined received conventions of social status. These Movements, which include the Women's, the Environmental, and the Black Movements, also contributed to the new awareness of the significance of emotion in social and cultural processes. A major concern of the New Social Movements has been that of identity. The politics of identity, in getting away from the idea that the political standing of persons is bequeathed to them by factors they are subordinate to and cannot influence, emphasized instead the conventional and customary as opposed to the natural elements of being. That is, they emphasized the cultural and social construction of the "person" and their "identity." Emotion, too, can be seen in this light. But if this is its only illumination the image is distorted, and the value of the concept for sociological research and analysis is lost: in the constructionist view emotion remains a consequence of other forces and its capacity for influencing social processes is neglected if not implicitly denied. [. . .]

References

Bedford, Errol. 1957. "Emotions." *Proceedings of the Aristotelian Society*, n.s. 57: 281–307.

Bendix, Reinhard. 1964. *Nation-Building and Citizenship*. New York: Wiley. 1974. *Work and Authority in Industry*. Second edn. Berkeley: University of California Press.

Bierstedt, Robert. 1979. "Sociological Thought in the Eighteenth Century." Pp 3–38 in *A History of Sociological Analysis*, ed. Tom Bottomore and Robert Nisbet. London: Heinemann.

Briggs, Jean L. 1970. *Never in Anger: Portrait of an Eskimo Family*. Cambridge, Mass.: Harvard University Press.

Ferguson, Adam. [1767] 1966. *An Essay on the History of Civil Society*. Edinburgh: Edinburgh University Press.

Gallie, Duncan, 1983. *Social Inequality and Class Radicalism in France and Britain*. Cambridge: Cambridge University Press.

Kemper, Theodore D. 1991. "An Introduction to the Sociology of Emotions." Pp. 301–49 in *International Review of Studies on Emotion*, vol. 1, ed. K. T. Stongman. New York John Wiley.

Kenny, Anthony. 1964. *Action, Emotion and Will*. London: Routledge & Kegan Paul.

Leventhal, Howard and Andrew. J. Tomarken. 1986. "Emotion: Today's Problems." *Annual Review of Psychology*, 37: 565–610.

Levy, Robert I. 1973. *Tahitians: Mind and Experience in the Society Island*. Chicago: Chicago University Press.

Lutz, Catherine and Geoffrey M. White. 1986. "The Anthropology of Emotions." *Annual Review of Anthropology*, 15: 405–36.

Macfie, A. L. and D. D. Raphael. 1976. "Introduction." Pp. 1–52 in *Adam Smith: the Theory of Moral Sentiments*. Oxford: Oxford University Press.

McCarthy, E. Doyle. 1989. "Emotions are Social Things: an Essay in the Sociology of Emotions." Pp. 51–72 in *The Sociology of Emotions: Original Essays and Research*

Papers, ed. David Franks and E. Doyle McCarthy. Greenwich, Conn.: JAI Press.

Middlemas, Keith. 1979. *Politics in an Industrial Society: the Experience of the British System Since 1911*. London: André Deutsch.

Neu, Jerome. 1977. *Emotion, Thought and Therapy: Hume and Spinoza, Theories of Emotion and Therapy*. London: Routledge & Kegan Paul.

Parsons, Talcott. [1937] 1968. *The Structure of Social Action*. New York: Free Press.

Ryle, Gilbert. 1949. *The Concept of Mind*. London: Hutchinson.

Smith, Adam. [1759] 1982. *The Theory of Moral Sentiments*. Oxford: Oxford University Press.

[1776] 1979. *An Inquiry in the Nature and Causes of the Wealth of Nations*. Oxford: Oxford University Press.

Solomon, Robert C. 1976. *The Passions*. Garden City, N.Y.: Anchor Press and Doubleday.

Swingewood, Alan. 1991. *A Short History of Sociological Thought*. 2nd edn. London: Macmillan.

Tomkins, Silvan S. and Carroll E. Izard. 1966. *Affect, Cognition, and Personality: Empirical Studies*. London: Tavistock.

Weber, Max. [1904] 1949. " 'Objectivity' in Social Science." Pp. 50–112 in *The Methodology of the Social Sciences*, ed. Edward A. Shils and Henry A. Finch. New York: Free Press.

[1917] 1967. *Ancient Judaism*. New York: Free Press.

Chapter 10

Erving Goffman

EMBARRASSMENT AND SOCIAL ORGANIZATION

[. . .]

Causes of embarrassment

EMBARRASSMENT HAS TO DO WITH unfulfilled expectations but not of a statistical kind. Given their social identities and the setting, the participants will sense what sort of conduct *ought* to be maintained as the appropriate thing, however much they may despair of its actually occurring. An individual may firmly expect that certain others will make him ill at ease, and yet this knowledge may increase his discomfiture instead of lessening it. An entirely unexpected flash of social engineering may save a situation, all the more effectively for being unanticipated.

The expectations relevant to embarrassment are moral, then, but embarrassment does not arise from the breach of *any* moral expectation, for some infractions give rise to resolute moral indignation and no uneasiness at all. Rather we should look to those moral obligations which surround the individual in only one of his capacities, that of someone who carries on social encounters. The individual, of course, is obliged to remain composed, but this tells us that things are going well, not why. And things go well or badly because of what is perceived about the social identities of those present.

During interaction the individual is expected to possess certain attributes, capacities, and information which, taken together, fit together into a self that is at once coherently unified and appropriate for the occasion. Through the expressive implications of his stream of conduct, through mere participation itself, the individual effectively projects this acceptable self into the interaction, although he may not be aware of it, and the others may not be aware of having so interpreted his conduct. At the same time he must accept and honor the selves projected by the other participants. The elements of a social encounter, then, consist of effectively projected claims to an acceptable self and the confirmation of like claims on the part of the others. The contributions of all are oriented to these and built up on the basis of them.

When an event throws doubt upon or discredits these claims, then the encounter finds itself lodged in assumptions which no longer hold. The responses the parties have made ready are now out of place and must be choked back, and the interaction must be reconstructed. [. . .]

There are many classic circumstances under which the self projected by an individual may be discredited, causing him shame and embarrassment over what he has or appears to have done to himself and to the interaction. To experience a sudden change in status, as by marriage or promotion, is to acquire a self that other individuals will not fully admit because of their lingering attachment to the old self. To ask for a job, as loan of money, or a hand in marriage is to project an image of self as worthy, under conditions where the one who can discredit the assumption may have good reason to do so. To affect the style of one's occupational or social betters is to make claims that may well be discredited by one's lack of familiarity with the role.

The physical structure of an encounter itself is usually accorded certain symbolic implications, sometimes leading a participant against his will to project claims about himself that are false and embarrassing. Physical closeness easily implies social closeness, as anyone knows who has happened upon an intimate gathering not meant for him or who has found it necessary to carry on fraternal "small talk" with someone too high or low or strange to ever be a brother. Similarly, if there is to be talk, someone must initiate it, feed it, and terminate it; and these acts may awkwardly suggest rankings and power which are out of line with the facts.

Various kinds of recurrent encounters in a given society may share the assumption that participants have attained certain moral, mental, and physiognomic standards. The person who falls short may everywhere find himself inadvertently trapped into making implicit identity claims which he cannot fulfil. Compromised in every encounter which he enters, he truly wears the leper's bell. The individual who most isolates himself from social contacts may then be the least insulated from the demands of society. And, if he only imagines that he possesses a disqualifying attribute, his judgment of himself may be in error, but in the light of it his withdrawal from contact is reasonable. In any case, in deciding whether an individual's grounds for shyness are real or imaginary, one should seek not for "justifiable" disqualifications but for the much larger range of characteristics which actually embarrass encounters.

In all these settings the same fundamental thing occurs: the expressive facts at hand threaten or discredit the assumptions a participant finds he has projected about his identity.[7] Thereafter those present find they can neither do without the assumptions nor base their own responses upon them. The inhabitable reality shrinks until everyone feels "small" or out of place. [. . .]

Domain of embarrassment

Having started with psychological considerations, we have come by stages to a structural sociological point of view. Precedent comes from social anthropologists and their analyses of joking and avoidance. One assumes that embarrassment is a normal part of normal social life, the individual becoming uneasy not because he is personally maladjusted but rather because he is not; presumably anyone with his combination of statuses would do likewise. In an empirical study of a particular social system, the first object would be to learn what categories of persons become embarrassed in what recurrent situations. And the second object would be to discover what would happen to the social system and the framework of obligations if embarrassment had not come to be systematically built into it.

An illustration may be taken from the social life of large social establishments—office buildings, schools, hospitals, etc. Here, in elevators, halls, and cafeterias, at newsstands, vending machines, snack counters, and entrances, all members are often formally on an equal if distant footing. . . . Cutting across these relationships of equality and distance is another set of relationships, arising in work teams whose members are ranked by such things as prestige and authority and yet drawn together by joint enterprise and personal knowledge of one another.

In many large establishments, staggered work hours, segregated cafeterias, and the like help to insure that those who are ranked and close in one set of relations will not have to find themselves in physically intimate situations where they are expected to maintain equality and distance. The democratic orientation of some of our newer establishments, however, tends to throw differently placed members of the same work team together at places such as the cafeteria, causing them uneasiness. There is no way for them to act that does not disturb one of the two basic sets of relations in which they stand to each other. These difficulties are especially likely to occur in elevators, for there individuals who are not quite on chatting terms must remain for a time too close together to ignore the opportunity for informal talk—a problem solved, of course, for some, by special executive elevators. Embarrassment, then, is built into the establishment ecologically.

Because of possessing multiple selves the individual may find he is required both to be present and to not be present on certain occasions. Embarrassment ensues: the individual finds himself being torn apart, however gently. Corresponding to the oscillation of his conduct is the oscillation of his self.

Social function of embarrassment

When an individual's projected self is threatened during interaction, he may with poise suppress all signs of shame and embarrassment. No flusterings, or efforts to conceal having seen them, obtrude upon the smooth flow of the encounter; participants can proceed as if no incident has occurred.

When situations are saved, however, something important may be lost. By showing embarrassment when he can be neither of two people, the individual leaves open the possibility that in the future he may effectively be either. His role in the current interaction may be sacrificed, and even the encounter itself, but he demonstrates that, while he cannot present a substainable and coherent self on this occasion, he is at least disturbed by the fact and may prove worthy at another time. To this extent, embarrassment is not an irrational impulse breaking through socially prescribed behavior but part of this orderly behavior itself. Flusterings are an extreme example of that important class of acts which are usually quite spontaneous and yet no less required and obligatory than ones self-consciously performed.

Behind a conflict in identity lies a more fundamental conflict, one of organizational principle, since the self, for many purposes, consists merely of the application of legitimate organizational principles to one's self. One builds one's identity out of claims which, if denied, give one the right to feel righteously indignant. Behind the apprentice's claims for a full share in the use of certain plant facilities there is the organizational principle: all members of the establishment are equal in certain ways qua members. Behind the specialist's demand for suitable financial recognition there is the principle that the type of work, not mere work, determines status. The fumblings of the apprentice and the specialist when they reach the Coca-Cola machine at the same time express an incompatibility of organizational principles.

The principles of organization of any social system are likely to come in conflict at certain points. Instead of permitting the conflict to be expressed in an encounter, the individual places himself between the opposing principles. He sacrifices his identity for a moment, and sometimes the encounter, but the principles are preserved. He may be ground between opposing assumptions, thereby preventing direct friction between them, or he may be almost pulled apart, so that principles with little relation to one another may operate together. Social structure gains elasticity; the individual merely loses composure.

Chapter 11

Susan Shott

EMOTION AND SOCIAL LIFE

A symbolic interactionist analysis

[. . .]

The socialization and construction of feeling

SOCIAL NORMS CLEARLY HAVE SUBSTANTIAL impact on the interpretation, expression, and arousal of emotion, a point succinctly made by Clifford Geertz (1973, p. 81): "Not only ideas, but emotions too, are cultural artificats." Whether emotional explanations are considered appropriate to a given situation, and which emotion, if any, is warranted, are suggested by social norms. [. . .]

There is a social framework that modifies the actor's experience, interpretation, and expression of emotion. This process of affective socialization can probably be described adequately by using basic assumptions about cultural and social influences common to most sociological (and anthropological) perspectives. . . . But there is another dimension of affective experience, the construction of emotion by the actor, which I believe can be best understood by applying a symbolic interactionist perspective. For this orientation focuses on the actor's definitions and interpretations and on the emergent, constructed character of much human behavior, both of which are central to the actor's experience of an emotion: . . . Moreover, the symbolic interactionist analysis to be presented here ties together a number of empirical studies of affect by attribution theorists.

Four major tenets of symbolic interactionism are especially appropriate for explicating the actor's construction of affect:

1. *Study of the actor's definitions and interpretations is essential for an understanding of human conduct* (Manis and Meltzer 1978, p. 8). When reflective human action is concerned, independent variables do not automatically influence dependent variables. Instead, their impact is mediated by interpretation and definition, which

are not just intervening variables but "formative or creative process[es] in [their] own right" (Blumer 1969 p. 135). Hence, definitions and interpretations are essential to social behavior and must be included in most sociological research.

2. *Human behavior is emergent, continually constructed during its execution* (Blumer 1969, p. 82). The meaning of an act is somewhat volatile, since acts are interpreted and defined continuously (by the actor and others) while being carried out. Consequently, human conduct is actively constructed and can be transformed in its making through reinterpretation and redefinition.

3. *The actions of individuals are influenced by their internal states and impulses in addition to external events and stimuli, for actors' perceptions and interpretations are shaped by the former as well as the latter* (Hewitt 1976, p. 47). Physiological or psychological impulses, once noticed, form the beginning of an act and motivate the actor toward its consummation (Mead 1938, pp. 3–8, 23–25). In no sense does the impulse determine the act, but it is a significant component of action and adds to its dynamic character.

4. *Social structures and normative regulation are the framework of human action rather than its determinant, shaping behavior without dictating it.* Structural features (culture, systems, stratification, roles, etc.) shape behavior only insofar as they influence the situations that are the setting of action and provide the symbols used to interpret situations; they do not determine human conduct. [. . .]

Social control and the role-taking-emotions

If there is any area in which the sociological relevance of sentiments is most evident, it may be that of social control; and symbolic interactionist theory is quite useful here, as well. One sort of feelings, which I shall call role-taking emotions, is really the foundation for the large part of social control that is self-control. Unlike other feelings, which do not *require* role taking for their evocation, role-taking emotions cannot occur without putting oneself in another's position and taking that person's perspective; Thus, an individual experiencing a role-taking sentiment (e.g., embarrassment or shame) has first cognitively taken the role of some real or imaginary other or the generalized other, which Mead (1934, p. 154) describes as "the organized community or social group which gives to the individual his unit of self." [. . .]

Role-taking sentiments are of two types: reflexive role-taking emotions, which are directed toward oneself and comprise guilt, shame, embarrassment, pride, and vanity; and empathic role-taking emotions, which are evoked by mentally placing oneself in another's position and feeling what the other feels or what one would feel in such a position. Reflexive role-taking feelings entail considering how one's self appears to others or the generalized other and, unless experienced empathetically, are directed toward oneself. . . . Both reflexive and empathic role-taking emotions, as I shall attempt to show in this section, are significant motivators of normative and moral conduct and, hence, facilitate social control. [. . .]

Three fundamental propositions of symbolic interactionism are particularly relevant to this area:

1. *Individuals have the capacity to treat themselves as objects* (Blumer 1969, p. 82).

Thought, in fact, is nothing more than internalized conversation with oneself and requires treating oneself as a social object. Thus, individuals can take themselves into account as factors in the situation (Hewitt 1976) and evaluate their actions and selves.

2. *The self-conceptions of actors and their capacity for mental self-interaction are derived largely from role taking (with specific others or the generalized other)* Hence, individuals often learn about, and experience, themselves *indirectly*, by taking toward themselves the attitudes of others; only in this manner can they become objects to themselves

3. *Social control is, in large part, self-control.* Because people can view themselves as others do, social control can operate in terms of self-criticism, exerting itself "intimately and extensively over individual behavior [and] serving to integrate the individual and his actions with reference to the organized social process of experience and behavior in which he is implicated" (Mead 1934, p. 255). The generalized other is particularly important for this kind of social control, since it is the means by which the attitudes of the community or group are incorporated within individuals and influence their thinking and conduct (Mead 1934, p. 155).

How do the reflexive role-taking sentiments facilitate social control? Most obviously, guilt, shame, and embarrassment check and punish deviant behavior; each, however, is evoked by different circumstances. Guilt is the feeling that accompanies the "negative self-evaluation which occurs when an individual acknowledges that his behavior is at variance with a given moral value to which he feels obligated to conform" (Ausubel 1955, p. 379). Hence, it is evoked when one commits or contemplates some "immoral" action, then takes the role of the generalized other (or some significant other) and accepts its perceived judgment of oneself as morally inadequate. Shame, however, does not stem from the sense of *moral* inadequacy that is the foundation of guilt; rather, it results from "an actual or presumed negative judgment of [oneself] resulting in self-depreciation vis-a-vis the group" (Ausubel 1955, p. 382). Riezler (1943, p. 459) suggests that shame occurs when one is forced, by taking the role of others . . . to see that others do not accept an idealized self-image that one has built up. Shame is not the same as embarrassment, even though embarrassment is often treated as a form of shame. . . . For shame is provoked by the realization that others . . . consider one's *self* deficient, while embarrassment arises from awareness that others . . . view one's *presentation* of self as inept. An inadequate self usually entails a bungled presentation of self; hence, shame is generally accompanied by embarrassment. The converse, however, is not true; embarrassment is not, as a rule, followed by shame. In Modigliani's (1968, p. 315) words, a "failure in self-presentation . . . does not undermine the individual's *general identity*; rather, it discredits a much more restricted *situational identity* which he is projecting into the current interaction."

Unlike other emotions that foster social control (such as fear), these emotions are frequently evoked even when others are not watching, when there is no threat of being caught in one's misdeed. Of these feelings, embarrassment seems to be the most closely linked with the actual presence of others, shame seems less connected to the presence of others, and guilt least tied to it. This may be due to the possibility that embarrassment is evoked most often by considering how one's self appears to specific others, guilt depends primarily on taking the role of the generalized other, and shame is intermediate in this respect. . . . In the final analysis, without our capacity to experience these sentiments, society as we know it would surely be impossible.

The same is true of pride and vanity, which often reward normative and moral conduct, and empathy, which moves us to feel joy or grief at another's situation and thereby ties us, at least momentarily, to that person. Pride and vanity accompany an enhanced self-conception that comes from taking the role of real or imaginary others or the generalized other and discovering approbation. Cooley (1964, p. 232) describes pride as the "form social self-approval takes in the more rigid and self-sufficient sort of minds; the person who feels it is assured that he stands well with others whose opinion he cares for." Vanity, unlike pride, is an unstable and transient emotion; it is the form social self-approval may take when one is not sure of one's self-image or the approval of others (Cooley 1964, p. 234). Vain persons are therefore more immediately dependent on others for their self-conceptions, which change each time they take the role of another. But, clearly, both pride and vanity may encourage normative and moral conduct (even when others are not actually present) by rewarding such behavior with pleasurable feeling. As I shall show below, empathy too tends to prompt moral behavior.

Returning to guilt, shame, and embarrassment, these feelings not only punish deviant behavior but also contribute to social control in a more positive fashion. A number of experiments have shown that guilt and embarrassment encourage altruistic conduct by those experiencing them. [. . .]

What seems to be common to these altruistic or reparative acts is an attempt to repair one's self-conception or self-presentation and convince others of one's moral worthiness or competence. Guilt is relieved when role taking with others or the generalized other enables people to see themselves once again as morally adequate. [. . .]

The motivation prompting altruistic conduct by embarrassed persons is in all likelihood, quite similar. People suffering embarrassment probably wish to convince others (or themselves) that they are really competent people, capable enough to assist others, and not the clods indicated by their inept or foolish performance. By repairing their situational identities in this fashion, they mitigate their unpleasant feelings of embarrassment. And just as transgressors are reluctant to interact with their victims, embarrassed individuals attempt to minimize interaction with those who have witnessed their inept performance (Brown and Garland 1971). [. . .]

All of the role-taking emotions, then, further social control by encouraging self-control; they are largely responsible for the fact that a great deal of people's behavior accords with social norms even when no external rewards or punishments are evident. The importance of this for social life is obvious: since it is impossible for a society to monitor and sanction everyone's behavior all the time, self-regulation must be the basis of much social control. While symbolic interactionists have long stressed this point . . . they have tended to focus only on the *cognitive* aspects of self-control, particularly role taking and self-interaction. But even though the abilities to take the role of the other and treat oneself as an object make role-taking emotions possible, these capacities are nearly useless for social control without their affective accompaniments. . . .

References

Ausubel, David P. 1955. "Relationships between Shame and Guilt in the Socializing Process." *Psychological Review* 62 (September): 378–90.

Blumer, Herbert. 1969. *Symbolic Interactionism*. Englewood Cliffs, N.J.: Prentice-Hall.

Brown, Bert R., and Howard Garland. 1971. "The Effects of Incompetency, Audience Acquaintanceship, and Anticipated Evaluative Feedback on Face-Saving Behavior." *Journal of Experimental Social Psychology* 7 (September): 490–502.

Cooley, Charles Horton, 1962. *Social Organization*. New York: Schocken.

———. 1964. *Human Nature and the Social Order*. New York: Schocken.

Geertz, Clifford. 1973. *The Interpretation of Cultures*. New York: Basic.

Hewitt, John P. 1976. *Self and Society*. Boston: Allyn & Bacon.

Manis, Jerome G., and Bernard N. Meltzer, eds. 1978. *Symbolic Interactionism*. 3d ed. Boston: Allyn & Bacon.

Mead, George Herbert. 1934. *Mind, Self, and Society*. Chicago: University of Chicago Press.

———. 1938. *The Philosophy of the Act*. Chicago: University of Chicago Press.

Modigliani, Andre. 1968. "Embarrassment and Embarrassability." *Sociometry* 31 (September): 313–26.

Riezler, Kurt. 1943. "Comment on the Social Psychology of Shame." *American Journal of Sociology* 48 (January): 457–65.

Chapter 12

Arlie Russell Hochschild

EMOTION WORK, FEELING RULES, AND SOCIAL STRUCTURE

[. . .]

WHY IS THE EMOTIVE EXPERIENCE of normal adults in daily life as orderly as it is? Why, generally speaking, do people feel gay at parties, sad at funerals, happy at weddings? This question leads us to examine, not conventions of appearance or outward comportment, but conventions of feeling. Conventions of feeling become surprising only when we imagine, by contrast, what totally unpatterned, unpredictable emotive life might actually be like at parties, funerals, weddings, and in the family or work life of normal adults.

Erving Goffman (1961) suggests both the surprise to be explained and part of the explanation: ". . . We find that participants will hold in check certain psychological states and attitudes, for after all, the very general rule that one enter into the prevailing mood in the encounter carries the understanding that contradictory feelings will be in abeyance. . . . So generally, in fact, does one suppress unsuitable affect, that we need to look at offenses to this rule to be reminded of its usual operation" (Goffman 1961, p. 23). If we take this passage seriously, as I urge we do, we may be led back to the classic question of social order from a particular vantage point—that of emotion management. From this vantage point, rules seem to govern how people try to try not to feel in ways "appropriate to the situation." Such a notion suggests how profoundly the individual is "social," and "socialized" to try to pay tribute to official definitions of situations, with no less than their feelings.

Let me pause to point out that there are two possible approaches to the social ordering of emotive experience. One is to study the social factors that induce or stimulate primary (i.e., nonreflective, though by definition conscious) emotions—emotions passively undergone. The other is to study *secondary acts* performed upon the ongoing nonreflective stream of primary emotive experience. The first approach focuses on how social factors affect what people feel, the second on how social factors affect what people think and do about what they feel (i.e., acts of assessment and management). Those who take the first approach might regard those who take the second as being "overly cognitive." But in fact the two approaches are compatible, and indeed the second, taken here, relies on some accumulation of knowledge garnered from the first. [. . .]

Emotion work

By "emotion work" I refer to the act of trying to change in degree or quality an emotion or feeling. To "work on" an emotion or feeling is, for our purposes, the same as "to manage" an emotion or to do "deep acting." Note that "emotion work" refers to the effort—the act of trying—and not to the outcome, which may or may not be successful. Failed acts of management still indicate what ideal formulations guide the effort, and on that account are no less interesting than emotion management that works.

The very notion of an attempt suggests an active stance vis-à-vis feeling. In my exploratory study respondents characterized their emotion work by a variety of active verb forms; "I *psyched myself up*. . . . I *squashed* my anger down. . . . I *tried hard* not to feel disappointed. . . . I *made* myself have a good time. . . . I *tried* to feel grateful. . . . I *killed* the hope I had burning." There was also the actively passive form, as in, "I *let myself* finally feel sad."

Emotion work differs from emotion "control" or "suppression." The latter two terms suggest an effort merely to stifle or prevent feeling. "Emotion work" refers more broadly to the act of evoking or shaping, as well as suppressing, feeling in onself. I avoid the term "manipulate" because it suggests a shallowness I do not mean to imply. We can speak, then, of two broad types of emotion work: *evocation*, in which the cognitive focus is on a desired feeling which is initially absent, and *suppression*, in which the cognitive focus is on an undesired feeling which is initially present. One respondent, going out with a priest 20 years her senior, exemplifies the problems of evocative emotion work: "Anyway, I started to try and make myself like him. I made myself focus on the way he talked, certain things he'd done in the past. . . . When I was with him I did like him but I would go home and write in my journal how much I couldn't stand him. I kept changing my feeling and actually thought I really liked him while I was with him but a couple of hours after he was gone, I reverted back to different feelings. . . ." Another respondent exemplifies the work, not of working feeling up, but of working feeling down:

> Last summer I was going with a guy often, and I began to feel very strongly about him. I knew though, that he had just broken up with a girl a year ago because she had gotten too serious about him, so I was afraid to show any emotion. I also was afraid of being hurt, so I attempted to change my feelings. *I talked myself into not caring about Mike . . .* but I must admit it didn't work for long. *To sustain this feeling I had to almost invent bad things about him and concentrate on them or continue to tell myself he didn't care. It was a hardening of emotions*, I'd say. It took a lot of

work and was unpleasant, because I had to concentrate on anything I could find that was irritating about him.

Often emotion work is aided by setting up an emotion-work system, for example, telling friends of all the worst faults of the person one wanted to fall out of love with, and then going to those friends for reinforcement of this view of the ex-beloved. This suggests another point: emotion work can be done by the self upon the self, by the self upon others, and by others upon oneself.

In each case the individual is conscious of a moment of "pinch," or discrepancy, between what one does feel and what one wants to feel (which is, in turn, affected by what one thinks one ought to feel in such a situation). In response, the individual may try to eliminate the pinch by working on feeling. Both the sense of discrepancy and the response to it can vary in time. The managing act, for example, can be a five-minute stopgap measure, or it can be a more long-range gradual effort suggested by the term "working through."

There are various techniques of emotion work. One is *cognitive:* the attempt to change images, ideas, or thoughts in the service of changing the feelings associated with them. A second is *bodily:* the attempt to change somatic or other physical symptoms of emotion (e.g., trying to breathe slower, trying not to shake). Third, there is *expressive* emotion work: trying to change expressive gestures in the service of changing inner feeling (e.g., trying to smile, or to cry). This differs from simple display in that it is directed toward change in feeling. It differs from bodily emotion work in that the individual tries to alter or shape one or another of the classic public channels for the expression of feeling.

These three techniques are distinct theoretically, but they often, of course, go together in practice. For example:

> I was a star halfback in high school. Before games I didn't feel the upsurge of adrenalin—in a word I wasn't "psyched up." (This was due to emotional difficulties I was experiencing and still experience—I was also an A student whose grades were dropping.) Having been in the past a fanatical, emotional, intense player, a "hitter" recognized by coaches as a very hard worker and a player with "desire," this was very upsetting. *I did everything I could to get myself "up." I would try to be outwardly "rah rah" or get myself scared of my opponents—anything to get the adrenalin flowing.* I tried to look nervous and intense before games, so at least the coaches wouldn't catch on. . . . When actually I was mostly bored, or in any event, not "up." I recall before one game wishing I was in the stands watching my cousin play for his school, rather than "out here." [. . .]

The smoothly warm airline hostess, the ever-cheerful secretary, the unirritated complaint clerk, the undisgusted proctologist, the teacher who likes every student equally, and Goffman's unflappable poker player may all have to engage in deep acting, an acting that goes well beyond the mere ordering of display. Work to make feeling and frame consistent with situation is work in which individuals continually and privately engage. But they do so in obeisance to rules not completely of their own making.

Feeling rules

We feel. We try to feel. We want to try to feel. The social guidelines that direct how we want to try to feel may be describable as a set of socially shared, albeit often latent (not thought about unless probed at), rules. In what way, we may ask, are these rules themselves known and how are they developed?

To begin with, let us consider several common forms of evidence for feeling rules. In common parlance, we often talk about our feelings or those of others as if rights and duties applied directly to them. For example, we often speak of "having the right" to feel angry at someone. Or we say we "should feel more grateful" to a benefactor. We chide ourselves that a friend's misfortune, a relative's death, "should have hit us harder," or that another's good luck, or our own, should have inspired more joy. We know feeling rules, too, from how others react to what they infer from our emotive display. Another may say to us, "You *shouldn't feel* so guilty; it wasn't your fault," or "You *don't have a right* to feel jealous, given our agreement." Another may simply declare an opinion as to the fit of feeling to situation, or may cast a claim upon our managerial stance, presupposing this opinion. Others may question or call for an account of a particular feeling in a situation, whereas they do not ask for an accounting of some other situated feeling (Lyman and Scott 1970). Claims and callings for an account can be seen as *rule reminders*. At other times, a person may, in addition, chide, tease, cajole, scold, shun—in a word, sanction us for "mis-feeling." Such sanctions are a clue to the rules they are meant to enforce.

Rights and duties set out the proprieties as to the *extent* (one can feel "too" angry or "not angry enough"), the *direction* (one can feel sad when one should feel happy), and the *duration* of a feeling, given the situation against which it is set. These rights and duties of feeling are a clue to the depth of social convention, to one final reach of social control.

There is a distinction, in theory at least, between a feeling rule as it is known by our sense of what we can *expect* to feel in a given situation, and a rule as it is known by our sense of what we *should* feel in that situation. For example, one may realistically expect (knowing oneself and one's neighbor's parties) to feel bored at a large New Year's Eve party and at the same time acknowledge that it would be more fitting to feel exuberant. However, "expect to feel" and "should ideally feel" often coincide, as below:

> Marriage, chaos, unreal, completely different in many ways than I imagined. Unfortunately we rehearsed the morning of our wedding at eight o'clock. The wedding was to be at eleven o'clock. It wasn't like I thought (everyone would know what to do). They didn't. That made me nervous. My sister didn't help me get dressed or flatter me (nor did anyone in the dressing room until I asked them). I was depressed. I wanted to be so happy on our wedding day. I never dreamed how anyone would cry at their wedding. A wedding is "the happy day" of one's life. I couldn't believe that some of my best friends couldn't make it to my wedding and that added to a lot of little things. So I started out to the church and all these things that I always thought would not happen at my wedding went through my mind. I broke down—I cried

going down. "Be happy" I told myself. Think of the friends, and relatives that are present. (But I finally said to myself, "Hey people aren't getting married, you are. It's for Rich [my husband] and you.") From down the pretty long aisle we looked at each other's eyes. His love for me changed my whole being. From that point on we joined arms. I was relieved and the tension was gone. In one sense it meant misery—but in the true sense of two people in love and wanting to share life—it meant the world to me. It was beautiful. It was indescribable.

In any given situation, we often invest what we expect to feel with idealization. To a remarkable extent these idealizations vary socially. If the "old-fashioned bride" above anticipates a "right" to feel jealous at any possible future infidelity, the young "flower child" below rejects just this right.

. . . when I was living down south, I was involved with a group of people, friends. We used to spend most evenings after work or school together. We used to do a lot of drugs, acid, coke or just smoke dope and we had this philosophy that we were very communal and did our best to share everything—clothes, money, food, and so on. I was involved with this one man—and thought I was "in love" with him. He in turn had told me that I was very important to him. Anyway, this one woman who was a very good friend of mine at one time and this man started having a sexual relationship, supposedly without my knowledge. I knew though and had a lot of mixed feelings about it. I thought, intellectually, that I had no claim to the man, and believed in fact that no one should ever try to *own* another person. I believed also that it was none of my business and I had no reason to worry about their relationship together, for it had nothing really to do with my friendship with either of them. I also believed in sharing. But I was horribly hurt, alone and lonely, depressed and I couldn't shake the depression and on top of those feelings I felt guilty for having those possessively jealous feelings. And so I would continue going out with these people every night, and try to suppress my feelings. My ego was shattered. I got to the point where I couldn't even laugh around them. So finally I confronted my friends and left for the summer and traveled with a new friend. I realized later what a heavy situation it was, and it took me a long time to get myself together and feel whole again.

Whether the convention calls for trying joyfully to possess, or trying casually not to, the individual compares and measures experience against an expectation often idealized. It is left for motivation ("what I want to feel") to mediate between feeling rule ("what I should feel") and emotion work ("what I try to feel"). Some of the time many of us can live with a certain dissonance between "ought" and "want," or between "want" and "try to." But the attempts to reduce emotive dissonance are our periodic clues to rules of feeling. [. . .]

References

Goffman, Erving. 1956. "Embarrassment and Social Organization." *American Journal of Sociology* 62 (November): 264–71.
———. 1961. "Fun in Games." Pp. 17–84 in *Encounters*. Indianapolis: Bobbs-Merrill.
Lyman, S., and Marvin Scott. 1970. *Sociology of the Absurd*. New York: Appleton-Century-Crofts.

Chapter 13

Theodore D. Kemper

POWER, STATUS, AND EMOTIONS

A sociological contribution to a psychophysiological domain

SOCIOLOGISTS HAVE GENERALLY ESCHEWED systematic inquiry into the emotions. This is understandable, in as much as sociologists ordinarily concern themselves with patterns of group organization and social structure. The emotions, on the other hand, are physiological and psychological phenomena, experienced-by and measured-in individual organisms. Even social psychology—which deals with the effects of social patterns on individuals—has concerned itself little with emotions per se, though many of the results of social psychological experiments are pertinent to the study of emotions. [. . .]

. . . The central contribution of a sociological approach to emotions is the specification of a comprehensive model of the social environment, as is detailed below. This allows for the formulation of empirically-based hypotheses linking variations in the social environment with varying emotions. . . .

Power and status as social environment

A remarkable convergence of theoretical and empirical work in the social sciences has gone relatively unremarked. I refer here to the oft-repeated findings that two central dimensions characterize social relationships between human actors. . . . The two dimensions are variously named but they refer unmistakably to relations of *power* and *status*. Power implies the ability to overcome the resistance of others when others do not wish to comply (cf. Weber, 1946, p. 181). Relationships can be *structured* in terms of power, so that there is a probability that in specified domains each actor can achieve his or her will to a certain extent despite the resistance of the other. There is also *process* power: this entails all the acts designed to overcome the resistance of the other, both actually and prospectively, including physical and verbal assaults, deprivations, threats, and the like.

Status refers to the compliance that actors voluntarily accord each other, unaccompanied by threat or coercion. As with power there are structural and processual aspects. Status structure in relationship indicates the probability of voluntary compliance with the desires and wishes of the other, whether actually or prospectively. As process, status entails the range of friendly, congenial, supporting, rewarding, ultimately, loving behavior that actors voluntarily accord each other. . . .

The particular utility of the power and status dimensions is that they permit the heuristic assumption that *all* social relations can be located in a two-dimensional power-status space, and that changes in social relations may be understood as changes in the power and status positions of actors. Actors relate to each other in structures of power and status, and in their interactions with each other express or change the relationship structure by acts that signify particular levels of power and status.

Granted this view of relationship, the following proposition is possible: *A very large class of human emotions results from real, anticipated, recollected, or imagined outcomes of power and status relations* (Kemper, 1978). This means that if we wish to predict or understand the occurrence of many human emotions we must look at the structure and process of power and status relations between actors. This approach encompasses both the distressful emotions—anger, depression, guilt, shame, anxiety—as well as the positive emotions—happiness, security, pride, righteousness, and love. . . .

One important assumption about power and status relations is that they are cross-culturally valid (cf. Triandis, 1972), hence universally applicable in the prediction of emotions. However, three things are not universal:

1. The specific cultural signifiers of particular levels of power and status outcomes. For example, Krout (1942, reproduced in Hinde, 1979, p. 60) indicates 15 different ways, distributed across 20 different cultures, of displaying *humility*, a condition expressing very low power-and-status for self, often in combination with accord of very high status (and probably very high power) to the other. Hence different concrete behaviors in different cultures may elicit and signify certain emotions.

2. Also not universal are the power and status levels of particular social positions, especially as defined by ascriptive category. For example, preliterate societies tend to respect older men for their wisdom and knowledge of the society's traditions. In modern societies, older men are ceded far less status.

3. Finally, specific social organizational and social structural patterns may exacerbate or inhibit the production of certain emotions. Marx (1964) proposed the link between capitalism and alienation. Blauner (1964) showed how this link is mediated by a particular form of technology and division of labor. Levy (1973) . . . reported the "hypocognition" of certain emotions among Tahitians (this means there is a limited vocabulary for these emotions). Depression is one of the hypocognated emotions, apparently rarely experienced among Tahitians. Why? Because, we see, in Levy's discussion, that the social organizational pattern does not frequently produce the kind of status-loss outcomes that are associated with depression. . . .

Universality of emotion does not mean that all societies experience the same amounts of different emotions. That would require that the social organization and the social structure of the societies be the same. Universality of emotions means that when particular social relational outcomes occur, the same emotions will result—regardless of how often such social relational outcomes occur in the society over-all.

I turn now briefly to three sociologically relevant considerations about emotions: their evolutionary survival value, emotions in the societal social structure, and emotions in interpersonal and micro-interaction.

A fundamental idea about emotions is that they have evolutionary survival value (Darwin, 1873; . . . Plutchik, 1980). . . . Biological survival entails not merely the survival of organisms, but the preservation of patterns of social organization, or perhaps change of pattern to a more adaptive form. . . .

Fear and anger energize flight or fight in the face of danger or threat from others. Love and attachment emotions help sustain commitment to pregnant women and to infants who can't forage or protect themselves; also to aged parents and other elder members of the group who may have wisdom to offer. Respect, and loyalty permit allegiance to leaders who manifest respect-worthy qualities that augment the survival prospects of the group. Guilt and shame allow for the exercise of relatively unsupervised self-control of impulses to aggression, malfeasance, and irresponsibility.

Durkheim (1965) emphasized the importance of religious sentiments (awe, respect, fear) in imparting a necessary force to moral commitments to other members of society. Further, Durkheim valued the "emotional effervescence" . . . that simple physical communion and common activity engender in people, giving them a sense of solidarity, security and strength via the identification with a larger social entity. . . . Hammond (1978) suggested that for Durkheim, emotions replace in humans the missing regulatory mechanism of instinct. Without emotions, presumably, humans would not bind themselves with sufficient constancy to any particular social-moral pattern, shunning others even if these are immediately instrumental i.e., immediately rewarded. . . . Hence it may be seen that emotions have not simply biological, but social survival value.

At the same time as we see the sociological facet of the biological phenomenon—the emotions—we must not proceed as far as have the sociobiologists in this area (e.g., Wilson, 1975). Sociobiologists presume to discover underlying biological processes and structures that support *particular* patterns of social organization, e.g., in relations between the sexes, hierarchy in society, etc. My proposal about the sociological relevance of the emotions is different. I view the emotions as capable of supporting extremely broad, even opposite, forms of social organization. Despite the great variability of cultural patterns and forms of societal organization, the same emotions undergird them. Hence we do not have direct biological determination of social patterns, but a case where social patterns—of whatever type—rely upon emotions for stability and support.

We may define *social structure* in society as a more or less stable distribution of power, status, and resources (usually wealth). Some have more, some less. Marx (1964) and Weber (1946) pointed out that these are potential bases of group formation, e.g., social classes and status groups, more or less conscious of their common interests and certainly aware of their standing relative to each other in the social structural dimensions. Two kinds of emotions are of interest here: *Integrating* emotions, which bind groups together, e.g., loyalty, pride, love; and *Differentiating* emotions, which maintain the differences between the groups, e.g., fear, anger, contempt, envy. [. . .]

Actual or threatened change in social structure—the previous arrangements of power, status, and wealth—produces extremely intense emotions. History records some of the most terrible cruelties and, we must assume, hatreds to have occurred at such times. Threatened groups are not only fearful, the fear may become a virtual paranoia. Groups on the rise may indulge themselves in the most extravagant confidence and hope. Nostalgia and depression are peculiarly appropriate for groups who sense their decline. Chekov was an exquisite literary recorder of the emotions of this phenomenon. Those already declassé maintain self-esteem through privately expressed contempt for the *nouveaux riches*. The succeeding class of par-venus or commissars must ride for some time a crest of extraordinary optimism and self-aggrandizement, even megalomania (see Kemper, 1978, p. 545). Bensman and Vidich (1962) detail systematically the possibilities here.

At the microinteraction level—interpersonal, moment-to-moment, etc.—emotions should operate both to integrate and differentiate, just as they do in the larger social structure. This is because the same descriptive categories can be applied at both levels: power, status, resources. Interaction consists of doing technical things together (cooperation in some form of divided labor), and of power and status relations. Emotions flow from the outcomes of the power and status relations. . . .

Moment-to-moment interaction and the ensuing emotions appear to be guided by three principles: First, there is *reciprocity*. This means that behaviors of one kind from actor A are likely to be followed by behaviors of a specific kind from actor B, with greater than chance probability. We may infer that the emotions evoked in B by the original actions of A provide some push for actor B's response. That response releases an emotion in turn in A, which leads to the start of another round in the interaction cycle. [. . .]

. . . This brings us to the second principle: *prior structure effects*, that is the influence on interaction and emotions of the existing social and personality structure. Gottman *et al.* (1977) found among distressed couples—those with a history (i.e., structure) of high-power, low-status interaction—that communication of disagreement was accompanied by negative affect; among the nondistressed by neutral affect. Among distressed couples messages sent with positive intent were more likely to be received as negative. Rausch *et al.* (1974) report similar findings. Among non-distressed couples, there was greater chance of power behavior from one partner to be answered with conciliatory or status behavior. Among distressed couples, power behavior was virtually always met with counterpower. [. . .]

A third principle of microinteraction that appears less distinctly is that of *devolution*. In interaction, things very often start well and end badly, or go downhill. Rausch (1965) found that interaction sequences tended to devolve over five exchanges from about 90% friendly to about 70–75% friendly. Loehlin's (1965) computer simulation of dyadic interaction found that even when his "personalities" were both essentially "positive" they reached a harmonious conclusion in a sequence of interactions only with some difficulty. . . . Love relations appear to be particularly vulnerable to movement into high-power sequences. Integrative emotions tend to be replaced by differentiating emotions in a somewhat predictable way (Houseknecht & Macke, 1981; Swensen, Eskew, & Kohlhepp, 1981). [. . .]

References

Bensman, J., & Vidich, A. Business cycles, class, and personality. *Psychoanalysis and Psychoanalytic Review*, 1962, *49*, 30–52.

Blauner, R. *Alienation and freedom*. Chicago: University of Chicago Press, 1964.

Darwin, C. *The expression of emotions in man and animals*. New York: Appleton, 1973.

Durkheim, E. *The elementary forms of the religious life*. (Translated by Joseph Ward Swain.) New York: Free Press, 1965. (Originally published 1915.)

Gottman, J., Markman, H., & Notarius, C. The topography of marital conflict: A sequential analysis of verbal and nonverbal behavior. *Journal of Marriage and the Family*, 1977, *37*, 461–477.

Hammond, M. Durkheim's reality construction model and the emergence of social stratification. *The Sociological Review*, 1978, *26* (New Series), 713–727.

Hinde, R. A. *Towards understanding relationships*. New York: Academic, 1979.

Houseknecht, S. K., & Macke, A. S. Combining marriage and career: The marital adjustment of professional women. *Journal of Marriage and Family* 1981, *43*, 651–661.

Kemper, T. D. *A social interactional theory of emotions*. New York: Wiley, 1978.

Levy, R. *Tahitians: Mind and experiences in the Society Islands*. Chicago: University of Chicago Press, 1973.

Lochlin, J. C. 'Interpersonal' experiments with a computer model of personality. *Journal of Personality and Social Psychology*, 1965, *2*, 580–584.

Marx, K. *Selected Writings in Sociology and Social Philosophy*. T. B. Bottomore and M. Rubel (Eds.), New York: McGraw-Hill, 1964.

Plutchik, R. *The emotions: A psycho-evolutionary synthesis*. New York: Harper and Row, 1980.

Rausch, H. L. Interaction sequences. *Journal of Personality and Social Psychology*, 1965, *2*, 487–499.

Rausch, H. L., Barry, W. A., Hertel, R. K., & Swain, M. A. *Communication, conflict, marriage*. San Francisco. Josscy-Bass, 1974.

Swensen, C. H., Eskew, R. W., & Kohlhepp, K. A. Stage of family life cycle, ego development, and the marriage relationship. *Journal of Marriage and Family* 1981, *43*, 841–851.

Triandis, H. C. *The analysis of subjective culture*. New York: Wiley, 1972.

Weber, M. From Max Weber: *Essays in sociology*. H. Gerth & C. W. Mills (Eds.), New York: Oxford University Press, 1946.

Wilson, E. C. *Sociobiology: The new synthesis*. Cambridge: Harvard University Press, 1975.

Chapter 14

Randall Collins

THE ROLE OF EMOTION IN SOCIAL STRUCTURE

HOW IMPORTANT ARE THE EMOTIONS in society? I would argue that they are quite fundamental. This is especially so if one conceives of emotion as a form of social energy which can take any state ranging from completely passive inactivity on through strong affectual arousal. The crucial mid-range of this continuum is a series of variations in social confidence, which manifest themselves in feelings of solidarity—membership in social groups. At their stronger levels, such feelings of confidence are important in the organization of property and authority.

Emotional energy not only upholds the social structure, but is produced by it. That is, social social structure *is* nothing more, on the most fine-grained empirical level, than repeated patterns of face-to-face interaction. These interactions have a *ritual* quality, which reproduce, increase, or decrease the emotional energies of individuals. Both the statics of repetitively reenacted social structure and the dynamics of social change are crucially mediated by the social production of emotions.

The following sociological theory of *interaction ritual* is based on the theories of Emile Durkheim (1947, 1954) and Erving Goffman (1959). I have suggested elsewhere (Collins, 1975, pp. 90–111) that it is consonant both with Darwinian animal ethology and with recent developments in cognitive micro-sociology, especially ethnomethodology. I have also attempted to show (Collins, 1975, pp. 49–89) how a variety of both hierarchic and egalitarian interactions produce the different emotional tones and cognitive propensities that make up the varieties of class cultures. The "marketplace" of such ritual interaction makes up social networks.

A fuller version of this discussion may be found in Collins (1981b).

Emotion as a micro basis of macro-sociology

Both neo-rationalist self-criticisms (Heath, 1976) and micro-sociological evidence (Garfinkel, 1967) agree that complex contingencies cannot be calculated rationally, and hence that actors must largely rely on tacit assumptions and organizational routine. But the actual structures of the social world, especially as centered around the networks upholding property and authority, involve continuous monitoring by individuals of each other's group loyalties. Because the social world can involve quite a few lines of authority and sets of coalitions, the task of monitoring them can be extremely complex. How is this possible, given people's inherently limited cognitive capacities?

The solution must be that negotiations are carried out implicitly, on a different level than the use of consciously minipulated verbal symbols. I propose that the mechanism is *emotional* rather than cognitive. Individuals monitor others' attitudes towards social coalitions, and hence towards the degree of support for routines, by feeling the amount of confidence and enthusiasm there is towards certain leaders and activities, or the amount of fear of being attacked by a strong coalition, or the amount of contempt for a weak one. These emotional energies are transmitted by contagion among members of a group, in flows that operate very much like the set of negotiations that produce prices within a market.

The underlying emotional dynamic, I propose, centers upon feelings of *membership in coalitions*. Briefly put: property (access to and exclusions from particular physical places and things) is based upon a sense of what kinds of persons do and do not belong where. This is based, in turn, upon a sense of what groups are powerful enough to punish violators of their claims. Authority is similarly organized: It rests upon a sense of which people are connected to which groups, to coalitions of what extensiveness and what capacity to enforce the demands of their members upon others. . . .

The most general explanation of human social behavior encompasses all of these. It should specify: What makes someone a member of a coalition? What determines the extensiveness of a coalition, and the intensity of bonds within it? How do people judge the power of coalitions? The answers to these questions, I am suggesting, determines the way in which groups of friends and other status groups are formed; the degree to which authority and property routines are upheld; and who will dominate others within these patterns. The basic mechanism is a process of emotional group identification that may be described as a set of interaction ritual chains.

A theory of interaction ritual chains

From a micro-translation viewpoint, all processes of forming and judging coalition memberships must take place in interaction situations. The main activity in such situations is conversation. But no one situation stands alone. Every individual goes through many situations: indeed, a lifetime is, strictly speaking, a chain of inter-action situations. (One might also call it a chain of conversations.) The people one talks to also have talked to other people in the past, and will talk to others in the future. Hence an appropriate image of the social world is a bundle of individual chains of interactional experience, criss-crossing each other in space as they flow along in time. The dynamics of coalition membership are produced by the emotional sense individuals have at any one point in time, due to the tone of the situation they are currently in (or last remember, or shortly anticipate), which in turn is influenced by the previous chains of situations of all participants.

The *manifest* content of an interaction is usually not the emotions it involves Any conversation, to the extent that it is taken seriously by its participants, focuses their attention upon the reality of its contents, the things that are talked about (Goffman, 1967, pp. 113–116). This may include a focus upon practical work that is being done. What is significant about any conversation from the point of view of social membership, however, is not the content, but the extent to which the participants can actually maintain a common activity of focusing upon that content. The content is a vehicle for establishing membership. From this viewpoint, any conversation may be looked upon as a ritual. It invokes a common reality, which from a ritual viewpoint may be called a "myth": in this case, whether the conversational "myth" is true or not is irrelevant. The "myth" or centent is a Durkheimian sacred object. It signifies membership in a common group, for those who truly respect it. The person who can successfully become engrossed in a conversational reality becomes accepted as a member of the group of those who believe in that conversational entity. In terms of the Durkheimian model of religious ritual, (Durkheim, 1954/1912; cf. Goffman, 1967), a conversation is a cult in which all believers share a moral solidarity. In fact; it *creates* the reference point of moral solidarity: those who believe are the good; defense of the belief and hence of the group is righteousness; evil is disbelief in, and even more so attack upon, the cognitive symbols that holds the group together. The cognitive symbols—however banal, particularized, or esoteric the conversational content may be—are important to the group, and defended by it, because they are the vehicle by which means the group is able to unify itself.

Not all conversations, however, are equally successful rituals. Some bind individuals together more permanently and tightly than others; some conversations do not come off at all. Among those conversations that do succeed in evoking a common reality, some of these produce a feeling of egalitarian membership among the conversationalists, while others produce feelings of rank differences, including feelings of authority and subordination. These types of variability, in fact, are essential for producing and reproducing stratified social order. Conversational interaction ritual, then, is a mechanism producing *varying* amounts of solidarity, varying degrees of personal identification with coalitions of varying degrees of impressiveness.

What, then, makes a conversational ritual succeed or not, and what kinds of coalitions does it invoke?

I suggest the following ingredients. (1) Participants in a successful conversational ritual must be able to invoke a common cognitive reality. Hence they must have similar *conversational* or *cultural resources*. A successful conversation may also be inegalitarian, in that one person does most of the cultural reality-invoking, the others acting as an audience; in this case we have a domination-and-subordination-producing ritual. (2) Participants must also be able to sustain a common emotional tone. At a minimum, they must all want to produce at least momentary solidarity. Again, the emotional participation may be stratified, dividing the group into emotional leaders and followers.

These two ingredients—cultural resources and emotional energies—come from individuals' chains of previous interactional experience, and serve to reproduce or change the pattern of interpersonal relations. Among the most important of the things reproduced or changed are feelings about persons' relationships to physical property, and to the coercive coalitions of authority. How individuals are tied to these is the crucial determinant of which coalitions are dominant or subordinate.

Conversational Resources.   Particular styles and topics of conversation imply memberships in different groups. At any point in time, the previous chain of interaction rituals that have been successfully negotiated have made certain conversational contents into symbols of solidarity. The range of these has been discussed elsewhere (Collins, 1975, pp. 114–131). For example, shop talk invokes membership in occupational groups, political and other ideological talk invokes contending political coalitions, entertainment talk invokes groups with various tastes, general discussion invokes different intellectual and nonintellectual strata, while gossip and personal talk invoke specific and sometimes quite intimate memberships. Again, it is not important whether what is said is true or not, but that it can be said and accepted as a common reality for that moment, that makes it an emblem of group membership. [. . .]

Emotional Energies.   Emotions affect ritual membership in several ways. There must be at least a minimal degree of common mood among interactants if a conversational ritual is to succeed in invoking a shared reality. The stronger the common emotional tone, the more real the invoked topic will seem to be, and the more solidarity will exist in the group Emotional propensities are thus a prerequisite for a successful interaction. But the interaction also serves as a machine for intensifying emotion, and for generating new emotional tones and solidarities. Thus emotional energies are important results of interactions at any point in the ritual chain. The emotional solidarity, I would suggest, is the payoff that favorable conversational resources can produce for an individual.

If successful interactional rituals (IRs) produce feelings of solidarity, stratification both within and among coalitions is a further outcome of emotional flows along IR chains. As noted, conversational rituals can be either egalitarian or asymmetrical. Both types have stratifying implications. Egalitarian rituals are nevertheless stratifying in that insiders are accepted and outsiders are rejected; here stratification exists in the form of a coalition against excluded individuals, or possibly the domination of one coalition over another. Asymmetrical conversations, in which one individual sets the energy tones (and invokes the cultural reality) while the others are an audience, are internally stratified.

The most basic emotional ingredient in interactions, I would suggest, is a minimal tone of positive sentiment towards the other. The solidarity sentiments range from a minimal display of nonhostility, up to warm mutual liking and enthusiastic common activity. Where do such emotions come from? From previous experiences in IR chains. An individual who is successfully accepted into an inter-action acquires an increment of positive emotional energy. This energy is mani-fested as what we commonly call confidence, warmth, and enthusiasm. Acquiring this in one situation, an individual has more emotional resources for successfully negotiating solidarity in the next interaction. Such chains, both positive and negative, extend throughout every person's lifetime.

Let us consider the variations possible within this basic model. The main conditions which produce emotional energy are these:

1. Increased emotional confidence is produced by every experience of success-fully negotiating a membership ritual. Decreased emotional confidence results from rejection or lack of success.

2. The more powerful the group within which one successfully negoti-ates ritual solidarity, the greater the emotional confidence one receives from it. The power of a group here means the amount of physical property it successfully claims access to, the sheer size of its adherents, and the amount of physical force (numbers of fighters, instruments of violence) it has access to.

3. The more intense the emotional arousal within an IR, the more emotional energy an individual receives from participating in it. A group situation with a high degree of enthusiasm thus generates large emotional increments for individuals. High degrees of emotional arousal are created especially by IRs which include an element of conflict against outsiders: either an actual fight, a ritual punishment of offenders, or on a lower level of intensity, symbolic denunciation of enemies (including conversational griping)

4. Taking a dominant position within an IR increases one's emotional energies. Taking a subordinate positions within an IR reduces one's emotional energies; the more extreme the subordination, the greater the energy reduction. [. . .]

References

Collins, R. *Conflict sociology*. New York: Academic Press, 1975.

Collins, R. On the micro-foundations of macro-sociology. *American Journal of Sociology*, 1981, *86*, 984–1014. (b)

Durkheim, E. *The division of labor in society*. Glencoc, Illinois: Free Press, 1947. (Originally published, 1893.)

Durkheim, E. *The elementary forms of the religious life*. Glencoe, Illinois: Free Press, 1954. (Originally published, 1912.)

Garfinkel, H. *Studies in ethnomethodology*. Englewood Cliffs, N.J.: Prentice-Hall, 1967.

Goffman, E. *The presentation of self in everyday life*. New York: Doubleday, 1959.

Goffman, E. *Interaction ritual*. New York: Doubleday, 1967.

Heath, A. *Rational choice and social exchange*. Cambridge: Cambridge University Press, 1976.

Chapter 15

Niklas Luhmann

INDIVIDUALITY OF PSYCHIC SYSTEMS

[. . .]

WHETHER AND UNDER WHAT SOCIETAL conditions can the individual's insistence on individuality as self-description be permitted or even dictated?

With this question, one can return to the history of how the semantics of individual/individuality/individualism developed. The hypothesis would be that the history of the concept mirrors a process in which individuals gradually become capable of referring to their individuality when describing themselves. Heroism could be seen as a first attempt at this—appropriate only to a few and perhaps inclined to discourage the many. Then followed a cult of genius, which no longer distinguished individual works and utterances solely from the perspective of their greater or lesser perfection, but took into account individuality-conditioned distinctions of execution and innovative quality, and socially secured these by "taste." The *homme universel* and alignment to the human universal was a transitional phase: it allowed everyone to be included, but it was still bound to cultural conditioning, which ultimately caused the individual to be subsumed in the universal. Accordingly, individuals that sought to conform to the individuality expected of them were forced into deviation: they identified their autopoiesis with a methodology of evil, with shocking normality, with avantgardism, revolution, a compulsive critique of everything established, and similar self-stylizations. But this, too, has devolved into imitable gestures and has thereby become unsuitable as a form for the self-description of the individual as an individual. . . . Does this history prove that the rise of the individual was a decline and that the expectation that the individual describe himself as an individual leads to meaninglessness? Or can we, blinded by the cultural imperative of value, not see correctly into which forms the individual decays when the differentiation of psychic and social systems has been carried so far that the individual can only use his individuality for self-description?

Generally, an individual psychic system exposes itself to the contingency of its environment in the form of *expectation*. . . . In consequence, the concept of expectation must be interpreted broadly to encompass both a psychical and a social use, as well as their interdependence. We can, for the moment, leave open the dependence of expectations on historical conditions, which later the nexus of the psychic and social formation of expectations. [. . .]

An expectation reconnoiters unknown terrain using a difference it can experience within itself: it can be fulfilled or disappointed, and this does not depend on itself alone.

The indeterminable environment, which does not enter at all into the closed operation of pure autopoiesis, is brought into the form of expectations so that it can express itself in a way that the system can understand and use operatively, in that the system projects an expectation and then records whether what was expected actually occurred or not.

Forming expectations is a primitive technique pure and simple. It involves almost no presuppositions. . . . It is only necessary for the expectation to be used autopoietically, namely, for it adequately to prestructure access to the connection between thoughts. It then offers subsequent experience as the fulfillment or disappointment of the expectation, thereby prestructuring a further repertoire of further behavioral possibilities. After a certain period of conscious life enriched by social experiences, completely random expectations cease to occur. In the normal succession that progresses from one thought to another, one no longer encounters anything perverse. One is forced to orient oneself to one's own history of consciousness, however unique it may be; and the determinacy of one's actual experience at any moment makes sure that arbitrary contrary expectations cannot be formed. Therefore socially standardized types are at one's disposal, to hold on to as a kind of rough orientation.

Expectations can be condensed into *claims*. This occurs by strengthening the self-commitment and vulnerability established and put into play in the difference between fulfillment and disappointment. This too is possible almost without involving pre-suppositions, though only with correspondingly increased risk. Similarly, the process of internal adaptation to fulfillment or disappointment is more complex and appears within the system as *emotion*. The transition from expectations to claims increases the chance and the danger that emotion will form, just as one can, conversely, cool down emotions by retreating to mere expectation. The boundary is fluid and can shift during the process; this concerns a single dimension, which can assume the quality of an expectation or a claim depending on how many internal interdependencies are at stake.

The distinction between expectations and claims makes it possible to pursue the question of what occurs psychologically when *individually* grounded claims are increasingly *socially* legitimated and when the social order finally incites individuals to put forward even their individuality as a claim—as the claim to recognition and as the claim to promoting what makes one happy. This "new right to be what one pleases" appears largely self-evident today. But how is it possible and how does it come about that an individual can ground a claim to individuality—can, so to speak, claim the *droit de seigneur*, "tel est mon plaisir"?

One must begin with the fact that claims must be offset by merits, because otherwise the balance would be upset and no social agreement would be possible. [. . .]

But what does all this mean for the individual? We had said that expectations organize episodes of autopoietic existence and claims reintegrate such episodes in the psychic system. For one thing, this implies that, if claims cannot be made routine, the individual is increasingly subject to the individual's own emotions. Thus modern society is more endangered by emotionality than one usually thinks. For another, individuals are encouraged to talk about themselves and their problems. If one accepts that an individual can justify claims not just by merit but by individuality alone, then the individual must provide self-descriptions. The blindly progressing autopoiesis of consciousness is insufficient for this; it must be "identified" as a point of reference for statements—that is, it must be capable of being handled as a difference from something else. [. . .]

As important as the linguistic forming of consciousness is social systems also influence psychic systems in other, less mediated ways. Above all, one must remember the fulfillment and disappointment of expectations and claims by which consciousness can be socially directed, although (and precisely because) it itself positions expectations in order to orient itself. In this way, for example, a kind of conscious certainty about judging and feeling can come about, something like taste, which proves itself in the objects and the social resonance of judging. One may then also be aware of the impossibility of expressing a judgment, indeed, may enjoy this as a kind of superiority.

Given the conceptual foundation of an autopoiesis based on consciousness, it is easy to gain access to a sphere of problems that until now have proved quite difficult for sociology (and therefore have hardly been treated), namely, the world of emotions. Emotions arise and grip body and consciousness when the autopoiesis of consciousness is in danger. This may have many kinds of causes, such as external danger, the discrediting of a self-presentation, and even new modes of conscious commitment that take consciousness itself by surprise, like love. Emotions are not representations that refer to the environment but *internal* adaptations to *internal* problem situations in the psychic system that concern the ongoing production of the system's elements by the system's elements. Emotions are not necessarily formed in an occasional and spontaneous manner; one can be more or less disposed to an emotion-laden reaction. Nevertheless, emotions are unstable because they die away when order is restored in the self-continuation of consciousness. Both, dispositionality and instability, are important givens for socially processing emotions when they arise, but these characteristics of emotion result from its psychic, not its social function.

In *terms of their function*, emotions can be compared to immune systems; they seem to assume an immunizing role for the psychic system. With unusual means, they secure the continuing performance of autopoiesis—here not the autopoiesis of life but of consciousness—in the face of problems that arise, and in doing so they use simplified procedures of discrimination, which permit decisions without considering the consequences. They can augment and weaken without direct reference to occurrences in the environment, depending on consciousness's own experience of itself.

Perhaps the most important insight, however, is that all emotions occur as essentially unitary and homogeneous. This results not only from increased inter-dependence with bodily occurrences, through which one experiences emotion, but also from the immunizing function, which, to guarantee autopoiesis against unforeseeable disturbances, cannot keep in store a separate emotion for everything that happens. One can establish in the biochemical domain that emotions occur as a unity, but emotions are more than interpreted biochemistry—they are the psychic system's self-interpretation with regard to whether its operation can continue.

The well-known variety of distinct emotions comes about only secondarily, only through cognitive and linguistic interpretation; thus it is socially conditioned, like the constitution of all complexity in psychic systems. This holds even more for everything one could designate a "culture of emotions": for refinements of the occasions and the forms of expression in which emotions take shape. Such trans-formations serve, on the one hand, to control emotions socially but, on the other, are burdened with problems of authenticity. Anyone who can say what he is suffer-ing already finds himself no longer entirely in the situation he would like to express. Thus special problems of incommunicability come into being—not of the emotions per se, but of their authenticity—which affect social systems and may burden psychic ones. [. . .]

PART TWO

Embodying affect

4. Emotions, selfhood and identity

SOCIAL SCIENTISTS HAVE devoted much attention to questions concerning selfhood and identity. On the one hand, they have documented historical changes as well as cultural relativity in the conceptualization of individuals and their and identity (see, e.g. Heelas and Lock 1981; Morris 1991, 1994; Hoffman, Sobel and Teute 1997; Turkle 1997; Seigel 2005). On the other hand, some have highlighted the particular salience of the category of the self to late modern forms of organization (e.g. Giddens 1991; Rose 1996). Selfhood and identity are intimately related to affective life. Different lived identity narratives, for instance, take up different evaluative orientations to the emotions in general or to specific affects. To give a stereotypical example, the warrior, the football hooligan and perhaps the city broker are, exceptions notwithstanding, apt to value the kind of self that can laugh in the face of danger, that is not sentimental in the face of the enemy pleading for pity, and that abhors weakness and timidity in general. An observer of their socialization practices, their routine interactions, and their typical heroes and fantasies might see that certain emotions and sentiments are elevated in value and encouraged (pride, courage, excitement, anger, disgust) whilst others are downgraded and scorned (fear, shame, pity, distress). To 'live' an approximation of such an identity would thus be to adopt particular evaluative orientations towards particular affective scenes of self and other, or to strive towards a form of life in which the likelihood of such a patterning of affects is enhanced. One might expect to find very different dynamics in play amongst members of the peace movement, environmentalists and human rights activists, again, exceptions notwithstanding. Emotions and our responses to them thus play a role in reproducing forms of subjectivity and the relations of power in which they are constituted.

Similar issues apply amongst those more 'elevated' forms of identity that touch upon aesthetic orientations and philosophies. For the romantic in the tradition of

Rousseau, Byron or Burke, the true self is associated with the deep, authentic feelings that alone reveal one's true nature, long hidden by the insincere layers of social pretentiousness. Salvation is not to be found in puny reason, but through following the passions. Here, emotionality *in general* plays the role of ethical source to the stream of selfhood. The opposite applies to those who resonate with the more norm-centered orientations of figures such as Hobbes and Kant. Here the true self is to be found precisely in an avoidance of such 'irrational' impulses which are thought to speak more of our animal heritage than of true, civilized humanity. Only a complete subjugation of 'the emotions' in general by reason will lead to the peace, order and stability that are prized. Whether our emotional experiences denote the truth of our being or its degradation, or something else entirely, thus depends upon the ways in which we narrate those encounters into wider scripts and narratives, and this in turn depends upon the complexities of our own experience and endowment, our socialization, our (gendered, raced and classed) positioning within ongoing strips of interaction, our relative power and status, and the broader social and cultural systems that provide the context for these. In our 'postmodern' days of reflexivity, irony, multiplicity and identity fragmentation, our evaluative (and emotional) relation to our affects has, arguably, become even more salient and troubled. This is due to the relative absence of explicit 'external' social dictates concerning who we are and should become (since any such dictates are increasingly packaged as 'choices').

In the introductory essay we remarked that Silvan Tomkins, from whose work the first extract in this sub-section has been drawn, is a key figure in the 'affective turn'. From the 1960s until his death in 1991, Tomkins offered a comprehensive social psychological theory grounded in a biological account of a small number of innate affects both positive (excitement and enjoyment), negative (shame, distress, disgust, fear, anger) and relatively neutral (interest). His work has been attractive to authors of the affective turn because, despite the biological nature and triggering mechanisms of these primary affects, Tomkins' theory holds that the affects can take on innumerable social objects and come to be subject to a good deal of social modification and social causation. Tomkins also developed a comprehensive theory of personality grounded in the motivational structure of the affect system and it is from this – his 'script theory' – that we have selected our extract. Affects are motivational since, all else being equal, we strive to maximize our experiences of positive affect and minimize the negative. But in the complexities of reality, of course, we involve ourselves in a range of much more complicated motivational narratives, and it is these that Tomkins calls 'scripts'.

A script is a regular way of organizing the relationships between a given number of *scenes*. A scene is a particular affective encounter: an infant smiles in pleasure at the face of her mother; a child recoils in fear at the snarl of a dog. Given that we need not initially *learn* how to experience affects, within the first few years of life any human being is likely to have experienced scenes of *excitement* and *enjoyment* as well as *surprise scenes, terrifying scenes, distressing scenes*, and so forth. A script, however, is a *set* of such scenes that has been co-assembled into a more complex form that serves to amplify certain affective aspects over others and to be associated with certain characteristic responses. An encounter with a snarling dog may be scripted by one person as a transient scene unlikely to recur, whilst for another it may be developed into a full blown phobia generalizing to canines of all shapes and sizes, and perhaps beyond. In the latter case, the fear scene is magnified through co-assembly with other fearful scenes, whilst in the former case a different script is at play. We are not neutral with respect to our scripts, since we tend to want to repeat and improve enjoyable, interesting or exciting scenes and to avoid, escape or limit the toxicity of scenes which are distressing, shameful, disgusting, infuriating or terrifying (316). In short, we aspire to command the scenes we wish to play. In practice, however, Tomkins show us that it is often the other way around: our scripts can come to define us.

In their book *Cool Rules*, Dick Pountain and David Robins offer an 'anatomy of an attitude'. Although they do not engage with Tomkins' work, the notion of 'cool' provides an interesting example of a script that has been highly influential in our modern mass-mediatized world, perhaps because it has been projected so forcefully via movies, jazz and pop-music, and the fashion industry. This indicates that scripts can be formed in a 'top-down' manner (e.g. via the emulation of popular cultural forms) as well as in a 'bottom-up' manner (e.g. via personal experiences), although it is of the essence of cool to escape any accusation of the former (since the 'truly cool' person just *is* cool). One of Pountain and Robins' definitions of cool is an oppositional attitude expressing defiance to authority. In the face of scenes that would scare, distress and humiliate others, the 'cool' individual shrugs their leather clad shoulders and oozes an 'I don't give a damn' nonchalance.

If the identity narrative of 'coolness' values a certain detachment from otherwise predictable emotional reactions, then the paper by Charles Morgan and James Averill (1992) 'True Feelings, the Self, and Authenticity: a psychosocial perspective' deals with the more romantic but equally prevalent script in which feelings are construed as the source of authentic identity. An unexpected episode of tearfulness may point the way to an unacknowledged loss and a moment of mystical rapture might reveal a spiritual truth. But what are true feelings? The context for this extract is an empirical study in which the first author surveyed 195 college students from the University of Massachusetts, Amherst using a series of questions about their experiences of 'getting in touch with true feelings'. In analyzing their findings, Morgan and Averill conclude that, according to their participants, true feelings can serve creative (e.g. helping to modify or restore a coherent sense of self), practical (e.g. helping to clarify values and guide decision making) and social (e.g. helping to make sense of relationships and one's place in society) functions. They also raise the issue of the extent to which a clamorous concern about 'who we really are' is a typically North American preoccupation reflecting its history of individualism.

Agneta Fischer and Jeroen Jansz's (1995) 'Reconciling Emotions with Western Personhood' applies an anthropological lens to western culture. They pose the question of whether or not a tension exists between the Western ideal of rational and self-contained personhood and what is often presented as the ordinary conception of emotions as irrational and involuntary forces. Compared to the extensive scholarship devoted by anthropologists to ordinary conceptions of emotion amongst so-called 'non-western' peoples, little is known about how ordinary westerners conceive of their affective life. Drawing upon interviews with Dutch men and women undertaken by Fischer, this article explores the 'emotion narratives' that are drawn upon to 'account' for emotional episodes of fear and anger. Through such emotion narratives, potentially discrediting episodes are rendered rationally intelligible and legitimate. In this way, any possible deviation from the rational, responsible and self-determining ideal of western personhood is mitigated by the image of rational, meaningful and potentially controllable emotional responses.

A selection of social science readings on emotions, selfhood and identity would be incomplete without explicit consideration of the affect we call shame. This is because shame is very much a 'self-conscious' affect (Tangney and Fischer 1995) implicating the role of a significant other into the self-conscious experience (Lewis 1992). As Tomkins (1963: 133) put it: 'In contrast to all other affects, shame is an experience of the self by the self. At the moment when the self feels ashamed, it is felt as a sickness within the self'. W. Ray Crozier's (1998) article 'Self-Consciousness in Shame: the role of the "other" ' begins by claiming that shame involves adopting the perspective of the other towards the self; that it is experienced on recognition that one's actions are given a specific interpretation by the other (irrespective of whether that interpretation is thought justified); and that it is distinct from embarrassment because it involves core aspects of the self. Whilst these propositions are by no means firmly established by the argument that follows, Crozier makes clear some of the complex relations between the experience of self-consciousness and the perspective of the other that have fascinated social theorists for many years.

References

Giddens, A. (1991) *Modernity and Self-Identity: self and society in the late modern age.* Stanford, CA: Stanford University Press.

Heelas, P. and Lock, A. (eds) (1981) *Indigenous Psychologies: an anthropology of the self,* Burlington, MA: Academic Press Inc.

Hoffman, R., Sobel, M. and Teute, F. J. (eds) (1997) *Through a Glass Darkly: reflections on personal identity in early America,* Chapel Hill, NC: University of North Carolina Press.

Morris, B. (1991) *Western Conceptions of the Individual,* London: Berg.

Morris, B. (1994) *Anthropology of the Self: the individual in cultural perspective,* London: Pluto Press.

Rose, N. (1996) *Inventing Our Selves: psychology, power and personhood.* Cambridge: Cambridge University Press.

Seigel, J. (2005) *The Idea of the Self: thought and experience in western Europe since the seventeenth century,* Cambridge: Cambridge University Press.

Turkle, S. (1997) *Life On the Screen: Identity in the Age of the Internet,* New York: Simon & Schuster Inc.

Chapter 16

Silvan S. Tomkins

REVISIONS IN SCRIPT THEORY

[. . .]

SCRIPT THEORY, AS A THEORY of personality, is built upon a particular theory of the innately endowed nature of the human being. Script theory assumes that the basic unit of analysis for understanding persons, as distinguished from human beings, is the *scene* and the relationships between scenes, as ordered by sets of rules I have defined as scripts. [. . .]

One class I labeled affluent scripts. These were basically scenes which were aesthetic in nature. They were scenes which were rewarding in and of themselves, not defined by affect per se but by their quality. The ocean is beautiful; a person is beautiful; music is wonderful; science is wonderful – not defined in affect terms. These are scenes of affluence and the critical question in describing a human being is what percentage of his life-space is taken up by affluent scripts. If it is small, it is a pity. If it is large, he is lucky. Most of us fall somewhere in between.

The next class of scripts was one step away from heaven. I called these damage-reparation scripts. They were defined as scenes which changed from affluence to damage, which could be repaired. One lost something of value, it might be recoverable; it might have been damaged, and could be recoverable. That was an optimistic kind of script in that it assumed that life could be beautiful, but sometimes it was damaged and could be recovered.

The next kind of script I called limitation-remediation. Here you confront those aspects of life which are less than ideal, but which must be confronted and can be confronted. Frequently, for most people in the world, this constitutes the realm of work. People think of play as aesthetic, as affluent, work as enforced. For many people, it is. They must work. They would rather not, or they would rather do something else. People vary radically in their limitation-remediation scripts, varying all the way from what I call commitment scripts to the resignation of slavery. If you are born a slave, you also have to script your life, and you resign yourself to be as good a slave as you know how to be. That is not much, but that is a limitation which you may face. Millions of people over thousands of years have faced lives less than perfect, to which they had to adapt in some way or another. This kind of script got at that large class of human concerns.

The next large class is what I called decontamination scripts. These were scenes in which some impurity is introduced-into a life. It may have been good before, or it may have always been bad, but is recognized by the individual as, not a permanent limitation, but an impurity, a contamination. This was the way Hitler regarded Jews in the life of Germany – a contamination, somehow to be purified.

The final group of scenes I call antitoxic. Now you can see we are going from bad to worse, which is the psychologist's way. In the anti-toxic script, we are dealing with scenes of intolerable punishment, which must be either eliminated, attenuated, escaped, or avoided – somehow destroyed. These are conditions that human beings find excessively toxic for one reason or another. They are exiled from their native land; they are put into chains. There are all kinds of conditions which they find intolerable. This is not their normal lot in life. It can happen at any time, to any of us. If we get cancer, that is very toxic. There is no way it cannot be. It is a disease that is very difficult to deal with, very painful, very life threatening. That is a toxic scene, and life is full of toxicity.

All of these types of scripts, and there are many different types under each of these classifications, were designed, . . . with no thought to affect. Then one day a light bulb went on in my head. I realized that each of these types of scripts, while very complex in affect structure and composition, nonetheless had a primary affect which matched extraordinarily well my understanding of the nature of each of the primary affects. That was a bonanza for me, because it was almost like an independent validation of both the script theory and the affect theory that they should hang together so nicely. Now that may be an insanity; it may be a self-delusion, but I tell it to you like it is in my mind. It was very exciting.

Let me tell you what those affects are and how they map onto these scripts. Obviously, with the affluent script, we are talking about the two major positive affects: excitement and enjoyment. Now, of course, excitement and enjoyment are two very different kinds of affluence. They can come into very serious conflict with each other, as they did, for example, in Tolstoy, and as they did in any number of people for whom one or the other of them is seen to be very dangerous and the other very pure. So I am not suggesting that either one of them is necessarily defined as affluent by all people, far from it. Puritans would not regard excitement as affluent. It is pretty close to consorting with Satan. But, nonetheless, the more excitement and/or enjoyment, the more affluence, and that is good.

With damage-reparative scripts there is a very happy coincidence with my understanding of the nature of shame, because, in my view, shame is an affect auxiliary, which is triggered by any perceived impediment to either excitement or enjoyment. I believe the toxicity of shame has been much exaggerated by shame theorists; shame is an affluent emotion. It arises only in the context of a strong bond with the other. You cannot be ashamed, per se, unless you find the other exciting or lovable or enjoyable in some way, and you wish to maintain that bond. Because if that is not the case, shame readily turns sour into disgust and dissmell and rage and sometimes fear. But if you stay with shame, if you see a face where shame is dominant, one thing you may be sure of is that that is a positively oriented human being, either one given to much love or much excitement. The shame response tells you that for the time being there has been an experienced impediment to that affluence. Thus the damage-reparative scripts map extraordinarily well to the dynamic structure of shame as I understand that affect to be. So if you have a script which speaks of a return to a promised land, as was true for Marx, and as is true in nuclear reparative scripts based upon sibling rivalry, then you know that bond, which was damaged by shame, is always believed to be reparable and recoverable. . . .

With limitation-remediation scripts we are dealing with permanent, serious problems, which, however, demand and lend themselves to remedy. That fits remarkably well with my understanding of the nature of distress. I have contrasted distress with terror. Terror is an emergency response which is urgent and costly and needs to be attended to immediately, whereas distress has the very fine property of motivating you in a negative scene but is not so punishing that you cannot utilize all of your resources to cope with that distressing state of affairs. Thus it fits very beautifully with the definitions of scripts dedicated to dealing with long-term bad situations, but situations which demand and which can be improved.

When we come to decontamination scripts, we are, of course, dealing very precisely with what I understand to be the dynamics of the drive auxiliary response of disgust. Disgust is the response of disenchantment. I stress both *dis* and *enchantment*. When you take something into your mouth which you thought was good enough to eat, and it turns out to be something you vomit out, you are disenchanted with that food and with that object, if you use it metaphorically. The status of disgust, of course, is quite different from that of an affect. It is a very strange status, because if I give you a very tasty dish which you enjoy, and a few minutes later I tell you that it came from the entrails of your neighbor, you are disenchanted and you may vomit. Now that is an innate nausea response to a learned stimulus – very strange. . . . It illustrates something of the ambiguity of . . . disgust, in that it can and does play a very powerful role in our lives because we react to scenes as if they were bad food, which once had been or were thought to be good. That is a very powerful motive.

We see it, for example, in an extraordinary way in the O'Neill family of which Eugene O'Neill, the playwright, was a member. They were all disgusted with each other because the mother became a dope addict, the father wasted his talent, the oldest son was an alcoholic, and Eugene O'Neill was sick and at times alcoholic. They tore each other apart in disgust, again and again. *Long Day's Journey into Night* probably will be the classic of shared, four-way disgust for all time to come. It is a very powerful play in which the major dynamic is shared disgust of people in love with each other and in disgust with each other. . . .

Finally, we come to the antitoxic scripts. These are mapped quite well onto terror, rage, and dissmell. We know the toxicity of terror. The body was not designed to live in terror. It is a very punishing response, which we have to get rid of as soon as possible. Rage is not like distress. . . . It is sufficiently more toxic so that it does not lend itself to fine, long-term use. If we get into a deep rage, our total resources are not always at our command. A muted rage may empower an organized life, but a hot rage rarely. Similarly, with dissmell; in contrast to disgust, dissmell is a very toxic response socially and otherwise, because it says the other is unfit for human consumption, basically. . . .

In dissmell you are moving yourself away from a bad-smelling object. . . . In contempt, . . . you move toward the object. . . .He means to hurt and he means to reject. That is what contempt is. It degrades the other. It is meant to. It is used in severely hierarchical relationships, when the one who has the power judges that the other is not only weak and can be abused but deserves to be, merits it, and asks for it. It is a rather ugly combination. It is the least attractive of human responses and it is very dangerous. Lynchings in this country were based upon it. The whites, endangered, were going to show the blacks their place and did it by killing, as an intimidation for other blacks, so that they should not be too "uppity." That is contempt. The other is judged less than human. This was also true in Hitler's Germany. The Jews were regarded as polluting the blood of the Aryan, and the only way to deal with that was to kill – six million of them. . . . So these . . . affects, . . . map extremely well onto scenes of extraordinary toxicity and danger for human beings. They exemplify the life in extremis. If you have to live your life terrified, dissmelling, and enraged, you are in big trouble and so are the people around you. . . .

Let me give you a little example, and I stress little, of the kind of illumination that one can get from the employment of such a set of categories and affects. I will contrast two people, both distinguished at the decontamination, antitoxic end of the scale. I refer to the philosopher Wittgenstein and the novelist Hemingway. Both, oddly enough, suffered from a very similar problem of gender identity. In the case of Wittgenstein, it was homosexuality. In the case of Hemingway, it was that his mother often dressed him as a girl and had him wear long curls long beyond the stage that might normally happen, and caused a great confusion in Hemingway's mind. So he started out with a deeply contaminated socialization. Did his mother want a boy? Did she want a girl? It certainly looked more like she wanted a girl, and he was interested in cross-sexed dressing games most of his life.

Hemingway's solution to the decontamination script was the general strategy of purification. If you have got an identity problem, one of the ways of handling a contaminated identity is to purify it. So he became ultramasculine, as we all know. A friend of mine, who was a fine athlete, an all-American football player, used to know Hemingway in Paris. He said Hemingway would always be bothering him to box with him, and that Hemingway could not box worth a damn. But he had to show that he was a man and used to bore my friend, who was, in fact, a very fine boxer. Hemingway's whole life history is an attempt, sadly, to prove something which he did not believe. . . .

The comparison with Wittgenstein is interesting because Wittgenstein also suffered from gender confusion and he seriously considered suicide. Three of his brothers had already suicided, and he talked of it much of his life. So he moved from a decontamination script to an antitoxic script. He saw no way to purify himself, so he moved over one rung on the scale to an antitoxic solution – he could destroy himself. But the fascinating thing about Wittgenstein is that at one point he learned about Freud. I do not know whether he was analyzed, or whether he just read it, but it radically changed him. It moved the script, which had started as decontamin-ation and had moved to anti-toxic, to remediation at the end, and that saved him. I will read to you his own account of it.

> Whenever you're preoccupied with something, with some trouble, or with some problem which is a big thing, as sex is, for instance, then no matter what you start from, the association will lead finally and inevitably back to that same theme. Freud remarks on how after the analysis of it, the dream appears so very logical and of course it does, and worse it often has the attractiveness of giving a sort of tragic pattern to one's life. It is all the repetition of the same pattern which was settled long ago, like a tragic figure carrying out the decrees under which the fates had placed him at birth. Many people have at some period serious trouble in their lives, so serious as to lead to thoughts of suicide. This is likely to appear to one as something nasty, as a situation which is too foul to be a subject of a tragedy. And it may then be an immense relief if it can be shown that one's life has the pattern rather of a tragedy, the tragic working out and repetition of a pattern.

In other words, this is a given limitation of the life condition over which you have very little control. But there is a dignity in seeing that this is an existential problem, and that enabled Wittgenstein to move from decontamination, to antitoxic, to remediation. It is not much, but enough to save his life.

I give you these two very small examples of the illumination that comes from the interaction between knowing what the dominant, primary affects are for large classes of scripts and how they may move around in development. Those changes are very difficult to deal with without some conceptual framework. I have found this framework to be quite illuminating in revealing the major outline of a life history. This is an example of what I mean when I say, if we have powerful enough theory, we can then go to the face and say, if you see this affect is dominant, look for such and such a class of preoccupation, and if it shifts, look for a shift in script formation. That is the utility of it.

Chapter 17

Dick Pountain and David Robins

COOL RULES

Anatomy of an attitude

[. . .]

HERE . . . IS A BASIS FOR a rough working definition of Cool that may serve until more of its properties are uncovered in later chapters. Cool is an oppositional attitude adopted by individuals or small groups to express defiance to authority – whether that of the parent, the teacher, the police, the boss or the prison warden. Put more succinctly, we see Cool as a *permanent* state of *private* rebellion. *Permanent* because Cool is not just some 'phase that you go through', something that you 'grow out of', but rather something that if once attained remains for life; *private* because Cool is not a collective political response but a stance of individual defiance, which does not announce itself in strident slogans but conceals its rebellion behind a mask of ironic impassivity. This attitude is in the process of becoming the dominant type of relation between people in Western societies, a new secular virtue. No-one wants to be good any more, they want to be Cool, and this desire is no longer confined to teenagers but is to be found in a sizeable minority even of the over-50s who were permanently affected by the '60s counter-culture.

This brings us to a second difficulty in defining Cool, namely its mutability. If Cool is not inherent in objects but in people, then what is seen as Cool will change from place to place, from time to time and from generation to generation. Those marketing managers at Levi Strauss desperately trying to 'crack the code of cool' know that their jeans were granted Cool status by an accident of history, and advertising alone cannot recapture it for them.

In any epoch, although Cool will have a particularly powerful meaning for teenagers, as an antidote to their ever-present fear of being embarrassed, being Cool forms part of a risky series of negotiations about becoming an individual while still being accepted into a group – it's about both individuality and belonging, and the tension between the two. Once acquired, Cool does not wear off quickly, and since in its modern form it appeared in the '50s, there are now at least four generations alive who have their own – often seriously clashing – definitions of what is Cool. Recent studies of under-30 drug users reveal that a significant number have parents who first experimented with drugs in the '60s and '70s (when they were Cool themselves) and who are now in a quandary about what to tell their children. Each succeeding generation feels that 'real' Cool is something pure and existential known only to them – it was founded in *their* time, in the jazz clubs of the '50s, or the hippy festivals of the '60s, or the punk explosion of the '70s. One component of Cool is certainly a retarded adolescence, inspired in part by a morbid fear of ageing – anyone who has been to a party where 50-somethings get down to the strains of 'Get Off of My Cloud' have had a glimpse of the *danse macabre*.

On the other hand, Cool is equally about teenagers behaving with precocious maturity (especially about sex and political cynicism), and older hipsters are discovering that the behaviour they employed as provocation in the '60s is now accepted as everyday routine: city streets, cafés, movie theatres and clubs thronged with exuberant youth for whom wearing hair long or sporting a nose ring is considered quite a mild social statement (it's easy to forget that in 'swinging London' in the '60s the burger joint was the only place open after 10.30pm). [. . .]

Cool is a rebellious attitude, an expression of a belief that the mainstream mores of your society have no legitimacy and do not apply to you. It's a self-contained and individualistic attitude, although it places high value on friendship within a tightly defined peer group – indeed it strives to displace traditional family ties, which are too intimate and intrusive to allow sufficient space for self-invention. Cool is profoundly hedonistic but often to such a self-destructive degree that it flirts with death: by accident, suicide or some ambivalent admixture of the two (for example, a motorcycle crash or auto-erotic strangulation). Cool was once an attitude fostered by rebels and underdogs – slaves, prisoners, political dissidents – for whom open rebellion invited punishment, so it hid its defiance behind a wall of ironic detachment, distancing itself from the source of authority rather than directly confronting it. In the '50s this attitude was widely adopted by artists and intellectuals who thereby aided its infiltration into popular culture, with the result that today it is becoming the dominant attitude, even (or perhaps especially) among the rich and privileged who can wield it as merely the latest in a long line of weapons with which to put down their 'social inferiors'. Contemporary Cool is equally at home in the tenement basement and the million-dollar loft conversion. At its most extreme, Cool can even be turned into a manipulative strategy for separating people from their families and encouraging dependency: 'control freaks' such as Charles Manson, David Khoresh of the Branch Dravidians (of Waco notoriety), the Reverend Jim Jones and gurus like the Bagwhan Shri Rajneesh have all deployed Cool as an aspect of their manipulative personas. [. . .]

The cool personality

. . . Cool is an attitude or personality type that has emerged in many different societies, during different historical epochs, and which has served different social functions, but is nevertheless recognizable in all its manifestations as a particular combination of three core . . . traits, namely narcissism, ironic detachment and hedonism.

Narcissism means an exaggerated admiration for oneself, particularly for personal appearance, which gives rise to the feeling that the world revolves around you and shares your moods. At its most positive such narcissism is a healthy celebration of the self, while even in its more negative manifestations it can be an effective adaptation to any oppressive circumstances that sap self-esteem. Such circumstances would appear to include not only the obvious experience of poverty, political repression and tyranny but even life in the celebrity-worshipping consumer democracies of the developed world. Of course to any puritan culture, narcissism appears as the sin of vanity.

Ironic detachment is a stratagem for concealing one's feelings by suggesting their opposite, for example feigning boredom in the face of danger, or amusement in the face of insult. Philosophers distinguish several types of irony, including Socratic irony, which involves saying less than one really means to lull an opponent into false security, while actually delivering a telling blow to his argument, and Romantic irony, a profound scepticism which questions the validity of everything (as exemplified in the aphorisms of Nietzsche). Cool irony partakes of both these meanings, making it a verbal weapon equally effective in aggression or defence, and crucial to the maintenance of a protective Cool persona. Irony allows one to give deep offence while ostensibly remaining civil, as in the black American tradition of 'shucking' speech used to address white authority figures, which offers a subservience so exaggerated that it becomes insolent. Jewish humour has a similar tradition of defensive-aggressive irony, and it was '60s comics such as Mort Sahl and Lenny Bruce, coming out of this tradition, who forged a new strain of 'sick humour', for example by deliberately using racial epithets as a way of defusing their power to hurt. This type of ironic humour now so suffuses modern Cool that displays of simple sincerity have become almost impossibly Uncool – Quentin Tarantino can make mopping splattered brains off a car seat seem genuinely funny.

Hedonism requires less explanation, except perhaps to point out that Cool hedonism tends toward the worldly, adventurous and even orgiastic rather than the pleasant. At its lightest, Cool hedonism is that pursuit of happiness enshrined in the American Constitution and described so well by de Tocqueville as 'a love of physical gratification, the notion of bettering one's condition, the excitement of competition, the charm of anticipated success'. [. . .]

The c word

A great source of confusion in understanding Cool is the word itself, which already has several closely related metaphorical usages, derived from its physical meaning of low temperature. For example, *The Oxford English Dictionary* offers this definition:

> Cool: to lose the heat of excitement or passion, to become less zealous or ardent. Not affected by passion or emotion, unexcited, deliberate, calm.

. . . while Jonathon Green in his *Dictionary of Slang* (1998) gives its vernacular usages as:

> Cool: late nineteenth century+: good or fine or pleasing; twentieth century: calm, self-possessed, aware and sophisticated; 1940+: fashionable, chic or with it.

These meanings accurately describe an important aspect of the Cool attitude, but at the same time they conceal its underlying transgressive elements, the ironic and defiant character that distinguishes it from many previous versions of nonchalance and savoir-faire. [. . .]

'Cool' in its meaning of 'good', 'fine' or 'fashionable' is now used as a universal term of approval among the young in North America and the UK (as well as in many non-English-speaking countries), right from children in primary school playgrounds up to college-age adults. [. . .] Does this then imply that 'cool' is a precise synonym for 'good' and has no deeper content? On the contrary, 'cool' always carries an extra, often barely perceived, connotation: describing something (a record, a movie, a soft drink) as 'cool' rather than 'swell' or 'dandy' makes the statement, in however small a way, that the person who utters it is Cool and not a nerd or a conformist. Of course the nine-year-old in primary school will not understand such connotations at first, but they will gradually absorb precisely what it is that makes some things Cool and others not in the eyes of their peers, so that merely using the word forms part of an unofficial, alternative process of socialization. [. . .]

The implication is that in many contexts 'cool' actually means the precise opposite of 'good'. If someone says 'It's cool to do coke' they don't mean that it's *good* citizenship to take cocaine, or *good* for your health to take cocaine: they mean it is intensely pleasurable to take cocaine, and that the fact that it's illegal makes taking cocaine more exciting and makes them Cooler in the eyes of their peers. This sort of ironic inversion of values underlies many other Cool-slang terms like the use of 'wicked' or traditionally unclean terms like 'shit' and 'funky' as terms of approval. [. . .]

In the USA controversy has surrounded the subcultural origins of the word *cool* rather than its etymology. Some have claimed the expression originated in the jazz club scene of the '30s: 'When the air of the smoke-filled nightclubs of that era became unbreathable, windows and doors were opened to allow some "cool air" in . . . By analogy, the slow and smooth jazz style that was typical of that late-night scene came to be called "cool". Cool was subsequently extended to describe any physically attractive male jazz musician, or aficionado who patronized such clubs.' This has the slightly bogus feel of a 'myth of origins', but what is certainly true is that music and sex played a major part in the derivation of Cool, as in the blues lyric 'Some like their man hot, but I like him cool.' In fact the word *cool* became attached to one particular style of jazz in the late '40s and '50s, compounding a confusion between the musical style and the attitude (which was exhibited by far more jazz musicians than ever played the style). Besides, the finger-clicking teenagers of *West Side Story* probably brought the word into the consciousness of more white, middle-class Americans than jazz ever did. Among the '60s hippies 'cool' took on a slightly narrower meaning – closer to its traditional implication of nonchalance – of a calming down to better deal with a problem, which has metamorphosed into the current usage 'to chill'. However, it was the hip-hop culture of the '80s and '90s that restored to 'cool' (or 'kool') those transgressive and defiant connotations that it still bears for many teenagers today. [. . .]

We would hypothesize further . . . that Cool is precisely one such mechanism that people use to short-circuit maladaptive comparisons and avoid depression. Sociological theories such as 'strain' theory support the idea that school students who feel that they are failing in the classroom, or who do not 'fit in' socially, adopt a strategy of disengagement from school activities, and develop anti-academic cliques, or subcultures, that provide an alternative route to self-esteem. By acting Cool you declare yourself to be a non-participant in the bigger race, for if you don't share 'straight' society's values then you can stop comparing yourself to them. Cool cannot abolish social comparisons entirely, but it can restrict their scope to your immediate peer group. Mods, rockers, skinheads, punks, hippies, crusties, goths: for several successive generations of marginalized and disaffected young people these subcultures, with their own rules, rituals and obligations, have provided a *magical* alternative to being written off as a hopeless loser in the rat race. In the language of youth subcultures, 'I'm cool' equates to 'I'm in control.'

So what Cool has offered to groups as disparate as field slaves, jazz musicians, disillusioned war veterans, Detroit street gangs, teenage runaways and middle-class high school dissenters is a kind of mental empowerment that their circumstances otherwise fail to supply. In this sense Cool is a subcultural alternative to the old notion of personal dignity, since dignity . . . is a quality that is validated by the established institutions of church, state and work. Cool, on the other hand, is a form of self-worth that is validated primarily by the way your personality, appearance and attitude are adjudged by your own peers. Nevertheless, the association between Cool, addiction and suicide suggests that as a *real* solution to living in a highly competitive society, it is only partially effective. Studies continue to show that the academic performance of many boys deteriorates rapidly between thirteen and nineteen as they come to see learning and academic success as 'girlish' and 'uncool', and this disabling tendency among boys is being accompanied by increases in the rate of suicide and attempted suicide. . . .

Cool detachment if pursued to its limit would lead to sociopathy and total isolation, but there is within it a countervailing tendency that unites close peer groups through a shared idea about what 'cool' means – precisely those self-invented codes of dress, hairstyle, ritual, attitude and slang that Majors and Mancini Billson call 'expressive styling'. But it is also this very tendency that opens the loophole through which the advertising industry has colonized Cool and used it to sell goods to the young (and not-so-young).

Cool's mechanism of social cohesion, the counterbalance to its distancing effect, involves sharing knowledge of some secret that is denied to members of respectable or mainstream society. This was the original meaning of that synonym for Cool, 'hip', which was used as in 'I'm hip to that.' The content of this shared secret may be many different things, from the appreciation of a certain style of music, to predilection for a particular illegal drug, participation in crime, or some forbidden sexual practice. However, in the background there is always the hint of a bigger, seldom-verbalized, more abstract secret, namely the perceived hypocrisy of 'straight' society. Cool people share a belief that society's taboos have no moral force for them, and that these taboos are in any case regularly broken by even its most supposedly respectable members. [. . .]

This quality of worldly knowingness is absolutely central to the Cool personality, which always wants to know everything and loathes secrecy, concealment and duplicity. In essence then the psychological core of Cool is self-invention coupled to a hyper-acute awareness of such self-invention by other people. It amounts to the creation of a calm psychic mask to hide inner disturbance, whether rage at racist mistreatment, anxiety in the face of competition or merely a furious urge for sexual conquest. It's no coincidence that Cool became the dominant attitude in a Hollywood where self-invention is a way of life. [. . .]

Reference

Tadesi, M. (1994) *Cool: the signs and meanings of adolescence*. Toronto. P. 37.

Chapter 18

Charles Morgan and James R. Averill

TRUE FEELINGS, THE SELF, AND AUTHENTICITY

A psychosocial perspective

[. . .]

IN HIS HISTORICAL EXAMINATION OF the idea of the self, Baumeister (1986, 1987) explores how a person's identity in contemporary society has become increasingly dependent on overtly ambiguous "metacriteria." Whereas once, for example, people typically derived identity from clear-cut religious and class expectations, now people more often define who they are in relation to "inner" needs and capacities, looking inward for markers of "authentic being" that may let them know themselves. "True feelings" are taken by many as exemplary markers in this search. However, as pervasive as such feelings are, we know very little about them. [. . .]

The problem of authenticity

> *True feelings are revealed from deep inside. Other experiences cover up your true feelings.*

> *True feelings were more important . . . intense. They bothered me more.*

> *They were kind of scary. I wasn't able to control them. They were going to happen if I wanted them to or not.*

In the domain of feeling, we characterize as "true" that which we experience as authentic. What, then, gives "true feelings" their authenticity? In this section, we examine some of the characteristic features that help distinguish "true feelings" from other, more commonplace emotional experiences. [. . .] As the above quotations from the study by Morgan (1989) suggest, "true feelings" are often characterized as (1) deep, (2) intense, and (3) passionate (in the literal sense of "beyond control"). These characteristics appear simple enough, but their simplicity is deceptive.

1. For the most part, as we have seen . . . "true feelings" are perceived not only as arising from deep inside ourselves, but as arising from a deeper source than the "ordinary" feelings of everyday life. It is in the "deep, dark regions" of our selves that society is presumed not to reside, and so feelings that we imagine as surfacing from this source are felt to be more "genuine" and "authentic," unvitiated by the influences of habit, expectation, and tradition. But, . . . the thematic content of "true-feeling" episodes, as well as the experienced feelings themselves, are drawn from the much vaster pool of cultural meanings. Ironically, it is our questionable perception of them as deep down, hidden, that lends them credibility, that "authenticates" them. As Trilling (1972, p. 161) notes, "to see society in ourselves is to feel inauthentic," and so for "true feelings" to feel "true," we must see them as arising from some culturally-devoid, socially-immune wellspring.

2. "True-feeling" episodes are intense experiences and the feelings they comprise are, more often than not, considered painful. (In comparison to ordinary feelings, 75.7% of subjects in the study judged "true feelings" as more intense; 61.3% judged them more painful.) It may be that intensity in this case reflects a state of disorganization, during which old patterns of thought and behavior are kept in abeyance, allowing the self-creative process to gain sway (Frank 1974). But be that as it may, intensity, painfulness, and struggle lend credibility to "true-feeling" experiences, enhancing our faith in their truthfulness. A belief in the authenticating power of suffering has a noble history that embraces epistemologies as diverse as Christianity and Freudianism. Sennett (1980) commented on the tendency of people in contemporary American society to seek moral legitimacy through suffering:

> Most of all, the ennobling of victims means that in ordinary middle-class life we are forced constantly to go in search of some injury, some affliction, in order to justify even the contemplation of questions of justice, right and entitlement in our lives. . . . The need to legitimate one's beliefs in terms of an injury or suffering to which one has been subjected attaches people more and more to the injuries themselves
>
> (p. 150).

3. Finally, "true feelings" are felt to be authentic insofar as they arise outside of a person's control. (In comparison to ordinary feelings, 60.7% of subjects claimed "true feelings" were "less under [their] control"). This presents a paradox. How can an experience that is free of personal control be considered true? Like many paradoxes, this one can be resolved at a higher level of analysis. The perception of "true feelings" as out of control can be seen largely as an artifact of a larger idea: the belief in the prehuman, organic nature of "true feelings," the belief, in short, in their fundamental "naturalness." [. . .]

In the Romantic Age, the glorification of organic being achieved new heights such that Schiller could write of the sophisticated person's need for "energizing beauty," the source of which is "the strength [man] brought with him from the state of savagery." This notion of a primordial inner strength still carries great weight in our culture (as the continued popularity of Jungian psychology attests, not to mention the current fascination with sociobiology). In "true-feeling" experiences we see reflected the belief in a transformational organic endowment. The search for the true, the authentic, thus becomes a search for the organic (a search, it must be noted, that acquires ever greater urgency as we experience the relentless demolition of our organic environment). In our erroneous perception of "true feelings" as free from the impingements of social and individual purpose, we see them as natural and organic and we read into them an otherwise elusive authenticity, a stay against the fragmentations of existence. Indeed, insofar as "true-feeling" experiences are self-enhancing, they foster a sense of transcendence over the disorientation and disconnection of our lives, that is, a sense of seamless being. And as we have seen, this can serve useful and adaptive purposes. But to the extent that our experiences of fragmentation, alienation, and disorientation are the products of cultural machinations beyond the self-constructive capacities of personal sensibilities, "true-feeling" experiences are merely one aspect of a perseverant cycle of loss and recovery, damage and repair. And the urgency in our search for authenticity, as well as the pervasiveness of "true-feeling" experiences themselves, may bespeak, to paraphrase Trilling, an increasing anxiety over the credibility of our very existence. By severing the authentic from the social, by seeking true being only in the depths of our selves, we are denied that sense of intersubjectivity whose absence has provoked these very severings and seekings, and whose recovery alone can restore lost meaning to our lives.

True feelings and the self

> Swarmed with problems and people for six weeks straight made me aware that I needed some time alone to pull myself together. I took a long walk by the fields resolving certain feelings and ideas that had bothered me for so long. It was enlightening.

> I had a boyfriend . . . he constantly manipulated me. Anything I liked, he hated. I thought we had some unbreakable commitment . . . [but] I realized I was dying inside . . . I was losing energy. . . . I really realized that he didn't love me, he loved me only when I was what he wanted me to be. . . . I was waking up for the first time. And when this true feeling really came out, I left him for good. Boom. That was it.

> True feelings help to form some answer to the question, who am I?

The near clamorous concern in our culture about "who we really are" has a long and intriguing history (Baumeister 1986, 1987; Ellenberger 1970; Marcuse 1966; Trilling 1972). And the extent to which this concern pervades and colors all aspects of contemporary American life is the subject of numerous books and articles (see, for example, Bellah, Madsen, Sullivan, Swidler, and Tipton 1985). "True-feeling" episodes (let alone this study itself!) are one more manifestation of this concern—

an especially emblematic manifestation in that the question of "true feelings" lies at the core of our beliefs about the self. We have presented evidence suggesting that beyond their self-affirming attributes, "true feelings" enable self-adaptive processes, providing, in a sense, creative solutions to problems in self-maintenance. In fact, "true-feeling" episodes bear striking parallels with creative processes in general, and an examination of these parallels may help further illuminate the nature of "true feelings" and their relation to the self.

Gordon (1989) noted that an essential distinguishing characteristic of emotional experience may be the sense of self-discovery. He suggested that through emotional experience we come to realize previously unseen capacities, leading to the expansion of our sense of self. In the experience of "true feelings," we have seen a similar relationship between self-discovery through emotional expression and the enlargement of self-adaptive capacities. We have suggested that the self-discovery born in "true feelings" is, in part, a creative solution to the turmoil, stasis, or confusion in a person's life. May's assertion (1975) that "creativity is one of the essential characteristics of self-discovery" further suggests the close relationship between creative acts and "true-feeling" experiences.

Most accounts of creativity (see May 1975; Rothenberg and Hausman 1976; Sternberg 1988) hold that the basic creative motivation is an innate need to make order out of chaos. (Stern's work [1985] provides empirical support for the fundamental pattern-seeking, order-creating propensities of humankind.) Crisis and disorder, then, provide the strongest occasion for both creative and "true-feeling" episodes. Moreover, in both kinds of episodes, the most common affective sequence is an early sense of turmoil and anxiety, an ensuing intensity of feeling, and a subsequent experience of relief and satisfaction. In creative acts the sense of ending or resolve is provided by the gratification of discovery. In "true-feeling" episodes, it seems to be the creation or discovery of aspects of self—and the gratification that ensues from self-understanding and change—that provides a sense of ending.

In order to make these observations more precise, we refer to the four stages of the creative process enumerated by Wallas (1926), namely, preparation, incubation, illumination, and verification. The first or preparatory stage entails the "hard, conscious, . . . and fruitless analysis" of a problem. In "true feelings," this corresponds to the conscious, often desperate, and mostly unsuccessful attempts, in the days and weeks before an episode, to make sense of inner conflict and find some means for resolving it. The second stage, incubation, is characterized by an absence of conscious effort. In the days, hours, or minutes just preceding a "true-feeling" episode, subjects often described a period of stasis and frustration. Unable to understand their turmoil or effect change, they became passive, at least momentarily forgoing conscious effort. In the experience of "true feelings," this stage, which may be similar to incubation, is followed by an often tumultuous sense of discovery and the experience of understanding and change—that is, of illumination.

The experience of illumination, whether in creative or "true-feeling" episodes, is marked by a conviction of validity that can be quite misleading. In the preceding section, we saw how "true feelings" are often experienced as deep, intense, and beyond personal control. Features such as these lend the experience an aura of authenticity. But no matter how "true" an experience may seem at the moment of illumination, a further step is required—verification. A creative discovery must be tested and refined in light of socially accepted standards. Similarly, "true feelings" require a period of verification, if only a moment in which the person's newly restored self is tested in the waters of cultural experience and social relations. This verification may come from internalized standards or external experience, but it is important in corroborating the "truth" of the feelings. . . .

It is in Arieti's (1976) elaboration of the processes occurring between stages two (incubation) and three (illumination) of the creative process that the relation between creativity and "true feelings" is most instructive. Arieti describes a kind of preconscious cognition which he calls the endocept and which he characterizes as "a primitive organization of past experiences, perceptions, memory traces, and images of things and movements" (p. 54). According to Arieti, artists who feel immobilized by their current forms of expression and who seek escape from the external impingements on their inner lives may find creative sustenance in a retreat to endoceptual experience. His research indicates that artists and non-artists alike move regularly between endoceptual and conceptual experience, but it is in moments of struggle that a problem-solving reliance on endoceptual structures becomes most manifest.

In the struggle characteristic of "true-feeling" episodes there may be a similar retreat from higher-order conceptual activity into a passively received, preverbal experiencing. Unlike Wallas's stage of incubation, this retreat (which may be experienced more as a "succumbing to") is not into unconscious activity, but into an almost preconscious intensity of imagery and feeling, a seeming jumble of cognitions, feelings, and sensations. For some of our subjects, the experience took on "a dreamy quality" (17.3% of subjects endorsed this descriptor), for others it was "nightmare-like" (17.9%), and for others it included a sense that "something false [was] being shed" (34.7%). For a majority, it was deep, intense, surprising, and beyond control. This endoceptual realm of experience can be seen as a kind of text: a history book of one's self; a dictionary of one's past. It is a text of memories and feelings, the components of self. And from this text, perhaps through an associative process imbued with problem-solving intention, new selves are composed, self-enhancement ensues, and meaningful understandings of the precipitating conflict are derived. "To find and constitute meaning" (Rothenberg 1979)—this is the creative process, in feelings as in poetry.

True feelings and the social order

> In high school I was a perfectionist. I was in a dance company. . . . I wanted to be thinner than anyone else. . . . I had bulimia for four and a half years because of this desire to look good. Then bulimia almost killed me. At that point the [true feelings] experience began and for the first time I went to my parents . . . we cried about it . . . and I realized people couldn't really love me unless I loved myself.

> A couple of months ago I was sitting in bed and my friend called . . . my friend who I'd had a relationship with for four years. He told me that he met someone

else . . . and did not want to see me anymore. After that . . . I was very mixed up for days, but after a while I got in touch with my true feelings about myself. I can deal with people and relationships better now.

I was put into a situation between two friends . . . one of which thought the other had betrayed a trust. I had to decide for myself . . . the truth . . . whether to remain neutral or take a side. I had to let my good judgment and values decide my stand, even if that meant giving up a friendship or possibly two.

I was in my room after my mother first explained to me that I was adopted. I felt like a "leftover" and that I wasn't really loved. I cried so hard. I was also angry. . . . The true feelings made me feel that I could go on to other things . . . and I felt stronger.

Current developmental research (e.g., Belenky, Clinchy, Goldgerger, and Tarule 1986; Jordan and 1986; Miller 1976; Stern 1985) suggests that our sense of who we are always exists within the dialectic of relationships, that there is no such thing as a self apart from the intrapsychic whisperings of our individual social histories and the interpersonal attunements of our current lives. We are each and always a self-in-relationship; and the self-amending process of "true-feeling" experiences, which we have seen as a kind of creativity in the service of the self, is at the same time a process of relocation, an attempt to locate one's self within a dramatically shifted, or shifting, relational matrix.

From infancy we are taught the meanings of our emotions, at first by parents and siblings and later by teachers, television, and friends. We are taught the general cultural forms of interpreting our feelings, as well as more idiosyncratic, familial forms. And we enlarge and refine these meanings within the context of subsequent experiences and relationships. Yet, however refined, our every emotion bears with it an imperative cultural history, a history which guides and governs the choice and expression of our feelings. During "true-feeling" episodes, we immerse ourselves in this history, in a sense "rummaging around" for a feeling or combination of feelings that will be our response to the turmoil, that will provide meaning not only for what has occurred but for what can occur. If we ultimately feel anger, it's not only a judgment about precipitating occurrences, it's a commitment to a way of under-standing the present: for example, by seeing one's self as an injured party, by condemning a particular person or action, by asserting one's boundaries in the face of shifting relationships. All "true feelings," from self-love and pride to anger and loss, establish the meaning of past and present events and create a context for future conduct. By establishing meaning they ameliorate confusion, by creating new contexts they enable commitment.

My friends and I were at the supermarket and there was a picket line. My friends started to go into the store and I said I didn't feel like it. They started teasing me and I just stood there . . . first embarrassed, then mad. My feelings came to me and I knew I wasn't crossing that line.

The commitment is to a way of being, a way of relating—in sum, to a set of values about the world, other people, and ourselves. For this young man whose friends were taunting him to cross a picket line, the conflict and confusion he initially experienced were signals that a choice would need to be made not only about his commitment to these friends but about his commitment to conflicting sets of values. The anger he soon experienced (as a "true feeling") helped guide his subsequent conduct, not only by giving the events meaning (delineating his friends as worth condemnation), but by creating a commitment to a particular way of being (as a person who complies and expects others to comply to particular standards) and way of behaving (not crossing the picket line).

In this case, the young man renewed his commitment to values which he already held dear, perhaps the values of his father and family. Another young man might just as easily have had a "true-feeling" experience that induced him to cross the picket line. If such were the case, the young man might still experience an initial confusion and conflict, even anger; but his anger might now reflect a judgment about picketers, and his commitment would be to his friends and their values and, more generally perhaps, to friendship rather than family. In neither case, it should be clear, would the "true feelings" arise from the depths of some pre-social "true" self. On the contrary, "true feelings," like all feelings, embody a history of social meanings, and their power to guide is based on that history. Ultimately we may break with that history, we may commit ourselves to values other than those we had previously held. But these new values, like old values, are still circumscribed by our view of who we are and who we wish to be, a view defined and constrained by what we have learned, experienced, and felt as members of particular social orders in a particular culture. [. . .]

References

Arieti, S. 1976. *Creativity: The Magic Synthesis*. New York: Basic Books.

Baumeister, R. F. 1986. *Identity: Cultural Change and the Struggle for Self*. New York: Oxford University Press.

———. 1987. "How the Self Became a Problem: A Psychological Review of Historical Research." *Journal of Personality and Social Psychology* 52: 163–176.

Bellah, R. N., R. Madsen, W. M. Sullivan, A. Swidler, & S. M. Tipton. 1985. *Habits of the Heart*. New York: Harper & Row.

Ellenberger, H. F. 1970. *The Discovery of the Unconscious*. New York: Basic Books.

Frank, J. D. 1974. *Persuasion and Healing* (rev. ed.). New York: Schocken Books.

Gordon S. L. 1989. "Institutional and Impulsive Orientations in Selectively Appropriating Emotions to Self." Pp. 115–135 in *The Sociology of Emotions: Original Essays and Research Papers*, edited by D. Franks and E. McCarthy. Greenwich, CT: JAI Press.

Jordan, J. V. and J. L. Surrey. 1986. "The Self-in-relation: Empathy and the Mother Daughter Relationship." Pp. 81–104 in *The Psychology of Today's Woman: New Psychoanalytic Visions,* edited by T. Bernay and D. W. Cantor. New York: Analytic Press.

Marcuse, H. 1966. *Eros and Civilization: A Philosophical Inquiry into Freud*. Boston: Beacon Press.

May, R. 1975. *The Courage to Create*. New York: Norton.

Miller, J. B. 1976. *Toward a New Psychology of Women*. Boston: Beacon Press.

Morgan, C. 1989. *True Feelings, the Self, and Authenticity: A Social Perspective*. Unpublished Masters Thesis, University of Massachusetts, Amherst.

Rothenberg, A. 1979. *The Emerging Goddess*. Chicago: University of Chicago Press.

Rothenberg, A. and C.R. Hausman, eds. 1976. *The Creativity Question*. Durham, NC: Duke University Press.

Sennett, R. 1980. *Authority*. New York: Knopf.

Stern, D. 1985. *The Interpersonal World of the Infant*. New York: Basic Books.

Sternberg, R. J. ed. 1988. *The Nature of Creativity*. Cambridge: Cambridge University Press.

Trilling, L. 1972. *Sincerity and Authenticity*. Cambridge: Harvard University Press.

Wallas, G. 1926. *The Art of Thought*. New York: Harcourt, Brace.

Chapter 19

Agneta H. Fischer and Jeroen Jansz

RECONCILING EMOTIONS WITH WESTERN PERSONHOOD

Emotions at odds with Western personhood?

WESTERN PHILOSOPHERS HAVE CHIEFLY TREATED emotions or passions as being in opposition to reason (cf. Pott, 1992; Solomon, 1976). In this dualist approach emotions have been described as irrational, involuntary or bodily forces, as 'diseases of the soul'. Although not all philosophers have advocated this line of thought, the dichotomy between passion and ratio has underlied Western philosophical thought ever since Plato and Socrates. . . .

This philosophical debate about the nature of emotions raises the question of how Western people in everyday life think and talk about their emotions. There is relatively little known about the way in which Western persons give meaning to their emotions in everyday life (examples of exceptions are Crawford *et al.*, 1992; Russell *et al.*, in press; Stearns and Stearns, 1986), whereas the number of studies of non-Western folk psychologies about emotions has increased enormously over the past few years. . . . Often, Western everyday conceptions have been contrasted with non-Western meaning systems, assuming that in Western culture emotional experiences are framed in terms of internal, bodily entities that disrupt rational behaviour (White, 1993). More specifically, emotions in Western culture have been associated with the following characteristics (cf. Averill, 1974, 1982, 1990): irrationality, corporeality, involuntarity and animality. [. . .]

These beliefs about the nature and workings of emotions necessarily imply that emotions are at odds with what is considered to be a normal and respectable person in Western society. Although there are various models of personhood in Western culture, there are shared conceptions of what a person is, as well as what a person ought to be. . . . These varieties of public models offer us examples that may inspire or frighten us. Most of these public models of being a person share three features that together form the dominant version of Western personhood (Dennett, 1978; Harré, 1983; Jansz, 1991). It is characterised first by *rationality*. Persons are assumed to, and have to be able to account for their words and actions in ways that meet standards of rational explanation. The second feature is *self-determination*. Persons can distance themselves from their contexts, and from their own immediate experiences. They are therefore able to consider alternatives, and to plan their actions according to their own preferences. . . . This self-determining feature is closely linked to the third characteristic: *Responsibility*. The organisation of Western societies is such that human beings are held individually responsible for what they say or do. . . . In sum, Western personhood pictures persons as rational agents, who are in charge of their own lives, are predictable and reliable, and responsible for their actions. Emotions, with their alleged irrationality, would seem to seriously undermine this cultural ideal of personhood. [. . .]

This being the case, how are people able to reconcile their emotions with the requirements of civilised behaviour in Western culture? Do people indeed judge their own or others' emotional behaviour as irrational? Do they think that they lack control over their emotions? Do they simply deny the presence of emotions? [. . .]

The social functions of emotion narratives

Not only because one might conceive of emotions as irrational, but also because they disrupt the ordinary course of social interaction, emotions almost always demand an account. [. . .]

Accounting is done in several ways. As a general rule, actors try to convince others that their behaviour is not as irrational, inappropriate, strange, unreasonable, or abnormal as it may appear at first sight. They often do so by presenting socially acceptable, agreed-upon and convincing reasons for their emotional behaviour in a story-like fashion (see Antaki, 1994; Jansz, in press): they tell an *emotion narrative*. Emotion narratives are characterised as authored, structured stories about emotional events. They are told from the perspective of the narrator, who generally employs a first person voice (Jansz, 1993; in press). Narrators present their own perspective of an emotional event and they try to convince their audience of the potential and plausible causes of their emotional reaction. In this way the protagonists set their own stories against the standards of what is considered to be intelligible and legitimate. An emotion narrative also has an ordered nature, that is, the elements in the narrative are sequentially organised. Studies of emotion knowledge, both in Western and non-Western countries, show that there is large consensus about the sequence of the major elements in an emotion narrative. Typically, an emotion narrative entails the following basic sequence: event→ emotion→(social) response (e.g. Lutz, 1988; Shaver *et al.*, 1987; White, 1990). This sequentiality generally results in a plot: the story ends in a denouement because the situation has been resolved, or because the emotion has been expressed, or because one has found a way to cope with the event or one's emotions. Another characteristic of emotion narratives is their intelligibility: they are intelligible in the sense that they provide reasons, arguments and thoughts that fit in the framework of shared cultural beliefs, rules and expectations. [. . .]

Telling emotion narratives is the primary strategy by which people try to solve the apparent conflict between emotion and personhood: emotion narratives not only describe emotional events, but also explain it and make one's emotions intelligible for others. Hence, the primary function of emotion narratives is the repair of a person's status as a responsible member of society (Shotter, 1984), and more specifically of his or her threatened identity. People generally do not like to be seen as a coward, a hothead, or a childish person. When experiencing or expressing emotions, people are concerned about how they will be evaluated, and whether their behaviour had good or bad consequences for their identity. Most people are generally aware of the fact that emotional behaviour may have either short- or long-term consequences for the characterisation and evaluation of who one is as a person. We presume that people will generally try to interpret and justify their emotions in such a way that they do not threaten the Western ideal of a person, or their specific identity. Knowing what an appropriate reaction is, a person can emphasise those elements in the story that make the emotional reaction the most natural and obvious one that was conceivable in that context. People will thus prevent being judged by others as irrational or primitive beings, or as cowards, or whiners. On the other hand, some emotion narratives are told so often and are so consistent across time that they become part of one's identity. One may, for example, find oneself a nervous, enthusiastic, or hot-tempered person. A second function of emotion narratives is restoration of the interrupted interaction. By giving acceptable reasons, explanations, or excuses for one's behaviour, the emotional and social balance in interactions is recovered: everything is returned to normal again. [. . .]

Narratives about anger

As expected, antecedent events were an indispensable element of anger narratives. Every story contained a description of the event that was perceived to be the just cause of one's anger or anger expression. This can be illustrated by the following example. Imagine a man who is very angry, because his wife's family reproached him and his wife for not attending the funeral of the wife's sister. Initially, one might think of the man's anger as being inappropriate, and that he should have felt guilty, or sad instead. Consider, however, the following narrative:

"I was on holiday with my family, somewhere in the middle of France. We rented a holiday home, the nearest village was 3 km further on, the nearest train station was 100 km away. While we were staying there, we got the message that my wife's sister was very ill and about to die. A sister with whom she was not very close, by the way. That same morning the car broke down, and we just had brought it to the garage when we received this message. Then we started calling and deliberating, are we going back, or not, and we decided to wait and see for the time being. Then the message came that she had died. My wife said: I want to go back, but how (she does not speak French)? Then I said, then I will go with you. By the way, I must tell you that before this holiday we had a very busy period, I worked myself to death. No, my wife said, I don't want that, you need this holiday. I will go on my own. I did not want that, for I was afraid that she would end up in Morocco. Then we called the son of the deceased sister, we are rather close to him, and he said he could understand very well why we would not come to the funeral (. . .): "You will be late for the funeral anyway". It did leave a negative mark on our holiday, of course. But then, we came home, and another sister did not even give us the chance to explain and she just was very mean to us. Well, then I exploded, and I said, that's enough, when you immediately start thinking the worst, if we don't even get the chance to explain that we were in the middle of nowhere, and that it was a miracle that the phone worked, and that we did not know in advance that the holiday home was in the middle of nowhere! I was terribly angry, and now, two years later, I still get angry about it."

Reading this narrative, it is easy to imagine that this man got mad. This story is not merely a description of what happened; the details of his story build up a credible account of his anger. He and particularly his wife were treated unfairly. This unfairness is stressed by providing various details of the antecedent events in order to convince the potential listener that he and his wife could not be blamed for their absence at the funeral: the car broke down, they were staying in the middle of nowhere, and they did not know in advance that the place was that isolated; she did not speak the language, and they did consult the wife's nephew. So, all in all, their good intentions were mistrusted and there should be no doubt that the wife's family's reproaches were extremely unfair. The function of this account is to repair the potential threat of his image as a rational and sensible man, and it probably removes potentially unpleasant feelings about his anger in that situation. The story keeps us from judging his anger as an irrational and uncontrolled reaction, and presses us to regard his anger as a reasonable reaction that serves the goal of putting his wife's family members in their proper place.

An interesting question is whether his wife's story would have been similar. From other studies we know that women's anger stories are different from men's (Campbell, 1993; Crawford et al., 1992). One very common ingredient of women's anger stories is their crying. Furthermore, compared to men, women seem to be less exclusively focused on the unfair and stupid behaviour of other persons, and seem to be more concerned with (the consequences of) their own feelings, and the very fact that they might lose control. Here is a typical example of a woman's anger narrative:

"I had some good friends for whom I did all kinds of things, taking care of their children and their animals, making clothes for them, and so on. Once I invited them for dinner; well I don't want to have anything in return for such things, but then they brought with them four twigs of flowers they picked from their own vase! I was so angry. Isn't that humiliating? Last year they were again on holiday and I had to go to the vet with their cat *twice*. He was already ill *before* they went on holiday, so in the end I had to let him consider letting him be put to sleep. I was

terribly angry then. I lay awake for nights, I couldn't sleep, because I
didn't know what to do about the cat, and then I went to the vet, but it
was such an agony for this animal. I was crying there, at the vet's place,
terrible."

The contents of this story are partly similar to the man's, in the sense that other
people are accused. Here too the antecedent events justify her anger. However,
there are also some interesting differences between this and the previous narrative
which seem illustrative for more general gender differences. Women more often
describe their feelings during the episode. In this case, for example, she mentions
the fact that she was extremely upset about the whole situation, that she could not
sleep, that she did not know what to do, and that she had been crying. In many other
stories women also refer to their feelings of powerlessness, their confusion about
the situation, their sense of incompetence and uncertainty about what to do. This
ambivalence in anger situations is often observed, and may be related to another
noticeable gender difference in anger stories: women tend to express some
empathy with the object of their anger. They try to look at the events from the
perspective of the other ('he is so miserable'), or they play down the faults or
stupidities of the other person ('I know she is like that, and I shouldn't get angry
about it'). An important function of these elements in women's stories may be the
mitigation of their own anger: because strong anger reactions are not in keeping
with their feminine identity, they try to tone it down by stressing their confusion
and ambivalence with respect to their own angry feelings.

 Despite these gender differences, however, both the men and the women
interviewed in this study generally provided rational accounts for their anger
reactions in terms of the antecedent events. Moreover, they considered their
expressions of anger to be quite appropriate, as well as their feelings. [. . .]

 People also mention other rationales for their anger expressions, which function as justifications for anger expressions in their stories. This is illustrated in the
following examples given by two women:

 "When you are very angry at a person, and when that is expressed, that
 is the time when it can be cleared up."

 "He should know how I feel. That is quite normal if you have to
 work together. When you know how the other person feels and he
 knows what is bothering you, you get to know each other better."

In both excerpts positive consequences of women's anger expression serve as
accounts for the fact that they expressed their anger The first account claims that
anger expression is right because it makes one's views or criticism of another
person more explicit. In the second account the focus is more on the woman's
personal relationship with another person and her commitment to this person. In
sum, people come up with a variety of reasons why they express their anger.
Interesting in this respect is that the effects of one's anger expression not only seem
to be expected, but are also *intended*. Anger expressions are largely described as if
they are voluntary and in the service of particular goals: one expresses one's anger

. . . *in order to* show others how you feel, or *in order to* improve one's relationship with another person.

Thus, the respectability of both men and women is restored by presenting themselves as actors who are in charge: when they get angry they have good reasons for doing so and they generally appear to be in control of their anger. In these stories, anger is seen as a functional emotion, which serves certain goals. Our assumption that rationality and self-determination are dominant characteristics of Western personhood, independent of gender, is supported here: both men and women generally present themselves as rational beings who have their anger under control, and express it intentionally.

Of course, we can also think of incidents in which one's anger is more extreme, and more likely to be interpreted as irrational and involuntary. Consider the following example.

> "I was so angry that I threw a cake at the man's head. Actually it was about nothing. (. . .) At that time I was more over-stressed than angry. I got a mist before my eyes, it was a kind of outburst inside myself and I just started to rant and rave. I could not think any longer what to do or say, it was just an explosion. I did not have myself under control any longer. (. . .) Afterwards I still think I was right, but, well you don't get any further, and maybe I should not have acted that extremely. But I could not help myself."

Here, the protagonist acknowledges that the antecedent event was a minor incident in which he was unjustly accused of something. However, he agrees that this is not a sufficient reason for his extreme behaviour ('actually it was about nothing') and he advances his being over-stressed as the real reason for the explosion. Apparently, this mental state is for him a more convincing account for throwing cakes than anger alone. It is also meant to explain why he could no longer control his behaviour: people who are under stress may act in a rather deviant way. The social advantage of claiming that one was over-stressed, instead of angry, is that being over-stressed refers to a temporary state of mental disturbance, so that it is implicitly claimed that he should not be regarded as fully accountable at that time. [. . .]

Narratives about fear

As in anger stories, antecedent events were the major ingredients of fear narratives. However, whereas the protagonist's identity is repaired by stressing the faults or unfair behaviours of *other persons* in anger narratives, in fear narratives it is the danger and inability to do something about the situation that is emphasised in order to account for one's fear. This is especially true if at face value the threat does not seem very serious, as exemplified in the following case.

> "Once I was very scared; it was a kind of unreal fear. My wife had a kind of sebaceous gland, just here, which had to be cut away surgically. At a certain moment I could not help thinking about various stories of

someone who also had a cosmetic surgery in order to cut away some lumps; and he never came to. I was really very worried that she would not awake from the anaesthesia."

This man accounts for his fear by referring to a true story of someone who died following similar surgery. The narrator appears to consider his fear to have been somewhat inappropriate ('it was a kind of unreal fear'); however, he tries to convince himself and the interviewer of the rationality of his fear by stressing the *reality* and *actuality* of the threat. This type of narrative is illustrative of the strategies used by men to protect their masculine identity (see also Crawford *et al.*, 1992): men try to justify their fears by claiming that the threat is real. However, we did not find support for the suggestion that men exaggerate the danger in fear episodes (Crawford *et al.*, 1992): men did not mention more dangerous events than women, nor did they go more into the details in describing the danger.

Although the description of antecedent events was the major type of justification given in fear stories, we also noticed another type of account, which is illustrated by the following example. This is provided by a man who is always very worried when his wife is late from her work.

"Well, she has to drive in heavy traffic, so then I ask myself, what has happened? You don't know what to do, you feel powerless, and, it is quite ridiculous, but you are already worrying about the future. The fear becomes stronger and stronger, but that happens automatically. I did not do anything to reinforce it. And, what can you do? You can take pills, or call other people, but I just let it go. I was the victim of my own fear."

The protagonist of the story blames the *nature* of the emotion. The fear is presented as an uncontrollable force that overwhelms him. As was the case with the angry outbursts, this involuntary and irrational nature of the fear is used to account for the obvious fact that the intensity of the emotion is out of proportion with the antecedent event. This man even admits that his reaction is ridiculous, but he stresses that it cannot be helped and that the increase in his fear is an automatic process that cannot be stopped. This accounting practice is far more typical of fear than of anger, and is used by men as well as women. Because of this uncontrollability, fear seems to be less acceptable, especially for men. Indeed, men more often maintained that there were no good reasons for their fear, although they considered it to be a reaction that could happen to anyone. Women, on the other hand, were more resigned and less upset; they clearly seemed to accept the irrationality and uncontrollability of the fear ('I just let it happen', 'If it comes, it comes'). [. . .]

All in all, the fear narratives, collected in this study, suggest that fear, to a greater extent than anger, is conceived of as an irrational and uncontrollable emotion. This applies more to men than to women. In the accounts of fear, no rationales were given for its expression, except those referring to the involuntary workings of the emotion. Hardly any positive consequences of fear expressions were advanced; people just wanted to be rid of this emotion. Both men and women argued that they almost always tried to suppress their fear, because they could hardly see any positive consequences of expressing their fear. The only positive social consequence that was mentioned, largely by women, was getting support from others.

Western personhood, gender and emotions

In this paper we have questioned the alleged conflict between the experience and expression of emotions and the normative characteristics of Western personhood: rationality, self-determination, and individual responsibility. The general presumption that Westerners, in contrast to some non-Western cultures, consider their emotions to be bodily, primitive impulses that are irrational and hard to control is difficult, if not impossible to maintain. We argued that emotions are not absent from Western personhood and that our cultural ideal of a person requires a form of 'bounded' emotionality: emotions should be felt and expressed within the strict boundaries of the social context. In contexts where emotional reactions are not suitable, however, repair work has to be done. In order to restore potential loss of personhood, people must demonstrate that their emotions are rational, although they may appear irrational. This is done by telling a well-ordered story about the emotional event, in which the narrator aims to convince the audience of the rationality, naturalness, or obviousness of his or her emotions. A narrative not only meets standards of rationality by providing reasons for one's emotions, but the very act of narrating also proves that one is once again in charge. . . .

The majority of narratives indeed pictured anger and, to a lesser extent, fear as quite rational emotions: they are rational first and foremost because respondents gave good reasons for their elicitation. Antecedent events were the most important components in the construction of a convincing story in which the person's own view on the 'rational or logical cause' of his or her emotions is outlined. [. . .]

References

ANTAKI, C. (1994). *Explaining and Arguing. The Social Organization of Accounts*. London: Sage.

AVERILL, J. R. (1974). An analysis of psychophysiological symbolism and its influence on theories of emotion. *Journal for the Theory of Social Behaviour*, **4**, 147–190.

AVERILL, J. R. (1982). *Anger and Aggression. An Essay on Emotion*. New York: Springer Verlag.

AVERILL, J. R. (1990). Inner feelings, works of the flesh, the beast within, diseases of the mind, driving force, and putting on a show: six metaphors of emotion and their theoretical extensions. In D. E. Leary (Ed.), *Metaphors in the History of Psychology*. Cambridge: Cambridge University Press, pp. 104–132.

CAMPBELL, A. (1993). *Out of Control. Men, Women and Aggression*. London: Pandora.

CRAWFORD, J., KIPPAX, S., ONYX, J., GAULT, U. and BENTON, P. (1992). *Emotion and Gender*. London: Sage.

DENNET, D. C. (1978). Conditions of personhood. In D. C. Dennet (Ed.), *Brainstorms*. Hassock: Harvester, pp. 267, 286.

HARRÉ, R. (1983). *Personal Being: A Theory for Individual Psychology*. Oxford: Blackwell.

JANSZ, J. (1991). *Person, Self and Moral Demands. Individualism Contested by Collectivism*. Leiden: DSWO-Press.

JANSZ, J. (1993). Het narratief als betekenisverlener [Narrative and meaning]. *Psychologie en Maatschappij*, **64**, 212–225.

JANSZ, J. (in press). Self-narratives as personal structures of meaning. In A. Oosterwegel and R.A. Wicklund (Eds.), *The Self in European and North American Culture: Development and Processes*. Dordrecht: Kluwer.

LUTZ, C. A. (1988). *Unnatural Emotions: Everyday Sentiments on a Micronesian Atoll and their Challenge to Western Theory*. Chicago: University of Chicago Press.

POTT, H. (1992). *De liefde van Alcibiades. Over rationaliteit en moties [Alcibiades' Love. On Rationality and Emotions]*. Amsterdam/Meppel: Boom.

RUSSELL, J. A., WELLENKAMP, J., MANSTEAD, A. S. R. and FERNANDEZ DOLS, J. M. (Eds.) (in press). *Everyday Conceptions of Emotion*. Dordrecht: Kluwer.

SHAVER, P., SCHWARTZ, J., KIRSON, D. and O'CONNOR, C. (1986). Emotion knowledge: further exploration of a prototype approach. *Journal of Personality and Social Psychology*, **52**, 1061–1086.

SHOTTER, J. (1984). *Social Accountability and Selfhood*. Oxford: Basil Blackwell.

SOLOMON, R. C. (1976). *The Passions: The Myth and Nature of Human Emotion*. Notre Dame, Indiana: University of Notre Dame Press.

STEARNS, P. N. and STEARNS, C. Z. (1986). *Anger: The Struggle for Emotional Control in America's History*. Chicago: Chicago University Press.

WHITE, G. M. (1990). Moral discourse and the rhetoric of emotion. In C. A. Lutz and L. Abu-Lughod (Eds.), *Language and the Politics of Emotion*. Cambridge: Cambridge University Press.

WHITE, G. M. (1993). Emotions inside out: The anthropology of affect. In M. Lewis and J. M. Haviland (Eds.), *Handbook of Emotions*. New York: The Guilford Press, pp. 29–41.

Chapter 20

W. Ray Crozier

SELF-CONSCIOUSNESS IN SHAME

The role of the 'other'

[. . .]

Self and other in shame

ONE WAY OF COMPARING DIFFERENT theoretical accounts of the role of the self in shame is to consider the emphasis they place upon self-evaluation of conduct relative to the individual's awareness of others' evaluations of conduct. Some accounts emphasise the individual's own assessment of his or her behaviour. Michael Lewis (1992) proposed a cognitive attribution model that defined shame as 'a consequence of a failure evaluation relative to the standards when the person makes a global evaluation of the self' (p. 75). In similar vein, Scherer (1993) offers a system for distinguishing among the fundamental emotions in terms of a series of 'stimulus evaluation checks'. Whether the individual judges him or herself to be the cause of a particular action and whether that action is compatible with the individual's self-image are classed as two of the evaluation checks for shame. According to each of these accounts, the person compares his or her action with some standard, and shame ensues from the combination of judgments that the action falls short and that he or she has caused or is responsible for it.

Each of these accounts involves the dual role for the self . . . the self; evaluates and is the object of evaluation. Other accounts introduce a further component, where the person perceives his or her behaviour through the eyes of another. This account is related to notions that shame is loss of standing, loss of face. It is linked to ideas of reputation, honour, dignity. This position has been adopted by influential philosophical accounts of shame, for example, those of Sartre (1943/1956) and Taylor (1985). Taylor writes of 'the agent's becoming aware of the discrepancy between her own assumption about her state or action and a possible detached observer-description of this state or action, and of her being further aware that she ought not to be in a position where she could be so seen, where such a description at least appears to fit' (p. 26). Some psychological accounts also emphasise the role of the 'other', for example, the theory of H.B. Lewis, cited above. Castelfranchi and Poggi (1990) distinguish between 'shame before oneself' and 'shame before the other', where the former concerns loss of self-esteem and the latter loss of esteem in the eyes of other. Harré (1990, p. 199) argues that shame is 'caused by the realisation that others have become aware that what one has been doing has been a moral infraction, a judgment with which I, as actor, concur'. Tangney *et al.* (1996, p. 1256) refer to 'public exposure (and disapproval) of some impropriety or short-coming'. Taylor (1985) has argued that it is the actor's realisation how his or her behaviour might be seen rather than the actual judgment made by another that is important. She provides the following example of an artist's model (1985, p. 61).

> A model who has been posing for an artist for some time comes to feel shame when she realizes that he no longer regards her as a model, but regards her as a woman.

The model does not have to share any opinion of her the artist might hold; she does not have to take an adverse view of her appearance; nor does she have to believe that there is anything blameworthy in her action. The shift from her being comfortable in the situation to being ashamed does not require any change in either her or the artist's behaviour, but only a change in her belief as to how she is being seen. While her exposure is to the artist in one sense (he is the only other person there), in the sense crucial for shame her exposure is to a particular view of her conduct. In shame, she identifies with that other view of herself, and the adverse judgment comes from herself: 'it [is] wrong for her to be so seen, at least at this time and by this audience. Being seen as she is seen is to be in a position in which no decent women should find herself . . . this is no fault of hers, but the question of responsibility is irrelevant to feelings of shame. However it may have come about, she is now in a false position and for this she is condemned' (Taylor, 1985, p. 61).

Some psychological theories also take the view that it is the actor's interpretation of a potential observer's view that is important. Semin and Manstead (1981) distinguish the self-image from the subjective public image. An emotional reaction is elicited by a discrepancy between these images occasioned by the recognition that some action unfairly reflects poorly on one's subjective public image. Higgins (1987) defines shame as a discrepancy between one's actual self and one's perception of how an ideal other would evaluate the self.

Accounts of shame that emphasise self-evaluation of behaviour relative to personal standards have a number of disadvantages. First, it is difficult in terms of their analysis to distinguish between shame, on the one hand, and depression and alternative kinds of negative self-evaluation, on the other; indeed, in one of the examples provided by M. Lewis to illustrate how the global self is involved in shame, a case where a patient forced his date to have sex, the patient actually says, "What's wrong with me? I'm depressed. Didn't feel like getting out of bed this morning." (1992, p. 72).

Second, the accounts attach too much importance to behaviour. As Sabini and

Silver (1997, p. 6) have argued, it is not behaviour itself but what the behaviour exposes to others about the self that is crucial for shame—an apparently trivial act can produce intense shame. Third, these accounts have difficulty in explaining cases of shame where there is no self-attribution of responsibility for wrongdoing. In the example of the artist's model the shift from being at ease in the situation to feeling shame requires only a shift in awareness, to the realisation that an adverse view of her behaviour can be entertained. Castelfranchi and Poggi (1990, p. 238) offer a similar example, of a man who has saved a woman from drowning and who is giving her mouth-to-mouth respiration when he realises that he is being observed by a passer-by. The man may feel shame if he becomes aware that he might appear as if he were taking advantage of the woman. Such examples are not difficult to generate. A personal example is when a fellow academic whom I did not know very well left me in charge of her bag. After a while I felt the need to go to the bathroom and I began to look through her bag to check if it contained anything valuable in order to decide whether or not it could safely be left, when she suddenly returned. Although she expressed neither surprise nor annoyance at my action I was immediately discomfited that she might think that I was looking for money or, perhaps even more shaming, taking a prurient interest in her private belongings. In all of these examples, the actor behaves in good faith and there is no self-evaluation relative to standards. What is crucial is the actor's attribution to the audience, the recognition and endorsement of the fact that his or her behaviour is being, or can be, judged in a manner that reflects badly upon him or herself. It is not necessary that an observer is actually present (in the case of the artist's model) or that an observer actually takes an adverse view of the actor's behaviour (in all three cases). This paper proposes a framework that can accommodate the different models that have been outlined. The framework is based on the assumption that shame (and embarrassment) entails a shift in perspective on the self, a perspective that is described in lay psychology as 'self-consciousness'.

Self-consciousness

The notion that people can shift perspective so that they seem to be viewing themselves from outside is not, of course, a new one. The Concise Oxford Dictionary refers in its definition of self-consciousness to a 'person embarrassed or unnatural in manner from knowing he is observed by others'. Harré (1983) defines it as the state where 'the normal intentionality of actions in which they are thought of as ends or outcomes is suspended and the self-conscious actor focuses on the actions he or she is performing'. The theory of objective self-awareness originally proposed by Duval and Wicklund (1972) seems to entail such a shift in perspective, and this is captured in the construct of public self-awareness developed by Carver and Scheier (e.g., Carver & Scheier, 1987). This construct was linked to shame by Buss (1980). Subsequently there has been criticism on logical and empirical grounds of the assumption that public self-attention results in the individual taking an external perspective on the self (Fenigstein, 1988, cited by Crozier, 1990; Fenigstein & Abrams, 1993). We propose here that there is a useful distinction to be drawn between two conceptions of self evaluation.

The first entails an individual's self-evaluation. We share the assumption of contemporary theories of the self-concept that it is multidimensional and hence any one of a number of discriminable aspects of the self can serve as the object of evaluation. These can include the kinds of evaluations which are emphasised by cognitive and attributional models of shame and related emotions of shyness and embarrassment, such as the evaluation of the self as a social actor and also the judgment that the individual's behaviour is discrepant from any standards that are relevant to him or her. An adverse self-evaluation gives rise to negative feelings, like regret, disappointment, depression. In everyday language such experiences can be labelled as shame, for example, one might express shame that one had arrived late for an appointment or had failed an examination.

However, it is proposed here that the self-conscious emotions are characterised by a shift in perspective where the individual views his or her own behaviour as if through the eyes of another. Many situations—walking across a public stage, arriving late at a social function, being (or feeling) conspicuous in appearance or dress, becoming aware that one is being talked about (including being praised, complimented or thanked), being in the presence of an authority figure, driving in front of a police car—produce self-consciousness of this kind. This often (perhaps always) has a distinctive phenomenological quality (including feeling 'small'). It seems often to be accompanied by blushing, even in the absence of adverse self-evaluation. Psychological theories need to consider the circumstances in which this state becomes shame, or embarrassment, or pride, or any of the other self-conscious emotions. It is proposed here that three factors are relevant to shame: the attribution to the other; the correspondence between the individual's judgment of behaviour and his or her perception of the other's judgment of that behaviour; the aspect of the self that is being judged, specifically whether some core aspect of the self is evaluated.

The other perspective

We have already indicated some theoretical accounts that include the notion of another perspective on the self. Further discussion in the literature has concerned whether shame is only experienced in an actual social situation, and whether the presence of an audience can help to distinguish shame from embarrassment. Buss (1980) claimed that no one is publicly self-focused unless there are others to observe them: 'Embarrassment and shame are both reactions to specific events in a social context' (1980, p. 162). Evidence and argument suggest the contrary position about shame. A survey reported by Tangney et al. (1996) found that participants recalled experiencing shame when they were alone. The analysis of shame provided by Taylor (1985) concluded that it was not essential that the observer was an actual or particular person, whether present or absent; the actor becomes aware of a particular view of his or her behaviour, and not necessarily of any particular individual holding that view.

Tangney et al. (1996) also reported that the presence of an observer helped differentiate shame and embarrassment. Recalled episodes of shame were signifi-cantly more likely than episodes of embarrassment to refer to occasions when the individual was on his or her own; that embarrassment elicited higher ratings on a scale assessing the extent to which participants felt that others were looking; that shame was more likely than embarrassment to be experienced in the presence of those who were close rather than acquaintances or strangers. Nevertheless, these are differences of emphasis, rather than categorical differences. We propose that shame and embarrassment both require the adoption of another perspective, and that this can take place whether the individual is alone or in company and whether the company is psychologically close or more distant. [. . .]

References

Buss, A.H. (1980). *Self-consciousness and social anxiety*. San Francisco: Freeman.

Carver, C.S. & Scheier, M.F. (1987). The blind men and the elephant: Selective examination of the public–private literature gives rise to a faulty perception. *Journal of Personality*, **55**, 525–540.

Castelfranchi, C. & Poggi, I. (1990). Blushing as a discourse: Was Darwin wrong? In *Shyness and embarrassment: Perspectives from social psychology* (ed. W.R. Crozier) pp. 230–251. New York: Cambridge University Press.

Crozier, W.R. (ed.) (1990). *Shyness and embarrassment: Perspectives from social psychology*. New York: Cambridge University Press.

Duval, S. & Wicklund, R.A. (1972). *A theory of objective self-awareness*. New York: Academic Press.

Fenigstein, A. & Abrams, D. (1993). Self-attention and the egocentric assumption of shared perspectives. Journal of Experimental Social Psychology, **29**, 287–303.

Harré, R. (1983). *Personal being*. Oxford: Blackwell.

Harré, R. (1990). Embarrassment: A conceptual analysis. In *Shyness and embarrassment: Perspective from social psychology* (ed. W.R. Crozier) pp. 181–204. New York: Cambridge University Press.

Higgins, E.T. (1987). Self-discrepancy: A theory relating self and affect. *Psychological Review*, **94**, 319–340.

Lewis, H.B. (1971). *Shame and guilt in neurosis*. New York: International Universities Press.

Lewis, M. (1992). *Shame: The exposed self*. New York: Free Press.

Sabini, J. & Silver, M. (1997). In defence of shame: Shame in the context of guilt and embarrassment. *Journal for the Theory of Social Behaviour*, **27**, 1–15.

Sartre, J.-P. (1943/1956). *Being and nothingness* (trans. H.E. Barnes). New York: Pocket Books.

Scherer, K.R. (1993). Studying the emotion-antecedent appraisal process: An expert system approach. *Cognition and Emotion*, **7**, 325–355.

Tangney, J.P., Miller, R.S., Flicker, L. & Barlow, D.H. (1996). Are shame, guilt, and embarrassment distinct emotions? *Journal of Personality and Social Psychology*, **70**, 1256–1264.

Taylor, G. (1985). *Pride, shame, and guilt: Emotions of self-assessment*. Oxford: Clarendon Press.

5. Emotions, space and place

HISTORICALLY, ISSUES OF space and place have been neglected by natural and social scientists of emotion. Like objects, space and place have a tendency to fade unnoticed into the background in favour of more obvious figures such as the particular individuals experiencing particular feelings, expressing them via their frowns, sighs, postures and gestures, or by talking about them. And yet, when writing about love and jealousy, a great novelist such as Proust draws our attention to the *places* in which Swann's feelings are played out and to the *settings* in which his encounters with Odette unfold (cf. Brown and Stenner 2001). Swann's jealousy is played out around the Verdurin salon and we sense that things 'feel different' outside of that particular milieu. He feels its pangs when it dawns on him how frequently Odette is now away from Paris. Some places are 'haunted' by Odette and some are the haunts of the 'young Swann' who predates the affair. Likewise, Proust shows us how the material objects populating spaces are woven into the relations configured by jealousy. The flowers accompanied by a note from Odette become so unbearable that Swann makes a detour to avoid them 'whenever he went in or out of the room'. When we begin to attend to them, space and place reveal themselves to be decisive ingredients in a social scientific understanding of affect.

Fortunately, this fact has not escaped geographers, who in recent years have contributed significantly both to the textual turn and to the affective turn by taking the spatial aspects of affect and emotion seriously. There are now, for instance, a number of editorials and special issues discussing 'emotional geographies' and 'spatializing affect' (Anderson and Smith 2001; Davidson and Bondi 2004; Davidson and Milligan 2004), and no shortage of heated debate (Thien 2005; Anderson and Harrison 2006) This move has required what MacKian (2004) calls a 're-subjectivization of space', since in what she calls 'simple modernity', space had been characterized by the removal of all subjectivity in favour of the objective space typified by the grid of the map. Some of this work has been spurred by practical and political interests such as feminist critique of masculine detachment and the spatial mediation of dynamics of inclusion and exclusion which have emotional impacts of relevance to class, race, disability and sexuality (Sibley 1995; Pain 1997; Dwyer 1999; Listerborn 2002). This work is often based upon the notion of space as a site of discursively mediated shared symbolic meaning. Geographical work in the affective turn, by contrast, sees in affect the possibility of attending to spatial encounters with 'a life and a force before and beyond . . . deliberative and reflective . . . representational thinking' (McCormack 2003: 490; see also McCormack 2007). This has spurred some geographers to articulate 'non-representational' theories of the spacing of affect that aim to 'engage with questions of materiality' and 'provoke a rethinking of the nature of . . . subjects . . . and the emergence of subjectivities from more or less unwilled affectual . . . assemblages' (Anderson and Harrison 2006: 334).

Our first extract is from Nigel Thrift's (2004) article 'Intensities of Feeling: towards a spatial politics of affect'. Thrift exemplifies the attempt to develop 'non-representational' theory proper to an 'affective turn' capable of moving beyond a discursive version of social constructionism. This paper is as much about politics as it is about space, but we include it in this sub-section because Thrift discusses issues he claims to be specific to the life of cities. Namely, he argues that the systematic engineering of affect is now central to the political life of Euro-American cities. If so, one can no longer understand politics in relation to a discursive or 'ideological' plan or regime, since the engineering of affect bypasses such higher order cognitive and linguistic processes. He examines four such 'developments' that enroll affect directly into the political life of cities: the proliferation of neo-liberal 'agencies of choice'; the enhanced mediating role of the 'screen'; the increased use of technologies of 'calculation in sensory registers' which permit a kind of corporeal communication; and the careful design of urban space to shape affective responses.

The second extract from Rani Kawale (2004) 'Inequalities of the Heart' exemplifies a social constructionist concern to challenge the 'naturalness' of heterosexuality through an analysis of the ways in which everyday places are 'felt'. She explores the notion of 'sexualized' emotional spaces through an examination of the accounts of the performance of emotion work given by a sample of lesbian and bisexual women in London. Heterosexuality, she points out, is an institutionalized phenomenon that regulates emotional expression through the mediation of law, religion and other institutions such as marriage. This regulation occurs in everyday *spaces* and *places* which thus take on emotional connotations that result in the 'spatial supremacy of heterosexuality'.

Our third extract from Mimi Sheller (2004) is also about the 'feeling' of everyday spaces, but in this case the focus in on what Sheller calls 'Automotive Emotions': feeling the car. Automotive emotions are about what it feels like to be 'in' the car, but such feelings are also influenced by the broader cultural and social meanings that particular types of car afford. Emotional investments in cars thus go beyond simple rational and economic calculations of costs and benefits since – as spaces embedded in broader personal, familial and national spaces – they include embodied experiences which often have deep affective resonances. This is something well understood by those who sell cars, who routinely dwell on the feeling of the driving experience and other passions that haunt our automobiles.

The final extract in this sub-section is from Ben Anderson's (2005) article, 'Domestic Geographies of Affect'. Anderson explores some of the affective dynamics involved in the operation of making judgements in mundane domestic spaces. He conducted research in 17 lower middle-class households in Sheffield, England. Part of this research involved eliciting accounts of how householders decide which music to play in their home. Denis, for example, selects a song which 'energizes' him after returning home from work. His partner Jenny doesn't like the song and leaves the room. On the basis of such seemingly mundane data, Anderson suggests that such judgements are made on the basis of what 'feels right' at a given moment and that what is 'felt' is based on how 'bodies' compose with other bodies (e.g. how a 'body' of music fits with particular people in particular moods in particular spaces and times). For Anderson, this shows that ordinary domestic space and time is brought into being by 'multiple, intersecting topologies of affect'.

References

Anderson, K. and Smith, S. (2001) 'Emotional geographies', *Transactions of the Institute of British Geographers*, 26: 7–10.

Anderson, B. and Harrison, P. (2006) 'Questioning affect and emotion', *Area*, 38 (3): 333–335.

Brown, S. and Stenner, P. (2001) 'Being affected: Spinoza and the psychology of emotion, *International Journal of Group Tensions*, 30 (1): 81–105.

Davidson, J. and Bondi, L. (2004) 'Spatialising affect; affecting space: an introduction', *Gender, Place and Culture*, 11: 373–4.

Davidson, J. and; Milligan, C. (2004) 'Editorial: Embodying emotion sensing space: introducing emotional geographies', *Social and Cultural Geography*, 5 (4): 523–532.

Dwyer, C. (1999) 'Contradictions of community: questions of identity for young British Muslim women, *Environment and Planning A*, 31: 53–68.

Listerborn, C. (2002) 'Understanding the geography of women's fear: toward a reconceptualization of fear and space', in L. Bondi, H. Avis, R. Bankey, A. Bingley, J. Davidson, R. Duffy, V. I. Einagel, A. M. Green, L. Johnston, S. Lilley, C. Listerborn, S. McEwan, M. Marshy, N. O'Connor, G. Rose. and B. Vivat, (eds) *Subjectivities, Knowledges and Feminist Geographies: the subjects and ethics of social research*. London and Lanham, MD: Rowman and Littlefield.

MacKian, S. (2004) 'Mapping reflexive communities: visualizing the geographies of emotion', *Social and Cultural Geography*, 5 (4): 615–631.

McCormack, D. P. (2003) 'An event of geographical ethics in spaces of affect', *Transactions of the Institute of British Geographers*, 26: 488–507.

McCormack, D. P. (2007) 'Molecular affects in human geographies', *Environment and Planning A*, 39: 359–377.

Pain, R. (1997) 'Social geographies of women's fear of crime', *Transactions of the Institute of British Geographers*, 22: 231–244.

Sibley, D. (1995) *Geographies of Exclusion*. London: Routledge.

Thien, D. (2005) 'After or beyond feeling? A consideration of affect and emotion in geography', *Area*, 37 (4): 450–456.

Chapter 21

Nigel Thrift

INTENSITIES OF FEELING

Towards a spatial politics of affect

[. . .]

OF COURSE, AFFECT HAS ALWAYS been a key element of politics and the subject of numerous powerful political technologies which have knotted thinking, technique and affect together in various potent combinations. One example is the marshalling of aggression through various forms of military trainings such as drill. [. . .]

Similar processes have been happening in many other arenas of social life, whether on a domestic or larger scale, sufficient to suggest that the envelope of what we call the political must increasingly expand to take note of 'the way that political attitudes and statements are partly conditioned by intense autonomic bodily reactions that do not simply reproduce the trace of a political intention and cannot be wholly recuperated within an ideological regime of truth' (Spinks, 2001, p. 23). In this section I want to illustrate how this envelope is expanding in cities by reference to four developments. The first of these developments consists of the general changes in the *form* of such politics which are taking place in the current era, changes which make affect an increasingly visible element of the political. In particular, I want to point towards so-called 'agencies of choice' and 'mixed-action repertoires' in line with a general move to make more and more areas of life the subject of a new set of responsibilities called 'choice'. As Norris (2002, p. 222) puts it:

> . . . Rising levels of human capital and societal modernization mean that, today, a more educated citizenry . . . has moved increasingly from agencies of loyalty to agencies of choice, and from electoral repertoires toward mixed-action repertoires combining electoral activities and pro-test politics. . . .

Many of these new forms of choice politics rely on an expansion of what has been conventionally regarded as the urban political sphere. For example, the political nowadays routinely takes in all manner of forms of culture–nature relation (e.g. environmental politics, animal rights politics, pro-choice or anti-life politics). In turn, this redefinition of what counts as political has allowed more room for explicitly affective appeals which are heavily dependent upon the media, as well as similar appeals which endeavour to reduce these affective impacts (e.g. by referring to science, by various means of deconstruction of the 'reality' of an image and so on). . . .

This brings me to the second development which is the heavy and continuing *mediatization* of politics. We live in societies which are enveloped in and saturated by the media: most importantly, it is difficult to escape the influence of the *screen* which now stares at us from so many mundane locations – from almost every room in the house to doctors' waiting rooms, from airport lounges to shops and shopping malls, from bars to many workplaces . . . from the insides of elevators to whole buildings – that it is possible to argue that the screen has taken on a number of the roles formerly ascribed to parent, lover, teacher and blank stooge, as well as adding a whole series of 'postsocial' relations which seem to lie somewhere between early film theory's brute translation of screen-ic force (Kracauer, 1960; Balasz, 1970) and cognitive film theory's later, more nuanced interpretation in which cognitive processes are strained through various conventions and styles (see Bordwell and Carroll, 1996; Thrift, 2004b). This mediatization has had important effects. As McKenzie (2001) has pointed out, its most important effect has been to enshrine the performative principle at the heart of modern Euro-American societies and their political forms. This has occurred in a number of ways. To begin with, the technical form of modern media tends to foreground emotion, both in its concentration on key affective sites such as the face or voice and its magnification of the small details of the body that so often signify emotion. Political presentation nowadays often fixes on such small differences and makes them stand for a whole. One line of movement can become a progression of meaning, able to be actualised and implanted locally. [. . .]

Thus, political presentation conforms increasingly to media norms of presentation which emphasize the performance of emotion as being an index of credibility. Increasingly, political legitimation arises from this kind of performance (Thompson, 2001). And, as a final point, these kinds of presentation chime with the increasingly 'therapeutic' form of selfhood which is becoming common in Euro-American societies (cf. Giddens, 1991; Rose, 1996). Indeed, Nolan (1998) argues that this therapeutic or 'emotivist' ethos is embedding itself in the structures of the American state to such a degree that it is becoming a key technology of governance, both challenging and to some extent replacing the affective background of older bureaucratic 'machine' technologies, by, for example, recognising emotional labour, emotion management and emotional learning as key skills (Smith, 2002). [. . .]

Thus, a series of heterogeneous knowledges of performance move to centre stage in modern societies which constitute a new 'disaggregated' mode of discipline, an emergent stratum of power and knowledge. These knowledges construct power in a number of ways – by delivering messages with passion, for example (indeed, it is often the force with which passion is delivered which is more important than the message), by providing a new minute landscape of manipulation (Doane, 2002), by adding new possibilities for making signs, and generally by adding new openings out of the event. But, most importantly, they provide a new means of creating 'fractal' subjects challenged to perform across a series of different situations in a way which demands not so much openness as controlled flexibility. As McKenzie (2001, p. 19) puts it:

> The desire produced by performative power and knowledge is not moulded by distinct disciplinary mechanisms. It is not a repressive desire: it is instead 'excessive', intermittently modulated and pushed across the thresholds of various limits by overlapping and sometimes competing systems. Further, diversity is not simply integrated, for integration is itself becoming diversified. Similarly, deviation is not simply normalised, for norms operate and transform themselves through their own transgression and deviation. We can understand this development better when we realise that the mechanisms of performative power are nomadic and flexible more than sedentary and rigid, that its spaces are networked and digital more than enclosed and physical, that its temporalities are polyrhythmic and non-linear and not simply sequential and linear. On the performative stratum, one shuttles quickly between different evaluative grids, switching back and forth between divergent challenges to perform – or else.

A third development is closely linked to mediatization and the rise of performance knowledges. It is the growth of new forms of calculation in sensory registers that would not have previously been deemed 'political'. In particular, through the advent of a whole series of technologies, small spaces and times, upon which affect thrives and out of which it is often constituted, have become visible and are able to be enlarged so that they can be knowingly operated upon. Though it would be possible to argue that outposts were already being constructed in this continent of phenomenality back in the seventeenth century with, for example, the growth of interest in conditioning the military body through such practices as drill, I would argue that the main phase of colonisation dates from the mid-nineteenth century and rests on four developments (Thrift, 2000). First, there is the ability to sense the small spaces of the body through a whole array of new scientific instruments which have, in turn, made it possible to think of the body as a set of micro-geographies. Second, there is the related ability to sense small bodily movements. Beginning with the photographic work of Marey, Muybridge and others and moving into our current age in which the camera can impose its own politics of time and space, we can now think of time as minutely segmented frames, able to be speeded up, slowed down, even frozen for a while. Third, numerous body practices have come into existence which rely on and manage such knowledge of small times and spaces, most especially those connected with the performing arts, including the 'under-performing' of film acting, much modern dance, the insistent cross-hatched tempo of much modern music, and so on. Special performance notations, like Labanotation and other 'choreo-graphics', allow this minute movement to be recorded, analysed and recomposed. Then, finally, a series of discourses concerning the slightest gesture and utterance of the body have been developed, from the elaborate turn-taking of conversational analysis to the intimate spaces of proxemics, from the analysis of gesture to the mapping of 'body language'. [. . .]

A fourth development which involves affect is the careful design of urban space to produce political response. Increasingly, urban spaces and times are being designed to invoke affective response according to practical and theoretical knowledges that have been derived from and coded by a host of sources. It could be claimed that this has always been the case – from monuments to triumphal processions, from theatrical arenas to mass body displays – and I would agree. In the twentieth century, it could be argued that much of the activity of the design of space was powered up again, becoming entangled with the evolution of knowledges of shaping the body (such as the microbiopolitics referred to above), often in a politics of the most frightening sort. But what I would argue is different now is both the sheer weight of the gathering together of formal knowledges of affective response (whether from highly formal theoretical backgrounds such as psychoanalysis or practical theoretical backgrounds like performance), the vast number of practical knowledges of affective response that have become available in a semi-formal guise (e.g. design, lighting, event management, logistics, music, performance), and the enormous diversity of available cues that are able to be worked with in the shape of the profusion of images and other signs, the wide spectrum of available technologies, and the more general archive of events. The result is that affective response can be designed into spaces, often out of what seems like very little at all. Though affective response can clearly never be guaranteed, the fact is that this is no longer a random process either. It is a form of landscape engineering that is gradually pulling itself into existence, producing new forms of power as it goes. [. . .]

References

BALAZS, B. (1970): *Theory of the Film. Character and Growth of a New Art*. New York: Dover Press.

BORDWELL, D., CARROLL, D. (eds) (1996): *Post-Theory. Reconstructing Film Studies*. Madison: University of Wisconsin Press.

DOANE, M.A. (2002): *The Emergence of Cinematic Time. Modernity, Contingency, The Archive*. Cambridge, MA: MIT Press.

KRACAUER, S. (1960): *Theory of Film. The Redemption of Physical Reality*. New York,

MCKENZIE, J. (2001): *Perform or Else. From Discipline to Performance*. New York: Routledge.

NOLAN, J.L.(1998): *The Theurapeutic State. Justifying Government at Century's End*. Albany, NY: New York University Press.

NORRIS, P. (2002): *Democratic Phoenix. Reinventing Political Activism*. Cambridge: Cambridge University Press.

SMITH, P. (ed.) (2002): 'Regimes of emotion', Special Issue of *Soundings* 20: 98–217.

SPINKS, T. (2001): 'Thinking the posthuman: literature, affect and the politics of style', *Textual Practice*, 15: 23–46.

THRIFT, N.J. (2000): 'Still life in nearly present time: the object of nature', *Body and Society*, 6: 34–57.

THRIFT, N.J. (2004b): 'Beyond mediation', in Miller, D. (ed.): *Materialities*. Durham, NC: Duke University Press.

Chapter 22

Rani Kawale

INEQUALITIES OF THE HEART

The performance of emotion work by lesbian and bisexual women in London, England

[. . .]

Feeling everyday places

EVERYDAY PLACES CLEARLY INCLUDE THE home. According to Valentine (1993a), Johnston and Valentine (1995) and Elwood (2000), the 'heteropatriarchal' parental home is a place where sexuality is under surveillance and lesbians do not always experience emotional comfort. Lesbians often actively conceal or suppress their identity or find discreet ways of resisting their invisibility in the home. Lesbian households, however, while not necessarily eliminating surveillance of sexuality, can offer lesbians emotional comfort. In my research, approximately 59 per cent of questionnaire respondents and 80 per cent of interviewees were out about their sexuality at home. They were likely to live alone or with same-sex partners and/or friends. However, 41 per cent of questionnaire respondents and 75 per cent of interviewees actively concealed their sexuality from their parents at home.[3] The interviewees described their homes in emotional terms and it was clear that Edwina (white Irish, lesbian, aged late twenties), Sunita (South Asian, lesbian, aged late twenties) and Sharada (South Asian, lesbian, aged late twenties) were concerned about the feelings and emotions of their parents:

> My parents wouldn't approve [of me being a lesbian] so therefore I'm 'in' at home . . . the only issue is not upsetting my parents. I'm living in their house rent-free because I'm a student and that's a courtesy that I've got to respect and [being out] would make me very unhappy so why bother? The only reason [why] I [would] want to tell them is to make them happy for me, that I've found someone or whatever. They're not going to be, [so] why bother? . . . [T]hey'll think I'll've gone a wrong

path . . . they wouldn't be able to stand what I'm doing, I'd be deviant,
wrong and it'd be 'their fault' and that's not fair.   (Edwina)

Rekha (South Asian, lesbian, aged late twenties) lived alone and explained that her girlfriend Sunita lived with her parents who were unaware of her lesbian sexuality. They did not allow Sunita to spend nights away from home so Rekha and Sunita met regularly on the scene to share some of their emotions and feelings for each other. Like Edwina, Sunita was eager to maintain an emotionally balanced atmosphere with her parents at home so she kept her sexuality a secret from them. They both performed surface acting such as deliberately changing topics of conversations with their parents away from their social lives, partners and marriage, and hiding lesbian and gay material. This helped them to avoid the fear of being accidentally 'found out' by their parents and also to protect their parents from feeling angry and upset. Many of my research participants lived in lesbian or bisexual (friendly) households, but whether they visited their parents' or other relatives' at home, or were visited by them in their own homes, the majority continued to conceal their sexuality from them even if they had already come out to them. Sharada lived with her brother who accepted her lesbian identity, and she was out to her mother. Yet she continued to hide her sexuality from her parents when they visited because, as she explained to me, 'they don't want to see it or know about it'. So a lesbian (friendly) household may offer emotional comfort but the feeling rules change according to who is present. However, whether a home is lesbian (friendly) or not, it certainly can be a site of emotional comfort for lesbians who, like Edwina, Sunita and Sharada, perform the emotion work of concealing their sexuality in the interest of their parents' feelings, and their own feelings.

Most employment organizations incorporate gendered performances and sexualized interactions among employees such that hegemonic heterosexuality remains powerful in them, and sexual minorities remain invisible (Burrell and Hearn 1989; Halford and Leonard 2001; Hall 1989; McDowell 1995; Schneider 1984; Valentine 1993a, 1993b; Witz, Halford and Savage 1996). Lesbians and gay men often pass as heterosexual in these environments by managing and negotiating multiple sexual identities (Valentine 1993b). The majority of my research participants negotiated and managed sexual identities at work and performed emotion work to avoid, for example, fear, anxiety and embarrassment of being found out or rejected by their colleagues. They were selective about who they came out to in order to avoid or minimize unwanted emotions in their colleagues and in themselves. Whether out or not, they often encountered awkward situations when colleagues expressed homophobic thoughts and opinions, hence the participants concealed and suppressed feeling offended, upset and angry by what may be regarded as surface acting. For example, Sujata (South Asian, lesbian, aged early twenties) adopted a 'liberal' stance at work when pointing out to colleagues that their homophobic comments were as unacceptable as they believed racist comments to be. Upset, anger or offence have no inherent meanings but expressing these emotions in response to homophobic comments at work was no option for Sujata as this would have effectively exposed her sexuality, something she considered to be unsafe.

Coming out to 'gay-friendly' colleagues does not necessarily guarantee a lesbian or bisexual woman can then express her sexuality at work in the same ways that heterosexual women can. Again, the performance of emotion work is required. For example, Kelly (white Australian, lesbian, aged mid-twenties) had been out at work for more than a year and developed a friendly rapport with her colleagues. She explained to me that two heterosexual female colleagues regularly described to her their weekends flirting with different men in pubs and bars. Kelly eventually decided to tell them about her night flirting with a woman in a lesbian bar and was 'shocked' by their facial and verbal expressions of disgust. It was not Kelly's sexuality that was reacted to unfavourably but her challenge to heterosexual norms around emotions and feelings. Her colleagues' stories relied on acts, gestures, emotions and feelings that adhered to heterosexual norms thus contributing to the heterosexualization of the workplace. Kelly's story, however, ruptured this space. So she intervened in her colleagues' 'surprise' and disgust and suppressed her own 'shock' and 'upset' by employing surface acting. She calmly responded to them

> Every weekend you guys go out and . . . try and pull . . . and I don't say anything about what I think. Why is it so gross that I might snog a woman? . . . I might think it gross to snog men all the time and I don't say anything, I don't go "ERRR! That's really gross" like a 5-year-old.
>
> (Kelly)

Like Sujata, Kelly frequently performed emotion work to maintain and (re)create an emotionally balanced working atmosphere for her colleague's sake and her own when similar conversations occurred at work.

Lesbians often hide their sexuality and pass as heterosexual in the streets (Green 1997; Valentine 1993a, 1993b), and the performance of surface acting helps to conceal emotions that would otherwise challenge heterosexual norms, as expressed to me by Megan (white Irish, lesbian, aged late twenties):

> [Lesbians] make so many allowances for straight people all the time. We don't hold hands on the road, we don't kiss in front of them, we don't snog in front of them, we don't talk about our relationship. I mean so many [lesbians] don't talk about their relationship for fear of embarrassing other [people], making other people feel awkward.
>
> (Megan)

This contrasts with Megan's one-off story about kissing her girlfriend outside a busy pub and being cheered on by some male punters. The act of two (in this case drunken) women kissing did not necessarily rupture the hetero-sexualized street because of the multiple ways in which it could be read. Megan's and her girlfriend's feelings and emotions were not read by the onlookers as being directed solely to each other but as transferable to heterosexual men.[4] However, when performers believe their emotional behaviour might be read as challenging heterosexual norms, they may also feel other emotions:

> [My girlfriend and I] now openly hug . . . have standing hugs in the middle of Tottenham Court Road and occasionally kiss each other as we're saying 'Bye', don't snog or whatever, and yet every time I split

from her I have this fleeting [thought] 'Shit! Is anyone ready to beat me
up on the street for doing that?'

(Rekha)

Rekha's feelings of love and affection for her girlfriend were entwined with fear and
anxiety of not being read as heterosexual by homophobic onlookers, and reminded
her of not adhering to heterosexualized feeling rules in the street. This is not to
suggest that same-sex couples can never feel or express love free of fear or anxiety
but that heterosexualized feeling rules means that such entwined emotions are
likely to occur among those who challenge these rules. In order for Rekha and her
girlfriend to remain safe from external forms of homophobia their emotions were
not to be read as rupturing the heterosexualized space. So rather than kissing
passionately they hugged, perhaps like sisters or best friends. '[T]he identity of
those present in a space, and thus the identity of the space being produced, can
sometimes be constructed by the gaze of others present rather than the performers'
(Valentine 1996: 149). Thus, spaces are not necessarily sexualized only by physical
behaviour, but by the reading of emotions attached to those bodily acts by
onlookers. Identities and emotions may not be recognized correctly by onlookers
and in neither Rekha's nor Megan's case were they knowingly under increased
threat from homophobic attack. Yet, the uncertainty of the possible readings means
that lesbians rarely overtly express their sexuality physically or emotionally in
everyday public places. [. . .]

References

Burrell, G. and Hearn, J. (1989) Sexuality of organisation, in Hearn, J., Sheppard, D.L.,
    Tancred-Sheriff, P. and Burrell, G. (eds) *Sexuality of Organisation*. London: Sage,
    pp. 1–27.
Elwood, S.A. (2000) Lesbian living spaces: multiple meanings of home, in Valentine, G.
    (ed.) *From Nowhere to Everywhere: Lesbian Geographies*. New York: Harrington Park
    Press, pp. 11–27.
Green, S.F. (1997) *Urban Amazons: Lesbian Feminism and Beyond in the Gender, Sexuality and
    Identity Battles of London*. London: Macmillan.
Halford, S. and Leonard P. (2001) *Gender, Power and Organisations*. Basingstoke: Palgrave.
Hall, M. (1989) Private experiences in the public domain: lesbians in organisations,
    in Hearn, J., Sheppard, L., Tancred-Sheriff, P. and Burrell, G. (eds) *The Sexuality
    of Organisation*. London: Sage, pp. 125–138.
Johnston, L. and Valentine, G. (1995) Wherever I lay my girlfriend, that's my home:
    the performance and surveillance of lesbian identities in domestic environments,
    in Bell, D. and Valentine, G. (eds) *Mapping Desire: Geographies of Sexualities*.
    London: Routledge, pp. 99–113.
McDowell, L. (1995) Body work: heterosexual gender performances in city work-
    places, in Bell, D. and Valentine, G. (eds) *Mapping Desire: Geographies of Sexualities*.
    London: Routledge, pp. 75–95.
Schneider, B. (1984) Peril and promise: lesbians' workplace participation, in Nardi,
    P.M. and Schneider, B.E. (1998) (eds) *Social Perspectives in Lesbian and Gay Studies: A
    Reader*. London: Routledge, pp. 377–389.

Valentine, G. (1993a) (Hetero)sexing space: lesbian perceptions and experiences of everyday spaces, *Environment and Planning D: Society and Space* 11: 395–413.

Valentine, G. (1993b) Negotiating and managing multiple sexual identities: lesbian time-space strategies, *Transactions of the Institute of British Geographers* 18: 237–248.

Valentine, G. (1996) (Re)negotiating the 'heterosexual street': lesbian production of space, in Duncan, N. (ed.) *BodySpace: Destabilizing Geographies of Gender and Sexuality*. London: Routledge, pp. 146–155.

Witz, A., Halford, S. and Savage, M. (1996) Organised bodies: gender, sexuality and embodiment in contemporary organisations, in Adkins, L. and Merchant, V. (eds) *Sexualising the Social: Power and the Organisation of Sexuality*. Basingstoke: Macmillan, pp. 173–189.

Chapter 23

Mimi Sheller

AUTOMOTIVE EMOTIONS

Feeling the car

C ARS ELICIT A WIDE RANGE of feelings: the pleasures of driving, the outburst of 'road rage', the thrill of speed, the security engendered by driving a 'safe' car and so on. They also generate intensely emotional politics in which some people passionately mobilize to 'stop the traffic' and 'reclaim the streets', while others vociferously defend their right to cheap petrol. Cars are above all machines that move people, but they do so in many senses of the word. Recent approaches to the phenomenology of car-use have highlighted 'the driving body' as a set of social practices, embodied dispositions, and physical affordances (Sheller and Urry, 2000; Dant and Martin, 2001; Edensor, 2002; Oldrup, 2004; Dant, 2004; Thrift, 2004). More encompassing approaches to the anthropology of material cultures have also resituated the car as a social-technical 'hybrid' (Michael, 2001; Miller, 2001a).[1] This article builds both on this work and on recent approaches in the sociology of emotions (Hochschild, 1983, 1997, 2003; Bendelow and Williams, 1998; Katz, 2000; Goodwin et al., 2001; Ahmed, 2004) to explore the ways in which the 'dominant culture of automobility' (Urry, 2000) is implicated in a deep context of affective and embodied relations between people, machines and spaces of mobility and dwelling, in which emotions and the senses play a key part.

Social commentators have long addressed the problem of car cultures in an explicitly normative manner concerned with the restitution of 'public goods' (the environemnt, human health, the social fabric of cities, democratic public cultures) that have been eroded by contemporary car and road systems (Jacobs, 1961; Nader, 1965; Sennett, 1990; Kunstler, 1994; Dunn, 1998). At stake in such debates is not simply the future of the car, but the future of the entire 'car culture' (and wider transportation system) in what might be characterized as 'societies of automobility' in which the 'coercive freedom' of driving shapes both public and private spaces of all scales and kinds (Sheller and Urry, 2000; Urry, 2004). Yet most practical efforts at promoting more 'ethical' forms of car consumption have been debated and implemented as if the intense feelings, passions and embodied experiences associated with automobility were not relevant.

Car cultures have social, material and above all affective dimensions that are overlooked in current strategies to influence car-driving decisions. The individual-istic 'rational choice' model, which is so influential as to be taken for granted in transportation policy debates, distorts our understanding of how people (and their feelings) are embedded in historically sedimented and geographically etched patterns of 'quotidian mobility' (Kaufman, 2000). Paying attention to the emo-tional constituents of car cultures, however, need not imply resorting to black-box causal explanations such as the popular yet ill-defined notions of 'automobile addiction' or a 'love affair' with the car (Motavalli, 2001). New approaches both to car cultures and to emotional cultures can aid us in shifting attention away from the counter-factual 'rational actor' who supposedly makes carefully reasoned economic choices, and towards the lived experience of dwelling with cars in all of its complexity, ambiguity and contradiction. [. . .]

Feeling the car

[. . .] Pleasure, fear, frustration, euphoria, pain, envy: emotional responses to cars and feelings about driving are crucial to the personal investments people have in buying, driving and dwelling with cars. Car manufacturers, of course, manipulate brand desire through the emotional resonance of their advertising campaigns; yet the 'thrill' of driving, the 'joy' of the road, the 'passion' of the collector, the nostalgia for retro designs are not simply lexicons of the advertising imagination. The 'feelings' being generated around cars can be powerful indicators of the emo-tional currents and submerged moral economies of car cultures. This affective relationship with cars is not only about pleasure-seeking, but also feeds into our deepest fears, anxieties and frustrations. The stomach-turning feeling of witnessing a car crash or the terrors and permanent anxiety produced by being in an accident are the dark underside of 'auto-freedom'. The very passions that feed into certain kinds of love for the car or joy in driving may equally elicit opposite feelings of hatred for traffic, rage at other drivers, boredom with the same route or anger at government transport policies (see Michael, 2001 for a discussion of road rage in terms of 'human–non-human hybridity').

An advertising campaign for the Lexus IS200 unsurprisingly proclaims: 'It's the feeling inside'. Emphasizing the leather seats, the automatic climate control and the digital audio system, the text makes clear that this slogan refers both to the 'feel' of the car interior and the feeling it produces inside the body that dwells within the car. The feel of the car, both inside and outside, moving or stationary, sensuously shapes and materially projects how motorists feel not only about cars but also about themselves and within themselves. These concerns can be traced back to Roland Barthes' reading of the mythology of the Citroen DS, in which he recognized the materiality of this particular car as marking a shift in the dominant car culture. Writing of the magic and spirituality of its lighter, less aggressive design, he describes a clear cultural shift from 'an alchemy of speed to a *gourmandise* of driving' (Barthes, 1957: 152). [. . .]

Of course, viewing cars as prosthetic extensions of drivers' bodies and fantasy worlds (Freund, 1993: 99; Brandon, 2002: 401–2) is the standard fare not only of motor shows and advertising, but also of youth cultures, pin-up calendars, pop lyrics and hip-hop videos. The 'love affair' with the car (Motavalli, 2001; Sachs, 2002), its sexualization as 'wife' or lover (Miller, 1997 [1994]: 238), suggests a kind of libidinal economy around the car, in which particular models become objects of desire to be collected and cosseted, washed and worshipped. Whether phallic or feminized, the car materializes personality and takes part in the ego-formation of the owner or driver as competent, powerful, able and sexually desirable. [. . .]

Being (in) the car

> It felt alive beneath my hands, some metal creature bred for wind and speed. . . . It ran like the wind. I ran like the wind. It was as though I became the car, or the car became me, and which was which didn't matter anymore.
>
> (Lesley Hazleton cited in Mosey, 2000: 186)

Macnaghten and Urry argue that there are ambivalent and contested 'affordances' that 'stem from the reciprocity between the environment and the organism, deriving from how people are kinaesthetically active within their world' (2000: 169; see also Costall, 1995). Driving can be included among the active corporeal engagements of human bodies with the 'sensed' world. Like other modes of mobility, such as walking, bicycling or riding trains, modes of driving also arise out of 'a specific time and place, and they have often developed in contrast to each other. They tend to have a history of both gendering and class' (Lofgren, 1999: 49). Driving, then, suggests many different kinds of affordances between varied bodies, cars and spaces. [. . .] For some the motion produces feelings of happiness, excite-ment or anticipation; others become fearful, anxious or sick to the stomach. These feelings are neither located solely within the person nor produced solely by the car as a moving object, but occur as a circulation of affects between (different) persons, (different) cars, and historically situated car cultures and geographies of automobility.

In what sense might we have 'embodied dispositions' towards the feeling of driving? At 6 weeks old my baby already expresses an excited anticipation of car rides. As I place her in the car seat (while still in the house) her countenance brightens and she looks around in expectation. As I fasten the seat into the back of the car she turns her face toward the window and looks expectantly for the show to begin as the car moves. During a ride she watches the window intently for as long as she can, until lulled to sleep. It is clear that many infants take pleasure in the kinaesthetic experience of the car ride, and develop an early orientation towards four-wheeled mobility within a car culture that soon enables them to play with toy cars, ride on child-sized cars, and learn to identify different kinds and brands of motor vehicles by the age of 2 years. At the same time, this seemingly 'instinctual' disposition is tightly coupled with a very particular car culture in which any moving vehicle is an extremely high-risk environment for children, shot through with legal interventions. The parent who places their infant in a car seat is faced with a warning of dire consequences (written in 11 languages in Europe): 'DO NOT place rear facing child seat on front seat with airbag. DEATH OR SERIOUS INJURY can occur.' This warning is an unnerving yet routine reminder of the need to cultivate a precise driving disposition oriented towards defensiveness, safety and security. Installing the child and the seat in the car correctly induces a sense of having taken security measures; it is a self-discipline that makes parents *feel* better about being in the car, as discussed in the following section on family cars and caring practices.[2]

Motion and emotion, we could say, are kinaesthetically intertwined and produced together through a conjunction of bodies, technologies and cultural practices (that are always historically and geographically located). Drawing on the research of Jack Katz on drivers in Los Angeles, Thrift suggests that we should:

> . . . understand driving (and passengering) as both profoundly embodied and sensuous experiences, though of a particular kind, which 'requires and occasions a metaphysical merger, an intertwining of the identities of the driver and car that generates a distinctive ontology in the form of a person-thing, a humanized car or, alternatively, an auto-mobilized person' (Katz, 2000: 33) in which the identity of person and car kinaesthetically intertwine.
>
> (Thrift, 2004: 46–7)

Human bodies physically respond to the thrum of an engine, the gentle glide through a gearbox, or the whoosh of effortless acceleration, and in some cases the driver becomes 'one' with the car (as in the quotation at the start of this section). Different emotional registers are produced through the variations in the embodied driving experience, which also have national variations. Some feel content with a smooth and silent ride (historically aligned with ideas of luxury, privilege and wealth), others prefer an all-wheel drive that shakes the bones and fills the nostrils with diesel and engine oil (historically aligned with ideas of adventure, masculinity and challenge). Although people also have 'embodied dispositions' towards walking, bicycling or riding a horse, it is the ways in which these dispositions become 'culturally sedimented', as Thrift puts it, that matter.[3] [. . .]

Today a further key change in the embodied feeling of cars is due to developments in digital control of the car and in mobile information technologies, which further transform the very ways in which we 'sense' the world. There is growing emphasis on the integration of information and communication technologies into the car (especially luxury cars), leading to a lacing of technologies of mobility with capacities for conversation, entertainment and information access (Sheller, 2004). Many aspects involved in directing the car as a machine have been computerized, while, simultaneously, car-dwellers have been insulated from the risky and dangerous environments through which they pass, seemingly protected by seatbelts, airbags, 'crumple zones', 'roll bars' and 'bull bars'. Features such as automatic gearboxes, cruise control, voice-activated entry and ignition, GPS-navigation, digital music systems and hands-free mobile phones all 'free' drivers from direct manipulation of the machinery, while embedding them more deeply in its sociality, producing what might be described as a 'cybercar' (Sheller and Urry, 2000, 2004; Sheller, 2004).[4]

The marketing of so-called 'smart' cars emphasizes not only their smaller size but also their enhanced capabilities for information or entertainment in congested urban areas, which will increasingly be designed as 'intelligent environments'.[5] [. . .]

Family cars, caring and kinship

[. . .] A key overlooked aspect of car cultures is the emotional investments people have in the relationships between the car, the self, family and friends, creating affective contexts that are also deeply materialized in particular types of vehicles, homes, neighbourhoods and cities. A recent advertising campaign for the Toyota Yaris points out that, 'You could end up loving it too much'; the Yaris is then shown in a variety of absurd yet believable social scenarios in which love is taken a bit too far (receiving postcards, being treated to a candle-lit bath, monopolizing a huge empty garage, etc.). Clearly cars have been deeply integrated into the affective networks of familial life and domestic spaces, as well as friendship networks and public sociability. As Simon Maxwell argues, policy discussions have neglected the 'positive social frames of meaning of car use associated with care and love for immediate others, as well as care for others within wider social networks' (Maxwell, 2001: 217–18). He finds that 'there are plural ethics associated with car use in everyday life, and intense negotiations between these ethical stances' (2001: 212). Such frames of meaning and ethics generate some of the feeling rules that govern the emotional cultures of car use, in which needs to manage personal identity, familial relationships, and sociability can easily override any ethical qualms about driving.

For example, driving offers many people a feeling of liberation, empowerment and social inclusion, while inability to drive may lead to feelings of social exclusion and disempowerment in cultures of automobility. A study of young suburban drivers in Britain suggests that 'the car is part of patterns of sociability' and the anticipation of new possibilities for such sociability generates 'an extraordinary and exciting moment of consumption' for young drivers (Carrabine and Longhurst, 2002: 192–3). In a large-scale survey study of the expressive dimensions of car use among English drivers, Stephen Stradling found that feelings of projection, pride, power, self-expression or independence, vary by age, class and gender: 'different kinds of persons obtain different kinds of psychological benefit from car use. Driving a car is particularly attractive to the young and the poor because of the sense of displayed personal identity it conveys' (Stradling et al., 2001; Stradling, 2002: 11). Along similar lines, Gilroy suggests that African-American flamboyant public use of cars makes up for feelings of status injury and material deprivation through 'compensatory prestige' (Gilroy, 2001: 94). [. . .]

Notes

1   The concept of hybridity has a complex history which ranges from colonial theories of race (Young, 1995) to debates about diasporic identities and multi-culturalism (Werbner and Modood, 1997) and the human–nonhuman hybrids

of studies of technoscience (Haraway, 1997), actor-network theory (Law and Hassard, 1999) and critical geography (Whatmore, 2002). This is not the place to discuss fully the implications of this theoretical genealogy, but it is worth noting that the discourse of hybridity is a powerful one within techno-cultures of automobility and is itself in need of careful analysis vis-à-vis its effects of denaturalization and renaturalization.

2   In other car cultures a blessing or a hidden charm might serve the same function of making the occupants of a vehicle feel they have taken appropriate safety precautions (see Verrips and Meyer, 2001 on protecting cars from witchcraft and ghosts in Ghana). Recent research carried out for the AA Motoring Trust suggests that up to two-thirds of child car seats used in the UK are in any case installed incorrectly thus providing little protection in accidents (http://www.aatrust.com/news/release_view.cfm?id=621).

3   Thus it is argued that electric motor vehicles and cars with fuel cells or hybrid power sources will have to *feel like* conventional cars and to deliver the same pleasures of driving: quick acceleration, speeds over 65 mph, and the capacity to drive at least 350 miles without recharging (Motavalli, 2001). It is for this reason that General Motors' electric EV-1 and Ford's Think are thought to have failed (Apcar, 2002; Duffy, 2002).

4   The Toyota/Sony Pod concept car even promises that it will:

> . . . measure your pulse and perspiration levels to gauge your stress levels. If you are becoming aggressive it will calm you with cool air and soothing music. It will even warn other drivers about your mental state by changing the colour of the strip-lights on the bonnet!
>
> (*RAC Magazine*, 2002: 14–15)

5   Such developments were already prefigured in the subcultures of car customization critized by Paul Gilroy (2001: 98–9), which produced 'road monsters' such as the GM Chevrolet Suburban 'macked out' with TV, video library, temperature controlled cup holders, digital compass and thermometer, invisible speakers in soundproof walls and a satellite-controlled security system.

References

Ahmed, S. (2004) *The Cultural Politics of Emotion*. Edinburgh: Edinburgh University Press.

Bendelow, G. and S. Williams (eds) (1998) *Emotions in Social Life: Critical Themes and Contemporary Issues*. London: Routledge.

Brandon, R. (2002) *Auto Mobile: How the Car Changed Life*. Basingstoke and Oxford: Macmillan.

Carrabine, E. and B. Longhurst (2002) 'Consuming the Car: Anticipation, Use and Meaning in Contemporary Youth Culture', *Sociological Review* 50(2): 181–96

Costall, A. (1995) 'Socializing Affordances', *Theory & Psychology* 5: 467–81.

Dant, T. (2004) 'The Driver-car', *Theory, Culture & Society* 21(4/5): 61–79.

Dant, T. and P. Martin (2001) 'By Car: Carrying Modern Society', in A. Warde and J. Grunow (eds) *Ordinary Consumption*. London: Harwood.

Dunn, J. (1998) *Driving Forces*. Washington, DC: Brookings Institution Press.

Edensor, T. (2002) 'Material Culture and National Identity', in *National Identities in Popular Culture*. Oxford and New York: Berg.

Freund, P. (1993) *The Ecology of the Automobile*. Montreal and New York: Black Rose Books.

Gilroy, P. (2001) 'Driving while Black', in D. Miller (ed.) *Car Cultures*. Oxford: Berg.

Goodwin, J., J. Jasper and F. Polletta (2001) *Passionate Politics: Emotions and Social Movements*. Chicago, IL and London: University of Chicago Press.

Hochschild, A.R. (1983) *The Managed Heart: Commercialization of Human Feeling*. Berkeley: University of California Press. Reprint, with new afterword, Berkeley: University of California Press, 2003.

Hochschild, A.R. (1997) *The Time Bind: When Work Becomes Home and Home Becomes Work*. New York: Metropolitan Books.

Hochschild, A.R. (2003) *The Commercialization of Intimate Life: Notes from Home and Work*. Berkeley: University of California Press.

Jacobs, J. (1961) *The Death and Life of Great American Cities*. New York: Random House.

Katz, J. (2000) *How Emotions Work*. Chicago, IL: University of Chicago Press.

Kaufman, V. (2000) *Mobilité quotidienne et dynamiques urbaines: la question du report modal*. Lausanne: Presses Polytechniques et Universitaires Romandes.

Kunstler, J. (1994) *The Geography of Nowhere: The Rise and Decline of America's Man-made Landscape*. New York: Touchstone Books.

Lofgren, O. (1999) *On Holiday: A History of Vacationing*. Berkeley and London: University of California Press.

Macnaghten, P. and J. Urry (2000) 'Bodies in the Woods', Special Issue 'Bodies of Nature', eds P. Macnaghten and J. Urry, *Body & Society* 6(3–4): 166–82.

Maxwell, S. (2001) 'Negotiations of Car Use in Everyday Life', in D. Miller (ed.) *Car Cultures*. Oxford: Berg.

Michael, M. (2001) 'The Invisible Car: The Cultural Purification of Road Rage', in D. Miller (ed.) *Car Cultures*. Oxford: Berg.

Miller, D. (1997 [1994]) *Modernity, An Ethnographic Approach: Dualism and Mass Consumption in Trinidad*. Oxford and New York: Berg.

Miller, D. (ed) (2001a) *Car Cultures*. Oxford: Berg.

Motavalli, J. (2001) *Forward Drive: The Race to Build 'Clean' Cars for the Future*. San Francisco, CA: Sierra Club Books.

Nader, R. (1965) *Unsafe at Any Speed: The Designer-In Dangers of the American Automobile*. New York: Grossman.

Oldrup, H. (2004) 'From Time-out to Self-control: Stories and Imagination of Automobility', PhD Thesis Series, Institute of Sociology, University of Copenhagen, Denmark.

Sachs, W. (2002) *For Love of the Automobile. Looking Back into the History of Our Desires*. Berkeley: University of California Press.

Sennett, R. (1990) *The Conscience of the Eye: Design and Social Life in Cities*. London: Faber and Faber.

Sheller, M. (2004) 'Mobile Publics: Beyond the Network Perspective', *Environment and Planning D: Society and Space* 22(1): 39–52.

Sheller, M. and J. Urry (2000) 'The City and the Car', *International Journal of Urban and Regional Research* 24: 737–57.

Sheller, M. and J. Urry (2004) 'The City and the Cybercar', pp. 167–72 in S. Graham (ed.) *The Cybercities Reader*. London and New York: Routledge.

Stradling, S. (2002) 'Persuading People Out of Their Cars', Presented to the ESRC

Mobile   Network,   http://www.its.leeds.ac.uk/projects/mobilenetwork/ mobilenet-work.html (accessed 15 May 2003).

Stradling, S.G., M.L. Meadows and S. Beatty (2001) 'Identity and Independence: Two Dimensions of Driver Autonomy', in G.B. Grayson (ed.) *Behavioural Research in Road Safety*. Crowthorne: Transport Research Laboratory.

Thrift, N. (2004) '*Driving* in the City', *Theory, Culture & Society* 21(4/5): 41–59.

Urry, J. (2000) *Sociology beyond Societies: Mobilities for the Twenty-first Century*. London and New York: Routledge.

Urry, J. (2004) 'The "System" of Automobility', *Theory, Culture & Society* 21(4/5): 25–39.

Chapter 24

Ben Anderson

DOMESTIC GEOGRAPHIES OF AFFECT

[. . .]

Feeling the making of a judgement

MAKING A JUDGEMENT IS AN ever-present part of those intimate encounters with the materialities of recorded music that frame, and enliven, a range of public and private space-times.

To begin to attune to how such practices of judgement emerge from within the day to day lives of specific homes I want to divert into the first event. Dennis, a 41-year-old engineer who lives with his partner and daughter, describes in a diary extract returning home from work on a weekday evening and making a series of judgments about what music to listen to.

> Got home from work—decided to play some music for a while before putting on supper—Jenny was busy in the garden so had some time to myself. Put on this album of folk songs but turned them off—didn't feel right. Skipped it forward to this one with a great melody, difficult to describe what it did—guess it energized me a bit, really like that song. Decided to flick onto the radio—heard some shit song on Radio Two so switched that off. End up listening to a brilliant album by a Modern artist James Green which is good for taking away the stress and making tea to: it moves about.
>
> (Listening diary extract: punctuation unchanged)

Dennis and I listen to the music described in the diary extract during a joint interview several days later:

> I played this, you know I'd been feeling a bit tired, long day at work we had loads of orders . . . and it'd tired me out so I needed something to boost me up. This song is good for that loads of . . . ummm . . . energy.

We listen to the end of the song. Dennis then switches the CD.

> I wouldn't normally play this but for some reason it, I was in a good
> mood as I was making tea and this makes me laugh and just . . . you
> know helped lighten the mood even more and get on and enjoy being at
> home after work.
>
> ('Listening-with', 17 December 2000)

Dennis hints at the presence of numerous practices of judgement that each serve to
create a set of (dis)connections between himself and the different music he heard/
listened to. Initially, on returning home, music is played and then turned off. It does
not *'feel right'*. He then skips forward to a different song and sings along. This
'energizes' him. Dissatisfied with the next song he switches to the radio. This is
turned off and he mentions how much he dislikes a song he had just heard. Finally,
he settles on an album because it *'is good for taking away the stress and making tea to'*.
Practices of judgement are here bound up with thought-imbued *feelings and emotions*
that enact the inscription, or modification, of value to a range of music. It is this
form of spontaneous immediate judgement, mixed into the incorporeal-
corporealities of the body, that is most critical to understanding how judgement is
of everyday life. Feeling a song in evaluative terms is not based on an already
decided preference, or taste, but instead is bodied-forth without deliberation from
within the 'immediacy of a given situation' (Varela 1999: 9). Making a judgement
does, of course, extend out from the immediate now into incipient feelings that
remember both latencies of what-has-been and tendencies of what has not-yet
come to be. It is also embedded in the more distanced circulations that fold
together to make up specific 'everyday lives': in the above case Dennis returns
home and prepares for an evening meal.

Feeling a judgement, embodying an evaluative stance that produces value,
therefore works through a number of proximate modifications of the body. In the
case of Dennis one song is, in his words, *'pretty boring, it's just slow . . . doesn't move
me'*. This change in the sense of movement folds into an effect in the visceral
register. The music comes to *'feel souless'*. It does not touch him. Given the proviso
that choice, and judgement, must always occur *from within* the patterns of 'everyday
life', we can specify that recorded music becomes entangled within the space-time
of the home through types of 'mundane metamorphosis' that emerge in 'responsive
recognition of the invisible dimensions that ground routine social interaction'
(Katz 1999: 323). These are passages in conduct specific to the movements of 'daily
life' that, in Katz's (1999: 335) words, are based on 'a sensual turning of one's
attention to regions of the body that, outside of one's own direct awareness, had
been employed to construct behavior'. Examples from this case include a side-
perception of a need to *'to take away the stress'* or *'to be energized'*. Bonds are therefore formed, responsively, from within a given situation between the materialities
of music and the body. This 'turning in' to an awareness of the body takes a number
of different forms and possesses a range of different forces. Each metamorphosis
is bound to, and emerges out of, the demands of the here and now. Music is
thereafter encountered, and judged, as 'appropriate' only if it 'promises' to create,
in Spinoza's term, 'good encounters'. In the above case music 'fits' with 'everyday

life' because it allows an augmentation: it gives energy or a boost (see Deleuze 1988).

Negative judgements, in comparison to the relations of agreement between the materialities of music and his body that Dennis describes, occur due to the lack of match between the materialities of music and the manner in which 'as emotions ebb and flow in experience, the person is absorbed into and withdraws from given regions and features of the world' (Katz 1999: 335). The conversations, periods of playing music together and more formalized interviews, were frequently enlivened with evaluative practices of talk that expressed a diminishing relation with music a diminishment that follows from the principle that 'when a body "encounters" another body, or an idea another idea, it happens that the two relations sometime combine to form a more powerful whole, and sometimes one decomposes the other, destroying the cohesion of its parts' (Deleuze 1988: 19).

To describe this process of decomposition we divert into a second example of how judgement is feeling-imbued. Below is an extract in which Jenny, Dennis's partner, discusses the event above. She listens to music that enables a 'pleasant' environment. Jenny and I have been talking about the music we dislike. She begins to talk about her husband's love of 'discordant' music, how she feels at times when he plays it, and what music she does 'like':

> Jenny: I don't like much of the modern stuff . . . like . . . well I don't know . . . I don't know what you'd call it even, and I don't like . . . modern composers either actually . . . it's too discordant, I don't like the odd squeaks and bangs and . . .

> Ben: no no, that's what I was going to ask you . . . you like tunes (yeah) and you like . . .

> Jenny: yes I like something that makes me feel nice and discordant sounds don't. Like Dennis' music that he had on yesterday when he got back from work . . . I mean I'm a bit of a nervous soul anyway . . . I mean, I jump when the phone rings . . . so . . . all . . . odd . . . noises . . . they [shivers and screws face up]

> Ben: they . . . make you . . .?

> Jenny: nervous . . . YES, makes me very uncomfortable, don't like it at all . . . I feel really on edge . . . unsettles me, I don't like . . . being unsettled, I like . . . calm, having a nice calm level.
> (Individual interview, 19 December 2000)

In a separate interview Dennis expresses how his judgement contrasts with Jenny's talk of the music he described in the previous diary extract and Jenny describes above:

> I guess I listened to that then because . . . well I'd had a dull day at work and wanted to liven things up a bit . . . I like the way it moves you

around loads . . . like you don't know what's coming next . . . it just
like . . . it's exciting and interesting . . . you keep noticing it.

('Listening-with', 17 December 2000)

Both positive and negative judgements about the relation between music and the
immediate situation begin from the same place: the affection of music, as sound, on
the (im)-material body by virtue of the enveloping function of the senses. Jenny
describes how she judges the 'fit' of music through embodied affections. She dislikes Dennis's music because it induces an '*uncomfortable*' background emotion that
leaves her '*unsettled*'. Negative judgements begin from such diminishments, i.e. a
real change in the distribution of intensities that works on and through the bodies of
those transformed. In contrast, for Dennis, functioning to alleviate a 'dulled' body,
the materialities of the same music resonate with a re-intensification of 'everyday
life': '*it's exciting and interesting . . . you keep noticing it*'.

The most common types of judgement that establish a disconnection with
music are those near constant practices of not-choosing a song, or album, because it
does not 'fit' or 'match' the immediate situation: so Dennis, for example, does not
choose music that does not enable him to '*lighten the mood . . . and enjoy being at home
after work*'. These practices of judgement co-exist with other practices of judgement
that by contrast involved deliberately choosing-not-to listen to a defined genre of
music or named artists/bands. Each participant, for example, could name a certain
genre of music that they would never listen to. Only occasionally, in response to
certain proximate affections, do practices of judgement take the form of such a
judgement-over music that is expressed in the act of naming music as 'good' or
'bad'. Key to such an encounter is that a relation is produced in which the affection
of music, and the dynamics of the situation, are felt to summon listening as an
event of judgement-over. Negative judgements-over music, rather than simply
not-choosing music, were notably bound up with the production of a range of
affects that act to enable distinction by expressing a relation that is suspended or
cut. Note, for example, the irritation that is expressed through Jenny's talk of the
'*discordant sounds*' of '*modern music*' or the indifference that animates Dennis' talk of
'*shit music*'. [. . .]

References

Deleuze, G. (1988) *Spinoza: Practical Philosophy*, trans. Hurley, R. San Francisco: City
   Lights Books.
Katz, J. (1999) *How Emotions Work*. Chicago: Chicago University Press.
Varela, F. (1999) *Ethical Know-how: Action, Wisdom, and Cognition*. Stanford, CA: Stanford
   University Press.

6. Emotions and health

THERE IS A long history of research on emotion in connection to various aspects of health and disease. As is the case for the study of emotion more generally, the contribution of social scientists to this field is relatively recent. It is beyond the scope of this volume to review the diversity of medical, psychiatric and psychological approaches to the relation between emotions and health. It is worth mentioning, however, that these have ranged widely. At one end of the spectrum we find experimental research on the psychophysiology of stress and immune responses (e.g. Vedhara and Irwin 2005; Evans *et al.* 2000); at the other end we find psycho-analytic approaches, informing hypotheses on organic disease as the affect-mediated expression of symbolic meanings (e.g. Chiozza 1998; Anzieu 1989). As we stressed in our introduction, there is no single uncontested way of constructing emotion: the medical, psychiatric, and psychological research in this sub-field reflects the diversity of meanings associated with the concept of 'emotion' itself. Important variations are equally evident in how social scientists have approached the connection between emotions and health. The variation occurs along different lines, and reflects different ways of relating to the work of clinical and experimental disciplines. Some social science research offers commentary, critique, and contextualization of medical con-structs (of the role of emotion in health and disease), in the interest of facilitating an understanding of the norms and values these implicitly reflect and promote (e.g. Riska 2000; Greco 2001). Additionally, research by social scientists may seek to complement, and eventually feed into, clinical expertise (e.g. Wilce 2003). The 'critical' and the 'complementary' orientations need not be mutually exclusive, and in many instances researchers in this field have a background in both social and clinical disciplines (e.g. Kleinman and Good 1985; Kleinman 1989). A further way in which social scientists have related to medical research on emotions and health is as a resource for the purpose of developing social theory, in the effort of revising assumptions concerning, for example, what a 'body' is (e.g. Wilson 2004; Lyon 1993). Selecting extracts for this section has been especially difficult in light of the richness, and indeed diversity, of materials available. While we have tried to provide a sense of this diversity through our selections, these should invite readers to explore further afield.

The first extract in this section is from a much cited article by Peter E. Freund, arguing for the relevance of an existential-phenomenological perspective in understanding the link between emotions and health. This article is a relatively early example of the 'affective turn', in the sense that it takes issue with the dichotomy opposing positivism and (social) constructionism as the only epistemological alternatives. Freund argues that sociologists of health and illness have either accepted a biomedical/mechanistic view of bodies, or treated biological and material processes as irrelevant – focusing instead on the study of medical knowledge (or *ideas* about bodies). The sociology of emotion, on the other hand, has been dominated by a 'pure' constructionism resulting in a very disembodied view of human emotions. Freund is also critical of so-called biopsychosocial approaches, in that they 'present very mechanistic . . . and . . . static views of mind, body and society', rather than offering 'textured descriptions of embodied subjectivity and the part played by the whole living body interacting in particular social networks'. In the biopsychosocial literature, attention to the body is characterized by an 'almost exclusive focus on neuro-hormonal activity', at the expense of other aspects of bodilyness, such as movement and facial expression (1990: 455). Against this background, Freund proceeds in this extract to outline some general features of what he calls the 'expressive body'. He defines a new agenda for the sociological study of distressful feelings, society, and health, focusing on key concepts such as those of 'dramaturgical stress' and 'emotional false consciousness'.

Our next selection is from a text by Alan Radley, a pioneer in the study of biographical, narrative and cultural aspects of the illness experience. Radley's text is included here as an example of a now vast body of literature in medical humanities. Already incorporated as an aspect of medical training in many programmes across the US, the UK and Australia, research in this area, broadly speaking, is intended to complement biomedical 'objectivism' through the interpretive analysis of the experience of suffering. Arguably, a longer-term ambition of the field as a whole is to contribute towards a tranformation of medical culture and practice, towards a greater ability to address the emotional components of health and disease processes. The extract included here explores the affective dynamics implicit in visual portrayals of suffering. What is it about certain images of suffering that leads the viewer to turn away? Or, conversely, what types of image succeed in reaching the viewer, and with what consequences? In this extract, Radley argues that the process whereby images of suffering achieve communication, overcoming horror and anxiety, binds the observer and the bearer of suffering into a 'reciprocal loop' that, if communication is successful, is transformative for both. Radley's piece is useful in highlighting how engagement with the affective dimensions of suffering always involves an ethical dimension.

The extract from Wilce and Price is drawn from a volume, edited by Wilce, entitled *Social and Cultural Lives of Immune Systems*. In this book, medical anthopologists engage in a rare form of dialogue with medical researchers in psychoneuroimmunology (PNI), offering a form of critique that is designed to feed into and improve (rather than deconstruct or contextualize) PNI hypotheses on the role of emotions in health and illness. The chapter from which this extract is drawn outlines an agenda for the research of 'local biologies', based on the premise that culturally variable images of bodies and healing are 'variably embodied within and across societies'. Their argument builds on experimental research that has demonstrated the immune-boosting efficacy of guided imagery and/or verbal disclosure, proposing that these interventions, and their effects, enact metaphors that are culturally specific. Contrasting examples are offered from a range of Asian contexts, to suggest that psychoneuroimmunology cannot proceed on the assumption of a 'universal, preconceptual, precultural human body that responds in predictable ways to the "same" emotions, meta-emotions, and behaviors'.

Our next extract is from an article entitled 'Disorders Without Borders? The expanding scope of psychiatric practice', a text that Nikolas Rose originally presented as the 18th Aubrey Lewis Lecture at the Institute of Psychiatry (King's College, London). In this piece Rose examines a number of hypotheses that might account for a seemingly uprecedented expansion in the prevalence of mental disorders (and particularly anxiety disorders, mood disorders, and impulse control disorders) in European and US societies. In an admirably synthetic presentation, Rose considers first the notion that there is simply 'more' mental disorder around today than in previous times; secondly, he considers the proposition that, through developments in psychiatric expertise, we have become better at recognizing existing mental disorder; thirdly, he examines the notion that the 'moral entrepreneurship' of the psychiatric profession may be the reason behind the perception of an increased rate of mental disorder; next, he considers 'today's favourite culprit – "Big Pharma"', and the idea that in pursuing market share, profit and stakeholder value, the industry may be distorting our perception and treatment of mental disorder; finally, Rose presents the case that an increase in the rate of mental disorder may arise from the fact that, in what he calls our 'Age of Freedom', vague discontents that are inherent in the human condition are being reshaped in a psychiatric form. This text is usefully read alongside the one by De Swaan on agoraphobia (see section 1, above).

The final extract in this section, by Elizabeth Wilson, exemplifies one of the ways in which engagement with the (natural) science of emotion can be productive of innovation in social theory. Wilson argues that the anti-biologism that characterizes most contemporary feminist theory has resulted in a premature dismissal of everything 'biological' as individualizing and reductive. In contrast to this orientation, Wilson proposes that 'effective political engagement with the contemporary life sciences requires ongoing intimacy with their data', and that such data holds the potential for rethinking 'conventional models of biological substrate and psychological malady'. Focusing on the example of 'new generation' antidepressants (SSRIs and SNRIs), she demonstrates how these drugs, contrary to the assumption that sees them as targeting the brain as if in a vacuum, actually implicate the whole body. Feminist historians and philosophers of the biosciences have critically claimed that these sciences espouse and reinforce problematic conceptual schemata, in so far as they privilege the centre over the periphery, or draw radical distinctions between (active) agents and (passive) vessels. If this can be said of the neurological and pharmacological sciences, writes Wilson, 'it seems to be despite the data they are generating, not because of them'. In relation to the brain, for example, the data suggest that this organ 'is always, necessarily implicated in relations with other organs and other extra-bodily systems'. Wilson's analysis makes room for the possibility, rarely avowed or explored in the literature, that there may be substantial areas of meta-theoretical compatibility between bio-medical research and approaches traditionally considered very distant from it, such as psychoanalysis.

References

Anzieu, D. (1989) *The Skin Ego*. New Haven, MA: Yale University Press.

Chiozza, L. A. (1998) *Hidden Affects in Somatic Disorders*. Madison, Connecticut: The Psychosocial Press.

Evans, P., Hucklebridge, F. and Clow, A. (eds) (2000) *Mind, Immunity and Health: the science of psychoneuroimmunology*. London: Free Association Books.

Greco, M. (2001) 'Inconspicuous anomalies: "alexithymia" and ethical relations to the self', *Health*, 6 (4): 471–492.

Kleinman, A. and Good, B. (1985) *Culture and Depression: studies in the anthropology and cross-cultural psychiatry of affect and disorder*. Berkeley: University of California Press.

Kleinman, A. (1989) *The Illness Narratives: suffering, healing, and the human condition*. New York: Basic Books.

Lyon, M. (1993) 'Psychoneuroimmunology: the problem of the situatedness of illness and the conceptualization of healing', *Culture, Medicine and Psychiatry*, 17 (1): 77–97.

Riska, E. (2000) 'The rise and fall of Type A man', *Social Science and Medicine*, 51: 1665–74.

Vedhara, K. and Irwin, M. (eds) (2005) *Human Psychoneuroimmunology*. Oxford: Oxford University Press.

Wilce, J. M. (ed) (2003) *Social and Cultural Lives of Immune Systems*. London: Routledge.

Wilson, E. (2004) *Psychosomatic: feminism and the neurological body*. Durham, NC: Duke University Press.

Chapter 25

Peter E. S. Freund

THE EXPRESSIVE BODY

Common ground for the sociology of emotions and health and illness

[. . .]

Emotional modes of being

[. . .] **I**T IS IMPORTANT TO UNDERSTAND that the 'schemata' or 'categories' by which we 'unconsciously' make sense of feeling are not static entities that simply reside in mind. These modes of experiencing feeling originate in the body's encounter with the world – in the same way that much cognition is an outcome of this process.

Johnson (1987) argues that the body is in the mind and that cognition arises out of this bodily experience. While it is the structure or meaning of feeling that come out of the relationship of the actor with existence, these meanings and structures are not to be seen as processes or entities divorced from bodilyness.

The meaning or structures of feelings originate pre-linguistically, though later in life they are refined by symbolic communicative activity. As Johnson notes:

> It is important to see that we are not considering here and how we might talk about our emotions, nor only how we might *conceptualise* our emotional experience. We are also describing the *structure of our experience* of emotions.
>
> (1987:89)

[. . .] The central nervous system in which such patterns are embodied involve an acting body and higher cognitive functions, the limbic and other components of the nervous system and 'mechanisms' that regulate movement. We are able to perceive meaning through a variety of sensory modalities (including proprioception). Information from one modality may at times be transposed to another one

(Dreyfus 1979:249). Thus we have the potential to 'see' voices and 'hear' colours (Merleau-Ponty 1962). [. . .]

The problem of a pure constructionism (or what Johnson [1987] would call 'idealism') or positivism (what he calls 'objectivism') is that they 'both assume that the organism and its environments are two wholly separate things, and then ask *how* the two are related, and which one is responsible for the structure of the world' (Johnson 1987:207). In the case of constructionism, it is disembodied talk and thought; in the case of positivism it is a neurophysiological 'substrate'. Thus the question of what comes first – neurohormonal arousal or the emotional meanings that we experience in environments is somewhat misleading (Buytendijk 1974:173).

A universal experience that accompanies embodiment is a sense of containment. This experience that our bodies are three dimensional containers emerges in our encounters with the external world of objects and persons who resist us, give way, etc.

> From the beginning we experience constant physical containment in our surroundings (those things that envelop us). We move in and out of rooms, clothes, vehicles and numerous kinds of bounded spaces. We manipulate objects, placing them in containers. In each of these cases there are repeatable spatial-temporal organisations. In other words, these are typical schemata for physical containment.
>
> (Johnson 1987:21)

Thus, many of our cognitive schemata emerge out of bodily activities of engaging the environment. Similarly, our ways of apprehending feelings, the basis of emotion, emerge in encounters with others. One might argue that there are *structural* isomorphisms on the level of meaning in our experience of the world of physical *and* social 'objects' (McCarthy 1984).

Initially our encounters with others consist of non-verbal gestures, touching and mirroring the other's expression (ie engaging in activities in which we align our rhythms with the bodily expressiveness of others) (Johnson 1987; Levin 1985). Our experience of physical containment leads us to develop an 'inside-outside' orientation (the degree and quality of this experience will vary historically and socioculturally) (Elias 1978). So gradually our interaction with others also leads us to develop a sense of self and of emotional boundaries that emerge out of others' responsiveness or non-responsiveness. Such experiences form the ground of our sense of ontological security or insecurity (Laing 1965; Levin 1985). Various feelings of bodily emotional and spatial boundedness are the basis of such metaphors as 'I feel vulnerable', 'I feel surrounded by friends', 'I'm touched by your expression of love', or 'I feel smothered by your love'. Feelings can be described in terms of the body's orientation in space, such as in the case of emotional balance. 'I feel on an even keel'. [. . .]

Buytendijk (1950) suggests a number of modes of feeling 'pleasant' or 'unpleasant'. These modes are the outcome of different ongoing conditions of existence. Modes of feeling may be broadly characterised as the experience of either obstructions or expansions in one's existence (in terms of access to the objects of our intention). Being pleased includes being with somebody or something – a felt sense of unity between self and other. It may be felt as a surging outward or movement outward of one's existence and an expansion of self. This mode may also be experienced as a process of assimilating objects outside of oneself.

In contrast, four modes of feeling unpleasant include (1) being thrown back or encountering resistance in one's encounter with others, (2) being subdued, (3) being injured, (4) losing a part of oneself, or abandoning all or a part of oneself.

In effect, these are different felt ways of feeling empowered or disempowered. These feelings are very much related to the conditions of existence encountered throughout one's biography. 'External' social structural factors such as one's position in different systems of hierarchy or various forms of social control can influence the conditions of our existence, how we respond and apprehend these conditions and our sense of embodied self. These conditions can also affect our physical functioning (Freund 1982).

Embodied subjectivity and physiological functioning

[. . .] Emotions are always in some ways embodied. It is one thing to argue that it is not essential for an emotion to be accompanied by 'felt' psychophysical sensations and quite another to argue that moods and emotional states do not have bodily accompaniments (Buytendijk 1974: 188).

The body may express emotions or emotionality through neurohormonal, musculo-skeletal physiological changes or through those aspects of bodilyness that involve exchanges of nutrients and other substances with the external environment (eg breathing). Altered neuro-hormonal reactivity, an inability to return to a state of rest or equilibrium, might affect blood pressure, coronary arteries, cholesterol levels and perhaps the immune system. Muscular tension and postural accompaniments might facilitate or aggravate orthopedic problems. Anxiety and related irregularities in patterns of respiration could amplify respiratory problems.

> A person may express a subliminal grasp of the world as overpowering, the self as inadequate before it, by assuming a stooped body posture. Years later the chronic back problems that result come before an orthopedic surgeon. Another body takes up the classic post of fight or flight in a stressful office situation. Over time the internal hypermobility leads to gastritis, high blood pressure, perhaps a heart attack. The over-secretion of acid, the construction of an artery exhibits the expressiveness of bodily movement no less than motions externally manifested.
>
> (Leder 1984:39)

Many of these paths for expression are being studied in bio-psychosocial research. Yet even these 'holistic' positivist approaches 'find themselves leaping from one level of discourse to another, describing the cortical-epinephrine pathways at one moment, the next the beneficial effects of spiritual belief' (Leder 1984:38–39).

[. . .]

Since the body is a means of expressing meaning, including socio-cultural meanings, it is not unrealistic to suppose that people might express somatically the conditions of their existence. Pain, for instance, can express a sense of an existence that weighs heavily on one or a sense of powerlessness. Kleinman defines somatisation (the expression of painful existence somatically) as 'the communication of personal and interpersonal problems in a physical idiom of distress and a pattern of behaviour that emphasizes seeking medical help' (1988:57). The fact that somatisation is the body's way of saying something about life doesn't mean that there aren't many ways to say the same thing 'physically'. Cultural (as one of many) factors can shape the language of the body. A perspective which argues that we can somaticise social-emotional existence does not necessarily lead to a specificity theory of psychosomatics (eg Alexander 1950). Emotional responses to maternal rejection in early childhood will not necessarily be expressed as asthma, and may not be physically expressed at all. [. . .]

Social status, control and physiology

There are no conditions that universally and automatically 'elicit' specific emotional responses. Individuals respond to situations on the basis of individual and cultural appraisals of 'what is going on'. There are, however, a number of social structural features that contribute to the *likelihood* that situations will evoke 'pleasant' or 'unpleasant' emotional modes of being. One's position in a system of social hierarchy and the activities involved in insuring social control are two features of social structure that influence feelings. These features may influence our physiology as well (Freund 1982).

Animal studies (and a few human ones) show an interplay between social structural position and patterns of neuro-hormonal reactivity or levels of neuro-transmitters such as serotonin (Freund 1988; Kemper 1987; Mazur 1985; Madsen 1985; Sapolsky 1982). A 'top banana' shows a different pattern of reacting to stress than a low status animal. [. . .]

A study by Madsen (1985) claims to distinguish human 'power seekers' (those showing Type A behaviour) from others on the basis of biochemical markers (serotonin levels). Yet, most studies are drawn from animal subjects and involve studying the activity of one chemical. In humans if there are biocultural correlates of status they probably involve complex and more subtle balances between a number of neurohormonal activities that dynamically interact with the individual's self-organising activities (Fausto-Sterling 1985:131). However, should these studies have anything to say about humans, the implications would be that one's position in any system of social hierarchy and the manner in which social relationships are managed both affect (and are affected by) biochemical states and other aspects of bodilyness. Certainly such hypotheses are well worth pursuing. [. . .]

A person's social position will determine the resources he or she has to protect the boundaries of their self and how they will come to define themselves. [. . .]

The structure of feelings is shaped by activities occurring within the context of socially organised emotional 'spaces'. Goffmans' use of spatial metaphors to describe this space and the politics of social communication (1959) are illustrative of one way to conceive of the topography of external and subjective social emotional space. Dramaturgical strategies of impression management, the sending of what others either intentionally or unconsciously make visible to us, are part of this topography that affects our conscious and unconscious subjective relationship to self and others. How does the display and concealment from others (and from oneself) of emotions by actors and their use of dramaturgical space interact with emotional modes of being and psyche soma? [. . .]

Dramaturgical stress

Self-presentational and role playing activities and the emotion work that accompanies them, can, in and of themselves, be stressful. If this stress is chronic, it may, for instance, affect neurohormonal regulation (Freund 1982). I have called this kind of stress dramaturgical stress (1982). One's social status affects the degree to which one has status shields available to one to protect the terrain of the self (Hochschild 1983). Status shields protect us against attacks on our self-esteem. A lack of status shields is a structural source of not feeling empowered (Franks 1989). Those who lack such shields are relatively powerless against the resistances and intrusions of others and have a decreased capacity to resist. Status shields protect one against another's aggression. The feelings of a lower status person are not accorded the same weight or taken as seriously as those of a higher status actor (Franks 1989) and thus they lack the status shields to protect themselves (Hochschild 1983:174). Having one's feelings ignored or termed as irrational is the analogue of having one's perceptions invalidated (Hochschild 1983:173). Both are more likely to be experienced by lower status persons and to be inflicted by those in power. The invalidation of one's feelings, however, may be more threatening than the invalidation of perceptions, since feelings as a form of information are experienced as the deeply authentic, existential ground of who we are. In general, the threats to ontological security are greater for those in dependent, subordinate positions. The lack of resources to protect oneself or to legitimate oneself further contributes to status-related insecurity. Less powerful people face a structurally built-in handicap in managing social and emotional information and this handicap may contribute to existential fear and anxiety.

Emotional false consciousness

The political use of status shields has consequences other than simply enhancing the stress of those who lack such shields. Such shields may be used by more powerful actors as a means of social control in various situations. The absence of shields for lower status actors means that they become more vulnerable to being socially redefined as the kind of people those in power expect them to be. They become more open to being 'constructed' as the kind of emotional beings, for instance, who get 'what they deserve'. Status shields of the more powerful may be used to shift the blame for the unpleasant emotionality experienced by, for instance, a subordinate away from themselves onto that less powerful person. Franks' pilot study

(1989) of battered women illustrates the ways in which these women defined situations in such a way as to blame themselves. To the extent to which they have internalised traditional gender expectations, they can be made to feel that it is *they* who have primary responsibility for what happened and for continuing the relationship, in order to, for example, keep the family together. Frank (1989) and Hochschild (1983) thus suggest that a person's status influences how status shields are used to validate the more powerful and invalidate subordinate actors as well as mute their attempt to resist. Ego's invisibility to more powerful others means that alter need not recognise boundaries and, in fact, ego can be made to feel responsible for such treatment.

Self blame and invalidation lead to depression and anxiety. Because of the greater ability of those in power to define situations, including emotional ones, depression and anxiety often come to replace anger in the experience of subordinate actors. These emotional states may, in turn, be physically expressed in, for instance, serotonin levels. Serotonin, a neurotransmitter, along with such substances as melatonin have been implicated in forms of depression (Wurtman and Wurtman 1989). I do not intend to reduce depression as a feeling to one or more neurotransmitters. Rather I want to suggest a more limited but nonetheless important role for biochemistry in emotions. Is it possible that the physical accompaniments of repeated experiences of depression eventually acquire some degree of 'functional' autonomy? [. . .]

Dramaturgical stress is particularly intense when there is a great discrepancy between a strongly held sense of self that one wishes to express and the displays of self that social relationships force on one (Freund 1982). Extreme dissociation between provoked feelings and their expression are subjective psychosomatic ways of coping with tensions found in social relationships. Work, for instance, may demand civility and often even 'sincere' displays of friendliness in the face of most uncivil conditions of exploitation and invalidation. Organisational pressures on workers (especially ones caught between the demands from customers for courteous civility and the demands to be nice to a pressuring boss) may be dealt with by splitting emotional physical appearances and the experienced structure of feelings. Sociological minorities, such as women, black people, gays and other minorities (such as people with disabilities) must often face situations in which they are ignored, patronised or abused but as a matter of survival or because of their socialised guilt (or fear) about displaying hostility, display a 'pleasant' acceptable face. Do such conditions engender depression (Zola 1982) even on physical symptoms such as elevated blood pressure (Harburg *et al* 1979; Harburg *et al* 1973)?

Contemporary forms of social control place demands on an actor's ability to manage not only emotional displays but increasingly their subjectivity as well (Stearns and Stearns 1986). Such emotion work involves not only surface acting but what Hochschild calls 'deep acting'. 'Deep acting' may become a part of one's workplace skills. It may be used to provide a service to a client or as a way of navigating the emotional waters of a tightly knit bureaucratic structure. Subordinate actors must also master the skills of anticipating, via emotional cues, the more powerful actor's emotional disposition. There is evidence that, in fact, lower status actors become more adept at such skills (Franks 1989; Henley 1977) – perhaps making them more vulnerable to identifying with the other (Franks 1989).

Emotional displays (a 'sincere' smile) may be the commodity that the actor produces as a service in the context of being a waiter, stewardess or bank teller. Such work, it is important to emphasise, involves the management not only of physical displays but of internal psycho-physical feelings. The self-regulation of emotions is expressed through the body and furthermore this regulation in turn may affect one's relationship to one's body. Hochschild speculates that the need to rework one's visceral responses leads one to 'disconnect' oneself from emotional signals. How is the stress of emotion work somaticised under invalidating or anger-eliciting situations in which displays and subjectivity must be reworked? These kinds of questions provide interesting possible areas of investigation for both a sociology of emotions as well as a sociology of health. [. . .]

References

Alexander, F. (1950) *Psychosomatic Medicine*. New York: W. W. Norton and Company, Inc.

Buytendijk, F. J. (1950) The phenomenological approach to the problem of feelings and emotions, in *Feelings and Emotions: The Mooseheart Symposium in Cooperation with the University of Chicago*, Martin C. Reymert, ed., New York: McGraw-Hill Company, Inc.: 127–141.

Buytendijk, F. J. (1974) *Prolegomena to an Anthropological Physiology*, Pittsburgh: Duquesne University Press.

Dreyfus, H. L. (1979) *What Computers Can't Do: The Limits of Artificial Intelligence*. New York: Harper and Row Publishers.

Elias, N. (1978) *The Civilizing Process, Volume I*. New York: Urizen Books.

Fausto-Sterling, A. (1985) *Myths of Gender*, New York: Basic Books, Inc.

Franks, D. D. (1989) Power and role taking: a social behavioralist's synthesis of Kemper's power and status model, in *The Sociology of Emotions: Original Essays and Research Papers*, D. D. Franks and E. D. McCarthy, (eds.), Greenwich, Connecticut: JAI Press: 153–177.

Freund, P. E. S. (1988) Bringing society into the body: understanding socialized human nature, *Theory and Society*, 17:839–864.

Freund, P. E. S. (1982) *The Civilized Body: Social Domination, Control and Health*. Philadelphia, PA: Temple University Press.

Goffman, E. (1959) *The Presentation of Self in Everyday Life*. Garden City, New Jersey: Doubleday-Anchor.

Harburg. E., Blakelock, E. H. and Roeper, P. J. (1979) Resentful and reflective coping with arbitrary authority and blood pressure, *Psychosomatic Medicine* 41, 189–202.

Harburg, E. T., Haunstein, L., Chare, C., Schull, W. and Shork, M. (1973) Socio-ecological stress, suppressed hostility, skin color and black-white male blood pressure: Detroit, *Psychosomatic Medicine*, 35:276.

Henley, N. M. (1977) *Body Politics*. Englewood Cliffs, NJ: Prentice Hall.

Hochschild, A. (1983) *The Managed Heart: Commercialization of Human Feeling*. Berkeley: University of California Press.

Johnson, M. (1987) *The Body in the Mind*. Chicago: University of Chicago Press.

Kemper, T. D. (1987) How many emotions are there? Wedding the social and the autonomic components, *American Journal of Sociology*, 93, 263–289.

Kleinman, A. (1988) *The Illness Narratives: Suffering, Healing and the Human Condition*. New York: Basic Books, Inc.

Laing, R. D. (1965) *The Divided Self*. Baltimore, MD: Penguin Books, Inc.

Leder, D. (1984) Medicine and paradigms of embodiment, *The Journal of Medicine and Philosophy*, 9, 29–43.

Levin, D. M. (1985) The Body Politics: political economy and the human body, *Human Studies*, 8:235–278.

Madsen, D. (1985) A biochemical property relating to power seeking in humans, *American Political Science Review*, 79, 448–457.

Mazur, A. (1985) A biosocial model of status in face to face primate groups, *Social Forces*, 64, 377–402.

McCarthy, E. (1984) Towards a sociology of the physical world: George Herbert Mead on physical objects, in *Studies in Symbolic Interaction*, N. K. Denzin (ed.), Greenwich, CT: JAI Press: 105–121.

Merleau-Ponty, M. (1962) *Phenomenology of Perception*. New York: Humanities Press.

Sapolsky, R. M. (1982) The endocrine stress-response and social status in the wild baboon, *Hormones and Behavior*, 1:279–292.

Stearns, C. Z. and Stearns, P. N. (1986) *Anger: The struggle for Emotional Control in America's History*. Chicago: University of Chicago Press.

Wurtman, R. J. and Wurtman, J. J. (1989) Carbohydrates and depression, *Scientific American*, 260, 68–75.

Zola, I. K. (1982) *Missing Pieces: A Chronicle of Living with a Disability*. Philadelphia: Temple University Press.

Chapter 26

Alan Radley

PORTRAYALS OF SUFFERING

On looking away, looking at, and the comprehension of illness experience

[. . .]

Pain, horror and looking away

IN ORDER TO DEAL WITH the question of what pictures of illness or suffering portray, it is necessary to ask about what they do *not* depict and what people avoid looking at. These two issues are closely related. Images of wounds, the ravages of disease and the effects of radical surgical treatment are examples of these exclusionary features. They constitute, in some sense, the stigma of disease that mark out sufferers as different. What those who have suffered bodily trauma do not wish to show and what other people do not wish to see coalesce in the fact that ill people live silently with the effects of serious disease. Before we can explore how portrayals of illness might break this silence, it is necessary to examine what it is that people are frightened of in depictions of the diseased or treated body. From what do we turn our eyes, and whom do we deny understanding beyond the pity that such pictures might evoke? [. . .]

There is a photograph of Dorothea Lynch (not reproduced here), taken by her colleague Eugene Richards, showing her lying in a hospital bed shortly after having undergone a mastectomy. This photograph is one of a number in a book chronicling her stay in hospital for treatment for breast cancer (Lynch and Richards, 1986). She lies on her back, naked to the waist, a doctor holding up her bandaged left arm so that the sutured wound is open to view. There are bandages covering a drainage tube in her side. What do we see in this photograph? At once too much and too little. By too much I mean that we see, in a literal sense, the body uncovered and the body deformed – a bare breast and the gash where a breast once was. This is a difficult picture to look at, and one that probably many would be pleased to cover by the turn of the page. It is not horrific by some standards, and yet the American Cancer Society refused to give such images to Lynch when she contacted them following her diagnosis because 'books with pictures of cancer treatments aren't considered suitable for non-medical people' (Lynch and Richards, 1986: 16).

The 'unsuitability' of such pictures – the fact that they are restricted – also gives them a fascination, so that one looks to see, to see more than one is normally able, or to see behind. Because of this, and because of Dorothea Lynch's partly clothed state and forced passivity, that looking soon feels intrusive and violent. It is a kind of looking without understanding that, in its frustration, draws the observer again and again to see what is not normally shown. However, the violence of the observer's gaze promotes (is repaid with) a power in the image so that it 'calls to' the eye. As Elkins (1996) puts it, in these cases 'the object stares back'.

What happens when we turn away from an explicit image of this kind? In turning away from the image the observer completes – in one particular way – the act of interpretation, inasmuch as it is developed at all. When we do this we remove the depiction from our view so that with its removal the 'difficulty' of its appearance is suppressed, if not entirely extinguished. In recognizing this, we are also acknowledging that the pain and the imagination involved are our own, that we, as observers, are caught up in the terrain that lies between the inexpressibility of pain and what is there pictured for us. The problem of the photograph of Dorothea Lynch – as with any photograph – is that we are used to reading these as if they were direct quotes from reality. Clearly, the photograph depicts Lynch's suffering, and it would appear to be her pain that is at issue. And yet the form of this suffering is not simply given in the photograph, is not there to be read out from its patterning of light and shade. The 'unmediated' form of the photograph with its stark presentation of the mundane world depicts her pain at the site of the surgical cutting of her body. And yet the wound in itself is insufficient to explain the observer's reaction, because it signifies (by the presence of 'the healthy breast') the absence of the part of the body that was. It is the presentational form of the depiction that evokes the horror, not merely the revelation of what is removed or deformed. To react to a photograph 'with horror' is to respond not only to a visual image, but to register in that denial the other's suffering in one's bodily shudder. That shudder can be seen as the reciprocating aspect of the depiction – however unintended – that reveals the complicity of the observer in the situation of the sufferer. We do not turn from the image as such, but from the depiction of that which exemplifies unbearable suffering. This points up a mode of representation that involves the 'setting forth' of the sufferer's situation. Such images do not 'refer away' to their significant object (pain) but are presentational in their standing as exemplars of this condition. (Just as one cannot [primarily] substitute the semantic content of the words 'I love you' for the saying [writing] of the words, so the same is true of the expression of suffering.)

Why, though, should people turn away from the difficult photograph? Put simply, it is unbearable. However, from what we have just said, it is not the visual image that is unbearable, but the apprehension of suffering that is instantiated in the observer who lacks the imaginative framework within which this pain can be given form. The photographic depiction of suffering stands as an example of pain *silence*, in the sense that it is inarticulate without an imaginative framework to give it form.

We might say, paradoxically, that such images evoke a silent scream in the observer, for whom this inarticulacy is made real. Unable to give form to the apprehension of suffering, the observer might have no recourse but to turn away from the image. And this often works precisely because the depiction of a wound, unelaborated by accompanying narrative or other presentational format, is trapped by its inarticulateness into the moment of viewing. We look and are horrified; we turn away and the image, and the feeling, are gone. This does not mean that photographic images are altogether forgettable. What is forgettable is an image that is presentationally inarticulate, or one that through lack of narrative commentary condemns it to the condition of being an instance, locked in time and space.

The idea of giving form to pain suggests that, whenever this is achieved, then the situation of the observer can be alleviated. We can then look with understanding. However, a caveat is in order here. For this proposal is misleading to the extent that it suggests that formlessness is the only problem. In fact, the presentation of the unwanted in the guise of the mundane (cloaked in ordinary objects) can actually heighten the sense of horror (Radley, 1999). The allusive portrayal of the unwanted and the feared unknown provides form for the expression of horror. In this situation, the conceptual dimension of the portrayal also provides its tangibility, its extensiveness out of the moment, so that (whether we wish it or not) the sense of that horror can be brought back to us at another time. We can less easily turn away from ideas ('in our heads') than from physically rendered images.

The issue of what is bearable in 'difficult' pictures of illness is therefore more than a question of what is seen. The reaction to the picturing of pain or to disfigurement associated with surgical treatment is not comprehensible as a visual issue, for the simple reason that the powers of horror invoke the absent, the unseen. What the observer turns away from is the visual image, but does so in the cause of turning off the formless fears and anxiety that the image opens up. The lack of mediation – the cultural frameworks of construction – that allow the observer to establish a coherent subjectivity are missing. These frameworks enable the image's meaning and the observer's perception through the repression of desires and fears, which would otherwise prevent any 'comfortable viewing' taking place.

'Difficult' images remain so, as one returns again to look at them, if they are deprived of frameworks that would enable the viewer to fashion a position with respect to them. This need not be a facile or comfortable position, but one that the artist/author might have fabricated. In the case of Dorothea Lynch's treatment for breast cancer, her partner Eugene Richards (himself a professional photographer) presents this photo-essay in the context of Lynch's own diary. This means that the photographs stand both as works in themselves and as illustrations of the text which refers to them. The narration around and with respect to the images releases each instance, each painful moment, from its time and space as it enables the viewer/reader to establish a position toward Lynch's illness experience. As we understand where, how and why things happen in her treatment – and in her actions – so the image of the mastectomy scar becomes bearable. That is, it becomes bearable for us insofar as we are able to comprehend how she bore it.

All this goes to show that picturing suffering is more than a matter of visual depiction, more than resemblance and revelation. What is at issue is the possibility of the observer sustaining a look, a look that is not overwhelmed by the stare of the object portrayed. This stare is the power of the image to overwhelm, to suffuse the observer with pity, horror or revulsion. How the look of the observer might be sustained is a question of *re-presenting* the suffering of the ill person, allowing pain to be given expressive form and thereby enabling the observer to reciprocate in the establishment of a compassionate understanding of the sick. How this re-presentation is achieved is the subject of the section to follow.

Picturing, possession and the transformation of suffering

In this section I shall discuss two images of individuals who have recovered from cancer, but whose bodies bear the marks of their surgical treatment. In doing this, I want to examine what it is that such images might achieve, what it is that they communicate and how they do so. For if pictures showing mastectomy scars are deemed horrific, then how can pictures with apparently similar content transcend this judgement? [. . .]

The self-portrait by Elissa Hugens Aleshire is drawn from the collection *Art.Rage.Us.* published by the Breast Cancer Fund of America (1998). It shows four images of her, three partial figures and one, centre-front, a complete figure. It is this figure that commands attention as it shows her naked to the waist, the scar of her missing right breast alongside the 'healthy' left breast. She looks straight ahead, into the mirror that (she tells us) she used in order to create the painting. It is an open look, what she terms in the accompanying comment 'the first real look at myself after surgery'. To the side and behind this central figure are three others. They are partly hidden, and in each case hide the missing breast. To the viewer's left she is shown wearing a blouse. To the right, and behind, we see only her face and a bare shoulder, her chest obscured by the two images in front. She holds her fingers to her chin, giving the impression of a quizzical attitude. The fourth figure, to the viewer's right, is only half in the picture, holding up her hand to cover the site of the missing right breast. By this device we are shown three part-figures whose anatomical completeness is preserved (by obscuration), and one whole figure who reveals that she is anatomically incomplete. The total picture works to suggest the achievement of self-recognition against the background of fear of revelation. In the course of this portrayal, the mastectomy scar so clearly depicted is given a different context. It is re-figured along with the artist as sufferer. This does not mean that its original (one might say, ab-original) power to evoke horror is entirely removed. (That this is not so can be demonstrated by showing the picture afresh to different viewers.)

Rather, the suffering that is indicated by the wound is given form, re-contextualizing the scar and giving it new meaning. The picture was not created by attempting to displace attention from the scar, but in contrast by facing it and refiguring it. As Elissa Aleshire comments:

> A week before the surgery, I had drawn a 'before' picture, and I prom-ised myself I would do an 'after'. It took about three months to work up to it. This painting was the first real look at myself after my surgery, and at first I was embarrassed to even show anyone. But in fact, the process

healed me, sitting in front of a mirror looking at an image that scared me.

(Breast Cancer Fund, 1988: 101)

This comment shows the act of painting to involve confrontation with the mastectomy scar in order that it might be transformed. In order to look beyond the scar, she had first to look at it. This indicates that horror is not dismissed in the course of such portrayals but that its powers are diminished in the course of being given a form, a shape. However, painting is not an objectification of horror as such (for then it could not 'heal') but the projection of the artist's recovery of herself from the grip of illness and its terrors. What the image achieves – using multiple figures – is a sense of coherence for Elissa Aleshire through an expressive portrayal of that recovery. The picture is an exemplification of her position – it stands forth as an open acknowledgement and acceptance of what is – while also being an expression of qualities that are elusive to specification. This is a key feature of all artistic works, in that they sensuously relate aspects of experience by setting forth properties that are metaphorically possessed (Goodman, 1968). The idea of metaphorical possession refers here to the figurative projection of a world (of illness) of which the image stands as if a fragment. As a fragment of such a figurative world (which in its assemblage of feelings is as real as any literal depiction), the image is bounded by a space-time of experience (looking at the picture, painting the picture) that sets it off from the mundane world. This does not imply a separation from the world of disease and surgery, but the fabrication of a way of being in relation to things, so that they are imbued with meanings that previously did not belong to them.

Although it is the image that metaphorically possesses the qualities of a recovering patient, it is the person (or in this case the artist) who is credited with those qualities. What comes to be possessed is possessed by her, and is achieved in the act of painting. Elissa Aleshire spells out this last point in her comment that 'the process healed me'. [. . .]

The imaged world of recovery (of illness-as-borne) is a fabricated one, dealing in metaphors, but it is not an ethereal one, in the sense of being wholly transcendent. It is fabricated by means of paint, and by virtue of remaining engaged with the mundane world that our bodies occupy. No transformation of suffering could be achieved by a portrayal that had wholly lost touch with the possibility of pain. To portray a 'world of suffering-as-borne' it is necessary that the picture remains an exemplar of pain, that it continues to show forth those features (the mastectomy scar) in the course of expressing the self-possession referred to above. This should not be thought of as the projection of any 'self' at all, but is an aesthetic judgement based upon the fact that the painting (as of Elissa Aleshire) does two things. It is experienced as a restoration of coherence, and as the expression of feelings that were previously inchoate. This experience is to be sought both in the act of painting (which 'heals') and in the contemplation of the image by others. Inasmuch as it is seen as coherent, the image is comprehended as a totality, and as such a fragment of the world to which it refers (i.e. it is a sample of 'illness-as-borne'). The image thus stands both in the mundane world (of paint, of media, of spaces of observation) and in the figurative world which it fabricates. And because the fabrication of this world requires work on the part of the artist, and the contemplative effort on the part of the viewer, its expressive potential is realized as the achievement of distance from horror and pain. That distance – which is common to all ascetic practice – is created by the practices of objectification (the skills of the artist) through which pain and horror can both be given communicative form.

To help address this issue of transformation we can examine another artwork, this time a photograph, taken by a third party (herself a cancer survivor) for an exhibition 'I'm so lucky' (Ogonowska-Coates and Robertson, 1998). This photo-exhibition was of cancer survivors and included this image of a man – Stefan Wahrlich – standing on a beach near a lake against the backdrop of a mountain range. He faces directly to camera, wearing only a pair of shorts, arms outstretched and standing on one leg. The other leg is visible only as a stump below his shorts, where it was removed as treatment for cancer of the bone. In the exhibition this image was displayed above a brief commentary explaining the background to his illness and his reactions to it.

Unlike the painting of Elissa Aleshire, Stefan Wahrlich's image is different in that its photographic form reveals this as a moment in time. At one level, the image is a record, an instance. And yet the pose is counterfactual by virtue of it both revealing the absent leg and defying that absence. This is a pose that is more than an alignment with what Goffman (1976) called 'schedules' for being pictured in such situations. Photo-schedules for cancer patients (especially with one leg amputated) do not exist, so that the portrayal in this image must make use of, in order to transcend, some of the conventions by which individuals might be pictured standing on a beach. In Stefan Wahrlich's case, the image conveys its meaning through this transcendence, wherein the achievement of balance, of the symmetry of his

arms, overcomes the literal instability that must follow from his having had a leg amputated. In this picture he does not just pose for the camera, but asserts his position vis-a-vis the world and the camera/observer. This image too is coherent and expressive, in that it exemplifies a world of 'suffering-as-borne' alluded to by qualities that it metaphorically possesses. It is these characteristics that entitle this photograph – along with Elissa Aleshire's self-portrait – to be called works, in that they achieve their meaning through figurative portrayal, which is the condition for any work to be deemed 'artistic'.

Scarry is helpful in defining such work and its artefacts as 'names that are given to phenomena of pain and the imagination as they begin to move from being a self-contained loop within the body to becoming the equivalent loop now projected into the external world' (Scarry, 1985: 170). This means that the private agony of suffering becomes social and sharable, resulting in the possibility of a collective outcome. Equally relevant to the argument here is her proposal that an artefact (e.g. a painting, a photograph) 'is a fragment of world alteration' (1985: 171). In the previous way that I have used the word, the artefact is a fragment of the world re-figured, not merely of a mundane world that has undergone change.

I introduce the concept of work here not only to identify once more the ontological status of images of suffering, but also to underline that the fabrication of such images is an achievement (we might call them 'works of illness'). It is in the act of *making* that the picture of 'suffering-as-borne' is given shape and form. This is more readily appreciated in respect of the painted portrait, where the laying on of paint and the construction of the image take time and rely upon the artist's skill. While the photographer clearly uses her skill in the assemblage of the pictured scene, we might see less easily how the photograph objectifies in the sense of a process of fabrication.

In order to try to unravel this problem, we need to see such work as involving both artist and model, for it is in the form of the pose captured by the camera that Stefan Wahrlich's world is to be apprehended. Instead of seeing it as a 'mere pose', we should recognize its mimetic power as a kind of static dance, in that the various countervailing tensions are held in a dynamic equilibrium in his balancing posture.

Considered as a (static) dance, what was originally an inchoate response to disease and its treatment is made visible; considered as the capturing of that dance, the photograph becomes the artefactual structure of this communicable act. We can understand Stefan Wahrlich's 'dance' as one that gives shape to his world of 'suffering-as-borne', that says 'this, *precisely, this*, is how it is'. There are, therefore, two possible levels of transformation, one concerning the bodily style in which the person's illness world is made visible, and one where this is given objective form in the material of paint or light-sensitive film. And because, as Goodman (1968) points out, expressive paintings deal not in shapes and colours but in sounds and feelings, so the portrait makes something else tangible through the medium of visual representation.

From horror to comprehension

While there can be no guarantee that any given observer will look in a contemplative way at either of the images discussed in the previous section, their expressive form provides the structure that makes this possible. Apprehension of the other's world of suffering ('suffering-as-borne') is the result of work by the observer, who must produce for himself or herself those structures that enable them to touch what the artist is able only to show. This is made difficult to the extent that the observer may recoil with horror from the sight of disease and its radical treatment. Comprehension can only follow from the transcendence of horror, made possible by the communicable transformation of pain as 'suffering borne'.

Portraits and photographs of suffering, considered as the objectification of ideas-with-feelings, are invested with the power to recreate in the observer that process of structuration. This 'reciprocal loop' completes the act of making, of externalizing suffering, one that is implicit in the act of production. That is, the comprehension of the sufferer's world is the logical conclusion (if that is not too final a word) of the artist's model's portrayal. The question then is what form does this act of comprehension take? And by attempting a description of it, can we say more about the form of signification involved in such portrayals?

What the observer comprehends when contemplating the picture is the illness world of the sufferer. Or rather, it is *the world re-made* by virtue of the sufferer's way of confronting the inevitability of disease and its treatment. For that reason, it is not pain or an objectified phenomenon that is grasped in these pictures, but rather the figuration of the sufferer by virtue of their role as authors of their world. It is suffering as an expressive form that is grasped, as signified through the metaphorical possession of qualities that the image exemplifies. This is achieved in the observer's act of sense-making, which is less a 'reading of the picture' than a willingness to engage their ab-original response to disease to its various forms of pictorial representation. For it is only by engaging his or her fear and anxiety to the imagined objects fashioned in the portrayal that the observer can move from a position of horror to one of apprehension. To comprehend another's suffering is not simply to see it 'for what it is', but to be brought within the relationship of artist-and-her-world that the picture expresses. It is only in the grounds of the observer's fear, anxiety and delight that such images achieve their potential. We are dealing here then, with a form of signification where the meaning appears elusive not because it is vague, but because it cannot be delimited. The *elusory* aspect of our embodiment as persons – which is the wider aspect of our ab-original shudder in the face of disease and death – is as necessary to explanations of comprehension as it is to explanations of horror (Radley, 1995). No adequate reason can be located on the canvas or in the print for what we see, because what we 'see' is grounded in our activity as observers. The engagement of the observer's fears, their transformation with respect to the figured world expressed by the image, is the necessary work for contemplation through which the reciprocating loop of comprehension is established. [. . .]

References

Breast Cancer Fund (1998) *Art.Rage.Us.: The Art and Outrage of Breast Cancer*. San Francisco: Chronicle Books.

Elkins, J. (1996) *The Object Stares Back: On the Nature of Seeing*. San Diego, CA: Harcourt Brace.

Goffman, E. (1976) 'Gender Advertisements', *Studies in the Anthropology of Visual Communication* 3(2): 69–154.

Goodman, N. (1968) *Languages of Art: An Approach to a Theory of Symbols*. Indianapolis: Bobbs-Merrill.

Lynch, D. and E. Richards (1986) *Exploding into Life*. New York: Aperture Foundation/ Many Voices Press.

Ogonowska-Coates, H. and I. Robertson (1998) *I Feel Lucky: Interviews and Photographs Celebrating Cancer Survivors*. Booklet to accompany photo exhibition 'I Feel Lucky', Palmerston North, New Zealand, February–March.

Radley, A. (1995) 'The Elusory Body and Social Constructionist Theory', *Body & Society* 1(2): 3–23.

Radley, A. (1999) 'The Aesthetics of Illness: Narrative, Horror and the Sublime', *Sociology of Health and Illness* 21: 778–96.

Scarry, E. (1985) *The Body in Pain: The Making and Unmaking of the World*. New York: Oxford University Press.

Chapter 27

James M. Wilce Jr and Laurie J. Price

METAPHORS OUR BODYMINDS LIVE BY

Culture, images, and imagination

IMAGINE A VERY SICK PERSON. Imagine her under the care of someone who helps her relax by suggesting she envision herself lying on a sunny beach. Picture another person suggesting that she imagine her T-cells killing, doing battle with, or just gobbling up bad cells – germs or cancer cells. We might even overhear such a guide telling the patient that if she does so, it will help her body to fight off her illness. Now imagine a woman in a less clinical setting, say, a self-help workshop centered on intensive personal journaling. The workshop leaders tell the woman there is evidence suggesting physical health benefits come to those who break through inner blocks and move beyond silent rumination on loss, stress, or trauma, by bringing themselves to write their most intimate feelings about the event.

Many readers will be able to envision such scenarios; some will have participated in similar ones. So, if we now propose to define "cultures," in part, as aids to the imagination, you might accept this as true in several senses. Sharing a particular culture means shared familiarity with a set of scenarios like those described above. It also means that participants in such events bring to them – and/or achieve within them – the imagination that the claims of caregivers and experts (e.g. about images and their therapeutic effects) make sense. Science involves the imagination, and the hard science and popular science invoked in the first paragraph involve plenty. But all science is cultural activity. It feeds upon and nourishes cultural images. Even textbooks in immunology draw upon images of such obviously sociocultural phenomena as class stratification, nation-states, and war (Martin 1994). And science produces images that enter the popular imagination. In the last several decades, through a trickling down of immunological research, the American public has come to imagine a range of diverse elements – the skin, IgA, and CD-4s – as a single system, the "immune system."

Cultures are not only aids to the imagination. We live by what we imagine; this must include our metaphors (Lakoff and Johnson 1980). In this chapter we make the even stronger claim that cultures help to shape actual bodies, partly by means of widely held models, images, and metaphors. Kirmayer has argued (1992) that metaphor not only arises out of embodied experience but, conversely, becomes embodied. Thus he calls for an investigation of "the psychophysiology of metaphor" (336). Much earlier, Moerman (1979) sought in metaphor at least a partial explanation for the efficacy of symbolic healing: "The construction of healing symbols *is* healing." This shaping potential of signs (images, metaphors, symbols) involves culturally particular multistory, reflexive, metalevel phenomena – e.g. feelings about feelings (metasentiment, meta-emotion; Gottman *et al.* 1996), and images of how images work. Imagine we "knew" that guided imagery had high curative efficacy with cancer and had reduced this "finding" to the relaxing effect of the image, which in turn was due to its association with sources of reassurance. This is to say that the image "relaxes" people in part because of a meta-imagination of the efficacy of images and symbols (Lévi-Strauss 1963), the assurance that certain images or imaginative acts carried therapeutic benefit. We propound just such a model of culture-as-multistory/metalevel phenomenon, and thus explain cultures' roles in mobilizing immune response and healing. To do so, we draw on ethnographic as well as experimental evidence.

[The] claim that immune systems have cultural and social lives is an inference from other sorts of evidence, too. No one who accepts the notion of the immune system denies that the life of such systems is embedded in the life of human populations. At one level, our claim that human immune systems (and psychoimmune systems) exist in relation to the empirical and symbolic life of societies is founded on the most fundamental insights of epidemiology – that health and disease have social contexts. The relationship is not one-way but mutual. We see the impact of immunity on social organization when we consider the disorder and cultural turmoil caused by depopulating plagues, including those brought on by colonial contact. On the other hand, the effects of subsistence and housing patterns on social networks and thus on patterns of disease and immunity are well known to epidemiologists. Physiological sociology (Barchas 1976) and anthropological field studies (Part II, this volume) have given us evidence that key immune mediators in the endocrine system may reflect social status and social experience. But human neuroimmunological process must be mediated by psychology and, therefore, by factors like culture that shape individual psychology. Measurable impacts of ideology and other dimensions of cultural life on immune function are less well studied than the more purely sociological factors – like the correlation between high stress and low socio-economic status – in human endocrinology. . . .

Popular notions of the self and its boundaries are not only specific to cultures, to political economies, and to the sorts of immune science generated therein. [. . .] These constructions of self, emotion, and expressivity might also be nonarbitrarily related to measurable processes in particular bodies in particular social formations. That entails a pressing research agenda, one foreshadowed by Frankenberg's (1986) call for a re-visioning of sickness as cultural performance (see Lock 1993: 142). We would suggest a reconsideration of *health and healing*, too, as performances of cultural potentialities. Culture – social experience and expectations as well as beliefs, images, metaphors, and meta-images – is embodied (Csordas 1990, Farnell 1996).

Our discussion to this point assumes that cultures have some degree of integration. We assume that members of social groups define themselves by a common orientation of their actions to a culture, a semi-shared, semi-integrated system of values and ideas. Moreover, evidence points to the importance, to those social actors, of feeling themselves to be in consonance with dominant cultural values and norms (Decker *et al.*, this volume). Dressler *et al.* (1998) have found evidence of a correlation between feeling, on the one hand, that one is achieving a successful lifestyle as it is defined locally, and one's physical and mental health on the other. "When the individual is continuously checking his or her own cultural consonance and finds it wanting, it is likely to be a frustrating and depressing circumstance. This is a process that is also expressed somatically" (Dressler *et al.* 1998: 440). [. . .]

Metaphor, minds, and bodies

When Johnson (1987) and Lakoff and Kövecses (1987) say that we live by certain metaphors of the body, they mean that cultural metaphors *reflect* innate biological, embodied experiences. Conversely, some psychoneuroimmunologists – including those who have encouraged guided imagery to fight cancer (Hall and O'Grady 1991) – go beyond this to hypothesize that images *change* somatic processes. We propose a revision of even that model, adding the proviso that culturally variable images of body and healing are variably embodied within and across societies. What we are proposing is "local biologies" (Lock 1998). [. . .]

The body is a rich metaphor for society (Scheper-Hughes and Lock 1987). Body metaphors – including those whose surface structure refers to individual somatic process – conventionally and most relevantly point to social processes. Cognitive linguists and anthropologists have carried out a large proportion of the studies of cultural metaphor to date (Lakoff and Johnson 1980). However, embodiment theorists who are not so wed to cognitivist models have contributed to the area as well (Farnell 1996; Lyon, this volume). We do not need to posit a conscious cognitive processing of cultural symbols through ritual, etc. in order to imagine that cultural metaphors are both enacted and enfleshed in individuals' bodies. It may be more accurate to picture actors doing with their bodies things that make sense in metaphoric ways because of a shared bodily group of action, cognition, and culture (Csordas 1990). Metaphor thus becomes an analytic tool – a way for anthropologists to talk about iconicity between bodily process or action on the one hand and cultural values on the other – rather than a trope to accurately represent the consciousness of actors.

Writing about trauma has a therapeutic efficacy that has been well demonstrated. Pennebaker and others (Pennebaker *et al.* 1989; Esterling *et al.* 1994; Petrie *et al.* 1995) have studied the benefits of writing (in private journal entries) about traumatic experience. Such interventions, and their effects, enact particular cultural metaphors that researchers have not made explicit as such. Writing exercises, and the conclusions drawn from them, reflect a wide-spread vision Westerners have of how language (written or spoken) communicates – a vision focusing on referentiality and neutrality that we can sum up with "the conduit metaphor." The title of a Pennebaker article, "Putting stress into words," metaphorically takes stress as a fluid-like thing that can be put in words as container-like things.

Words achieve many things, including performing and reshaping selves and social realities, as Booth and Davison imply (this volume). Yet Western folk and philosophical images of language tend to reduce its function to reference to pre-existing objects, including emotions metaphorized as (fluid) things. This imagination of communication also separates message form from message function, treating form as a neutral, non-obstructing conduit through which semantic notions flow unaffected (Reddy 1993). The metaphor reproduced in studies of trauma-writing by Pennebaker (this volume) and colleagues (Booth and Davison, this volume) is that of bodies as containers and emotions as fluids to be poured out into neutrally referring words before their pressures damage the container. We view language differently. Words are not neutral conduits for objectifiable fluid-like feelings. Rather, words and gestures perform quite magically; the performative (as opposed to merely referential or reflective) power of language is certainly central to ritual of all sorts, including healing ritual (Tambiah 1979). It is precisely the performative power of words and other human signifying acts to unite bodies and cultural images that must be studied in an investigation of PNI-relevant therapeutic interventions across cultures.

Psychoneuroimmunology, or PNI, has taken for granted a universal, preconceptual, precultural human body that responds in predictable ways to the "same" emotions, meta-emotions, and behaviors. Such behaviors include reprocessing trauma by writing it, or participating in a guided imagery intervention for cancer patients – one centering on military images of the immune system. By contrast, we propose that sociocultural contexts that discourage verbalizing of trauma or paying any attention at all to cancer (even through "positive" imagery) might engender local psychoimmunologies for which such acts have a neutral or even negative impact on immune function.

"Healthy" expressive "release" of negative affect: a cultural metaphor in comparative perspective

Lakoff and Johnson (1980) pioneered a useful example of an approach to culturally particular images and metaphors – though their work generally fails to draw on actual occurrences in natural discourse. They explored in some detail the "body as container" metaphor common in European languages. Lakoff and Kövecses (1987) link this master metaphor with specific English metaphors for anger. The idioms "bursting with anger" and "barely containable rage" evoke the container metaphor, while indirectly supporting notions that it is better to "let it out" in a controlled way. Lakoff and Kövecses claim that the association of anger with metaphors of contained heat *reflects* embodied experience and is thus likely to prove universal at least in outline (ibid.: 220f). Given a model that holds idioms to be part of an integrated semantic network (Good 1977), we could take it as a working hypothesis that anyone who experiences anger as threatening them with "bursting" might experience, along with anger, another tension over the risk such anger posed to their "container." We can also hypothesize that those who "live" such metaphors might feel the release of tension and anger to be health-inducing.

We are not arguing that Americans share conscious notions linking catharsis with *immune function* per se, though that might be true (Martin 1994). Rather, we are asserting two things: first, we claim that broader images that implicitly link a "contained" emotion with risk, and expression with health are culturally salient. Second, we point to the likelihood that such tropes are themselves embodied in a process whereby cultural signs (metaphors, idioms, images) somehow join with physiology (Moerman 1979; Dow 1986; Csordas 1988, 1990; Csordas and Kleinman 1990; Kirmayer 1992; and cf. Barchas 1976, Lyon 1993).

Re-evaluation Counseling (RC, also called "Co-counseling") is a popular movement in the US based on the conviction that emotional discharge is essential for psychological and social well being. Founded in the 1960s, RC is now practiced by many thousands of North Americans (including co-author Price), and has organizations in many other locales around the world. After a multiweek training program, people learn how to be both counselor and counselee. They exchange roles on a regular basis, typically halfway through a given session. In RC theory, when people have distressing experiences, they need to discharge the distress with the attention of another individual, someone who is listening carefully and supportively, but not "telling them what to do." "Discharge" is signaled externally when the person being counseled begins to cry or sob, tremble with cold perspiration, laugh loudly, shout, talk in a fully engaged way, or move around vigorously. RC offers a cultural model that explicitly mandates expression of emotions, and periodic catharsis, a model endorsed by at least a portion of the general population in North America.

Anthropologists argue that such cultural models need to be seen in broad, global, comparative perspective. Theoretical links between local models of self and emotion on the one hand and social structure on the other, were made by Michelle Rosaldo (1984). Arguing that "cultural idioms provide the images in terms of which our subjectivities are formed, and . . . these idioms themselves are socially ordered and constrained," Rosaldo left us a strong form of the social constructionist argument in relation to metaphors of emotion and containment or control. She proposed that the expression of anger is viewed as destructive in "brideservice" or hunter-gatherer societies, whereas in "more complex, tribal . . . 'bridewealth' groups . . . 'anger' held within may work to other people's harm in hidden, witchlike ways." Extending this, it seems clear that in the postindustrial West – and perhaps in classical Greece, given Aristotle's vision of catharsis – it is the one with "unresolved" or "repressed" anger and grief who feels at risk. This anthropology of self must be taken into consideration in any account of PNI – specifically, any account of how writing about trauma might enhance immune function – that presumes to cover the diversity of human societies.

Metaphors and images that involve the activity of immune systems are a subset of metaphors for the body and emotion that have been well studied (Scheper-Hughes and Lock 1987; Desjarlais 1992). We focus on a particular metaphor that seems to have power over our conceptions and even our physiologies (Pennebaker *et al.* 1989): "Rid the body/container of dangerous repressed emotion"

(Lakoff and Kövecses 1987). It exemplifies the subset of cultural models that link body and emotion vis-à-vis health and immunity, and on another implicit meta-image, namely, that active, assertive imaging can engender positive emotions and bodily states (Kiecolt-Glaser *et al.* 1985). Both involve something like "catharsis," an ancient notion in the West (Scheff 1979) with new manifestations in popular health and immune metaphors.

Hall and O'Grady, reviewing experimental psychosocial interventions designed to enhance immunocompetence, mention a general benefit from relaxation or simply from the relaxation dimension of a guided imagery exercise, a benefit measurable in several clinical populations. The content of the imagery also counts for something. Some images may have "noxious" effects on some participants; but this is true, more generally, of psychological interventions in conditions like cancer – they run the risk of burdening the patient with a sense of responsibility for a condition that is in fact a cultural metaphor for that which is out of control (Balshem 1991). Hall and O'Grady cite such potential noxious consequences as the induction of a sense of burdensome responsibility for the disease or healing (cf. Sontag 1978). Particular individuals may resist particular images, recoiling at the aggressiveness of imagining "the self's" cells killing "other" cells. One Catholic priest in a study of the effects of imagery in cancer treatment substituted a weed-pulling image for it (Hall and O'Grady 1991). The potential for people to generate any such images arises in the post-1970s' sociocultural environment in which the notion of an "immune *system*" per se has gelled and has captured the popular imagination (Martin 1994). Moreover, the potential for embodying the very images that immune sciences present us (as they trickle down through *National Geographic* and *Time* (Haraway 1993; Martin 1994) – including the commonly militaristic ones – is real (Napier 1996: 335f).

The body and emotions provide ample subjects and objects for culture-specific troping or image-building. . . . Such tropes or images are often invented and propagated through public discourse. Whatever else they might be, scientific discussions of "emotions" are also discourses, and thus cultural products. The experience of an emotion is not precultural, not ultimately separable from cultural discourses about it, including social evaluations of the emotion (Roseman *et al.* 1995). And the *expression* of emotion cannot be understood apart from the histories of response to it – predictable and therefore expected verbal and gestural responses to equally stereotyped verbal and nonverbal expressions. [. . .]

Disharmony, distress, and coping: Western and Asian models

Literary sources of Western meta-imagery of coping

If our readers share a sense that it is a good thing to cry or to tell one's woes, the notion might well be traced back to *Poetics*, in which Aristotle meta-imagines enacted images of tragedy exercising a purifying or cathartic effect on the audience. Scheff (1979) links Aristotle's reflections on drama with psychotherapeutic theories of "emotion work." The historiography of more recent Western cultural theories of emotional imagery and the meta-image of therapeutic re-experience or expression must include the work of Shakespeare. Some psychological anthropologists regard him as a source of insight into "universal" human nature and emotions. More likely, his work resonates with us because he helped to reproduce or re-present fundamental Western cultural themes. Consider Shakespeare's Thirtieth Sonnet:

> When to the sessions of sweet silent thought
> I summon up remembrance of things past,
> I sigh the lack of many a thing I sought
> And with old woes new wail my dear time's waste:
> Then can I drown an eye, unused to flow
> For precious friends hid in death's dateless night,
> And weep afresh love's long-since-cancell'd woe,
> And moan the expense of many a vanisht sight:
> *Then can I grieve* at grievances foregone,
> And heavily from woe to woe *tell* o'er
> *The sad account* of fore-bemoaned moan,
> Which I new pay as if not paid before.
> But if the while I think on thee, dear friend
> All losses are restored, and sorrows end.
> (1938: 1228, emphasis added)

The sonnet embraces the need to "grieve at grievances" – and not forego or repress grieving – and "heavily from woe to woe tell o'er the sad account of fore-bemoaned moans." We find the same metasentiment in *Macbeth* (IV, iii).

Macduff is finally told the truth about the murder of his wife and children. Malcolm, standing by, says:

> Merciful heaven! –
> What, man! ne'er pull your hat upon your brows;
> *Give sorrow words*: the grief that does not speak
> Whispers the o'er – fraught heart, and bids it break.
> (1938: 879, emphasis added)

Shakespeare inherited – but, more saliently, passed on to countless Western audiences – a cultural meta-image of cathartic disclosure of images and feelings too awful to bear within. His poems and his dramatic characters counsel verbal disclosure – giving sorrow words. The images of interiority (one's insides as the seat of feeling), of hearts that can break unless relieved of emotion objects/fluids over-filling them, and of narrative as catharsis/therapy, come down to us as powerful cultural affirmations. Shakespeare leaves most of the responsibility for coping with the sufferer himself. As much as these metasentiments stir us, we must recognize that they are not universal. That is made clear by contrasting meta-sentiments from other traditions.

Coping with cancer: a Japanese oncology manual

Consider Japanese oncologists, whose writings invoke idioms of conflict and support in describing gentle disclosure of cancer diagnoses. We Western readers might skip to the end of the script and presume that the Japanese idiom parallels American oncology's experiments with guided imagery in which patients may be left alone with their imaginations, but not left without guidance – may in fact be encouraged to use aggressive images. American cancer patients are told to relax, *turn inward*, and draw on and enhance inner strength by envisioning their good cells defeating the invading cancer cells (Hall and O'Grady 1991). In contrast, the Japanese oncologists' *Manual of Terminal Care for Cancer Patients* guides physicians thus: "[I]nform your *patients you are a co-fighter in this process . . . [Say,]* 'Probably, *we* have a long term fight.'" A later "lesson" suggests, "Another example of demonstrating empathy and being a 'co-fighter' is to touch the abdominal area, perhaps thus indicating a visceral core, and ask 'how is the *common* enemy?' . . . or [suggest] '*We* deal with the enemy with deliberateness'" (cited by Good *et al.* 1994: 859, emphasis added; and see Good *et al.* 1993). While American researchers recognize the therapeutic value of social support, a great gap separates those Japanese meta-images of joint social effort from the individualistic metaphors governing the American metacommunicative practice of guided imagery. Pronouns help mark the contrast – Japanese physicians are told to say "we" to convey a subtly *different* military metaphor suggesting *common* engagement in the struggle against cancer.

Costs and benefits of withholding words in South Asia

The Bangladeshi use of the metaphor "holding something in your abdomen" invites our attention for its deceptive appearance to Westerners. A very situated example arises from a moot, country "court," or conflict-resolution meeting that Wilce attended and recorded during his Bangladeshi fieldwork (Wilce 1996). As I (Wilce) listened to negotiations that followed a violent confrontation needing redress in my field village, I sensed the tensions were still palpable and violence was still possible. At one point, my curiosity was piqued when my friend Jalu Miah gave his testimony and the mediators of the confrontation responded: they framed his revelation as something that had emerged from his abdomen! What Jalu revealed was that he had been threatened with a gun. My mind quite naturally – and mistakenly – heard his testimony and the mediator's reframing thereof in terms of cathartic disclosure of his personal trauma. My misimpression arose, in particular, from the question one of the mediators asked Jalu: "How could you have held the word of testimony in your *pet* (abdomen) so long?" But the South Asian ethnotheory implicit therein metaphorically casts the abdomen as a repository for secrets. Thus the chairman chides the aggrieved Jalu for his tardiness in speaking. But the Bangladeshi body metaphor is *not* a parallel to our own ethnotheory of emotion which makes the body a dangerous place to store anger or grief as reified emotion-things. Rather, the mediator upbraided Jalu for impeding the "physiological processes" of the body politic by withholding his testimony until that point. At least from the perspective of those mediating the dispute, for Jalu to hold in his *pet* information needed to "disentangle" a problem (Watson-Gegeo and White 1992) was a social offense; Jalu had been part of the social problem rather than contributing to its social resolution.

This metaphor is not isolated. Locally, it appears in Bengali literature, where women are sometimes characterized as being *unable* to store secrets in their *pet*. We find a parallel even more relevant to the consideration of emotion and its storability – though it comes from the western side of South Asia – in idioms used by women who have spoken with Veena Das about being victims of torture and rape during communal violence in the Punjab. Do they tell the stories again and again in an attempt to cleanse themselves by disclosing or verbally "refining" their traumatic experience? Quite the contrary. Das says the women consider memories of rape a kind of "poisonous knowledge" – memories that dare not be retraced – "[N]one of the metaphors used to describe the self that had become the repository of poisonous knowledge emphasized the need to give expression to this hidden knowledge" (1996: 84). Rather, these women keep the pain and its story inside their abdomens, hiding the stories as babies are hidden in the womb. The "repression" hardly suggests agency at all, let alone virtue. The Punjabi metaphor suggests both. Agency is suggested in two senses, first in terms of the women's choice and visceral struggle to hold things inside. Then, according to Das the abdomen is also made to represent a uniquely female bodily power – the ability to transform a germ into something safe or even good, something such as occurs in pregnancy (1996: 85). The perspective distilled in the metaphor of these Punjabi women contrasts starkly with post-Freudian (but pre-Foucaldian) Western sensibilities about repression.

When we compare South Asian abdomen metaphors with Western metaphors that involve similar "hiding" of words "inside," we see differences in the "text," "upshot," or ideological shading of the metaphors. The value polarities are switched when we move from Western tropes of "getting it all out" to the Punjabi women's hope to keep it "in" and transform "it." Even when disclosing was valorized as it was in the country court discourse recorded by Wilce, it was for the sake of the health of the body politic, not Jalu's body. Admittedly, we lack even ethnographic evidence as to whether the physiological and immunological processes of these women reflect their sense of the positively transformative potential of holding secrets, or whether they would at least feel themselves to be at risk if they brought their secrets out of their abdomens.

Evidence of that sort comes from ethnographic work in Indonesia.

Setres, abdomens, and sorcery in Indonesia

Berman's fieldwork in Java (1998) shows how men and women exercise careful control, especially when speaking Javanese, over how they express emotion. Javanese use the term, *setres*, borrowed from English (stress), to designate a phenomenon so dreadful that it is able to kill, at least in the case of very young children. Parents are, obviously, motivated to protect their children from this threat. Thus, Javanese and Americans share the word "stress," a belief that it can damage one's health, and a concern to manage it. There the similarity ends. Where at least middle class Americans (see Kusserow 1999) encourage their children, as Shakespeare wrote, to "give sorrow words," Javanese parents work hard to desensitize children to sudden changes. That is, instead of training them to be aware of and express feelings, they train them early to maintain poise and equanimity, to rise above emotional lability (Berman 1998).

For decades, anthropologists concerned with culture's role in relation to illness and health have described "culture-bound syndromes" (Simons and Hughes 1985), a concept useful in theorizing American and Indonesian illness patterns. Most so-called culture-bound syndromes — like *amok* and *latah* — presented in the literature lend themselves to psychological or behavioral rather than somatic interpretation. Exceptional accounts include anorexia nervosa in the US (Swartz 1985) and Balinese "pregnancy with stones." Wikan (1990) describes the Balinese syndrome involving a bloating of the abdomen with very hard lumps. It is understood to be caused by sorcery and can lead to death. Key to understanding it, however, is a set of images we could consider metaphoric if they weren't so real to the Balinese. The first is a body-ideal-image in which a flat stomach represents discipline and self-control, linchpins of a Balinese value system. The bloated stomach, by contrast, is the very image of failure to live up to Balinese ideals of hard work and self-denial (Wikan 1990: 258). It is feared, not only because of those moral-aesthetic connotations, but also because of its interpretability as a sign of a sorcerer's attack. That is, the abdomen becomes the site in which Balinese might involuntarily be made to embody status-conflict and social tensions as they boil over in that curse called "pregnancy with stones." Wikan writes:

> If, as Hahn and Kleinman [1983] assert, the mindful body [Scheper-Hughes and Lock 1987] responds to its biopsychosocial environment in terms of cultural expectations and beliefs that facilitate or impede nocebo [noxious beliefs] and placebo effects, then pregnancy with stones might be seen as peculiarly Balinese: a culturally constructed expression of particular fears and despairs. It embodies basic Balinese concepts of beauty, morality, and interpersonal evil. The physical embodiments of fears work, to quote Hahn and Kleinman, to retard "integrated biopsychical processes, demoralizing, *reducing immunological competence* and physiological activation" . . . Conversely, contact with a *balian* [traditional healer] might activate hope, and with it, the person's internal therapeutic system.
>
> (Wikan 1990: 258f, emphasis added)

Wikan's evidence that bodies take on local shapes reflecting local emotions points to the link between physiological (and (psycho)immune) processes and societies that we are claiming is mediated by cultural metaphors. [. . .]

Conclusion

Anthropology can enhance understandings of immune function to the extent that it convinces various publics of the relevance of ethnography along with other forms of research. Together, the several forms of research we have drawn on help us envision a cultural psychoimmunology. They illuminate how variable are cultural models of self, illness, healing, and immunological function. They point to possible embodiments of these divergent metaphors. We have argued for a deep cultural consonance, a model that joins two seemingly incomparable sorts of findings. It joins ethnographic accounts of cultural metaphors and verbal images that body-minds "live by" on the one hand, with experimental evidence from the US that indicates that interventions can teach patients a therapeutic embodiment of images (even of the conduit metaphor). Further research to find measurable immuno-logical reflections of culturally constructed metaphors of body and emotion is a project worth pursuing. Although such research remains to be done, we have put forward a hypothesis that reflects and moves beyond the experimental evidence of Pennebaker and colleagues, and the set of ethnographic case studies we reviewed. That hypothesis is that acts (e.g. writing, disclosing, or hiding words in one's abdomen) that are felt to be consonant with dominant values of one's culture are stress-reducing and thus beneficial.

This hypothesis is a step toward a cultural immunology. A cultural model of (psycho)immunology helps correct imbalances and could thus be part of clinical interventions aimed at enhancing hope. Such a model responds critically to the metaphorical linking (in the self-help literature, for instance) of cancer (or illness in general) with personal failure (Sontag 1978; DiGiacomo 1992; Martin 1993), a link that reproduces Western individualism and reifies agency to the point of blaming the victim for disease. Yet, even critical medical anthropology has the opportunity to build, *with hope*, a sort of multistory edifice on its own partly phenomenological roots. The first "story to be built" is to demonstrate links between body, mind, society, and political economy and healing in cultural specific ways, without collapsing one into another (body into society, etc.; Cone and Martin, this volume). But a second story can be added to this building; a critical anthropology can also be clinically relevant in shaping therapeutic practice, e.g. guiding the training of physicians who are faced with choices about metaphorizing cancer, AIDS, or the common cold. The dilemma for such an applied/critical anthropology becomes that of supporting patients' hopes while avoiding an uncritical reproduction of the *hope in technology* which defines US oncology's "discourse on hope" (Good *et al.* 1990). A PNI that takes cultural variability seriously could not succumb so to a highly particular cultural model (hope in technology). It is a matter of recognizing the sense in which self-healing is both resistance to and a reflection of other technologies of the self and health. [. . .]

References

Balshem, M. (1991). Cancer, control, and causality: talking about cancer in a working-class community. *American Ethnologist, 18*(1), 152–172.

Barchas, P. (1976). Physiological sociology: interface of sociological and biological processes. *Annual Review of Sociology, 2*, 299–333.

Berman, L. (1998). *Speaking through the silence: narratives, social conventions, and power in Java*. New York: Oxford University Press.

Cone, R. and Martin, E. (2003) 'Corporeal flows the immune system, global econ-omies of food, and new implications for health' in J. M. Wilce (ed.) *Social and Cultural Lives of Immune Systems*, Routledge.

Csordas, T. (1988). Elements of chrismatic persuasion and healing. *Medical Anthropology Quarterly, 2*(2), 121–142.

—— (1990 [1988]). Stirling Award Essay: Embodiment as a paradigm for anthropology. *Ethos, 18*(1), 5–47.

—— and Arthur Kleinman (1990). The therapeutic process. In T. M. Johnson and C. F. Sargent (eds), *Medical anthropology: contemporary theory and method.* New York: Praeger.

Das, V. (1996). Language and the body: transactions in the construction of pain. *Daedalus, 125*(1), 67–91.

Desjarlais, R. R. (1992). *Body and emotion: the aesthetics of illness and healing in the Nepal Himalayas.* Philadelphia: University of Pennsylvania Press.

DiGiacomo, S. M. (1992). Metaphor as illness: postmodern dilemmas in the representation of body, mind and disorder. *Medical Anthropology, 14*(1), 109–137.

Dow, J. (1986). Universal aspects of symbolic healing: a theoretical synthesis. *American Anthropologist, 87*(1), 56–69.

Dressler, W. W., Balieiro, M. C., and Dos Santos, J. E. (1998). Culture, socio-economic status, and physical and mental health in Brazil. *Medical Anthropology Quarterly, 12*(4), 424–446.

Esterling, B. A., Antoni, M. H., Fletcher, M. A., Margulies, S., and Schneiderman, N. (1994). Emotional disclosure through writing or speaking modulates latent Epstein-Barr virus antibody titers. *Journal of Consulting and Clinical Psychology, 62*(1), 130–140.

Farnell, B. (1996). Metaphors we move by. *Visual Anthropology, 8*(2–4), 311–335.

Frankenberg, R. (1986). Sickness as cultural performance: Drama, trajectory, and pilgrimage root metaphors and the making of disease social. *International Journal of Health Services, 16*(4), 603–626.

Good, B. (1977). The heart of what's the matter: the semantics of illness in Iran. *Culture, Medicine, and Psychiatry, 1*(1), 25–58.

Good, M.-J. D., Good, B., Schaffer, C., and Lind, S. E. (1990). American oncology and the discourse on hope. *Culture, Medicine, and Psychiatry, 14*(1), 59–79.

—— , Hunt, L., Munakata, T., and Koybayashi, Y. (1993). A Comparative analysis of the culture of biomedicine: disclosure and consequences for treatment in the practice of oncology. In P. Conrad and E. B. Gallagher (eds), *Health and health care in developing countries: sociological perspectives* (pp. 180–211). Philadelphia: Temple University Press.

—— , Munakata, T., Koybayashi, Y., Mattingly, C., and Good, B. J. (1994). Oncology and narrative time. *Social Science and Medicine, 38*(6), 855–862.

Gottman, J. M., Katz, L. F., and Hooven, C. (1996). Parental meta-emotion philosophy and the emotional life of families: theoretical models and preliminary data. *Journal of Family Psychology, 10*(3), 243–268.

Hahn, R., and Kleinman, A. (1983). Belief as pathogen, belief as medicine. *Medical Anthropology Quarterly, 14*(4), 16–19.

Hall, N. R. S. and O'Grady, M. P. (1991). Psychosocial interventions and immune function. In R. Ader, D. L. Felten, and N. Cohen (eds), *Psychoneuroimmunology* (2nd edn). San Diego: Academic Press.

Haraway, D. (1993). The biopolitics of postmodern bodies: determinations of self in immune system discourse. In S. Lindenbaum and M. Lock (eds), *Knowledge, power, and practice: the anthropology of medicine and everyday life* (pp. 364–410). Berkeley: University of California Press.

Johnson, M. (1987). *The body in the mind*. Chicago: University of Chicago Press.

Kiecolt-Glaser, J. K., Glaser, R., Williger, D., Sout, J., Messick, G., Sheppard, S., Ricker, D., Romisher, S. C., Briner, W., Bonnell, G., and Donnerberg, R. (1985). Psychosocial enhancement of immunocompetence in a geriatric population. *Health Psychology, 4*(1), 25–41.

Kirmayer, L. J. (1992). The body's insistence on meaning: metaphor as presentation and representation in illness experience. *Medical Anthropology Quarterly, 6*(4), 323–346.

Kusserow, A. S. (1999). De-homogenizing American individualism: socializing hard and soft individualism in Manhattan and Queens. *Ethos, 27*(2), 210–234.

Lakoff, G. and Johnson, M. (1980). *Metaphors we live by*. Chicago: University of Chicago Press.

Lakoff, G. and Kövecses, Z. (1987). The cognitive model of anger inherent in American English. In D. Holland and N. Quinn (eds), *Cultural models in language and thought* (pp. 195–221). Cambridge: Cambridge University Press.

Lock, M. (1993). Cultivating the body: anthropology and epistemologies of bodily practice and knowledge. *Annual Review of Anthropology, 22,* 133–155.

—— (1998). Menopause: lessons from anthropology. *Psychosomatic Medicine, 60*(4) (Special Issue: Cross-Cultural Research), 410–419.

Lyon, M. (1993). Psychoneuroimmunology: the problem of the situatedness of illness and the conceptualization of healing. *Culture, Medicine, and Psychiatry, 17*(1), 77–97.

Martin, E. (1993). Histories of immune systems. *Culture, Medicine, and Psychiatry, 17*(1), 67–76.

—— (1994). *Flexible bodies: the role of immunity in American culture from the days of polio to the age of AIDS*. Boston: Beacon.

Moerman, D. E. (1979). Anthropology of symbolic healing. *Current Anthropology, 20,* 59–80.

Napier, A. D. (1996). Unnatural selection: social models of the microbial world. In S. A. Plotkin and B. Fantini (eds), *Vaccinia, vaccination, vaccinology: Jenner, Pasteur and their successors* (pp. 335–340). Paris: Elsevier.

Pennebaker, J. W. (1989). Confession, inhibition, and disease. *Advances in Experimental Social Psychology, 22,* 211–244.

—— , Barger, S. D., and Tiebout, J. (1989). Disclosure of traumas and health among Holocaust survivors. *Psychosomatic Medicine, 51*(5), 577–589.

Petrie, K. J., Booth, R. J., Pennebaker, J. W., Davison, K. P., and Thomas, M. G. (1995). Disclosure of trauma and immune response to a hepatitis B vaccination program. *Journal of Consulting and Clinical Psychology, 63*(5), 787–792.

Reddy, M. (1993). The conduit metaphor: a case of frame conflict in our language about language. In A. Ortony (ed.), *Metaphor and thought* (pp. 164–201). Cambridge: Cambridge University Press.

Rosaldo, M. Z. (1984). Towards an anthropology of self and feeling. In R. A. Shweder and R. A. LeVine (eds), *Culture theory: essays on mind, self, and emotion* (pp. 137–157). Cambridge: Cambridge University Press.

Roseman, I. J., Dhawan, N., Rettek, S. I., Naid, R. K., and Thapa, K. (1995). Cultural differences and cross-cultural similarities in appraisals and emotional responses. *Journal of Cross-Cultural Psychology, 26*(1), 23–48.

Scheff, T. J. (1979). *Catharsis in healing, ritual, and drama*. Berkeley: University of California Press.

Scheper-Hughes, N. and Lock, M. (1987). The mindful body: a prolegomenon to future work in medical anthropology. *Medical Anthropology Quarterly*, *1*(1), 6–41.

Shakespeare, W. (1938). Sonnet 30. In Oxford University Press (ed.), *The works of William Shakespeare gathered in one volume* (p. 1228). New York: Oxford University Press.

Simons, R. C. and Hughes, C. (eds). (1985). *Culture-bound syndromes: folk illnesses of psychiatric and anthropological interest*. Dordrecht: D. Reidel.

Sontag, S. (1978). *Illness as metaphor*. New York: Farrar, Strauss, Giroux.

Swartz, L. (1985). Anorexia nervosa as a culture-bound syndrome. *Social Science and Medicine*, *20*(7), 725–730.

Tambiah, S. J. (1979). A performative approach to ritual. *Proceedings of the British Academy*, *65*, 113–169.

Watson-Gegeo, K. and White, G. M. (eds). (1992). *Disentangling: the discourse of interpersonal conflict in Pacific Island societies*. Stanford: Stanford University Press.

Wikan, U. (1990). *Managing turbulent hearts: a Balinese formula for living*. Chicago: University of Chicago.

Wilce, J. M. (1996). Reduplication and reciprocity in imagining community: the play of tropes in a rural Bangladeshi moot. *Journal of Linguistic Anthropology*, *6(2)*, 188–222.

Chapter 28

Elizabeth A. Wilson

THE WORK OF ANTIDEPRESSANTS

Preliminary notes on how to build an alliance between feminism and psychopharmacology

. . . **O**NE OF THE CENTRAL DIFFICULTIES in generating a useful dialogue between feminism and psychopharmacology is the anti-biologism of contemporary feminist theory. It has become axiomatic that culture rather than nature is the proper sphere for feminist politics. This presumption underpinned the success of social constructionism as the premier mode of feminist analysis in the social sciences in the 1990s. Indeed, the turn against biological explanation was so conceptually lucrative for feminism that it now seems a non-sense to think of biology as a site of transformation or innovation (Wilson, 2004b). This schism between politics and biology remains a significant obstacle for feminist work in the current psychocultural climate. Without conceptual interest in how biology invents, transforms, crafts, redistributes, incorporates and bequeaths, fem-inists will remain perplexed by the character of psycho-pharmaceutical events.

In this commentary, I offer a preliminary analysis of how feminism and psychopharmacology could be brought into a more dynamic and fruitful alliance. I will argue that close attention to pharmacological data opens up new avenues for analysing the embodiment of melancholy.

Pharmacokinetics

Let me begin with a prosaic but important datum about the new antidepressant medications: they are all administered orally.[1] That is, they are manufactured in tablet form, and they are swallowed. While it is the case that most pharmaceuticals are administered orally, there is particular significance in the oral administration of antidepressants: there is an intimate connection between the gut and depression, making intervention via the gut an especially felicitous means of treatment for depressed mood (Wilson, 2004a). While conventional neuroscientific and psychiatric texts often posit a direct link from drug to brain, close attention to the details of drug absorption, distribution, metabolism and excretion (what is called the drug's pharmacokinetics) shows that the viscera are also essential to how disorders of mood become instantiated and how they can be treated. Rather than validating a single, central site of determination for mood (the brain), the pharmacokinetics of antidepressant drugs shed light on how depression is distributed, in both organic and psychic registers, all through the body.

What are the pharmacokinetic trajectories of an antidepressant? For any orally administered drug, the gastrointestinal (GI) tract is the site at which the drug is absorbed into the body, and GI distress (nausea, delayed gastric emptying and constipation) is a commonly experienced adverse effect. Because oral administration of drugs is so widespread, management of the gut's response to drugs has become a crucial part of pharmaceutical research. For example, there are numerous technologies available for controlling where in the GI tract drugs are released. Tablets can be specially coated so that they don't dissolve in the stomach but will dissolve in the intestine; or pills can be manufactured to float on the gastric juices, thus extending their time in the stomach (Jantzen and Robinson, 2001). In most cases, the gut itself is not the target of therapeutic action; the drug is being released into the body some distance from its intended site of action (Katzung, 2001). The pathways from the gut to that target site are often circuitous, and it is these pathways that have arrested my critical interest.

A drug like an antidepressant that is intended for the central nervous system (CNS) must first pass from the gut lumen into the bloodstream. Once it has passed though the gut mucosa, the drug is transported via the portal vein to the liver where enzymes remove a certain amount of the drug (this is called first-pass clearance). From the liver, the remaining percentage of the drug moves into general (systemic) circulation in the body, where it is distributed into the fluid inside and between the cells of the body's tissues and organs. The brain is targeted rapidly, as are the liver, kidneys and other organs that are well supplied with blood. Eventually (this can take anywhere from several minutes to several hours) muscle tissue, the remaining viscera, the skin and the body's fat will also be infused with the drug (Wilkinson, 2001).[2] The first thing to note, then, is that the physiological itinerary of an antidepressant takes in every organ of the body. Might we not wonder about antidepressant effects of drug action at these other sites?

The passage of a drug from systemic circulation into the brain is also quite intricate. The brain is protected by a barrier that prevents the transit of large molecules and potentially toxic solutes from the blood into the brain itself (Begley, 2003). Serotonin, for example, cannot pass the blood-brain barrier (it is too large). Even though there are significant reservoirs of serotonin in the rest of the body,[3] the brain must synthesize its own serotonin from other, smaller molecules that are able to cross the blood-brain barrier. To put this in quotidian form: it isn't possible to increase serotonin levels in the brain simply by ingesting more serotonin. One of the ways in which the blood-brain barrier functions is simply obstructive—the cells that make up the walls of the brain's capillaries are so tightly packed together that drugs are not able to pass between these cells into brain tissue, as they would in other parts of the body (Begley, 2003). Prevented from passing *between* cells, drugs must pass *through* the cells, and to do this they require some assistance from a chemical transport system. One of the most widely used methods for getting drugs across the blood-brain barrier is to make them lipid-soluble—the more lipophilic a drug is, the more readily it will cross the blood-brain barrier (Wilkinson, 2001). SSRIs are small molecules that are lipophilic, and they readily pass across the blood-brain barrier (Brøsen and Rasmussen, 1996).

Once inside the brain, SSRIs (selective serotonin reuptake inhibitors) are thought to increase the amount of serotonin that is available for neurotransmission (by inhibiting its reuptake in the synapse); and in turn this increase in serotonin is thought to elevate mood. It has been conventional (in both biopsychiatric texts and the political literatures that agitate against them) to focus on this particular destination of an antidepressant—as though the cerebral synapse were an antidepressant's natural or most important coalface. My interest has been diverted elsewhere—to the many biological sites and processes implicated in the ingestion of an antidepressant pill. It seems to me that too narrow a focus on the brain occludes other important events in antidepressant metabolism, making it difficult to think anew about the nature of body-mind relations.

Body and brain

There are two issues I would like to draw out of these data that may help inform feminist theories of body and mind.

First, drugs work with the whole body. While antidepressants may be intended for the brain, their therapeutic effects are gleaned from a wide variety of responses in other organs. Given that SSRIs and SNRIs (serotonin-norephinephrine reuptake inhibitors) are widely distributed in the body by systemic circulation and that they work effectively on synapses in the CNS, it would seem likely that they are also targeting the synapses of the nerves in the peripheral nervous system, especially the gut. Any pharmaceutical alleviation of dysthymic symptomatology, then, cannot be attributed solely to effects in cortical and subcortical structures in the brain, it must also include the soothing and animating effects on the viscera (Wilson, 2004a, 2004b). Pharmacokinetic data support models of the body in which simple lines of cause and effect (drug to brain to mood) are refracted; and these data are immensely valuable for feminism, as it argues for more dynamic and expansive accounts of the body. Close observation of these data finds not biological determinism but biological overdeterminism.

Even though the viscera are not mentioned as target sites for SSRI action in psychiatric or pharmacological texts, the effective pharmaceutical treatment of depression requires engagement with the organic periphery as well as the brain. Perhaps because the gut is the delivery system for these drugs, it has been thought of as simply a conduit for drug action and not as a participant in the drug's therapeutic effects. Conceptual schemata that privilege the centre over the periphery, or that draw radical distinctions between (active) agents and (passive) vessels have been the target of ongoing feminist intervention (e.g., Keller, 1995). If the neurological and pharmacological sciences have been particularly forceful sites for reinforcing these problematic conceptual structures, it seems to be despite the data they are generating, not because of them. Indeed, the neurological and pharmacokinetic data on anti-depressants strongly indicate that the body as a whole is implicated in depressive states. The viscera aren't mere transfer stations for agents that will have their effects elsewhere. Rather, the liver and the gut provide the bioaffective tone of depressions: if your depressions are agitated, or soporific, or angry, or anorectic that is due in no small part to the attitude of the visceral organs. It appears that the co-assembly of these traits with cognitive and ideational schemata (suicidality, hopelessness, guilt) is what generates a depressive condition serious enough to warrant intervention and treatment.

The second issue I would like to consider in the pharmacokinetic data concerns the brain and its interface with extra-cerebral systems. Just how isolated and autocratic is the brain? Are the biological bases of dysthymic states exclusively cerebral? Neurological and pharmacological descriptions of the blood-brain barrier often stress the sequestration of the brain: 'a major function of the [blood-brain barrier] is that of neuroprotection. Over a lifetime the CNS will be exposed to a wide range of neurotoxic metabolites and acquired xenobiotics, which may cause cell damage and death' (Begley, 2003: 84). Notions of the brain as an autonomous, self-contained organ are common enough in both the scientific and popular imaginary. However, the pharmacological work on the blood-brain barrier seems less interested in the defensive and segregating nature of the barrier, than in its function as a system of transportation and communication with the outside. As we follow these data, we find that the brain is always, necessarily implicated in relations with other organs and other extra-bodily systems; the blood-brain barrier is one particularly intensive site for such xenobiotic transmissions.

For example, the brain doesn't manufacture serotonin internally and independently of the body. Rather, the synthesis of serotonin requires ongoing commerce between the brain and the gut and the cultural milieu. The basic building block of serotonin is tryptophan, an amino acid that is small enough to cross the blood-brain barrier. Tryptophan is an essential amino acid, which means it cannot be manufactured by the body—it must be supplied to the body as part of the diet. Chocolate, bananas, milk, meat and fish are all high in tryptophan. The production of CNS serotonin is further complicated by the amount of carbohydrate that is ingested in the diet. If the diet is heavy in carbohydrates (bread, cake, icecream), the body will produce insulin in order to control high blood sugar. The insulin will remove most of the other amino acids from the blood, reducing competition at the blood-brain barrier, and allowing a disproportionate amount of tryptophan to pass from the blood to the brain (Wurtman *et al.*, 2003). This means that levels of serotonin in the brain are dependent on a number of extra-cerebral systems: for example, enzymes in the liver, conditions in the gut lumen, and the psychocultural milieu governing diet. No one of these systems entirely governs serotonin traffic. Rather, serotonergic activity is an overdetermined network of relations among organs, and among biological and cultural and psychological systems.

Any regulation of the serotonergic system—including the ingestion of SSRIs to regulate mood—must grasp this network logic in order to be successful. A narrow focus on the brain as the sole biological source of psychological malady will obstruct the lines of connection that tie organ to organ, and that underpin the biological possibility of recovery. To paraphrase Winnicott (1964)—there is no such thing as a brain, there is always a brain and another system. My hypothesis is this: the biological disintegration of mood is a breakdown not of the brain *per se*, or of the liver or the gut—it is a breakdown of the relations among organs. The pharmaceutical treatment of depression has to be the management—not of a place or a centre or even a neurological pathway—but of an organic capacity to connect. When they work, SSRIs reiterate the serotonergic networks that traverse the body and reanimate the natural affinities among organs. Effectively administered, SSRIs can promote a profound, long-lasting, organic empathy.

Biological politics

Of course, feminists have argued that psychopharmaceuticals are often not effectively administered. There is also extensive debate in the feminist and affiliated literatures about whether antidepressants, in particular, work in the manner promoted by pharmaceutical manufacturers (e.g. Healy, 2004). These critics tend to emphasize the social motivations for keeping women medicated; they are critical of the practices of pharmaceutical companies and the doctors who collude with them, and they remain dubious about the efficacy of pharmaceutical treatments for conditions they diagnose as essentially cultural in origin (e.g. Griggers, 1997; Zita, 1998). In this short commentary, I have taken a different approach to the nexus of feminism and psychopharmaceuticals—one that is more directly engaged with the biological substrata of psychological disequilibrium. This orientation is governed by my conviction that effective political engagement with the contemporary life sciences requires ongoing intimacy with their data. It is my expectation that close, conceptually rigorous attention to biological detail will procure more dynamic models of depression than we have hitherto suspected.

Notes

1   The new generation antidepressants include the selective serotonin reuptake inhibitors (SSRIs) Prozac/fluoxetine, Zoloft/sertraline, Paxil/paroxetine, Celexa/citalopram, and Luvox/fluvoxamine. As well as the SSRIs there are new 'atypical' antidepressants that came onto the US market around the same time: Serzone/nefazodone, Effexor/venlafaxine and Wellbutrin/bupropion. These drugs are more heterogeneous in their pharmacological action—they are less specific to the serotonin system and act on other neurotransmitter systems, specifically nor-epinephrine (Potter and Hollister, 2001). They are sometimes called third generation, heterocyclic or serotonin-norepinephrine reuptake inhibitors (SNRI) antidepressants. Prozac/fluoxetine is manufactured in liquid and oral form. The other SSRIs and the other atypical antidepressants are only manufactured in oral form (Potter and Hollister, 2001). Some of the well-established tricyclic antidepressants (e.g. Elavil/amitriptyline and Tofranil/imipramine) can be administered by injection: 'Intramuscular administration of some tricyclic antidepressants (notably amitriptyline and clomipramine [Anafranil]) can be performed under special circumstances, particularly with severely depressed, anorexic patients who may refuse oral medication or ECT' (Baldessarini, 2001: 463).

2   Each of the SSRI antidepressants varies in terms of how much of the drug reaches systemic circulation. This is called a drug's bioavailability. The bioavailability of Paxil/paroxetine is around 50%, for example, Prozac/fluoxetine has a reasonably high bioavailability (70%) and Luvox/fluvoxamine is even higher (greater than 90%) (Potter and Hollister, 2001). The differences in bioavailability are further amplified by the fact that the metabolites of the SSRIs (i.e. the substances produced by metabolism of the drug in the liver and elsewhere) can also have antidepressant effects. The metabolite of fluoxetine (norfluoxetine), for example, is four times more potent as a serotonin reuptake inhibitor than is fluoxetine itself.

3   Ninety-five percent of the body's serotonin is stored outside the CNS—in the blood and in the extensive network of nerves that encases the gut (Wilson, 2004b). In fact, serotonin was first discovered in the blood, where it was understood to be a vasoconstrictor (thus the name sero-tonin: a serum agent affecting vascular tone). It was some years before it was located in the brain and accepted as a neurotransmitting substance, in both the central and peripheral systems (Gershon, 1998).

References

Baldessarini, R. (2001). Drugs and the treatment of psychiatric disorders: Depression and anxiety disorders. In Hardman, J. & Limbird, L. (Eds), *Goodman and Gilman's The pharmacological basis of therapeutics*, 10th edn, 447–483. New York: McGraw-Hill.

Begley, D. (2003). Understanding and circumventing the blood-brain barrier. *Acta Paediatrica Supplement, 443*, 83–91.

Gershon, M.D. (1998). *The second brain*. New York: Harper-Perennial.

Griggers, C. (1997). *Becoming woman*. Minneapolis: University of Minnesota Press.

Jantzen, G. & Robinson, J. (2001). Sustained- and controlled-release drug-delivery systems. In G. Banker, & C. Rhodes (Eds) *Modern pharmaceuticals*, 4th edn, 501–528. New York: Marcel Dekker.

Katzung, B. (2001). *Basic and clinical pharmacology*, 8th edn. New York: McGraw-Hill.

Keller, E.F. (1995). *Refiguring life: Metaphors of twentieth-century biology*. New York: Columbia University Press.

Potter, W. & Hollister, L. (2001). Antidepressant agents. In B. Katzung, (Ed.), *Basic and clinical pharmacology*, 8 edn, 498–511. New York: McGraw-Hill.

Wilkinson, G. (2001). Pharmacokinetics: The dynamics of drug absorption, distribution, and elimination. In Hardman, J. & L. Limbird (Eds) *Goodman and Gilman's The pharmacological basis of therapeutics*, 10th edn, 3–29. New York: McGraw-Hill.

Wilson, E.A. (2004a). Gut feminism, *differences: A Journal of Feminist Cultural Studies, 15*(3), 66–94.

Wilson, E.A. (2004b). *Psychosomatic: Feminism and the neurological body*. Durham, NC: Duke UP.

Winnicott, D.W. (1964). *The child, the family and the outside world*. Harmondsworth: Penguin.

Wurtman, R. Wurtman, J. Regan, M. McDermott, J. Tsay, R. & Breu, J. (2003). Effects of normal meals rich in carbohydrates or proteins on plasma tryptophan and tyrosine ratios. *American Journal of Clinical Nutrition, 77*, 128–132.

Zita, J. (1998). *Body talk: Philosophical reflection on sex and gender*. New York: Columbia University Press.

Chapter 29

Nikolas Rose

DISORDERS WITHOUT BORDERS?

The expanding scope of psychiatric practice

[. . .]

An expanding problem

... IN 2001 THE WORLD HEALTH ORGANIZATION (WHO) published *Mental health: New understanding, new hope*, to draw attention to the public health issues raised by rates of mental disorders across the world. It estimated that more than 25 per cent of people are affected by mental disorders at some point in their lives. It claimed that depression affects over 340 million people worldwide. It predicted:

> By the year 2020, if current trends for demographic and epidemi-ological transition continue, the burden of depression will increase to 5.7% of the total burden of disease, becoming the second leading cause of DALYs [disability adjusted life years] lost. Worldwide it will be second only to ischemic heart disease for DALYs lost for both sexes. In the developed regions, depression will then be the highest ranking cause of burden of disease.
>
> (WHO, 2001: 30)

Other reports paint a similar picture. In the US, in June 2005, Kessler and his colleagues, on the basis of a household survey of over 9,000 people, using a diag-nostic interview, reported that, in any one year, 26.2 per cent of adult Americans reported having symptoms that would qualify them for a *DSM-IV* diagnosis of mental disorder, with the anxiety disorders leading at 18.1 per cent, followed by mood disorders, notably depression, at 9.5 per cent and impulse control disorders at 8.9 per cent—a total of over 57 million Americans diagnosable with mental disorder in any one year (Kessler *et al.*, 2005). . . . And they concluded that 'About half of Americans will meet the criteria for a *DSM-IV* disorder sometime in their life, with first onset usually in childhood or adolescence' (Kessler *et al.*, 2005a).

The belief that around half of the population will meet the criteria for a mental disorder at some time in their life was originally proposed by Kessler and his colleagues a decade ago (Blazer *et al.*, 1994; Kessler *et al.*, 1994; Wittchen *et al.*, 1994). It is not a peculiarly American perception. In 2005, a Task Force of the European College of Neuropsychopharmacology on 'The Size and Burden of Mental Disorders in Europe' reported the results of a series of studies that aimed 'to reach a consensus on what we know about the size, burden and cost of "disorders of the brain" in each European country and—ultimately—in Europe as a whole' for a total of 20 mental and neurological disorders (Wittchen *et al.*, 2005: 355). The results were truly alarming. . . .

Some 27 per cent or 82.7 million of the adult European Union (EU) population (18–65 years of age):

> . . . is or has been affected by at least one mental disorder in the past 12 months. Taking into account the considerable degree of comorbidity (about one third had more than one disorder), the most frequent disorders are anxiety disorders, depressive, somatoform and substance dependency disorders. . . . Only 26% of cases had any consultation with professional health care services, a finding suggesting a considerable degree of unmet need.
>
> (Wittchen and Jacobi, 2005: 357)

And the editorial of this special issue summed up the situation thus:

> Even though only a restricted range of all existing mental and neurological disorders from the *ICD 10* or the *DSM-IV* was considered, there is clear evidence that more than one-third of the adult EU population is or has been affected by at least one disorder in the past year, or 50% of the EU population . . . if lifetime risk is considered. . . . [M]ental disorders are associated with immense costs of over 290 billion Euros, the majority of which were not healthcare costs.
>
> (Wittchen *et al.*, 2005: 355–356)

The message is self-evident—we need more research, earlier diagnoses, better treatment, and education and training of policy makers and the public about this public health problem. This report was one basis for the European Commission (EC) Green Paper, *Improving the mental health of the population: Towards a strategy on mental health for the European Union*, which estimated that 'mental ill health costs the EU an estimated 3%–4% of GDP, mainly through lost productivity' (EC Health and Consumer Protection Directorate-General, 2005: 4) and proposed a strategy to promote the mental health of all (2005: 8). It would be difficult to disagree. But how has this perception arisen at the start of the twenty-first century? A perception of a Europe, indeed a world, so ravaged by mental ill health that a diagnosable mental disorder afflicts every third person each year, of whom probably two-thirds remain undiagnosed and untreated. Is it, perhaps, something to do with those 'risk factors' identified by the WHO and repeated in that Green Paper—access to drugs and alcohol; displacement; isolation and alienation; lack of education, transport, housing; neighbourhood disorganization; peer rejection; poor social circumstances; poor nutrition; poverty; racial injustice and discrimination; social disadvantage; urbanization; violence and delinquency; war; work stress; unemployment (WHO, 2004b: 21). A doleful and familiar list, it is true. But can these travails have really become more intense, in this, the most wealthy and healthy of all parts of this planet in the most wealthy and healthy century of human existence. If not that, then what? Has the population of Europe, indeed the world, always been so beset by undiagnosed mental illness? Or, as I will suggest, do these figures arise from something else? [. . .]

Accounting for expansion

How should we make sense of such data? Can it really be that half of us, over our lifetimes, will suffer from a mental disorder? Of course, we wouldn't be surprised if half of us, in our lifetimes, suffered from a physical disorder—indeed we would be surprised if this was not so. And we would want to make health services available to all and be scandalized if only a quarter of those conditions were treated. Yet we are troubled by such a perception of prevalence of mental disorders. Why? Is this a residue of an earlier age of stigma? A throwback to an earlier age of anti-psychiatry? A suspicion of the very idea of a mental disorder? A belief that this perception serves some interests but not others? A specific worry about drug treatment? Or is it, perhaps, the sense that the very idea of normality or mental health is at stake.

In what follows, I would like to explore five interlinked hypotheses that might account for the perceptions of the rates of mental disorder that I have sketched.

- *first*, that, in reality, there is more mental disorder today than in previous times;
- *second*, that we are more aware of mental disorder and better at recognizing it;
- *third*, that this arises from what the sociologists term 'moral entrepreneurship' on the part of psychiatrists as passionate advocates for a cause they believe in: a neglected source of misery only they can identify and conquer;
- *fourth*, today's favourite culprit, 'Big Pharma'—that it is the pharmaceutical companies, in a cynical search for market share, profit and shareholder value, who, in a multitude of ways, are distorting our perception and treatment of mental disorder;
- *fifth*, that this arises from a reshaping of our discontents in a psychiatric form—perhaps even a psychiatrization of the human condition itself.

Hypothesis 1: There is just more of it about

The perception that mental disorder is on an alarming upward trend because of the conditions of modern life has been a recurrent theme since at least the birth of psychiatry in the nineteenth century. Aubrey Lewis himself points this out in his classic paper on Social Psychiatry, which he delivered in 1957:

> It has long been customary to assert that mental disorder is on the increase, because of the more and more complex strains which society imposes on its members. A hundred and thirty years ago the psychiatrist Esquirol read a paper in Paris on the question: 'Are there more madmen today than there were forty years ago?' There was then widespread alarm at 'the [f]rightful increase of insanity', which people said menaced France with calamity. In his admirable review Esquirol showed that the alleged increase was spurious; more people had come into hospitals, but . . . the reputation of the asylums had changed from that of cruel prisons to humanely conducted hospitals. Many quiet patients who would not formerly have been sent to these institutions were now admitted and came willingly. Hence the apparent increase.
>
> (in Lewis, 1967a: 263)

Most social scientists are similarly unconvinced that the rise in psychiatric diagnoses reflects a 'frightful increase' in mental disorder. There is good evidence that poverty, poor housing, stressful working experiences and the like are associated with increased rates of psychiatric morbidity. But I don't think we can extrapolate historical trends from this, or agree that contemporary social conditions are more pathogenic than those of earlier times. To be blunt, the question 'Is there more mental disorder today than before?' is impossible to answer because our own notions of normality and mental disorder are inescapably historically and culturally specific.

Hypothesis 2: We are just better at recognizing it

Do mental disorders simply await their recognition by adequate diagnostic schemes? I don't think so. Our perception of 'mental disorder' today bears little relation to that in other times and places. From the mid-nineteenth to the mid-twentieth century, the walls of the asylum marked a distinction between two empires, that of madness and that of nervous disorders, the property of different explanatory systems, different institutions, different cultural understandings, different authorities. This distinction weakened in the mid twentieth century, with the unlocking of wards, day hospitals, out-patient provision and so forth. From the 1980s, community psychiatry multiplied the sites for the practice of psychiatry—in psychiatric wards in general hospitals, special hospitals, medium secure units, day hospitals, out-patient clinics, child guidance clinics, prisons, children's homes, sheltered housing, drop-in centres, community mental health centres, domiciliary care by community psychiatric nurses, schools and, of course, in the general practitioner's surgery. This blurred the distinction between psychiatric professionals who treated the mentally ill and those who treated what once were termed 'neuroses'—the complaints of those who were unable to function according to the norms and expectations of the various departments of life. In short, more and more people and problems were opened up to the diagnostic gaze and therapeutic interventions of psychiatry (Rose, 1986).

This changing territory of psychiatry has been embodied in diagnostic manuals and classifications across the second half of the twentieth century. Many of a psychoanalytic persuasion in the US, and many social psychiatrists in the UK, argued that that there was no clear distinction between normality and mental illness, that, as Karl Menninger put it, 'most people have some degree of mental illness at some time, and many of them have a degree of mental illness most of the time' (Menninger *et al.*, 1965: 33). This expansion of the psychiatric gaze, embodied in the first and second *Diagnostic and Statistical Manuals* published in 1952 and 1968, was one element in criticisms that psychiatry was simply medicalizing difference and was an apparatus of social control. Some suggest that the publication of *DSM-III* in 1980 was a response to that criticism (Wilson, 1993). It stressed that that diagnosis must be based on a pattern of symptoms that was not merely an expectable response to an event, but a manifestation of a dysfunction in the person: 'Neither deviant behavior . . . nor conflicts that are primarily between the individual and society are mental disorders unless . . . a symptom of a dysfunction in the person' (American Psychiatric Association, 1980). In a moment I will question the success of that attempt to avoid psychiatrizing problems of living. But *DSM-III* does not restrict the scope of mental disorder. Its claims to provide neutral empirical descriptions of symptom patterns did quite the reverse. It implied that psychiatrists could diagnose as mental disorders, things ranging from troublesome conduct in children to men's problems in getting an erection. The diagnostic manuals of our own age are analogous to those that arose from the nineteenth-century asylums—they suggest some fundamental connections between all those under the gaze of the psychiatrist in our own Age of Freedom.

These changes were accompanied by another—a contested and partial unification of treatment in the form of psychiatric drugs. This is not the place to tell that history, or the ways in which drugs became part of the treatment for almost all conditions within the expanded psychiatric system. Not is it the place to discuss the implications of the new brain sciences and the suggestion that variations in the neurotransmitter system underpin not only frank mental disorders but also variations in personality, as well as transient fluctuations in mood or conduct. Here I want to note just one consequence. We now have a group of loosely related drugs that claim to treat not just major psychotic breakdowns, but the minor troubles that impair people's capacity to think, feel or act in the ways in which they or others would want them to. This makes it possible to believe that all these conditions have a 'family resemblance'—that conditions from autistic disorder to zoophilia are varieties of the same sort of thing.

Hypothesis 3: Psychiatrists as 'moral entrepreneurs'

Undoubtedly proclamations by public health bodies about the personal and social harm from untreated mental disorders stem from genuine concerns. Frank Ayd's 1961 book *Recognizing the depressed patient* has often been cited as contributing both to the increase in diagnoses of depression and to its framing as a condition treatable with drugs. Ayd had carried out the clinical trials for amitryptiline as an antidepressant for Merck who held the patent, and Merck distributed his book widely. As Emily Martin (2005) has pointed out, drawing on his interview with David

Healy, Ayd was a passionate believer in the need for psychiatric drugs to alleviate mental illness: in 1957, he 'spoke of the emerging psychopharmacology as a "blessing for mankind" '—and his wife sometimes compared him to John the Baptist preaching the coming thing (Healy, 1996: 85). In those days, pharmaceutical companies were viewed as ethical allies with public health professionals in the defeat of disease: on the evidence of the recent success of new drugs for physical conditions, their prospects to improve the human condition, in alliance with psychiatrists, seemed enormous.

The sociologist Howard Becker coined a term for such campaigns—'moral entrepreneurship' (Becker, 1963). This is not meant to disparage them, but merely to describe their evangelical quality and the many characteristics shared by such campaigns for righting wrongs. Today, after years in the doldrums, biological psychiatrists and psychopharmacologists are excited, perhaps with good reason, about their capacity to treat and perhaps even to cure. This excitement goes hand in hand with endeavours to convince us of the seriousness of the problem to which these treatments are a solution. But we need to interrogate this way of formulating the problem and its solution.

I have suggested that these alarming figures arise, in part at least, from the methods of inquiry themselves—epidemiological surveys using diagnostic interviews. WHO asserts that psychiatric diagnoses, today, are not just reliable but also valid. The debate over diagnosis in psychiatry has run for centuries, and so have arguments over its desirability, reliability and validity. Critics suggest that many diagnoses, especially those 'on the borders', are judgements of social deviance or problems of living that have no place in psychiatry, or that they misrecognize intelligible responses to social situations as symptoms of individual psychopathology (Double, 2002; Wakefield, 1992). *DSMs* from the 1980s claimed to answer this criticism. But their criteria for personality disorder and many other disorders explicitly require an assessment of the conduct, mood or thoughts in question against a norm of social functioning, or a norm of appropriate responses to a particular situation such as sexual attraction or bereavement. These diagnostic manuals thus capture behaviour that, as Jerome Wakefield puts it, 'need not originate in dysfunctions' and some that is 'clearly the result of conflict with others or with society' (1997: 635).

DSM-IV stipulates that diagnoses should not be made where patterns of behaviour are responses to external conditions, rather than reflecting a dysfunction within the individual. Wakefield himself, in his research on conduct disorder, suggests that *clinicians* can make that distinction. But he also points out that while *DSM-IV* says this, the items in its diagnostic checklist, for conduct disorder and many other disorders, concern only the behaviour of the individual (Wakefield *et al.*, 2002). How, then, can those using such checklists avoid 'false positives'? *DSM-IV* tries to deal with this by adding a 'clinical significance criterion', of the form 'The symptoms cause clinically significant distress or impairment in social, occupational, or other important areas of functioning' (Spitzer and Wakefield, 1999: 1857). But the epidemiological surveys that generate such high prevalence rates are not conducted by clinicians in clinical settings. *Even in clinical settings*, evidence shows that initial medical diagnoses depend a great deal upon the background expectations and beliefs of the doctor, and are shaped by such issues as the gender, age, race, social background and demeanour of the patient. The same is true in psychiatry, where diagnoses may also be shaped by prior information available to the diagnostician as to the background of the proto-patient, their pathway to the clinic, their previous history and so forth. Further, in sites outside the clinic there are often incentives to diagnose, rather than not to diagnose.

Consider, for example, ADHD. [Olfson and colleagues] suggest that the overall observed increase might have arisen as a result of the recognition by the US Department of Education, in 1991, that ADHD was a disability that conferred eligibility for special education. This, combined with awareness campaigns and the activities of ADHD advocacy groups, increased the willingness of school teachers and others to identify the condition, the use of school-based clinics to diagnose it and the take-up of assessment instruments to make the diagnosis (Olfson *et al.*, 2003). [. . .]

Psychiatric diagnoses today take place in a climate where ideas of risk, precaution, prevention are in the ascendant. We know from other examples—for instance, screening programmes for breast cancer or prostate cancer—that the health consequences of screening are ambiguous—widespread screening generates false positives, leading to many being brought within the scope of treatment and started on the career of patient who would never, in fact, suffer from or be troubled by that condition. Historians of medicine identify many similar examples of 'diagnostic creep', often elicited by the technology itself—diagnostic tools elicit signs that are taken as evidence of pathologies that would previously have been invisible, and these 'proto-diseases' are themselves taken to require treatment (Rosenberg, 2003). No wonder, then, that many are so concerned with the widespread use of diagnostic tests that transform malaise into psychiatric classifications requiring treatment. Such tests are now found in self-help form on internet websites, in checklist form in schools and clinics, and in screening programmes such as those proposed by George W. Bush's New Freedom Commission on Mental Health. And such screening and testing is often proposed or supported by pharmaceutical companies (Lenzer, 2004).

Hypothesis 4: Big Pharma

This leads me naturally to my fourth hypothesis—Big Pharma is to blame. The industry, it is claimed, uses its wealth, its lobbyists, its tame psychiatrists, the cunning of the marketing profession to influence governments, regulators, researchers, medical practitioners and patients. Its aim is simply to increase markets, not merely by selling new cures for old diseases, but constructing new diseases to fit the products that claim to treat them. There has, of course, been much controversy over the safety and efficacy of the new generation of psychopharmaceuticals. Critics also suggest that the pharmaceutical companies promote the illusion that their different drugs are each targeted to a specific condition, a claim that has more to do with marketing products to fit discrete *DSM-IV* diagnoses than any actual evidence of such specificity. This is not the place to evaluate these arguments: I want to make some different points.

Pharmaceutical companies certainly seek to increase the use of their products through influencing the prescribing practices of doctors, though most doctors claim to resist this influence. They also act directly on potential patients as consumers of their products. In the United States, the use of 'direct to consumer' advertising for psychopharmaceuticals has come under particular scrutiny—especially advertisements relating to mild to moderate depression, anxiety disorders, conditions such as pre-menstrual dysphoric disorder and even bipolar disorder. Such advertising seeks not just to market a drug, but to reshape the potential patient's understanding and presentation of their condition to their doctor in the form of a particular *DSM* disorder for which a specific drug has been licensed and marketed. Disorder and remedy are mutually aligned. There is some evidence that that physicians today feel under pressure from patients to prescribe particular drugs. Certainly, in medicine as in consumption more generally, we are seeing a phenomenon that is driven, in part at least, by the reshaping of demand.

Pharmaceutical companies seek to increase demand for their products in many ways. They fund, and sometimes set up, campaigning groups for particular conditions. They support and sometimes initiate disease awareness campaigns for conditions where they have the patent for the treatment. These campaigns point to the misery caused by the apparent symptoms of this undiagnosed or untreated condition, and interpret available data so as to maximize beliefs about prevalence, shaping malaise into a specific clinical form. Such campaigns often involve the use of public relations firms to place stories in the media, providing victims—sometimes celebrities—who will tell their stories and supplying experts who will explain them in terms of the new disorder. For example Roche's 1997 campaign for its antidepressant Auroxix (moclobemide) for the treatment of social phobia in Australia involved the use of the public relations company to place stories in the press, an alliance with a patients group called the Obsessive Compulsive and Anxiety Disorders Federation of Victoria, funding a large conference on social phobia and promoting maximal estimates of prevalence (Moynihan, Heath *et al.*, 2002). These are not covert tactics—as a quick glance at the 'Practical Guides' published on the web by the magazine *Pharmaceutical Marketing* will show.

There is, therefore, some evidence for Hypothesis 4—that Big Pharma is responsible. But I think this is only part of the picture. This is not to say that there is not corrupt practice, to condone the non-disclosure or manipulation of the results of clinical trials, or to deny that some doctors, and some public health officials, and all pharmaceutical companies, have a vested interest in promoting the beliefs in the widespread prevalence of disorders, the damage wrought to individuals and society by their inadequate or partial treatment, and their ready and effective treatability by drugs. But I think that we need, at the very least, to situate it in a wider context.

Hypothesis 5: The psychiatric reshaping of discontents

The shaping of discontent today certainly has novel features, including the role of the pharmaceutical industry and the massive capitalization of ill health. But at any time and place, human discontents are inescapably shaped, moulded, given expression, judged and responded to in terms of certain languages of description and explanation, articulated by experts and authorities, leading to specific styles and forms of intervention. What, then, is specific to today?

As Simon Wessely points out, experiencing symptoms is the rule, not the exception:

> In one early survey 14% of a community sample reported having no symptoms at all. . . . An American study of healthy university students taking no medication found that no fewer than 81% had experienced at least one somatic symptom during the previous three days. . . . Over a six week period 43% of normal American women reported at least one somatic symptom . . . whilst women in South London experienced symptoms on one day out of three, chiefly headache and fatigue. . . . A population based survey of the Nordic countries will report that up to 75% of subjects experienced at least one subjective health complaint in the last 30 days—with more than 50% experiencing tiredness, and 33% muscular pain.
>
> (1997)

He is reviewing evidence on somatic symptoms. But as he recognizes, experiencing a symptom is not, as it were, a 'raw feel'. And perhaps at least a part of the pool of malaise available to be recoded as physical illness is also available to be recoded in psychiatric terms. It might be recoded by those carrying out public heath surveys with a gaze attuned to the symptomatic. It can be recoded by proto-patients themselves, once categories such as generalized anxiety disorder or pre-menstrual dysphoric disorder become available to them. It can be recoded by medical market research agencies seeking to chart and delineate potential markets for their products. And it can be recoded by psychiatrists and general practitioners.

Such recoding depends on two things—a norm against which experience can be judged as abnormal, and a set of beliefs and words to enable it to be understood and communicated. These disorders on the borders, I suggest, are experienced and coded as such, by individuals and their doctors, in relation to a cultural norm of the active, responsible, choosing self, realizing his or her potential in the world though shaping a lifestyle. And they are given form by the availability of categories such as depression, panic, social anxiety disorder and ADHD.

For our disorders on the borders, we can think of a term such as depression—which exists in a zone of transaction between experts and lay people—as a 'problem/solution complex': it simultaneously judges mood against certain desired standards, frames discontents in a certain way, renders them as a problem in need of attention, establishes a classification framework to name and delineate them, scripts a pattern of affects, cognitions, desires and judgements, writes a narrative for its origins and destiny, attributes it meaning, identifies some authorities who can speak and act wisely in relation to it and prescribes some responses to it. These are powerful condensations, ways of making aspects of existence intelligible and practicable.

It is too simple to see actual or potential patients as passive beings, acted upon by the marketing devices of Big Pharma who invent medical conditions and manipulate individuals into identifying with them. The process is more subtle. Companies explore and chart the experienced discontents of individuals, link these with the promises held out by their drugs, and incorporate those into narratives that give those drugs meaning and value. It is this intertwining of products, expectations, ethics and forms of life, that I think is involved in the development and spread of psychiatric drugs. In engaging with these images and narratives, in the hopes, anxieties and discontents they shape and foster, individuals play their own part in the medicalization of problems of living.

Today, health has become a central ethical principle, and it is not surprising that discontents so often find their expression in medical or psychiatric terms. Over the first 60 years or so of the twentieth century, human beings came to understand themselves as inhabited by a deep interior psychological space, to evaluate themselves and to act upon themselves in terms of this belief. But over the past half century, human beings have also come to see themselves as 'biological' creatures— to understand ourselves, speak about ourselves and act upon ourselves as the kinds of beings whose characteristics are shaped by our biology. This development—I call it somatic individuality—is reshaping the borders of normality and pathology, of mental illness and mental health. We are coming to think of ourselves as individuals whose moods, desires, conduct and personalities are shaped, in part, by the particular configuration of our neurochemistry, and which can therefore be moderated or modulated by acting upon that neurochemistry, acting upon our brains through drugs.

This new way of thinking has not effaced older religious or psychological styles of thought about our discontents. Unlike in many other disorders, the claim that psychiatric disorders have a biological basis is hotly contested. On the one hand, many individuals refuse to think of their conditions in these terms. On the other hand, there is much evidence to suggest that many still see mental disorders as different in kind from physical illness, excluded and stigmatized. But nonetheless, I think these changes that I have tried to document, shaped by many different factors, do indicate that we are witnessing a 'psychiatrization' of the human condition. In shaping our ethical regimes, our relations to ourselves, our judgements of the kinds of persons we want to be, and the lives we want to lead, psychiatry, like the rest of medicine is fully engaged in making us the kinds of people who we have become.

Conclusion

The borderlines of illness have long been subject to debate: are headache, insomnia, back pain and the like diseases, symptoms of diseases or inescapable conditions of life itself? Who should decide—doctors, medical administrators, patients themselves? Where are the boundaries between conditions for which an individual is to be accorded responsibility, and those for which responsibility is to be located elsewhere—in the organs, in fate, in heredity (Rosenberg, 2003)? And medicine has always practised beyond disease—in childbirth, infertility, grief and much more. Why does the extension of medicine trouble us for some problems and not others? Why is it preferable to place some aspects of life under one description—as a problem of living for example—rather than another—as a condition that can be alleviated by drugs?

I have taken my distance from some critics. But I do still think that, for these disorders on the borders and their treatment with drugs, there are grounds for concern. They arise from a particular way in which these different processes are interlinked in current conditions—the extension of diagnostic categories, the perception of the public health problems generated by untreated mental disorder, the demands for disease recognition, moves to screening, fears of risk and hopes for prevention by early intervention at a presymptomatic level, and the widespread use of the simple prescription of pharmaceutical remedies. All this, I think, serves to lower the threshold at which individuals are defined, and define themselves, as suitable cases for treatment. It increases the numbers of those who enter upon a 'moral career' as a person suffering from a treatable condition, and reduces the age at which many enter upon this career. These are powerful mechanisms for recruiting individuals, turning them from non-patients to proto-patients, to actual patients. They are powerful mechanisms for retaining individuals within this domain. No walls are now needed to sustain a lifetime career under the psychiatrist. Whether or not the drugs cause more damage than they cure, whether or not this generates careers for psychiatric researchers, demands for psychiatric professionals, satisfaction for public health professionals or profits for pharmaceutical companies, we have yet to count the costs of this way of organizing and responding to discontents in our own Age of Freedom. [. . .]

References

American Psychiatric Association (1980). *Diagnostic and statistical manual of mental disorders: DSM III*. Washington, DC: American Psychiatric Association.

Ayd, F. (1961). *Recognizing the depressed patient, with essentials of management and treatment*. New York: Grune & Stratton.

Becker, H.S. (1963). *Outsiders: Studies in the sociology of deviance*. New York: Free Press of Glencoe; London: Collier-Macmillan.

Blazer, D.G., Kessler, R.C., McGonagle, K.A., & Swartz, M.S. (1994). The prevalence and distribution of major depression in a national community sample—The National Comorbidity Survey. *American Journal of Psychiatry, 151*(7): 979–986.

Double, D. (2002). The limits of psychiatry. *British Medical Journal, 324*(7342): 900–904.

EC (European Commission) Health and Consumer Protection Directorate-General (2005). *Improving the mental health of the population: Towards a strategy on mental health for the European Union* (Green Paper). Brussels: European Commission.

Healy, D. (1996). *The psychopharmacologists: Interviews by David Healy*. London, Chapman & Hall.

Kessler, R.C., Berglund, P., Demler, O., Jin, R., Merikangas, K.R., & Walters, E.E. (2005). Lifetime prevalence and age-of-onset distributions of *DSM-IV* disorders in the National Comorbidity Survey Replication. *Archives of General Psychiatry, 62*(6): 593–602.

Kessler, R.C., Chiu, W.T., Demler, O., & Walters, E.E. (2005). Prevalence, severity, and comorbidity of 12-month DSM-IV disorders in the National Comorbidity Survey Replication. *Archives of General Psychiatry 62*(6): 617–627.

Kessler, R.C., McGonagle, K.A., Zhao, S., Nelson, C.B., Hughes, M., Eshleman, S. *et al.* (1994). Lifetime and 12-month prevalence of *DSM-III-R* psychiatric-disorders in the United-States—Results from the National ComorbiditySurvey. *Archives of General Psychiatry, 51*(1): 8–19.

Lenzer, J. (2004). Bush plans to screen whole US population for mental illness. *British Medical Journal, 328*(7454): 1458.

Lewis, A.J.S. (1967a). *Inquiries in psychiatry: Clinical and social investigations*. London: Routledge & Kegan Paul.

Martin, E. (2005). *Pharmaceutical virtue*. Bergen: Vital Matters.

Menninger, K.A., with Mayman, M., & Pruyser, P. (1965). *The vital balance: The life process in mental health and illness*. New York: Viking.

Moynihan, R., Heath, I., & Henry, J. (2002). Selling sickness: The pharmaceutical industry and disease mongering. *British Medical Journal, 324*(7342): 886–891.

Olfson, M., Gameroff, M.J., Marcus, S.C., & Jensen, P.S. (2003). National trends in the treatment of Attention Deficit Hyperactivity Disorder. *American Journal of Psychiatry, 160*(6): 1071–1077.

Rose, N. (1986). Psychiatry: The discipline of mental health. In P. Miller & N. Rose (Eds), *The Power of Psychiatry*, 43–84. Cambridge: Polity Press.

Rosenberg, C. (2003). What is disease? In memory of Owsei Temkin. *Bulletin of the History of Medicine, 77*: 491–505.

Spitzer, R.L., & Wakefield, J.C. (1999). *DSM-IV* diagnostic criterion for clinical significance: Does it help solve the false positives problem? *American Journal of Psychiatry, 156*(12): 1856–1864.

Wakefield, J.C. (1992). The concept of mental disorder—On the boundary between biological facts and social values. *American Psychologist, 47*(3): 373–388.

Wakefield, J.C. (1997). Diagnosing *DSM-IV*. 1. *DSM-IV* and the concept of disorder. *Behaviour Research and Therapy, 35*(7): 633–649.

Wakefield, J.C., Pottick, K.C., & Kirk, S.A. (2002). Should the *DSM-IV* diagnostic criteria for conduct disorder consider social context? *American Journal of Psychiatry, 159*(3): 380–386.

Wessely, S. (1997). Psychological, social and media influences on the experience of somatic symptoms. ESF Workshop on 'Cognitive Functions as Mediators of Environmental Effects on Health', 15–17 September.

WHO (World Health Organization) (2001). *Mental health: New understanding, new hope*. Geneva: WHO.

WHO (World Health Organization) (2004b). *Prevention of mental disorders: Effective interventions and policy options, summary report*. Geneva: WHO.

Wilson, M. (1993). *DSM-III* and the transformation of American psychiatry: A history. *American Journal of Psychiatry, 150*(3): 399–410.

Wittchen, H.U., & Jacobi, F.(2005). Size and burden of mental disorders in Europe—a critical review and appraisal of 27 studies. *European Neuropsychopharmacology, 15*(4): 357–376.

Wittchen, H.U., Jönsson, B., & Oleson, J. (2005). Towards a better understanding of the size and burden and cost of brain disorders in Europe. *European Neuropsychopharmacology, 15*(4): 355–356.

Wittchen, H.U., Knauper, B., & Kessler, R.C. (1994). Lifetime risk of depression. *British Journal of Psychiatry, 165*: 16–22.

PART THREE

Political economies of affect

7. Emotion in work and organizations

ONE OF THE AREAS WHERE the sociological and socio-psychological study of emotions has been most readily embraced and most keenly developed is that of research on work and organizations. Contrary to the assumption, prevalent until recently, that emotional expression is incompatible with the instrumental goal orientation of work life — and thus 'deviant' when and where it occurs — it is now increasingly acknowledged that emotion 'is not simply an adjunct to work; rather, it is the process through which members constitute their work environment by negotiating a shared reality' (Putnam and Mumby, 1993: 36). Arlie Hochschild's seminal book *The Managed Heart* (1983) is widely credited with laying the ground for subsequent research on emotions in organizations. In this much-cited work, Hochschild proposed that feelings themselves are the object of 'management' in both private and commercial contexts, and that the capacity for managing feeling through 'emotion work' could be commercially exploited as 'emotional labour' to produce surplus value. From this initial impetus, research on the role of emotion in the context of different institutional and corporate enviroments, and/or in relation to particular occupations has flourished and diversified, not only thematically but also methodologically (Fineman 2005; Fisher and Ashkanasy 2000; Domagalski 1999). The study of emotion management as part of work roles is only one of a whole range of issues addressed by this research. Broadly speaking, research may vary through a focus on the structural determinants and behavioral consequences of *transient* moods (Weiss and Cropanzano 1996), as distinct from *dispositional* affect (or 'trait affectivity') (Staw *et al.* 1996). Alternatively, the focus may be on the emotional repertoires of specific occupational or corporate cultures, to suggest that particular emotional orientations to the world, or 'affective subject positions', can be institutionally produced (see, e.g. Watson 1999 on the police). Research may also adopt a thematic focus on issues like conflict, in connection with negotiating organizational change, work/life balance, among other situations or variables (Jordan 2006). A significant amount of research has explored the gendered dimensions of emotion at work (see, e.g. Lewis and Simpson 2007; Hochschild and Ehrenreich 2002).

The first extract in this section addresses the relatively neglected topic of emotion work in connection with 'race'. Kiran Mirchandani's argument draws on anti-racist feminist theory to propose not only a focus on 'racial silences' in the literature on emotion work, but also a methodological critique of dominant approaches in the field. The argument is based on Mirchandani's review of the abundant literature on emotion work in its gendered dimensions, and on her analysis of the experiences of an ethnically diverse group of women who are small-business owners (the latter not included in this extract from her article). Contemporary debates on emotion work, she proposes, tend to rely on racially homogenous samples and on the implicit methodological assumption that workers are, by default, white. They also tend to assume that interactions themselves are racially homogenous. This normalization of whiteness, argues Mirchandani, is symptomatic of a more fundamental problem. Norms of emotional display and management relative to race, class, and gender hierarchies are studied as a function of (static and fixed) identities, whereas they should be analysed as a function of specific locations that are 'relational and shifting'.

The following extract, by Stephen Fineman, also offers a set of critical methodological reflections, this time directed at the recent growth in quantitative techniques for the study of emotion at work. The extract outlines the reasons for the increasing appeal of psychometric techniques in this area of research, and some negative consequences of 'boxing' emotion through metrication. While numbers tend to convey an impression of dispassionate objectivity and order, the practice of measuring emotion in an organizational context, Fineman argues, is 'no neutral act'. The extract focuses on the discussion of the construct of 'emotional intelligence', as an illustration of how experts use measurements to ascribe positive and negative value to individuals on the basis of their emotional intelligence quotients (EQ). In the concluding section of the article, not included here, Fineman presents alternative ways of 'knowing' emotions that are at risk of being marginalized by the field's 'moving hegemonically' in the direction of quantification. He points to narrative and discursive methods (otherwise well represented in social scientific research on the emotions — and elsewhere in this volume) as ways of addressing the complexities and nuances of affective experience that quantification tends to reduce and exclude.

Our third extract in this section illustrates a different use for quantitative investigation in the study of emotion at work. Using survey techniques, Reeves and colleagues explore the psychological ramifications of euthanasia-related work in the context of animal shelters. A particular point of interest of this piece lies in addressing the relatively neglected dimension of emotion in situations of interaction across species, rather than exclusively among humans. The result of the study by Reeves and colleagues indicate that 'perceived euthanasia-related strain is prevalent among shelter employees' and is associated with a number of other dimensions of stress, conflict, and ill-being. The extract concludes with a wide range of indicative suggestions for future research.

The fourth and final extract in this section is by Allen Smith and Sherryl

Kleinman, and looks at emotion management in the context of the profession of medicine. The physical intimacy involved in medical work can be associated with strong emotional experiences, ranging from feelings of sexual arousal to disgust and revulsion. This is countered by a professional ideology of 'affective neutrality'. The authors begin by considering that, while this ideology is strong in medicine, emotion management is neither explicitly taught nor collectively talked about by students in training. Based on ethnographic fieldwork in a medical school, Smith and Kleinman then illustrate the resources students employ to manage their feelings. The 'affective socialization' of doctors relies on mostly implicit and informal strategies that both illustrate and reproduce the culture of modern Western medicine.

References

Domagalski, T. A. (1999) 'Emotions in organizations: main currents', *Human Relations*, 52 (6): 833–852.

Fineman, S. (2005) 'Appreciating emotions at work: paradigm tensions', *International Journal of Work, Organization and Emotion*, 1 (1): 4–19.

Fisher, C. D. and Ashkanasy, N. M. (2000) 'The emerging role of emotions in work life: an introduction', *Journal of Organizational Behavior*, 21 (2): 123–129.

Hochschild A. R. (1983) *The Managed Heart: commercialization of human feelings*. Berkeley, CA.: University of California Press.

Hochschild, A. R. and Ehrenreich, B. (eds) (2002) *Global Woman: nannies, maids and sex workers in the new economy*. New York: Metropolitan Press.

Jordan, P. J. (2006) 'Editorial: emotions and coping with conflict', *Journal of Management and Organization*, 12 (2): 98–100.

Lewis, P. and Simpson, R. (eds) (2007) *Gendering Emotions in Organizations*. New York: Palgrave Macmillan.

Putnam, L.L., Mumby, D.K. (1993) 'Organizations, emotion and the myth of rationality', in S. Fineman (ed.), *Emotion In Organizations*. London: Sage.

Staw, B.M., Bell, N.E., Clausen, J.A. (1986) 'The dispositional approach to job attitudes: a lifetime longitudinal test', *Administrative Science Quarterly*, 31: 56–77.

Watson, S. (1999) 'Policing the affective society: beyond governmentality in the theory of social control', *Social and Legal Studies*, 8 (2): 227–251.

Weiss H.M., Cropanzano R. (1996) 'Affective events theory: a theoretical discussion of the structure, causes and consequences of affective experiences at work', *Research in Organizational Behavior*, 18: 1–74.

Chapter 30

Kiran Mirchandani

CHALLENGING RACIAL SILENCES IN STUDIES OF EMOTION WORK

Contributions from anti-racist feminist theory

[. . .]

HOCHSCHILD'S STUDY OF THE EMOTION work of flight attendants marks the beginning of the development of a multifaceted literature on the emotion work which is required in many paid work jobs. As summarized in Tables 1 and 2, there have been three distinct types of work that have been characterized as 'emotion work': the management of self-feeling, the work of making others feel a certain way, and the effort involved in giving definition to one's work. These three forms of emotion work are interconnected. For example, making others feel a certain way may be a way for a worker to define her or his work. Similarly, promoting certain definitions of one's work may be a way of managing one's own feelings.

Hochschild terms emotion work done for a wage as 'emotion labour' and defines this as 'the act of trying to change in degree or quality an emotion or feeling' (1979: 561). The emotion labour of flight attendants thus involves 'trying to feel the right feeling for the job' (Hochschild 1983: 118). As Fineman notes, 'emotional "labour" is the buying of an employee's emotional demeanor; the individual is being paid to "look nice", smile, be caring, be polite' (1996: 546). Theorists also provide evidence of the fact that workers may experience stress and inauthenticity when there is a disjuncture between the way in which they are expected to feel and the way in which they actually feel (Ashforth and Humphrey 1993; Fineman 1995; Erickson and Wharton 1997; Thoits 1990).

According to Hochschild (1983), many jobs require workers to produce a particular emotional state in another person. Bill collectors, for example, do emotion labour to deflate customers' status and evoke gratitude or fear in clients. Building on the work of Hochschild, Daniels (1987: 109) notes that emotion work involves four interrelated behaviours: '(1) attending carefully to how a setting affects others in it . . .; (2) focusing attention through ruminating about the past and planning for the future; (3) assessing the reasonableness of preliminary judgements . . .; (4) creating a comfortable ambience'. Daniels' definition suggests that emotion work involves not only monitoring one's own reactions to situations, but also caring for others and establishing links between people and events. James (1989) similarly argues that emotional labour is a social process which is involved in dealing with other people's feelings. Examples include being available for others, interpreting their needs and providing a personal response.

Other theorists have focused on the emotion labour involved in defining one's work. Nelson and Barley (1997), for example, examine the emotion work of paid and volunteer emergency medical systems personnel. Paid workers emphasized the highly skilled, commodifiable qualities of emergency medical work, while volunteers stressed the humanitarian and caring nature of the same work. Fine (1996), in a similar way, demonstrates the strategies used by restaurant cooks to define their work as worthy of respect and professionalization.

Caring, professionalism and acting: gender dimensions of emotion work

Researchers have documented the nuanced ways in which emotion work is structured by gender processes. The focus of this literature is on the gendered assumptions implicit in certain jobs, and the mechanisms through which women's work is often devalued. As Steinberg and Figart (1999: 17) note, service organizations which require the constant display of friendliness often hire women to fill these roles on the assumption that women are better at displays of warmth. Theorists note that doing emotion work is fundamentally an act of doing gender in the context of 'women's allegedly greater facility with emotions — the feminine capacity to console and comfort, flatter, cajole, persuade and seduce' (Frith and Kitzinger 1998: 300). Pierce similarly argues that paralegal work, which involves deference and caretaking, is feminized; this is 'not simply because women do it but because taking care of others is constructed as something that women are well constructed to do' (1995: 24).

Table 1 Types of Emotion Work Explored in the Literature

Theorist	Sample	Examples of Types of Emotion Work Explored
Aronson (1992)	Women who care for their elderly mothers	-internalizing resentment that their affection for mothers is questioned by service providers -drawing boundaries in relation to mothers about the extent to which it was possible for them to provide care -dealing with inner conflicts as a result of the incongruence between their ability to provide care and expectation that it is their responsibility to do so
Aronson and Neysmith (1996)	Home-care workers	-breaking rules in official job descriptions by giving gifts, providing after-hours care, personalizing relations with care receivers

Table 1—*Continued*

Theorist	Sample	Examples of Types of Emotion Work Explored
Bellas (1999)	Academics	-performing in the classroom -relating personal experiences in classrooms -displaying positive emotions and controlling negative emotions vis-a-vis students -diffusing volatile situations -advising students
Clark (1990)	Theoretical	-using emotions strategically to elicit emotions in others during face-to-face interactions in order to mark one's place in the interaction
Fine (1996)	Restaurant kitchens	-justifying and legitimating their work to the public
Fineman (1995)	Helping professionals (theoretical)	-maintaining an emotional distance from the client in order to appear professional -creating the desired emotional impression or expression
Fineman (1996)	Theoretical	-suppressing or representing private feelings to achieve a socially acceptable emotional face -looking nice, smiling, being polite
Ghidina (1992)	Custodial workers	-asserting the value of the work -redefining work traditionally known as 'dirty' work
Gubrium (1989)	Caregivers of Alzheimer's patients	-managing self-feeling against audience expectations
Hall (1993)	Waiters and waitresses	-smiling, deferring to customers
Heimer and Stevens (1997)	Social workers in a neonatal unit	-transforming people into clinical material (integrating parents into the hospital routine) -coping with variability -helping parents deal with the strain of having a premature child -managing the risk of lawsuits by parents or the state against the hospital
Hochschild (1979, 1983, 1990)	Flight attendants and bill collectors	-feeling the right feeling for the job -managing/changing feelings through surface and deep acting
James (1993)	Doctors, nurses and relatives of cancer patients	-anticipating, planning, pacing, timetabling and troubleshooting -managing negative feelings in a way that results in a neutral or positive outcome -ongoing work of managing emotions is done by relatives, nurses and junior doctors
Kahn (1993)	Social science agency	-caregiving -balancing attachment and detachment from others

Theorist	Sample	Examples of Types of Emotion Work Explored
Kunda and Van Maanen (1999)	Managers and professionals	-building a market of their own
Leidner (1999)	Interactive service workers (McDonalds servers and insurance salespeople)	-smiling, making eye contact, remaining calm -being enthusiastic -trying to persuade customers to listen to the sales pitch
Lois (2001)	High risk takers (volunteer search and rescue group)	-accepting the unknown -suppressing feelings in high-risk situations -releasing and redefining feelings
Nelson and Barley (1997)	Paid and volunteer emergency medical teams	-differential construction of emergency medical teams' work (as commodity or community focus) -promoting own point of view through marginalizing others
Pierce (1995)	Litigators and paralegals	-dominating through intimidation (litigators) -using strategic friendliness (litigators) -showing deference and providing emotional care to attorneys (paralegals) -managing resentment about being treated as if one is stupid (paralegals)
Rafaeli and Sutton (1991)	Bill collectors and criminal interrogators	-using a mixture of positive and negative emotional displays to construct five 'emotional contrast strategies'
Rae (1998)	Paid caregivers of persons with Altzeimer's	-managing own emotions in relation to receipients' inability to control their emotions -managing guilt -managing tension in family life of patient
Thoits (1990)	Theoretical	-coping with emotional deviance (when feelings deviate from what is expected in a given situation)
Van Maanen and Kunda (1989)	Disneyland employees and employees of a high tech firm	-participating in organizational rituals. -conforming to particularistic standards of appearance, being nice.
Wharton and Erickson (1993)	Service sector workers (professional and non-professional)	-binding the group together through integrating emotions -conveying authority through masking emotions. -provoking client compliance through displays of anger, irritation
Wisely and Fine (1997)	Portrait painters	-recognizing the character of the client being portrayed -negotiating the worker-client relationship
Wolkomir (2001)	Gay and ex-gay Christian support groups	-redefining situation and authenticating self -promoting participation in groups -sustaining members' commitment

Theorists also note that male- and female-dominated occupations require workers to perform different kinds of emotion work. Flight attendants, therefore, may feel annoyance and tiredness, but are expected to have a *'sincere* smile' when serving passengers (Hochschild 1983: 120). Doctors or counsellors may feel deeply about a client's situation, but they are required to be cool and controlled in their response (Fineman 1994: 19). Emotion work is, therefore, needed to deal with the outcome of the gap between real and right feeling, and individuals often have to manage the resentment (Pierce 1995) or conflict (Aronson 1992) which they feel as a result of this gap.

Table 2 Dimensions of Emotion Work

Management of self-feeling	*Making others feel a certain way*	*Defining one's work*
Aronson (1992)	Bellas, (1999)	Aronson (1992)
Bellas (1999)	Clark (1990)	Aronson and Neysmith (1996)
Fineman (1995, 1996)	Fine (1996)	Fine (1996)
Gubrium (1989)	Fineman (1995, 1996)	Ghidina (1992)
Hochschild (1979, 1983, 1990)	Heimer and Stevens (1997)	Heimer and Stevens (1997)
Leidner (1999)	Hochschild (1979, 1983, 1990)	James (1993)
Lois (2001)	James (1993)	Nelson and Barley (1997)
Pierce (1995)	Kahn (1993)	Wisely and Fine (1997)
Rae (1998)	Nelson and Barley (1997)	
Steinberg and Figart (1999)	Pierce (1995)	
Thoits (1989)	Rafeli and Sutton (1991)	
Van Maanen and Kunda (1989)	Steinberg and Figart (1999)	
Wharton and Erickson (1993)	Van Maanen and Kunda (1989)	
Wolkomir (2001)	Wharton and Erickson (1993)	
	Wisely and Fine (1997)	

Accompanying the gendering of emotion work is a frequent de-skilling of this work. Hochschild distinguishes emotion work from emotion labour in terms of pay and location, that is, emotion work is unwaged work done in the private sphere, while emotion labour is work in the public sphere done for a wage. A number of other theorists, however, have noted that there is often considerable overlap between these two categories, and that it is not always easy to separate the paid and unpaid, or public and private parts of a job (see, for example, Gubrium 1989; Mirchandani 1998, 1999, 2000; Uttal and Touminen 1999). Tancred notes that it is often assumed that 'women are born with certain "natural" skills which require neither talent nor training, and which are merely part of their "natural," "feminine" behaviour' (1995: 17). Hall argues that much of the service work done by women is considered an extension of women's roles in the home. Restaurants, for example, construct and legitimate a gendered image of the server as deferential servant (Hall

1993: 455). Adkins's study of hotel managers similarly illustrates the ways in which managers are expected to be male, but married managers are seen to be more reliable because it is assumed that men cannot be counted on to carry out many of the essential, routine tasks required for the job. These tasks are the hidden and unpaid responsibilities of managers' wives (1995: 76).

These discussions of emotion work have allowed writers to illuminate the relationships between discourses of rationality and gendered structures within organizations. Theorists note that the emphasis on rationality within organizations has resulted in the fact that emotions have often been 'written out' (Fineman 1994: 1), treated as 'handicapped appendage[s] to reason', or understood as com-modities (Mumby and Putman 1992: 471; James 1989: 130). Swan argues that given the historical association between women and emotionality, this discourse of rationality within organizations has unique effects on women managers: 'to be a "proper" manager requires that a woman reproduces an account of herself in terms of attributes which commonly represent a type of masculinity' (Swan 1994: 105; Seron and Ferris 1995). For example, women cite crying as an unprofessional and a 'girlie' thing to do (Swan 1994: 105). Thoits similarly notes that individuals' feelings may deviate from their required emotional displays, giving rise to 'emotional deviance' (1990: 181). Such deviance is likely when individuals hold multiple roles 'that have mutually contradictory feeling expectations' (Thoits 1990: 188). In so far as women's professional work requires emotional masking, while their family emotion work requires integrative emotions (Wharton and Erickson 1993: 471), emotional deviance for women in professional jobs in likely to be high.

The insights generated through the studies discussed above have furthered our understanding of the gender dimensions of emotion work as well as documented the nature of the emotion work done by women in a variety of contexts. In much of this analysis, there is an attempt to move away from biological understandings of gender. [. . .] At the same time, . . . much of the analysis has been based on a concept of a 'universal woman'. Little attention is paid to the ways in which women are socially located within a multitude of hierarchies which coincide with and construct gender differences.

Racial silences and the normalizing of whiteness

Contemporary debates on emotion work, as outlined in the sections above, normalize whiteness in two ways: first, through the reliance on racially homo-geneous samples in empirical studies, and second, through the assumption that workers are, by default, white.

While empirical knowledge on emotion work has increased substantially in the past two decades, studies continue to draw on samples that are only, or pre-dominantly white (see, for example, Bulan et al. 1997; Lois 2001; Pierce 1995; Seery 2000; Wharton 1993; Wolkomir 2001). This has led to the masking of a number of important forms of emotion work. Lee-Treweek's (1997) analysis of nursing auxiliary work, for example, provides a nuanced and complex understand-ing of the ways in which workers deal with the often violent and demeaning treatment they receive from patients and nurses. Given what we know about the prevalence of racism in the health-care sector (Calliste 1996), it would be worth exploring how auxiliary workers who are women of colour do emotion work to deal simultaneously with the low status of their work and the racial stereotypes of their background. Similarly, Rafaeli and Sutton's (1991) discussion of the work done by bill collectors and criminal interrogators to undermine their victims' emotional defences by being nasty is likely to have been different if their analysis had included male black interrogators (in the context of the stereotype of 'the violent black man'). Pierce's (1995) account of the nurturing done by female paralegals raises questions about how this work would be different if either the paralegals or the attorneys they were caring for were of Asian, African or Hispanic descent; and her research on the treatment of people of colour in law firms suggests that challenging the deeply racialized nature of this setting involves considerable emotion work (Pierce, 2003).

Not only have studies relied primarily on white samples, but much of the analysis of emotion work to date has been based on the *assumption* of racially homogeneous interactions, and on the assumption that the dominant ethnic group does not possess a 'race' (Anthias 1998). Theorists frequently do not provide the racial characteristics of samples on which analyses of emotion work are developed (see, for example, Fine 1996; Hall 1993; Rae 1998), making it difficult to theorize the ways in which this work is racialized. For example, in the introduction to a recent special issue on emotion work in the *Annals of the American Academy of Political and Social Science*, Steinberg and Figart comment on the ways in which cultural norms often structure the allocation of people to different jobs. They note:

> 'Gender is implicated within these social norms, which vary by culture. In the United States, for example, where service organizations emphasize emotional displays of friendliness, women are more likely to be hired to work in these organizations because it is believed that, on average, they smile and display more warmth than men do. Yet, in Muslim culture, such displays are restricted by employees because they would provoke a sexual response.'
>
> (Steinberg and Figart 1999: 17–18)

While this is an interesting analysis, it does not provide much insight into the emotion work done by Muslim women who may be working in service organizations in the USA, or by non-Muslim women working in organizations with some Muslim customers. As Glenn argues, this normalizing of whiteness in studies of gender occurs when white women are positioned as the 'universal female subject' (1999: 3). [. . .]

Interlocking hierarchies: race, class and gender

[. . .] Rather than identifying the separate impact of race, gender and class on individuals' lives, feminist anti-racist theory stresses the need to develop understandings of how these forms of stratification intersect and overlap. [. . .]

Friedman argues, for example, that individuals do not hold fixed race, gender and class identities, nor do they confront static social divisions. She provides the following example to illustrate her point:

'In relation to white people, Leslie Marmon Silko and Paula Gunn Allen are women of colour, Native Americans and partially white. In relation to women of colour, they are Native American. In relation to Native Americans, they are members of the Laguana Pueblo. In relation to each other, they are individual women who characterize the Laguna Pueblo culture in startlingly different ways.'

(Friedman 1996: 125)

[. . .] The focus on the interlocking nature of race, class and gender raises two issues which can be used to extend our understandings of emotion work. First, rather than possessing particular ethnicities, class positions and gender traits, individuals occupy social locations which are relational and shifting. The work of recognizing, managing and participating in these shifting relations of difference requires emotion work which is done in conjunction with the work of managing one's own feelings, making others feel a certain way and defining one's work. Second, *both* racial majority and racial minority groups do emotion work which is racialized, that is, which is situated within hierarchies of racial privilege and disadvantage. As Razack argues, 'it is vitally important to explore in a historically and site specific way the meaning of race, economic status, class, disability, sexuality, and gender as they come together to structure women in different and shifting positions of power and privilege' (1998: 12). Women do emotion work to maintain privilege or to challenge disadvantage in conjunction with the emotion work they do as part of their jobs. [. . .]

Conclusions

[. . .] The focus on the gendered nature of emotion work needs . . . to be understood in the context of the interactions between gendered processes and other processes of stratification. Two types of projects would further facilitate this exploration.

First, it would be useful to document the ways in which past understandings of the emotion work done by flight attendants, service workers, nurses, lawyers, and so on change when racially diverse groups of these workers are placed at the centre of analysis. While much of the research to date has been concerned with the connections and distinctions between 'emotion labour' (that is, the management of feelings which are done as part of one's job) and 'emotion work' (family or unpaid work), the experiences of racially diverse groups of people is likely to reveal that the emotion work of dealing with inequity is seldom remunerated and yet a fundamental part of paid work. Through such an analysis, new understandings of emotion work (based not only on pay or location of work) can be advanced.

A second set of projects which would extend our understanding of emotion work could focus on processes of racialization which may be present even in racially homogeneous occupations. Rather than an absence of stratification, workers in homogeneous work settings may, in fact, do emotion work to exert privilege and exclusion, which would be worthy of further study. These explorations would contribute to the theoretical and empirical understanding of the emotion work involved in living and working in contemporary urban societies with coexisting, multiple and interlocking forms of stratification.

References

Adkins, Lisa
1995   *Gendered work — Sexuality, family and the labor market*. Buckingham: Open University Press.
Anthias, Floya
1998   'Rethinking social divisions: Some notes towards a theoretical framework'. *The Sociological Review* 63: 505–533.
Aronson, Jane
1992   'Women's sense of responsibility for the care of old people: "But who else is going to do it?" '. *Gender and Society* 6: 8–29.
Aronson, Jane, and Sheila M. Neysmith
1996   ' "You're not just in there to do the work": Depersonalizing policies and the exploitation of home care workers' labor'. *Gender and Society* 10: 56–77.
Ashforth, Blake E., and Ronald H. Humphrey
1993   'Emotional labor in service roles: The influence of identity'. *Academy of Management Review* 18: 88–115.
Bellas, Marcia
1999   'Emotional labor in academia: The case of professors'. *Annals of the American Academy of Political and Social Science* 56/1: 96–110.
Bulan, Heather F., Rebecca J. Erickson, and Amy S. Wharton
1997   'Doing for others on the job: The affective requirements of service work, gender and emotional well-being'. *Social Problems* 44 (May): 235–256.
Calliste, Agnes
1996   'Antifeminism, organizing and resistance in nursing: African Canadian women'. *Canadian Review of Sociology and Anthropology* 33/3: 368–390.
Clark, Candace
1990   'Emotions and micropolitics in everyday life: Some patterns and paradoxes' in *Research agendas in the sociology of emotions*. T. D. Kemper (ed.). New York: SUNY Press.
Daniels, Arlene Kaplan
1987   'Invisible work'. *Social Problems* 34/4: 403–415.
Erickson, Rebecca J., and Amy S. Wharton
1997   'Inauthenticity and depression: Assessing the consequences of interactive service work'. *Work and Occupations* 24/2: 188–213.
Fine, Gary A.
1996   'Justifying work: Occupational rhetorics as resources in restaurant kitchens'. *Administrative Science Quarterly* 41: 90–115.
Fineman, Stephen
1994   'Introduction' in *Emotions in organization*. S. Fineman (ed.). London: Sage.

Fineman, Stephen
1995   'Stress, emotion and interaction' in *Managing stress: Emotion and power at work*.
       T. Newton (ed.). London: Sage.
Fineman, Stephen
1996   'Emotion and organizing' in *Handbook of organization studies*. S. R. Clegg,
       C. Hardy and W. R. Nord (eds). London: Sage.
Friedman, Susan S.
1996   'Beyond white and other: Relationality and narratives of race in feminist
       discourse. *Signs* 21/1: 109–157.
Frith, Hannah, and Celia Kitzinger
1998   ' "Emotion work" as participant resource: A feminist analysis of young
       women's talk in interaction'. *Sociology* 32/2: 299–321.
Ghidina, Marcia J.
1992   'Social relations and the definition of work: Identity management in a low-
       status occupation'. *Qualitative Sociology* 15/1: 73–85.
Glenn, Evelyn-Nakano
1999   'The social construction and institutionalization of gender and race: An inte-
       grative framework' in *Revisioning gender*. M. M. Ferree, J. Lorber and B. B. Hess
       (eds). Thousand Oaks, CA: Sage.
Gubrium, Jaber F.
1989   'Emotion work and emotive discourse in the Alzheimer's disease experience'.
       Current Perspectives on Aging and the Life Cycle 3: 243–268.
Hall, Elaine J.
1993   'Smiling, deferring and flirting — Doing gender by giving "good service" '.
       Work and Occupations 20/4: 453–466.
Heimer, Carol A., and Michelle L. Stevens
1997   'Caring for the organization: Social workers as frontline risk managers in neo-
       natal intensive care units'. *Work and Occupations* 24: 133–163.
Hochschild, Arlie R.
1979   'Emotion work, feeling rules and social structures'. *American Journal of Sociology*
       85: 551–575.
Hochschild, Arlie R.
1983   *The managed heart*. Berkeley: University of California Press.
Hochschild, Arlie R.
1990   'Emotion management: A perspective and path for future research' in *Research
       agendas in the sociology of emotions*. Theodore D. Kemper (ed.), 117–142. New
       York: University of New York Press.
James, Nicky
1989   'Emotional labour: Skill and work in the social regulation of feelings'. *The
       Sociological Review* 37: 15–42.
James, Nicky
1993   'Divisions of emotional labour: Disclosure and cancer' in *Emotions in organiza-
       tions*. S. Fineman (ed.). London: Sage.
Kahn, William A.
1993   'Caring for the caregivers: Patterns of organizational caregiving'. *Administrative
       Science Quarterly* 38: 539–563.
Kunda, Gideon, and John Van Maanen
1999   'Changing scripts at work: Managers and professionals'. *Annals of the American
       Academy of Political and Social Science* 56/1: 64–76.

Lee-Treweek, Geraldine
1997   'Women, resistance and care: An ethnographic study of nursing auxiliary work'. *Work, Employment and Society* 11/1: 47–63.
Leidner, Robin
1999   'Emotion labour in service work'. *Annals of the American Academy of Political and Social Science* 56/1: 81–95.
Lois, Jennifer
2001   'Peaks and valleys: The gendered emotional culture of edgeworkers'. *Gender and Society* 15/3: 381–406.
Mirchandani, Kiran
1998   'Protecting the boundary: Teleworker insights on the expansive concept of "work"'. *Gender and Society* 12/2: 167–186.
Mirchandani, Kiran
1999   'Legitimizing work: Telework and the gendered reification of the work/non-work dichotomy'. *Canadian Review of Sociology and Anthropology* 36/1: 87–107.
Mirchandani, Kiran
2000   ' "The best of both worlds" and "Cutting my own throat": Contradictory images of home-based work'. *Qualitative Sociology* 23/2: 159–182.
Mumby, Denis K., and Linda L. Putman
1992   'The politics of emotion: A feminist reading of bounded rationality'. *Academy of Management Review* 17/3: 465–486.
Nelson, Bonalyn J., and Stephen R. Barley
1997   'For love or money? Commodification and the construction of an occupational mandate'. *Administrative Science Quarterly* 42/4: 619–653.
Pierce, Jennifer
1995   *Gender trials: Emotional lives in contemporary law firms.* Berkeley: University of California Press.
Pierce, Jennifer
2003   ' "Racing for innocence": Whiteness, corporate culture, and the backlash against affirmative action'. *Qualitative Sociology* 26/1: 53–70.
Rae, Hazel M.
1998   'Managing feelings: Caregiving as emotion work'. *Research on Aging* 20/1: 137–160.
Rafaeli, Anat, and Robert J. Sutton
1991   'Emotional contrast strategies as means of social influence: Lessons from criminal interrogators and bill collectors'. *Academy of Management Journal* 34/4: 749–775.
Razack, Sherene
1998   *Looking white people in the eye.* Toronto: University of Toronto Press.
Seery, Brenda
2000   'Women's emotion work in the family: Relationship management and the process of building father-child relationships'. *Journal of Family Issues* 21/1: 100–128.
Seron, Carole, and Kerry Ferris
1995   'Negotiating professionalism: The gendered social capital of flexible time'. *Work and Occupation* 22/1: 22–47.
Steinberg, Ronnie J., and Deborah M. Figart
1999   'Emotional labour since *The Managed Heart'. Annals of the American Academy of Political and Social Science* 56/1: 8–26.

Swan, Elaine
1994   'Managing emotion' in *Women in management*. M. Tanton (ed.). London: Routledge.

Tancred, Peta
1995   'Women's work: A challenge to the sociology of work'. *Gender, Work and Organization* 2/1: 11–20.

Thoits, Peggy A.
1990   'Emotional deviance: Research agendas' in *Research Agendas in Sociology of Emotions*. T. D. Kemper (ed.). New York: SUNY Press.

Uttal, Lynet, and Mary Tuominen
1999   'Tenuous relationships: Exploitation, emotion and racial ethnic significance in paid child care work'. *Gender and Society* 13/6: 758–780.

Van Maanen, John, and Gideon Kunda
1989   ' "Real feelings": Emotional expression and organizational culture'. *Research in Organizational Behavior* 11: 43–103.

Wharton, Amy S.
1993   'The affective consequences of service work: Managing emotions on the job'. *Work and Occupations* 20/2: 205–232.

Wharton, Amy S., and Rebecca J. Erickson
1993   'Managing emotions on the job and at home: Understanding the consequences of multiple emotional roles'. *Academy of Management Review* 18/3: 457–486.

Wisely, Nancy, and Alan Fine
1997   'Making faces: Portraiture as a negotiated worker-client relationship'. *Work and Occupations* 24/2: 164–187.

Wolkomir, Michelle
2001   'Emotion work, commitment and the authentication of the self: The case of gay and ex-gay Christian support groups'. *Journal of Contemporary Ethnography* 30/3: 305–334.

Chapter 31

Stephen Fineman

GETTING THE MEASURE OF EMOTION – AND THE CAUTIONARY TALE OF EMOTIONAL INTELLIGENCE

[. . .]

EMOTION PENETRATES AND DEFINES MANY of the processes and consequences of organizing. These include the subjective meanings of work, leadership, decision making, negotiation, motivation, ethical conduct, communication, gender and ethnic relationships. More sharply, emotion draws attention to the psychological injuries of working, such as harassment, bullying, violence, stress and emotional labour (e.g. see Fineman, 2003a). Emotion's potential multifacetedness suggests that any one approach to understanding 'it' will be just that – one approach. It is necessarily partial, meaningful only in terms of the philosophy that informs it, the medium through which it is conveyed and the receiving audience.

. . . Such strictures have been broadly side-stepped by mainstream organizational researchers of emotion, schooled principally in reductionist research (e.g. see Ashkenasy et al., 2000; Diener et al., 1999; Parrott & Hertel, 1999; Weiss & Brief, 2001). Metrication is a principal hallmark of their endeavours, reflecting a long history of psychometrics – the transformation of psychological qualities into quantities. Their aim is to make the inchoate tangible through quantification. Size matters. Emotion is 'unrolled' and divided into convenient units, which are then susceptible to different forms of statistical manipulation. As a 'variable', emotion can then be correlated, or causatively linked, with other variables – such as pride with job satisfaction, fear with labour turnover, anxiety with absenteeism (e.g. see de Dreue et al., 2001; Weiss & Brief, 2001). [. . .]

No academic discipline has exclusive rights to emotion. It has been differently colonized by biologists, anthropologists, historians, sociologists, psychoanalysts, neurologists and several different branches of psychology (e.g. clinical, evolutionary, educational, organizational, psycholinguistics). And emotion is not, by any means, the sole province of the sciences. Poetry, creative literature, music, drama and the visual arts have long been custodians of emotion – being at the very soul of their endeavours. Such an impressive array reveals something of the centrality of emotion in human affairs. Measurement, of course, marks out some of them, but non-measurement characterizes many others. In the latter we have reported stories and speech, contextualized observations of behaviour, particular observations, ethnographies, free-form diaries, drawings, interpretations of symbols, textual analyses of secondary data (e.g. autobiographies, letters, official reports), action research and phenomenological analysis (Domagalski, 1999; Fineman, 1993b, 2000b; Reason & Bradbury, 2000). These all generate 'broad band' data, representing feeling and expressed emotion in dynamic, socially situated, form. They contrast to the measure's inclination to pre-box, or freeze, emotion.

Emotion, then, has many possible representations, of which reconstructed feeling on researcher-led scales are one – but a dominant one. As Sturdy (2003) points out, this tends to privilege one form of emotion knowledge (e.g. statistical trends, numerical profiles) and silences others (e.g. personal meanings, interpersonal dynamics). Even if the representation feels/appears crude, remote from the daily circuits of 'real-time' feeling and its ambivalences ('*Am I a 1, 2 or 3 on this item? 'I'm sometimes a bit of each'; 'I can't really remember how I "felt last week"* '), the scale, nevertheless, speaks authoritatively for itself. The conventions of validity and reliability, and their numerical signifiers (*'internal consistency r = .78', 'correlation with other, similar, measure r = .42'*), take on a life, and justificatory rhetoric, of their own.

There is a socially constructed, collusive, comfort in numbers. They are abstractions that symbolize authority and 'fact' in ways that other representations often fare less well in social scientific and other professional communities (Iedema et al., 2003). [. . .] The doubting or uneasy researcher eventually ceases to doubt or feel uneasy: '*It's just how we do it'; 'it's what my supervisor recommends', 'it's the only way to get published'*. The researchers' understanding of their own feelings and emotions, their own phenomenological realties, are split-off from their 'subjects', via measurement. Reflexiveness and experiential validity are squeezed out. What is lost – the fine texture, the tensions, the heat, the contradictory sensations, the subtle postures, the negotiations, the interconnections between researcher and researched – are neither noticed nor mourned, at least not publicly.

. . . Such issues are compounded when emotion measurement and control spills beyond the researcher's own community tangibly to affect the ordering and valuing of other people's work lives. Emotion becomes defined as a valuable, and instrumental, 'item' for commercial success. There is, for example, the prizing of people with high self-esteem in the workplace – '*the prime determinant of organizational and personal success in the Information Age*' (Branden, 1988, back cover). In customer-service industries (fast food, airlines, hotels, theme parks, call centres), employee 'enthusiasm', and 'smiles' have become part of the product, to be monitored and measured (e.g. Hochschild, 1983; Leidner, 1991; Talwar, 2002; Wasko, 2001). Happiness has followed a similar route (Lubyomirski & Lepper, 1999), now incorporated into the offerings of management consultants – as one consultancy advertises:

> Measure worker happiness and improve business success. Seeking organizations who value worker happiness. This long-term process/tool can

be the catalyst for positive change in organizations and improve communication.

The point here is not that self-esteem, enthusiasm and happiness are unworthy pursuits (although all reflect a cultural valuation of particular emotion states). The concern is about encapsulating what might plausibly be regarded as complex, shifting and micro-contextual phenomena, on measuring instruments, and the power that this invests in the measurers or their sponsors. What, we may ask, are the effects on those who fail to 'measure up' on the emotions prescribed? [. . .]

When a dynamic social or psychological phenomenon is framed as a quantity or position, it acquires particular political force – because of the symbolic significance attached to numbers. There are, for instance, the life opportunities or constraints that tend to follow an individual's level of measured intelligence or academic grades (Kamin, 1997; Montague, 1999). [. . .] Counting, per se, creates a convenient, durable, and often seductive, shorthand of value or worth. Its authority appears to derive from several sources: a reduction in ambiguity, making the complex and inchoate appear meaningful and manageable; the pervasiveness of natural sciences where numbers are commonly taken as an indication of precision and truth; and a cultural predilection to arrange people (organizations, products, events, services) in hierarchical order to identify/create winners and losers, high status and low status, eligible and non-eligible.

Together, these influences can lock people into numbers – and hold them there. [. . .] Emotion, when exposed to such measurement, along with marketplace demands and consultant interventions, is precariously poised as a commodity to exploit. It also creates conditions of self-fulfilling prophecy, where the authority of the measure and its categories ('low self-esteem', 'unhappy', 'neurotic', 'anxious', 'stressed') can permeate individuals' self-perceptions in ways they find hard to contest or resist. Emotional intelligence illustrates this particularly well. [. . .]

Emotional intelligence has emerged from a challenge to the supremacy of cognitive, 'IQ', intelligence. It has early roots in the idea of 'multiple' intelligences, which includes 'emotional sensitivity' (Gardner, 1993), and from findings from brain sciences on the role of emotion in thinking and problem solving (Bechara et al., 2000). Mayer and colleagues have been prominent in developing these insights into a conception of emotional intelligence as,

> an ability to recognize the meanings of emotions and their relationships, and to reason and problem-solve on the basis of them.
>
> (Mayer et al., 1999: 267)

From relatively quiet and cautious beginnings, emotional intelligence has rapidly been adopted by academic practitioners, heavily promoted by management consultants and extensively extolled in trade magazines and newspapers. [. . .]

All emotional intelligence measures are based on author-contrived domains and response categories, each one reflecting its own, particular, rendition of emotional intelligence. Some authors attempt to gauge emotional intelligence through hypothetical events. For example, a test item in the Multifactor Emotional Intelligence Scale (Mayer et al., 1988) describes a car hitting a dog and asks the testee to decide 'how likely the owner felt ashamed about not being able to have better trained the dog'. Other items require the rating of emotions portrayed in pictorial faces, and making emotional judgements on what, for example, someone feels 'when their emotion grows even past happiness and they are out of control' . . . (see review in Ciarrochi et al., 2001).

The most common measures of emotional intelligence are of the self-report kind, how people perceive their own emotional abilities, competence or sensitivity. In Cooper and Sawaf's (1977) 'EQ Map' we have, for example, 'I change my emotional expression depending upon the person I am with' and, 'I can recognise emotions in others by watching their eyes' (pp. 331–2). Total scores are summarized as *'optimal'*, *'proficient'*, *'vulnerable'* or *'cautionary'*. The Boston Ei Questionnaire (Chapman, 2001) asks 25 questions, including 'How well can you concentrate when you are feeling anxious?' and 'Are you able to demonstrate empathy with others' feelings?'. For Chapman, a high total score is an indication that *'you seem to shape up pretty well'*, but a low score means *'oh dear!'*. Bar-On's EQi scale contains items such as 'I have good relations with others' and 'I'm fun to be with', 'I'm sensitive to the feelings of others' (Bar-On, 1997). Bar-On includes three factors considered as 'facilitators' of emotional intelligence – happiness, optimism and self-actualization (Bar-On, 2000; Bar-On & Parker, 2000). The Emotional Competence Inventory (Boyatzis et al., 2000) is based on reports of 'self-awareness', 'self-management', 'social awareness' and 'social skills'. In addition to the above measures there are numerous self-report questionnaires on the Web offering instant 'EQ' readouts, typically coupled with the promotion of a consultancy service. An extensive review of available measures by Matthews et al. (2002) fails to find evidence of convergent validity (triangulation).

All such techniques are highly abstracted representations of the multicued, real-time settings where 'emotionally intelligent' judgements may occur. They also assume that *reportable* emotional knowledge, judgement or decisions are predictors of emotionally intelligent action. In a real-time event we may, for instance, intuitively act in an 'emotionally intelligent' manner, but be unable to report on our own or others' emotions, especially on questions that are general, hypothetical, or both. Furthermore, if we accept a psychoanalytic portrait of reality, there is reason to believe that we often do not know what feelings impel what actions, however hard we try. And when we do think we know, there is now considerable evidence that our thinking is rarely, if ever, emotion free: cognition and affect interpenetrate (Bechara et al., 2000; de Sousa, 1987; Fineman, 1996, 2003a; Forgas, 2000).

. . . Measuring emotional intelligence, and assigning people an ordinal value of their worth, is no neutral act. Although emotional intelligence researchers might argue the niceties of their particular approach, and claim impartiality in mapping an 'interesting field', emotional intelligence has now become appropriated, heavily impregnated with a value stance of the sort: 'high emotional intelligence is good; low emotional intelligence is not good' (Fineman, 2000a; Paul, 1999). The mapmaker and map user are complicit in shaping the direction of the field. This is baldly revealed in the caveats and evaluations that attend the summary of results on EQ-type measures, and in the aggressive propagation of the view that positive emotions produce 'winners' and 'stars'. For Goleman, emotionally intelligent managers are enthusiastic, optimistic, honest, energetic, hopeful and persistent;

they also exude empathy, composure and self-assurance (Goleman, 1966, 1988) – an Americanized portrait of 'positive mental attitude', or as Matthews et al. (2002) suggest, characteristics that are '. . . little more that a dating-agency of desirable qualities' (p. 531).

Universal prescriptions for managerial success have eluded researchers for many decades, and it would be prudent to regard emotional intelligence in such historical light. In current, popular, renditions of emotional intelligence, the place of 'bad' feelings, such as rage, jealousy, anxiety, guilt, boredom, revenge, disgust and hurt are given little voice, even though these feature in many political portraits of corporate life and have, on occasions, produced remarkably successful business or organizational results – evidenced in the reputation of, for instance, Henry Ford, Sam Goldwin, and Jack 'Neutron' Welch of General Electric. Arguably, it would sometimes be emotionally intelligent to be angry, pessimistic, hurtful, envious or vengeful. Mayer reflects:

> When, in the dark days of World War II, Winston Churchill offered the British people 'Blood, sweat and tears', he was not nice and it was not optimistic but it was arguably quite emotionally intelligent. It is for these reasons (and the fact that a century of personality research contradicts the likelihood) that EI researchers who hope to somehow live up to the popular claims about success by studying the positive aspects of personality are likely to be disappointed.
>
> (Mayer, 2001: 16)

Paul's sentiments accord with this view: 'Should a child from a minority ethnic or religious group be forced to engage in trust-building activities with classmates who tease him? Should kids from abusive homes feel compelled to "share their feelings" with the entire class?' (1999: 7).

The emotional intelligence lens offers little insight into how emotions are valued performatorily in different national cultures and across ethnicity and gender. Current applications of emotional intelligence can be seen as a 'discourse technology' (Fairclough, 1989), appropriating social scientific, or quasi-scientific, knowledge, to promote a particular value system, or doctrine, on emotions. It is the counting of *certain* emotions that, supposedly, count. Its 'capture' is well described by one enthusiastic devotee – a senior executive in a global financial services organization:

> EI [emotional intelligence] . . . is an evolutionary path towards getting a blend between acting and executing tasks in a particular way, with a spirit that pervades everything that the organisation does . . . it is about getting people in the organisation to deliver the corporate values, to feel good about themselves, about each other and more importantly, to project that passion to sell products in a sincere way.
>
> (Chapman, 2001: 102)

The subtext here is that the emotionally less intelligent need correcting in some way (typically through training). Emotional intelligence is a leverage point for more sales. [. . .]

The 'less' emotionally intelligent are exposed to the apparent authority of 'their' test score – and to a scorer who has a vested interest in demonstrating that emotional intelligence 'works'. Emotional intelligence measurement creates a form of knowledge through which the worker is defined, and can also come to define him or herself. It renders the emotionally intelligent, and 'unintelligent', visible and more governable (Miller & Rose, 1990). [. . .]

References

Ashkenasy, N.M., Hartel, C.E.J. & Zerbe, W. (Eds). *Emotions in the workplace: Research, theory and practice*. Westport, CT: Quorum Books, 2000.

Bar-On, R. *The Emotional Quotient Inventory (EQi): A test of emotional intelligence*. Toronto: Multi-Health Systems, 1997.

Bar-On, R. Emotional and social intelligence: Insights form the Emotional Quotient Inventory (EQ-i). In R. Bar-On & J.D.A. Parker (Eds), *The handbook of emotional intelligence*. San Francisco, CA: Jossey Bass, 2000.

Bar-On, R. & Parker, J.D.A. (Eds). *The handbook of emotional intelligence*. San Francisco, CA: Jossey-Bass, 2000.

Bechara, A., Damasio, H. & Damasio, A.R. Emotion, decision making and the orbitofrontal cortex. *Cerebral Cortex*, 2000, *10*, 295–307.

Boyatzis, R.E., Goleman, D. & Rhee, K.S. Clustering competence in emotional intelligence. In R. Bar-On & J.D.A. Parker (Eds), *The handbook of emotional intelligence*. San Francisco, CA: Jossey-Bass, 2000.

Chapman, M. *The emotional intelligence pocketbook*. Arlesford: Management Pocketbooks, 2001.

Ciarrochi, J., Chan, A., Caputi, P. & Roberts, R. Measuring emotional intelligence. In J. Ciarrochi, J.P. Forgas & J.D. Mayer (Eds), *Emotional intelligence in everyday life*. Philadelphia, PA: Psychology Press, 2001.

Cooper, R.A. & Sawaf, A. *Executive EQ*. London: Orion Business, 1977.

De Dreue, C.K.W., West, M.W., Fischer, A.H. & MacCurtain, S. Origins and consequences of emotions in organizational teams. In R. Payne & C.L. Cooper (Eds), *Emotions at work*. Chichester: Wiley, 2001.

De Sousa, R. *The rationality of emotion*. Cambridge, MA: MIT Press, 1987.

Diener, E., Suh, E.M. & Smith, H.L. Subjective well-being: Three decades of progress. *Psychological Bulletin*, 1999, *125*, 276.

Domagalski, T.A. Emotion in organizations: Main currents. *Human Relations*, 1999, *52*, 833–47.

Fairclough, N. *Language and power*. Harlow: Longman, 1989.

Fineman, S. An emotion agenda. In S. Fineman (Ed.), *Emotion in organizations*. London: Sage, 1993b.

Fineman, S. Emotion and organizing. In S. Clegg, C. Hardy & W. Nord (Eds), *Handbook of organization studies*. London: Sage, 1996.

Fineman, S. Commodifying the emotionally intelligent. In S. Fineman (Ed.), *Emotion in organizations*, 2nd edn. London: Sage, 2000a, pp. 101–15.

Fineman, S. Emotional arenas revisited. In S. Fineman (Ed.), *Emotion in organizations*, 2nd edn. London: Sage, 2000b, pp. 1–24.

Fineman, S. *Understanding emotion at work*. London: Sage, 2003a.

Forgas, J.P. (Ed.). *Feeling and thinking: The role of affect in social cognition*. Cambridge: Cambridge University Press, 2000.

Gardner, H. *Multiple intelligences*. New York: Basic Books, 1993.

Goleman, D. *Emotional intelligence*. London: Bloomsbury, 1966.

Goleman, D. *Working with emotional intelligence*. London: Bloomsbury, 1988.

Hochschild, A. *The managed heart*. Berkeley: University of California, 1983.

Iedema, R., Braithwaite, J. & Sorensen, R. The reification of numbers: Statistics and the distance between self, work and others. *British Medical Journal*, 2003, *326*, 771.

Kamin, L.J. *The science and politics of IQ*. Harmondsworth: Penguin, 1997.

Leidner, R. Serving hamburgers and selling insurance: Gender, work and identity in interactive service jobs. *Gender and Society*, 1991, *5*, 154–77.

Lubyomirski, S. & Lepper, H.S. A measure of subjective happiness: Preliminary reliability and construct validity. *Social Indicators Research*, 1999, *46*, 137–55.

Matthews, G., Zeider, M. & Roberts, R.D. *Emotional intelligence: Science and myth*. Cambridge, MA: MIT Press, 2002.

Mayer, J.D., Caruso, D. & Salovey, P. The Multifactor Emotional Intelligence Scale: MEIS. Department of Psychology, University of New Hampshire, 1988.

Mayer, J.D., Caruso, D. & Salovey, P. Emotional intelligence meets traditional standards for an intelligence. *Intelligence*, 1999, *27*, 267–98.

Mayer, J.D., Ciarrochi, J. & Forgas, J.P. Emotional intelligence in everyday life: An introduction. In J. Ciarrochi, J.P. Forgas & J.D. Mayer (Eds), *Emotional intelligence in everyday life*. Philadelphia, PA: Psychology Press, 2001.

Miller, P. & Rose, N. Governing economic life. *Economy and Society*, 1990, *19*(1), 1–31.

Montague, A. *Race and IQ*. New York: Oxford University Press, 1999.

Parrott, G.W. & Hertel, P. Research methods in cognition and emotion. In T. Dalgleish & M. Power (Eds), *Handbook of cognition and emotion*. Chichester: Wiley, 1999.

Paul, A.M. *Promotional intelligence*. Salon.com, 1999. Available at: http://archive.salon.com/books/it/1999/06/28/emotional/print.html

Reason, P. & Bradbury, H. (Eds). *Handbook of action research – Participative enquiry and practice*. London: Sage, 2000.

Sturdy, A. Knowing the unknowable? – Discussion of methodological and theoretical issues in emotion research and organizational studies. *Organization*, 2003, *10*, 81–105.

Talwar, J.T. *Fast food, fast track*. Boulder, CO: Westview Press, 2002.

Wasko, J. *Understanding Disney: The manufacture of fantasy*. Malden, MA: Blackwell, 2001.

Weiss, H.M. & Brief, A.P. Affect at work: A historical perspective. In R.L. Payne & C.L. Cooper (Eds), *Emotions at work*. Chichester: Wiley, 2001.

Chapter 32

Charlie L. Reeve, Steven G. Rogelberg, Christiane Spitzmüller and Natalie DiGiacomo

THE CARING–KILLING PARADOX

Euthanasia-related strain among animal-shelter workers

It's very difficult when we are inundated from spring until fall. Every single person who walks through the door has one more litter of kittens. And you only have X number of cages in your facility, and they are already full. So the animal may come in the front door and go out the back door in a barrel.

(Shelter employee, as reported in Arluke & Sanders, 1996)

I think it's [animal euthanasia] made me an angry person. I want to be alone most of the time. I drink sometimes to numb the stress of the day. I eat and sleep more than I feel I need. I used to feel that my work was helping "save" the world. Not anymore. It doesn't seem to end. Although I believe that euthanasia isn't the worst thing that can happen to an animal, it's taking a toll on my life!

(Anonymous shelter employee, personal communication, April 6, 2002)

THE MAGNITUDE OF PET OVERPOPULATION in the United States appears to make animal euthanasia a tragic and necessary reality. Each year, an estimated 4 to 12 million companion animals are euthanized (cf. "HSUS pet overpopulation estimates," 2000; Nassar, Talboy, & Moulton, 1992; Olson, 1990). Although some have medical problems severe enough to preclude adoption and warrant euthanasia, many of the animals euthanized are healthy but unwanted.

Most typically, the job of performing euthanasia on unwanted animals falls in the hands of animal-shelter workers. Though no large-scale effort has been made to investigate this population, numerous ethnographic investigations and media reports have suggested that individuals performing animal euthanasia are at increased risk of emotional mismanagement, physical ailments such as high blood pressure and ulcers, unresolved grief, depression, as well as substance abuse and even suicide (e.g., Arluke, 1994; Arluke & Sanders, 1996; Fogle & Abrahamson, 1990; Frommer & Arluke, 1999; Hart & Mader, 1995; Rollin, 1986; Sanders, 1995; "Shelter workers," 2000).

These anecdotal reports certainly seem to suggest that shelter workers are experiencing a severe form of work strain stemming from what Arluke (1994) calls a *caring–killing paradox*. That is, if suitable homes are not found in a timely manner, shelter workers are expected to euthanize animals for which they have been providing care and protection. Consistent with this notion, Rollin (1986) argued that shelter workers are exposed to a type of stressor qualitatively different from the typical types of physical, task, and role-process stressors studied in the work-stress literature: a "moral" stressor. Namely, shelter workers, most of whom enter the occupation because they want to help animals (Rollin, 1986), are faced with a daily contradiction between their ideal occupational selves (i.e., protectors of animals) and the reality of having to kill healthy but unwanted animals. The effects of this stressor are likely to be amplified given the social stigma attached to the killing of companion animals.

There is reason to believe that the thousands of people charged with performing animal euthanasia in the United States are a potentially at-risk population. In view of the magnitude of the pet overpopulation problem, limitations on governmental and private funding for the creation of shelter facilities, and the persistence of pet abandonment and relinquishment, the need for performing euthanasia is unlikely to decrease in the near future. Taken together, it behooves applied psychologists to address the dearth of substantive empirical research aimed at understanding and helping individuals and shelter management deal with euthanasia-related issues.

As the first quantitative investigation of this topic, the purpose of the current study is to gain preliminary empirical evidence of the prevalence and correlates of euthanasia-related strain among shelter workers. As any single field study in a new area of inquiry can make only limited advances, a secondary purpose of this study is to sensitize the applied research community to this unique population and to provide a stepping stone for the additional research required to understand fully the psychological ramifications of performing animal euthanasia. [. . .]

Discussion

The current study shows evidence that animal euthanasia is an important source of job strain for animal-shelter employees. First, when asked, most employees reported feeling strain as a result of their involvement with euthanasia. The prevalence of these ERS perceptions supports the suggestion by prior qualitative studies that euthanasia is a significant stressor for animal-shelter employees. Further, among a group of people who all work in the same general sheltering environment, the results show a clear pattern of differences in stress and well-being between those who are involved directly with euthanasia and those who are not directly involved. Most notably, those who are directly involved in euthanasia reported significantly higher levels of work stress, stress-related somatic complaints, and WFC, and lower levels of satisfaction with the work that they actually do. Likewise, among those who are engaged in euthanasia, the results demonstrate that perceived ERS was correlated significantly to a number of well-being-related outcomes beyond that resulting from the variance shared with generalized work stress.

Taken as a whole, these results, which are summarized in Table 1, indicate that among individuals for whom conducting animal euthanasia is part of their job, it is a salient, unique source of work stress that has a negative impact on their well-being. These findings should be of additional importance to shelter management in that poor physical and affective well-being can lead to absenteeism and turnover (Chen & Spector, 1992; Hendrix Ovalle, & Troxler, 1985; Wright & Cropanzano, 1998).

It is interesting to note that there was variability on ERS and the well-being indexes for employees involved in euthanasia activities. This suggests that not all employees are affected by euthanasia involvement to the same extent. The observed diversity of reactions to a common stressor is not surprising and is consistent with a body of research from differential psychology in general, and work stress in particular, showing that the appraisal of a stressor as a threat depends on one's

Table 1 Summary of Hypotheses and Results

	Hypothesis	Significant findings
1.	Individuals involved in euthanasia activities, compared to shelter workers not involved in euthanasia activities, will experience more work-to-family conflict, somatic complaints, substance use, work stress, and less job satisfaction	Mostly supported; significant differences in general job stress, work-to-family conflict, overall job satisfaction, and satisfaction with work itself, but not substance use
2.	Perceived ERS will be associated positively with work-to-family conflict, somatic complaints, and substance use; and negatively with overall job satisfaction.	Fully supported
3.	Individuals who perceive higher levels of ERS will report higher overall stress.	Fully supported
4.	Perceived ERS will be associated positively with work-to-family conflict, somatic complaints, and substance use; and negatively with overall job satisfaction after controlling for the variance as a result of overall work stress.	Mostly supported; significant correlations with overall job satisfaction, work-to-family conflict, and somatic complaints, but not substance use
5.	Attitudes toward the necessity of euthanasia (scored positively) will be correlated negatively with ERS and positively with indicators of well-being.	Mostly supported; significant correlations with ERS, overall job satisfaction, work-to-family conflict, and somatic complaints, but not substance use

Note. ERS = euthanasia-related strain.

personal resources (Lazarus & Folkman, 1984). A variety of personal and organizational/situational factors have reliable and important influences on the propensity to experience stress and the ability to cope with stress, presumably by buffering or depleting one's personal resources.

The current analyses suggest that variance in ERS and well-being is associated with individual, work, and organizational differences. For instance, we found that employees' attitudes toward euthanasia were associated significantly with perceived ERS. Individuals who are more apt to evaluate euthanasia as necessary and acceptable, given the magnitude of the overpopulation of unwanted pets, appear to perceive experiencing less strain from their euthanasia involvement. It is possible, however, that this association is a consequence, rather than an antecedent, of differences in the euthanasia response. That is, those who have difficulty dealing with euthanasia may eventually develop negative attitudes toward it, whereas those who do not experience ERS may come to hold a more positive evaluation of the acceptability of euthanasia.

Clearly, the roles of many more individual differences in explaining variation in ERS necessitate investigation. For pragmatic reasons, the current study was limited in the number of scales that could be administered to participants who were "on the fly" at these conferences. This is clearly a limitation of the current study. However, we made the decision to forgo the assessment of many of these variables in the interest of increasing our response rate, believing it more important to gain reliable information about a little rather than unreliable information about a lot. Future research should continue to investigate associations between individual characteristics and ERS. For example, the general work stress literature has indicated that a number of personality characteristics (e.g., hardiness, locus of control) are related to differences in susceptibility to emotional and psychological strain, as well as coping responses (Costa, Somerfield, & McCrae, 1996; Hahn, 2000; Havlovic & Kennan, 1995; Kobasa, 1982; Krohne, 1996; Lefcourt, 1992). Information such as this potentially could be used to identify employees who may be more resilient (or alternatively, to screen for those who may be especially susceptible) to the adverse effects of performing animal euthanasia.

Our investigation of the work-related factors and well-being suggests that there is a difference between the total amount of time a person is engaged in euthanasia and how this time is distributed over the course of the work week. For example, the results show that the numbers of hours engaged in euthanasia per week was associated with increased substance use. Similarly, the frequency of conducting euthanasia was associated positively with WFC. These results suggest that the more a person is engaged in euthanasia overall, the worse the impact on well-being.

On the other hand, among those who perform euthanasia, the impact on well-being appears to be associated with differences in how shelters schedule this time. That is, those who engage in fewer, longer sessions report less substance use and WFC compared to those who conduct more frequent, shorter sessions. This may suggest that frequent, short euthanasia sessions are more emotionally taxing in the aggregate than infrequent, but longer sessions. Findings such as these clearly indicate the need for further, more detailed investigations of the ramifications of variations in euthanasia work processes.

The results also indicate that organizational differences are associated with differences in well-being. Specifically, the pattern of results indicated that shelter type (private vs. government/municipal) was associated with differences primarily in work satisfaction indicators, whereas shelter size was associated primarily with stress-related indicators (e.g., ERS, overall stress, WFC). While the current study is not able to investigate the specific shelter factors that are associated with these differences, the finding that organizational size was inversely associated with stress-related indicators of well-being is consistent with our initial suggestion that larger shelters may have more social and financial resources to help employees deal effectively with ERS (e.g., shelter size may act as a proxy for variables that may moderate or directly influence the experience of stress). However, future research will be needed to identify specific characteristics associated with these outcomes.

As stated earlier, this study was seen as an effort to lay a foundation for further study, rather than an attempt for a comprehensive assessment of all euthanasia-related influences. Although a full discussion of potential future research in this area is well beyond the scope of this paper, we provide a few suggestions for general directions. First, staying within the organizational psychology framework from which we approached this study, future research can be thought of as emphasizing either breadth or depth. That is, one stream of future research needs to expand the breadth of the nexus of variables associated with ERS. For instance, a variety of organizational-level variables might be related to differences in the ambient level of ERS across organizations. Likewise, as pointed out earlier, future studies need to better sample the domain of individual differences to better understand the full range of antecedents of ERS. Moreover, the potential for interactions and person—environment correspondence requires investigation.

On the other hand, rather than casting a wide net, it also would be useful for future studies to take a more focused, in-depth approach by focusing on a smaller sample (e.g., a single shelter) across time and using a full range of research techniques (e.g., surveys, interviews, workplace observation, experience sampling techniques, experimental designs). As one example, additional interviews with some of the participants regarding how management can help employees suggests that the following interventions may be worth studying for their potential to reduce ERS or its effects: (a) establishing internal support or discussion groups; (b) provision of professional counseling; (c) management sponsorship of self-care behaviors (e.g., vouchers or discounts to health clubs, sponsored non-work gatherings or entertainment, scheduling "quiet time" into workers' schedules); (d) job redesign (e.g., rotation of duties); (e) increased euthanasia technical training; and (f) public awareness initiatives (e.g., increased focus on the prevention of animal overpopulation, general public education of euthanasia policies and procedures). A focused approach, though limited in other respects, is an appropriate way to evaluate the effectiveness of interventions such as these.

Second, we believe that the investigation of animal-shelter employees affords an opportunity to apply a variety of theoretical perspectives. To take but a single example from the management literature, Ashforth and Kreiner's (1999) model of dirty work would seem highly applicable to this population. In addition to the personal struggle to deal with and reconcile the caring—killing paradox, shelter workers as a group are often confronted with the social stigma of doing *dirty work*; that is, work that is mandated, yet morally stigmatized by society (Hughes, 1951,

1962). By engaging in work that is regarded as morally tainted (e.g., "sinful") by society, negative attributions likely may be attached to shelter workers themselves, which, in turn, may add more strain by frustrating their desire to construct a positive sense of self and to seek social validation (Ashforth & Kreiner, 1999). The point here is that this is merely one of many valuable theoretical perspectives that potentially could be brought to bear on this issue to better understand the ramifications of euthanasia-related work.

Finally, over the past three decades, animal-welfare issues appear to have moved from the fringe into the mainstream of social conscience. This makes salient questions such as whether increased social awareness increases or decreases the stress of euthanasia-related work. On the one hand, perhaps increased awareness alleviates stress as a result of greater public understanding of the role that shelter workers play and the problems they face, as well as increasing donations and volunteer help. On the other hand, perhaps greater awareness enhances the stress by increasing the saliency of the social stigma attached to this work. Likewise, shelter workers might experience a sense of hopelessness if they perceive increased social concern, but fail to observe a concomitant decrease in pet overpopulation.

We believe that the myriad of research questions that remain will require multi-disciplinary answers. Many of these questions require an integrated consideration and understanding of social problems, workplace dynamics, individual mental health, death and dying, animal handling, and human-animal interactions. Clearly, this requires extending the umbrella of participation to fields outside of psychology, such as sociology, thanatology, and ethics. Albeit based on limited exposure, we believe that our colleagues across psychology and other social sciences will be pleasantly surprised with how willing the animal-sheltering community is to embrace researchers' ideas and to participate in substantive research endeavors.

This study is the first systematic attempt to investigate quantitatively the impact of animal euthanasia on shelter workers' well-being. The findings demonstrate that euthanasia-related work is significantly related to a number of well-being outcomes of accepted importance in applied psychology. Further, the comparative analyses between those who are and those who are not subjected to euthanasia-related activities at work show substantial differences in various indicators of well-being. Taken together, these results suggest that understanding and working to ameliorate or cope with ERS is of importance, not only for individual well-being, but for organizational effectiveness as well.

References

Arluke, A. (1994). Managing emotions in an animal shelter. In A. Manning & J. Serpell (Eds.), *Animals and human society* (pp. 145–165). New York, NY: Routledge.

Arluke, A., & Sanders, C. R. (1996). The institutional self of shelter workers. In A. Arluke & C. R. Sanders (Eds.), *Regarding animals* (pp. 82–106). Philadelphia, PA: Temple University Press.

Ashforth, B. E., & Kreiner, G. E. (1999). "How can you do it?" Dirty work and the challenge of constructing a positive identity. *Academy of Management Review, 24,* 413–434.

Chen, P. Y., & Spector, P. E. (1992). Relationships of work stressors with aggression, withdrawal, theft, and substance abuse. *Journal of Occupational and Organizational Psychology, 65, 177–184.*

Costa, P. T., Somerfield, M. R., & McCrae, R. R. (1996). Personality and coping: A reconceptualization. In M. Zeidner & N. S. Endler (Eds.), *Handbook of coping: Theory, research, applications* (pp. 44–61). New York, NY: John Wiley and Sons.

Fogle, B., & Abrahamson, D. (1990). Pet loss: A survey of the attitudes and feelings of practicing veterinarians. *Antrhozoös, 3,* 143–150.

Frommer, S. S., & Arluke, A. (1999). Loving them to death: Blame-displacing strategies of animal shelter workers and surrenderers. *Society and Animals, 7,* 1–16.

Hahn, S. E. (2000). The effects of locus of control on daily exposure, coping, and reactivity to work interpersonal stressors: A diary study. *Personality and Individual Differences, 29, 729–748.*

Hart, L. A., & Mader, B. (1995). Pretense and hidden feelings in the humane society environment: A source of stress. *Psychological Reports, 77, 554.*

Havlovic, S. J., & Keenan, J. P. (1995). Coping with work stress: The influence of individual differences. In R. Crandall & P. L. Perrewé (Eds.), *Occupational stress: A handbook* (pp. 179–192). Washington, DC: Taylor & Francis.

Hendrix, W. H., Ovalle, N. K., & Troxler, R. G. (1985). Behavioral and physiological consequences of stress and its antecedent factors. *Journal of Applied Psychology, 70,* 188–201.

HSUS pet overpopulation estimates. (2000). Retrieved February 18, 2000, from http://www.hsus.org/programs/companion/ overpopulation/op_faq.html

Hughes, E. C. (1951). Work and the self. In J. H. Rohrer & M. Sherif (Eds.), *Social psychology at the crossroads* (pp. 313–323). New York, NY: Harper and Brothers.

Hughes, E. C. (1962). Good people and dirty work. *Social Problems, 10, 3–11.*

Kobasa, S. C. (1982). The hardy personality: Toward a social psychology of stress and health. In J. Suls & G. S. Sanders (Eds.), *The social psychology of health and illness* (pp. 3–32). Hillsdale, NJ: Lawrence Erlbaum.

Krohne, H. W. (1996). Individual differences in coping. In M. Zeidner & N. S. Endler (Eds.), *Handbook of coping: Theory, research, applications* (pp. 381–409). New York, NY: John Wiley and Sons.

Lazarus, R. S., & Folkman, S. (1984). *Stress, appraisal, and coping.* New York, NY: Springer.

Lefcourt, H. M. (1992). Perceived control, personal effectiveness, and emotional states. In B. N. Carpenter (Ed.), *Personal coping: Theory, research, and application* (pp. 111–113). New York, NY: Praeger.

Nassar, R., Talboy, J., & Moulton, C. (1992). *Animal shelter reporting study: 1990.* Englewood, NJ: American Humane Association.

Olson, P. N. (1990). Concerned about euthanasia of healthy homeless animals. *Journal of the American Veterinary Medical Association, 196,* 10.

Rollin, B. E. (1986). Euthanasia and moral stress. *Loss, Grief, and Care, 1,* 115–126.

Sanders, C. R. (1995). Killing with kindness: Veterinary euthanasia and the social construction of personhood. *Sociological Forum, 10, 195–214.*

Shelter workers suffer from dealing in death. (2000, May 15). *The Washington Times,* p. A2.

Wright, T. A., & Cropanzano, R. (1998). Emotional exhaustion as a predictor of job performance and voluntary turnover. *Journal of Applied Psychology, 83, 486–493.*

Chapter 33

Allen C. Smith, III and Sherryl Kleinman

MANAGING EMOTIONS IN MEDICAL SCHOOL

Students' contacts with the living and the dead

How do I set aside 25 years of living? Experience which made close contact with someone's body a sensual event? Maybe it's attraction, maybe disgust. But it isn't supposed to be part of what I feel when I touch a patient. I feel some of those things, and I want to learn not to.

(Third-year, male medical student.)

[. . .]

THE IDEOLOGY OF AFFECTIVE NEUTRALITY is strong in medicine; yet no courses in the medical curriculum deal directly with emotion management, specifically learning to change or eliminate inappropriate feelings (Hochschild 1983). Rather, two years of participant observation in a medical school revealed that discussion of the students' feelings is taboo; their development toward emotional neutrality remains part of the hidden curriculum. Under great pressure to prove themselves worthy of entering the profession, students are afraid to admit that they have uncomfortable feelings about patients or procedures, and hide those feelings behind a "cloak of competence" (Haas and Shaffir 1977, 1982). Beneath their surface presentations, how do students deal with the "unprofessional" feelings they bring over from the personal realm? Because faculty members do not address the problem, students are left with an individualistic outlook: they expect to get control of themselves through sheer willpower.

Despite the silence surrounding this topic, the faculty, the curriculum, and the organization of medical school do provide students with resources for dealing with their problem. The culture of medicine that informs teaching and provides the feeling rules also offers unspoken supports for dealing with unwanted emotions. Students draw on aspects of their experience in medical school to manage their emotions. Their strategies include transforming the patient or the procedure into an analytic object or event, accentuating the comfortable feelings that come from learning and practicing "real medicine," blaming patients, empathizing with patients, joking, and avoiding sensitive contact. [. . .]

The students' problem

As they encounter the human body, students experience a variety of uncomfortable feelings including embarrassment, disgust, and arousal. Medical school, however, offers a barrier against these feelings by providing the anesthetic effect of long hours and academic pressure.

> You know the story. On call every third night, and stay in the hospital late most other evenings. I don't know how you're supposed to think when you're that tired, but you do, plod through the day insensitive to everything.
>
> (Third-year male)

Well before entering medical school, students learn that their training will involve constant pressure and continuing fatigue. Popular stories prepare them for social isolation, the impossibility of learning everything, long hours, test anxiety, and the fact that medical school will permeate their lives (Becker, Geer, Hughes, and Strauss 1961). These difficulties and the sacrifices that they entail legitimate the special status of the profession the students are entering. They also blunt the students' emotional responses.

Yet uncomfortable feelings break through. Throughout the program, students face provocative situations—some predictable, others surprising. They find parts of their training, particularly dissection and the autopsy, bizarre or immoral when seen from the perspective they had "for 25 years" before entering medical school.

> Doing the pelvis, we cut it across the waist. . . . Big saws! The mad scientist! People wouldn't believe what we did in there. The cracking sound! That day was more than anxiety. We were really violating that person . . . Drawn and quartered.
>
> (First-year male)

> I did my autopsy 10 days ago. That shook me off my feet. Nothing could have prepared me for it. The person was my age . . . She just looked (pause) asleep. Not like the cadaver. Fluid, blood, smell. It smelled like a butcher shop. And they handled it like a butcher shop. The technicians. Slice, move, pull, cut . . . all the organs, insides, pulled out in 10 minutes. I know it's absurd, but what if she's not really dead? She doesn't look like it.
>
> (Second-year female).

The "mad scientist" and the "butcher" violate the students' images of medicine.

Even in more routine kinds of contact, the students sometimes feel that they are ignoring the sanctity of the body and breaking social taboos.

Much of the students' discomfort is based on the fact that the bodies they have contact with are or were *people*. Suddenly students feel uncertain about the relationship of the person to the body, a relationship they had previously taken for granted.

> It felt tough when we had to turn the whole body over from time to time (during dissection). It felt like real people.
>
> (First-year female)

> OK. Maybe he was a father. But the father part is gone. This is just the body. That sounds religious. Maybe it is. How else can I think about it?.
>
> (First-year male).

When the person is somehow reconnected to the body, such as when data about the living patient who died is brought into the autopsy room, students feel less confident and more uneasy.

Students find contact with the sexual body particularly stressful. In the anatomy lab, in practice sessions with other students, and in examining patients, students find it difficult to feel neutral as contact approaches the sexual parts of the body.

> When you listen to the heart you have to work around the breast, and move it to listen to one spot. I tried to do it with minimum contact, without staring at her tit . . . breast . . . The different words (pause) shows I was feeling both things at once.
>
> (Second-year male)

Though they are rarely aroused, students worry that they will be. They feel guilty, knowing that sexuality is proscribed in medicine, and they feel embarrassed. Most contact involves some feelings, but contact with the sexual body presents a bigger problem. [. . .]

Students also feel disgust. They see feces, smell vomit, touch wounds, and hear bone saws, encountering many repulsive details with all of their senses.

> One patient was really gross! He had something that kept him standing, and coughing all the time. Coughing phlegm, and that really bothers me. Gross! Just something I don't like. Some smelled real bad. I didn't want to examine their axillae. Stinking armpits! It was just not something I wanted to do.
>
> (Second-year female).

When the ugliness is tied to living patients, the aesthetic problem is especially difficult. On opening the bowels of the cadaver, for example, students permit themselves some silent expressions of discomfort, but even a wince is unacceptable with repugnant living patients.

To make matters worse, students learn early on that they are not supposed to talk about their feelings with faculty members or other students. Feelings remain private. The silence encourages students to think about their problem as an individual matter, extraneous to the "real work" of medical school. They speak of "screwing up your courage," "getting control of yourself," "being tough enough," and "putting feelings aside." They worry that the faculty would consider them incompetent and unprofessional if they admitted their problem.

> I would be embarrassed to talk about it. You're supposed to be professional here. Like there's an unwritten rule about how to talk.
>
> (First-year female)

[. . .]

The "unwritten rule" is relaxed enough sometimes to permit discussion, but the privacy that surrounds these rare occasions suggests the degree to which the taboo exists. At times, students signal their uncomfortable feelings—rolling their eyes, turning away, and sweating—but such confirmation is limited. Exemplifying pluralistic ignorance, each student feels unrealistically inadequate in comparison with peers (yet another uncomfortable feeling). Believing that other students are handling the problem better than they are, each student manages his or her feelings privately, only vaguely aware that all students face the same problem. [. . .]

Emotion management strategies

How do students manage their uncomfortable and "inappropriate" feelings? The deafening silence surrounding the issue keeps them from defining the problem as shared, or from working out common solutions. They cannot develop strategies collectively, but their solutions are not individual. Rather, students use the *same* basic emotion management strategies because social norms, faculty models, curricular priorities, and official and unofficial expectations provide them with uniform guidelines and resources for managing their feelings.

Transforming the contact

Students feel uncomfortable because they are making physical contact with people in ways they would usually define as appropriate only in a personal context, or as inappropriate in any context. Their most common solution to this problem is cognitive (Hochschild 1979; Thoits 1985). Mentally they transform the body and their contact with it into something entirely different from the contacts they have in their personal lives. Students transform the person into a set of esoteric body parts and change their intimate contact with the body into a mechanical or analytic problem.

> I just told myself, "OK, doc, you're here to find out what's wrong, and that includes the axillae (armpits)." And I detach a little, reduce the person for a moment . . . Focus real hard on the detail at hand, the

fact, or the procedure or the question. Like with the cadaver. Focus
on a vessel. Isolate down to whatever you're doing.

(Second-year female)

[. . .] Students also transform the moment of contact into a complex intellectual puzzle, the kind of challenge they faced successfully during previous years of
schooling. They interpret details according to logical patterns and algorithms, and
find answers as they master the rules. [. . .]

The patient is really like a math word problem. You break it down into
little pieces and put them together. The facts you get from a history and
physical, from the labs and chart. They fit together, once you begin to
see how to do it . . . It's an intellectual challenge.

(Third-year female)

Defining contact as a part of scientific medicine makes the students feel safe.
They are familiar with and confident about science, they feel supported by its
cultural and curricular legitimacy, and they enjoy rewards for demonstrating
their scientific know-how. In effect, science itself is an emotion management
strategy. By competing for years for the highest grades, these students have
learned to separate their feelings from the substance of their classes and to
concentrate on the impersonal facts of the subject matter. In medical school they
use these "educational skills" not only for academic success but also for emotion
management. [. . .]

The scientific, clinical language that the students learn also supports intel-
lectualization. It is complex, esoteric, and devoid of personal meanings. "Palpating
the abdomen" is less personal than "feeling the belly." [. . .]

Further, the structure of the language, as in the standard format for the presentation of a case, helps the students to think and speak impersonally. Second-year
students learn that there is a routine, acceptable way to summarize a patient: chief
complaint, history of present illness, past medical history, family history, social
history, review of systems, physical findings, list of problems, medical plan. In many
situations they must reduce the sequence to a two- or three-minute summary.
Faculty members praise the students for their ability to present the details quickly.
Medical language labels and conveys clinical information, and it leads the students
away from their emotions.

Transformation sometimes involves changing the body into a nonhuman object.
Students think of the body as a machine or as an animal specimen, and recall earlier,
comfortable experiences in working on that kind of object. The body is no longer
provocative because it is no longer a body.

After we had the skin off (the cadaver), it was pretty much like a cat or
something. It wasn't pleasant, but it wasn't human either.

(First-year female)

(The pelvic exam) is pretty much like checking a broken toaster. It
isn't a problem. I'm good at that kind of thing.

(Second-year male)

> You can't tell what's wrong without looking under the hood. It's dif-
> ferent when I'm talking with a patient. But when I'm examining them
> it's like an automobile engine . . . There's a bad connotation with that,
> but it's literally what I mean.
>
> (Third-year male)

[. . .] The curriculum supports these dehumanizing transformations by eliminating the person in most of the students' contact with the body. Contact is usually indirect, based on photographs, X-rays (and several newer technologies), clinical records, diagrams, and written words. Students would have to make an effort to reconnect these images to the people they remotely represent. [. . .]

Accentuating the positive

As we hinted in the previous section, transforming body contact into an analytic event does not merely rid students of their uncomfortable feelings, producing neutrality. It often gives them opportunities to have *good* feelings about what they are doing. Their comfortable feelings include the excitement of practicing "real medicine," the satisfaction of learning, and the pride of living up to medical ideals.

Students identify much of their contact with the body as "real medicine," asserting that such contact separates medicine from other professions. As contact begins in dissection and continues through the third-year clinical clerkships, students feel excited about their progress. [. . .]

> This (dissection) is the part that is really medical school. Not like any
> other school. It feels like an initiation rite, something like when I joined
> a fraternity. We were really going to work on people.
>
> (First-year male)

[. . .] Eventually students see contact as their responsibility and their right, and forget the sense of privilege they felt at the beginning. Still, some excitement returns as they take on clinical responsibility in the third year. All of these feelings can displace the discomfort which also attends most contact.

Contact also provides a compelling basis for several kinds of learning, all of which the students value. They sense that they learn something important in contact, something richer than the "dry facts" of textbooks and lectures. Physicians, they believe, rely on touch, not on text. [. . .]

Laughing about it

[. . .] By redefining the situation as at least partially humorous, students reassure themselves that they can handle the challenge. They believe that the problem can't be so serious if there is a funny side to it. Joking also allows them to relax a little and to set ideals aside for a time.

Where do students learn to joke in this way? The faculty, including the residents (who are the real teachers on the clinical teams), participate freely, teaching the students that humor is an acceptable way to talk about uncomfortable encounters in medicine. [. . .]

Unlike the students' other strategies, joking occurs primarily when they are alone with other medical professionals. Jokes are acceptable in the hallways, over coffee, or in physicians' workrooms, but usually are unacceptable when outsiders might overhear. Joking is backstage behavior. Early in their training, students sometimes make jokes in public, perhaps to strengthen their identity as "medical student," but most humor is in-house, reserved for those who share the problem and have a sense of humor about it.

Avoiding the contact

Students sometimes avoid the kinds of contact that give rise to unwanted emotions. They control the visual field during contact, and eliminate or abbreviate particular kinds of contact. [. . .]

Keeping personal body parts covered in the lab and in examinations prevents mold, maintains a sterile field, and protects the patient's modesty. Covers also eliminate disturbing sites and protect students from their feelings. Such non-professional purposes are sometimes most important. Some students, for example, examine the breasts by reaching under the patient's gown, bypassing the visual examination emphasized in training. [. . .]

Conclusion

Medical students sometimes feel attracted to or disgusted by the human body. They want to do something about these feelings, but they find that the topic is taboo. Even among themselves, students generally refrain from talking about their problem. Yet despite the silence, the culture and the organization of medical school provide students with supports and guidelines for managing their emotions. Affective socialization proceeds with no deliberate control, but with profound effect. [. . .]

The . . . emotion management strategies used by the students illustrate the culture of modern Western medicine. In relying on these strategies, the students reproduce that culture (Foucault 1973), creating a new generation of physicians who will support the biomedical model of medicine and the kind of doctor-patient relationship in which the patient is too frequently dehumanized. Students some-times criticize their teachers for an apparent insensitivity to their patients, but they turn to desensitizing strategies themselves in their effort to control the emotions that medical situations provoke. These strategies exclude the patient's feelings, values, and social context, the important psychosocial aspects of medicine (Engel 1977; Gorlin and Zucker 1983). Contradicting their previous values, students reinforce biomedicine as they rely on its emotion management effects. [. . .]

It would be unfair to conclude that medical training is uniquely responsible for the specific character of the students' emotion management problem and for its unspoken solution. The basic features of the culture of medicine are consistent with the wider cultural context in which medicine exists. Biomedicine fits with the emphasis in Western culture on rationality and scientific "objectivity." In Western societies the mind is defined as superior to the body, and thoughts are defined as superior to feelings (Mills and Kleinman 1988; Tuan 1982; Turner 1984). Not surprisingly, students know the feeling rules of professional life before they arrive at medical school. Childhood socialization and formal education teach them to set aside their feelings in public, to master "the facts," and to present themselves in intellectually defensible ways (Bowers 1984). Medical situations provide vivid challenges, but students come equipped with emotion management skills that they need only to strengthen. [. . .]

References

Becker, H., B. Geer, E. Hughes and A. Strauss. 1961. *Boys in White*. New Brunswick, NJ: Transaction.

Bowers, C. 1984. *The Promise of Theory: Education and the Politics of Cultural Change*. New York: Longmans.

Engel, G. 1977. "The Need for a New Medical Model: A Challenge for Biomedicine." *Science* 196(4286):129–36.

Foucault, M. 1973. *The Birth of the Clinic: An Archaeology of Medical Perception*. New York: Pantheon.

Gorlin, R. and H. Zucker. 1983. "Physicians' Reactions to Patients: A Key to Teaching Humanistic Medicine." *New England Journal of Medicine* 308(18):1059–63.

Haas, J. and W. Shaffir. 1977. "The Professionalization of Medical Students: Developing Competence and a Cloak of Competence." *Symbolic Interaction 1:71–88.*

———. 1982. "Taking on the Role of Doctor: A Dramaturgical Analysis of Professionalization." *Symbolic Interaction* 5:187–203.

Hochschild, A. 1979. "Emotion Work, Feeling Rules, and Social Structure." *American Journal of Sociology* 85(3):551–75.

———. 1983. *The Managed Heart*. Berkeley: University of California Press.

Mills, T. and S. Kleinman. 1988. "Emotions, Reflexivity, and Action: An Interactionist Analysis." *Social Forces* 66(4):1009–27.

Thoits, P. 1985. "Self-Labeling Processes in Mental Illness: The Role of Emotional Deviance." *American Journal of Sociology* 91:221–49.

Tuan, Y.-F. 1982. *Segmented Worlds and Self: Group Life and Individual Consciousness*. Minneapolis: University of Minnesota Press.

Turner, B. *The Body and Society*. 1984. New York: Basil Blackwell.

8. Emotions, economics and consumer culture

EMOTIONS ARE CENTRAL to economic processes of production and consumption and, more generally, to processes of decision-making. This is increasingly recognized among theorists of economic behaviour, an area traditionally dominated by models that assume a rational, self-interested actor as their norm. Recent years have seen a proliferation of studies of emotion, for example in connection with buying behaviour for marketing purposes (O'Shaughnessy and O'Shaughnessy 2002); in relation to the management of uncertainty in the context of global financial institutions (Pixley 2004); or for the purpose of revising theoretical models of risky choice behaviour (Pilz 2007). Theorists of consumer culture, on the other hand, have long recognized that commodities are invested with symbolic meaning; practices of consumption are emotionally significant in so far as they bear on the construction of individuals' identity and forms of belonging (Dittmar 2007; Sassatelli 2007; Slater 1997).

The first extract in this section is drawn from Colin Campbell's *The Romantic Ethic and the Spirit of Modern Consumerism* (1987). Campbell is one of a number of scholars who have argued against 'productivist' historical narratives – namely narratives that implicitly privilege the historical role of production, and that present consumer culture as emerging only at the beginning of the twentieth century, as a consequence of the industrial revolution. Campbell builds on Weber's thesis relating the protestant ethic of rationality, industry and emotional control to the rise of capitalism. He argues that a second 'ethic' associated with Sentimentalism and then Romanticism proper (both with roots in eighteenth-century English Puritanism), combined with the former to facilitate the industrial revolution. Campbell's longer term view thus suggests that this more 'emotionalist' Puritan strand is a key cause of the modern economy and not, as typically thought, merely its effect. He thus attempts to explain the consumer revolution of eighteenth-century England in terms of the spread of an 'emotionalist' ethic. Campbell sees in this ethics the origins of more recent forms of hedonism based on the endless creation of 'wants' through the imputation of ultimately illusory meanings and images onto a mass-produced procession of commodities.

The second extract is drawn from Danny Miller's *A Theory of Shopping* (1998) and was selected as something of a counterbalance to those writers who stress the illusory, shallow and hedonistic values associated with consumption. It is based on anthropological fieldwork conducted in London and informed by the idea that, if we are to talk of the meaning of everyday consumption practices, then we had better talk to those doing the consuming. Drawing on the example of Mrs Wynn, Miller makes the case that much ordinary, working class supermarket shopping can be construed as a form of 'love making'. That is to say, the minutiae of daily purchasing decisions and actions are framed within broader and higher aims and values, such as sensitive care for one's family.

Love figures also in our third extract, from Daniel Lefkowitz's article 'Investing in Emotion: love and anger in financial advertising' (2003). In this piece Lefkowitz examines the television commercials for financial services companies that were shown during the late 1990s in the US. Lefkowitz finds that these ads frame and construct the financial services by way of discourses and images associated either with loving nurturance and care, or with anger and violence. He adopts a discursive approach that sees emotions as culturally constructed within 'performative texts', such as these TV commercials.

Our last extract is from an article by Jon Elster published in 1998, a pioneer in attempting to bridge the gap between emotion theory and economic theory – two fields, Elster wrote, 'that seem to exist in near-complete isolation from each other'. The article as a whole accordingly proposes 'a general way of incorporating emotion into the toolkit of economics'. Elster reviews the psychology of emotion and extracts a 'cost-benefit model of emotions'; this model concentrates on the motivational dynamics of affects such as shame and guilt and promises to be of use in explaining and predicting behaviour. He suggests that emotions can shape the 'reward parameters' for 'rational choice' (e.g. by changing people's preferences or acting as psychic costs or benefits). However, he also suggests that emotions can shape the very ability to make rational choices, either on a short term (a brief episode of anger) or a long term (a lifelong hatred) basis.

References

Dittmar, H. (2007) *Consumer Culture, Identity and Wellbeing: the search for the 'good life' and the 'body perfect'*. Hove: Psychology Press.

O'Shaughnessy, J. and O'Shaughnessy, N. J. (2002) *The Marketing Power of Emotion*. New York: Oxford University Press.

Pilz, F. (2007) *Emotions and Risky Choice: an experimental and theoretical study from the economic psychological perspective*. Saarbrücken: VDM Verlag

Pixley, J. (2004) *Emotions in Finance: distrust and uncertainty in global markets*. Cambridge: Cambridge University Press.

Sassatelli, R. (2007) *Consumer Culture: history, theory and politics*. London: Sage.

Slater, D. (1997) *Consumer Culture and Modernity*. Cambridge: Polity.

Chapter 34

Colin Campbell

THE ROMANTIC ETHIC and THE SPIRIT OF MODERN CONSUMERISM

Most attempts to describe the general development of modern thought tend to pay exclusive attention to the growth of rationalism. The result is a picture quite incompatible with historical facts and the world as we know it.

Karl Mannheim

THE *OXFORD ENGLISH DICTIONARY* DEFINES the word 'romantic' as meaning 'marked by or suggestive of or given to romance; imaginative, remote from experience, visionary, and (in relation to literary or artistic method) preferring grandeur or passion or irregular beauty to finish and proportion'. None of these connotations would appear to have much to do with those activities which are generally covered by the heading 'consumption'. The selection, purchase and use of goods and services are all forms of everyday action which, on the contrary, we commonly tend to view as rather dull and prosaic matters, except perhaps on those rare occasions when we purchase a major item like a house or a car. It would appear, therefore, that consumption, being a form of economic conduct, should be placed at the opposite pole of life from all that we generally regard as 'romantic'. The reasonableness of this contrast is deceptive, however; something which becomes apparent once we recognize that there is one significant modern phenomenon which does indeed directly link the two.

This, of course, is advertising, for even the most cursory examination of the pages of glossy magazines and the contents of television commercials will serve to reveal how many advertisements are concerned with the topic of 'romance', or with images and copy which deal with scenes which are 'remote from everyday experience', 'imaginative' or suggestive of 'grandeur' or 'passion'. And it is not just romance in the narrow sense which features so prominently in conjunction with perfume, cigarettes or lingerie advertisements – it is also that the pictures and stories used are typically 'romantic' in the broader sense of being exotic, imaginative and idealized; whilst the very purpose of advertisements, of course, is to induce us to buy the products which are featured: in other words, to consume.

The fact that basically 'romantic' cultural material is commonly used in advertisements in this fashion has often been noted and hence one could say that a general awareness of the link between 'romanticism' and 'consumption' already exists. The assumption which has largely prevailed among social scientists, however, indeed among academics and intellectuals in general, has been that it is the advertisers who have chosen to make use of this material in an attempt to promote the interests of the producers they represent, and consequently that the relationship should be seen as one in which 'romantic' beliefs, aspirations and attitudes are put to work in the interests of a 'consumer society'. That view is challenged in the pages that follow (although not dismissed) where it is argued that the reverse relationship should also be taken seriously, with the 'romantic' ingredient in culture regarded as having had a crucial part to play in the development of modern consumerism itself; indeed, since consumption may determine demand and demand supply, it could be argued that Romanticism itself played a critical role in facilitating the Industrial Revolution and therefore the character of the modern economy. [. . .]

The problem posed at the beginning of this book was that of accounting for the consumer revolution which accompanied the onset of industrialization in eighteenth-century England. Noting that economic historians had identified the importance of rising demand as a crucial factor initiating that revolution, and located its principal cause in a 'new propensity to consume', the origins of this propensity were then taken as the focus of discussion. Whilst the evidence showed that this stemmed from changes in values and attitudes, being in some way related to such innovations as the rise of modern fashion, romantic love and the novel, it soon became clear that existing accounts of these changes were either reductionist or circular. This problem was then shown to be a general feature of those theories of consumer behaviour current within the social sciences, with neither the instinctivist, manipulationist nor Veblenesque perspectives supplying satisfactory explanations of that dynamic generation of new wants which is so characteristic of modern consumerism. Indeed, these perspectives were seen to be seriously deficient in their ahistorical treatment of the subject, as well as in their common tendency to regard wanting as an irrational, involuntary and 'unworthy' form of behaviour.

It therefore proved necessary, in order to resolve this historical problem, not only to provide a more adequate conceptualization of the nature of modern consumerism, but to develop a theory which, while not reducing this aspect of human conduct to a matter of instinctive impulsiveness or environmental manipulation, nevertheless compensated for the inability of utilitarianism to consider the question of the origin of wants. The solution adopted was to turn to a hedonistic model of human action, and eschewing the misleading habit of treating this term as a synonym for utility, focus upon that feature of human conduct in which pleasure and not satisfaction is the goal. Recognition of the fundamental and extensive differences between behaviour directed toward these two ends, and hence the fact that individuals living above the level of subsistence are likely to be faced with a choice between them, made it possible to distinguish traditional from modern hedonism. The former was identified as a preoccupation with sensory experience, with 'pleasures' regarded as discrete and standardized events, and in the pursuit of which there is a natural tendency for the hedonist to seek despotic powers. Modern hedonism is marked, in contrast, by a preoccupation with 'pleasure', envisaged as a potential quality of all experience. In order to extract this from life, however, the individual has to substitute illusory for real stimuli, and by creating and manipulating illusions and hence the emotive dimension of consciousness, construct his own pleasurable environment. This modern, autonomous, and illusory form of hedonism commonly manifests itself as day-dreaming and fantasizing. [. . .]

Hedonistic self-interest and romantic idealism

The manner through which genuinely idealistic or moral action might decay over time into a mere hedonistic self-concern is readily appreciated, and has already been referred to in discussing the decline of the cult of sensibility. There it was suggested that an exaggerated display of sentimentality might not indicate either genuine feelings of pity or concern, nor lead to appropriate benevolent or sympathetic action, being mainly a symptom of self-love. Joyce Tompkins provides a good description of this phenomenon:

> again and again we find that enormity of self-congratulation with which the weeper at once luxuriates in the beguiling softness of tears and compliments himself on his capacity for shedding them, seeing in his mind's eye not only the object of his attention [that is whatever prompted the display of emotion] but himself in a suitable attitude in front of it.

Even earlier, we had occasion to note what David Fordyce called that 'self-approving joy' which is open to the benevolent man, and which Isaac Barrow dubbed 'virtuous voluptuousness'. Crane labelled it 'egoistic hedonism' of the kind that leads individuals to 'entertain themselves with pleasant Reflections upon their own Worth' It is especially easy to see how Puritanism might lead to this kind of hypocrisy and self-love, given the repeated injunctions to examine one's spiritual condition, coupled with the urgent need to have confirmation of one's status as a member of the elect. Such continual reflection on oneself and one's conduct was bound to provide ample opportunities for self-admiration.

It generally requires a greater effort, on the other hand, to recognize how it is that action of an essentially hedonistic kind may also develop into ethical and idealistic forms. Here it is critically important to recognize that ideals are necessarily implicated in that variety of imaginatively mediated hedonism which has been taken to constitute the spirit of consumerism, and this for the simple reason that perfected or 'idealized' images naturally offer the greatest pleasure. This is clearly revealed in both Walter Mitty's and Billy Liar's fantasies for in each case idealized self-images are the central means through which pleasure is attained. Obviously, if it is pleasant to contemplate perfect images, then it is especially pleasant to contemplate ourselves as embodying that perfection. Walter Mitty obtains pleasure from his fantasies because he envisages himself as a dare-devil flying ace or world-famous surgeon, whilst the heroine of Virginia Woolf's story 'sees' herself as the epitome of beauty. We may choose to regard such day-dreams as evidence of self-love, or even childishness, but one cannot escape the fact that they do involve the imaginative realization of ideals, and, as such, can, under appropriate circumstances, become the basis for self-idealistic activity in reality. Conduct directed at realizing perfection in oneself arising out of imaginative exercises of this kind thus manifests a mixture of hedonistic and idealistic features. Striving to make oneself beautiful is perhaps the most obvious and common example of such behaviour, and although it can justifiably be labelled 'self-interested', it also con-stitutes 'idealism' in the sense of being activity aimed at fulfilling an ideal. Such self-directed idealism becomes especially important, however, when the moral rather than the aesthetic dimension is the focus of attention.

Morally idealized self-images can be just as much sources of pleasure as aesthetic ones, as Simone de Beauvoir revealed in her autobiography. There she disclosed how, as a child, she played fantasy games with her sister, using exemplary figures as the basic props for their hedonism. She describes how, in the course of playing these character games, she often imagined herself to be Mary Magdalene, 'drying Christ's feet with her long hair', or alternatively, a heroine such as Joan of Arc, or Geneviève de Brabant, women who 'only attained to bliss and glory in this world or in the next after sufferings inflicted on them by males'. These roles enabled her to enjoy all manner of imaginary sufferings, and 'revel in the delights of misfortune and humiliation', her 'piety' disposing her 'towards masochism'. Here we can see how encouraging children to emulate 'saintly' figures provides ample opportunity for self-illusory hedonism. Although Simone de Beauvoir shared these games with her sister it is also clear that she could easily have acted them out in isolation, or even covertly; the pleasure itself deriving from the 'fatefulness' of the situations accompanying the achievement of saintliness, as well as the simple con-templation of oneself in an idealized persona.

However, whilst the habit of identifying with ideal images may be embarked on in the first instance largely because of the opportunities which this provides for imaginative pleasure-seeking, the hedonist's sense of identity can easily become so moulded by this process as to come to depend upon a belief in a real similarity. Although the element of pretence remains – there is usually no desire to *be* the person imagined, and certainly not to actually experience their fate – the pleasure gained from contemplation of the idealized self-image encourages the belief that one possesses similar qualities. This can only be regarded as true, however, if the individual obtains some external proof, and this must necessarily take the form of conduct in the world. In order to bolster and protect the idealized self-image the individual must now engage in some character-confirming conduct; it becomes necessary to 'do good' in order to retain the conviction that one is good. Hence the irony by which 'disinterested', idealistic action eventually becomes required in order to protect the ideal self-image which the pursuit of pleasure has been instrumental in constructing.

A similar result can occur if imagination is put to work realizing the ideal in all those with whom one comes into contact, thereby casting oneself in the role of a pathetic and worthless person. The emotional satisfactions provided by such self-denigration and debasement are similar to those which were noted earlier to derive from Calvinism Goethe makes the melancholic young Werther declare that 'Our imagination, impelled by nature to assert itself, nourished by the fantastic images of the poet's art, invents a hierarchy of being of which we are the lowest, while everyone else appears more splendid, more perfect. Although there may be a perverse tendency in some people for conduct to be directed to the 'realization' of such 'masochistic' anti-ideals, the use of imagination in this way typically works to assist the development of idealism for it is the real self which is judged unfavourably as consequence of these comparisons. The dreamer realizes only too well how he is failing to live up to his own ideal image, whilst on the other hand, 'everyone else appears more splendid, more perfect'. In either case, however, whether the ideal is projected onto the self or onto others, awareness of the ever-widening gap between that ideal and the nature of the real self becomes a critical feature of life.

A central problem for the imaginative hedonist, therefore, is his awareness of this widening disjunction between the constructed ideal and the experienced reality; the more the hedonistic impulse causes images to be idealized, the greater the discrepancy becomes between these and the real-self. It is as if the pleasures gained by dreaming on the ideal are 'taken out' of those experienced in reality, which is judged to be more and more unsatisfactory in consequence. In this case, however, the reality which is thus 'degraded' is the individual's perception of himself as a virtuous person, leading to a deepening sense of worthlessness and demoralization. Indeed, for the morally sensitive, inner-directed person the power-ful feelings of guilt which are generated may spark off intense self-condemnation. This, then, in turn, adds an extra intensity to the need for reassurance that one is indeed good.

It can be seen from this analysis how forms of self-illusory hedonism can link up with a self-centred, moral idealism; while the search for pleasure may itself lead to the generation of guilt and a consequent need for signs of one's goodness. It merely remains to observe that since virtue is usually defined in terms of conduct which does transcend concern with the self, or at least involves some subordination of self to a higher goal, it is nearly always necessary actually to perform some genuinely disinterested act in order to obtain such reassurance. Self-interested hedonism and altruistic idealism are thus connected via images of the self as 'virtuous', with, in both cases, character-confirming conduct acting as the critical fulcrum around which behaviour turns.

The concept of character forms a common thread running through the multi-tude of modern vocabularies which are applicable to human actions. Used to refer to that aspect of behaviour for which individuals accept responsibility, it enables all action to be viewed as moral, with judgements made about the 'goodness' of each individual actor in the light of prevailing ideals. It is not suggested here, however, that it is people's direct desire to 'do the good thing' which is most affected by changes in conceptions of the good, the true and the beautiful, so much as the indirect effect exerted via the need for character confirmation. It is the need people have to be convinced that they are good which is crucial, something which is especially relevant in the case of those social groups which have inherited a tradition of moral inner-direction, and hence are attuned to the importance of membership of a moral elite or 'elect'.

By recognizing that social conduct is typically a composite product of hedonistic self-interest and altruistically inclined idealism, with an overriding concern with self-image serving to articulate the two, it becomes possible to see how the spirit of modern consumerism and the romantic ethic might be connected; hedonistic concerns leading into self-idealism and ethical preoccupations creating opportunities for hedonism. Indeed, the two forms are not merely connected but must be seen as inextricably interlocked, bound together by processes through which a desire for pleasure develops into a genuine concern for ideals, and ethical impulses 'degenerate' into mere narcissism. If, then, such individual processes are aggregated and viewed in macro-social terms as socio-cultural movements, it becomes possible to perceive how a modern consumerist outlook and a romantic ethic may be linked in both generative and degenerative directions; that is to say, by tendencies for periods of commercial dynamism to develop into idealistic 'reformations', and idealistic upheavals to degenerate into sentimentalistic self-seeking. As there is no good reason for assuming that a one-way trend governs such changes, it would seem reasonable to postulate a *recurso* pattern of generation-degeneration-regeneration to have typified the past two hundred years. Thus, if Romanticism did originally make modern hedonism possible, then the spirit of hedonism has subsequently also functioned to give rise to further outbursts of romantic fervour.

This is a conclusion which allows us to observe that the Romantics were not necessarily wrong in assuming that people could be morally improved through the provision of cultural products that yielded pleasure. Nor indeed were they wrong in seeing this process as one which relied upon individuals dreaming about a more perfect world. Such activity can reasonable be viewed as creating opportunities for the generation of idealism. This is only one possible outcome, however, of encouraging people to pursue imaginative pleasure, and would seem to depend for its success upon the prior acceptance of a more general romantic outlook. For it is also clear that where this is absent, and largely materialistic and utilitarian beliefs prevail, then it seems only too likely that romantic poems, novels and music, will be employed as little more than the raw material for a leisure and recreation industry; with dreams used less to raise the vision of an imaginatively apprehended ideal world with which to counter this one, than to overcome boredom and alienation. As we have had occasion to note, however, irony pervades the human condition, connecting intention and consequence in strange and unanticipated ways, hence while romantics may sometimes have assisted commercialism, commercial interests may also have unwittingly acted so as to promote romanticism.

Chapter 35

Danny Miller

A THEORY OF SHOPPING

FOR MANY PURPOSES THE MAIN division in the street where I conducted fieldwork lies between the council estates on one side and the private housing on the other. But the significance of this division cannot always be assumed. Although she lives in an owner-occupied maisonette, Mrs Wynn comes across immediately as quintessentially working class. Her husband is an electrician but has been unemployed for several months owing to an injury. She is a child-minder, taking into her home other people's children while they are out working. Between his injury and the fact that someone recently ran into their car while it was parked outside their house, they were not having an easy time of it. Nevertheless, as often proved to be the case, her concerns in shopping bear little upon the contingencies of the moment, and relate more to longer-term issues surrounding the personal development of each member of the family. She was pretty fed up with the consequences of these unexpected events, but shopping as a topic drew her back to things that at one level were more mundane. But these were relationships which she cared about a great deal and was constantly thinking about and forming strategies to deal with. In conversation she notes:

A My husband is quite fussy vegetable wise and he's a big meat eater, but yes I've been doing a lot of stir fries because I found I could get him to eat a lot more vegetables if I do stir fries, and he likes Chinese. He likes spicy stuff. He's got a lot better than when I first met him because his mum's Irish and over cooked every-thing and was pretty basic and he's got so much better in the years.

Q Do the kids eat the same as him?

A No. Jack my son's got very fussy, definitely in the last year. I would say he's a good vegetable and fruit eater but he's the basic chips and burger and I'm afraid so.

Q Do you cook separately for them?

A Pasta he loves pasta. Yes, and separate times as well.

Later on in the same conversation she notes:

A I try not to buy a lot of convenience [foods]. I do buy meat that is marinated and stuff like that and then think what can I do with it, but now and again I will sit down and get my books out and have a look. I did it last week just because I was getting a bit tired of things. But also what I will do is buy the sauces and the stirfry things, stuff like that, and then just add it to everything so it makes a bit of difference, but I seem to get stuck doing the same things over and over again. So, every now and then, I've got to get my books out to remind myself or think of some new things.

Q Is it you that's bored?

A No. He will say as well, we've had this a bit too much. I'm a great chicken eater and he says chicken again!

Later still she starts discussing the purchase of clothing for the family, making it clear that she buys her husband's clothes. She notes that out of preference he would just wear some old T-shirts, and often would then go on to use these as cloths during his work. It's not just his clothing she buys. In practice she prefers not to let him do any of the shopping. She feels that if she lets him shop, then he misses things on the list she has made, or buys, himself things like biscuits on a whim.

A So it's more hard work. I'd rather him stay here and look after the children and I'll do it. Then it's a break for me and you know. These views were reiterated when we were out shopping in a local supermarket. She again noted the problems with getting her children to eat what she wants them to eat rather than what they would choose for themselves. She claimed to be quite strict with the children that she was paid to look after, but with respect to her own children, she tended to be much more lenient – 'anything for a bit of peace and quiet.' Again and again her actual purchases are related back to household preferences. When she buys mint-flavoured lamb at the butcher's she notes in passing that this had gone down really well the week before and that she had been asked to get it again. Equally, some jam tarts purchased previously because they were under offer (going cheap) had been well received. The only exceptions to this orientation to the household in her shopping come with the purchase of some bread rolls and frankfurters for a friend who will be coming round for tea. Also at another point in our expedition she buys a fancy ice cream called Vienetta which she declares is 'a treat for herself'.

By no means all the shoppers I accompanied were like Mrs Wynn, but she is representative of a core of households. She should anyway be quite a familiar figure from many previous feminist studies of the housewife. The feminist perspective on such housewives will be discussed below, but many researchers have acknowledged that which would be clearly evident here. However oppressive the outside observer might find this subsumption of the individual to her husband and children, the housewife herself insists that she merely expresses thereby a series of responsibilities and concerns with which she strongly identifies and of which she is generally proud.

Mrs Wynn acknowledges that she is constantly monitoring, even researching, the desires and preferences of her household. These include both foundational goods which are expected to be constantly present and available in the house, but also transient desires which arise from a preference for at least a subsidiary element of change and innovation. But she would by no means regard herself as merely the passive representative of these desires. Indeed if she merely bought what the other members of her household asked for, shopping would be relatively easy. The problem is that she wishes to influence and change her husband and children in quite a number of ways. She is constantly concerned that they should eat healthier foods than those they would choose for themselves. By the same token she wants them to wear either better quality or at least more respectable clothes than those they prefer. She sees her role as selecting goods which are intended to be educative, uplifting and in a rather vague sense morally superior. It is precisely their unwillingness to be uplifted by her shopping choices that creates the anxieties and battles of shopping. In vindicating their decisions, such housewives often lay claim to a wider perspective than that of other family members. They see themselves as having the foresight to prevent the embarrassment and disdain that others might feel if they let their families dress as they choose, or determine their own food choices.

Of course, all these efforts could be reduced to her interests. It could be argued that she is buying better clothes because she feels she will be made to suffer the opprobrium of criticism by others if she doesn't. She buys healthier foods because she would have to look after the person who otherwise becomes ill. But for us to try to figure out whether the constant hassle of arguing with her family, in order to persuade them to adopt her preferences, actually pays some kind of long-term dividend is the kind of daft calculation we may safely leave to economists, socio-biologists and their ilk. There is no reason to suppose that Mrs Wynn engages in any such weighing up of cost or benefit. As far as she is concerned, the reasons that she researches their preferences and equally that she then tries to improve upon them are the same. Both are assumed by her to represent the outcome of a responsibility so basic that it does not need to be made explicit or reflected upon. In short, her shopping is primarily an act of love, that in its daily conscientiousness becomes one of the primary means by which relationships of love and care are constituted by practice. That it is to say, shopping does not merely reflect love, but is a major form in which this love is manifested and reproduced. This is what I mean to imply when I say that shopping in supermarkets is commonly an act of making love.

One could use other terms than love. Care, concern, obligation, responsibility and habit play their roles in these relationships. So also may resentment, frustration and even hatred. Can these latter be the ingredients of something we may properly term love? As long as it is clear that we understand by this term 'love' a normative ideology manifested largely as a practice within longterm relationships and not just some romantic vision of an idealized moment of courtship, then the term is entirely appropriate. Love as a practice is quite compatible with feelings of obligation and responsibility. [. . .] The term is certainly justified by ethnography in as much as these shoppers would be horrified by the suggestion that they did not love the members of their family or that there was not a bedrock of love as the foundation of their care and concern, though they might well acknowledge some of these other attributes as well.

I never knew Mrs Wynn well enough to be able to gain a sense of the more intimate moments within her household. I don't know how free she felt about expressing her love in explicit forms. In general, a reticence with regard to more overt expressions of emotion is regarded as a typically British characteristic, and was commented upon by those born elsewhere. But this reticence about love need not imply its absence, so much as its being essentialized as so natural that it becomes embarrassing to feel the need to express it. One consequence of this reticence is that love has come to be primarily objectified through everyday practices of concern, care and a particular sensitivity to others, within which shopping plays a central role.

During the course of this essay the term 'love', which first appears here as the common term by which relationships are legitimated will become used to represent a value that leads us towards the problems of cosmology and transcendence. These terms are not intended to obfuscate or make complex some simple phenomenon. They merely remind us that within a largely secular society almost all of us still see ourselves as living lives directed to goals and values which remain in some sense higher than the mere dictates of instrumentality. Daily decisions are constantly weighed in terms of moral questions about good and bad action indicated in traits such as sensitivity as against style, or generosity as against jealousy. Though these may not be made explicit, the accounts we use to understand each others' actions depend on the continued existence of cosmology as a realm of transcendent value.

The terms 'cosmology' and 'transcendent' suggest values that are long lasting and opposed to the contingency of everyday life. They are intended to imply that although we focus upon the particular persons, children, partners and friends who occupy our concerns at a given moment of time, the way we relate to them is much influenced by more general beliefs about what social relations should look like and how they should be carried out. At one level then, love is a model of one particular type of identification and attachment. It is one we are socialized into and constantly informed about. This ideal is then triggered by an individual, such as a family member who makes it manifest. A relationship then builds its own specificity and nuance which (sometimes) goes well beyond the transcendent model with which we started. When the term 'love' is used, as here, in a more general sense, actual relationships are found to develop on the basis of much wider norms and expectations which pre-exist and remain after the relationship itself.

The term 'love' then indicates more than a claim to affection made during courtship. It stands for a much wider field of that to which life is seen as properly devoted. In later parts of this essay it will be more closely related back to devotional practices in which the term 'cosmology' is more obviously appropriate since the context is more clearly that of religion. The ethnography suggested that just as devotion is the taken-for-granted backdrop to the carrying out of religious rites in other times and places, so in North London love remains as a powerful taken-for-granted foundation for acts of shopping which will be argued to constitute devotional rites whose purpose is to create desiring subjects.

I would call Mrs Wynn a housewife, even though for the present she is the sole wage-earner of the family, because, for her, housewifery is her principal *raison d'être*. As feminist research has made clear, a person such as Mrs Wynn is more likely to view her earnings as simply part of her housewifery than as a job equivalent to that which her husband would be engaged in were he fit. As someone who identifies with being a housewife, the requests made by her family for particular foods are not viewed with resentment but are in fact desired by her. [. . .]

Chapter 36

Daniel Lefkowitz

INVESTING IN EMOTION

Love and anger in financial advertising

[. . .]

On the Structure of Commercials

IN ANALYZING THE DISCOURSE OF television commercials, it is
important to note that modern ads focalize emotion rather than information.
As Tony Schwartz observes:

> If you are selling a kitchen drain cleaner, the advertising effort might
> involve building an association in the listener's mind between the *real*
> annoyance of a stopped-up sink and the *real* relief of unclogging it, in the
> context of the product.
>
> [Schwartz 1973:71]

Advertisements thus obscure how they function—and they do so in multiple ways.
In Williamson's (1978) Freudian terms, viewers fail to recognize an ad's latent
message because they are kept busy thinking about its manifest content. Ads work
because viewers respond emotionally to ideas suggested by the ad, while believing
that they are responding to information actually stated in the ad. [. . .]

Finance and Family: Love

The juxtaposition of love and anger was a striking pattern in advertising for financial
services at the turn of the millennium. Individual commercials rarely thematized
both emotions together, but when advertising for the industry as a whole is considered, the juxtaposition stands out. Many commercials from that time period

situated investing in the home and the family by representing investment as love. By contrast, many other commercials situated investing in violence, conflict, and revolution by representing investment as anger. As I explain further below, the theme of anger later disappeared from financial-services ads, whereas the theme of love remained prominent. In order to adequately contextualize the discourse of investing-as-anger, I will begin by looking at an ad that represents investing as love.

The Raymond James commercial called "Playground" features an elderly white-haired man taking a little girl to the playground. The ad begins with a close-up image of two clasped hands—one large, one small. The camera then pulls back to reveal the face of a young girl. The girl lets go of the larger hand, turns her back to the camera, and runs toward a playground where other children are playing. At the playground, the girl plays happily with other children. The ad then shows the girl returning, running toward the camera and approaching an elderly man who is sitting on a swing. The girl embraces the old man in a warm hug, and he turns a contented smile toward the camera, the final shot, the camera pans upward and to the right, over the man's shoulder, settling on an image of blue sky and white cloud, where the company's name, "Raymond James," and the ad's tag line, "You first," are displayed.

Like the Ameritrade ad . . . , this commercial's appeal to the viewer is entirely indirect—through the mechanism of desire. Little in this ad directly relates to the services Raymond James provides or asserts that Raymond James provides such services better than other companies. Rather, the advertisement depicts a morally charged site of desire (sunny day, loving grandchild, carefree retirement, etc.) and establishes in the viewer's memory a resonant association between his or her desires and the company's name (Schwartz 1973).

The "Playground" commercial can be seen as a parable that suggests a simple moral message: Investing with Raymond James keeps families together. This moral is communicated through the ad's three-part structure: separation as dilemma: reunification as solution (through retirement planning with Raymond James): and familial love as the desired outcome. A brief analysis—diagrammed in Table 1—highlights the complex poetics of this ad.

The thematic opposition of separation and unity is established through the imagery of making and a breaking physical embrace (hand holding and hugging). The ad begins and ends with images of physical embrace; in between are images of separation. The visual image of separation coincides with the onset of narration. The deep, sonorant male voice of the narrator reinforces the representation of separation by breaking the primal silence of the earlier images. The voiceover narration reinforces this image as well.

Table 1 Parable structure of Raymond James commercial "The Playground."

Episode	Narrative Function	Themes	Imagery (plot elements)
Act One	Dilemma	Separation → Fear	Hands part; girl leaves caretaker.
Act Two	Solution	Unity → Security	Girl returns: tension ends.
Act Three	Mythical Result	Family → Love	Girl and grandfather hug.

In a world of opportunity.
How do you find the financial advisor who's right for you.

The words *in a world of opportunity* establish the tension at the root of the parable's dilemma. The idea of opportunity suggests a tension between desire (for something good to happen) and fear (of the risk involved). The ad sets up a parallel between the opportunities and risks facing a young child (making new friends on the playground, but having to leave the familial embrace) and those facing an investor (making money, but having to take financial risks). The ad then reinforces this symbolic connection between the (child's) playground scene and the (adult's) investment world by describing the search for a financial advisor in terms of personal relationship *(right for you)*.

Narration and audio effects construct risk by performing fear. The ad begins in silence. The first sound we hear (before the narration begins) is a rhythmic squeak that continues in the background throughout much of the commercial. The squeak is a grating, unpleasant sound that establishes tension. Voicing over images of (unheard) children at play, the narrator continues:

Do you want one who works for the oldest company?
    Or the youngest.
Do you want one with the fastest growing company?
    Or the most deeply rooted in tradition.

These phrases are paired as couplets. The pairing is accomplished through the parallelism of juxtaposing antonymous meanings (old–young. growing–traditional), the alternation of rising and falling intonations (marked in the transcript by the question mark and comma respectively), and the systematic alignment of the vocal phrases with cuts in the visual images of children at play. The world of opportunity (growing up and making money) is thus portrayed as simultaneously desirable and threatening.

The third part of the commercial suggests a resolution to the tension. The narration continues:

Or do you simply want one who listens to you.
Like you.
Are the only investor in the world.
Raymond James.
You first

This narrative resolution coincides with several other semiotic resolutions. The girl returns to hug her grandfather. The squeak, which began when the girl left the grandfather's hand, stops precisely at the moment when girl and grandfather embrace. At this juncture the viewer can recognize for the first time that the squeak comes from the swing the grandfather is sitting on. The children's play, which until that point had been seen but not heard, is now heard but not seen.

This commercial elaborates the performance of the emotions of happiness, fear, and love. Happiness is performed through repeated visual images of children smiling, laughing, playing, and of the grandfather smiling toward the camera. Fear, enacted through the audio channel, is performed through the unpleasant, rhythmic squeak. Love is performed by the hand holding and hugging that frame the ad's beginning and end. The advertisement's implied analogy, that Raymond James financial advisors care for their clients just as a grandfather cares for his grand-daughter, completes the moral: Investing with the sponsor enables parental love, keeps families together, and makes children value their family.

Finance and Anger

The Raymond James commercial described above is typical of a wide range of financial services ads that situate investing in the family by linking investment to nurturing love. A longstanding ad campaign for the Allstate Insurance Company had as its tag line "You're in good hands with Allstate." Banks often advertise their loans by suggesting that they help send the viewer's children to college. In a survey of seventy financial-services commercials that aired in March and April of 2001, roughly half conformed to this general pattern. [. . .]

References

Schwartz, Tony
   1973   The Responsive Chord. Garden City, NY: Anchor Press.
Williamson, Judith
   1978   Decoding Advertisements: Ideology and Meaning in Advertising. London: Marion Boyars.

Chapter 37

Jon Elster

EMOTIONS AND ECONOMIC THEORY

[. . .]

Emotions and interest

FROM THE POINT OF VIEW of economic theory, the most interesting issue concerning the emotions may be the nature of the interaction between emotion and other motivations. Among the latter, I shall only consider material self-interest ("interest" for short), although similar problems arise for the relation between emotions and impartial motivations. For instance, a wealthy liberal might on impartial grounds prefer to send his children to a public school, but his emotional attachment to the children might induce a preference for a better-quality private education.

The cost-benefit model of emotions

By far the most common way of modeling the interaction between emotions and interests is to view the former as psychic costs or benefits that enter into the utility function on a par with satisfactions derived from material rewards. In this perspective, the only relevant aspect of the emotions is their *valence*. We may use Becker's analysis of beggar-induced guilt to illustrate two ways in which the pleasure and pain associated with the emotions may enter into the utility function. First, the guilt itself is a cost. Even if I do not have any money with me, I may cross the street to avoid coming face to face with a beggar whose visible misery would induce the unpleasant feeling of guilt. Second, the guilt may induce behavior that is costly in the material sense. If I do have money with me, I know that if I come face to face with the beggar I would give him something to alleviate my guilt. More accurately, I would give up to the point where the marginal utility of money in alleviating my guilt equals its marginal utility for other purposes. (If crossing the street is costly, this would also have to be taken into account.)

In other analyses, the encounters that trigger the emotion is taken for given and not subject to choice. The question of choice arises only because the agent has to weigh emotional satisfaction against other satisfactions, as in the choice of the amount to give to the beggar. In modeling envy, we may assume that the agent is willing to invest resources in making the rival worse off up to the point where he derives more utility from making himself better off (Hirshleifer 1987). In modeling altruism, we can make a similar assumption (Becker 1976, chs. 12 and 13). Economic analyses of regret (David Bell 1982; Graham Loomes and Robert Sugden 1982) also assume that agents weigh satisfaction from actual outcomes and emotions generated by counterfactual beliefs. Strictly speaking, none of these analyses need to rely on valence, in the sense of subjective feelings of pleasure and pain. All that is needed is that we can draw indifference curves that reflect the tradeoffs involved. We may think of emotional valence as the underlying mechanism behind these tradeoffs, but it need not be directly reflected in the formal analysis. In a modeling perspective, "emotional altruism" is indistinguishable from "reason-based altruism." In the following I assess the usefulness of this approach with respect to guilt, shame, envy, indignation, love, vindictiveness, hatred, and contempt.

Guilt

Let us assume that a person is tempted to steal a book from the library. If he feels guilty about doing it, he may abstain. If he steals the book and then feels guilt, he may return the book to the library. On the Becker-Frank assumption that guilt is to be modeled as a cost, both the abstention from stealing and the return of the book would be explained by a simple cost-benefit analysis. This approach has the great advantage that it allows us to account for the undeniable existence of a tradeoff between moral emotions and self-interest. The world is not made up of two exclusive and exhaustive categories, those who would steal a book whenever there was no risk of detection and those who would never do so. Many people would go ahead and steal the book if but only if its value to them was sufficiently high or its value to others sufficiently small. To model such behavior, we could talk "as if" guilt and interest add up to an inclusive utility, with the marginal disutility from guilt being an increasing function of (say) the number of people on the waiting list for the book and the marginal utility from interest a decreasing function of (say) the time the agent expects to use the book.

Whether or not this model of the interaction between emotion and interest is predictively adequate, I submit that it is basically flawed. If guilt were nothing but an anticipated or experienced cost, an agent whose guilt deters him from stealing or retaining the book should be willing to buy a guilt-erasing pill if it was sufficiently cheap. *I submit that no person who is capable of being deterred by guilt would buy the pill.* In fact, he would feel guilty about buying it. For him, taking the pill in order to escape guilt and be able to steal the book would be as morally bad as just stealing it. He would not see any moral relevance between stealing the book in a two-step operation (taking the pill to steal the book) and stealing it in a onestep operation. There is a strict analogy between this argument and a point that I have made elsewhere (Elster 1997), viz. that a person who discounts the future very highly would not be motivated to buy a pill that would reduce his rate of time discounting. To want to be motivated by remote consequences of present behavior *is* to be motivated by remote consequences of present behavior. Similarly, to want to be immoral *is* to be immoral. A person willing to take the guilt-erasing pill would not need it.

We need, therefore, a model that can account for the tradeoff between guilt and interest and yet does not imply that a reluctant agent would buy the guilterasing pill. I conjecture that the model would involve some kind of non-intentional psychic causality rather than deliberate choice. To illustrate what I have in mind, I shall sketch a model drawn from catastrophe theory, along the lines of a model of the relation between personal opinion and conformism proposed by Abraham Tesser and John Achee (1994). In a catastrophe model, the surface describing the behavior of a dependent variable as a function of two independent variables folds in on itself in a cusp. Within a certain range, a given constellation of the independent variables is thus consistent with several values of the dependent variable.

Suppose that the agent is initially unwilling to steal the book, but that as its value to him increases he finally decides to do so. Suppose conversely that the agent has stolen the book, but that as its value to others increases he finally returns it to the library. In the first case, suppose that its value to others is 10 and that he decides to steal it just when its value to him reaches 15. In the second case, suppose that its initial value to him is 15 and the initial value to others is 6. On the cost-benefit model, he would return it when its value to others reaches 10. On the catastrophe model, he might not do so until its value to others reached 15. The reason for this asymmetry is found in the mechanism of dissonance reduction (Leon Festinger 1957). An individual who is subject to several motivations that point in different directions will feel an unpleasant feeling of tension. When on balance he favors one action, he will try to reduce the tension by looking for cognitions that support it; when he favors another, he will look for cognitions which stack the balance of arguments in favor of that action. . . . Thus the timing of the switch in behavior will be path-dependent.

Dissonance theory is more realistic than the cost-benefit model in that it views individuals as making hard choices on the basis of *reasons* rather than on the basis of introspections about how they feel. Although the person who has stolen the book but feels guilty about it may try to alleviate his guilt, he would do so by coming up with additional reasons that justify his behavior rather than by accepting a guilt-erasing pill. It is a fundamental feature of human beings that they have an image of themselves as *acting for a reason*. Guilt, in this perspective, acts not as a cost but as a psychic force that induces the individual to rationalize his behavior. Beyond a certain point, when the arguments on the other side become too strong and the rationalization breaks down, a switch in behavior occurs. Although we may well say that the switch occurs when the guilt becomes unbearable, we should add that the point at which it becomes unbearable is itself influenced and in fact delayed by the guilt. This *dual role of emotions in decision making* is an important phenomenon to which I shall return.

As indicated, the "tension" in this example would be guilt if the person on balance preferred to steal the book, and perhaps regret if he preferred to abstain from stealing it. As psychologists have not considered emotions as sources of cognitive dissonance and of dissonance reduction, the argument involves an extension of dissonance theory as usually stated. Yet there seems to be no reason why emotions could not be sources of dissonance. Although it is descriptively accurate that dissonance theory places the "emphasis on the individual's concept of *what he is* rather than his concept of *what he should be*" (Festinger and Dana Bramel 1962, p. 271), this limitation on the scope of the theory seems arbitrary. As economists are now incorporating dissonance theory into their framework (George Akerlof and William Dickens 1982; Rabin 1994), the incorporation of guilt and other self-evaluative emotions (E. Tory Higgins 1987) into dissonance theory would also lead to their incorporation in economics.

Shame

An analysis of shame will allow me to suggest further alternatives to the simple cost-benefit model. Empirically, we know that people can take extreme actions when targeted by social ostracism. The case of the Navy Admiral who killed himself when it was shown that he was not entitled to decorations he was wearing (Peter Boyer 1996) is one example. The five Frenchmen who killed themselves in June 1997 after they had been caught in a crackdown on pedophilia is another. The two explanatory issues that arise are, first, whether the decisive factor was fear of material sanctions or rather an emotion of shame; and, second, assuming it was shame, whether it can simply be modeled as a cost.

In these dramatic cases few would dispute that the emotion of shame must have been a decisive factor. It is not generally accepted, however, that social norms in general operate through the emotion of shame. Many writers (Aker- of 1976; Robert Axelrod 1986; Didier Abreu 1988; James Coleman 1990) have argued that social norms work through material sanctions, involving higher-order sanctions of those who fail to sanction norm-violators or non-sanctioners. [. . .]

I would like to go beyond my earlier arguments, however, to assert that the material sanctions themselves are best understood as vehicles of the emotion of contempt, which is the direct trigger of shame. When a person refuses to deal with someone who has violated a social norm, the latter may suffer a financial loss. More important, he will see the sanction as a vehicle for the emotions of contempt or disgust, and suffer shame as a result. The material aspect of the sanction that matters is *how much it costs the sanctioner to penalize* the target, not how much it costs the target to be penalized. (Thus the phrase "This hurts me more than it hurts you" may be intended to add to the punishment, not to soften it.) The more it costs the sanctioner to refuse to deal with the target person, the stronger will the latter feel the contempt behind the refusal and the more acute will be his shame. Although high costs to the sanctioner often go together with high costs for the target, as when the sanctioner renounces on the opportunity for a mutually profitable business transaction, this need not be the case; and even when it is the case, my claim is that the costs to the sanctioner are what makes the sanction really painful to the target. It tells him that others see him as so bad that they are willing to forego valuable opportunities rather than have to deal with him.

The second question concerns the mode of operation of shame in shaping behavior. According to the cost model, present and future shame enters into the utility function on a part with material costs and benefits. A person who has been publicly exposed to contempt might compare three options: suicide, moving elsewhere to take up a new profession with a new name, and sticking it out in the expectation that the contempt of others and the feeling of shame will fade after a while. If the immediate feeling of shame is immense, suicide might well be preferable to the discounted present value of the other options. It would be hard to refute this account, as the disutility of shame can always be stipulated to be arbitrarily high. I believe it is at least equally plausible, however, to assume that shame induces a temporary heightening of the discounting rate. With respect to drugs, Becker (1996, p. 329) argues that "A habit may be raised into an addiction by exposure to the habit itself. Certain habits, like drug use and heavy drinking, may reduce the attention to future consequences—there is no reason to assume discount rates on the future are just given and fixed." The argument seems equally applicable to strong emotions. Alternatively, we might follow Loewenstein (1996) and argue that shame, like other visceral factors, undermines our ability to predict future subjective states. When one is in intense pain or suffering from intense shame, it is hard to imagine that the state will not last forever.[11] The overwhelming desire is for immediate release. By continuity, a shame of less intense strength will also have a causal effect on the evaluation and perception of other rewards *over and above its own role as a (negative) reward*. This is another instance of the dual role of emotion in decision making. [. . .]

References

ABREU, DIDIER. "On the Theory of Infinitely Repeated Games with Discounting," *Econometrica*, Mar. 1988, *56*(2), pp. 383–96.

AKERLOF, GEORGE. "The Economics of Caste of the Rat Race and Other Woeful Tales," *Quart. J. Econ.*, Nov. 1976, *90*(4), pp. 599–617.

AKERLOF, GEORGE A. AND DICKENS, WILLIAM T. "The Economic Consequences of Cognitive Dissonance," *Amer. Econ. Rev.*, June 1982, *72*(3), pp. 307–19.

AXELROD, ROBERT. "An Evolutionary Approach to Norms,"*Amer. Polit. Sci. Rev.*, Dec. 1986, *80*(4), pp. 1095–1111.

BECKER, GARY S. *The economic approach to human behavior*. Chicago: U. of Chicago Press, 1976.

BELL, DAVID. "Regret in Decision Making Under Uncertainty," *Operations Research*, Sept./Oct. 1982, *30*(5), pp. 961–81.

BOYER, PETER. "Admiral Boorda's War," *The New Yorker*, Sept. 16, 1996.

COLEMAN, JAMES S. *Foundations of social theory*. Cambridge, MA: Harvard U. Press., 1990.

ELSTER, JON. Review of Becker (1996), *U. of Chicago Law Rev.*, 1997, *64*, pp. 749–64.

FESTINGER, LEON. *A theory of cognitive dissonance*. Stanford, CA: Stanford U. Press, 1957.

FESTINGER, LEON AND BRAMEL, DANA. "The Reactions of Humans to Cognitive Dissonance," in *Experimental foundations of clinical psychology*. Ed.: ARTHUR J. BACHRACH. New York: Basic Books, 1962, pp. 254–79.

HIGGINS, E. TORY. "Self-discrepancy: A Theory Relating Self and Affect," *Psychological Review*, July 1987, *94*(3), pp. 319–40.

HIRSHLEIFER, JACK. "On the Emotions as Guarantors of Threats and Promises," in *The latest on the best*. Ed.: JOHN DUPRÉ. Cambridge, MA: MIT Press, 1987, pp. 307–26.

LOEWENSTEIN, GEORGE. "Out of Control: Visceral Influences on Behavior," *Organizational Behavior & Human Decision Processes*, Mar. 1996, *65*,(3) pp. 272–92.

LOOMES, GRAHAM AND SUGDEN, ROBERT. "Regret Theory: An Alternative Theory of Rational Choice under Uncertainty," *Econ. J.*, Dec. 1982, *92*(368), pp. 805–24.

RABIN, MATTHEW. "Cognitive Dissonance and Social Change," *J. Econ. Behav. Organ.*, Mar. 1994, *23*(2), pp. 177–94.

TESSER, ABRAHAM AND ASCHEE, JOHN. "Aggression, Love, Conformity, and Other Social Psychological Catastrophes," in *Dynamical systems in social psychology*. Eds.: ROBIN R. VALLACHER AND ANDRZEJ NOWAK. New York: Academic Press, 1994, pp. 96–109.

9. Emotions and the media

IN 1950, IN HIS landmark study of American character, David Riesman wrote that '[I]ncreasingly, relations with the outer world and oneself are mediated by the flow of mass communications' (1950: 21). Fifty years later German sociologist Niklas Luhmann confirms Riesman's proposition: 'whatever we know about our society, or indeed about the world in which we live', he writes, 'we know through the mass media' (2000:1). By extension we might say that, today, the mass media – those institutions which disseminate communication widely via copying technologies such as printing and broadcasting – mediate not only what we know but, on that basis, also much of what we *feel*. A number of prominent social theorists interested in the relationship between culture and capitalism have addressed the media as a key factor in the emergence of what is variously called a 'culture of narcissism' (Lasch 1979), an existential 'waning of affect' (Jameson 1991), or a climate of 'post-emotionalism' (Meštrović 1997). What these accounts have in common is the view that the massive impact of the media on our lives is associated with new forms of psychological depthlessness. Lasch proposed that the media and advertising industries, along other 'agencies of mass tuition', had taken over many of the socializing functions previously performed by the family. Through its cult of celebrity, and by translating everything into a form of entertainment, the media had played a substantial role in fostering 'narcissistic dreams of fame and glory', encouraging 'the common man to identify himself with the stars and to hate the "herd" ', making it 'more and more difficult for him to accept the banality of everyday existence' (1979: 21). For Jameson, the 'waning of affect' is associated with a dream-like life of 'pseudo-events', sustained by the artificial stimuli of televised experience. Meštrović's 'post-emotional' type is one whose capacity for experiencing genuine emotions has ostensibly given way to the consumption of 'vicarious' (or second-hand) emotions, useless feelings that bear no relation to action.

More recently, media theorists have argued that emotions have become more conspicuous in media culture, suggesting a global trend towards 'emotionalization'. As we noted in our general introduction, this trend is associated with the emergence of 'factual television' and its sub-genres (talk shows, docu-soaps and docu-dramas, and reality TV), and with an erosion of the distinction between information and entertainment. Against this background, an important focus of interest for researchers has been the media portrayal of human suffering (both individual and collective), and its social significance. Do media images of distant suffering generate 'compassion fatigue', or do they facilitate the emergence of a progressive humanitarian conscience (see e.g. Moeller 1999; Tester 2001; Cohen 2001; Boltanski 1999)? Are tabloid talkshows and docu-dramas a modern form of 'freakshow', or do they offer platforms for subjects whose voices would otherwise remain unheard (see e.g. Dovey 2000; Shattuc 1997; Gamson 1998; Lunt and Stenner 2005)?

In our first extract, Birgitta Höijer (2004) examines Swedish and Norwegian audience reactions to television news and documentary reporting of human suffering in the Kosovo war. She is interested not just in the extent of voiced compassion for victims of such conflicts, but also in how 'worthiness' for compassion is worked up in practice via notions and images of 'ideal' victimhood. Although she finds some support for the cynical view of post-emotional spectators expressing 'kitsch emotional reactions to serious problems' (Meštrović 1997), her participants – and especially the women – also appeared to express genuine 'moral compassion at a distance' (Höijer 2004: 528).

The emotions evoked and shaped by the mass media are, of course, not only the worthy and fine ones of which we are proud. In the second extract 'Chav Mum, Chav Scum: class disgust in contemporary Britain', Imogen Tyler (2008) examines the emotional characteristics – and disgust in particular – associated with the figure of the 'chav' in British newspapers, TV comedy and internet fora. It is likely that relations of social class were mediated by emotions like disgust long before modern mass media came upon the scene. Mass media, however, contribute to the generation and circulation of highly condensed forms that Tyler refers to as 'figures'. Like 'the immigrant', 'the terrorist' or 'the pedophile', the chav is a symbolically over-determined figure expressive of a dense knot of class-based emotional reactions. Comparable to Moscovici's 'social representations', such highly mediatized figures make for rapid and easy communication at the cost of the reinforcement of class distinctions and the scapegoating of abject groups.

In the third extract 'Talking Alone: reality TV, emotions and authenticity' (2006), Minna Aslama and Mervi Pantti look at the various ways in which 'real life' emotional encounters are staged within reality TV shows. Very often this staging takes the form of a monologue in which an individual expresses their innermost feelings, while alone with the camera. The authors draw attention to the paradox involved in the idea that the more authentically one can express true emotions, the more saleable they are as a media commodity.

The final extract is from *Film Structure and the Emotion System* by Greg Smith (2003). He draws upon a growing tradition of work which analyses the relationship between motion pictures and emotion (Carroll 1990; Tan 1996; Grodal 1997). Ed Tan (1996), for instance, defines film as an 'emotion machine'. Deriving a model of emotion from cognitive and neuropsychological research, Smith argues that the structure of successful films is conditioned by the need to engage the human emotion system. His 'mood-cue' approach attends to the usually unnoticed ways in which coordinated sequences of filmic cues (facial expressions, music, costume, lighting, camera technique, set design, etc.) invite the creation of a general mood state that in turn makes the eliciting of shorter-term intense emotional states more likely. The key is thus the establishment of reciprocal relations between mood (a longer term state of diffuse preparation for specific emotional experience) and the experience of specific emotions.

References

Boltanski, L. (1999) *Distant suffering: morality, media and politics*. Cambridge: Cambridge University Press.

Cohen, S. (2001) *States of Denial: knowing about atrocities and suffering*. Oxford: Polity.

Dovey, J. (2000) *Freakshow: first person media and factual television*. London: Pluto Press.

Gamson, J. (1998) *Freaks Talk Back. Tabloid shows and sexual non-conformity*. Chicago, IL: University of Chicago Press.

Jameson, F. (1991) *Postmodernism, Or, the Cultural Logic of Late Capitalism*. Durham, North Carolina: Duke University Press.

Lasch, C. (1978) *The Culture of Narcissism*. New York: W. W. Horton.

Luhmann, N. (2000) *The Reality of the Mass Media*. Cambridge: Polity.

Lunt, P. and Stenner, P. (2005) 'The Jerry Springer Show as an Emotional Public Sphere', *Media, Culture and Society*, 27 (1): 59–81.

Meštrović, S. (1997) *Postemotional Society*. London: Sage.

Moeller, S. D. (1999) *Compassion Fatigue: how the media sell disease, famine, war and death*. London: Routledge.

Riesman, D. (2001 [1950]) *The Lonely Crowd: a study of changing American character*. New Haven, MA: Yale University Press.

Shattuc, J. M. (1997) *The Talking Cure. TV talk shows and women*. New York: Routledge.

Tester, K. (2001) *Compassion, morality and the media*. Buckingham: Open University Press.

Chapter 38

Birgitta Höijer

THE AUDIENCE AND MEDIA REPORTING OF HUMAN SUFFERING

[. . .]

Audience reactions

IN THE FOLLOWING, THE DISCUSSION will be based on two sets of empirical studies of audience reactions. One set of studies focused on violent news in general and combined brief telephone interviews carried out with a representative sample of Swedes (in total 500 interviews) with in-depth personal interviews with a variety of individuals (Höijer, 1994, 1996). The other set of studies consisted of focus group interviews about the Kosovo War with different groups of citizens in Norway and in Sweden (Höijer and Olausson, 2002). Thirteen groups were run in Norway and 11 in Sweden, and the female and male informants were recruited from different occupational sectors and age levels. Kosovo-Albanian and Serb immigrants were also interviewed.

Extent of compassion

Although it is a risky and uncertain task to determine the extent of compassion for victims of distant suffering among the audience in general, I shall here present some figures indicating a division of the audience into those who express some type of compassion and those who are more or less indifferent. Further, there are different reactions among different segments of the audience.

The results in Table 1 are based on telephone interviews in which the public answered open-ended questions about their reactions to pictures of victims for violence (conflicts, war and so on) in news reports. Table 1 shows that half of the respondents (51 percent) said that they often or quite often do react to the pictures of distant suffering.[1] About a quarter of the public (23 percent) said they were

Table 1 Audience's reactions to pictures of suffering on television news (%)

	Gender			Age in years					
	Total	M	W	15–19	20–29	30–39	40–49	50–64	65–99
React often or quite often	51	41	59	28	37	49		49	54	68
React only sometimes	14	17	12	22	14	16		17	13	9
Do not react at all	23	32	16	41	31	22		19	25	14
Other answers or do not know	7	6	8	4	6	7		12	7	5

Notes:
Number of respondents: 554.
Source: From Höijer (1994).

totally indifferent and do not react at all, and 14 percent said they react some-times but very seldom. Some (7 percent) gave unclear answers that could not be categorized. The table also shows gendered differences and differences among age groups. Women react with compassion more often than men, and elderly people much more often than younger people. Feelings of pity, sadness and anger were reported, and women especially also said that they sometimes cried, had to close their eyes or look away, because the pictures touched them emotionally. [. . .]

Compassion is dependent on visuals

The compassion that the audience expresses is often directly related to the docu-mentary pictures they have seen on television. When asked about their spontaneous impressions of the Kosovo War most of the audience groups interviewed started to talk about the television pictures of streams of refugees or pictures of crying people in refugee camps, especially pictures of children and elderly people:

> 'It was what I saw of live pictures on television that made the strongest impression, all the innocent people, all those who cried.'

> 'I have terrible memories of children stepping on board buses and sitting by the windows crying.'

> 'I remember that I saw crying people on television. They had lost someone in their family and they could not find them again. There were a lot of people and it was very crowded on the gravel roads along which they were walking.'

Pictures, or more precisely our interpretations of pictures, can make indelible impressions on our minds, and as a distant audience we become bearers of inner pictures of human suffering. Especially when emotional pictures are shown repeatedly over time, as for instance the pictures of the refugees from Kosovo, they have a long-term impact on our collective memories. When the audience say

'You never get rid of all the crying children and the elderly' they emphasize the penetrative power of pictures.

The impact of photographic pictures is not least due to the truth-claim connected with them. They are perceived as truthful eye-witness reports of reality. The audience very rarely questions the reality status of documentary pictures, or sees them as constructions of situations or events (an exception from this is discussed under the heading 'distantiation'). Documentary pictures are instead experienced as if they give direct access to reality and they therefore insist upon being taken seriously. It is hard to deny the burnt corpses from the massacre in Stupni Do, the swollen bodies floating in the rivers of Rwanda and Burundi, the crying children in refugee camps, the endless lines of refugees forced to leave their homes in Kosovo, injured people from the conflict in the Middle East lying on the ground or being carried away on stretchers.

Compassion is dependent on ideal victim images

The audience accept the dominant victim code of the media and regard children, women and the elderly as ideal victims deserving compassion. When describing their emotional reactions the groups interviewed about the Kosovo War unanimously talked about these categories of civilian people:

> 'It makes a really strong impression to see children and elderly people, and women, infirmly wandering about. You start thinking about how it is for them.'

> 'I felt so terribly sorry for them. [. . .] Seeing all the elderly people and the children. They are so tired that they can hardly walk.'

> 'I saw a news item from an empty village and there was an old, old woman left there. She could not go on any longer. I thought it was so terrible for her.'

A condition for being moved is that we as audience can regard the victim as helpless and innocent, and this was sometimes also explicitly pointed out by participants in the study: 'I was most affected by the fact that innocent people were stricken.'

A news item about a crying middle-aged man in a refugee camp in Macedonia who, in front of the television camera, begged to be brought to Norway challenged this cultural conceptualization of a worthy victim. In most of the interviewed groups they considered the man distasteful and selfish and they charged him with bad behaviour. They also thought he was not behaving in a manly way:

> I thought it was a shame to behave as he did when you think about all the pregnant women and sick people. They need to be helped and he should have begged for them. He should have said: 'Please help them!'

A man in his prime is not worthy of our compassion since we do not regard him as helpless and innocent enough. Instead he should be active in fighting the enemy or helping the helpless ones. Elderly men are conceptualized differently since they are considered weak and have a right to be cared for. In one of the groups this was underlined by an utterance about the middle-aged man who begged to be taken to Norway: 'If he had been an old man over seventy'.

Witnessing remote suffering on television we are thus especially moved by pictures of children, women and elderly as victims. A child is, however, the most ideal victim in the perspective of compassion. When a child shows his/her feelings by crying or looking sad, we may feel pity both through our own memory of being open and vulnerable to the treachery of adulthood, and in terms of our adult identity – our desire to protect the child. When the child stares into the photographer's camera she or he may be perceived as looking directly at you as an audience, reminding you of her or his vulnerability and innocence.

Forms of compassion

Boltanski (1999) distinguishes between three forms of emotional commitment in relation to distant suffering: the mode of denunciation, the mode of sentiment, and the aesthetic mode. The first refers to a perspective in which compassion (pity in Boltanski's terminology) is combined with indignation and anger and turned into an accusation of the perpetrator. The suffering is considered as unjust. In the mode of sentiment there is no search for a perpetrator to accuse. Instead attention is focused on the victim and a benefactor. The suffering is experienced as touching and compassion is tender-hearted and sympathizes with the victim's gratitude at receiving help from a doctor, a nurse or humanitarian workers. The aesthetic mode is described by Boltanski (1999: 115) as a third possibility, which 'emerges from the criticism of the first two. It consists in considering the unfortunate's suffering as neither unjust nor as touching, but as sublime.' As examples he discusses paintings, for instance those by Goya, in which the horrible and the grotesque sides of the unfortunate's suffering is revealed.

Looking at audiences' responses to televised distant suffering we may quite clearly recognize the mode of denunciation and the mode of sentiment. It is harder to identify the aesthetic mode as a form of compassionate reading. There are, however, two other forms of compassion, which may be identified. In one, compassion is combined with feelings of shame and in the other with feelings of powerlessness. This gives us four forms of compassion identified in audience reactions. Below they are named tender-hearted compassion, blame-filled compassion, shame-filled compassion and powerlessness-filled compassion:

Tender-hearted compassion focuses on the suffering of the victims and the responses of pity and empathy it gives rise to in oneself as a spectator: 'It breaks my heart when I see refugees. They are coming in thousands and they tell what they have been through. It's so terrible'; 'I felt pity for them when they stood there in the mud and the cold weather. They had very little food and you could see the fear in their eyes.'

Blame-filled compassion brings up the suffering of the victims in combination with indignation and anger: 'I became angry when I saw the many innocent people and civilians who died and were stricken by the conflict.' The indignation may be directed towards someone seen as responsible for the excesses. In political conflicts it is often a person in power more than the specific perpetrator who executed the violent act. In the Kosovo Conflict Milosevic was an ideal enemy to accuse. He was conceived of as having an evil disposition, of being dangerous, powerful and inhuman both by the media and by the audience (Höijer et al., 2002): 'He is evil, manipulative, and stark mad'; 'He is a terrible man, a psychopath.'

Shame-filled compassion brings in the ambivalence connected with witnessing the suffering of others in our comfortable lives and the cosiness of our living room. Shame is 'an emotional state produced by the awareness that one has acted dishonourably or ridiculously' and 'knowledge of the transgression by others' is part of the emotional state (Reber, 1985: 313, 695). Concerning distant suffering you know that you have transgressed the moral obligation to help suffering others. 'I had such a bad conscience and I almost did not manage to watch any more terrible scenes on television. And they weren't just scenes, it was reality.'

In the feelings of shame there may also be a component of anger or denunciation directed at oneself for being passive and not engaging in the destinies of the remote victims: 'I get furious with myself because I do nothing. You can't say that you do not have time. It's a question of priority. Certainly there is more to do.'

Being an immigrant from an area in conflict makes the shame even more pronounced. In relation to the Kosovo conflict immigrants from the Balkans experienced a specific deep shame related to questions of identity and solidarity:

> We helped our relatives with money as best as we could. But you constantly had the feeling that it wasn't enough. The only right way to help was to go down there. But I didn't and I really feel that I failed. I left my people in the lurch and I can't look them in the eye.

Powerlessness-filled compassion arises from a subjective awareness of the limits of the media spectator's possibilities to alleviate the suffering of the victims. It brings forth sentiments of impotence and powerlessness: 'You feel so helpless and there is so little you can do. You can of course give some money but that will not stop the war'; 'I got a feeling that it would never stop and I experienced so much impotency.'

The various forms of compassion may take different forms in the individual spectator, and they may also be represented simultaneously in the same person. A spectator may for instance feel tender-hearted compassion, blame a perpetrator *and* experience powerlessness in relation to the same news story or reported encroachment. In the representative telephone interview study, 62 percent reported that they often or quite often had sentiments of sadness when watching news pictures about violence against civilians, and the same number, 62 percent, reported sentiments of anger. This study was not totally compatible with the face-to-face interviews, however, so one should not draw too strong conclusions about the extension of different types of compassion.

Distantiation from compassion

Far from everyone in the audience feels compassion with the victims of war and other conflicts. There are also different ways of turning one's back on the suffering of distant others. One strategy, though not a common one, is to reject the truth claim of the news reporting. Criticizing the news in general may also be a way of shifting focus away from the humanitarian tragedies. Another strategy is to dehumanize the victims in some way, or just to become numb or immune to remote human suffering. [. . .]

Sometimes, . . . a critical propaganda perspective may be strong and take over. This was the case when the interviewed Serbian immigrants, especially the male groups, saw the news about Kosovo-Albanian refugee streams. The news pictures were regarded as have been staged for propaganda purposes:

> On television all pictures may be arranged. They show the same strong pictures over and over again. They showed dreadful pictures, for instance they broadcast the same family on a horse-drawn cart several times. And they said that thousands of Kosovo-Albanians were hiding in the forest. But to me the pictures seemed incredible, arranged.

A more common critical perspective, which creates a distance from the human suffering, is to criticize the news in general for commercialism and sensationalism. News media give a distorted picture, according to this view, by paying too much attention to violence and human misery:

> The news reporting is focusing more and more on dead bodies and acts of violence. It seems to be the only thing of news value, and that can be quite disturbing. Especially when they are reporting from hotbeds of war. If nobody has been shot or blown to pieces there are no reports. It makes you quite critical of the media.

Another way to form a distance is to apply an us-them perspective in which the culture, mentality and way of living and behaving of the others, that is, the suffering people, are dehumanized. With stereotyped thought figures such as 'In the Balkans they think only of vendetta', 'It is a totally different culture from ours', 'It is something about their temperament', empathy is turned away and the lack of involvement is rationalized and legitimized. Why bother about people who are primitive and uncivilized and not like us, civilized citizens in democracies? 'Personally I felt no compassion for the people down there', as one man who was interviewed about the Kosovo War said, 'I think they only have themselves to blame. There have been problems in the Balkans ever since World War I. They are no angels!'

Just becoming numb or immune to the pictures and reports about human suffering on a large scale is also quite a common reaction: 'I cannot engage in it any longer. A dead body no longer touches me.' Being fed with news about suffering may in the end lead to feelings of satiation and numbness. A common reaction among the audience of the Kosovo War was that pity for the victims gradually decreased over the period of the growing humanitarian disaster. According to NATO propaganda, the war was going to last for just a few days. Instead it lasted for 78 days and during this period the audience were repeatedly exposed to images of seemingly endless streams of refugees. The powerlessness over the situation, the never ending number of victims, the difficulty of understanding the Balkan situation and ethnic conflicts, and the inability of the media to give a background, made the audience less interested, numb and even immune to the human suffering. 'In the end you could not manage it any more', was one way of expressing how time undermined the feeling of compassion. [. . .]

References

Boltanski, L. (1999) *Distant Suffering: Morality, Media and Politics*. Cambridge: Cambridge University Press.

Höijer, B. (1994) *Våldsskildringar i TV-nyheterna. Produktion, utbud, publik*. Stockholm University: Department of Journalism, Media and Communication, No. 5.

Höijer, B. (1996) 'The Dilemmas of Documentary Violence in Television', *Nordicom Review* 1: 53–61.

Höijer, B., S.A. Nohrstedt and R. Ottosen (2002) 'The Kosovo War in the Media – Analysis of a Global Discursive Order', *Conflict & Communication Online* 1(2): www.cco.regener-online.de

Reber, A.S. (1985) *The Penguin Dictionary of Psychology*. London: Penguin Books.

Chapter 39

Imogen Tyler

"CHAV MUM CHAV SCUM"

Class disgust in contemporary Britain

The reason Vicky Pollard caught the public imagination is that she embodies with such fearful accuracy several of the great scourges of contemporary Britain: aggressive all-female gangs of embittered, hormonal, drunken teenagers; gym slip mums who choose to get pregnant as a career option; pasty-faced, lard-gutted slappers who'll drop their knickers in the blink of an eye . . . these people do exist and are every bit as ripe and just a target for social satire as were, say, the raddled working-class drunks sent up by Hogarth in Gin Lane.

(James Delingpole 2006, p. 25)

Disgust and contempt motivate and sustain the low ranking of things, people, and actions deemed disgusting and contemptible.

(William Miller 1997, p. xiv)

Introduction

IN THE LAST THREE YEARS a new vocabulary of social class has emerged in Britain. The word "chav," alongside its various synonyms and regional variations, has become a ubiquitous term of abuse for white working-class subjects. This article explores the emergence of the grotesque and comic figure of the chav within a range of contemporary British media: primarily television comedy, Internet fora, and newspapers. Bringing together current sociological research on social class and recent feminist theoretical writing on emotions, I consider how social class is emotionally mediated, focusing on the role played by disgust reactions in the generation and circulation of the chav figure. . . . Concentrating on the figure of the female chav and the vilification of young white working-class mothers, I explore how the "chav mum" is produced through disgust reactions as an intensely affective figure that embodies historically familiar and contemporary anxieties about sexuality, reproduction and fertility and "racial mixing." . . . I argue that the level of disgust directed at the chav is suggestive of a heightened class antagonism that marks a new episode in the dirty ontology of class struggle in Britain. [. . .]

The figure of chav

Chav, and its various synonyms and regional variations (including Pikey, Townie, Charver, Chavette, Chavster, Dumbo, Gazza, Hatchy, Hood Rat, Kev, Knacker, Ned, Ratboy, Scally, Scumbag, Shazza, Skanger), have become ubiquitous terms of abuse for the white poor within contemporary British culture. Since 2003 we have seen the emergence of an entire slang vocabulary around chav, which includes terms such as chavellers cheques (giro and benefit payments), chavtastic, chaving a laugh (laughter at chavs), chavbaiting, chavalanche (large group of chavs), chavalier (chav car), chavspeak, chavspotting and acronyms, such as "Council Housed And Violent," "Council Housed And Vile," and "Council House Associated Vermin." Folk etymologies have sprung up to explain the term: some sources suggest that the term chav might derive from a distortion of a Romany word for a child, (chavo or chavi), or that it may have originated in the Medway town of Chatham. Others argue that chav is an historical East End of London term for child, while others suggest it emerges from the term charver, long used in the north east of England to describe the disenfranchised white poor (see Nayak 2003). As criminologists Haywood and Yar argue, all these etymological accounts suggest that the term chav "has always been connected with communities who have experienced social deprivation in one form or another" (2006, p. 16). In current parlance, the term chav is aligned "with stereotypical notions of lower-class" and is, above all, "a term of intense class-based abhorrence" (Haywood & Yar 2006, p. 16).

Chav news

One of the primary sites within which the chav figure has been constituted is newspapers. Writing in *The Edinburgh Evening News* in 2004, the year in which disgust and fascination with chavs peaked in the British press, journalist Gina Davidson pronounces:

> And we will know them by their dress . . . and trail of fag ends, sparkling white trainers, baggy tracksuit trousers, branded sports top, gold-hooped earrings, "sovvy" rings and the ubiquitous Burberry base-ball cap. Throw them together, along with a pack of Regal, and you have the uniform of what is being described as the UK's new underclass— the chav. Call them what you will, identifying them is easy. They are the sullen youths in hooded tops and spanking-new trainers who loiter listlessly on street corners and shopping malls, displaying an apparent

lack of education and an all too obvious taste for fighting; the slack-jawed girls with enough gold or gold-plated jewellery to put H Samuel out of business. They are the dole-scroungers, petty criminals, football hooligans and teenage pram-pushers.

(2004, p. 14)

Davidson's invocation of "dole-scroungers, petty criminals, football hooligans and teenage pram-pushers" illustrates how the chav figure comes to embody in a condensed form a series of older stereotypes of the white poor. In particular, the use of phrases such as "petty criminal" and "dole-scroungers," conjures up debates from the 1980s and 90s about the rise of a socially excluded "underclass." However, one of the things that distinguishes the figure of the chav from previous accounts of the underclass is the emphasis on the excessive consumption of consumer and branded goods. Indeed, within news media accounts of the chav, this figure is primarily identified by means of his or her "bad," "vulgar" and excessive consumer choices—cheap brands of cigarettes, cheap jewellery, branded sports tops, gold-hooped earrings, sovereign-rings, Burberry baseball caps. As Hayward and Yar argue "the 'chav' phenomenon recapitulates the discursive creation of the underclass, while simultaneously reconfiguring it within the space of commodity consumption" (2006, p. 16). Certainly, it is arguable that changes in the configuration of social class in Britain and shifts in traditional markers of social class (such as accent or education) have made it more difficult to ascertain class difference. In the context of shifting class definitions, the vilification of the chav can be interpreted as a symptom of a middle-class desire to re-demarcate class boundaries within the context of contemporary consumer culture. However, the attempt to demarcate class difference through practices of consumption is not a new phenomenon. Moreover, it is important to note that depictions of the white working class have always pivoted on appearance and, in particular, on a perceived excess of (bodily) materiality. Indeed, newspaper accounts of chavs vividly recall Victorian and Edwardian accounts of the dangerous, immoral, and libidinal lower classes. As Keith Haywood and Majid Yar note:

just as was the case in the 19th century, when terms such as "moral wretch," "degenerate poor," "depraved nomad," and "savage outcast" all ultimately came to be incorporated under the umbrella term "dangerous class," the word "chav" is increasingly acting as a ubiquitous structural category—a soft semantic target for those keen to rebadge the underprivileged and socially excluded among us as a new form of feckless underclass.

(2006, p. 17)

Within news media accounts of chavs, older iconographies of the excess and horror of the lower classes are reanimated within a rush of descriptions of sullen, hooded, loitering, unemployed, pram-pushing, intoxicated youths. Through the figure of chav a new publicly sanctioned wave of middle-class contempt for the lower classes is bodied forth. Consider for instance, the following extract from a *Sunday Telegraph* article titled "In Defence of Snobbery":

> It's official: the classless society is finished. After decades in remission, the most infamous of British vices—snobbery—is making a comeback . . . They are the non-respectable working classes: the dole-scroungers, petty criminals, football hooligans and teenage pram-pushers. They are also the kind of people one would not dare mock face-to-face . . . Chavs are often poor, but they are not weak: on the contrary, they are in the cultural ascendant. They are tough enough to take a little ribbing. And for the rest of us—too frightened to take them on in person—there is a delicious release to be had from laughing at them.
>
> (Jemima Lewis 2004, p. 23)

In this article, journalist Lewis argues that mockery of chavs marks the return of traditional snobbery. Identifying herself as middle class she identifies the chav as "the non-respectable working classes." Contrary to claims that "directly articulated" class distinctions have disappeared, this overt class-naming demonstrates how the emergence of the figure of the chav is part of a resurgence of the explicit naming of social class within British media. Lewis's article is indicative of the many thousands of descriptions of chavs published within British newspapers since 2003, accounts in which class differences are not seen as irrelevant, outmoded or shameful to articulate but are openly and aggressively explored through virulent unapologetic stereotyping. [. . .]

Broadsheet newspaper articles on chavs tend to fall into two groups: articles by journalists such as Burchill that are highly critical of the new vilification of the working classes and articles by journalists such as Lewis that overtly celebrate this "new snobbery" and offer vivid descriptions of the "delicious release" afforded by class disgust. From 2003 onwards, these two opposing broadsheet positions on chavs have been played out in an ever growing series of articles which—through response and counter-response—struggle over and simultaneously invent the figure of the chav.

In a 2006 *The Times* article titled, "A conspiracy against chavs? Count me in" Delingpole mocks the "hand-wringing prose" of "humourless, Polly Toynbee-style Lefties" who defend chavs. Delingpole describes chavs as "disgusting, selfish, violent underclass specimen[s]" and articulates his class disgust in terms of "a socially necessary" snobbery. As he writes:

> As a member of probably the most discriminated-against subsection in the whole of British society—the white, middle-aged, public-school-and-Oxbridge educated middle-class male—I see no reason why . . . the Vicky Pollards and the Waynes and Waynettas of our world have got it coming to them. If they weren't quite so repellent, we wouldn't need to make jokes about them, would we? The function of satire is not only to make us laugh, but also, with luck, to draw our attention to the things that are wrong with the world and help mock them into extinction.
>
> (James Delingpole 2006, p. 25)

[. . .]

Menninghaus argues that laughing at something is "an act of expulsion" that closely resembles the rejecting movement of disgust reactions. Disgust and laughter are, he notes "complementary ways of admitting an alterity" (2003, p. 11). Like disgust, laughter is community-forming, it is often contagious and it generates proximity. Laughter is always shared with a real or imagined community. [. . .] In the case of laughter at those of a lower class, laughter is boundary-forming. It creates a distance between "them" and "us," asserting moral judgments and a superior class position. As Miller notes, "Laughing habits turn out to be one of the crucial clues we use to get a fix on a person's moral and social competence" revealing an individual's "social place" and their aspirations, where they would like to be placed (1997, p. 83). . . . Laughing at chavs is a way of naming, managing and authorising class disgust, contempt, and anxiety. The expression of class disgust within newspaper articles on chavs is deliberate and self-conscious, it is a feigned disgust performed both for our entertainment and as a means of asserting middle-class identity claims. In the online vocabulary of chav-hate, we can further discern the ways in which class disgust is performed in ways that are community-forming.

Chav online

The website, *urbandictionary* (n.d.) is an online slang dictionary that functions as an unofficial online authority on English language slang. *Urbandictionary* was created and is owned by a former computer science student Aaron Peckham, who launched the site in 1999 to compare slang used by students in California. *Urbandictionary* is modelled on an internet forum in which (unregistered) users post definitions of new or existing slang terms, which are then reviewed by volunteer editors before being published. Visitors to the site vote on definitions (which can include images and sounds) by clicking a thumb-up or thumb-down icon and these postings are then ranked according to the votes they have accured: The tag line of *urbandictionary* is "Define your World." The website currently hosts 300,000 definitions of slang terms and is ranked as one of the 2,000 highest web traffic sites in the world. The site profile states that 65 per cent of the users are under 25. There were 368 definitions of the term chav posted on the site at the time of writing this article, and I have listed below a small number of indicative phrases taken from some of the most highly ranked posts.

Chavs . . . the cancer of the United Kingdom

They live in estates, feeding off our taxes through benefits, which they spend on countless rings, thick gold chains, cigarettes and alcohol.

Chav: a type of person who lacks the intelligence to be able to speak or write proper english, uses words, if they are proper words such as "blingin," "mingin" etc

Favourite jobs of chavs: drug dealer, McDonalds worker, prostitute, page 3 "model."

Disgusting, dirty, loud, ugly, stupid arseholes that threaten, fight, cause trouble, impregnate 14 year olds, ask for money, ask for fags, . . . steal your phones, wear crap sports wear, drink cheap cider and generally spread their hate.

A social underclass par excellence. The absolute dregs of modern civilization

The only good chav is dead one. The only thing better than that is a mass grave full of dead chavs and a 24 hour work crew making way for more.

All chavs are disgusting scum.

(*urbandictionary* n.d.)

As Ahmed notes, "to name something as disgusting is performative" in that "it generates the object that it names" (2005, p. 93). We can see how disgust is both performative and performed in the internet forum *urbandictionary*. This disgust speech generates a set of effects, which adhere to, produce, and embellish the disgusting figure of the chav: chavs are white, live on council estates, eat junk food, steal your phones, wear crap sports wear, drink cheap cider, they are the absolute dregs of modern civilisation; a social underclass *par excellence*, chavs are disgusting. The dictionary format is significant here because—like the accompanying veneer of irony—it grants a strange authority to the dehumanising bigotry of the posts. *Urbandictionary* illustrates how class disgust is not simply felt but actively generated through repetition. Through the repetition of this disgusted response, the negative properties attributed to chavs make this figure materialise as representative of a group that embodies those disgusting qualities, a group that is "lower than human or civil life" (Ahmed 2005, p. 97). As users add to and build a comprehensive definition of "the chav" within the *urbandictionary* site, they interact with one another and a conversational environment emerges. The voting system works on this site as a form of peer authorisation that encourages users to invoke more and more intense and affective disgust reactions. As Ngai suggests, disgust involves an expectation of concurrence, and disgust reactions seek "to include or draw others into its exclusion of its object, enabling a strange kind of sociability" (2005, p. 336). This sociability has a particular specificity within online communities in which anonymity gives community members license to express their disgust in extreme and virulent ways. The interactivity of these internet forums, and the real and illusory immediacy they transmit, makes online forums intensely affective communal spaces/places within which disgust reactions can be rapidly shared and accrued. [. . .]

Chav mum

There is a repeated emphasis within news media and internet forums on the sluttish behaviour and multiple pregnancies of the female chav. Many of the *urbandictionary* (n.d.) posts focus on the spectacle of the chavette's excessively reproductive body.

Human equivalent of vermin . . . Most reproduce by the age of 14, sometimes younger.

[Chavs] are almost always white, and very skinny, where the chavettes are usually overweight, with large stretchmarks on their stomachs from excessive baby having, a chavette will have one baby every year from the age of 13.

The chavettes have . . . a large 3 seater second hand pushchair, with 3 different coloured children in, all at different stages in the chav develop- ment, with caps already fitted and ears pierced.

Whilst young unwed working-class mothers have always been a target of social stigma, hatred, and anxiety, the fetishisation of the chav mum within popular culture has a contemporary specificity and marks a new outpouring of sexist class disgust. The gossip website *popbitch* famously determined celebrity chav mothers as "pramface." Now a popular term of abuse, *urbandictionary* (n.d.) defines pramface as, "a woman who looks so young she ought to be pushing a pram around a council estate in the shittiest part of town." The chav mum or pramface, with her hoop earrings, sports clothes, pony tail ("Croydon facelift") and gaggle of mixed race children, is the quintessential sexually excessive, single mother: an immoral, filthy, ignorant, vulgar, tasteless, working-class whore. This figure of chav mum circulates within a wide range of media, celebrity media, reality television, comedy pro- gramming on British television, consumer culture, print media, literature, news media, films, and "chav hate" websites. [. . .]

The mass vilification and mockery of the chav mum can be understood in relation to what Wilson and Huntington (2005, p. 59) have argued is the emergence of a new set of norms about femininity, in which the ideal life trajectory of middle- class women conforms to the current governmental objectives of economic growth through higher education and increased female workforce participation. We can clearly ascertain how the chav mum figures middle-class values through disgust for the sexuality and excessive reproduction of the lower classes within this thread of comments, take this post: "If YOU think that's an acceptable life and ambition for a young girl in this day and age of supposed equality, you might as well just lie in the gutter and open your legs right now." The chav mum represents a thoroughly dirty and disgusting ontology that operates as a constitutive limit for clean, white, middle- class, feminine respectability: "an acceptable life and ambition for a young girl in this day and age of supposed equality." However, the comic and disgusting chav mum is haunted by another figure, that of the infertile white middle-class middle- aged woman. For whilst the chav mum represents a highly undesirable reproductive body, this figure can also be read as symptomatic of an explosion of anxiety about dropping fertility rates amongst the white middle classes. Indeed, the disgust for and fascinated obsession with the chav mum's "easy fertility" is bound up with a set of social angst about infertility amongst middle-class women, a group continually chastised for "putting career over motherhood" and "leaving it too late" too have children. The figure of the chav mum not only mocks poor white teenage mothers but also challenges middle-class women to face their "reproductive responsibilities."
[. . .]

References

DAVIDSON, GINA (2004) 'Sites to check out if you chav what it takes', *The Edinburgh Evening News*, 4 Feb., p. 14.

DELINGPOLE, JAMES (2006) 'A conspiracy against chavs? Count me in', *The Times*, 13 April, p. 25.

HAYWARD, KEITH & YAR, MAJID (2006) 'The "Chav" phenomenon: Consumption, media and the construction of a new underclass', *Crime, Media, Culture*, vol. 2, no. 1, pp. 9–28.

LEWIS, JEMMIA (2004) 'In defence of snobbery', *The Daily Telegraph*, 1 Feb., p. 23.

MENNINGHAUS, WINFRIED (2003) *Disgust: Theory and History of a Strong Sensation*, trans. Howard Eiland & Joel Golb, State University of New York Press, New York.

MILLER, WILLIAM (1997) *The Anatomy of Disgust*, Harvard University Press, Cambridge, MA.

NAYAK, ANOOP (2003) *Race, Place and Globalization: Youth Cultures in a Changing World*, Berg, Oxford.

NGAI, SIANNE (2005) *Ugly Feelings Literature, Affect, and Ideology*, Harvard University Press, Cambridge.

Chapter 40

Minna Aslama and Mervi Pantti

TALKING ALONE

Reality TV, emotions and authenticity

Introduction

INTEREST IN THE EMOTIONS OF other people seems to be very much a part of contemporary culture, as is a pressure to reveal emotions and talk about them in both private and public forums (Lupton, 1998). We are supposedly living in a 'confessional' (Foucault, 1978) or 'therapeutic' culture (Furedi, 2004) that celebrates individual feelings, intimate revelations and languages of therapy. The role of the media and particularly television as a central public site for confessing one's innermost feelings has been rightly stressed by media scholars (e.g. Dovey, 2000; Gamson, 1998; Living-stone and Lunt, 1994; Shattuc, 1997; White, 1992, 2002). After all, recent decades have seen an eye-catching rise of genres and programmes that offer opportunities for the public display of once-private feelings. Accordingly, we have witnessed an increase in the number of ordinary people who are willing to speak in a confessional voice (White, 2002). Confessional and therapeutic strategies are perhaps most prominent in reality television – although certainly they are not absent from informative genres such as the news either – where the outbreaks of raw emotion figure prominently in the attraction and popularity of the genre (see Grindstaff, 1997). [. . .]

The prominence of free-flowing, confessional talk in talk shows has attracted considerable attention (e.g. Livingstone and Lunt, 1994; Lunt and Stenner, 2005; Masciarotte, 1991; Shattuc, 1997; White, 1992) but the study of the strategies used in displaying 'real emotions' through confessional discourses in reality TV is still relatively unexplored. We hope to contribute to the understanding of the production of self-disclosure through a formal analysis of selected international and domestic dating, competition and lifestyle-oriented reality shows broadcast on Finnish television between 2002 and 2004. When conducting the study in early 2004, we wished to review the array of programmes aired at that time on the four

Finnish nationwide TV channels (two public broadcasting channels, YLE1 and YLE2; two commercial channels, MTV3 and Nelonen). The periods sampled comprised the last week of October 2003 (week 43; 26 October–1 November 2003) and the last week of January 2004 (week 4; 25–31 January 2004). We also wanted to include one entire season of a Finnish adventure show broadcast in summer 2002. We have examined altogether 39 episodes of reality programmes, as follows:

- *The Bachelor* (USA);
- *The Bachelorette* (USA);
- *Expedition Robinson* (Sweden);
- *Extreme Escapades* (*Suuri seikkailu*, Finland, all 30 episodes);
- *Faking It* (UK);
- *Fat Club* (UK);
- *Idols* (Finland);
- *Popstars* (Finland);
- *Shipmates* (USA); and
- *Temptation Island* (USA).

It should be noted that the so-called makeover reality shows appeared *en masse* on Finnish screens only in late 2004. Genre labels such as 'dating show', 'lifestyle show' or 'competition show', which are quite vague, draw attention to the fact that reality TV is an extremely complex concept that unites a variety of programmes and subcategories (see Holmes and Jermyn, 2004). All our programmes belong to the 'third phase' of reality programming, mixing the earlier 'action/incident' programmes (e.g. the BBC's *999*) and 'docusoap' formats (e.g. the BBC's *Hotel* and *Airport*) with gameshow interest in tests and challenges and incorporating elements of the talent contest (Corner, 2004). [. . .]

Reality television in the age of commodified and managed emotions

> Right now I'm so sad. My heart is broken. I go from a limo towards the man I'm in love with thinking I'm going to spend the rest of my life with him. Next minute I was walking away with nothing. I'm just so mad and shocked and really sad. I feel so alone.
>
> (Kelly Jo, *The Bachelor* (USA), broadcast in Finland, 2003)

Reality television's rise to prominence among contemporary television formats resonates with the validation of emotional talk in politics and culture. Attributes such as 'confessional', 'therapeutic' and paradoxically 'postemotional' (Mestrovic, 1997) that have been ascribed to the times in which we are living are related to the notion that we are witnessing an emergent preoccupation with emotions and authenticity of the self (see Furedi, 2004; Giddens, 1991). According to Furedi (2004: 30), 'therapeutic culture promotes not simply emotionalism but emotionalism in an intensely individualized form'. Certainly, an essential part of the strategies of finding the authentic self is the confession of one's innermost feelings to others. Indeed, Mestrovic (1997: 71–100) claims that there is a special industry today, the authenticity industry, by which ordinary people as well as celebrities – such as 'the postemotional President Clinton' – can disclose intimate feelings. Television, accurately named as a 'therapy machine' (White, 2002), is the major institution among these therapeutic mechanisms in contemporary society. [. . .]

It is not difficult to see reality TV as a part of this authenticity industry. It must use strategies that encourage people to express and manage their emotions and problems, since it depends on the belief that 'real' emotions and conflicts will arise. [. . .]

Interestingly, although most reality programmes involve scores of participants, they interact surprisingly little in larger groups and the multiparty situation can be divided roughly into two main categories. One is the casual 'dinner-table talk' or other similar small-scale talking that occurs when a group is planning a wood-gathering excursion, or waiting for the next competition to begin. This communicative situation is common in programmes such as *Survivor* or in its Swedish and Finnish sister programmes, the *Expedition Robinsons*. The only programme in our sample where such conversation has a central role is the *Fat Club* (UK, broadcast in Finland in 2002): in that show, participants are often filmed while dining together for the simple reason that food and dieting are the main ingredients of the show.

The second multiparty situation is the town hall meeting of the new millennium, the Tribal Council (and its multiple equivalents), which feature in *Survivor* and its many clones. These situations consist of a quick assessment, guided by the host, of the episode's events (as well as of personal plotting and politicizing), followed by some kind of ceremony. The council meeting seems to be a central element of reality television, since it also appears in singles' shows such as *Paradise Hotel* and in the weighing session in *Fat Club*. The main purpose, evidently, is to create suspense over the prospect of winning and losing. Perhaps not dramatic and intimate enough on their own, these segments are relatively short compared to the duration of most reality TV episodes. Although statements with strong feelings are uttered when one of the participants is voted out, in a multiparty situation verbal comments are kept short while the camera shows the tears in close-up. After all, it is usually the follow-up of the situation featuring participants talking alone that is the point of highest drama: one-by-one the participants step in front of the camera and proclaim their difficult decisions, broken hearts or remark on the joy of revenge.

The multiparty conversation may be too public and official a situation or simply too hard to control for the purpose of most reality shows. Instead, the dialogue – the very foundation of the television drama – emerges in several variants. Many reality programmes, dating shows in particular, include two-party conversations that have little to do with the carnivalistic shocker fights of some talk shows; instead they follow the melodramatic scenes known from soap operas – even to the extent of visualization by means of traditional shot/reverse-shot camera work. These talk situations involve declarations of love, honesty, friendship and the like; they convey a semi-official tone of declaring some kind of a vow while the other party silently listens, thus coming close to the monologue situation and its multiple modifications.

First, the confrontational dialogue: a kind of verbal duel is clearly in place to support the competitive aspect in the shows. Consider the following example:

Annelie: We meet again. [tries to hug Charlie]

Charlie: Don't you hug me. It's a Judas kiss. Let's not pretend. You deceived me, voted me out . . . you stabbed me in the back and now we should pretend to be friends?

Annelie: This doesn't have to be this hard. I didn't like you either. But there's such a thing as good manners. I follow my way and you, yours.

Charlie: I think honesty is what matters.

Annelie: Don't you want to hear the news [from the camp]?

Charlie: You talk if you want. I'm not interested in chatting. I've managed to be away from all that plotting for a few days now. There is no room here for intrigues and lies. This is a duel. It started from the first moment on. [Charlie walks away]

Annelie [alone]: What an asshole. I knew it from the beginning. The poor man won't have it easy.
(Expedition Robinson (Sweden), broadcast in Finland, 2003)

At the core, the underlining purpose of confrontations seems to be to allow the display of anger, rage, accusations and all kinds of negative emotions. In dating shows, the confrontation may have little to do with winning or losing but is included simply to facilitate the melodramatized presentation of feelings, a propos of *Jerry Springer*. Toni gives a prime example in her discussion with Keith after a dinner at the *Paradise Hotel*:

Toni: If you ever disrespect a woman again like you did tonight, so help me God, I'm gonna flare up on you.

Keith: This can't be true.
(Paradise Hotel (USA), broadcast in Finland, 2004)

Besides these two types that seem to dominate the dialogue in reality television, other supporting dialogue conventions can be found. One is a news-like interview, conducted by the host. The Finnish adventure show *Extreme Escapades* (*Suuri seikkailu*, 2002, 2003) made an art of making references to sports interviews: after challenges, the host questions participants with clichés such as: 'How do you feel now?' Interestingly, the interviewees' role as 'professional athletes' evoked some of the most colourful expressions of joy or disappointment from Finns, otherwise somewhat lacking in emotional expression, since emotions were connected to factual statements about how hard it was to climb a hill or what kind of strategy was used when crossing a stream (Aslama and Pantti, forthcoming 2006). In a similar vein, the Finnish version of *Popstars* (2002) included 'professional interview sessions' in the recording studio during which the members of the girl band-to-be seemed to try to construct their image furiously as serious musicians.

Although interviews remain more the exception than the rule in reality shows, they also play a role in dating shows such as *The Bachelor*, when the host poses simple questions: 'Are you ready?'; 'How did you arrive at this decision?' In this context, the interview brings a more factual contrast to the melodramatic declaration. Although no clear line can be drawn between a more factual or official and a more intimate interview situation, another supporting type of interview dialogue that emerges could be called the 'therapy interview'. This kind of talk situation has been made famous already by talk shows (Bruun, 1994; Murdock, 2000): here, the journalist gives subtle, supporting cues to the participant, so that they can work through difficult situations. In the Finnish version of *Survivor, Robinson* (2004), the therapy talk was given its own weekly 30 minutes. As the show had been recorded some six months in advance, the producers could stage therapeutic interviews in which the participant voted out in a given week appeared in their own way to analyse their key strategies and emotions in hindsight.

Yet another form of dialogue is the one between the expert assessor and the assessed. Shows such as *Idols* are built largely on this way of talk:

> I'm your fan. You've been damn good from the start. And I, somehow . . . I want to thank you . . . your whole attitude, that humility that you've had all along the way . . . I think it's incredibly great. The man comes here, sings, leaves. That really hits me, deep down inside. I'm gonna cry soon, but you get all the points because of that humility and the attitude, how you approach singing. Rock 'n' roll!
>
> (Hannu, music producer and member of the jury,
> *Idols* (Finland), 2003)

The above example poignantly illustrates the kind of assessment required in reality programmes: emotional expression that does not solicit a reply. Often, situations that appear to be dialogues are either wellprepared, witty one-liners solicited by the host, or monologues where the other participants serve merely as an audience, waiting for their own monologue. Regardless of the type or origin of the reality show and, accordingly, of the action taking place (be it a worm-eating competition or a hot date), the dramatic culmination comes when participants face the camera alone.

Talking alone

> Up to now I have kept my mouth shut about 95 percent of the events in our camp [i.e. haven't talked about them to the teammates] and, in turn, told 95 percent of everything directly to the camera. The first time I said something directly to somebody here I realized that I should have kept quiet even then.
>
> (Nina, *Extreme Escapades* (Finland), 2002)

Traditionally, in drama as well as prose, single-person speech situations have served to reveal the inner life, secret thoughts and feelings of the characters. Interestingly, reality shows have reintroduced this out-of-date staged talk situation into the context of television. Indeed, it can be argued that it is precisely the monologue that is at the core of reality television, as it provides for those moments when emotions run free and a person's true self appears. We argue that the specific moments of talking alone are used on the whole as a truth-sign of direct access to the 'real'.

Reality television has produced a multitude of variations of the monologue. The most obvious may be the staged confession, which is illustrated by Kristen in the following:

> [Crying] It's kind of all set in . . . like things might get to the end. And it really bothers me a lot because I met lot of true friends and I don't want, I don't want to leave. I cried tonight knowing that Tommy was the only person I ever wanted truly to know what I was about. I love him to death for being that person.
>
> (Kristen, *Temptation Island* (USA), broadcast in Finland, 2002)

This is a talk situation that *The Real World* made famous in the early the 1990s and which has figured subsequently in most reality television formats worldwide. The confession clearly borrows its video-diary expression from factual genres, specifically from 'performative documentary' (e.g. Nichols, 2001). Indeed, a form of monologue could be called the 'diary confession', as it is used in a documentary manner to encounter events rather than reveal the speaker's inner secrets, as for example in *Faking It*. In the following, 22-year-old Sian, a student of classical music, is to be transformed into a top DJ:

> I've always felt that maybe I'm entering into an old profession. So yeah, I think it's quite an advantage for me to actually explore youth and what young people are enjoying doing . . . When I woke up this morning I felt sick and thought about not coming . . . for a second. Then I just thought, yeah well, let's do it now, I've got to do this now. And I'm quite excited.
>
> (Sian, *Faking It* (UK), broadcast in Finland, 2004)

If distinctions are to be made, a video diary includes a narrative purpose: it develops the story. In contrast, a confession may look the same visually, but the content and form of talk resemble more closely the melodramatic declaration – as their main content, confessions feature emotional revelations, speculations and analyses.

Arguably, a confession resembles therapy talk, but a distinction can be made: clearly, the therapeutic situation is conducted with someone (even if the 'therapist's' questions may be omitted in the final version), whereas the confession is a self-induced examination of one's prior actions and, even more importantly, of one's thoughts, feelings and relationships with others. Christy, who has taken part in a dating cruise with Roger on *Shipmates*, illustrates this:

Roger likes me and I would bet my life on the fact that he does. If you like me, you like me. You need to be upfront with me and tell me that you like me. Don't play games with me; leave that back in elementary school, where you learned it. Roger does not have what it takes to be a part of me.

(Christy, *Shipmates* (USA), broadcast in Finland, 2003)

A dialogical variant of the confession is the video greeting. It differs from confession in that the former is directed to the audience directly, whereas the latter makes them eavesdroppers on a monologue targeted at a certain someone within the programme (be it another participant or relative, etc.). The analysis that Christy offers alone in the confessional monologue takes the following form when directed at someone special:

Roger, I just want to say to you, while it hasn't (or these haven't) been the best days of my life, I have had a decent time. I think it could have been better had you been more honest, more upfront and more frank with your feelings. I think that you like me; you told me that you do.

(Christy, *Shipmates* (USA), broadcast in Finland, 2003)

A talk situation that Murdock (2000) defines as the 'sales pitch' also resembles the confession: often the pitch is present more or less explicitly in reality television shows, especially in the kind in which audiences have the power to vote for or against competitors. The purpose of pitching in this context is to ensure one's enrolment (such as the showreels of the aspiring inmates of *Paradise Hotel*) or one's survival, to promote oneself as the most socially, psychologically and/or physically competent contestant. The Finnish *Idols* provides an example that is both typical for the situation and typically subdued, representing Finnish communicative culture (see Aslama and Pantti, forthcoming 2006):

I like to teach and I like that line of work, but somehow I feel I'm not living to my full potential doing that. I want something else still. I'm no longer 15 years old, I have life experience. And I believe that I have good prerequisites to endure this [competition and stress] and enjoy everything this brings along. The thing is, regardless of everything, I have my feet on the ground.

(Maria, teacher, *Idols* (Finland), broadcast 2003)

[. . .]

References

Aslama, M. and M. Pantti (forthcoming 2006) 'Flagging Finnishness: Reproducing National Identity in the Reality Television Series *Extreme Escapades*', *Television and New Media*.

Bruun, H. (1994) 'Snakkeprogrammet. Inkredsning av en TV-genre' ['Talk Show. Incarnation of a TV Genre'], working paper. Aarhus: University of Aarhus.

Corner, J. (2004) 'Afterword: Framing the New', in S. Holmes and D. Jermyn (eds) *Understanding Reality Television*, pp. 290–9. London: Routledge.

Dovey, J. (2000) *Freakshow: First Person Media and Factual Television*. London: Pluto Press.

Foucault, M. (1981[1976]) *The History of Sexuality: Volume I, an Introduction*. Harmondsworth: Penguin.

Furedi, F. (2004) *Therapy Culture: Cultivating Vulnerability in an Uncertain Age*. London: Routledge.

Gamson, J. (1998) *Freaks Talk Back. Tabloid Shows and Sexual Nonconformity*. Chicago, IL: University of Chicago Press.

Giddens, A. (1991) *Modernity and Self-Identity. Self and Society in the Late Modern Age*. Cambridge: Polity Press.

Grindstaff, L. (1997) 'Producing Trash, Class and the Money Shot', in J. Lull and S. Hinerman (eds) *Media Scandals*, pp. 164–201. Cambridge: Polity Press.

Holmes, S. and D. Jermyn (2004) 'Introduction: Understanding Reality TV', in S. Holmes and D. Jermyn (eds) *Understanding Reality Television*, pp. 1–32. London: Routledge.

Livingstone, S. and P. Lunt (1994) *Talk on Television. Audience Participation and the Public Debate*. London: Routledge.

Lunt, P. and P. Stenner (2005) '*The Jerry Springer Show* as an Emotional Public Sphere', *Media, Culture and Society* 27(1): 59–82.

Lupton, D. (1998) *The Emotional Self. A Sociocultural Exploration*. London: Sage.

Masciarotte, G. (1991) 'C'mon Girl: Oprah Winfrey and the Discourse of Feminine Talk', *Genders* 11(Fall): 81–110.

Mestrovic, S. (1997) *Postemotional Society*. London: Sage.

Murdock, G. (2000) 'Talk Shows: Democratic Debates and Tabloid Tales', in J. Wieten, G. Murdock and P. Dahlgren (eds) *Television Across Europe: A Comparative Introduction*, pp. 198–220. London: Sage.

Nichols, B. (2001) *Introduction to Documentary*. Bloomington: Indiana University Press.

Shattuc, J.M. (1997) *The Talking Cure. TV Talk Shows and Women*. New York: Routledge.

White, M. (1992) *Tele-advising: Therapeutic Discourse in American Television*. Chapel Hill: University of North Carolina Press.

White, M. (2002) 'Television, Therapy and the Social Subject; or, The TV Therapy Machine', in J. Friedman (ed.) *Reality Squared. Televisual Discourse on the Real*, pp. 313–21. New Brunswick, NJ: Rutgers University Press.

Chapter 41

Greg M. Smith

THE MOOD CUE APPROACH

GIVEN THE FLEXIBILITY OF THE emotion system, it would seem difficult for a mass-media form to elicit emotional responses with any degree of consistency across a wide range of viewers. If social and cultural differences create diverse emotion scripts and prototypes, then audience members can be using very different prototypes when emotionally assessing the same stimuli. [. . .]

How can films be structured to elicit dependable responses from a wide variety of audience members, as noted in the desiderata? [. . .]

The central assertion: the interaction between mood and emotion

I argue that the primary emotive effect of film is to create mood. Generating brief, intense emotions often requires an orienting state that asks us to interpret our surroundings in an emotional fashion. If we are in such an emotionally orienting state, we are much more likely to experience such emotion, according to my theory.

Film structures seek to increase the film's chances of evoking emotion by first creating a predisposition toward experiencing emotion: a mood. Films rely on being able to elicit a lower-level emotional state, which can be established with less concentrated cuing than would be required for emotion. The first task for a film is to create such an emotional orientation toward the film.

To sustain a mood, we must experience occasional moments of emotion. Film must therefore provide the viewer with a periodic diet of brief emotional moments if it is to sustain a mood. Therefore, mood and emotion sustain each other. Mood encourages us to experience emotion, and experiencing emotions encourages us to continue in the present mood.

Film structures attempting to elicit mood can take advantage of the various means of access to the emotion system. [. . .] Filmic cues that can provide emotional information include facial expression, figure movement, dialogue, vocal expression and tone, costume, sound, music, lighting, mise-en-scène, set design, editing, camera (angle, distance, movement), depth of field, character qualities and histories, and narrative situation. Each of these cues can play a part in creating a mood orientation or a stronger emotion.

Films, however, cannot dependably rely on using single emotion cues. There is considerable variation among individual viewers' emotion systems, and single cues might be received by some viewers and missed by others. Films therefore provide a variety of redundant emotive cues, increasing the chance that differing audience members (with their differing preferences of emotional access) will be nudged toward an appropriate emotional orientation.

As a brief and simple example of how film cuing works, let us examine how Alfred Hitchcock coordinated emotion cues in a familiar scene from *Psycho*. When Marion and Norman share a meal in Norman's parlor, redundant cues begin to alert us that something is wrong with this young man and that we should begin to fear for Marion's safety. Dialogue connects Marion (who "eats like a bird") and the birds that Norman stuffed and placed on the wall, suggesting that perhaps Marion might receive the same fate as the birds. The narrative situation places Marion alone in the hotel with Norman, a man whom she only barely knows. Low angles make Norman more menacing, particularly when he is framed with the birds (lit from below to create elongated shadows). His stuttering, given the norm of perfect Hollywood diction, can be seen as a hint of deeper troubles. The close-up of Norman when he bitterly describes a madhouse, along with the orchestral music in a minor key, further alerts us that Norman is a man to be feared. The cues are not so foregrounded that we are certain Norman will do something evil, but they are coordinated enough to signal to the viewer that they should be fearful.

Redundant cues collaborate to indicate to the viewer which emotional mood is called for. The viewer need not focus conscious attention on each of these elements. Some of these cues activate the associative network of the emotions, and this creates a low level of emotion. If a film provides a viewer with several redundant emotive cues, this increases the likelihood of moving the viewer toward a predispositionary mood state.

Once that mood is created, it has a tendency to sustain itself. A mood is not entirely self-perpetuating, however. If we do not find any opportunities to experience these brief emotions, our particular mood will erode and change to another predispositionary state. It requires occasional moments of strong emotion to maintain the mood. A critic should look for these occasional moments of strong cuing that bolster an audience's emotional orientation. [. . .]

The first step for the mood-cue approach is for the critic to pay close attention to the way that emotion cues act together to create mood at the beginning of a film. The approach assumes that the film will use coordinated sets of cues to signal an emotional orientation toward the film as a whole. [. . .]

Coordinated cuing: the emotion marker

Narrative provides a series of diegetic goals and obstacles, and goal achievements and obstacles frequently provide the necessary mood-reinforcing payoffs. We rejoice when the protagonist achieves a goal or subgoal; we are sad, fearful, or anxious when a goal is frustrated. Goals and obstacles are highly foregrounded in the narrative, and so they create highly marked opportunities for moments that are significant both narratively and emotionally.

Almost every narratively significant moment has the potential to provide some emotional payoff, but not every emotional payoff is narratively significant. The classical Hollywood cinema frequently uses what I call "emotion markers," configurations of highly visible textual cues for the primary purpose of eliciting brief moments of emotion. These markers signal to an audience traveling down the goal-oriented path of a narrative, cuing them to engage in a brief emotional moment.

The emotion marker is not there simply to advance or retard the narrative's progress. Neither is the emotion marker an informative device offering more detail about the story or offering authorial commentary on the diegesis. The primary purpose of an emotion marker is to generate a brief burst of emotion. Often such moments could be excised from a film with little or no impact on the achievement of narrative goals or the state of story information.

These markers do fulfill an important emotive function in the text, however. For the viewer engaged in an appropriate mood, they give a reward that helps maintain that predisposition toward expressing emotion. Few texts can rely only on narratively significant moments to provide mood-sustaining emotion. Most have to provide markers to shore up the mood the text has created, even if the markers have little or no effect on the overt diegetic aim: the character's achievement of a goal.

An example will help illustrate this, and I have selected the opening of a film that densely packs obstacles to the steamrolling forward progress of its action-oriented, protagonist-centered narrative: Steven Spielberg's *Raiders of the Lost Ark*. *Raiders* is an exercise in putting one obstacle after another in front of Indiana Jones's (Harrison Ford) attempt to find the Ark of the Covenant and save the world. These retarding moments endanger the hero, allying the audience with him and providing the audience with traditional adventure serial pleasures such as fear and excitement. Yet even a film with as many exciting hairpin escapes as *Raiders* uses emotion markers to provide even more emotional payoffs.

The opening sequence of the film follows Jones through the jungle and into a boody-trapped cave in search of a golden statue. The mood is suspenseful, apprehensive of the imminent attacks of jungle savages or the swift triggering of hidden death traps. The musical score is an unsettling mix of unusual melodic intervals and percussion; the environment is full of deep shadows, and the camera tracks behind Jones. One of Jones's trail guides tries to shoot him from behind, and Jones saves himself with a quick lash of his whip, establishing his character's skill with the weapon. That whip helps Jones and his remaining guide cross over a deep pit, only to have their support slip, almost plunging the guide to his death. This whip-and-pit obstacle must be crossed again on their way out of the cave. These obstacles use multiple emotion cues (musical stingers, facial close-ups, etc.)

to signal emotional expression of fear, both serving important narrative functions (impeding progress toward the goal and providing the setup for future narrative occurrences) and providing emotional payoffs.

Along the way there are moments that are just as emotionally marked without serving such significant goal-oriented narrative function. One of the guides traveling through the thick jungle uncovers a grotesque stone idol and screams, accompanied by the loud flapping of a flock of flushed birds and a musical stinger. Clearly this is a concentrated organization of emotion cues coordinated to prompt a startle reflex in the viewer, yet unlike the previously discussed emotional elicitors, this emotion marker neither hinders nor helps the protagonist's progress toward his goal, nor does it provide new story information. What this moment does do is provide a reliable burst of congruent emotion that helps maintain the sequence's suspenseful mood. This is the primary purpose of the stone idol scare.

It is difficult to argue, given the interconnected nature of narrative, that any moment has absolutely no bearing on goal progress or story information. The stone idol scare may have some minor contribution to the state of story information (letting us know that Jones is near the place where the golden treasure is housed), but clearly the functionality of this narrative incident exceeds its narrative informativeness. The main purpose of the stone idol is to shout "Boo!" at the audience. It is a sort of red herring that marks this moment as fearsome, bolstering the mood's predisposition toward emotion (a necessary function given the structure of the emotion system).

The appearance of tarantulas on Jones's and the guide's backs in the cave is another emotion marker. Here the case is a bit less clear-cut. One could argue that the tarantulas are an obstacle to Jones's progress, but their function as obstacles is minor compared with the emotional effect called for. Jones merely brushes the spiders off, making them an extremely minor obstacle (and the only obstacle that is not reencountered when Jones and the guide race back out of the cave). The tarantuals' primary function is to elicit disgust or fear in the audience, relying on common societal associations with hairy spiders. Their emotional function greatly exceeds their goal-oriented function.

Note that both of these emotion markers are fairly simple and reliable devices. The startle reflex when hearing a loud noise is impossible to suppress, even if one becomes accustomed to hearing artillery fire daily. The disgust reaction at seeing a hairy spider is as widespread and dependable today as it was on my elementary school playground. When choosing emotion markers to buoy the mood, the film-makers relied on some of the more dependable and simple emotional elicitors. Emotion markers in general tend to be uncomplicated and direct.

Also note that these markers need not elicit exactly the same emotions for them to continue the mood. The stone idol may prompt a fearful startle reflex, and the tarantulas may elicit disgust. What is required is that the emotion markers prompt emotions that are congruent with the suspenseful mood. Emotions are not sharply discrete entities; one cannot argue that a cue must elicit either fear or disgust and not both. Disgust is associated with fear, and when one pathway is activated, the other is often triggered as well. Filmmakers need not be concerned that they elicit precisely the same emotion throughout a sequence. Because of emotional interconnections, related emotions serve to maintain the mood. [. . .]

Cues are the smallest unit for analyzing a text's emotional appeals. Emotion cues are the building blocks that are used to create the larger structures such as emotion markers. Mood is sustained by a succession of cues, some of which are organized into larger structures (narrative obstacles, emotion markers), some of which are not. [. . .]

Brief prototypes: mixing genre microscripts

Genres are composed of narrative and iconographic patterns, but they also specify patterns of emotional address, providing the viewer with scripts to use in interpeting a genre film. How does a particular genre structure its use of emotion cues, mood, and emotion markers?

The most significant genre scripts with relation to emotion are not the broad expectations for the overall shape and form of a film, but genre microscripts, intertextual expectation sets for sequences and scenes. We approach a film with an enormous collection of microscripts we have gathered from real-world experience and from encounters with other genre texts, scripts for feuding lovers, showdowns, fight sequences, romantic reconciliations, chases, and stalkings. These microscripts encourage the viewer to anticipate what will happen next narratively, stylistically, and emotionally. Because emotions tend to be brief microlevel phenomena, smaller generic units tend to be more useful guides for the emotion system.

We do not interpret the mood of the *Raiders of the Lost Ark* opening based solely on its emotion cues. Instead we recognize it as a sequence in which we follow a protagonist into hostile territory. The threat of off-screen savages is rooted in experiences with other jungle adventure movies or with westerns and stalker films. Genre signposts of mise-en-scène (dark jungle), cinematography (tracking camera following the protagonist as he walks), and so forth quickly orient us toward the appropriate emotionally prototypical script to use in this particular narrative situation. The schemata for generic sequences contain information about the kinds of emotion cues usually used in such sequences and how those cues are arranged, and these schemata guide us in making hypotheses concerning what emotional events will soon occur. Emotion cues confirm or question our initial choice of a script, modifying or supporting or escalating our mood.

Such genre microscripts are primarily tools to help us recognize which emotional responses are called for. By themselves, such scripts can serve a purely cognitive function: cuing us to identify an appropriate emotion. Recognizing and labeling an emotion are not the same as experiencing it, but consciously labeling an emotion state is an important factor in shaping most emotional experiences because conscious thought is one of the primary inputs into the emotion system outlined in the previous chapter.

By combining such genre microscripts with coordinated patterns of emotion cuing, however, a film can make an emotional appeal to its audience that exceeds the purely cognitive. Coordinated emotion cues associatively encourage the viewer toward a mood, and when we note genre microscripts that are consonant with our mood, we are encouraged to do more than simply recognize these emotion scripts. We are encouraged to feel, to execute these scripts in our own emotion systems.

Again, a text provides only an invitation to feel, not an irresistible prescription. If mishandled, genre microscripts can derail the emotional appeal established by the mood. When used in conjunction with other emotion cuing patterns, however, they can make complicated emotional appeals, as the following case study illustrates.

Sequences do not always use cues that are consonant with traditional genre expectation. A film can leave out cues that we would normally anticipate or use emotion cues that are associated with other genres. In this way filmmakers can play with the emotional possibilities of a genre, sometimes blending components of different genres into a complex emotional mix.

Ivan Reitman's *Ghostbusters* is an example of such a genre blend. *Ghostbusters* is ostensibly a comedy that contains numerous elements from the horror film. Examining sequences from this film illustrates how an individual film makes a unique emotive mix out of our various generic expectations. This short case study is meant to be indicative of how a critic might examine the complex interactions among genre microscripts.

The first scene in *Ghostbusters* is a recognizable one from the horror/stalker genre. A lone woman is being followed from behind by a dollying camera. When the camera follows such characters performing ordinary actions (the kind of actions usually elided in narrative film), we are encouraged to hypothesize that offscreen forces are going to threaten her (otherwise such insignificant action would not be shown).

And yet this particular tracking shot does not fit perfectly into the genre prototype. The woman is clearly middle-aged, not young. The lighting in the library stacks is high key with no menacing shadows (unlike the dark jungle in the opening of *Raiders*). The nondiegetic music is bouncy and playful, although the oboe melody maintains some associations with unsettling music generally heard in such sequences (like the music in *Raiders*'s opening).

In addition, viewers have probably brought some genre expectations for comedy with them to the film. Publicity, promotion, previews, reviews, and the star images of Bill Murray, Dan Ackroyd, and Harold Ramis all signal that an appropriate mood for *Ghostbusters* is a comedic one.

Given this mix of competing genre schemata, it is difficult to decide which mood is called for. Some emotion cues (cinematography, for example) point to a tense mood from a horror film. Some cues (lighting and casting) undermine those expectations, and some cues (music) point simultaneously toward horror and a lighter mood like the comic. The scene ends with some poltergeist activity, the woman running toward the camera while screaming, a quick fade to white, and the loud beginning of the upbeat title music, providing a coordinated burst of cues to signal the end of the scene with little definite information on the emotional state appropriate for this sequence.

This scene is followed by a broadly comic scene in which Peter Venkman (Bill Murray) tries to seduce a young woman during an ESP experiment. Here the cuing is clear: we are expected to laugh. Once we have this clear mood information, the parapsychologists are called to the library stacks we've just seen in the previous sequence to investigate a ghost sighting.

Once again we are shown the stacks, and the difference between this scene and the previous library stack scene is instructive. The film presents us once again with the same mix of emotion cues as before – light oboe music, high-key lighting, camera following characters through the stacks – but a comic mood has been established, and this influences how we read the scene. In addition, Venkman makes regular humorous remarks, further reinforcing the comic mood.

Now that a comic mood is clearly signaled, the text is free to present more strongly marked horror cues than before, knowing that the comic mood strongly predisposes us toward laughter, not fear. Unlike the previous library stack scene, this scene actually shows the ghost (accompanied by a generically expected zither sound). Most importantly, the scene ends with the ladylike ghost suddenly transforming into a death's head that rushes toward the camera. The effect is briefly horrific, inducing a dependable startle reflex, but the predisposition to laugh that has been reinforced many times over the last two scenes reasserts itself. We are cued to laugh over the upbeat music that follows, laughing at ourselves for flinching after someone says "Boo!" [. . .]

PART FOUR

Affect, power and justice

10. Emotions and politics

IN THIS SECTION WE HAVE gathered examples of work that addresses emotion in the context of political action and communication. As Goodwin, Jasper and Polletta remark in their introduction to a recent collection entitled *Passionate Politics* (2001), emotions were once at the centre of the study of politics, but only in so far as their 'irrational' character might explain the behaviour of those who engaged in political action outside formal political institutions. Emotions were invoked in connection with the transforming influence of the 'mob' or 'crowd' on individuals otherwise presumed rational, or to account for the type of personality that might be susceptible to 'brainwashing' or recruitment into subversive political activism. A more sympathetic stance towards protest movements, evident among many academic political analysts from the 1970s, only meant that they turned away from the study of emotions in politics altogether, to produce accounts based on structural, rationalistic and organizational models. Even the recent cultural turn 'has taken a cognitive form, as though political participants were computers mechanically processing symbols' (Goodwin *et al.* 2001: 1). The collection edited by Goodwin and colleagues testifies to an emerging trend in the opposite direction. One of the effects of the engagement with questions of emotion on the part of social scientists more generally has been to highlight that emotions cannot simply be regarded as the opposite of rationality – the construction of emotion as the opposite of reason, as Lutz (1986) among other anthropologists has argued, is culturally specific and itself ideologically laden. Once emotions are acknowledged as not only compatible with, but as an active ingredient of rational action, they also become recognizable as a central factor in political analysis, and no longer as a residual one. Goodwin and colleagues highlight that emotions have been, in fact, implicit in many of the key concepts employed by scholars to theorize social movements, such as the concepts of *frame* and *framing* (including motivational framing), that of *social networks* (which consist of affective bonds as well as shared ideologies and beliefs) and of *collective identity* (likewise, consisting of affective bonds as much as of ascribed characteristics such as sexual preference, nationality, race, class, or gender).

The first extract in this section is by Barry Richards, and addresses a broad change in the forms of political communication in recent years, towards what he calls an 'emotionalization' of politics. This emotionalization, Richards argues, stems partly from the increasing influence of popular culture on the sphere of politics (among others), and from the tendency for people to relate to politics in the 'mode of consumption'. If the domain of popular culture has always, to some extent, been associated with passion and with and emotional release, the contemporary emotionalization of politics is characterized by reflexivity as much as by emotional expression. This concern with the need to acknowledge and reflect upon often complex feelings distinguishes contemporary 'emotionalization' from carnivalesque catharsis, on the one hand. On the other, this concern with reflecting upon feelings also disinguishes contemporary 'emotionalization' from the traditional ways in which politicians have invoked emotions to influence public opinion in the context of political appeals. Elsewhere in the article, Richards examines how this insight may be applied in the empirical study of political communications, proposing that political ads and campaigns may be studied, as have commercial ads, as forms of emotional communication. He argues that, although emotions and their management are ubiquitous in the conduct of politics, this is rarely an explicit item in the discourse of politicians. Political communication could be developed to better convey the complexity and ambivalence of the emotional labor involved in the conduct of politics, in the interest of facilitating 'supportive and creative relationships' that are crucial to a 'vigorous and enabling democratic ethos'.

In the second extract, Anne-Marie Fortier examines the role of emotions in the press media response to the publication of the Parekh Report on 'The Future of Multi-Ethnic Britain' (2000). The Report recommended that Britain should rethink its 'national story' and identity in light of the historical legacies of imperialism, and triggered a controversy played out through the emotional categories of pride and shame. Instead of focusing on questions of history and reckoning with the past, the debate effectively became a tug-of-war for the claim to legitimate patriotism. Fortier examines how, in the context of this controversy, shame was 'evoked, rejected and projected on to particular subjects' deemed 'unpatriotic' and thereby construed as targets of legitimate anger. This refusal and externalization of shame, she argues, facilitates a 'sanitized' attachment to the nation through the maintenance of a guilt-free national story. At the same time, however, it precludes the possibility of regarding 'dissent' from such a story as an act of national attachment and thus produces new forms of exclusion from the national collective. The notion of a 'happy' (sanitized) multiculturalism thus relies on deflecting the anger that may be justifiably experienced and expressed by dissident subjects towards the nation (or collective self), by making these the object of legitimate anger on account of their alleged lack of patriotism. At the same time, it relies on deflecting accusations of *historical* racism and collective shame by attributing racism to individual extremists. In this way, paradoxically, the (dissident) subjects who *are ashamed* are positioned alongside the (racist) subjects who *are the source of 'our' shame*, outside the national community.

In the second part of the article, not included here, Fortier goes on to examine how membership of the multicultural collective for individuals from ethnic minorities is conditional on their declarations of pride, whereas membership is taken for granted for those (white Britons) assumed to be racially neutral. It is only through such declarations that the ethnic minority subject achieves 'unmarked' status. Yet the multicultural collective relies on the embodied 'otherness' of ethnic minority subjects, which 'must stay in place as "other" in order to claim the *multi* of multiculturalism'. The very recognition of 'others' as legitimate speaking subjects, in other words, 'reconstitutes them as "other" through a double process of de-racialization and re-racialization'.

The third extract in this section examines hope as a 'technology of governance', namely a collective sensibility that can be steered in various directions by governing agencies. Authors Shearing and Kempa focus on the example of Robben Island Museum – a former prison to the political opponents of apartheid, situated on a small island off the coast at Cape Town – as a device for celebrating and promoting public hope for a new South Africa. Based on interview and ethnographic data gathered between 1998 and 1999, the analysis examines the Museum's educational aim to offer an 'authentic and relatively unmediated experience' of the hopeful mindset experienced by the political prisoners, which is regarded as essential to their eventual success in overturning the apartheid regime. The methods employed by the management team and by tour guides – for example, the refusal to exclusively use professionally trained guides, or to provide them with scripts – reflect the emphasis placed on facilitating personal engagement, as distinct from trasmitting a uniform message. The authors propose an interesting contrast between Robben Island Museum and the Museum of Tolerance that commemorates the Holocaust in Los Angeles. Their informants, who themselves invoked the contrast, likened the Museum of Tolerance to an 'emotions factory' where visitors are manipulated into experiencing particular feelings. The experience of visitors to Robben Island, by contrast, is constructed to suggest the possibility of personal reinvention, through which the collective reinvention of South Africans is imagined as possible.

In the fourth extract, Deborah Gould examines the role of emotional ambivalence in shaping lesbian and gay responses to the AIDS crisis in the US, and the emergence of militant AIDS activism. Her study refers to Reddy's concept of 'emotives' (see Reddy in section 2, above) and offers an empirical illustration of how emotional experience itself, as residually but significantly distinct from emotional discourse, provides a 'reservoir of possibilities for change'. In this case, lesbian and gay ambivalence – oscillating between pride and shame, feelings of attraction and rejection *vis-à-vis* mainstream society – mediated the possibility of a range of responses to the crisis, each of which can be read as a 'resolution' to the ambivalence itself. Gould traces the transition from an emphasis on self-sufficiency and volunteerism, associated with feelings of defiant pride, towards forms of militant activism that mobilized feelings of indignation, anger, and grief for the purposes of a more confrontational politics. At a theoretical level, the study offers a significant contribution to the study of social movements, contradicting the dominant model in this field according to which the emergence of social movements is linked to moments of expanded political opportunity. Militant AIDS activism, she argues, emerged with the tightening of political opportunities, fuelled by the emotional impact of that very tightening. Similarly, she proposes that attention to emotions enhances understanding of how different ways of interpreting or 'framing' a problem may or may not resonate with individuals, and thereby succeed (or not) in motivating them for action.

References

Goodwin, J., Jasper, J. M. and Polletta, F. (2001) 'Introduction: why emotions matter', in J. Goodwin, J. M. Jasper and F. Polletta (eds) *Passionate Politics: emotions and social movements*. Chicago and London: University of Chicago Press.
Lutz, C. (1986) 'Emotion, thought, and estrangement: emotion as a cultural category', *Cultural Anthropology*, 1 (3): 287–309.

Chapter 42

Barry Richards

THE EMOTIONAL DEFICIT IN POLITICAL COMMUNICATION

ONE CONTRIBUTION THAT SOCIOLOGY CAN make to the study of political communication is to identify broad social and cultural changes which are influencing the democratic process and so are likely to have effects on political communication. This impact may be indirect, via changes in the societal context within which communications take place, or more direct, by affecting the aims or content of communications. [. . .]

Drawing upon the sociology of emotion, this article will argue that a cultural trend that may be called "emotionalization" has already transformed the context for political communications, and that the style of many of these communications needs to be adapted to this new context, with implications for their aims and content.

In summary, the argument is as follows. First, as a consequence of social changes which—as a key feature of the "postmodern"—have weakened the boundaries between different spheres of life, politics is now interwoven with popular culture. By this, I mean that modes of engagement and judgment which characterize our experience of popular culture are now increasingly applied to our experience of politics, though our awareness of this development and of its implications for political communication is as yet limited.

Second, since popular culture is substantially about feeling, about the expression and management of emotion (Richards, 1994; Elias & Dunning, 1986), the incursion into political experience of the values of popular culture means that we now seek certain kinds of emotionalized experience from politics that we have not done in the past. This can have one of two consequences. Either politics, and particularly the communication of politics to the public, begins to offer more of these experiences in tune with the concerns of popular culture, or it becomes increasingly alien to the preoccupations of the majority of the public, and the democratic deficit grows.

The democratic deficit has been the object of much commentary and analysis in recent years. Here it is understood as a growing disinterest in or distaste for politics, and is seen to be in part a function of an emotional deficit in political communications—that is, the failure of these communications to satisfy the contemporary taste for certain kinds of affective experience. The revitalization of democracy therefore requires that the everyday business of political debate at all levels, and of presenting politics to the public, acquires something of the emotionally compelling narratives offered by, for example, television soap operas.

To the objection that democracy should be a rational contest, and that emotionality is antithetical to a balanced and mature political process, there is a simple rejoinder (though following it through in practice may be very complex). This is that much contemporary psychology, and much common sense, recognizes that far from being an oppositional dichotomy, the relationship between feeling and reason is one of deep interconnection and complementarity. To invite emotional engagement is to facilitate rational discourse, not to banish it.

Sociologically, this argument posed so far in terms of *popular* culture can be put in another way, which is that we inhabit a *consumer* culture in which there is a cultivated prominence of feeling (Campbell, 1987; Featherstone, 1991). Forms of social participation which do not embrace and build on this key feature of contemporary experience will decline. Marketing—especially advertising—has developed in part as an expertise in addressing the emotionality of the consumer, often via highly aestheticized imagery, with the aim of giving goods and services the power to generate strong and attractive emotional resonance in the public mind. "Political marketing," if it is to achieve its ambitions, will need to do the same with politics, both generically for the whole domain of politics and for the particular "brands" available within it. [. . .]

Politics, popular culture, and emotion

Much recent controversy about political communication has tended to focus around the nature and consequences of promotional techniques in contemporary politics (e.g., Wernick, 1991; Franklin, 1994; Scammell, 1995; Ansolabehere & Iyengar, 1997; Jones, 1999). The high profile critiques of spin, media manipulation, and presentational packaging take us directly to questions about the fundamental nature of politics in the present day. As Street (1997) has pointed out, they require us to ask about the relationship between culture and politics. How is politics influenced by culture? It may be suggested that politics has been influenced by a culture of marketing. In a sense that is true, but this is too narrow a way of putting it. It is not a case of one specific cultural influence—marketing or promotionalism—impacting from "outside" on politics as a particular sphere which, in theory at least, could resist this influence.

Instead, as Ryfe (2001) and Schudson (2001) remind us, politics *is* culture. It is therefore a case of broad cultural changes unfolding partly *within* politics, as in many other spheres of life. [. . .]

The broad cultural changes which are transforming politics can be described and analyzed in various ways. The specific feature to be taken here as a starting point—because it is assumed to be a fundamental one—is, crudely put, the increasing influence in politics (though it affects other spheres also) of popular culture (Street, 2001; Dorner, 2003). There are complex drivers of this trend, which I cannot go into here: the proliferation of mass media; the vigor and creativity of popular culture in areas such as music, sport, humor, and other forms of entertainment; and perhaps most basically a deep historical trend toward the democratization of life.

Commonplace illustrations of this influence as it affects politics abound. Political broadcasts, rallies, sometimes whole campaigns take theme tunes from pop music. . . . The more televisual the political process has become, the more "we 'read' our politicians through their gestures and their faces, in the same way that we read performers on television" (Street, 2001, p. 5). . . . Overall, the democratic process is now played out on a stage where—alongside traditional resources from ideology, ritual, and the values of older civic cultures—there are scripts, actors, and props which could be seen as "borrowed" from popular culture (though in fact they soon become part of the political fabric itself). . . .

From the point of view of individual politicians or parties, this process brings tensions and possibilities for failure. The song may not be right for some target audiences, or the stylistic gesture may backfire (as in the derision which greeted the public appearance of then Conservative Party leader William Hague in a baseball cap). Indeed, it might be argued, drawing on these negative examples, that popular culture cannot really be infusing politics as suggested, because if it were then politics would be much more popular than it is. The problem we face is, after all, the unpopularity of electoral politics.

This, however, takes us to the main point: The unpopularity of politics can be attributed in part to the failure of political actors (from national leaders and their advisors to local activists), and of the professional communicators they work with, to respond and adapt sufficiently to the ways in which popular culture has now transformed society. While the experience of citizens has been transformed, the modes of political address to them have not always matched these transformations. Despite all of the hype about spin and about politicians' enslavement to the media, and despite the undoubted energy with which control of media agendas has been pursued, political communications often remain unattuned to some key dimensions of this new cultural reality. In particular, there is an *emotional deficit* in contemporary political communications, a lack of crafted, sustained attention to the emotional needs of the audience. There is at best only an implicit and patchy recognition that popular culture is an emotionalized culture dense with desires and anxieties.

The popular has always to some extent been a domain of passion, and of emotional release. There are, however, particular qualities to the present pre-occupation with feeling. It is not a carnivalesque festival of pure expression or catharsis. It is more reflective, and is as much concerned with the management of feelings as with their expression. It is therefore better described as a "therapeutic" rather than "emotionalized" culture, since in its most positive and developed forms it is characterized by reflexivity as well as by expressivity, by the conjoining of emotion with thought (Richards & Brown, 2002). This is what differentiates it from earlier types of public emotionality. In some respects, the rise of popular culture has involved a simple or quantitative emotionalization of everyday life, as may be observed in, for example, aspects of the uninhibited mourning seen after the death of Princess Diana. But typically this emotionalization is qualitatively different from earlier forms, and is characterized by particular concerns with acknowledging and reflecting upon feelings, both in private and in public (e.g., Walker et al., 1995).

The distinctive nature of this development can be highlighted if we consider it in terms of Elias's theory of the "civilizing process" (e.g., Wouters, 1986). Therapeutic culture is not a remissive reversal of the increasing restraint placed upon us by the civilizing trend, but on the contrary a further stage of the internalization of restraint through the capacities for self-monitoring and self-management which it promotes. The expressive, disinhibitory aspects which are required for this—and which may sometimes appear, at least on the surface, to be the major component of the trend—are best thought of as a "controlled de-controlling," a psychic loosening necessary in order to build firmer structures overall. [. . .]

Despite . . . the profusion of commentary on these trends, the coming of the therapeutic is not much acknowledged in political discourse. One implicit patch of recognition is in the rise of political marketing. As noted earlier, the development of popular culture is inseparable from the development of consumer culture, and contemporary emotionalization is both cause and effect of marketing communications. Despite the influence of some rationalistic models in marketing, most marketers have always known their audience to be emotional, in the sense of being influenced by paralinguistic cues and nonrational message content.

It is important to note that this is a matter of human nature, not necessarily of human weakness. Paying deliberate and systematic attention to factors such as the dress, demeanor, and general personality image of political figures is a much-derided practice. It may indeed not be a most edifying contribution to political culture, but it is a recognition of the importance now of the impression that politicians as persons make on citizens as persons. Policy alternatives come with persons attached to them, and the public are quite legitimately interested in the emotional qualities of these persons. At root here is an old question, that of trust: Can this person be trusted? We now ask this question in ways informed by psychological understandings, and we seek answers that tell us about the person as an emotional being. In a promotional culture, there will inevitably be some overlap or convergence of political campaigning with emotionally oriented marketing techniques in the effort to win trust in individual politicians, and this should not be summarily dismissed as superficial or cynical manipulation. [. . .]

Political communications as emotional labor

Of course, it has long been recognized that voters choose leaders on the basis partly of their personalities, though the older term "character" would for some be a more acceptable way of stating this. We know that we are presented with choices between candidates as objects of trust as well as between parties with different policies, and trustworthiness is a question of individual character. However, this factor of trust is now becoming increasingly personalized, as alternative bases of trust in party traditions (whether based in economic interest, ideology, or vague sentiment) become ever weaker.

We now need more than the capacity to trust politicians' role, since we can rely less on cultural and institutional role structures (whether patrician, technocratic, democratic, or whatever). So political leaders have, to an increasing extent, the task of presenting themselves as *persons* to be trusted for their intrinsic qualities.

This does not mean that we are at the end of ideology, but that we are amidst a cultural transformation in which ideology and politics in the traditional sense are becoming more enmeshed with the personal, with psychological considerations and emotionality. Emotional qualities are increasingly registered and scrutinized, and judgment of them is part of the political process. Those involved in communicating with the public must do so in ways cognizant of the new emotionality.

Traditional political considerations are not now occluded, nor is public life being asymmetrically invaded by the private and personal. The public is not necessarily degraded, nor any less capable of participating in a humane and inclusive civic culture. But traditional separations between domains are no longer viable. There is a compression together in the same social and psychic spaces of the personal, feeling subject and the public figure. The personality of the politician is bound up with the policies she or he represents, and voting is a complex choice between packages of pragmatic, ideological, and emotional values.

One aspect of this development is that politicians now have a clear and major piece of "emotional labor" (to use the term introduced by Hochschild, 1983; see also, e.g., Smith, 1992) to perform. They must present themselves as individual persons of a particular emotional makeup, who (to use terminology developed earlier in the study of group dynamics, as in, e.g., Parsons & Bales, 1955) can offer themselves as social-emotional, expressive leaders as well as task-oriented leaders. More is demanded of leaders than previously. They must now be seen as attuned to newly dominant values of expressivity and spontaneity. But our contemporary cultural concerns are not just with the expression of emotions but also with the *management* of emotions. So politicians must also be seen to offer some containment of the emotions of their public. Like other social institutions and cultural forms, politics is drawn into the circulation of feelings and has to contribute to the emotional labor of containing the feelings circulating in the public domain.

In one sense, this has always been the case; the historical shift is complex, and leadership has always been an exercise in feeling management, as has sometimes been apparent (one thinks, for example, of Churchill in the U.K. and Eisenhower in the U.S.). Now, however, there is pressure to offer such leadership very deliberately. Much effort is expended in presentation to achieve this, to encompass within it all aspects of the leader's life and self, and to ensure that these in turn encompass the relevant therapeutic agendas in personal philosophy and policy values. Moreover, there is a fundamental new quality to the emotional role of political leaders. This lies in the much greater potential for awareness of the emotional dimensions of everyday life, and in the increased self-questioning and self-examination characteristic of our therapeutic times. Acknowledgment of error and vulnerability, and honesty about failure and disappointment, for example, are now more widely recognized as important in the conduct of everyday life, but are still remarkably rare in the discourse of politicians.

With this awareness comes greater scope for choice, and for the deliberate management of feelings in certain ways to achieve certain outcomes. Politicians are managers, not only in the technocratic sense of their management of the national economy but also in the sense that they (among other public figures) are charged with the management of massive national reserves of feeling.

To recognize this, and to speak of the possibility that this emotional management might be conducted artfully, is not to invoke a nightmare of social engineering. As in small face-to-face groups, and as in organizations, so it is at the level of national culture: The effective management of emotional dynamics can lead to the development of supportive and creative relationships, and to a vigorous and enabling democratic ethos. The argument is not for a rush into "personality politics," but for the enrichment of politics with communication practices that carry emotional narratives.

One thing that was new about "New" Labour (Richards, 2000) was the attention paid to the emotional tasks of political leadership, to intuiting the anxieties of the public and seeking to respond to them. Some of the emotional attentiveness comes from Tony Blair's own self. He is the first U.K. leader with a social self formed during the 1960s, and so has styles of thought and speech that are attuned to the reflexive and emotionalized modes of today. And some of this attentiveness comes from the much-criticized practices of communication and image management. Evaluations of these differ, from left and right condemnations of the cynicism of spin to other, more complex and potentially favorable assessments. But beneath these arguments we can see wide acceptance that the political scene is more about emotions and their management than it used to be, and that politicians and their advisors are intensely involved in certain kinds of emotional labor, particularly the mass-mediated management of public feeling. This labor at its best fosters a creative approach to political communication, one that inverts the 1960s slogan that "the personal is political" and redefines politics as interwoven with the domains of the personal and wired into the emotional circuitry of popular culture.

References

Ansolabehere, S., & Iyengar, S. (1997). *Going negative: How political advertisements shrink and polarize the electorate*. New York: Free Press.

Campbell, C. (1987). *The romantic ethic and the spirit of modern consumerism*. Oxford: Blackwell.

Dorner, W. (2003). Political identities in the US and Germany. *Media Tenor, 3*, 74–77.

Elias, N., & Dunning, E. (1986). *Quest for excitement: Sport and leisure in the civilising process*. Oxford, England: Blackwell.

Featherstone, M. (1991). *Consumer culture and postmodernism*. London: Sage.

Franklin, B. (1994). *Packaging politics: Political communications in Britain's media democracy*. London: Edward Arnold.

Hochschild, A. (1983). *The managed heart: The commercialisation of human feeling*. Berkeley: University of California Press.

Jones, N. (1999). *Sultans of spin*. London: Victor Gollancz.

Parsons, T., & Bales, R. (Eds.). (1955). *Family, socialization and interaction process*. New York: Free Press.

Richards, B. (1994). *Disciplines of delight: The psychoanalysis of popular culture*. London: Free Association Books.

Richards, B., & Brown, J. (2002). The therapeutic culture hypothesis: A critical discussion. In T. Johansson & O. Sernhede (Eds.), *Lifestyle, desire and politics: Contemporary Iidentities* (pp. 97–114). Gothenburg: Daidalos.

Richards, B. (2000). The real meaning of spin. *Soundings, 14*, 161–170.

Ryfe, D. M. (2001). History and political communication: An introduction. *Political Communication, 18*, 407–417.

Scammell, M. (1995). *Designer politics: How elections are won*. Basingstoke: Macmillan.

Schudson, M. (2001). Politics as cultural practice. *Political Communication, 18*, 421–431.

Smith, P. (1992). *The emotional labour of nursing*. Basingstoke: Macmillan.

Street, J. (1997). *Politics and popular culture*. Cambridge, England: Polity.

Street, J. (2001). *Mass media, politics and democracy*. Basingstoke: Palgrave.

Walker, T., Littlewood, J., & Pickering, M. (1995). Death in the news: The public invigilation of private emotion. *Sociology, 29*, 579–596.

Wernick, A. (1991). *Promotional culture: Advertising, ideology and symbolic expression*. London: Sage.

Wouters, C. (1986). Formalisation and informalisation: Changing tension balances in civilising processes. *Theory, Culture and Society, 3*, 1–18.

Chapter 43

Anne-Marie Fortier

PRIDE POLITICS AND MULTICULTURALIST CITIZENSHIP

[. . .]

A NEO-ETHNIC VERSION OF NATIONAL identity has emerged in Britain: one based as a common hybridity. Gerd Baumann's remark about the US can be paraphrased here: 'It is the multiethnic hybridity of many [British] citizens that is used to argue for a shared neoethnic endorsement of national unity. If everyone's ancestry were "mixed", then everyone's present identity would be the same: superethnically [British].' (1999, p. 34) Still primarily ethnicized, the new nation is now re-imagined as the result of a timeless mixing of cultures, in a typical melting-pot assimilationist stew where differences are dissolved and assimilated into a palatable diversity (see Hage 1998). Following Sara Ahmed's lead (2000, p. 97), this article is framed by a wider interest in what happens to the definition of 'national culture' when 'minority cultures' are not only let in, but redefined as *integral* to the nation itself? With respect to my immediate concerns here, a corollary question is: *who* are the legitimate multicultural subjects entitled to belong to the national community and to speak in its name? [. . .]

A key aim of this article is to consider the role of emotions in policing the terms of belonging and entitlement to citizenry. I consider emotions as they are taken up and circulated in the press, that is, I discuss the effects of displays of emotions on the kind of national community, and national subject, that is being imagined. What I am interested in here is the way in which the resort to the emotional register of shame interpellates people in a particular way. By tracing how shame is evoked, rejected and projected on to particular subjects, I trace how shame is linked to the process of identity formation not only of 'self', but also of 'other', *within* the national collective. [. . .]

The politics of pride and shame

The Parekh Report was the result of the work of 'the Commission on the Future of Multi-Ethnic Britain', established in January 1998 by the Runnymede Trust, an independent think-tank devoted to promoting racial justice. 'The Commission's remit was to analyse the current state of multi-ethnic Britain and to propose ways of countering racial discrimination and disadvantage' (Runnymede Trust 2000, p. viii). The report's main intervention was in areas of social policy, offering extensive recommendations for policy developments in a range of areas, from policing through to education, the arts and immigration, to name a few. This was, then, an extensive and comprehensive document. Yet the response to the report ignored all matters of social policy and rather focused on 'the report's questioning of the exclusionary implications of the category "British".' (Neal 2003, p. 60). Thus, when the 373-page report was released in October 2000, one short passage was the focus of much media attention:

> Britishness, as much as Englishness, has systematic, largely unspoken, racial connotations. Whiteness nowhere features as an explicit condition of being British, but it is widely understood that Englishness, and there-fore by extension Britishness, is racially coded . . . Unless these deep-rooted antagonisms to racial and cultural difference can be defeated in practice, as well as symbolically written out of the national story, the idea of a multicultural post-nation remains an empty promise.
> (Runnymede Trust 2000, pp. 38–9)

Because of its association with white supremacy, white privilege, imperialism, and its historical position at the centre of British political and cultural life, the Parekh Report rejects Englishness as an appropriate label for the re-imagined multi-ethnic nation. In turn, it reluctantly takes on Britishness as the best available term to designate the common terrain of belonging that 'communities' share. 'Britishness is not ideal', the report states, 'but at least it appears acceptable, particularly when suitably qualified – black British, Indian British, British Muslim, and so on.' (Runnymede Trust 2000, p. 38)

[. . .] The Parekh Report was calling for an acknowledgement of the historical legacies of imperialism in the constitution of a racially connoted idea of Britishness, as well as in shaping present conditions of racism within broader social relations and social inequalities. Implicit in this proposal, was the acknowledgement that we are not only subjects of history, but also agents of history – revisiting the past might allow for the creation of different futures. But critiques were quick to seize this and see it as an 'assault on national pride', a 'promot[ion of] national guilt', a 'brain-washing exercise designed to destroy our sense of nationhood', an 'attempt to destroy our centuries-old culture', and 'to rewrite our history'. In response, they endeavoured to recover the glories of British history, and its numerous achieve-ments. Boadicea, the Magna Carta, the abolitionist movement, Waterloo, VE Day: these events were indiscriminately listed and hailed as evidence of the enduring British values of fairness, resilience, tolerance, democracy and decency. [. . .]

The Parekh Report's call to revise the national story, as well as the outcry this has triggered, were *both* wedded to the project of asserting a 'new' Britain, but with different ways of relating to the 'old' one. What is the role of the 'new' as a way of writing history? What is it that people are trying to recover, forget, or erase? What is at stake in refusing to acknowledge the terrors of the past? Clues may be found in pride politics that dominated the controversy. Indeed, the public outcry against the report evacuated questions of history and reckoning with the past, and rather centred on the search for, and prosecution of, those who might be held accountable for what was perceived as a generalized loss of pride and patriotism among Britons. The report was thus seen as part of a wider problem. The question of pride and patriotism dominated much of the debate, which was marked by mutual blaming and shaming in a tug-of-war over who held the highest patriotic moral ground.

At one end, conservative rightists accused Lord Parekh and the commissioners of the report, along with the Labour government, the 'chattering classes' and the 'Islingtonian intelligentsia', for being 'ashamed of our history and feel the need to apologise.' At the other end, Jack Straw, then Home Secretary, reacted by distancing himself and the government from the Parekh Report in the face of criticism that he and his Labour colleagues were unpatriotically ashamed of being British. 'I am proud to be English and proud to be British', he declared. 'I am proud of what I believe to be the best of British values'. And he added that 'Unlike the Runnymede Trust, I firmly believe that there is a future for Britain and a future for Britishness.' He then joined the collective admonition of blame by pointing the accusative finger for lack of patriotism to the political left: 'Given the Left's tendency to wash their hands of the notion of nationhood', he wrote in *The Observer*, 'it's unsurprising our perception of Britishness became a conservative one.'

Pride in Britishness became a resonating mantra that rang through the arguments against the recommendations of the Parekh Report that Britain should rethink its 'national story' and identity. Letters and articles succeeded each other in claiming love and pride in Britain, and disclaiming any shame or guilt whatsoever. 'I am a Sri Lankan Tamil who came here thirty years ago. I show my British passport with pride, not shame'; 'In Sydney it felt great being British, and that should never be taken away . . . to compete for your country is about taking pride in where you come from'; 'I'm proud to be British and call myself British. If you're not proud to be British then you're living in the wrong place'; 'I am proud to be British. I have done well by being in Britain. We are still the country that everybody respects'; 'I am proud of being British. I have no guilt about it.'

Running through these exhortations of pride is one refrain: the repelling of shame and of national guilt. The politics of pride deployed in response to the Parekh Report seek to *eradicate shame*: pride in 'our' history, in 'our' country, in 'our' passports, is repeatedly rehearsed by way of *sanitising the attachment to the nation under a veneer of guiltless pride*, one which knows no shame or guilt. Thus both shame and guilt are closely linked, and the attacks on Lord Parekh and his co-commissioners treat shame and guilt equally: as repulsive, unwanted and illegitimate affects to be eradicated from the collective body. Some theorists, such as Axel Honneth (1992) or Elspeth Probyn (2000, following Silvan Tomkins) have discussed how the repelling of shame is about self-affirmation whereby the once shamed subject/body is now declaring its self-pride – for example, in Lesbian/

Gay/Bisexual/Transgender Pride, or the Fat Pride movement (Probyn 2000, pp. 125–43). But here, in contrast, the refusal of shame is also a *refusal* to make it 'ours' in the first place, a refusal to interiorize it in the national body, a refusal to consider that shame might be a feature of the attachment to the nation. Shame is not evoked as something 'we' no longer want to feel; it is rejected as something 'we' have not – and should not have – internalized in the first place. Shame, here, is exteriorized, rejected, pushed out, and projected on to those who are guilty of unpatriotic feelings or acts. Shame is replaced by anger expressed against 'them' who are seen as being ashamed of 'us'-the-nation, and against 'them' who shame 'us'-the-nation. Invested in the process of eradicating shame from the collective body is, paradoxically, a process of splitting the national collective, between patriots and unpatriotic culprits.

First, the 'unpatriotic' liberal and leftist who questions the national story and the notion of a historically fair, just and inclusive Britain. [. . .]

By turning dissent into a shameful act, the very possibility of thinking of dissent not only as a democratic act, but as an act of national attachment, is undermined. The issue at stake in dismissing dissent as an unpatriotic act is the preservation of the stories of a national identity; dissent, here, should not be tied to ideas that shake the national story.

In addition, the scorn against the unpatriotic dissident is also about the maintenance of a guilt-free national story. As stated earlier, the Parekh Report's recommendation to rewrite the national story of Britain as an imperial force was rejected by critics as 'promot[ing] national guilt'. Reckoning with the history of racism – that is, reckoning with Britain as *historically* racist – could potentially clear a space for the expression of anger by many of Britain's citizens. What is threatening to the white subject, as Gunaratnam and Lewis (2001) suggest, is the black subject's anger. The shame of white people's history of racism is averted through anger against those subjects, white or black, whose own anger is threatening to effect 'white guilt' (Gunaratnam and Lewis 2001, p. 143). Thus, we could begin to make sense of the predominance of black faces that were seen to declare their pride in Britishness in October 2000: the refusal of shame is also about silencing their anger. . . .

To be sure, the positions alluded to above (the angry black subject and the shamed white subject) are not complete or static. But in the press debates around the Parekh Report, the rejection of shame was inextricably related to the rejection of perceived accusations of racism. A sanitized 'happy' multiculturalism requires the eradication of unwanted unhappy subjects, including those whose anger might be justified but which can be managed and re-directed away from the nation (the collective self) and on to individualized selves. Thus, a second unpatriotic culprit hovered in the background of the pride/shame debate: the intolerant racist thug, emblematically represented by the flag waving white BNP activist's 'ugly face of patriotism'. This figure, however, was more often explicitly evoked by politicians themselves, rather than journalists or other commentators. In the midst of the 'patriotism tug-of-war' mentioned above, Jack Straw felt compelled to urge the British left 'not [to] leave patriotism to [the] far right', and to 'reclaim national pride from racists and xenophobic football thugs'. So, the pride/shame debate was in part a struggle between politicians and activists over who lays claims to 'real patriotism' and, crucially, to the right to 'author' the nation; a struggle between politicians and activists. But the same threatening figure was evoked when commentators repeatedly rejected the Parekh Report's statement about the racial connotations of Britishness. Though racism was recognized by some as part of British life and institutions, the general outcry was against the assumption that *individual* Britons are racists. Being British is NOT being racist, we were insistently told, *because* 'we' are tolerant: 'we' have black friends and have welcomed and absorbed migrants and their cultures for centuries.

As Robin Wiegman has noted, the well-intentioned liberalist turn towards tolerance, inclusion and diversity is characterized by a disaffiliation from the more overt forms of racism and racial violence (in Chow 2002, p. 13), associated here with the white working-class BNP activist or football hooligan. The darker side of history is evacuated by ascribing the origins and sources of racism and intolerance to individual acts, singular bodies, or within specific localities and sub-cultures. The shameful subject, the bad citizens, the racists, are held solely accountable for hate crimes. Exhortations of pride project shame on to outcast subjects who are a source of revulsion for the 'decent majority'. They, the racists, are the source of 'our' shame: the meanings of shame are seen to *originate* from, and *reside* in, the actions of these subjects (Butler 1997). Conversely, the confinement of shame and guilt on to individual bodies allows for the nation and its 'decent majority' to emerge as naturally tolerant and inclusive. Wider questions of collective accountability and self-examination are concealed, indeed evacuated in the creation of injurious subjects (Butler 1997). [. . .]

References

AHMED, SARA 2000 *Strange Encounters. Embodied Others in Postcoloniality*, London, Routledge

BAUMANN, GERD 1999 *The Multicultural Riddle*, London: Routledge

BUTLER, JUDITH 1997 *Excitable Speech. A Politics of the Performative*, London: Routledge

CHOW, REY 2002 *The Protestant Ethnic and the Spirit of Capitalism*, New York: Columbia University Press

GUNARATMAN, YASMIN and LEWIS, GAIL 2001 'Racialising emotional labour and emotionalising racialised labour: anger, fear and shame in social welfare', *Journal of Social Work Practice*, vol. 15, no. 2, pp. 131–48

HAGE, GASSAN 1998 *White Nation. Fantasies of White Supremacy in a Multicultural Society*, Annandale (Aus.) and West Whikham (UK): Pluto and Comerford & Miller

HONNETH, AXEL 1992 'Integrity and disrespect. Principles of a conception of morality based on the theory of recognition', *Political Theory*, vol. 20, no. 2, pp. 187–201

NEAL, SARAH 2003 'The Scarman Report, the Macpherson Report and the Media: how newspapers respond to race-centred social policy interventions', *Journal of Social Policy*, vol. 32, no. 1, pp. 55–74

PROBYN, ELSPETH 2000 *Carnal Appetites. FoodSexIdentities*, London: Routledge

RUNNYMEDE TRUST 2000 *The Future of Multi-ethnic Britain. The Parekh Report*, London: Profile Books

TOMKINS, SILVAN 1995 'Shame-humiliation and contempt-disgust', in E. Kosofsky and A. Frank (eds), *Shame and its Sisters*, Durham, NC: Duke University Press, pp. 133–78

Chapter 44

Clifford Shearing and Michael Kempa

A MUSEUM OF HOPE: A STORY OF ROBBEN ISLAND

[. . .]

A SIZABLE AMOUNT OF LITERATURE HAS been published about the cultivation of collective sensibilities. The authors of these works have widely acknowledged that liberal modes of governance that attempt to govern through the freedom of subjects are dependent upon constituting political actors who are capable of exercising such freedom responsibly (Garland 2001; O'Malley 1992; O'Malley and Palmer 1996; Rose 1996; Rose and Miller 1992). Thus, liberal governments are constantly engaged in constituting sensibilities in their citizens that will enable them to govern with efficiency and a light touch—although Barry Hindess (2001) reminds us that this light touch can quickly become a heavy fist when governments are faced with those actors who have failed to assimilate the requisite sensibilities. As scholars drawing upon the work of Michel Foucault have detailed so well, the cultivation of sensibilities for responsible liberal citizenship is often achieved through governmental mechanisms such as systems of surveillance, sanctions, and rewards that shape the mind through shaping conduct and that, conversely, shape conduct through shaping consciousness (e.g., Burchell, Gordon, and Miller 1991; Dean 1999; Foucault 1977, 1991). Other theoretical traditions, such as that inspired by the work of Pierre Bourdieu, in taking up the theme of the shaping of conduct through shaping sensibilities remind us of the importance for liberal governance of technologies that seek to act on the figurative plane to shape consciousness—through mobilizing such symbolic resources as stories and iconic images with the intention of promoting desired ways of thinking and feeling (e.g., Bourdieu and Wacquant 1992; Shusterman 1999; see also other traditions such as those represented by Boal 2000). [. . .]

In exploring Peter Drahos's (2004) question of whether constituted hope— and in particular a politically constituted hope in the form we have just outlined—

can be a positive force, we examine the work that is being undertaken at the Robben Island Museum in South Africa. . . . The Robben Island Museum is one of the initiatives that the South African government is supporting to promote a hope sensibility within South Africans in the context of that country's ongoing political transition from apartheid to what is hoped will be a fully established, inclusive, and prosperous democracy.

Like most museums, Robben Island is a site for the preservation and exhibition of objects thought to be of lasting value. But as a site designed to promote a hope sensibility, it is also more than that. It belongs to a class that we might think of as "governance museums"—that is, museums that are concerned with promoting sensibilities rather than with simply exhibiting valued objects. In these museums, the exhibits are intentional vehicles for shaping consciousness. Another example of a governance museum, which we will have more to say about later, is the Museum of Tolerance in Los Angeles that exhibits and interprets the Holocaust. If we think beyond museums to symbolic sites more generally, we might think of Robben Island as a site of "figurative governance"—that is, as an instance of figurative sites designed to shape sensibilities that it is hoped will promote a desired future by promoting certain ways of thinking and therefore acting across the population. [. . .]

Robben Island and the Robben Island Museum

Robben Island has a long history as a place of exclusion, having served a variety of carceral purposes over its history including the confinement of mutinous sailors, lepers, the mentally ill, and tribal leaders who fought against the colonization of southern Africa (see Buntman 1996a, 1996b, 1997; Deacon 1996; Strange and Kempa 2003). The apartheid government put the site to use as a prison where it attempted to isolate the leading political opponents of apartheid. This is where Nelson Mandela spent eighteen of his twenty-seven years as a political prisoner.

Robben Island, as a prison, was designed as a place that would cultivate a sensibility of hopelessness among those who resisted, or who might resist, apartheid governance. It is worth noting that *apartheid* in Afrikaans means "separateness." . . . The technique of isolating the political opponents of apartheid at Robben Island can be understood as consistent with a broader ideology of governing through separateness—in this case, by isolating the leaders of the resistance to apartheid, the government sought to "crush the spirit of the people" by "crushing the struggle itself" (Ahmed Kathrada, personal communication, August 1998). [. . .]

As history has shown, the strategy of governing through separateness has proven to be a spectacular failure. The history of the island through the apartheid years is one of sustained resistance and surprising political activity among the prisoners and, surreptitiously, between the prisoners and the struggle movement back on the mainland (for academic accounts, see Buntman 1996a, 1996b, 1997; Deacon 1996; Hutton 1994; Rioufol 1999, 2000; for prisoners' accounts, see Alexander 1994; Dlamini 1984; Mandela 1994). Embodying the slogan of "each one teach one," the prison gained the moniker of the "University of Robben Island" among those involved in the struggle as many people learned to read and write, while others went on to attain "diplomas" in history, economics, and law signed by Nelson Mandela. The island remained throughout a center for political debate—and it is widely reported by former inmates and acknowledged in academic accounts that the philosophy of inclusive governance that eventually came to form the basis of the new democratic South Africa was refined between groups at Robben Island (see Buntman 1996a, 1996b).

. . . As we will elaborate in a moment, Robben Island Museum celebrates and builds upon the failure of the apartheid designers' plans and programs to create the sense of hopelessness and acceptance of separateness between racial groups that was intended, as well as the triumph of an inclusive vision for governance that was refined within the walls of the prison.

It is important to note that the transformation of the site into a museum was largely a foregone conclusion within resistance circles as apartheid began to crumble in the late 1980s. The African National Congress government established the "Future of Robben Island Committee" in 1995, chaired by Ahmed Kathrada, which reviewed some two hundred public submissions as to the fate of the island. In response, . . . the committee reported to the cabinet in September 1996 and recommended that the island become a museum. The government agreed. Along with an additional major initiative—The Truth and Reconciliation Commission—Robben Island was to be developed as a central pillar in the government's program of renewal, nation building, and reconciliation. [. . .]

The museum displays not simply the physical artifacts of the island but also, much more important, the lives and experiences of the political prisoners. It is these lives and experiences, as much as the physical features of the island, that constitute the preserved and exhibited objects thought to be of lasting value by the South African government and the museum's directors and employees.

Mandela's hope

We turn now to elaborate upon the hope of the political prisoners of Robben Island, namely, a hope for a New South Africa that Mandela has come to epitomize. A critical feature of this hope was what a New South Africa should not be. . . . This negative vision was a key element in the resistance by prisoners to the technologies of apartheid designed to promote hopelessness that is now celebrated in and through the museum. What South Africa should not be is a place that responds in kind to apartheid by mirroring apartheid.

The culture of political resistance that the museum celebrates centers on a deliberate refusal by the political prisoners to respond in kind to the actions of warders and their superiors. They refused to respond to hatred with hatred. They refused, as they have expressed it, to be less as human beings than they could be—a total rejection of the notion of separateness along lines of "difference" drawn across (imaginary) racial groups. It is this refusal, more than anything else, that Mandela has come to represent.

It is perhaps this refusal to respond to hatred with hatred, more than any other single factor, that made a negotiated transition in South Africa possible

(Deegan 2000). It is this refusal that now stands at the center of the vision of a New South Africa. This refusal is what the Robben Island Museum has been, and is being, designed to exhibit and, through this, to celebrate as a "way of being" worthy of South Africans. It is the hope that this sensibility will indeed become a defining sensibility of South Africans and a sensibility that will spread and found a new nonracist, harmonious, and prosperous society; that is the hope of Robben Island.

This sensibility that the Robben Island Museum has been designed to constitute has been beautifully expressed by Ahmed Kathrada (1997), in a statement made at the time that the Future of Robben Island Committee reported to the government in 1996:

> We will not want Robben Island to be a monument to our hardship and suffering. We would want it to be a monument reflecting the triumph of the human spirit against the forces of evil, a triumph of freedom and human dignity over repression and humiliation; a triumph of wisdom and largeness of spirit against small minds and pettiness; a triumph of courage and determination over human frailty and weakness; a triumph of non-racialism over bigotry and intolerance; a triumph of the new South Africa over the old.
>
> (pp. 10–11)

As this statement makes clear, both a positive and a negative side are on the coin of meaning that Robben Island as a museum seeks to embody and express. This positive side that the refusal noted above draws forth is nicely captured by a southern African concept that expresses the "largeness of spirit" to which Kathadra refers. This is the concept of *ubuntu*—a concept that is deeply rooted in Nguni culture (i.e., the culture of southern Africans who speak linguistically similar languages, including Xhosa and Zulu).

. . . Ubuntu . . . means that we all belong to a unified "bundle of life"—a person with ubuntu "is diminished when others are tortured or oppressed, or treated as if they were less than who they are" (Tutu 1999, 34–35).

What is important to note here, and this is something we will come back to, is that the hope of Robben Island is deeply grounded in the experience of South Africans—both through Nguni culture and through the experience of the islanders. Mandela's hope thus integrates a widespread African sensibility with a more specific sociopolitical one that is oriented toward a New South Africa.

This brings us back to the question of authentic hope and the possibility of authenticity where sensibilities are deliberatively constituted through governmental programs. Does a politically cultivated sensibility that draws upon deeply rooted cultural sensibilities discredit these sensibilities, or does this cultural embedding promote authenticity? Is it possible to constitute a sensibility that strives for a public vision, for a public hope, without diminishing the autonomy and freedom of those whose sensibility is being shaped? More generally, can a public hope be constituted toward political reinvention that is normatively desirable?

[. . .] The technologies employed by the museum were founded on a single overriding assumption—namely, that the most persuasive reason that South Africans can have for maintaining a sensibility of hope and a vision of ubuntu during the difficult times that lie ahead is the fact that the prisoners who struggled against apartheid under extraordinarily difficult conditions were able to cultivate, sustain, and practice a sensibility of ubuntu and a hope for a new South Africa that embraced this. From this assumption follows the premise that a museum experience that simply exposed South Africans to this prison reality—rather than imposing it upon them—would be a powerful force in cultivating a hope sensibility for a New South Africa. Given this conclusion, the museum designers and managers have sought to structure visits to the island to promote as much as possible a direct experience of the prisoners' hope sensibility and its accompanying way of being.

What is required, from this point of view, is an authentic and relatively unmediated experience of the hopeful life that was regarded as essential to the experience of the political prisoners—the experience of Mandela being the totemic instance. A critical reason for simply making the reality of prisoners' sensibilities available to visitors was also that to do otherwise would undermine the freedom and largeness of mind that ubuntu requires. To manipulate an acceptance of ubuntu would be to contradict the spirit of ubuntu. [. . .]

The idea of facilitating a direct and unmediated experience appears, judging by other academic accounts, to be in sharp contrast to the experience designed by the management of the Museum of Tolerance where, as Lisus and Ericson (1995) observe, guides anticipate the visitors' experience with a voice-over designed to interpret what they see before they experience it. Guides, they write, provide "moral interpretations of the exhibitry" in ways that parallel the "journalist's voice-over in television" (Lisus and Ericson 1995, 3). Indeed, the director of the Robben Island Museum made clear that his team was aware of other museums that seek to shape a future rather than simply exhibit a past. One of these museums mentioned explicitly in our interviews with Robben Island management was the Museum of Tolerance. The director of the Robben Island Museum and his staff appear to share the conclusions drawn by Nicola Lisus and Richard Ericson that at the Museum of Tolerance visitors were being "entertained into submission" (p. 8) and that the site had become an "emotions factory" (p. 18). The Robben Island Museum staff stood firm in the belief that this undermined the freedom to choose that they believed was essential to transmitting the message of hope in a gentle manner that reflected ubuntu values. . . .

In commenting on lessons learned for the Robben Island Museum from their interpretations of the Museum of Tolerance, the director of Robben Island noted that for him, the other experience is

> like a tunnel, you follow the story of the Holocaust and there is no way of escaping out of the story. You come in the tunnel and you had to go out the other side and, if one is not feeling emotionally strong that day or you want out of it, you can't. And I think that's a lesson for me about Robben Island: you mustn't force a story onto people. You must allow people to opt out depending on where they are at.
>
> (Personal communication, December 1999)

Consistent with this approach, the management of the Robben Island Museum had, at the time of the research, refused to provide scripts for tour guides. Furthermore, rather than use exclusively professionally trained guides, the museum has undertaken an outreach program to employ ex-prisoners as guides and simply encouraged them to tell their stories. The use of ex-prisoners as guides has made, in the words of the director,

> concrete our vision of making [Robben Island] a living museum and a new kind of museum—a place of engagement and education rather than it being a fixed narrative [for] a passive observer.
> (Personal communication, December 1999)

[. . .]

In outlining the methods they were employing to inspire visitors into adopting a hope sensibility, the tour guides spoke of the importance of drama in their presentations and the need to tailor their narratives to their audience—to their political consciousness and their historical sophistication as these became apparent in the course of tours. One had, they emphasized, to talk to people who had supported apartheid (who were sometimes reluctant to acknowledge the brutality of apartheid) differently to foreigners who were often apocalyptic in expectations about South Africa's future. So too one needed to speak to black South Africans, who continue to live in the aftermath of apartheid, differently. A tour guide and former political prisoner elaborates,

> [Some Afrikaners] come with a totally negative attitude, and you can see it, because the body language tells you. Instead of listening to you, the guy would turn his back, you know, or sneer, or walk away—show disinterest—or talk while you're talking. These are the tell-tale signs, and your question is now, "I want to reach that person, what am I going to do?" If it means altering slightly, so you actually snare that person, then you do so. You're not just like a parrot—that you turn on and then just babble. You learn to read your audience. You're not going to alter the facts, but you present the facts in such a way that you are able to send over . . . positive messages, because the negative is always there.
> (Tour Guide 2, personal communication, December 1999)

While the line may at times be fine between a process of invitation and an "emotions factory," Robben Island, we suggest, remains consistently on the side of engagement and education at a pace appropriate to the state of preparedness of an individual visitor.

The understanding of the history that informs the museum's objectives of assembling an inclusive narrative is of great importance in evaluating the nature of their program for inspiring hope. As the museum develops, it is very crucial to Robben Island that it

> remains a platform for critical debate and lifelong learning. Because that's one of the big legacies that we inherited from Mandela and all

> those thousands of prisoners who argued amongst each other within
> [political] organizations, between organizations and obviously they
> contested the whole apartheid ruling class version of history. . . . So
> that notion of critical debate, contestation is very important.
>   (Director, personal communication, December 1999)

This insistence on the island as a space for deliberation that may and does lead to
different conclusions is critical to the issue of constructing a sensibility that is
authentic in the sense that Peter Drahos (2004) sees private and collective hopes
as being authentic. Authentic hope in Drahos's sense is hope that "leads into a cycle
of expectation, planning, and action that sees the agent explore the power of her
agency." [. . .]

While a "pilgrimage" to Robben Island may not be as orchestrated an
experience as a visit to the Museum of Tolerance is regarded as being, it is clearly
not an entirely unmediated experience either. Indeed, the very notion of a completely unmediated experience is an ideal type—there are very few if any such
experiences. Rather, the idea of an unmediated experience stands at an end of a
continuum where the other end is a completely manipulated experience. Everywhere along the continuum, our experience is constructed to varying degrees. So
the question is not whether our experience is constructed but rather how it is
constructed and toward what ends? Is what is happening facilitation, . . . or is it
about the constitution of a submissive consciousness?

Perhaps at this point, it might be useful to reflect on what we take to be
Foucault's conception of freedom as a space for personal reinvention (Foucault
1997). [. . .]

The hope being constituted on the island, as well as the conditions and
technologies used, has deep deliberative roots in the history of the prison itself,
the broader struggle movement against apartheid, and the indigenous southern
African culture more generally. In Drahos's (2004) terms, the public hope is deeply
rooted in individual and collective hope. This is reflected in the work of the
museum staff in their insistence that visitors should be invited (but not compelled)
to share in the inspiration of the island and to experience the range of voices that
comprised the islanders. To return to Foucault (1997), we conclude that the
Robben Island Museum has been, and is being, constituted as a space that invites
the possibility of personal reinvention and, through this, the collective reinvention
of South Africans.

References

Alexander, Neville. 1994. *Robben Island prison dossier 1964–1974*. Cape Town, South
    Africa: University of Cape Town Press.
Boal, Augusto. 2000. *Theatre of the oppressed*. London: Pluto Press.
Bourdieu, Pierre, and Loïc J. D. Wacquant. 1992. *An incitation to reflexive sociology*.
    Cambridge, UK: Polity.
Buntman, Fran L. 1996a. Resistance on Robben Island 1963–1976. In *The island: A
    history of Robben Island 1488–1990*, edited by Harriet Deacon. Cape Town, South
    Africa: Mayibuye Books.

——. 1996b. How best to resist? Robben Island after 1976. In *The island: A history of Robben Island 1488–1990*, edited by Harriet Deacon. Cape Town, South Africa: Mayibuye Books.

——. 1997. The politics of conviction: Political prisoner resistance on Robben Island, 1962–1991, and its implications for South African politics and resistance theory. Ph.D.thesis, University of Texas at Austin.

Burchell, Graham, Colin Gordon, and Peter Miller, eds. 1991. *The Foucault effect: Studies in governmentality*. Chicago: University of Chicago Press.

Deacon, Harriet, ed. 1996. *The island: A history of Robben Island 1488–1990*. Cape Town, South Africa: Mayibuye Books.

Dean, Mitchel. 1999. *Governmentality: Power and rule in modern society*. London: Sage.

Deegan, Heather. 2000. *The politics of the New South Africa*. New York: Longman.

Dlamini, Moses. 1984. *Hell-hole Robben Island: Reminiscences of a political prisoner*; Nottingham, UK: Spokesman.

Drahos, P. 2004. 'Trading in public hope' ANNALS, AAPSS, 592, March 2004 pp. 18–38.

Foucault, Michel. 1977. *Discipline and punish: The birth of the prison*. New York: Vintage Books.

——. 1991. Governmentality. In *The Foucault effect: Studies in governmentality*, edited by Graham Burchell, Colin Gordon, and Peter Miller. Chicago: University of Chicago Press.

——. 1997. The ethics of the concern of the self as a practice of freedom. In *Michel Foucault: Ethics, subjectivity and truth: The essential works of Foucault 1954–1984*, edited by Paul Rabinow. Vol. 1. New York: The New Press.

Garland, David. 2001. *The culture of control: Crime and social order in contemporary society*. Chicago: University of Chicago Press.

Hindess, Barry. 2001. Not at home in the empire. *Social Identities* 7 (3): 363–77.

Hutton, Barbara. 1994. *Robben Island: Symbol of resistance*. Bellville, South Africa: Mayibuye Books.

Kathrada, Ahmed. 1997. Opening address: The Robben Island exhibition, Esiqithini. In *Robben Island timeline*, edited by Harriet Deacon, Nigel Penn, Andre Odendaal, and Peter Davison. Cape Town, South Africa: Mayibuye Books.

Lisus, Nicola A., and Richard V. Ericson. 1995. Misplacing memory: The effect of television format on Holocaust remembrance. *British Journal of Sociology* 46 (1): 1–19.

Mandela, Nelson. 1994. *Long walk to freedom*. London: Abacus.

O'Malley, Pat. 1992. Risk, power, and crime prevention. *Economy and Society* 21:252–75.

O'Malley, Pat, and Darren Palmer. 1996. Post-Keynesian policing. *Economy and Society* 25 (2): 137–55.

Rioufol, Veronique. 1999. The making of a new past for a "new" South Africa: The commemoration of Robben Island. Master's thesis. Department of Political Studies, University of Cape Town, South Africa.

——. 2000. Behind telling: Post-apartheid representations of Robben Islands past. *Kronos* 26:22–41.

Rose, Nikolas S. 1991. *Governing the soul: The shaping of the private self*. London: Routledge.

——. 1996. The death of the social? Refiguring the territory of government. *Economy and Society* 25(3): 327–56.

Rose, Nikolas, and Peter Miller. 1992. Political power beyond the state: Problematics of government. *British Journal of Sociology* 43 (2): 173–205.

Shusterman, Richard, ed. 1999. *Bourdieu: A critical reader*. Oxford, UK: Blackwell.

Strange, Carolyn, and Michael Kempa. 2003. Shades of dark tourism: Alcatraz and Robben Island. *Annals of Tourism Research* 30 (2): 386–405.

Tutu, Desmond. 1999. *No future without forgiveness*. London: Rider.

Chapter 45

Deborah Gould

ROCK THE BOAT, DON'T ROCK THE BOAT, BABY: AMBIVALENCE AND THE EMERGENCE OF MILITANT AIDS ACTIVISM

[. . .]

DARRELL YATES RIST SUGGESTS A connection between what I am calling ambivalence and lesbian and gay politics:

> Whatever the state of our 'gay pride,' our politeness sticks to us all. It oozes from a well of acquiescence deep within, down where we still can't *quite* believe that we're as good as straights and deserve *all* of the heterosexual prerogatives: kissing lovers on the street, holding hands in front of Mom and Dad . . ., *marrying*. This politeness, which we nurture as though it were a virtue, emanates from dark convictions—lying dogmas we grew up with—that tell us we aren't quite right. . . . When it comes to taking hold of freedom, our politeness shuts us out.
>
> (Rist 1987: 54)

Rist intimates that lesbian and gay self-hatred and self-doubt emanate from, and animate, a deep concern with social acceptance that translates into political quiescence. In arguing that gay shame persists and sometimes trumps gay pride, Rist reminds us that prior to making political demands, lesbians and gay men must believe that they deserve to be treated better. Shame and self-doubt potentially gnaw away at any such conviction even while gay pride and indignation about homophobia might bolster it. Ambivalence about dominant society also introduces uncertainty into any political course of action; lesbians and gay men want to accommodate to, but also to confront, society's norms, values, and institutions.

Lesbian and gay political discourse reveals a relationship between lesbian and gay politics and ambivalence about self and society. As is true of most identity-based politics, lesbian and gay politics in large part revolve around questions of lesbian and gay selves in relation to society—who are we and how are we treated in relation to others; where do we fit in this society and where do we want to fit; how might we best achieve our goals? Given such concerns it is no surprise that the language of lesbian and gay politics is saturated with emotions about self and society. Emotions justify and explain lesbian and gay political actions (e.g., "our rage made us turn to civil disobedience"); are blamed for and credited with lesbians' and gay mens' political stands vis-à-vis dominant society (e.g., "our shame makes us too accommodating in the political realm"); are invoked to advocate one strategy over another (e.g., "if we're proud, we'll act responsibly and take care of our own"); are evoked to condemn and discourage those who engage in a politics of respectability as well as those who disregard such politics (e.g., "gay men who condemn promiscuity are self-hating"; "promiscuous gay men are self-hating"); are linked to specific political acts (e.g., "our leaders should feel ashamed about groveling for crumbs"); are credited with political successes (e.g., "our calm, reasonable tone made them respond to our demands").

In short, emotions suffuse lesbian and gay political discourse, proclaiming how, in light of specific political actions, lesbians and gay men supposedly feel, should feel, should not feel, will feel, about themselves and about society. Various, and sometimes conflicting, emotions are incessantly reiterated, indicating both an instability in how lesbians and gay men feel about themselves in the context of a hostile society as well as conscious and less than fully conscious attempts to affect those feeling states and thereby influence lesbian and gay politics. It seems clear that this highly emotional language of politics—in its focus on the relationship of lesbian and gay selves to society—is centrally engaged with lesbian and gay ambivalence, with all of its instabilities. [. . .]

Ambivalence and early lesbian and gay responses to AIDS

Throughout the AIDS epidemic, the evocation and expression of certain emotions have produced constellations of feelings and of emotion rules and norms that have effectively, if only temporarily, helped to "resolve" lesbian and gay ambivalence; these processes helped to shape lesbian and gay responses to AIDS. For example, during the first years of the AIDS epidemic, the prevalent and already existing ambivalent emotion culture animated feelings and articulations of shame ("our perverted sexual practices are killing us") linked to fear ("we now will surely be rejected by family, friends, and society"), and submerged the few early articulations of anger directed at the government. In bolstering negative feelings about homosexuality and appealing to a strong desire for social acceptance, this constellation of emotions heightened lesbian and gay concerns about respectability and assimilation into society, providing a "resolution" to lesbian and gay ambivalence that encouraged a nonconfrontational political response to AIDS that consisted mostly of service provision and lobbying.

During the mid-1980s, this emotion culture shifted slightly. There was an increase in expressions of anger about the government's inadequate response to AIDS. However, lesbian and gay ambivalence worked to delink that anger from militant political activism and channeled it instead in the direction of an internally oriented community pride that encouraged lesbians and gay men to continue on the commendable path of nobly, responsibly, and quietly taking care of their own in the face of little outside help. This constellation of emotions discouraged militant activism, pointing instead toward volunteerism, community-based service provision, and lobbying. The following example, where anger was articulated and elicited, but quickly defused and directed toward compassion rather than activism, illustrates these dynamics. At an AIDS memorial candlelight procession in Chicago, one speaker asked the crowd, "Are you mad? Are you angry?" He continued by saying that he was "pissed" because no one outside the lesbian and gay community was doing anything about AIDS. The crowd loudly agreed with him. He then concluded by advising: "Take your anger and turn it into love for your brothers." Perhaps following his suggestion, the procession concluded with marchers singing the refrain "We are a gentle, angry people" from Holly Near's song, "Singing for our Lives" (Cotton 1985). In this period, editorials in Chicago's lesbian/gay newspaper *Gay Life* consistently criticized the government's homophobic and negligent response to AIDS, but rather than calling for activism, the editorials all simply commended the community for its strength in the face of such adversity. A typical editorial angrily indicted the government, but issued no activist call and instead focused on an inward-directed pride: "Where others might have caved in under the pressure of the killer AIDS, our community has grown in strength during this tremendous crisis. . . . June is Gay and Lesbian Pride Month, and in Chicago we can truly be proud" ("Off to a Good Start," 1985).

The repeated invocations to feel pride might have been animated by a desire to bolster lesbian and gay self-esteem and to fight the greater stigma attached to homosexuality in the context of AIDS; they also might have been motivated by a need to increase the resource and volunteer base to fight AIDS. Equally important, however, seems to be the role that such elicitations of pride played in submerging a growing anger; each time anger began to be articulated, pride about the community's response to AIDS was immediately evoked and affirmed as the proper emotion to feel amidst this dire crisis. Regardless of their intent, the political effect of these expressions of pride was to submerge anger and to encourage an inward orientation that trumpeted volunteerism and community self-help rather than a more externally oriented activist response. When "gay pride" was first coined as a slogan by lesbian and gay liberationists in 1969, it was linked to militant activism. In the mid-1980s, it had an altogether different flavor. In a moment when a public health epidemic intensified gay shame and fear of social rejection, and when government response to AIDS was negligent at best and punitive at worst, gay pride now encouraged volunteerism, remembrance of the dead, relative quietude despite the government's glaring failures, and a stoic nobility in the face of a deadly epidemic, rather than confrontational or oppositional politics.

According to Reddy, because emotives can alter feelings, emotive conventions strongly influence individual and community-wide emotions over time. The evidence suggests that lesbian and gay communities' emotive conventions very much affected feelings about AIDS, largely submerging anger for the first four or five years of the crisis by rechanneling it toward fear of social rejection, shame, community pride, and tranquil nobility whenever it threatened to surface. The promotion of certain emotives over others, however, did not rid lesbian and gay communities of anger; it simply reduced its expression and seemingly reduced the feeling itself. But as Reddy points out, individuals vary in their responses to emotive convention. That variation "provides an initial reservoir of possibilities for change . . . that can be drawn upon when ideological, economic, or political factors put pressure on the system" (Reddy 1997: 334–35). In other words, emotive conventions are subject to contestation, particularly in times of crisis.

The management of a growing anger

Specific events in San Francisco and New York and comments of lesbian and gay leaders at the end of 1985 reveal the beginning of a shift in the mood of lesbians and gay men. At the end of October, nine individuals camped out in front of the old Federal Building in San Francisco to protest the government's response to AIDS. Two gay men with AIDS chained themselves to the doors. Their continuous vigil grew over the succeeding months (Hippler 1986: 42–47). Meanwhile, activists in New York City who were "fearful, angry and frustrated over mushrooming AIDS hysteria" (Freiberg 1985: 14) formed the Gay and Lesbian Anti-Defamation League (GLADL). More than six hundred lesbians and gays attended a mass meeting called by GLADL to discuss AIDS hysteria stirred up by the media and politicians; the next day one hundred protested outside City Hall during a committee hearing on closing gay sex establishments. In December, five hundred lesbians and gay men joined GLADL in a demonstration against the sensationalistic, antigay AIDS coverage of the *New York Post* (Freiberg 1985, 1986a). These more oppositional politics were not yet widespread, but their occurrence indicated a shifting emotional climate and the growing instability of accommodationist politics.

Comments made at a meeting of elected and appointed lesbian and gay officials by the executive director of the National Gay Task Force, Virginia Apuzzo, and by Massachusetts representative Barney Frank revealed their awareness of rumblings among some lesbians and gay men for more militant action. Apuzzo's comments indicated her perception that widespread ambivalence about self and society had translated into anxiety about lesbian and gay expressions of anger and militant political practices. She attempted to alleviate lesbian and gay anxieties about rocking the boat:

> For those of us who have earned . . . the respect and regard of [the political] system, we must be willing to spend it on this issue. We must be willing to mount a multiple offensive on what is coming down on us. Yes, we must negotiate. Yes, we must lobby. Yes, we must litigate. . . . But we must also remember where we come from, and return to allowing that rage to be expressed and not think for a minute that there is something not respectable about that.
>
> (Walter 1985: 11)

Frank, in contrast, tried to dampen the anger and steady the boat: "The political system has responded better [to the AIDS crisis] at this point than I would have hoped. . . . [That means] in my judgment, that the political course of action that has been chosen [by the lesbian and gay community] is correct" (Walter 1985: 13).

Although there was movement toward greater militance, Frank's cautionary note was the more typical expression during this period. [. . .]

Events and a new constellation of emotions

In the middle of 1986, there was a marked and widespread shift in lesbian and gay rhetoric about the AIDS crisis. In the context of everincreasing AIDS deaths, government failure to address the crisis, and growing calls for more repressive AIDS legislation, the U.S. Supreme Court's *Bowers v. Hardwick* decision, announced in June 1986, was a turning point, an event that, primarily as a result of its emotional effects, animated a transformation in lesbian and gay political responses to AIDS.

Comparing gay sex to "adultery, incest, and other sexual crimes," the Court upheld a Georgia statute that denied homosexuals the constitutional right to engage in consensual, private sexual acts (Walter 1986). Lesbians and gay men experienced the decision as "a declaration of war" (Deitcher 1995: 140). Deitcher writes that "news of the *Hardwick* decision was enough to awaken the radical in most apolitical queers. . . . Protests erupted in cities across the country as the news reached communities in which frustration and rage had been mounting over the loss of lovers and friends, the accelerating rate and intensity of bias-related violence, and the unprecedented challenge to queer social identity that the epidemic posed" (148–49). Accounts of the demonstrations remind one of Durkheim's notion of "collective effervescence," brimming with the emotional energy generated by the amassing of large numbers of people who see themselves as in some way connected. In New York City, lesbians and gay men "took to the streets for two angry, militant demonstrations," the largest since the 1970s; many engaged in civil disobedience. [. . .] Lesbians and gay men across the country angrily called for "active resistance," "riots," "massive protests," "law-breaking," another "Stonewall," a "return to the streets." The shift in lesbians' and gay men's emotional and political discourse is remarkable; militant language like this almost never appeared in the lesbian and gay media during the first five years of the AIDS epidemic.

The new militance grew quickly, delineating a politics that linked emotions such as indignation, anger, self-respect, fear of death and inaction, and grief to militant, confrontational AIDS activism. This new cluster of emotions prevailed over the previous evocations of pride about the community's self-help, faith in the government's goodwill, and stoicism in the face of death. Lesbian and gay newspapers both recorded and helped to generate the shifting emotion culture, running ever more op-eds and articles that indicted the government, articulated a growing anger, expressed dissatisfaction with the lesbian and gay community's moderate response to AIDS, and suggested the need for more confrontational AIDS activism. Militant AIDS activist groups began to emerge. [. . .]

Why did the *Hardwick* ruling—which, following McAdam (1982), we should consider as a tightening in political opportunities—provoke such a militant response by lesbians and gay men, and why did the ruling prompt lesbians and gay men to embrace militant AIDS activism? For years, lesbians and gay men had suffered through punitive AIDS legislation, inadequate AIDS funding, calls to tattoo and quarantine people with AIDS (PWAs), and so on; in response, they had strongly criticized, lobbied, held candlelight vigils, and sometimes protested, but lesbian and gay militance after *Hardwick* was much more pronounced, widespread, and lasting. One explanation for the response to *Hardwick* may be found in Jasper's (1997) concept of "moral shock." *Hardwick* was experienced as an *unexpected* and *outrageous* legal decision, particularly to lesbians and gay men who believed in American democracy's proclamation that equality was the law of the land. In denying them basic rights, the ruling confronted lesbians and gay men with the extent of their outsider status, forcing them to reconceptualize the U.S. as the land of justice for all—except "queers." In tandem with the government's inadequate response to AIDS, the ruling confounded the sense of belonging to dominant society and the sense of entitlement to citizen rights and privileges felt by many members of the lesbian and gay community, particularly those who were white, male, and middle class. They were newly indignant that their rights could be so thoroughly abrogated. As Jasper argues, a moral shock "helps a person think about her basic values and how the world diverges from them" (106) and can propel that person into political activism. Two pressing questions remain unanswered, however. First, given their past experiences with numerous indignities, why did lesbians and gay men experience *Hardwick* as a moral shock? Second, why did they respond with militant activism? As Jasper writes, "responses to moral shocks vary greatly. Most people, in most cases, resign themselves to unpleasant changes" (106) and do not embrace militant activism even in the face of such a shock.

   To understand lesbians' and gay men's experiences of and political reactions to *Hardwick*, then, we must consider the context in which the ruling occurred as well as the already shifting emotion culture that both derived from and reinforced lesbian and gay understandings of that context. By the middle of 1986, lesbians and gay men were facing a horrific and devastating social, political, and health crisis. *Hardwick* was announced five years into the AIDS epidemic when the number of AIDS cases reported to the Centers for Disease Control (CDC) had surpassed 30,000, more than half of whom had already died (CDC 1997: 14). President Reagan had yet to utter the word "AIDS" in public. Lyndon LaRouche's initiative to quarantine persons testing HIV-positive had recently garnered well over the required 394,000 signatures to be placed on the California ballot, and other state legislatures were increasingly considering similar laws (Freiberg 1986c: 10; Fall 1986: 9). Emanating from the highest echelons of the state and amidst increasingly repressive legislation, government negligence, and the ever-increasing AIDS deaths, the *Hardwick* ruling shocked lesbians and gay men into a greater recognition of the life-threatening nature of state-sponsored and socially sanctioned homophobia. As I have argued, in the year prior to *Hardwick*, lesbians and gay men were increasingly feeling anger toward the government; the shift in the emotion culture then reigning in lesbian and gay communities was occurring quite gradually, however. The *Hardwick* ruling greatly quickened the pace, shattering the previous "resolution" to ambivalence and the concomitant constellation of emotions that had prevailed in lesbian and gay communities during the first years of the AIDS epidemic. The ruling radically transformed lesbians' and gay men's feelings about self and society, accelerated a shift in their emotion norms and rules, and provoked a new "reso-lution" to lesbian and gay ambivalence, all of which stimulated new understandings of the AIDS crisis and encouraged militant activism. To understand why *Hardwick* animated lesbians and gay men to embrace militant AIDS activism, then, requires an investigation of the ruling's emotional effects.

First and foremost, *Hardwick* amplified shifts in lesbian and gay community emotion cultures that had already begun to occur as a result of the mounting deaths and the government's negligent and punitive handling of the AIDS crisis. A new configuration of emotions is apparent in lesbian and gay activist documents and newspapers after *Hardwick*. Indignation, born from a sense of entitlement betrayed, was pronounced, complementing frequent expressions of self-respect; anger and animosity toward the government were increasingly articulated; fear about the consequences of lesbian and gay *in*action was heightened. Emotions like shame, pride in the community's self-help, fear of social rejection, and tranquil nobility in the face of death and government negligence, which had previously dominated and had encouraged community-based service provision, volunteerism, candlelight vigils, and lobbying, were rarely elicited or articulated during this period. The now-normative emotion culture offered a new constellation of emotions about self and society—i.e., a new "resolution" to lesbian and gay ambivalence—that encouraged militance and profoundly shook up the orthodoxy of political moderation and accommodation that had dominated lesbian and gay politics since the mid-1970s.

Although itself not directly about AIDS, *Hardwick* punctuated and gave new meaning to the ongoing epidemic; it crystallized and heightened feelings about and interpretations of the epidemic that had previously been more or less inchoate. By exposing the state's willingness, even eagerness, to exclude an entire class of people from constitutional protections, the *Hardwick* ruling encouraged a more politicized analysis of the government's response to AIDS, making it increasingly difficult to reduce the epidemic to a string of individual deaths and to isolated feelings of grief. Before the ruling, a number of lesbians and gay men had begun arguing that the government's response to the AIDS crisis was proof that gay men were seen as expendable; as the highest court in the land was now willing to espouse homo-phobic justifications in denying privacy rights to a group of citizens, who was to say that quarantine of HIV-positive people would not now be implemented? If state and society saw homosexual love (and thus homosexual lives) as criminal, they certainly would not suddenly become concerned about homosexual deaths. After *Hardwick*, framings of AIDS that invoked the Nazi holocaust and accused the government of genocide by intentional neglect became more resonant. Lesbians' and gay men's growing fear, grief, and anger supported an interpretation of AIDS as genocide, and, at the same time, this new and apocalyptic framing amplified those very emotions. [. . .]

It should be clear that there was nothing inevitable about the response of lesbians and gay men to the *Hardwick* decision, and there was no necessary connec-tion between *Hardwick* and the emergence of militant AIDS activism. To understand why *Hardwick* amplified lesbian and gay anger at state and society rather than shame about homosexuality, and why it encouraged confrontational politics rather than more lobbying or paralysis born of despair, we need to consider the context of shifting emotions and political subjectivities that lesbians and gay men were experiencing when the ruling occurred. As stated above, the Court's decision was announced at a moment when the prevailing lesbian and gay emotion culture was already shifting as a result of other, more gradual processes and occurrences—a steady (although of course alarming) increase in cases and deaths, government inaction, and repressive legislation—that had by then spanned five years. Similarly, pockets of more militant AIDS activism were already slowly beginning to emerge to protest the closing of gay bathhouses, the growing AIDS hysteria in the media, and government inaction. *Hardwick*, then, had the impact that it did because it occurred at a moment when anger toward the government was increasingly being articulated and felt, and because some lesbians and gay men were beginning to channel that anger into more militant politics. [. . .]

In conclusion, I'd like to suggest how my analysis of the emergence of ACT UP might assist our studies of social movements more generally. First, an exploration of the role played by emotions and emotives in the negotiation of an intense ambivalence among a marginalized group of people helps to explain why and how a movement can emerge in the context of few political opportunities, and perhaps even in response to such a context. Second, my analysis suggests the important role that emotions and their expression play in interpretive processes, including framing as well as less purposive activities. Scholars point to the important role that framing activities play in movement emergence and development, but their accounts typically emphasize the cognitive rather than emotional components of framing. Moreover, scholars tend to define framing as a strategic, purposive activity and fail to link it to broader, less intentional, interpretive processes. Perhaps as a result of both their cognitive bias and the emphasis they place on strategic behavior, the crucial question of frame resonance often remains unanswered. What seems to be missing in the current conceptualization of framing is a consideration of interpretive processes that include conscious, strategic thinking as well as less than fully conscious or purposive processes, all of which are always saturated with emotions; we need to consider how people make sense of themselves, their situations, and their political options and then explore how those emotion-saturated understandings affect their political actions. [. . .]

References

Cotton, J. (1985) 'Marchers remember losses to AIDS', *Gay Life*, 30 (1): 5.

Deitcher, D. (1995) 'Law and desire', in D. Deitcher (ed.) *The Question of Equality: lesbian and gay politics in America since Stonewall*. New York, NY: Simon and Schuster.

Fall, J. A. (1986) 'LaRouche group seeks AIDS quarantine referendum; gay and lesbian community forms coalition to defeat measure', *New York Native*, 16 June: 9–10.

Freiberg, P. (1985) 'Gay anti-defamation league forms in New York: activists outraged by Cuomo's policies, media sensationalism', *Advocate*, 24 December: 14–15.#

Freiberg, P. (1986a) 'Gays protest *N. Y. Post* homophobia', *Advocate*, 7 January: 16–17.

Freiberg, P. (1986c) 'LaRouche AIDS initiative', *Advocate*, 19 August: 10–11, 20.

Hippler, M. (1986) 'The vigil: a profile in gay courage', *Advocate*, 15 April: 42–47.

Jasper, J. M. (1997) *The Art of Moral Protest: culture, biography, and creativity in social movements*. Chicago: University of Chicago Press.

Reddy, W. M. (1997) 'Against constructionism: the historical ethnography of emotions', *Current Anthropology*, 38: 327–351.

Rist, D. Y. (1987) 'Drawing blood', *Advocate*, 14 April: 52–59, 108–111.

Walter, D. (1985) 'Openly gay elected and appointed officials hold "historic" meeting', *Advocate*, 24 December: 10–13.

Walter, D. (1986) 'High court upholds sodomy law', *Advocate*, 5 August: 10.

11. Emotions and law

NOTHING COULD SEEM further from the topic of emotion than the discourse of the law, with its highly formal normative procedures and its traditional respect for neutrality, rationality and objectivity. When lawyers write of emotions in legal processes, they typically construe them as a 'messy' contrast to the hard legal categories and rules that, in a sense, tackle the important job of 'containing' and regulating this mess. Cool and neutral justice can thus be contrasted with hot vengeance (Solomon 1999), and the clarity of a formal decision with respect to legal guilt can be contrasted with the unpredictable perturbations of moral guilt. This perceived distance from affect, of course, is itself relevant to social scientists, since it results from what is actually a rather intimate relation between law and emotional scenes (e.g. of conflict and violence). Much of law, it might be said, processes and sorts out conflicts which are often highly emotional. Emotions are thus, in a sense, at the origins of law, and are ever present at its borders (e.g. at the interface between legal processes and the broader society). Stenner (2005a, 2005b) thus writes of the 'emotional cooling' that is effected when what might otherwise be purely personal disputes and conflicts are shifted into the register of the norms of legal discourse, and he shows how legal right is in intimate dialogue with the sense of moral right.

Research into law and emotions has proliferated in the last decade or so. From the mid 1990s there has been a steady stream of publications addressing both the general relationships between law and emotion (e.g. Bandes 1999; Posner 2001) and more specific matters such as the emotional content of victim impact statements (Bandes 1996), the role of particular emotions such as disgust (Miller 1997), sympathy (Feigenson 1997), or shame (Massaro 1997) in legal judgement and/or punishment (Nussbaum 2004). In a recent special issue of the journal *Law and Human Behaviour* on the topic of emotion in legal judgement and decision making, Maroney (2006) argues that the subject of law and emotion now has a sufficient critical mass of activity (special issues, conference symposia, etc.) to be given the status of a distinct research field equivalent to others such as 'law and psychology'. Taking stock of this movement, Maroney identifies a number of distinct strands of interest. Some scholars, for example, analyze how particular emotions might be reflected in law, as in arguments over whether disgust is a legitimate basis for legal rule making ('emotion-centred' approach). Others apply a particular theory of emotions to some legal issue (an 'emotion-theory' approach). Others find particular theories of emotion implicitly embedded in particular legal theories (a 'theory-of-law' approach), and still others explore how the performances of particular legal actors might be influenced by emotions (a 'legal actor' approach), and so on.

Our first extract is from Kathy Laster and Pat O'Malley's 'Sensitive New Age Laws'. Published in 1996, the full paper begins by identifying two broad social 'tendencies' that have influenced late twentieth-century legal processes. On the one hand, processes of administrative rationalization and proceduralization that reflect neo-liberal concerns with optimizing resource efficiency have resulted in an increased depersonalization and bureaucratization of justice. On the other hand, there has also been an increased emphasis on questions of emotionality, spirituality and the value of the non-rational associated with a world organized around personal lifestyle choices, self-expression and emotional fulfillment. Currently, they argue, both technocratic *and* emotional tendencies co-exist and compete for discursive space with the old enlightenment vision of a rationally governed legal system playing a decisive role in social progress. In the selected extract, Laster and O'Malley illustrate the reassertion of emotionality in law in relation to rape, domestic violence, and psychological distress in Australian criminal law.

In addressing law and the emotions we should thus always keep in mind that we are concerned with the very practical and worldly enterprise of *regulating conduct*. Subjecting human conduct to rules is not just a matter of shaping behaviour but also involves the regulation of values and feelings, and hence the generation and management of emotional experience and expression. This theme is picked up in the second extract drawn from Bettina Lange's (2002) article 'The Emotional Dimension in Legal Regulation'. Lange sees emotions as a crucial 'link concept' between the legal realm and society more generally. She examines the sense in which emotions can be both at the *source* of legal regulation and its *effect*. These relationships, she argues, are becoming more important in today's 'emotionalized' societies. Consider, for example, the emotionalized criminal justice debates that took place around the release of the young killers of the toddler James Bulger in the UK.

'Affective Versus Effective Justice' by Arie Freiberg (2001) deals with the broader question of crime prevention policies and argues that successful policies must address the deeper affective aspects of the social place and meaning of crime. Any response to crime, it is argued, contains instrumental and emotional dimensions, and also expressive dimensions involved in the production of social cohesion. Rationalist approaches tend to ignore that latter two elements and hence fail to compete with crime prevention policies designed to emotively resonate with the deep seated psychosocial needs of the public. In the extract included, Freiberg endorses such an affective turn by contrasting instrumental approaches to crime policy with symbolic/affective approaches.

The fourth extract is from an article by anthropologist Yael Navaro-Yashin, entitled 'Make-Believe Papers, Legal Forms and the Counterfeit: affective inter-actions between documents and people in Britain and Cyprus' (2007). In a version of the affective turn inspired by the tradition of Actor Network Theory, Navaro-Yashin studies the affective circulations enabled and enacted by way of identity verification and travel documents. Documents, of course, are the life-blood of legal and adminis-trative process, but are not usually associated with emotions. Based on a study of the interactions which Turkish Cypriots have with legal forms and papers, this article suggests that they can be psychically charged phenomena involved in the flow of emotional energy within and between collectives.

The final extract by Susanne Karstedt, 'Emotions and Criminal Justice' (2002) critically develops the theme of the 'emotionalization of law'. She describes it as a process which has transformed criminal justice globally in the last decade. Emotions such as anger, disgust and shame, for example, have been re-introduced into criminal procedures and are increasingly recognized as 'barometers' of social morality. Karstedt is deeply concerned with some of these developments, and particularly with the idea that legal institutions might require the expression of 'authentic emotions' from the individuals caught up with them. This notion gives a new political urgency to the question of whether or not particular emotions are 'natural' responses and to the relations between emotions and evaluative judgment more generally.

References

Bandes, S. (1996) 'Empathy, narrative, and victim impact statements', *University of Chicago Law Review, 63,* 361, 365, 371, 372.

Bandes, S. (ed) (1999) *The Passions of Law.* New York: New York University Press.

Feigenson, N. R. (1997) 'Sympathy and legal judgment: a psychological analysis', *Tennessee Law Review, 65,* 1, 15, 16, 68, 69.

Maroney, T. A. (2006) 'Law and emotion: a proposed taxonomy of an Emerging Field', *Law & Human Behavior*, 30:119–142

Massaro, T. (1997) 'The meanings of shame: implications for legal reform', *Psychology, Public Policy, and Law,* 3: 645.

Miller, W. I. (1997) *The Anatomy of Disgust.* Cambridge, Massachussetts: Harvard University Press.

Nussbaum, M. C. (2004) *Hiding from Humanity: Disgust, shame, and the law.* Princeton, NJ: Princeton University Press.

Posner, E. A. (2001) 'Law and the emotions', *The Georgetown Law Journal, 89,* 1977.

Solomon, C. (1999) 'Justice v. vengeance: on law and the satisfaction of emotion', in S. Bandes (ed) *The Passions of Law.* New York: New York University Press.

Stenner, P. (2005a) 'Rights and emotions, or: on the importance of having the right emotions', *History and Philosophy of Psychology,* 7 (1).

Stenner, P. (2005b) Emotions and rights: On the interpenetration of the psychic and the social. In A. Gülerce, I. Steauble, A. Hofmeister, G. Saunders and J. Kaye (Eds), Theoretical Psychology. Toronto: Captus Press.

Chapter 46

Kathy Laster and Pat O'Malley

SENSITIVE NEW-AGE LAWS

The reassertion of emotionality in law

[. . .]

THE INCORPORATION OF THE EMOTIONAL into law and legal rhetoric is manifest in an wide array of areas of law, some of which we will turn to later in the paper, but it is perhaps best illustrated by dramatic reforms to the law of rape. In Australia, and elsewhere, rape law is now predicated on a concern with human dignity. Historically, rape was a property crime and accordingly treated seriously (Smart 1989). Husbands and fathers were entitled to extract due compensation and punishment for *their* loss. For a woman too, the consequences of rape were devastating since marriage prospects largely determined her future. Rape also subjected women to the risk of pregnancy and hence risk to their lives, either through unsafe abortion or death in childbirth. The birth of an illegitimate child destroyed not only a woman's social standing but her economic viability (Laster 1989, 1994; Allen 1990). Now, however, in law the social harm is to a far greater extent envisaged in terms of the harm to the emotional well-being or consciousness of self of the individual woman. Changes in attitudes to sexuality have been linked to the much greater weight placed on emotional well-being. Ironically, the law now treats rape as a devastating crime at a point in history when the effect of the crime is *materially* least injurious.

The legal definition of rape now focuses not on the physical or material harm to the victim, but on the affront to human dignity of non-consensual sex. The unequal position of women is acknowledged both in law and in community education campaigns with the onus on the more powerful partner (usually men) to establish that the woman did, indeed, 'freely' or happily participate in sexual relations. Thus, the new definition of rape holds physical harm to be irrelevant — the only valid basis for establishing the crime is the absence of 'free consent' to an act of penetration. The new generation of legislation explicitly requires the judge in a rape trial to direct the jury that absence of physical injury should not be regarded as evidence of consent [see for example, *Crimes Act* 1958 (Vic), Section 37(b)(ii)] and any psychological pressure exerted on the victim "because of fear of harm of any type" to them or someone else (e.g. Section 36) is sufficient to vitiate consent. In recognizing the possibility of rape within marriage, the legislation places a premium on the sexual autonomy of women [Section 62(2)]. Women are, under the new definition of rape, also entitled to change their mind. Refusal to "withdraw from a person who is not consenting on becoming aware that the person is not consenting or might not be consenting", is a significant concession to the sensibilities of (usually) women even during the sex act [Section 38(2)(b)].

At the same time, the ideological justification for adversial process in criminal cases was undermined *inter alia* by accusations from the feminist movement that women were systematically degraded and demeaned by the legal system, most notably in rape trials. The arguments are by now well-known, with many case studies illustrating the 'secondary victimization' (e.g. Greenberg & Ruback 1985: 611) experienced by women subjected to the trauma of giving evidence in court. The Australian Law Reform Commission, justifying the introduction of new measures for receiving evidence in sexual assault cases, gave one woman's account of her experience giving evidence at a committal against two of her colleagues who had allegedly raped her after leaving their annual Christmas party.

> In the court room I gave evidence for four hours. They asked me why I did not fight back, why I had so many drinks, why I had asked them to help me find a taxi and not someone else. Apart from the (sexual assault) counsellor . . . I was the only woman in the room. When their barrister asked me whether I am a vegetarian, I was confused, and upset. I said, "No". He then asked me if I ate meat. I said, "Yes". When he then asked me why I did not bite off their penises, I became distressed and looked around the court room. At that moment I realised that this was not their trial. The magistrate, like all the others, looked at me, waiting for my response.
>
> (Australian Law Reform Commission 1994: 28).

In subsequent law reforms, deference to the emotional well-being of victims and witnesses was allowed to override concerns that adversarial truth-certifying mechanisms were necessary to ensure fair outcome for defendants. In Victoria, for example, legislative amendments now allow children under the age of 18 years, intellectual disabled people, as well as victims in sexual offence cases, to give evidence through alternative arrangements where, in the view of the court, the witness in giving evidence is likely to "suffer severe emotional trauma; or to be so intimidated or stressed as to be severely disadvantaged as a witness" [Section 37C of the *Crimes Act* 1958 (Vic) (as amended)]. These changes include giving evidence through closed circuit television, using screens to remove the defendant from the witness's direct sightline, allowing a person to sit beside the witness to provide emotional support, requiring counsel to be seated, or not robed, while examining or cross-examining the witness and excluding non-essential personnel from the court room while the witness is giving evidence [Section 37C(3) *Crimes Act* 1958 (Vic)].

The same concern with victims' sensibilities has also brought new restrictions on the nature of questions which can be put to witnesses in sexual assault cases. Thus, for example, evidence relating to general reputation of the complainant's chastity cannot be admitted, nor can complainants be cross-examined about their sexual activities without leave of the court [Section 37A(1) and (2) *Crimes Act* 1958 (Vic)]. The emotional state of victims after experiencing sexual assault is now taken into account in the judge's instructions to the jury in sexual assault cases.

In this new era, the indignity experienced by women because of their powerless position has also led to the legislative development of new civil harms, notably sexual harassment. From the late 1970s, sexual harassment came to be defined broadly and subjectively as "any repeated and unwanted sexual comments, looks, suggestions or physical contact that you find objectionable or offensive and that causes you discomfort on your job" (Evans 1978: 203). Such behaviour must be dealt with by law because like all forms of victimhood, it is a collective phenomena, a condition of the relationship between the powerful and the powerless which is relational and socially constructed, rather than the province of the individual woman. There is, in law, no need to rely on proof of violence or indeed of any loss suffered by the woman as a consequence of the harassment. Rather, the emphasis is on the implied emotional harm and hurt to feelings and the sense of dignity which such behaviour engenders (Stanko 1995).

In Victoria, sexual harassment is accommodated within the civil law through equal opportunity legislation. It is linked to discriminatory behaviour in the course of employment, in the provision of goods and services and accommodation. In the context of employment, it is unlawful for an employer 'knowingly' to permit an employee to be harassed with sexual advances; or to be importuned or harassed with persistent sexual suggestions or innuendo whilst acting in the course of their employment [*Equal Opportunity Act* 1984 (Vic), Section 20(1)(b)(i) and (ii)]. Here, as elsewhere, the legal prohibition on sexual harassment has allowed women, for the first time, to define women's injuries (MacKinnon 1987). As in the United States (*Harris* v. *Forklift Systems* (1993) 114 S. Ct. 367), the Equal Opportunity Commission and the Equal Opportunity Board have been prepared to accept that harm need not be material nor do the circumstances need to be so severe so as to cause a nervous breakdown.

Other aspects of procedure have also been changed in terms of this rethinking of emotionality. For example, the arbitrary legal cut-off point for 'harm' has been challenged in the light of 'late onset' diseases, including emotional or psychological damage. Courts have been pressed to acknowledge the long-term effects of child-hood sexual abuse, and the 'repressed memory syndrome' is being used to bring both civil and criminal actions which would otherwise be statute-barred because of the Statute of Limitations. The Canadian Supreme Court in the case of *KM* v. *HM* (96 D.L.R. 4th 289) applied a more liberal interpretation arguing that a cause of action accrues at the moment when the victim becomes fully cognisant of the abuse and makes the connection between past acts and present injuries. The legislature in British Columbia acted swiftly to abolish the Statute of Limitations in cases of sexual abuse. The psychological effects of child sexual abuse is also increasingly being accepted as a mitigator for later, adult behaviour. In Victoria for example, a 21-year-old woman physically and sexually abused as a child by her stepfather was given a suspended jail sentence for running him down with her car. The judge acknowledged that she had been traumatizedby her childhood experience and was still 'suffering' when she committed the offences (*Melbourne Age* 4.11.93).

Women are not the only group to make such new demands. From the 1960s, combating racial discrimination and inequality have been the main catalysts for a range of laws which seek to change public attitudes and behaviour. In Australia, imminent federal legislation to amend the Racial Discrimination Act will bring under its umbrella "extreme behaviour in public which offends, insults or intimidates another person because of their race, colour or national or ethnic origin" Similar legislation exists already in three other Australian states (*Melbourne Age* 1.11.94). In supporting parallel measures designed to deal with 'hate propaganda', the Supreme Court of Canada described such publications as "a serious attack on psychological and emotional health" (*R* v. *Zundel* (1992) 95 DLR (4th) 202). [. . .]

Aboriginal people too have made use of the common law's extension of a right to remedy resulting from psychological distress. In Victoria, police recently shot dead a 41-year-old Aboriginal woman with a psychiatric history. The relatives of the dead victim are now pursuing an action for nervous shock based on the insensitivity of the police in the way in which they were informed of the death. In an ironic twist, the Police Association has also declared its support for common law action for negligence brought by the police officers involved in the shooting. The action, against the Government, claims a failure to train them adequately and seeks compensatory damages for the emotional harm caused to them by the publicity associated with the case (*Melbourne Age* 7.10.94). Litigation by both sides has been facilitated by a series of Australian cases expanding the class of persons entitled to claim for nervous shock (Mullany & Handford 1993). It is significant that while these two groups linked their claims to broader concerns (on the one hand the treatment of Aboriginal people by the criminal justice system, on the other, the conditions of work for police officers), emotional harm has been chosen as the umbrella for the legal airing of the political grievances of both groups.

In the past decade, such concerns have given rise to the comparatively new tort of intentional infliction of emotional distress. In the U.K., Section 57 of the Race Relations Act 1976 allowed that 'damages in respect of any unlawful act of discrimination may include compensation for injury to feelings", and in *Alexander* v. *The Home Office* ([1988] IRLR 190, at 193) it was argued that awards for damages for injury to feelings under the Act, should not be trivial in comparison to damages for any material harm. This contrasts quite markedly with previous conditions where the old tort of 'nervous shock' required 'recognizable psychiatric illness' and was set about by all manner of arbitrary limitations such that distress and grief were not actionable *per se* (e.g. *Hinz* v. *Berry* [1970] 2 QB 40 at 42). [. . .]

References

Allen, J. (1990) *Sex and Secrets*. Oxford University Press: Melbourne.

Australian Law Reform Commission (1994) *Equally Before the Law: Justice for Women*, Report No 69, Part 1. AGPS: Canberra.

Evans, L. (1978) Sexual harassment: women's hidden occupational hazard. In *The Victimisation of Women* (Roberts-Chapman, J. & Gates, M., Eds). Sage: Beverley Hills.

Greenberg, M. & Ruback, B.R. (1985) A model of crime victim decision-making. *Victimology: An International Journal* **10**, 600–616.

Laster, K. (1989) Infanticide: a litmus test for feminist criminological theory. *Australian and New Zealand Journal of Criminology* **22**(3), 151–166.

Laster, K. (1994) Arbitrary chivalry: women and capital punishment in Victoria, 1842–1967. In *A Nation of Rogues: Crime, Law and Punishment in Colonial Australia* (Philips, D. & Davies, S., Eds). Melbourne University Press: Melbourne, pp. 166–186.

MacKinnon, C. (1987) *Feminism Unmodified: Discourses on Life and Law*. Harvard University Press: London.

Mullany, N. & Handford, P. (1993) *Tort Liability for Psychiatric Damage. The Law of Nervous Shock*. Allen & Unwin: Sydney.

Smart, C. (1989) *Feminism and the Power of Law*. Routledge: London.

Stanko, E. (1995) Reading danger: sexual harassment, anticipation and self-protection. In *Violence Against Women* (Hester, M., Kelly, L. & Radford, J. Eds.). (forthcoming).

Chapter 47

Bettina Lange

THE EMOTIONAL DIMENSION IN LEGAL REGULATION

THIS ARTICLE SUGGESTS THAT EMOTIONAL processes are one aspect of legal regulation. Sociological analysis has made important contributions to the understanding of regulatory processes. It has shown the significance of a range of contextual factors, beyond formal law, in shaping the design and implementation of legal regulation. It has, however, been limited by focusing on cognitive aspects and by neglecting emotional dynamics of social action. [. . .]

An analysis of emotions allows to identify close interrelationships between a legal and a social realm because emotions are a crucial 'link concept'. On the one hand, emotions are clearly anchored in a private sphere of civil society, but, on the other hand, they are also involved in the creation of social structures, such as forms of governance and law. . . . First, legal regulation can be the source of emotions. Secondly, legal regulation can be the outcome of emotional processes. Thirdly, 'regulatory law in action' can be understood as the interaction between regulatory state law and the 'laws of emotions'.

1. Legal regulation as the outcome of emotional processes

In Western legal systems legal regulation is often considered as the outcome of cognitive processes. Rational discussion is usually focused upon in accounts of the production of legal regulation. For example, political lobbying, an important aspect of the creation of legal regulation, is often described as a process in which various actors try to assert their self-interests and in that sense act rationally. Even where politicians act as advocates on behalf of other groups, this behaviour can still be described as rational. According to public-choice theories of regulation, politicians acting on behalf of interest groups act rationally because they can expect to maintain or be voted into positions of political power in return.

Furthermore, institutions for the production of legal regulation, such as parliaments and their specific procedural rules for debate, are meant to ensure that legal regulation is produced on the basis of rational criteria. [. . .]

Not just cognitive but also emotional processes are important in the formation of legal regulation. Both from a 'top-down' and a 'bottom-up' perspective, emotions are significant for explaining how legal regulation is produced. . . . Legal regulation 'in action' is composed of small-scale, social orders which are established during the practical implementation of state legal regulation. So far, the literature on legal regulation has focused on the cognitive dimension of these small-scale social orders. For example, actors' interpretations of formal legal regulation feed into the establishment of these social orders. Mundane social orders, however, can also be an element of these small-scale social orders. Some sociologists have argued that emotional processes are key to understanding how such mundane social orders become established. Collins, in analysing Garfinkel's work,[1] suggests that the limits of human cognitive abilities are essential for an explanation of how the micro elements of mundane social order, such as rules governing conversations or encounters between family members, are established. Social actors employ a range of practices in order not to recognize that mundane social order is established in a rather arbitrary fashion. Hence social actors keep up conventions because emotions buttress them, not because they have evaluated these conventions as valid and consciously support them. This insight was generated through experiments conducted by Garfinkel. During these, participants showed strong negative emotions when the experiment revealed to the respondents that they were constructing their own social world in an arbitrary and conventional way, rather than responding to an exterior, objective reality. . . .

Also, from a 'top down' perspective legal regulation can be perceived as the outcome of emotional processes. In this approach legal regulation is equated with formal, regulatory state law. On the most simple level the feelings that social actors have about the issues which are legally regulated can influence the form and content of legal regulation. For example, the expression of emotions, such as fear about health or aversion to interference with the 'laws of nature', are part of debates about the regulation of GMOs and can feed into its design. Moreover, emotion can feed into the establishment of cognitive constructs on the basis of which a law-making debate is conducted. For example, notions of romantic love can help to explain the different legal regulation of same-sex and heterosexual relationships. . . . Emotions also inhere in large-scale social structures, such as the state and systems of governance. Legal regulation, in turn, reflects the nature of these large-scale social structures. For example, . . . resentment is a key ingredient of class structures. Economic structures, such as a differential distribution of resources, or cognitive constructs, such as class consciousness, are not sufficient to explain the social phenomenon of class. Emotions, such as resentment, also construct class. Furthermore the control and management of emotions can be important for the maintenance of systems of governance. . . . Scheff has explored how shame and anger sequences can inform collective behaviour and influence international relations between states.[2] Also, anthropologists have argued that states can become involved in the construction and strategic management of emotions and legal regulation bears the imprint of the 'emotional economy' of a state.[3] To conclude, this section has argued that legal regulation can be the outcome of emotional processes. The next section will suggest that legal regulation can also give rise to emotional processes.

2. Legal regulation as giving rise to emotional processes

The idea that legal regulation can give rise to emotional processes has been discussed in particular in the context of enforcement. Particular types of law may lead to specific emotions. Regulatory or coercive law may elicit fear. For example, . . . the power of school inspectors to recommend school closures generated levels of fear among the regulated unknown in business regulation. [. . .]

    This section suggests, however, that any legal regulation can give rise to the full range of emotions, not just negative emotions, such as shame and fear. According to Kemper's social interactional theory, emotions are a response to environmental stimuli. These stimuli are produced in social relationships between individuals. Kemper considers power and status distributions as key aspects of these relationships. Changes in their distribution lead to the production of emotions. The feelings produced vary depending if the self or the other person are seen as the source of one's excessive, sufficient or insufficient status or power. For example, if one actor perceives the status others grant to him or her as adequate then this actor will feel secure. When a person, however, thinks that too much status is allocated to them by another person then the emotion produced is shame. This, however, can be 'extrojected' in the form of hostility or anger towards the other.

    Legal regulation can impact directly on the distribution of power and status among social actors. For instance, command-and-control regulation, can enhance the power of regulators, or where devices of 'creative compliance' are successfully used it can enhance the power of the regulated. Even where legal regulation is not enforced in practice, simply its existence can affect the distribution of power and status between social actors. For example, bargaining between regulators and regulated can occur in the shadow of the 'big stick' of sanctions. According to Kemper, status exists when social actors possess positive attributes in response to which other social actors grant voluntary compliance with the demands of such actors. For example, regulators are sometimes perceived as providers of expert consultancy advice by the regulated. The regulated at times comply voluntarily with regulators' demands because regulators are attributed status on the basis of their knowledge and expertise. Legal regulation can affect the distribution of status between the regulated and regulators. For example, the invocation of criminal sanctions can lead to status loss. According to Kemper, the perception of the distribution of status between social actors as adequate, insufficient or excessive, in turn, leads to the production of emotions. Understanding how legal regulation generates emotions is important because emotions can help to explain social dynamics between the regulated and the regulators. For example, anger might lead to behaviour which is directed at change, while security might underpin behaviour which is aimed at the preservation of the status quo between regulated and regulators. [. . .]

Notes

1   H. Garfinkel, *Studies in Ethnomethodology* (1967).
2   T. Scheff, *Microsociology: Discourse, Emotion, and Social Structure* (1990) 76–8.
3   H. Jenkins and M. Valiente, 'Bodily Transactions of the Passions: El Calor among Salvadorean Women Refugees' in *Embodiment and Experience: The Existential Ground of Culture and Self*, ed. T. Csordas (1994) 163–82..

Chapter 48

Arie Freiberg

AFFECTIVE VERSUS EFFECTIVE JUSTICE

Instrumentalism and emotionalism in criminal justice

IMPRISONMENT RATES IN AUSTRALIA, ENGLAND and the United States are now at their highest levels in decades. Although crime rates in the United States have fallen over the last decade, the rate of imprisonment in that country continues to accelerate, with no signs of its diminution (Tonry, 1999a). In Australia, although the rate of some crimes is increasing, particularly some crimes of violence and burglary, the increase in the rate of imprisonment far exceeds increases in crime rates. Popular opinion tends to be supportive of this trend, if not to have created it. Politicians, adept at sensing and amplifying public moods, have encouraged the view that a rising punitive sentiment is an appropriate and under-standable public response to crime. While the policy of fighting crime by increasing imprisonment rates has been described as foolish, misguided, irrational or uninformed, it has, nonetheless, captured the public imagination.

Although what some term a 'rational' crime policy – that is, one directed at finding and implementing effective crime prevention or crime control policies – plays an important role in government policy, such a response appears to have failed to strike a chord in the heartland of the community. Either the message is wrong or it has not been not been sold well enough. Despite growing investments in such policies crime prevention policies are regarded by many as defensive, reactive or irrelevant. Noting the dominance of law and order rhetoric in public discourse, Sutton (1997) has argued that the primary challenge facing crime pre-vention strategies is to seize the opportunity to 'develop philosophies and programs which could compete with law and order at both the symbolic and the practical levels' (Sutton, 1997: 17). His argument is that the search for, or even the attain-ment of, technical perfection in crime prevention policies would not make them politically or popularly successful because technical or rational crime control policies fail to address some of the deeper emotional or affective dimensions of crime and its place in our society. The failure of crime prevention, the argument runs, will lie not so much in a failure to prevent crime, but in its failure to capture the public imagination, to tap into the deeper psycho-social forces which have driven the recent wave of popular punitiveness and which underlie the criminal justice system generally.

Recent commentators have noted that in the latter part of the 20th century, an emotional, non-rational, expressive trend in law and society has emerged in contradiction to the formal, rational, administrative and routinized forms of law which came to be termed 'technocratic justice' (Laster and O'Malley, 1996; Garland, 2000). The purpose of this article is to argue that . . . crime prevention strategies are more likely to be successful if they recognize and deal with the roles of emotions, symbols, irrationalism, expressionism, non-utilitarianism, faith, belief and religion in the criminal justice system. The article contends that criminology must deal with the *affective* as well as the *effective*, with both the instrumental and sentimental aspects of penal policy (Garland, 2000).

Rational/instrumental approaches to crime policy

Modern penal policy, a product of the Enlightenment, seeks to understand crime and its control in a scientific, dispassionate manner. It requires an examination of the nature and extent of crime, reported and unreported, its economic and social impact, the means used to combat it: in particular their effectiveness and cost. Sentencing policy looks to utilitarian matters such as deterrence and incapacitation, although non-utilitarian aspects such as desert are major features, reflecting a concern with abstract concepts of 'fairness' and 'justice'. As Garland summarizes it, in a rational system, science replaces belief, calculation replaces commitment and knowledge replaces tradition and sentiment as leading determinants of action. He states: 'In consequence, social practices and institutions become more instrumentally effective, but at the same time they become less emotionally compelling or meaningful for their human agents' (Garland, 1990: 179).

Crime prevention seems to be the quintessential 'rationalist' approach to crime policy. Whether it be early intervention strategies, social or situational approaches or routine activities theories and the like, crime prevention appears primarily as a technical approach to social problems. Find the problem, invent the solution: identify 'the problem child' or family and provide more parental, educational or medical support; improve street lighting, design better suburbs, cars or locks; ensure better access to education and health services; create a neighbourhood watch system and so on (Homel et al., 1999). Dry, functional, worthy and basically, unexciting. In Weberian terms, the transition is from the charismatic to the bureaucratic (Garland, 1990: 183).

Symbolic/affective approaches

[. . .]

Symbols

Criminal justice policy not only has an instrumental dimension, but also contains symbolic and expressive elements (Scheingold, 1984: xiii; Gusfield, 1986: 180). At the symbolic level, government actions symbolize power, status and value positions. Contentious issues such as crime, drugs, alcohol, civil rights, religion, sex and others generate considerable heated and emotional responses, often regarded as 'irrational', but they are only so if they are only seen as pragmatic rather than symbolic issues. Gusfield's work on temperance movements concluded that political decisions in relation to these matters could best be understood in terms of social dramas in which the outcomes were statements or symbols of changes in power or status (Gusfield, 1986). Symbolic acts – legislation, court decisions, sentencing are essentially forms of rhetoric, functioning to organize the perceptions, attitudes and feelings of observers, a series of persuasive devices. Preference for one outcome over another confers status upon one group and possibly degradation upon another.

Under this non-instrumental approach, political struggle is not just about conflicts of interest but become 'vehicles of catharsis' taking on almost magical aspects. It is not a case of classifying action as 'rational' or 'irrational' but more of understanding it as an expression of emotion arising from decisions made about the distribution of power, prestige, respect and honour in society. In the 1930s, Harold Lasswell described politics as the process by which the irrational bases of society are brought out into the open (cited in Gusfield, 1986: 182). This model of politics, termed psychological expressivism, sees the political process as an arena into which 'irrational' impulses are projected. Criminal justice policy is but one player in this area which also 'trades in images, archetypes and anxieties', representing what Garland calls 'a politicized discourse of the unconscious' (Garland, 1996: 461).

Emotions

[. . .] The urge to punish the criminal is deep-seated and probably universal (Tyler and Boeckmann, 1997: 238). Public vengeance may be disapproved of, but it has not disappeared as a private emotion (Garland, 1990: 27). Durkheim argued that the shock of violation of social norms outrages people and produces in them the emotions of anger and indignation together with a desire for revenge which modern, technicist responses to crime fail to recognize or acknowledge. As Garland writes:

> To think of punishment as a calculated instrument for the rational control of conduct is to miss its essential character, to mistake superficial form for true content. The essence of punishment is not rationality or instrumental control – though these ends are super-imposed upon it – the essence of punishment is irrational, unthinking emotion fixed by a sense of the sacred and its violation.
>
> (Garland, 1990: 32)

But the punishment response is more complex than simply the urge to avenge (Newman, 1995). Punishment can give pleasure to those inflicting it while in others it may evoke responses of pity and compassion. Freudian accounts of punishment point to the roles of aggression, displacement and sublimation while socio-psychological theorists of crime and culture note the emotional ambivalence we show towards crime when we both condemn, and are attracted to, crime and punishment and their representations in books, films, plays, news broadcasts and the like. We show similar complex ambivalence towards criminals and revolutionaries, the 'romantic outlaw' phenomenon (Duncan, 1996; Goodrich, 1999: 118) which not only reflects our desire for excitement, the seductions of crime, as Katz termed it (Katz, 1988), but our ambivalence towards authority, our admiration for those who step beyond the bounds and our mixed feelings about responsibility, freedom, routine and about the sacred and profane (Duncan, 1996).

The psychological and psychoanalytic literature indicates that these emotions, beliefs and assumptions, often unconscious, influence our actions in ways that we are unaware. Emotions can be channelled, aroused and organized by rituals and ceremonies: the rituals of the courtroom, the scaffold and the prison, what Garfinkel called 'degradation ceremonies'. As Garland observes: 'The penal process . . . must be seen as a means of evoking, expressing, and modifying passions, as well as an instrumental procedure for administering offenders' (Garland, 1990: 67). [. . .]

Public opinion

It appears that in many western countries public opinion has become more punitive over recent years. Previously unthinkable punishment policies are now not only thought, but enacted in legislation (Tonry, 1999b: 1752). Support for more punitive measures such as three strikes laws, mandatory and minimum sentences, indefinite sentences, sexual psychopath laws, truth in sentencing, boot camps and capital punishment appears to be growing (Tyler and Boeckmann, 1997: 238). In 1965 48 percent of Americans polled thought that the courts were not harsh enough on criminals. In the following decade this increased to 78 percent and has stayed there (Gaubatz, 1994: 2). Another aspect of punitiveness is the willingness to abandon procedural safeguards designed to protect the individual (Tyler and Boeckmann, 1997: 243).

To recognize the growth in punitive policies, is not, of course, to concede that all of the people support all of these policies at all times. Public opinion is neither monolithic nor stable. There is a significant body of research which suggests that 'the public' has complex and multifaceted views on punishment and that there are significant groups in the community who, at any time, are interested in rehabilitation, remorse and reparation (Cullen, 1982). The work of Julian Roberts and others has consistently found that when provided with details of individual cases which set out the circumstances of the offence and the offender, respondents to surveys are often more lenient than the sentencers whose sentences were condemned in the abstract (Roberts, 1992; Hough, 1996). There is also evidence that supports the notion that stereotypes play a role in public support for tough sanctions: as people learn more about the offender than just the crime, they become more willing to embrace non-punitive sanctions.

The relationship between the public and the political process is a complex one. 'Populist punitiveness' that is, the ability of politicians to draw from, feed upon, amplify and shape public attitudes and feelings is regarded as a cynical exercise in vote buying or power maintenance, but this explanation tells only part of the story (Bottoms, 1995). While politicians and others gain access to the mass media, this does not guarantee success in shaping public opinion. The claims of political contestants must resonate with the public, who will not always be responsive to every claim. Further, responsiveness will change with the times. An important question is 'why are some policies supported at one time and not another' (Tonry, 1999b: 1752)? People's circumstances shape their beliefs: people will believe different things under different circumstances. What is enduring and timeless and what is sensitive to change (Tonry, 1999b: 1755)?

Garland has recently argued that the increase in popular support for punitive policies is rooted in major social changes which include the wider exposure of the professional middle classes to crime, the declining influence of social expertise and a consequent loss of faith in criminal justice professionals, the growth and legitimation of the victims' movement, which Robert Hughes has characterized as the 'culture of complaint' (Hughes, 1994), the changes in everyday life of the middle classes resulting from increases in crime as well as the impact of the mass media upon popular perceptions of crime (Garland, 2000). He suggests that these profound changes have led to alterations in social routines, cultural practices and collective sensibilities and have produced a more intense emotional investment in crime and criminal justice policy. [. . .]

References

Cullen, Frances T. (1982) *Reaffirming rehabilitation*. Cincinnati, OH: Anderson Publishing Co.

Duncan, Martha G. (1996) *Romantic outlaws, beloved prison: The unconscious meanings of crime and punishment*. New York: New York University Press.

Garland, D. (1990) *Punishment and modern society*. Oxford: Clarendon Press.

Garland, David (1996) 'The limits of the sovereign state: Strategies of crime control in contemporary society', *British Journal of Criminology* 36: 445–71.

Garland, David (2000) 'The culture of high crime societies: Some preconditions of "law and order" policies', *British Journal of Criminology* 40: 347–75.

Gaubatz, Kathlyn (1994) *Crime in the public mind*. Ann Arbor, MI: University of Michigan Press.

Goodrich, Peter (1999) 'Book review', *Punishment and Society* 1: 118–21.

Gusfield, Joseph R. (1986) *Symbolic crusade: Status politics and the American temperance movement*, 2nd edn. Urbana, IL: University of Illinois Press.

Homel, Ross et al. (1999) *Pathways to prevention: Developmental and early intervention approaches to crime in Australia*. Canberra: National Crime Prevention, Attorney-General's Department.

Hough, Michael (1996) 'People talking about punishment', *The Howard Journal* 35: 191–214.

Hughes, Robert (1994) *The culture of complaint: The fraying of America*. New York: Warner Books.

Katz, Jack (1988) *Seductions of crime: Moral and sensual attractions in doing evil*. New York: Basic Books.

Laster, Kathy and Pat O'Malley (1996) 'Sensitive new-age laws: The reassertion of emotionality in law', *International Journal of the Sociology of Law* 24: 21–40.

Newman, Graeme (1995) *Just and painful: A case for the corporal punishment of criminals*, 2nd edn. New York: Harrow & Heston.

Roberts, Julian (1992) 'Public opinion, crime and criminal justice', in Michael Tonry (ed.) *Crime and justice: A review of research*, Vol. 16. Chicago, IL: University of Chicago Press.

Scheingold, Stuart (1984) *The politics of law and order: Street crime and public policy*. New York: Longman.

Sutton, Adam (1997) 'Crime prevention: The policy dilemmas – a personal account', in Pat O'Malley and Adam Sutton (eds) *Crime prevention in Australia*. Sydney: The Federation Press.

Tonry, Michael (1999a) 'Why are US incarceration rates so high?', *Overcrowded Times* 10(3): 1, 8–15.

Tonry, Michael (1999b) 'Rethinking unthinkable punishment policies in America', *UCLA Law Review* 46: 1751.

Tyler, Tom R. and Robert J. Boeckmann (1997) 'Three strikes and you are out, but why? The psychology of public support for punishing rule breakers', *Law and Society Review* 31: 237–65.

Chapter 49

Yael Navaro-Yashin

MAKE-BELIEVE PAPERS, LEGAL FORMS AND THE COUNTERFEIT

Affective interactions between documents and people in Britain and Cyprus

THIS ARTICLE IS ABOUT THE affective interaction which a group with a specific history has fashioned with various complexes of law and state-craft. I study Turkish-Cypriots as they relate to and transact documents produced by several different administrative structures and practices. The focus on Turkish-Cypriots is significant, as they have been subjects and 'citizens', since 1983, of an unrecognized state, the 'Turkish Republic of Northern Cyprus' (TRNC), which is considered illegal under international law Documents produced by this 'state' for identity verification and travel, then, form a centrepiece of my enquiry here, where I explore what it means, affectively, to deal with internationally unrecognized forms of certification. Identity cards and passports issued by the 'TRNC' are technically not recognized anywhere outside Northern Cyprus, and yet there have been a set of state practices in place whereby people have had to organize their lives whilst verifying it through these documents.

But there is something peculiar about 'TRNC' documents in that they are both real and unreal, present and absent. On the one hand, they exist and there is an administrative practice in place in Northern Cyprus that requires them. On the other hand, these documents mean little once one leaves Northern Cyprus, as they, like the state which manufactures them, are not recognized. Following my Turkish-Cypriot informants who often called their polity a 'make-believe state' (*uyduruk devlet*), I name the papers of the 'TRNC' make-believe papers, with the intention of emphasizing their performative and phantasmatic quality. [. . .] I do not introduce the category of the 'make-believe' just as a device to distinguish the illegal regime in the 'TRNC' away from its legal counterparts, but in order to illuminate the phantasmatic aspect of politics, including those in legal regimes, more generally. People believe in the fictions that they make, or fictions have potency and real effects. Under the 'TRNC', an illegal state, this phantasmatic aspect of politics is only more evident because this state practice is not recognized by the international system: everyone draws attention to the manufactured aspect of reality here. However, my argument is that such 'make-believe' styles can be studied, if with more careful observation, in legal regimes and other administrative practices, too.

. . . I am then interested in contrasting these documents with forms and papers produced by three other administrative entities with which Turkish-Cypriots interact in the contemporary period. These are: Britain, where they have travelled as immigrants or asylum-seekers; the Republic of Cyprus, from where they have recently been reclaiming their rights, as citizens, to obtain legally recognized identity cards and passports; and the underground passport mafia in which Turkish-Cypriots are involved, along with others, where they produce and sell forged documentation and passports to citizens of Turkey or others who would otherwise be blocked from access to the European Union. [. . .]

Against the connotations which the term 'legal' might invoke, documentary practices in Britain do not entice affects of calm, security and quietude among Turkish-Cypriots. In other words, the legal procedures and regulations of western Europe, or the European Union more broadly, incite affectivities among those at its margins, which are not represented or imagined in formal portrayals of 'the law' in Europe. In turn, what I have called the 'make-believe' documents of the illegal state in Northern Cyprus, against what the category 'illegal' might imply, bring out feelings of familiarity among Turkish-Cypriots in the vein of what Michael Herzfeld (1997) has called 'cultural intimacy'. [. . .]

Legal forms: Britain

. . . I begin my story of the affective life of documents through . . . the story of a Turkish-Cypriot man, Fuat, who felt fear and panic whenever he received a letter in the post from a local British administrative body. He would not open the envelopes on his own; rather, he attended one of the community centres where Turkish translators would decipher for him the contents of the letter. Most of the time, the contents would be mundane: a reminder to renew a parking permit from the local council or a blank form from the Inland Revenue asking about the ages of children in the household in order to provide child tax credit. In a rush of anxiety, Fuat would go to the Cypriot community centre in Hackney, where a Turkish-speaking social worker would, through the act of translating, mediate between the British state apparatus and the local Turkish-Cypriot community. There was nothing more piercing in Fuat's psychical experience of the political than those moments of enforced accountability to the apparently rationalized structure of the British welfare state. [. . .] He said he felt rushes of panic each time he had to fill out another document or write another letter to a British authority. He did not fill in the forms, nor did he learn to write letters the way a 'proper' British citizen would learn to do. He asked the translators to do this for him in periodic attempts to contain his anxiety. The letters to the local authorities would be posted straight from the community centre and the original correspondence would be kept in a file under Fuat's name in a filing cabinet at the centre. Those pieces of paper produced, as if by magic, such powerful psychical effects in Fuat's subjective experience of the British state apparatus that he did not dare bring them back home. Filed away in the community centre to pacify their phantasmatic power were all of Fuat's correspondence with the Home Office, social benefit forms, as well as household electricity, gas and water bills, all kept for him by the translators in a safe box. [. . .]

. . . What is important to observe, having taken the British example on board, is the psychical and phantasmatic quality of documents as they are used and exchanged in west European contexts. Correspondence with state bodies through the means of letters in the post, the practice of letter-writing in itself, as well as the filing and saving of such documents for future reference may appear like a neutral, mundane, as well as benign activity from the point of view of those acculturated within the domains of west European complexes of law and statecraft. It may even appear that nothing could be more removed from the spectrum of affect than the clerical side of statecraft. Scholarly works on bureaucracy would have it as such as well, crafting portraits of rationalized western administrative apparatuses, leaving no space for the study of affect. For example, in recent anthropological work on policy documents and their implementations, organizations, 'networks' and 'audit cultures', administrative procedures in west European and other contexts are studied as emergent forms of rationalized practice (see Riles, 2000; Strathern, 2000).

Consider the image of the filing cabinet in the Cypriot community centre holding correspondence with state bodies for Turkish-Cypriots. Such rooms, full of files kept for immigrants who do not know how to engage, in writing, with bodies of British authority, abound in the ghettos of London. They are not, in this case, necessarily specific to Turkish-Cypriots. But the filing cabinet in the community centre, in my analysis, emblematizes a containment and management of explosive affectivity in immigrants' interactions with the complex of British law and statecraft. The Turkish translator, employed as a social worker, endeavours to mediate the relation between the Turkish-Cypriot immigrants and the documents from British state institutions. In the practice of translation by social workers, there is an attempt to pacify and calm the affects transmitted by the documents or the ways in which they are taken in by immigrant subjectivities. The translators assist immigrants in coping with British modes of statecraft by handling their documents for them. The filing cabinet in the community centre, as an object this time, serves a similar purpose. Its seemingly rationalized appearance, gray and containing boring file documentation, goes against its psychical weight and phantasmatic quality for the immigrants. I therefore propose to bear this file cabinet in mind as an analytical motif, a symbol for the study of contained affectivity in the domains of European statecraft and bureaucracy. Documents produced by this specific complex of west European law, 'legal forms' as I have tentatively labelled them, generate nervous affectivity when they are held and transacted by immigrant Turkish-Cypriots. It is to this 'non-rational' underside of apparently rationalized state functions (see Aretxaga, 2005; Navaro-Yashin, 2002) that I would like, again, to draw attention here. [. . .]

Make-believe documents: the 'Turkish Republic of Northern Cyprus'

[. . .] Since 1963, the moment of the break-up of the Republic of Cyprus into ethnically segregated enclaves following inter-communal conflicts with

Greek-Cypriots, Turkish-Cypriots have been governed by several consecutive administrative practices, none of which was recognized as a 'state' under international law. The most recent of these complexes of law and administration is the 'Turkish Republic of Northern Cyprus', declared independent in 1983, to the alarm of the Republic of Cyprus (the Greek side). The 'TRNC' is called a 'pseudo', 'illegal', or 'pirate' state in international legal documents. In this section, I study the wider nexus of documentary practices of the successive Turkish-Cypriot administrations, with specific attention to the 'TRNC'.

In its sophisticated mimicry of other state practices, the 'TRNC' acts as governing body and sovereign power over a population of about 200,000 people. As in other state practices, transactions under this polity are verified by reference to documents. In all of its institutions, including, for example, the Office of Title Deeds, the Electricity Unit, the Tax Office, the Maps Department, the Post Office, and the Immigration Office, the illegal state has created documents of sorts bearing its logo. These documents are highly loaded symbolically because, at each instance of their use and exchange, they do not only represent specific identities and transactions, but also declare the legitimacy of the 'TRNC'.

Unrecognized by the UN and isolated, to a great degree, from international transactions, Turkish-Cypriots who have remained as subjects of the 'TRNC', or who continue to have interests in Cyprus, have had to organize their lives by using and employing internationally unrecognized documents now for decades. . . . Most of these documents, and especially the most symbolically significant ones like the title deeds, identity cards, passports, and stamps, are not recognized or considered 'legal' anywhere in the world outside Northern Cyprus or Turkey. From the point of view of international law, these documents are considered fabrications. They certainly do not carry the symbolic status, weight, and legitimacy of 'legal' documents. They do not provide access to certain practices and transactions outside Northern Cyprus the way 'legal' documents do. In other words, they don't perform the magic which documents effect when they are recognized as internationally valid. These documents work as reference points for bureaucratic transactions only within the confines of Northern Cyprus. Because they are not considered 'legal' (and therefore 'real') outside the zones of this self-declared polity, I construe them as 'make-believe' documents for the purposes of this analysis.

Imagine a population internally communicating with one another through the medium of make-believe documents for several decades and an economy organized around these documents. For example, and most significantly, after the flight of Greek-Cypriots from the north of the island with the arrival of Turkish troops in 1974 and the arrival of Turkish-Cypriot refugees from the south of the island which became 'the Greek side', the makeshift Turkish-Cypriot administration of the period allocated houses, land and property legally belonging to Greek-Cypriots to Turkish-Cypriots who had arrived from villages and towns in the south. This was done through what was called a 'point system', where a council of elderly men from each town and village designated the value of the property each family should be allocated on the basis of the size of their previous belongings in the south. But the Turkish-Cypriot administrative body did not only consider itself to be temporarily settling down the refugees or providing shelter for them. Knowingly defying international law on property and settlement, it considered the transaction permanent and, by allocating property to Turkish-Cypriot refugees, it made its subject population party to its operations. In return for the houses and land that were allocated to them – property which, still, under international law belongs to Greek-Cypriots – Turkish-Cypriots were granted 'title deeds' by the Turkish-Cypriot governing body. Recently these title deeds have been bearing the logotype of the 'TRNC', standing as symbols for the unrecognized state, but also operating as vehicles for asserting its existence. Since 1974, there has been a whole economy around 'make-believe' title deeds. Property belonging to Greek-Cypriots has been bought, sold, rented, and transacted through the use of these 'make-believe' deeds, which are treated as valid documents by the 'TRNC'. So there is a reality, certainly a physicality, to 'make-believe' documents.

. . . What I want to draw attention to . . . is the Turkish-Cypriots' consciousness or awareness of the 'make-believe' quality of the documents they employ for identity verification, economic, or transactional purposes. These documents, like others, generate specific kinds of affectivity among the persons who employ them. If many Turkish-Cypriots inhabit Greek-Cypriot property and hold 'TRNC' brand title deeds, they are not content or at peace with this. They hold these deeds with trepidation. Many Turkish-Cypriots are acutely conscious that they are living on other people's property and do not feel that they really own it, in spite of the 'TRNC' deeds. In other words; they hold the 'TRNC' deeds and have conducted transactions with them, and yet, they do not feel at ease with these documents. They know that these deeds are not considered legal outside the confines of Northern Cyprus, and they are even bothered by and despise these documents.

. . . Documents are ideological artefacts; they are not neutral. But if in certain situations the ideology of documents is not evident to their transactors, under the internationally unrecognized administration in Northern Cyprus, the symbolic content of documents is known to its users. [. . .] On the occasion, particularly, of documents which do not carry out their function, such as 'TRNC' passports, Turkish-Cypriots ridicule the documents in their hands. [. . .]

Documents of the 'illegal' administration incite contempt, evoke unease and encourage wit among Turkish-Cypriots. Remarkably they do not instigate fear, panic or anxiety. Having been used and transacted now under various transitional administrations, documents of the governing entities in Northern Cyprus are familiar ground for Turkish-Cypriots. Turkish-Cypriots have been using versions of such 'make-believe' documents now for decades, for all sorts of administrative and other purpose. They know how to interpret and manipulate, or, if necessary, to reverse the undesirable effects of these documents. We could say that through their wit and irony about it, Turkish-Cypriots have made the Turkish-Cypriot polity a sort of 'home'. . . . And the ironic stance of the Turkish-Cypriots vis-a-vis their 'state' and its physical representations, as well as their sharp criticisms of it, are possible within a context of normalization and familiarity.

Legal forms: the Republic of Cyprus

Imagine a situation where a group of people was forced to abandon their rights to internationally recognized and legal citizenship and assume certificates issued by an unrecognized administrative body. Indeed, Turkish-Cypriots, having been blocked from access to southern Cyprus from the time of Turkey's invasion in 1974, and facing tremendous difficulties in international mobility due to the unrecognized status of their passports, never forgot their entitlements to citizenship rights under the Republic of Cyprus. It could be argued that in their interactions with 'TRNC' documents, Turkish-Cypriots enact an implicit comparison with Republic of Cyprus papers which they know are fully and internationally valid. [. . .]

Turkish-Cypriots have maintained, to this day, a consciousness of their entitlements to Republic of Cyprus documents. In other words, their ambiguous relation with 'TRNC' papers has developed with a subtext of knowledge about their rights to legal citizenship of the Republic of Cyprus. Though technically in Greek-Cypriot hands, the Republic of Cyprus, under international law, is the only recognized state representing both Greek-Cypriots and Turkish-Cypriots. . . .

Through the decades when access across the border with south Cyprus was banned, Turkish-Cypriots found ways to apply for passports from the Republic of Cyprus either through middlemen who secretly operated across the border or by applying for passports through Cypriot embassies and consulates in other countries. [. . .]

In Turkish-Cypriot folk language, Republic of Cyprus passports are called 'Greek passports' ('*Rum pasaportu*'). Turkish-Cypriots know that they have rights to obtain Republic of Cyprus documents because the Republic was meant, since its foundation, for both the Greek and Turkish communities in Cyprus. And the massive move to apply for updated Republican documentation is a way of reclaiming these rights as citizens of the Republic. On the one hand this rush could be interpreted as a way of retrieving a lost, yet 'authentic' identity, while at the same time obtaining 'legal' forms to replace or complement the unrecognized and 'illegal' documents of the 'TRNC'. However, I would argue that aside from the elderly population of Turkish-Cypriots who would have a memory of interacting with Republican papers, for most Turkish-Cypriots of the younger generations, Republican documents felt less 'authentic' (even if 'legal' and internationally valid) than their 'TRNC' documents which have been much normalized through decades of use in Northern Cyprus. The term 'Greek passport' precisely expresses this feeling of remove from the documents in the very practice of claiming them. As they rush to obtain passports from state offices in south Cyprus, Turkish-Cypriots feel that the Republic of Cyprus belongs to Greek-Cypriots. The passport has been personified and allocated an 'ethnicity'. The passionate desire to obtain 'Greek passports', as well as other Republican documentation, should not be simply interpreted as a pragmatic and economical move on the part of Turkish-Cypriots. In other words, Turkish-Cypriots are not neutrally lining up to get Republican passports simply because the Republic is a member of the European Union and these passports guarantee international access without visa requirements. For a group of people whose access to the world was blocked for decades – due to the border, embargoes on the 'TRNC', and its lack of recognition – 'Greek passports' symbolized an 'opening up' or a liberation. 'This place has opened up' many Turkish-Cypriots would say, in reference to the freeing of access across checkpoints through the border after decades of bans on movement. The passports also signified a reunion with a time past, with repressed memories and a bifurcated life. Therefore we could interpret that, though branded 'Greek' and held at some distance, Republican documents have been claimed by Turkish-Cypriots as a way of overcoming decades of blocks and repression. We could even go as far as saying that for Turkish-Cypriots, applications for 'Greek passports' are a political act, a willing or unwilling commentary, through a relation with objects, on their state of discontent as subjects of an unrecognized regime in the North. [. . .]

Affective documents: conclusions

[. . .] In this article, I have studied not representations, but objects, physical things, as phenomena which generate affect. I argue that state-like structures make themselves evident to the persons who inhabit their domains in the form of materialities. Documents are one of the most tangible phenomena which induce state-like affects. Here I use the word 'tangible' on purpose, to mean both 'that [which] can be clearly seen to exist' and 'that [which] you can touch and feel' (*Oxford Advanced Learner's Dictionary*, 2004: 1328). I carry the study of affect and the political, then, to yet another domain, to the study of objects. [. . .]

References

Aretxaga, B. (2005) *States of Terror: Begoña Aretxaga's Essays*. Reno, NV: Center for Basque Studies.

Herzfeld, M. (1997) *Cultural Intimacy: Social Poetics in the Nation-State*. London and New York: Routledge.

Navaro-Yashin, Y. (2002) *Faces of the State: Secularism and Public Life in Turkey*. Princeton, NJ: Princeton University Press.

Riles, A. (2000) *The Network Inside Out*. Ann Arbor: University of Michigan Press.

Strathern, M., ed. (2000) *Audit Cultures: Anthropological Studies in Accountability, Ethics and the Academy*. London: Routledge.

Chapter 50

Susanne Karstedt

EMOTIONS AND CRIMINAL JUSTICE

Emotions and penal law

EMOTIONS PERVADE PENAL LAW AND the criminal justice system. Offenders, victims and witnesses bring their emotions to the courtroom, criminal courts deal with crimes of passion, and their decisions can occasion public outrage and anger, or feelings of vengeance among victims. Offenders feel shame and remorse when they have transgressed the laws, and offences provoke feelings of moral disgust. At the same time, victims as well as offenders elicit our compassion and sympathy.

Law has by no means been blind to this invasion of emotions into its very realm. It explicitly references and grants legitimacy to emotions through legal defences (as in crimes of passion); by establishing specific categories of behaviour like 'hate crimes', or by restricting the admission of evidence that might influence the emotions of jury members and judges (as, for example, in victim statements—see Posner, 2000). Legal institutions and in particular the criminal justice system are the very institutions in society that are designed to deal with the most intense emotions and emotional conflicts, with individual as well as collective emotions. The criminal courts and procedures are a prominent institutional space and institutional mechanism for emotions in society.

The particular position of penal law and the criminal justice system in the emotional space delineated by societies has long since captured the imagination of social theorists, and figures prominently in the work of Durkheim and Elias. Both realized that penal law was deeply embedded in the emotional culture of societies, and intricately linked to the structural and institutional patterns of society. Consequently, decisive changes in the 'morality' (Durkheim) and 'mentality' (Elias) of societies are at the roots of the historical development of penal law and punishment, and criminal justice illuminates—or more technically, indicates—subterranean shifts in the emotional culture of societies. Interestingly, both of these theorists interpreted the historical change from traditional to modern society as a pathway that continuously and consistently limited and changed the role of emotions in the public sphere, and, as a result, modes of penal law and punishment. Modern societies, highly differentiated and interdependent, rely on other and more subtle mechanisms to ensure compliance with norms than the crude and simple arousal of moral and collective emotions by criminal proceedings and the (public) execution of sanctions.

In jurisprudence, the history of penal law and criminal justice is in fact cast as a process that has more strictly confined and more precisely outlined the space of emotions, and limited the amount of emotionality that is admitted in courts. The conventional story of modern penal law portrays a narrowly delineated list and proper roles for emotions in the legal realm, so that emotions do not intrude into the true preserve of law: reason (Bandes, 1999a: 2). Such a juxtaposition of reason and emotion, one deeply embedded in modern thought, seems within the normative framework of jurisprudence to ignore vital facets of the actual role of emotions in law and legal procedures (see Douglas, 1993). The edifice of penal law itself is erected on a strong undercurrent of emotions: the fear of sanctions, that should instil compliance, or vengeance that is to be channelled by legal procedures (Elster, 1999). Popular wisdom as well as criminological theory have both established fear of sanctions as a cornerstone and powerful mechanism of the criminal justice system, the thing that makes it work.

Far from precluding rational action, emotions may facilitate a 'rational response'—for example, to the experience of injustice. The 'handling of emotions' within the criminal justice system is not a priori 'rational', neither in its procedural arrangements nor with regard to its final outcomes, but designed according to specific functions. Both offenders and victims react by no means in principle emotionally, but make 'rational decisions' when dealing with the criminal justice system: offenders try to find ways of beating the system, or victims weigh the advantages and disadvantages of invoking the law (Poletta, 2001).

During the last decade, the secular process of restricting the space of emotions in the penal realm seems to have taken a turn towards bringing emotions back in. A process of 're-emotionalization of law' or the 'reassertion of emotionality in law' (Laster and O'Malley, 1996) spread around the globe, and has changed the criminal justice system in many ways. The 'return of emotions' to criminal justice and penal policies has occurred in two arenas: the emotionalization of public discourse about crime and criminal justice, and the implementation of sanctions in the criminal justice system that are explicitly based on—or designed to arouse—emotions. Both developments corresponded to the changing space of emotions and the emotional culture of late modern societies, and it can be assumed that these processes have fuelled one another. [. . .]

The 'return of emotions'

'The Return of Shame'—as described in a *Newsweek* article in 1995—has brought back an emotion to the criminal justice system that had been dismissed as hopelessly old-fashioned during previous decades. Judges in the United States were the first to remake the courts and the criminal justice system as a public space of emotions. Offenders were ordered by courts to wear T-shirts in public that identified them as thieves. Young offenders had to apologize on their knees to their victims with members of the community present. Sexual offenders had to erect signs on their front lawn warning the public about the inhabitant; another court order sent the victims of a burglary to the house of the offender to take from it what they liked (see Massaro, 1991, 1997; Anderson, 1995; Karstedt, 1996). What is striking about these sentences, is not only the explicit use of emotion, but the way it is done, the great emphasis placed on their publicness. The thin line between shame, humiliation and stigmatization was consistently ignored, and the question of whether shame has the impact intended if imposed in such ways never asked. . . . The effects of constant and public terrorization of norm-violators by an emotional mechanism (which the judges assumed to be shame) on the offender and/or watching spectators was never questioned in these cases. The revival of shame in the first instance came with 'episodic, almost whimsical bursts of judicial, legislative or prosecutorial inspiration' (Massaro, 1991: 1940), which were nonetheless the first and most visible signs of the return of emotions.

The influential movement of restorative justice in criminology and criminal justice is based in contrast on a theoretical concept. In his book *Crime, Shame and Reintegration* (1989), Braithwaite carefully developed a theoretical argument to the effect that shaming the offence, but not the offender, will reintegrate the offender into the community. In indigenous procedures of 'conferencing' from New Zealand and Australia he found settings in which shaming and reintegration could simultaneously work. In particular, he gave the victims a strong role and presence in these procedures. Their participation should make the process of shaming powerful and lasting. The conferences were designed to allow for emotional experiences and expressions of shame, remorse, guilt and anger, but also of sympathy and forgiveness. The fact that procedures of restorative justice have become the most successful reform movement in criminal justice world-wide shows that the return of emotions has struck a cord in the criminal justice system and with the public. In instances as diverse as drunk driving, teenage shoplifting and domestic violence (as well as in the Truth and Reconciliation Commissions for perpetrators of past regimes) emotions were brought back into legal procedures and made an essential part of them. While restorative justice brought victims to centre-stage, it made it perfectly clear that justice is relational, something that establishes an emotional connection between the victim, the offender and the often neglected actors who actually impose the punishment. [. . .]

Disgust, anger, shame: some cautious notes on the use of emotions in criminal justice

The recent discourse about law and emotions has been dominated by three emotions—disgust, anger and shame. Though this discourse lingers between constructionist perspectives and assumptions about 'primordial' emotions, between a constitutive, functionalist and indicative role of emotions for law and morality, there is nonetheless a strong consensus that emotions could and should be used in the legal sphere and in lawmaking more than in the past.

As noted above, legal theorists have identified disgust as a legitimate and valuable barometer of societal morality (Bandes, 1999a: 4; Kahan, 1999; Posner, 1999, 2000). Disgust should and could have a legitimate place in the legal arena. It has been argued that law should shape the cognitive contents of the emotion by leading us to feel disgust for heinous but not sufficiently punished acts like racial violence or hate crimes (Kahan, 1999; see Poletta, 2001 for a critique). In particular, the latter—more constructionist—perspective is in line with conclusions from emotion theory. Nonetheless, it has to be stressed here that universal components in the emotion process are embedded into concrete cultural settings which define the content of moral rules, and thus the situations when disgust is elicited. Cross-cultural studies in more than 35 countries show that feelings of disgust are mostly and universally related to moral evaluations and events of violation of moral norms, in contrast to anger, which is related to experiences of injustice (Scherer, 1991, 1997).

However, the fuelling of emotions of disgust has led societies to treat marginalized groups as if they were less than human, and in particular has instigated racial violence amounting to genocide (Nussbaum, 1999). In his book *Ordinary Men*, Browning (1992) shows how the members of a police battalion in occupied Poland voiced their disgust about the Jewish population, and how they used this emotion in their moral legitimation of the mass murder in which they participated. These emotions had been consistently fuelled among the population during the Nazi Regime (and before), and this process was related to laws that step-by-step deprived the Jewish population in Germany of their civil and finally human status. Most infamous in this process were the Nuremberg Laws issued in 1936, which prohibited marriages between Jews and other Germans, and barred Jews from employing German girls in their households and businesses with accompanying propaganda that Jews were paedophiles. Existing moral norms and the emotions attached to them were thus used to direct emotional reactions of disgust towards the marginalized group. Disgust is 'brazenly and uncompromising judgmental' (Nussbaum, 1999: 21) and therefore comes with a powerful potential for disruptive and violent consequences. As much as it might be 'necessary . . . for perceiving and motivating opposition to cruelty' (Nussbaum, 1999: 21), disgust is also heavily implicated in the commission of cruelty. Using it in the legal realm as a 'barometer of social morality' deprives the law of much of its own potential of establishing justice and fairness.

Anger is the emotion most clearly linked to concerns and values about justice and fair treatment (Frijda, 1996; Mesquita et al., 1997; Scherer, 1997). Notwithstanding cultural differences with regard to the intensity and the display of anger, the emotional link seems to be universal. We get angry when we and others are not treated fairly, or are humiliated, or when our social position and self-esteem are hurt. Legal procedures have a central role in society as they provide justice, both channelling such feelings and simultaneously arousing them. Anger of victims of crime might be linked to such a sense of 'unfair' treatment by fellow citizens. But it is much less clear how 'anger about crime' is aroused in those who have not been a victim and who have no personal experience of crime (Farrall, 2001). What kind of concerns and emotional experiences are involved, and what are the underlying emotion components and processes, when a majority of the population declares that they are 'angry about crime'? Before designing 'affective crime prevention policies' (Freiberg, 2001) that take into account such emotional processes, we need to establish which kind of emotion and emotion process are involved, if at all.

Shame, remorse and guilt are emotions most closely linked to the criminal justice system and the community it represents. Among them shame is defined as the emotion that is embedded in the bonds to groups and communities, and therefore a visible physiological reaction—blushing—is attached to it. Shame is a tremendously complex emotion, dependent on specific contexts, related to a range of other emotions, and actions (Lewis, 2000). Violations of self-esteem, humiliation and stigmatization cause shame as well as anger, varying with the context and the concerns. Obviously, legal procedures have the potential to evoke shame in offenders, but like other modern institutions they do not *require* particular emotional reactions. The return of shame might have counterproductive consequences when shame interferes with procedural justice and fairness, and causes anger and defiance.

Legal institutions are not based on a small number of basic emotions, but on different and contradictory ones. Processes of punishment are linked to feelings of disgust as well as being embedded in emotions of sympathy. Any efforts to bring one of these to the forefront, and make it the foundation of criminal justice procedures, will necessarily ignore the range of moral sentiments which are involved in the individual as well as in the collective. The fact that emotional reactions are attached to moral norms does not necessarily imply the strategic use of emotions in, for example, defining laws against hate crimes or violations of human rights. The complex and complicated role and space of emotions within the legal system does not allow for easy solutions.

References

Anderson, Digby (ed.) (1995) *This Will Hurt. The Restoration of Virtue and Civic Order*. London: The Social Affairs Unit.

Bandes, Susan A. (1999a) 'Introduction', in S. Bandes (ed.) *The Passions of Law*. New York: New York University Press.

Braithwaite, John (1989) *Crime, Shame and Reintegration*. Cambridge: Cambridge University Press.

Browning, Christopher (1992) *Ordinary Men: Reserve Police Battalion 101 and the Final Solution in Poland*. New York: HarperCollins.

Douglas, Mary (1993) 'Emotion and Culture in Theories of Justice', *Economy and Society* 22(4): 501–15.

Elster, Jon (1999) *Alchemies of the Mind. Rationality and Emotions*. Cambridge: Cambridge University Press.

Farrall, Stephen (2001) 'Anger, Fear and Victimisation: Emotional Responses without Emotions', paper presented at joint meetings of Law and Society Association and Research Committee on the Sociology of Law (ISA), Central European University, Budapest, July.

Freiburg, Arie (2001) 'Affective Versus Effective Justice. Instrumentalism and Emotionalism in Criminal Justice', *Punishment and Society* 3(2): 265–78.

Frijda, Nico H. (1996) 'Passions: Emotion and Socially Consequential Behavior', in R. Kavanaugh, B. Zimmerberg and S. Fein (eds) *Emotion. Interdisciplinary Perspectives*, pp. 1–27. Mahwah: Lawrence Erlbaum.

Kahan, Dan M. (1999) 'The Progressive Appropriation of Disgust', in S. Bandes (ed.) *The Passions of Law*, pp. 63–79. New York: New York University Press.

Karstedt, Susanne (1996) 'Recht und Scham', *Neue Kriminalpolitik* 8(4): 22–5.

Laster, Kathy and Pat O'Malley (1996) 'Sensitive New-Age Laws: The Reassertion of Emotionality in Law', *International Journal of the Sociology of Law* 24(1): 21–40.

Lewis, Michael (2000) 'Self-Conscious Emotions: Embarrassement, Pride, Shame and Guilt', in M. Lewis and Jeanette M. Haviland-Jones (eds) *Handbook of Emotions*, 2nd edn, pp. 623–36. New York: Guilford Press.

Massaro, Toni M. (1991) 'Shame, Culture, and American Criminal Law', *Michigan Law Review* 89(6): 1880–944.

Massaro, Toni M. (1997) 'The Meanings of Shame', *Psychology, Public Policy, and Law* 3(4): 645–704.

Mesquita, Batja, Nico H. Frijda and Klaus R. Scherer (1997) 'Culture and Emotion', in J.W. Berry, P.R. Dasen and T.S. Saraswathi (eds) *Basic Processes and Human Development. Handbook of Cross-Cultural Psychology*, vol. 2, pp. 255–97. Boston, MA: Allyn & Bacon.

Nussbaum, Martha C. (1999) ' "Secret Sewers of Vice": Disgust, Bodies and the Law', in S. Bandes (ed.) *The Passions of Law*, pp. 19–62. New York: New York University Press.

Poletta, Francesca (2001) 'The Laws of Passion. Reviewing Bandes's *The Passions of Law*', *Law and Society Review* 35(2): 467–94.

Posner, Richard A. (1999) 'Emotion Versus Emotionalism in Law', in S. Bandes (ed.) *The Passions of Law*, pp. 309–29. New York: New York University Press.

Posner, Richard A. (2000) *Law and the Emotions*. John M. Olin Law and Economics Working Paper No. 103. Chicago, IL: The Law School, University of Chicago.

Scherer, Klaus (1991) 'Die Emotionalen Grundlagen des Gerechtigkeitsgefuehls', in D. Frey and G. Koehnken (eds) *Bericht ueber den 37. Kongress der Deutschen Gesellschaft fuer Psychologie in Kiel 1990*, pp. 411–20. Goettingen: Hogrefe.

Scherer, Klaus (1997) 'The Role of Culture in Emotion-Antecedent Appraisal', *Journal of Personality and Social Psychology* 73(4): 902–22.

12. Compassion, hate, and terror

THE TWENTIETH CENTURY was a century of profound suffering. Rummel (1996) estimates that 170 million people were murdered by governments, and by the end of the century around 2,800 million people were living below the World Bank's $2/day poverty line, with 18 million dying each year from poverty related causes (Pogge 2002). The start of the twenty-first century looks no better, with inequalities widening globally and warfare rife. In this context, non-governmental organizations struggle to draw public attention to the mass suffering caused by war, material scarcity, oppression and natural disasters and human rights organizations strive to document and disseminate a seemingly endless flow of atrocities (Cohen 2001). Compassion, hate, and terror are emotional terms that frequently appear in the media today, particularly after the 9/11 events. There can be little doubt they have become key metonyms for aspects of contemporary geo-political reality, and this fact has not escaped the attention of social scientists (Nussbaum 1996; Kleinman *et al.* 1997; Das 1997; Moeller 1999; Das *et al.* 2000; Wilkinson 2005).

There is something uniquely modern about the mutual implication of compassion, hate, and terror in a distinctly political form. In her classic book *On Revolution* (1963: 79) Hannah Arendt argues, for instance, that the realities of the French revolution 'cannot be understood without taking into account the crucial role compassion had come to play in the minds and hearts of those who prepared and those who acted [in it]'. Compassion, she argues, became the driving force of the revolutionaries once the Jacobins, led by Robespierre, had seized power. The notion of consent as a prerequisite of government gave way, she argues, to Rousseau's notion of the *volonté générale* (general will) and, for Robespierre, the unifying principle of the general will 'was the compassion of those who did not suffer with those who were *malheureux*', namely, the 'people' (the phrase *le peuple* became an equivalent for misfortune and unhappiness). Legitimate political power thus became identified with 'the capacity to suffer with the "immense class of the poor", accompanied by the will to raise compassion to the rank of the supreme political passion and of the highest political virtue' (1963: 75). Since compassion was associated with uncorrupted human nature, self-interest became cast as the source of all depravity and of an ever-present inhuman enemy within. In this context, far from being an openness to the concrete suffering of particular others, compassion transformed into the abstract form of pity which, as Arendt puts it, 'has proved to possess a greater capacity for cruelty than cruelty itself' (1963: 89). She thus controversially traces a direct line from a politics of pity to the hatred of the reign of terror enacted in the name of Robespierre's 'Republic of Virtue' (cf. Boltanski, 1999; Barker, 2007).

Compassion towards the suffering of others 'in general' can, it seems, lead to a re-doubling of suffering through the provision of a warrant for hate and terror. What appears to be the highest good thus merges with, and becomes seemingly indissociable from, the gravest bad. This frustrating Orwellian confusion in which words appear to take on the opposite of their ordinary meaning is, unfortunately, an all too common experience amongst those who have lived and died on the wrong side of regimes of terror. This is the very theme of Marguerite Feitlowitz's (1998) book *A Lexicon of Terror: Argentina and the legacies of torture*, from which our first extract is drawn. Regimes such as the one that came to rule Argentina during the mid 1970s invariably construe themselves as operating in the name of virtue, and have a powerful interest, not just in construing the targets of terror as 'delinquent', 'criminal', 'subversive' and otherwise 'immoral' and deserving of their fate, but also in convincing their victims that this is the case. Language itself thus becomes a painful and fraught minefield of confusion, as when the word 'persuasion' becomes identified with acts of torture. Feitlowitz thus sets about constructing a lexicon of terror which bears witness to some of the perversions of language that were wrapped up in the suffering inflicted upon so many victims of the regime. 'I am convinced', writes Feitlowitz, 'that we will not begin to grasp what happened in Argentina unless we gain a sense of how these words were *lived*.'

In the second extract, Lauren Berlant (2004) scrutinizes some of the issues at stake in the recent re-branding of the US Republican Party as 'compassionate conservatism'. Berlant associates the rise of this rhetoric of compassion with the shrinkage of state welfare provisions and their replacement with neo-liberal notions such as the 'dignity' of labour (associated with welfare-to-work programmes) and tax cuts. Berlant draws attention to the selective nature of this supposed 'humane recognition', which prioritizes, for example, conventional family structures and religious orientations. Berlant thus suggests that compassion might be better thought of as a 'social and aesthetic technology of belonging' rather than some authentic, organic emotion.

This theme is picked up in our third extract from Judith Butler's (2004) book *Precarious Life: The Powers of Mourning and Violence*. Butler is interested in whether a basis for community can be found in our responses to loss and our sense of vulnerability, particularly in the context of political violence. Through loss, Butler suggests, we gain a tenuous sense of a 'we' that binds humanity together. She wishes to challenge the notion of a self-contained and intact individual with no fundamental need of others, and in this sense her work chimes with a long tradition of others, such as Turner (1993), who argue for the legal, political and moral importance of a conception of 'human frailty'. The definition of 'humanity' is thus at issue in such arguments, and a contrast is implied between a militaristic conception based on a fantasy of independent mastery (and the subsequent denial of vulnerability) and a feminist conception in which the 'I' is nothing without its relations to the 'Other'. Butler thus raises important questions such as, practically speaking, 'What counts as human?', 'Whose lives count as lives?' and 'What makes for a grievable life?'

The extract from social psychologists Elaine Hatfield and Richard Rapson is concerned to address the part played by what they call 'primitive' forms of 'emotional contagion' in the forms of hatred now associated with words such as 'Serbia and Bosnia', 'Cambodia', 'Rwanda', 'Palestine and Israel' and 'Kenya'. This is a controversial topic, since notions such as emotional contagion are still associated, by many academics, with the conservative sentiments of early crowd psychology (cf. Blackman and Walkerdine 2001). Hatfield and Rapson agree that the cultural, historical and political factors informing the calculative and rational considerations of combatants are always very relevant. They argue, however, that the analysis of such rational motives needs to be supplemented with a recognition of the emotional dynamics involved. They are particularly interested in the tendency for people to 'catch' and 'mimic' the emotions of those around them, and they provide some interesting historical examples of the ways in which collectivities can be swept up into what used to be called mass 'hysteria'.

The final extract is from Natan Sznaider's *The Compassionate Temperament* (2001). For Sznaider, compassion as an organized effort to lessen the suffering of strangers is a distinctly modern form of moral sentiment. However, Sznaider seeks to challenge the view that it can thus be 'unmasked' as an insidious form of power and control. He asserts instead that being able to recognize barbarism and to sympathize with its victims is an important part of modern society that can be observed in a range of modern developments (the book deals at length with responses to cruelty against children). Sznaider thus offers a counternarrative to the more typical academic stories of the erosion of moral solidarity under modernity, and seeks to avoid what he thinks of as the nihilistic and cynical rejection of compassion.

References

Arendt, H. (1963) *On Revolution*. Harmondsworth: Penguin.

Barker, V. (2007) 'The politics of pain: a political institutionalist analysis of crime victims' moral protests', *Law & Society Review*, 41 (3): 619–664.

Blackman, L. and Walkerdine, V. (2001) *Mass Hysteria: critical psychology and media studies*. Basingstoke and New York: Palgrave.

Boltanski, L. (1999) *Distant Suffering: morality, media and politics*. Cambridge: Cambridge University Press.

Cohen, S. (2001) *States of Denial: knowing about atrocities and suffering*. Cambridge: Polity.

Das, V. (1997) 'Sufferings, theodicies, disciplinary practices, appropriations', *International Journal of Social Science*, 49: 563–72.

Das, V., Kleinman, A., Ramphele, M. and Reynolds, P (eds) (2000) *Violence and Subjectivity*. Berkeley: University of California Press.

Kleinman, A., Das, V. and Lock, M. (eds) (1997) *Social Suffering*. Berkeley: University of California Press.

Moeller, S. D. (1999) *Compassion Fatigue: how the media sell disease, famine, war and death*. London: Routledge.

Nussbaum, M. C. (1996) 'Compassion: the basic social emotion', *Social Philosophy and Policy*, 13 (1): 27–58.

Pogge, T. (2002) *World Poverty and Human Rights*. Cambridge: Polity.

Rummel, R. J. (1996) 'The Holocaust in comparative and historical perspective, in A. J. Jongman (ed) *Contemporary Genocides: causes, cases, consequences*, Leiden: PIOOM.

Turner, B. (1993) 'Outline of a theory of human rights', *Sociology*, 27 (3): 489–512.

Wilkinson, I. (2005) *Suffering: a sociological introduction*. Cambridge: Polity. Geography and emotion.

Chapter 51

Marguerite Feitlowitz

A LEXICON OF TERROR

Argentina and the legacies of torture

[. . .]

"**WHAT WORDS CAN YOU NO** longer tolerate? What words do you no longer say?" In this way, I gathered entries for "A Lexicon of Terror," a record of the changes wrought in the Argentine language by the perpetrators of the Dirty War. [. . .]

Language as it was used in the camps was a form of torture. What follows are entries for a lexicon of terror, based on interviews I conducted or from testimony given at the trial of the ex-commanders or to human rights organizations. This lexicon gives a detailed picture of daily life in the camps and the thinking that went into their creation. It is no accident that official "germ theories" concerning "subversion" yielded a host of tortures bearing medical names. The accounts are harrowing. But testimony fulfills the sacred obligation to bear witness, and however discomfiting it may be for us, our pain, though great, is minor compared with that of the victims. We lack the right to turn away. After years of taking testimony, I am convinced that we will not begin to grasp what happened in Argentina unless we gain a sense of how these words were *lived*. . . .

Desaparecido / a (n. Something that or someone who disappeared). The concept of individuals made to vanish originated with the Nazis, as part of the doctrine of Night and Fog. "The prisoners will *disappear* without a trace. It will be impossible to glean any information as to where they are or what will be their fate." (Marshall Keitel, explaining Hitler's decree to his subordinates.) In Argentina the model sequence was disappearance, torture, death. "The first thing they told me was to forget who I was, that as of that moment I would be known only by a number, and that for me the outside world stopped there." (Javier Alvarez, CONADEP file no. 7332) Most *desaparecidos* spent day and night hooded, handcuffed, shackled, and blindfolded in a cell so cramped it was called a "tube." Some were given jobs. When their shifts were over, they were returned to their tubes where again they were hooded, cuffed, shackled, and blindfolded. Or they were sent to be tortured. Or they were murdered.

Ana María Careaga was sixteen at the time of her disappearance. She was recently married and three months' pregnant. "As soon as we arrived at the camp, they stripped, and began torturing me. The worst torture was with the electric prod—it went on for many hours, with the prod in my vagina, anus, belly, eyes, nose, ears, all over my body. They also put a plastic bag over my head and wouldn't take it off until I was suffocating. When I was on the verge of cardiac arrest, they called in a doctor who gave me pills. Then I had convulsions, lost consciousness. So he gave me something else and that brought me round. I wanted to die, but they wouldn't let me. They 'saved' me only so they could go on torturing me.

"They were always saying, 'We have all the time in the world.' 'You don't exist. You're no one. If someone came looking for you (and no one has) do you think they'd ever find you *here?*' 'No one remembers you anymore.' The impunity they had. One would go eat, another would take his place, then he would take a break, and another would replace him."

"The worst," she told me, "—so often I find myself saying 'the worst'; it was all 'the worst'—was after they moved me to the infirmary. The camp I was in was in the basement of the Sub-Prefecture of the Federal Police in the neighborhood of La Boca, Buenos Aires. A big police station in a busy neighborhood. There were small air holes between the ceiling and the walls, from which I could hear people walking by, cars and buses passing, life going on as usual—with us disappeared in a torture center. In the afternoon, when the sun was at a certain angle, I could see on the floor the shadows of the people passing by, getting in and out of their cars. Yes, that I think was the worst. To be so close to them, for them to be so close to us, and yet so far away."

Trasladar (v. to transfer, to move). To take prisoners away to be killed. *Traslado / a* (n. transfer). *Trasladado / a* (n. one who had been transferred, one who was a transfer, one who had "got his ticket"). "You quickly learned that you were in the pit for only a limited period of time, difficult to predict. Then, transfer.

"The most terrible thing was that this period was indeterminate. It was impossible to conquer the fatalism and to understand that the visible end of the road was a dark point, a leap into the void, transfer. . . .

"There were various indications that a transfer would be happening soon. A week before, there would be a lot more intelligence officers coming and going, filling out forms. At first we didn't know what these forms were about.

"Another sign had to do with women. They'd check out all of them to see if they were pregnant; pregnant women were [usually] not transferred.

"The transfers didn't happen on schedule, but they happened in the same way. Movement began around two or three in the afternoon. And there was a special crew (all of whom were called Peter—*Pedro*—after the saint who has the keys to heaven).

"The 'lock' called out the code names of those compañeros who had been selected. They had to [exit their cells] and form a single-file line in the passage-way, still shackled and 'walled up' [*tabicados*, see below]. They had to leave behind any clothes: 'Where you're going everyone gets the same uniform,' or 'You're going North, you don't need all those clothes.' [The northern zones of South America are warmer.] Many compañeros were transferred in the dead of winter in only their underwear.

"A doctor . . . always accompanied the transfer. . . . All of the transfers were injected with Pen-Naval, a strong sedative. Then they were loaded onto trucks, from there into an airplane from which they were thrown alive, though unconscious, into the sea." (From testimony given to Amnesty International by Oscar Alfredo González and Horacio Guillermo Cid de la Paz)

Lisandro Cubas, a survivor of the Navy Mechanics School, testified that, "In general, where the fate of transfers was concerned, the officers forbade it being mentioned. . . . [The crew] said previously [before the use of airplanes] the method had been to shoot people and burn the corpses in the Navy Mechanics School ovens or bury them in common graves in cemeteries in the province of Buenos Aires." (CONADEP file no. 6974)

For survivors of the clandestine camps, *trasladar* carries more terror, more grief, than any other single word. "Tension reached untold heights for most of the prisoners. It produced a strange mixture of fear and relief, given that one both dreaded and longed for the transfer that on the one hand spelt certain death, and on the other meant the end of torture and agony. One [also] felt . . . fear of death, though not the fear of any death—which most of them could have faced with dignity—but of that particular death which is dying without disappearing, or disappearing without dying. A death in which the person dying had no part whatsoever . . . as though dying being already dead, or like never dying at all." (CONADEP file no. 2819) At the trial of the ex-commanders a survivor on the stand told the judge, "Sir, it is very hard for me to use the word 'transfer,' because it was employed when they took someone we would never see again. So I will use the word only to refer to those persons, and in all other cases, must use the word 'move.' "

Asado (n. barbecue). Traditionally closely associated with *parrilla*. From the testimony of Jorge Carlos Torres, a seaman stationed at the Navy Mechanics School: "I knew that the bodies of the dead prisoners were taken away from the school in green trucks to the sports field at the far end, the other side of the Avenida Lugones, on the river bank. Two people were in charge of each truck and I once heard them say to the NCO on guard duty that they had come 'to have a barbecue,' which was a way of describing the job. . . . At night the bonfires of burning bodies could be seen. During the day this area was filled in with earth to extend the sports ground; I imagine this was how the remains of the bonfires were covered over. This is the field where I found a blue plastic bag. When I opened it I saw there was a fetus and some liquid inside."

[. . .]

Botín de Guerra (n. war booty). Belongings, including cars, houses, and land, taken from *desparecidos* and detainees.

La Cacha n. nickname for La Cachavacha, a television witch who made people disappear. The name of a camp in Buenos Aires Province.

[. . .]

Enfermería (n. infirmary). In El Vesubio, a central hall with three or four small torture chambers, all decorated with swastikas. In Campo de Mayo, the infirmary was near the operating theater. Although medical attention was given to the bodies of *desaparecidos*, they were psychically tortured: "There one would have to witness the torture and even death of others, as they tried to force prisoners to talk. The length of torture depended on how far the interrogator wished to go." (Juan Carlos Scarpati, CONADEP file no. 2819)

[. . .]

La Favela (n. Portuguese for "shantytown"). Camp in the upper story of the Provincial Police headquarters in Santa Fe. At the time, Brazil had more shantytowns than Argentina. Moreover, many of the inhabitants of the *favelas* were black or of mixed race, which further incited prejudice among Argentines.

Grupo de Tareas (n. task force). Group that carried out kidnappings, torture, and other terror operations. Syn. *la patota* (the gang).

Huevera (n. egg carton). Torture chamber in the ESMA whose walls were lined with egg cartons to blunt the sounds.

Inmobilaría (n. real estate agency). Agency in the ESMA that falsified property deeds and defrauded prisoners of land, houses, and apartments whose ownership was then transferred to navy personnel.

[. . .]

Leonera (n. lion's cage). "So called because it was the place where new arrivals were 'softened up.' It was like a collective cell where five to ten compañeros would be lying on the floor in very bad shape after torture. The first hour they used the electric prod without asking us anything. To quote them: 'This is to soften you up so we understand each other.' " (Oscar Alfredo González and Horacio Guillermo Cid de la Paz)

Marcadores (n. markers). Prisoners who had "broken" under torture and who then agreed to cruise (see *crucero*) with their enforcers, and mark (identify) individuals (acquaintances, friends, intimates) for kidnap.

[. . .]

Números (n. pl. numbers). La Perla slang for lower-ranking personnel who assisted in operations and other types of work. They generally came from other provinces, notably La Rioja and Catamarca. Patricia Astelarra remembered certain *números* staying on to watch torture sessions "out of morbid pleasure."

[. . .]

Pacto de Sangre (n. blood pact). Pact among officers, all of whom had participated in acts of kidnap, torture, and / or murder.

[. . .]

Quirófano (n. operating theater). Torture chamber. . . .

[. . .]

Rectóscopo (n. rectoscope). Anal torture device invented by Julio Simón, the extremely sadistic anti-Semite known as Julián the Turk.

[. . .]

Submarino (n. submarine; traditional Argentine children's treat consisting of a chocolate bar slowly melting in a cup of warm milk). Form of torture in which the prisoner's head was held under water befouled with urine and feces. When the victim was on the verge of suffocation, his head would be raised and then dunked again. After hours of being tortured by five men, Teresa Celia Meschiati "tried to kill [herself] by drinking the foul water in the tub . . . but [she] did not succeed.

[. . .]

Tubo (n. tube). Tiny, narrow, prisoners' cell. Too low to stand, too low for some to sit up straight, too short for some prisoners to stretch out.

[. . .]

Los Verde (n. the green ones). Young NCOs assigned to guard the prisoners; usually 16–20 years old.

[. . .]

Zona Libre (n. free zone). Area cleared and secured by police and military in preparation for an *operación*. Syn. *luz verde* (green light); *zona liberada* (liberated area).

Chapter 52

Lauren Berlant

COMPASSION (AND WITHHOLDING)

THERE IS NOTHING CLEAR ABOUT compassion except that it implies a social relation between spectators and sufferers, with the emphasis on the spectator's experience of feeling compassion and its subsequent relation to material practice. [. . .] In the context of the United States where these essays are written, the word *compassion* carries the weight of ongoing debates about the ethics of privilege—in particular about the state as an economic, military, and moral actor that represents and establishes collective norms of obligation, and about individual and collective obligations to read a scene of distress not as a judgment against the distressed but as a claim on the spectator to become an ameliorative actor.

This national dispute about compassion is as old as the United States and has been organized mainly by the gap between its democratic promise and its historic class hierarchies, racial and sexual penalties, and handling of immigrant populations. The current debate takes its particular shape from the popular memory of the welfare state, whose avatar is Lyndon Johnson's Great Society, with its focus on redressing those legal, civic, and economic inequities that acted, effectively, like disenfranchisement. Now the Republican Party of the twenty-first century brands itself with the phrase "compassionate conservatism" and insists that there is a moral imperative to change our image of the kinds of state and personal actions that demonstrate compassion for those people whose suffering can be deemed to be social.

In particular, its advocates seek to replace the grand gestures of the Great Society welfare state with a melodrama of the overtaxed and the underemployed, those whose dignity must be restored to them by tax cuts and welfare-to-work programs. If an expanding liberal state used laws and programs to animate the technology of amelioration, the compassionately conservative state wants to limit these mechanisms severely and in particular to shift its economic obligations from redressing poverty to protecting income by taking less from and giving less back to workers and citizens. Compassion can be said to be at the heart of this shrinkage, because the attendant policies relocate the template of justice from the collective condition of specific populations to that of the individual, whose economic sovereignty the state vows to protect.

Great Society ideology had presumed that the social realities of privilege did not require individual intentions and practices to contribute directly to inequality. Nor were one's particular experiences deemed authentic evidence of whether undemocratic practices were organizing life. Instead, the Johnson administration argued that unjust inequalities were objective and enabled by state sanction, such that the state must alter its economic, juridical, and bureaucratic rules and practices toward equality while also placing demands on smaller institutions to make the same changes.

In contrast, currently reigning Republican thought resituates who the subject of compassionate action ought to be. No longer is the icon of structural damage any member of a historically and structurally subordinated population but rather the working citizen—that is, the person who works for a living, especially for his family's living. (By "his" I point to the crisis of paternal value that this particular state ideology seeks to ameliorate.) But what happens to those who do not work, do not work steadily, or do not belong to heterosexual nuclear families? The aim of current state policy is to impel these people to work harder and to enter nuclear families, at which point state entitlements will step in to protect their economic interests. The more successful one is at these practices, the more one is protected by the state put forward by this administration.

In other words, compassionate conservatism advocates a sense of dignity to be derived from labor itself—of a particular sort. No longer casting a living wage, public education, affordable housing, and universal access to economic resources as the foundation of the individual and collective good life in the United States, the current state ideology sanctifies the personal labor of reproducing life at work, at home, and in communities. That is, income-producing labor is deemed valuable chiefly in the context of its part in making smaller-scale, face-to-face publics. The Republican view supports the amassing of corporate wealth on the theory that such wealth will produce investments that make the jobs that workers need to maintain their zones of intimacy.

What links these zones conceptually is no longer the American Dream of social mobility as such but faith, faith in the highly symbolized, relatively immobile structures of intimate attachment from the family and the nation to God. Faith in such a project of social membership is seen to provide the moral tone of a state and a nation; at the same time, when compassionate action is necessary to alleviate social suffering, it is seen as at best a local response put out by individuals and smaller institutions toward people who live somewhere, sharing an everyday life. The problem of social interdependence is no longer deemed structural but located in the faith that binds to itself a visible, lived-in community.

In this view all occupants of the United States are local: we cultivate compassion for those lacking the foundations for belonging *where we live*, and where we live is less the United States of promise and progress or rights and resources than it is a community whose fundamental asset is humane recognition. Operating powerfully is a presumption that the local is the same thing as the communal, both experientially and institutionally. This remediation of national life away from the federal state does not blank out the nation but sees patriotism as a feeling of abstract intimacy practiced from the ground up. In asking individuals and local institutions to take up the obligation to ameliorate the suffering that used to be addressed by the state, compassionate conservatives see themselves as moral actors: for rather than imposing solutions from on high, as it were, compassionate conservatives believe that local institutions will best be able to serve the less fortunate persons *who come forward for help*. All social membership is voluntary in this view. By insisting that society's poorest members can achieve the good life through work, family, community participation, and faith, compassionate conservatives rephrase the embodied indignities of structural inequality as opportunities for individuals to reach out to each other, to build concrete human relations.

In the new good life imagined by the contracting state, the capitalist *requirement* that there be a population of poorly remunerated laborers-in-waiting or those who cobble together temporary work is not deemed part of a structural problem but rather a problem of will and ingenuity, and if poverty becomes severe enough for action to be asked for, the individuals caught in that bind are left to themselves and to their community. [. . .]

In operation, compassion is a term denoting privilege: the sufferer is *over there*. You, the compassionate one, have a resource that would alleviate someone else's suffering. But if the obligation to recognize and alleviate suffering is more than a demand on consciousness—more than a demand to *feel right*, as Harriet Beecher Stowe exhorted of her white readers—then it is crucial to appreciate the multitude of conventions around the relation of feeling to practice where compassion is concerned. In a given scene of suffering, how do we know what does and what should constitute sympathetic agency?

Not only is this volume about the present moment, but the present moment haunts its investigations of the compassionate emotions, their aesthetic conventions, their place in political theories, and their centrality to modern subjectivites. This is a peculiarly modern topic, because members of mass society witness suffering not just in concretely local spaces but in the elsewheres brought home and made intimate by sensationalist media, where documentary realness about the pain of strangers is increasingly at the center of both fictional and nonfictional events. The Freudian notion of *Schadenfreude*, the pleasure one takes in the pain of another, only begins to tell the unfinished story of the modern incitement to feel compassionately—even while being entertained.

Some readers might feel that to think about compassion as a social and aesthetic technology of belonging and not an organic emotion is to demean its authenticity and its centrality to social life. No one in this volume says that compassion is merely stupid, naïve, or a narcissistic mirror in which the privileged can express to themselves their worthiness. This worry—that critique seeks to befoul its object—is especially acute in response to writing on what we might call the humanizing emotions: compassion, sentimentality, empathy, love, and so on. But scholarly critique and investigation do not necessarily or even usually entail nullifying the value of an affirmative phrase or relation of affinity. It is more likely that a project of critique seeks not to destroy its object but to explain the dynamics of its optimism and exclusions. If we challenge the affirmative forms of culture, it is not to call affirmation wrong but to see how it has worked that forms of progress also and at the same time support destructive practices of social antagonism. Social optimism has costs when its conventional images involve enforcing normative projects of orderliness or truth. This kind of bargaining demands scrutiny, in that desires for progress in some places are so often accompanied by comfort with other social wrongs. Such contradictions were as much a part of the Great Society as of the compassionately conservative one.

Nonetheless, it makes sense that people object when analysis of the intimate emotions makes those desires for attachment seem equally like instruments of suffering. In the liberal society that sanctions individuality as sovereign, we like our positive emotions to feel well intentioned and we like our good intentions to constitute the meaning of our acts. We do not like to hear that our good intentions can sometimes be said to be aggressive, although anyone versed in, say, the history of love or imperialism knows volumes about the ways in which genuinely good intentions have involved forms of ordinary terror (think about missionary education) and control (think of state military, carceral, and police practices). We do not like to be held responsible for consequences we did not mean to enact. We can feel bad about it; we can feel compassionately toward those who suffer: why isn't it enough to have meant well, or not to have meant badly? [. . .]

No doubt many readers of this volume will not feel comfortable in the faith-based society that is now being offered as the ground of the good. But this does not mean that they are somehow superior to or untouched by the contemporary culture of true feeling that places suffering at the center of being and organizes images of ethical or honorable sociality in response. When the response to suffering's scene is compassion—as opposed to, say, pleasure, fascination, hopelessness, or resentment—compassion measures one's value (or one's government's value) in terms of the demonstrated capacity not to turn one's head away but to embrace a sense of obligation to remember what one has seen and, in response to that haunting, to become involved in a story of rescue or amelioration: to take a sad song and make it better. [. . .]

The aesthetics of compassion—the cultivation of the senses toward a more nuanced and capacious engagement with scenes of human activity—opens a hornet's nest of problems about what responses should be desired and when private responses are not only insufficient but a part of the practice of injustice. Compassion turns out not to be so effective or a good in itself. It turns out merely to describe a particular kind of social relation, as I suggested in this essay's first sentence. Indeed, it would be possible to make an argument about the image of the human the compassion archive provides for us that could bring down on our heads the whole project of feeling committed to compassion.

As I have worked through this volume, I have been struck by an undertone accompanying the performance of compassion: that scenes of vulnerability produce a desire to withhold compassionate attachment, to be irritated by the scene of suffering in some way. Repeatedly, we witness someone's desire to not connect, sympathize, or recognize an obligation to the sufferer; to refuse engagement with the scene or to minimize its effects; to misread it conveniently; to snuff or drown it out with pedantically shaped phrases or carefully designed apartheids; not to rescue or help; to go on blithely without conscience; to feel bad for the sufferers, but only so that they will go away quickly. In this book's archive, the aesthetic and political spectacle of suffering vulnerability seems to bring out something terrible, a drive not to feel compassion or sympathy, an aversion to a moral claim on the spectator to engage, when all the spectator wants to do is to turn away quickly and harshly.

I thought about calling this volume *Coldness and Cruelty*, but that title has been taken and it might confuse the issue by making compassion seem like a bad thing. Yet the relation of compassion to sadism seen generally cannot be overlooked. There was no way to call this volume *Withholding*, either: there is no elastic enough affective term for the variety of refusals archived here. [. . .]

What is the relation between becoming capaciously compassionate and becoming distant from responsibility for what one experiences directly and indirectly about the populations relegated to social negativity? What if it turns out that compassion and coldness are not opposite at all but are two sides of a bargain that the subjects of modernity have struck with structural inequality? Normatively, the bargain would go like this: the experience of pain is pre-ideological, the universal sign of membership in humanity, and so we are obligated to be responsible to it; but since some pain is more compelling than some other pain, we must make judgments about which cases deserve attention. Justice is objective; it seeks out the cold, hard facts against the incoherent mess of feeling. But we must be compelled to feel right, to overcome our aversions to others' suffering by training ourselves in compassionate practice. This discipline is a discipline of our judgment, phrased as the cultivation of our visceral sense of right. This logic only seems circular. Actually, the moral elevation of compassion is reversed when we raise questions about the scale of suffering, the measures of justice, or the fault of the sufferers. The modern social logic of compassion can as easily provide an alibi for an ethical or political betrayal as it can initiate a circuit of practical relief.

This, then, is a book not just about the optimism of fellow feeling nor the privileged pedagogies of social coldness. It is about an emotional complex that has powerfully material and personal consequences. As George Eliot demonstrates in *Middlemarch*:

> Some discouragement, some faintness of heart at the new real future which replaces the imaginary, is not unusual, and we do not expect people to be deeply moved by what is not unusual. The element of tragedy which lies in the very fact of frequency, has not yet wrought itself into the coarse emotion of mankind; and perhaps our frames could hardly bear much of it. If we had a keen vision and feeling of all ordinary human life, it would be like hearing the grass grow and the squirrel's heart beat, and we should die of that roar which lies on the other side of silence. As it is, the quickest of us walk about well wadded with stupidity.

Chapter 53

Judith Butler

VIOLENCE, MOURNING, POLITICS

I **PROPOSE TO CONSIDER A** dimension of political life that has to do with our exposure to violence and our complicity in it, with our vulnerability to loss and the task of mourning that follows, and with finding a basis for community in these conditions. [. . .]

. . . I propose to start . . . with the question of the human. . . . We start here not because there is a human condition that is universally shared—this is surely not yet the case. The question that preoccupies me in the light of recent global violence is, Who counts as human? Whose lives count as lives? And, finally, What *makes for a grievable life*? Despite our differences in location and history, my guess is that it is possible to appeal to a "we," for all of us have some notion of what it is to have lost somebody. Loss has made a tenuous "we" of us all. And if we have lost, then it follows that we have had, that we have desired and loved, that we have struggled to find the conditions for our desire. We have all lost in recent decades from AIDS, but there are other losses that afflict us, from illness and from global conflict; and there is the fact as well that women and minorities, including sexual minorities, are, as a community, subjected to violence, exposed to its possibility, if not its realization. This means that each of us is constituted politically in part by virtue of the social vulnerability of our bodies—as a site of desire and physical vulnerability, as a site of a publicity at once assertive and exposed. Loss and vulnerability seem to follow from our being socially constituted bodies, attached to others, at risk of losing those attachments, exposed to others, at risk of violence by virtue of that exposure.

I am not sure I know when mourning is successful, or when one has fully mourned another human being. Freud changed his mind on this subject: he suggested that successful mourning meant being able to exchange one object for another, he later claimed that incorporation, originally associated with melancholia, was essential to the task of mourning. Freud's early hope that an attachment might be withdrawn and then given anew implied a certain interchangeability of objects as a sign of hopefulness, as if the prospect of entering life anew made use of a kind of promiscuity of libidinal aim. That might be true, but I do not think that successful grieving implies that one has forgotten another person or that something else has come along to take its place, as if full substitutability were something for which we might strive.

Perhaps, rather, one mourns when one accepts that by the loss one undergoes one will be changed, possibly for ever. Perhaps mourning has to do with agreeing to undergo a transformation (perhaps one should say *submitting* to a transformation) the full result of which one cannot know in advance. There is losing, as we know, but there is also the transformative effect of loss, and this latter cannot be charted or planned. One can try to choose it, but it may be that this experience of transformation deconstitutes choice at some level. I do not think, for instance, that one can invoke the Protestant ethic when it comes to loss. . . . I think one is hit by waves, and that one starts out the day with an aim, a project, a plan, and finds oneself foiled. One finds oneself fallen. One is exhausted but does not know why. Something is larger than one's own deliberate plan, one's own project, one's own knowing and choosing.

Something takes hold of you: where does it come from? What sense does it make? What claims us at such moments, such that we are not the masters of ourselves? To what are we tied? And by what are we seized? Freud reminded us that when we lose someone, we do not always know what it is *in* that person that has been lost. So when one loses, one is also faced with something enigmatic: something is hiding in the loss, something is lost within the recesses of loss. If mourning involves knowing what one has lost (and melancholia originally meant, to a certain extent, not knowing), then mourning would be maintained by its enigmatic dimension, by the experience of not knowing incited by losing what we cannot fully fathom.

When we lose certain people, or when we are dispossessed from a place, or a community, we may simply feel that we are undergoing something temporary, that mourning will be over and some restoration of prior order will be achieved. But maybe when we undergo what we do, something about who we are is revealed, something that delineates the ties we have to others, that shows us that these ties constitute what we are, ties or bonds that compose us. It is not as if an "I" exists independently over here and then simply loses a "you" over there, especially if the attachment to "you" is part of what composes who "I" am. If I lose you, under these conditions, then I not only mourn the loss, but I become inscrutable to myself. Who "am" I, without you? When we lose some of these ties by which we are constituted, we do not know who we are or what to do. On one level, I think I have lost "you" only to discover that "I" have gone missing as well. At another level, perhaps what I have lost "in" you, that for which I have no ready vocabulary, is a relationality that is composed neither exclusively of myself nor you, but is to be conceived as *the tie* by which those terms are differentiated and related.

Many people think that grief is privatizing, that it returns us to a solitary situation and is, in that sense, depoliticizing. But I think it furnishes a sense of political community of a complex order, and it does this first of all by bringing to the fore the relational ties that have implications for theorizing fundamental dependency and ethical responsibility. If my fate is not originally or finally separable from yours, then the "we" is traversed by a relationality that we cannot easily argue against; or, rather, we can argue against it, but we would be denying something fundamental about the social conditions of our very formation. [. . .]

What grief displays . . . is the thrall in which our relations with others hold us, in ways that we cannot always recount or explain, in ways that often interrupt the self-conscious account of ourselves we might try to provide, in ways that challenge the very notion of ourselves as autonomous and in control. I might try to tell a story here about what I am feeling, but it would have to be a story in which the very "I" who seeks to tell the story is stopped in the midst of the telling; the very "I" is called into question by its relation to the Other, a relation that does not precisely reduce me to speechlessness, but does nevertheless clutter my speech with signs of its undoing. I tell a story about the relations I choose, only to expose, somewhere along the way, the way I am gripped and undone by these very relations. My narrative falters, as it must.

Let's face it. We're undone by each other. And if we're not, we're missing something.

This seems so clearly the case with grief, but it can be so only because it was already the case with desire. One does not always stay intact. One may want to, or manage to for a while, but despite one's best efforts, one is undone, in the face of the other, by the touch, by the scent, by the feel, by the prospect of the touch, by the memory of the feel. And so, when we speak about "my sexuality" or "my gender," as we do and as we must, we nevertheless mean something complicated that is partially concealed by our usage. As a mode of relation, neither gender nor sexuality is precisely a possession, but, rather, is a mode of being dispossessed, a way of being *for* another or *by virtue of* another. It won't even do to say that I am promoting a relational view of the self over an autonomous one or trying to redescribe autonomy in terms of relationality. Despite my affinity for the term relationality, we may need other language to approach the issue that concerns us, a way of thinking about how we are not only constituted by our relations but also dispossessed by them as well.

We tend to narrate the history of the feminist and lesbian/gay movement, for instance, in such a way that ecstasy figured prominently in the sixties and seventies and midway through the eighties. But maybe ecstasy is more persistent than that; maybe it is with us all along. To be ec-static means, literally, to be outside oneself, and thus can have several meanings: to be transported beyond oneself by a passion, but also to be *beside oneself* with rage or grief. I think that if I can still address a "we," or include myself within its terms, I am speaking to those of us who are living in certain ways *beside ourselves*, whether in sexual passion, or emotional grief, or political rage.

I am arguing, if I am "arguing" at all, that we have an interesting political predicament; most of the time when we hear about "rights," we understand them as pertaining to individuals. When we argue for protection against discrimination, we argue as a group or a class. And in that language and in that context, we have to present ourselves as bounded beings—distinct, recognizable, delineated, subjects before the law, a community defined by some shared features. Indeed, we must be able to use that language to secure legal protections and entitlements. But perhaps we make a mistake if we take the definitions of who we are, legally, to be adequate descriptions of what we are about. Although this language may well establish our legitimacy within a legal framework ensconced in liberal versions of human ontology, it does not do justice to passion and grief and rage, all of which tear us from ourselves, bind us to others, transport us, undo us, implicate us in lives that are not are own, irreversibly, if not fatally. [. . .]

To grieve, and to make grief itself into a resource for politics, is not to be resigned to inaction, but it may be understood as the slow process by which we develop a point of identification with suffering itself. The disorientation of grief— "Who have I become?" or, indeed, "What is left of me?" "What is it in the Other that I have lost?"—posits the "I" in the mode of unknowingness.

But this can be a point of departure for a new understanding if the narcissistic preoccupation of melancholia can be moved into a consideration of the vulnerability of others. Then we might critically evaluate and oppose the conditions under which certain human lives are more vulnerable than others, and thus certain human lives are more grievable than others. From where might a principle emerge by which we vow to protect others from the kinds of violence we have suffered, if not from an apprehension of a common human vulnerability? I do not mean to deny that vulnerability is differentiated, that it is allocated differentially across the globe. I do not even mean to presume upon a common notion of the human, although to speak in its "name" is already (and perhaps only) to fathom its possibility. [. . .]

Chapter 54

Elaine Hatfield and Richard L. Rapson

EMOTIONAL CONTAGION

Religious and Ethnic Hatreds and Global Terrorism

"**WHY CAN'T THE PALESTINIANS AND** Israelis craft a peaceful solution to the current crisis?" political commentators ask. To many, the accords seem so straightforward. In the end – whether the peace process takes 1 year, 10 years, or 1,000 years – Palestinians and Israelis must find some way to share the Promised Land. [. . .]

It is our hope to provide a few insights into the powerful forces that unite people and divide them from their fellows. We hope to provide a better understanding of the factors that provide a shared vision, push emotions to a fever pitch, and contribute to people's perplexing and unrelenting willingness to engage in Holy Wars – no matter how wasted the effort, horrendous the costs, and how devastated a suffering humanity. . . .

Defining emotional contagion

Emotional contagion is defined as:

> The tendency to automatically mimic and synchronize expressions, vocalizations, postures, and movements with those of another person and, consequently, to converge emotionally.
>
> (Hatfield, Cacioppo, & Rapson, 1993, p. 5)

[. . .]

Mechanisms of emotional contagion

The process of emotional contagion is thought to involve three steps: (1) Mimicry, (2) Feedback, and, consequently, (3) the Experience of Emotional Contagion.

Step 1: mimicry

Proposition 1: In conversation, people automatically and continuously mimic and synchronize their movements with the facial expressions, voices, postures, movements, and instrumental behaviors of others.

[. . .]

Step 2: feedback

Proposition 2: Subjective emotional experience is affected, moment-to-moment by the activation and/or feedback from facial, vocal, postural, and movement mimicry.

[. . .]

Step 3: emotional contagion

Proposition 3: Consequently, people tend, from moment-to-moment, to "catch" others' emotions.

[. . .] Since in this paper we are focusing on the impact of contagion on religious and ethnic hatreds and global terrorism, we briefly review a sampling of the historical research on "hysterical contagion."

[. . .]

The dancing manias of the Middle Ages

In the Middle Ages, in the wake of the Black Death, dancing manias, redolent of mass hysteria, swept throughout Europe. Harold Klawans (1990) set the scene of generalized "sorrow and anxiety" that drove people "to the point of hysteria":

> [The bubonic plague, the infamous Black Death] appeared [in the 12th century,] an illness far worse than any of the others. . . . It was an epidemic of unprecedented proportions that broke over Europe in a great wave. Entire villages were exterminated. Fields became neglected. Soon famine complicated the pestilence. And just as the plague receded and the population and economy began to recover, another wave struck.

From 1119 to 1340 – a period of 221 years – the plague ravaged Italy sixteen times. No words can fully describe its horrors, but the people who witnessed them, who lived in those days so full of the uncertainty of life, of sorrow, and of anxiety, were driven to the point of hysteria.

It was at that point that the dancing mania began and spread like a contagion. Today, most historians view this phenomenon as a form of mass hysteria (Klawans, 1990, pp. 236–237).

One writer (reported in Hecker, 1837/1970) described the twelfth-century scene this way:

The effects of the *Black Death* had not yet subsided and the graves of millions of its victims were scarcely closed, when a strange delusion arose in Germany, which took possession of the minds of men, and, in spite of the divinity of our nature, hurried away body and soul into the magic circle of hellish superstition. It was a convulsion which in the most extraordinary manner infuriated the human frame, and excited the astonishment of contemporaries for more than two centuries, since which time it has never reappeared. It was called the dance of St. John or of St. Vitus, on account of the Bacchantic leaps by which it was characterized, and which gave to those affected, while performing their wild dance, and screaming and foaming with fury, all the appearance of persons possessed. It did not remain confined to particular localities, but was propagated by the sight of the sufferers, like a demoniacal epidemic, over the whole of Germany and the neighboring countries to the northwest, which were already prepared for its reception by the prevailing opinions of the times.

So early as the year 1374, assemblages of men and women were seen at Aixla-Chapelle who had come out of Germany, and who, united by one common delusion, exhibited to the public both in the streets and in the churches the following strange spectacle. They formed circles hand in hand, and appearing to have lost all control over their senses, continued dancing, regardless of the by-standers, for hours together in wild delirium, until at length they fell to the ground in a state of exhaustion. They then complained of extreme oppression, and groaned as if in the agonies of death, until they were swathed in cloths bound tightly round their waists, upon which they again recovered, and remained free from complaint until the next attack. This practice of swathing was resorted to on account of the tympany which followed these spasmodic ravings, but the by-standers frequently relieved patients in a less artificial manner, by thumping and trampling upon the parts affected. While dancing they neither saw nor heard, being insensible to external impressions through the senses, but were haunted by visions, their fancies conjuring up spirits whose names they shrieked out; and some of them afterward asserted that they felt as if they had been immersed in a stream of blood, which obligated them to leap so high. Others, during the paroxysm, saw the heavens open and the Saviour enthroned with the Virgin Mary, according as the religious notions of the age were strangely and variously reflected in their imaginations. Where the disease was completely developed, the attack commenced with epileptic convulsions.

(pp. 1–2)

The dancing mania spread from town to town. In Cologne, 500 joined the wild revels; in Metz, 1,100 danced. Priests tried to exorcise the devils. Sufferers traveled to the Tomb of Saint Vitus in southern France to be cured. Paracelsus, a sixteenth-century physician and alchemist, devised a harsh but effective treatment for the dancing mania: He dunked the victims in cold water, forced them to fast, and condemned them to solitary confinement. The hysterical outbreaks began to subside.

The historical record abounds in descriptions of mass emotional effusions inspired by superstition and charismatic demagogues. (Modern-day tent and TV evangelists are masters of the art of contagion, as were such orators as Adolph Hitler.) However, even supposedly "reasonable" folk are not immune to the spread – witness the next case from "The Age of Reason."

The great fear of 1789

In the eighteenth century, the *philosophes* of the Enlightenment championed the cause of science and reason over ignorance, superstition, and tyranny. Much intellectual leadership came from such French writers as Voltaire, Montesquieu, Rousseau, and Diderot, who challenged the traditional legal, moral, hierarchical, and religious foundations of French society. By 1789, large sections of France's professional and middle classes had been converted to these revolutionary ideas, and they became active in trying to achieve the changes in French society that they thought necessary. In fact, some of these advocates of reason began to try to force social change.

Reason and persuasion soon gave way to hate and terror. Rumors began to circulate that the Royal Court and aristocracy were plotting to take over Paris by counterforce. People fled Paris in fear. As they trudged along country roads on their way to the French countryside, they spread rumors of an impending assault on the provinces by a mercenary army of criminals and foreigners in the pay of the aristocracy.

France became gripped by an almost universal panic. Fear bred fear. Local authorities and citizens became convinced that the criminal army was not just on the march, but was at the door. This led to the breakdown of local government, the arming of the poor, and food riots, and furnished a dramatic impetus to revolution in the provinces (Bernstein, 1990; Cook, 1974; Headley, 1971; Lefebvre, 1973).

After the storming of the Bastille in 1789, historians described the years that later ensued as the Reign of Terror – a term suggesting that emotional contagion may have a life well beyond the walls of the laboratory.

The New York City draft riots of 1863

New York City, in the hot summer of 1863, was a place of extremes. The Civil War had brought ever greater wealth to a few and increasing poverty to many. Wartime inflation eroded the buying power of the poor. The city's struggling immigrant population lived in run-down, crowded tenements. Immigrants, especially the Irish, were outraged at the use of blacks to replace striking Irish longshoremen.

New York was an antiwar city, controlled by a local Democratic political machine, which had lost power and influence to the national Republican "war" party. The city's Democratic press and politicians skillfully played up the theme that Northern white workers were betraying their own best interests by fighting to free slaves who would then compete for their jobs.

In the midst of this, a national military draft commenced during the summer of 1863. The new law permitted a commutation of military service for anyone who could pay a $300 fee. This set the stage for viewing the draft as a symbol of Republican over Democrat, national over local government, native over immigrant, and rich over poor.

The first 1,236 names of New York City drafted men appeared in the morning papers at the same time that casualty lists from Gettysburg (the bloodiest battle ever fought on the North American continent) were posted around the city. Early the next morning, men, women, and boys began to move along streets carrying the weapons of the poor – crowbars and clubs. Mobs quickly formed and grew, caught up in and carried away with anger.

Four days of subsequent uncontrolled violence – including the lynching and burning of 12 blacks – left 119 persons dead and 306 injured. Forty-three regiments of union troops had to be stationed in and around the city to ensure order (Church, 1964; McCague, 1968).

The era of mass media

Research on emotional contagion has focused on the effect of interpersonal inter-actions; there is, however, historical evidence to suggest that the dissemination of emotions does not always require direct physical contact or proximity. As rumors spread, emotions may accompany them. Mass communications – films, newspapers, radio, and (particularly) television – can transmit people's emotions far beyond their geographical perimeters. Our very image of the mob is linked inextricably with notions of the spread of anger, leading to the out-of-control behaviors of murder, lynchings, and large-scale destruction. We see daily on television the pictures of weeping and angry crowds mourning the death of a Palestinian guerrilla or an Israeli child, a murdered leader and her mournful followers, or the defiant and angry opposition. We replay the weekend of mourning by an entire nation (perhaps even the entire world) on the assassination of John F. Kennedy. Are these instances of emotional contagion, or are these phenomena too complicated to be so labeled? Historical examples cannot be tested in the laboratory, but they do hint at the reality of emotional contagion and suggest that it may have occurred on a large scale in many historical eras. They also suggest that the mass media of our day may possess power even greater than generally realized because of their potential to precipitate the spread not just of information and entertainment, but also of emotions. [. . .]

References

Bernstein, I. (1990). *The New York City draft riots*. New York: Oxford University Press.
Church, W. F. (Ed.). (1964). *The influence of the enlightenment on the French revolution: Creative, disastrous or non-existent?* Lexington, MA: D. C. Heath.
Cook, A. (1974). *The armies of the streets: The New York City draft riots of 1863*. Lexington, KY: University of Kentucky Press.

Hatfield, E., Cacioppo, J. T., & Rapson, R. L. (1993). *Emotional contagion* (p. 5). New York: Cambridge University Press.

Headley, J. T. (1971). *The great riots of New York 1712 to 1873*. New York: Dover.

Lefebvre, G. (1973). *The great fear of 1789* (trans. J. White). New York: Pantheon.

McCague, J. (1968). *The second rebellion: The story of the New York City draft riots of 1863*. New York: Dial Press.

Chapter 55

Nathan Sznaider

THE COMPASSIONATE TEMPERAMENT

COMPASSION—THE ORGANIZED CAMPAIGN TO lessen the suffering of strangers—is a distinctly modern form of morality. It played a historically important role in the rise of modern society, and it continues to play an important role today. And if we understand the nature of compassion and its connection to social structure, we can explain many social movements today that otherwise seem accidental, unprecedented, and postmodern.

The idea that the sight of suffering imposes a duty to ameliorate it seems like it should be a very old notion but is in fact a very recent one. There is a big distance between a duty that once bound saints and one that is now considered incumbent on all reasonable people. So little was suffering considered an evil before the nineteenth century that the guardians of morality paraded the spectacular suffering of evildoers before the public as a means of improvement. Public hangings continued until the end of the eighteenth century. And during the Reformation, often thought of as the first turning on the road toward modernity, people whose only crimes were doctrinal were routinely burned in the city squares of Europe's capitals.

The movement to reform such cruelties reflected a change in the conception of human nature. No longer were public displays of cruelty thought to be salutary. They were thought rather to be brutalizing—to the people who watched them. The idea that we must remove "brutalizing" conditions in order to "civilize" people developed in tandem with the development of capitalism. Coeval with the rise of capitalism and its "dark satanic mills," as William Blake described it, was a qualitatively new outpouring of compassion.

Compassion is the moral self-organization of society. It is the first moral campaign not organized by the church or the state. The structures of modernity are what make this self-organization of society possible. And the moral sentiments that result from this process constitute qualitatively new social bonds.

My argument in a nutshell is that it is in the nature of modernity to foster compassion. Despite the historical record, this is a minority view among today's intellectuals. Most tend to think of modernity as corrosive of moral sentiments. They see clearly the way in which modernity breaks down older social bonds, but they are much less attentive to the way in which it builds new ones. And when waves of compassion break out into demands for political action, they are forced to consider it an atavism, an excuse, a subterfuge, or an irrelevancy. [. . .]

I have tried to show that compassion as moral sentiment and as humanitarian praxis exists. I used the example of children and the emergence of compassion toward them. But can we really claim that modern society is a compassionate society? Has our century not been the century of horror, mass extermination, genocide, the cruelest and most callous conduct mankind has ever seen? Do not the ovens of the extermination camps in the 1940s cry out that compassion is not a feature of modernity, especially argued by those who see the Holocaust even as the logical consequence of modernity? How can the attempt to curb violence against children compare to these horrors? Is it enough to just have a language that gives us the opportunity to recognize these horrors as such and cry out in lamentation about evil? Is that all that is left?

Clearly this has been the century of cruelty, and it also has been the century of compassion. If we understand the moral foundations of modern society as the interplay between compassion and barbarism that results from the world's moving between a communal morality and a universal one, then we will be able to see not only the breakdown of ethics but also its construction and the processes that accompany both of them. The French Revolution also played a key role in the history of compassion. It produced the Declaration of the Rights of Man, perhaps the founding document in the history of human rights, and in its armies the ideal of equality literally conquered Europe. But the French Revolution was also the site of horrific cruelty. How can these two things be reconciled? Hannah Arendt gives a direct answer: compassion has no place in politics, and when it enters, it leads to cruelty. She believes that modernity begins with the mobs of the French Revolution, and climaxes in the mobs of totalitarianism (Arendt 1963). For her, compassion is not politics. I have shown that it is. Compassion abolishes distance between people, so says Arendt (see also Canovan 1992 and Hansen 1993), but it is exactly distance that can create the kind of public compassion that Arendt would consider an oxymoron. Suffering people, children, animals do not have to be turned into abstract masses. The danger exists; sentimentality always lurks in the back of compassion, but it is not intrinsic to it. For Arendt, at the base of compassion is disdain for the real suffering of people. It is the cause that becomes important, the first step to totalitarianism. Compassion cannot make one free. Arendt might be right here. Compassion was not meant to make one free. But does it imprison us? Her theoretical influence empowered an entire tradition suspicious of modern forms of politics that do not share the highmindedness of the Athenian polis. Arendt's line of thought comes to its consequence by trying to show not only how much totalitarianism is a sign of modernity, but even more: that the realm considered the evilest of all by most people, Nazi Germany and the concentration camps, the world where compassion ended, is a consequence of modernity. The entering of compassion into politics begot the most cruelty of all, the world of the concentration camp. Does that mean that the modern temperament is rather barbarian, as Mestrovic (1993) argues? Can the Holocaust be considered the breakdown of compassion? Is barbarism the true face of modernity? Thus, the critics of modernity argue, the breakdown of civilization is part and parcel of the processes of rationalization and bureaucratization. Arendt hinted to this view; Horkheimer and Adorno radicalized it in their *Dialectics of the Enlightenment* (1971). Foucault and Bauman continued this view of modernity. For Foucault (1965, 1977), humanitarian actions, which I analyzed above, are expressions of discipline and violence. For Bauman (1989), the attempt in modernity to create order—and public compassion does, of course, exactly that—is a form of violence with the worst consequences. But is this true? Can it not be argued that modernity is a form of consciousness and being that is aware of its potential for cruelty and that tries to overcome it in a process of civilization? But in order to do this, it needs concepts of civility, which in turn ask for the recognition of other people's suffering (i.e., compassion). Incomplete as it might be when faced with the cruelties of this world, this state of mind and action is only possible in a modernity of a special kind, namely in a democratic market society.

The question remains whether we talk about "modernity in general" or whether we talk about "peculiar German history" when talking about the Holocaust. I would like to suggest that "modernity" the way Bauman understands it is too weak a concept to try to encompass such an event as the Holocaust. This complete breakdown of civilization, and with it the breakdown of compassion, was first of all an event that involved Germans and Jews. The German Nazis identified themselves with the heroic life, which they contrasted with "Jewish parasites" and mundane everyday life. Nothing scared them more than the perceived decline of heroic ethics, which they identified—and rightly so—with the rise of commercial capitalism. But for them, commercial capitalism was embodied in the Jew. The decline of heroic ethics implied at the same time a "feminization" of culture. But the "feminization" of culture very often meant to the Nazis the Judaization of culture as well. Anti-Semitic imagery not only identified the Jew with the soulless spirit of capitalism, but also as an incomplete man, a woman actually. Hence, for many who identified the commercial spirit with a decline of manly heroism, the identification of Jews and women was almost complete. In more sophisticated forms, one can observe these tendencies in German sociology as well. The hatred of the bourgeois and his spirit was clear in the works of German social thinkers like Tönnies, Sombart, and Scheler, often mixed with anti-Semitism as well.

Elias, in his study titled *The Germans* (1996), points out that even during the end of the nineteenth and beginning of the twentieth century, the social status of rich bankers and merchants was significantly lower than that of high civil servants and military men. The predominance of the duel in German society is a case in point. Elias talks about the bourgeoisified warrior ethos of Wilhelmine German society. This military ethos was also dominant in the industrial spheres of lives. Many written testimonies speak about the parallels of running a factory with the same military discipline as running an army camp. This may not have been typical only for Germany, but there it was hegemonic. Opposed to this notion of Germanness rooted in the soil, defended by warriors ever willing to die an honorable death and fight without mercy and compassion, was the "homeless," the global, the commercial, in short, the "feminine" Jew. Remaining in the framework of Elias and his distinction between "*Kultur*" and "*Zivilisation*," the Jew was representative of civilization and the German of culture. The Jew represented money and abstraction; in short, in the anti-Semitic German mind, the Jew stood for rootless capitalism. I have shown that one can think of money and "alienated" relations also in terms of impersonal relations between people. Obligations are anonymous and are turned into services. Money therefore tends to extend a concept of equality, insofar as the perception of inequality becomes based upon differences in person. This means that the predominance of money relations can unintentionally also foster moral relations like compassion between strangers. The analysis of the metropolis is a case in point. While it was Simmel (1900) who analyzed the "metropolis" as the site of freedom fostered by commercialized and depersonalized relations between people, the very same "metropolis" was analyzed by German sociologists like Sombart (1911) and Tönnies (1965) as the site of alienated and cold relations, as the site where Jews rule. Thus Sombart, in his *Jews and Capitalism*, wrote, "Now the modern city is nothing else but a great desert, as far removed from the warm earth as the desert is, and like it forcing its inhabitants to become nomads" (1911, 423, translation mine). And, of course, Sombart believed the Jews to be natural inhabitants of the desert, and by extension of the city. During Word War I, Sombart, in his *Händler und Helden* (Merchants and Heroes; 1915), took England to be the merchant nation (i.e., civilization) par excellence, while the Germans represented concrete heroism (i.e., culture).

Indeed, something different was going on in Germany. In *The Germans* (1996), Elias speaks about functional democratization, the emergence not only of a middle class, but of middle-class values. In Germany, the aristocratic concept of honor and glory outweighed bourgeois concepts of self-interested economic behavior. What I tried to show above is that a modern notion of compassion arises out of these bourgeois, so-called self-interested actions. Can we, therefore, speak of a German "special path" to history, a notion that seems to be increasingly discredited among historians and social scientists? I believe we should not dismiss Germany's "special path" right away. Elias (1996) talked about "honor" in the context of the duel, a habit that increasingly became discredited in countries outside of Germany as an atavistic residue of aristocratic conduct, while in Germany itself (as shown by Frevert 1991 and McAleer 1994) dueling became part of the habitus of a feudalized bourgeoisie. Clearly, honor and death are very much connected in the notion of the "honorable death." Honor is a positional good (in the words of Charles Taylor 1992); my honor is another's disgrace. My honorable death is somebody else's disgraceful death. Cassirer (1946) has shown how this aristocratic thinking is the bridge to racism and anti-Semitism. As Elias pointed out often enough in *The Germans*, the way from aristocratic to National Socialist concepts was short enough. While middle classes in other countries, especially in the Anglo-Saxon contexts, developed notions of institutionalized compassion, counteracting in many ways the brutalities and excesses of modern life and colonialism, in Germany the brutalization of the middle classes prevented this notion of compassion from emerging as a cultural value.

The major challenge to this view has been launched by Zygmunt Bauman. For Levinas (1990), the social is an extension of the interpersonal. Bauman (1989) misreads Levinas as propagating a presocial morality, a morality that withstands socialization, that withstands society. Levinas's "being with others" is transformed in Bauman to a moral principle that opposes socialization. By that, Bauman looks at the individual as outside of society, even as opposed to society. This view is ahistorical. It overlooks the historical and structural preconditions for the emergence of individualism (as was done by Elias 1978). Levinas (1990) speaks about the existential modality of interaction between people, a view that has been treated sociologically by Mead (1962), Elias (1978), and Habermas (1962). Bauman also "de-Judaizes" Levinas, neglecting completely the point that for Levinas ethics is Jewish ethics. Jewishness is the particularistic identity that is by nature universalistic. It is about religious identity. It is about identifying the deepest roots of Jewishness with modernity, not as something foreign, but as something the Jews invented. It is the antithesis to the above mentioned German habitus. Recall how Sombart compared the city to the desert and located the Jew in both those sites. As opposed to this, the German lives in the concrete forest. Forest and desert have been the archetypal opposites of Germans and Jews. This is true not only in the anti-Semitic mind. Levinas in *Difficult Freedom* (1990) tells us that the Jewish person discovers other people before he discovers landscapes. He is at home in a society before he is at home in a house. To be a Jew means to be free, to be disconnected, to be without roots. In the words of Levinas: "Man is no tree and mankind no forest" (36). This abstract relation to the other is confused by Bauman with an asociological point of view. Simmel, Mead, and Elias knew otherwise. And so did the Nazis.

What I want to say with all this is that it was not modernity that killed the Jews during the Holocaust in the most brutal manner. What killed the Jews was the direct opposite to their being, namely the Germans. To be a German meant first of all to be not a Jew. For Germans to be Germans, the Jew had to die, and not only die the normal death of an enemy, but a death without honor. A death without compassion. Think about how Jews were carried in wagons all over Europe for weeks just for the sole purpose of being killed. They were denied an "honorable death." I think Goldhagen (1996) in his very controversial study has put his finger on that. It was not "indifference" that killed the Jews, but an active, voluntaristic demand to torture and to annihilate them. Think of Auschwitz as a cosmopolitan society of uprooted Jews, speaking dozens of languages, having not much in common besides being Jews. This was the nightmarish civilization that German culture created. A world without compassion and without ethics. The very antithesis of modernity. To be modern means not to be barbaric. To be modern means to be able to recognize barbarism as such, to have a concept of it, to be able to name it. Compassion is key to this.

References

Arendt, Hannah. 1958. *The Human Condition*. Chicago: University of Chicago Press.
———. 1963. *On Revolution*. New York: Viking.
Bauman, Zygmunt. 1989. *Modernity and the Holocaust*. Cambridge: Polity Press.
Canovan, Margaret. 1992. *Hannah Arendt: A Reinterpretation of Her Thought*. Cambridge: Cambridge University Press.

Cassirer, Ernst. 1946. *The Myth of the State*. New Haven: Yale University Press.

Elias, Norbert. 1978. *The Civilizing Process*. Edmund Jephcott, trans. Reprint, New York: Pantheon. Orig. pub. 1939.

———. 1996. *The Germans*. Cambridge: Polity Press.

Foucault, Michel. 1965. *Madness and Civilization*. New York: Random House.

Frevert, Ute. 1991. "Bourgeois Honor: Middle Class Duelists in Germany from the Late Eighteenth Century to the Early Twentieth Century." In *The German Bourgeoisie*, ed. David Blackbourn and Richard J. Evans. London.

Goldhagen, Daniel Jona. 1996. *Hitler's Willing Executioners*. New York: Random House.

Habermas, Jürgen. 1962. *Strukturwandel der Öffentlichkeit*. Darmstadt: Neuwied.

Hansen, Phillip. 1993. *Hannah Arendt: Politics, History and Citizenship*. Standford: Stanford University Press.

Horkheimer, Max, and Theodor Adorno. 1971. "Juliette oder Aufklärung und Moral." In *Dialektik der Aufklärung*. Reprint, Frankfurt: Fischer. 93. Orig. pub. 1944.

Levinas, Emmanuel. 1990. *Difficult Freedom*. Baltimore: Johns Hopkins University Press.

McAleer, Kevin. 1994. *Duelling: The Cult of Honor in Fin-de-Siecle Germany*. Princeton: Princeton University Press.

Mestrovic, Stjepan. 1993. *The Barbarian Temperament*. London: Routledge.

Simmel, Georg. 1900. *Philosphie des Geldes*. Berlin: Humbolt.

Sombart, Werner. 1911. *Die Juden und das Wirtschaftsleben*. Leipzig: Duncker.

Guide to further reading

This collection of annotated references is intended as a resource for further study on each of the areas addressed in the different Parts of the Reader. We have also included a section specifically devoted to the 'affective turn'. As the literature in each of these areas is rapidly expanding, the list aims to be suggestive and illustrative rather than comprehensive.

General

Armon Jones, C. (1991) *Varieties of Affect*. London: Harvester Wheatsheaf. (A sustained argument about the intentionality and rationality of emotional states by an influential figure in the development of a social constructionist account of affect.)

Averill, J. (1982) *Anger and Aggression: an essay on emotion*. New York: Springer-Verlag. (Based on empirical and theoretical work on anger, this volume is also a classic example of a social constructionist approach to emotion in general.)

Calhoun, C. and Solomon, R. (eds) (1984) *What is an Emotion? Classic readings in philosophical psychology*. Oxford: Oxford University Press. (A collection drawing together classic readings on emotion by Aristotle, Descartes, Spinoza, Hume, Darwin, James and Freud; the last two sections include readings by twentieth-century European and Anglo-American philosophers.)

Damasio, A. R. (1999) *The Feeling of What Happens: body and emotion in the making of consciousness*. New York: Harcourt Brace. (An influential neuroscientific account based on the distinction between 'emotion' as physical process and 'feeling' as conscious experience.)

De Sousa, R. (1987) *The Rationality of Emotion*. Cambridge, MA: MIT Press. (An interesting and influential philosophical argument from within a broadly cognitive tradition concerning the ways in which emotional vocabularies are learned via the application of paradigmatic scenarios from early life experience.)

Frijda, N. (1993) *The Emotions*. Cambridge: Cambridge University Press. (A classic and highly influential text in the psychology of emotions that takes a cognitive 'information processing' approach to emotions as events related to concern-based appraisals that modify states of action-readiness.)

Griffiths, P. (1997) *What Emotions Really Are: the problem of psychological categories*. Chicago: University of Chicago Press. (This text presents a psychoevolutionary approach to emotion with a critical review of alternative existing models. One chapter is dedicated to the discussion of social constructionism.)

Kagan, J. (2007) *What is Emotion? History, measures and meanings*. New Haven: Yale University Press. (An overview of emotions by a Harvard emeritus professor of psychology, integrating findings from anthropology, biology, and psychology.)

Katz, J. (2000) *How Emotions Work*. Chicago: University of Chicago Press. (This book combines hermeneutic, phenomenological and interactionist accounts of emotion with evolutionary theory and is particularly strong with respect to the communicative functions of emotional scenes. Chapters concentrate on anger, laughter, crying and shame through a series of imaginative studies involving 'pissed off' drivers, fun-fair distorting mirrors, whinging children and confessing murderers.)

LeDoux, J. (1999) *The Emotional Brain*. London: Phoenix. (An influential text on the neurophysiology of emotions drawing upon a wealth of experimental data in support of a thesis for the primacy of affect with respect to 'higher' forms of cognitive processing).

Nussbaum, M. (2001) *Upheavals of Thought: the intelligence of emotions*. Cambridge: Cambridge University Press. (A provocative contribution to the debate around the rationality of emotions by a prominent US philosopher.)

Oatley, K. and Jenkins, J. M. (1996) *Understanding Emotions*. Oxford: Blackwell. (A textbook written by two well-established psychologists that impressively spans across a broad range of disciplines and considers emotions as functional elements in a broadly developmental context.)

Panksepp J. (1998) *Affective Neuroscience: the foundations of human and animal emotions*. Oxford: Oxford University Press. (An attempt to define a new field of neuroscience based on the study of affect.)

Parkinson, B., Fischer, A. H. and Manstead, A. S. R. (2005) *Emotion in Social Relations: cultural, group, and interpersonal processes*. Hove: Psychology Press. (An overview and intergration of a large amount of empirical data demonstrating the implication of emotions in social events and in the allignment of relationships bewteen people.)

Parrott, G. W. (2001) *Emotions in Social Psychology: key readings*. Philadelphia: Psychology Press. (A collection of influential articles on the nature of emotions and ther role in social psychological phenomena.)

Rorty, A. O. (ed.) (1980) *Explaining Emotions*. Berkeley: University of California Press. (An edited collection with contributions from numerous influential authors that tackles the classification of emotions from neurophysiological, psychological and philosophical perspectives.)

Scherer, K. and Ekman, P. (eds) (1984) *Approaches to Emotion*. Hillsdale, NJ: Erlbaum. (A classic collection edited by two prominent psychologists of emotion which brings together the work of many of the most influential psychologists of emotion of the twentieth century.)

Solomon, R. (1976) *The Passions*. New York: Anchor/Doubleday. (An influential account of the passions which takes issue with their construction in contradistinction to rationality.)

Solomon, R. (ed.) (2004) *Thinking about Feeling: contemporary philosophers on emotion*. Oxford: Oxford University Press. (A collection of essays by contemporary Anglo-American philosophers with interdisciplinary interests.)

Affective turn

Ball, K. and Restuccia, F. (eds) (2007) *Traumatizing Theory: the cultural politics of affect in and beyond psychoanalysis*. New York: Other Press. (A collection of essays that go beyond psychoanalysis in rethinking the cultural significance of traumatic anxiety, melancholy, and the representation of suffering in testimony, self-narration, and politics.)

Blackman, L. and Cromby, J. (2007) *International Journal of Critical Psychology*. Special issue on 'Affect and Feeling'. 21. (A collection of essays from authors critical of mainstream experimental psychology.)

Brennan, T. (2003) *The Transmission of Affect*. Ithaca: Cornell University Press. (This book addresses the belief that the emotions and energies of one person or group can be absorbed by or can enter directly into another. The author details the relationships among affect, energy, and "new maladies of the soul," including attention deficit disorder, chronic fatigue syndrome, codependency, and fibromyalgia.)

Deleuze, G. (1988) *Spinoza: practical philosophy*. San Franscisco, CA: City Lights Books. (Authoritative discussion of Spinoza's conception of affect that decisively influenced the affective turn.)

Massumi, B. (2002) *Parables of the Virtual: movement, affect, sensation*. Durham, NC: Duke University Press. (A key reference for the 'affective turn', Massumi renews and assesses William James's radical empiricism and Henri Bergson's philosophy of perception through the filter of the post-war French philosophy of Deleuze, Guattari, and Foucault.)

Miller, W. I. (1998) *The Anatomy of Disgust*. Cambridge: Harvard University Press. (Presents disgust in relation to the drawing of boundaries and points to the dependency of democracy upon class boundaries organised via disgust.)

Ngai, S. (2005) *Ugly Feelings: literature, affect and ideology*. Cambridge: Harvard University Press. (Makes the case that 'unprestigious' negative affects such as envy, irritation and paranoia are particularly diagnostic of late modern culture and discusses curiousities such as 'animatedness' and 'stuplimity'.)

Redding, P. (1999) *The Logic of Affect*. Ithaca: Cornell University Press. (Makes a historical case for the relevance of the idealism and German *Naturphilosophie* to the contemporary psychology of affect).

Riley, D. (2005) *Impersonal Passion: language as affect*. Durham, NC: Duke University Press. (A feminist theorist and poet, Riley examines the emotionality of everyday language.)

Sedgwick, E. K. and Frank, A. (eds) (1995) *Shame and its Sisters: A Silvan Tomkins Reader*. Durham, NC: Duke University Press. (A collection of the work of Silvan Tomkins with some original essays from other authors using his work.)

Sedgwick, E. K. (2003) *Touching Feeling: affect, pedagogy, performativity*. Durham, NC: Duke University Press. (Best known for her work in queer theory, this author drawns upon the phenomenology of emotion and the work of Tomkins to develop the notion of affects as motivators of performativity.)

Terada, R. (2003) *Feeling in Theory: emotion after the 'death of the subject'*. New Haven MA: Harvard University Press. (A poststructuralist and deconstructive perspective on the relation between emotion and subjectivity, engaging debates in philosophy, literary criticism, psychology and cognitive science.)

Ticineto Clough, P. and Halley, J. (2007) *The Affective Turn: theorizing the social*. Durham, NC: Duke University Press. (A collection of essays on the 'affective turn', addressing the implications of this movement for theorizing new configurations of bodies, technologies and matter.)

Emotions, history and civilization

Bound Alberti, F. (ed) (2006) *Medicine, Emotion and Disease, 1700–1950*. London: Palgrave Macmillan. (An edited collection of contributions from scholars working on the history of medicine who address medical constructions of the relation between emotion and disease.)

Bourke, J. (2006) *Fear: a cultural history*. Shoemaker and Hoard. (A survey of fear in the 'long twentieth century').

Cubbitt, C. (2001) *Early Medieval Europe*. Special issue on 'The history of emotions: a debate'. 10 (2). (A collection of five articles along with an introduction dealing with broadly historiographical issues around the study of emotions in Medieval Europe.)

James, S. (1999) *Passion and Action: the emotions in seventeenth-century philosophy*. Oxford: Oxford University Press. (This book examines the role of emotions in seventeenth-century philosophical understandings of the mind-body relation and of the reasoning / action interface. It provides a grounding in Aritotelian and Thomist conceptions of passion and action before concentrating on Descartes, Melebrance, Hobbes and Spinoza.)

Oatley, K. (2004) *Emotions: a brief history*. Oxford: Blackwell. (An attempt to synthesize ancient and modern accounts of affect by a prominent cogntive psychologist. Combines a conventional notion of history with evolutionary and developmental 'histories'.)

Reddy, W. (2001) *The Navigation of Feeling: a framework for the history of emotions*. Cambridge: Cambridge University Press. (A theory of emotions and historical change, drawing on multidisciplinary sources, and critical of strong constructionist approaches to emotion. The theory is applied in an investigation of Revolutionary France).

Rosenwein, B. H. (ed.) (1998) *Anger's Past: the social uses of an emotion in the Middle Ages*. Ithaca: Cornell University Press. (A collection of essays on the meaning and uses of anger in medieval Europe).

Rosenwein, B. H. (2006) *Emotional Communities in the Early Middle Ages*. Ithaca: Cornell University Press. (A study of emotional discourse in the Early Middle Ages and a contribution to the debates among historians and social scientists about the nature of human emotions. The author proposes the notion of 'emotional communities' and explores it through various case studies.)

Sorabji, R. (2000) *Emotion and Peace of Mind: from Stoic agitation to Christian temptation*. Oxford: Oxford University Press. (A study of ancient Greek views on passions and their influence on the subsequen Christian tradition of scholarship.)

Stearns, C. and Stearns, P. (1986) *Anger: the struggle for emotional control in America's history*. Chicago: University of Chicago Press. (The text inaugurating 'emotionology' as a field of study for historians. The authors trace the development of anger over two centuries beginning with premodern colonial America, drawing on diaries and popular advice literature.)

Stearns, P. (1989) *Jealousy: the evolution of an emotion in American history*. New York: New York University Press. (Particularly interesting with respect to the role played by psychological knowledge in transforming the cultural meanings of jealousy to suit early twentieth-century social arrangements.)

Stearns, P. (1994) *American Cool: constructing a twentieth-century emotional style*. New York and London: New York University Press. (An interesting application of Stearns' notion of shifting forms of emotionology to the notion of 'cool'.)

Stearns, P. (2006) *American Fear: the causes and consequences of high anxiety*. New York: Routledge. (A study of how Americans have traditionally coped with and managed their anxieties in the past, and how the media, businesses, and the government have historically used fear to manipulate the consumers and the public. Stearns argues that controlling fear has become a significant problem in American society.)

Zeldin, T. (1982) *A History of French Passions*. Oxford: Clarendon Press. (An attempt to explain the idiosyncracies of the French with respect to a range of issues such as national identity, taste in art, notions of happiness, friendship and quality of life, etc.)

Emotions and culture

Abu-Lughod, L. (1999) *Veiled Sentiments: honour and poetry in a Bedouin society*. Berkeley: University of Chicago Press. (A poststructuralist informed social constructionist account based on ethnographic work in a Bedouin society.)

Boelstorff, T. and Lindquist, J. (eds) (2004) *Ethnos*. Special issue on 'Bodies of emotion: rethinking culture and emotion through Southeast Asia'. 69 (4). (A collection of articles illustrating the role of emotions in the turn to embodiment amongst anthropologists.)

Briggs, J. L. (1970) *Never in Anger: portrait of an Eskimo family*. Cambridge: Harvard University Press. (An influential anthropological study of the Inuit with some observations about the cultural pressure to contain aggression.)

Grima, B. (1992) *The Performance of Emotion among Paxtun Women*. Austin: University of Texas Press. (Based on ethnographic fieldwork among an Islamic, Paxto-speaking group living in both Afghanistan and Pakistan. Concentrates on ritualistic stories of grief and sadness.)

Hardman, C. (2000) *Other Worlds: notions of self and emotion among the Lohorung Rai*. Oxford: Berg. (An ethnographic study of the Lohorung Rai of Eastern Nepal.)

Harré, R. (ed.) (1989) *The Social Construction of Emotion*. Oxford: Blackwell. (A much cited interdisciplinary collection of essays on the social construction of emotion.)

Hovland, I. (ed) (2007) *Anthropology Matters*. Special issue on 'Fielding Emotions'. 9 (1). (A collection of articles dealing with various methodological and theoretical issues concerning the study of emotion and the role of emotion in the research process.)

Kitayama, S. and Markus, H. R. (eds) (1994) *Emotion and Culture: empirical studies of mutual influence*. Washington, DC: American Psychological Association. (An approach to emotion and culture drawn from the empirical traditions of cross cultural psychology.)

Lutz, C. A. (1988) *Unnatural Emotions: everyday sentiments on a Micronesian atoll and their challenge to Western theory*. Chicago: University of Chicago Press. (An ethnography of emotional life on a Pacific island and an exemplary study in the constructionist tradition.)

Lynch, O. M. (ed.) (1990) *Divine Passions: the social construction of emotion in India*. Berkeley: University of California Press. (A collection of papers largely specializing on the role played by religion in shaping emotional expression in India.)

Manstead, A. S. R. and Fischer, A. H. (eds) (2002) *Cognition and Emotion*. Special issue on 'Culture and emotion'. 16 (1). (Eight articles presenting cross-cultural analyses of various aspects of emotion. The introductory essay by the editors reviews key positions on the 'universality-specificity' dichotomy.)

Milton, K. and Svašek, M. (eds) (2005) *Mixed Emotion: anthropological studies of feeling*. Oxford: Berg. (This book attempts a concise introduction to the anthropology of emotions which is sensitive to the connections between emotions, memory, consciousness, identity and politics.)

Milton, K. (2002) *Loving Nature: towards an ecology of emotion*. London: Routledge. (A social anthropologist explores the meanings of nature in Western societies and culture, particularly in relation to how emotional commitments towards nature are developed.)

O'Nell, T. D. (1998) *Disciplined Hearts: history, identity and depression in an American Indian community*. Berkeley and Los Angeles: University of California Press. (An enthopsychological study of depression among the Flathead Indian people of Montana, by a medical anthropologist.)

Rosaldo, M. Z. (1980) *Knowledge and Passion: Ilongot notions of self and social life*. Cambridge: Cambridge University Press. (An ethnography of a group of hunters and horticulturists from Northern Luzon in the Philippines with a focus on the practice of headhunting.)

Shweder, R. A. and LeVine, R. A. (eds) (1984) *Culture Theory: essays on mind, self, and emotion*. Cambridge: Cambridge University Press. (An influential collection of articles articulating the relationship between culture and psychology with a particular emphasis on emotion.)

Stewart, K. (2007) *Ordinary Affects*. Durham, NC: Duke University Press. (An example of the 'affective turn' in anthropology.)

Wierzbicka, A. (1999) *Emotions across Languages and Cultures: diversity and universals*. Cambridge: Cambridge University Press. (A contribution to the debate on the universality or cultural specificity of emotions from a linguistics approach.)

Wulff, H. (ed.) (2008) *The Emotions: A Cultural Reader* Oxford: Berg. (A collection of work that highlights some of the theoretical and methodological issues at play in the cultural construction of emotion.)

Emotions and society

Barbalet, J. (2001) *Emotions, Social Theory, and Social Structure*. Cambridge: Cambridge University Press. (A study of the role of emotions such as fear, resentment, shame and confidence in social processes.)

Barbalet, J. (ed.) (2002) *Emotions and Sociology*. Oxford and Malden, MA: Wiley-Blackwell. (A collection of eight essays on emotions by sociologists from five countries, each focusing on a specific subfield including political sociology, economic sociology and the sociology of science.)

Becker, D. (ed.) (2004) *Soziale Systeme*. Special issue on 'Wozu Gefühle?'. 10 (1). (A special issue critically addressing Luhmannian theory in relation to emotions with articles in German and English.)

Bendelow, G. and Williams, S. J. (eds) (1998) *Emotions in social Life: critical themes and contemporary issues*. London: Routledge. (An edited collection designed to illustrate the value of taking an emotions perspective in sociological research and social theory.)

Denzin, N. (1984) *On Understanding Emotion*. San Francisco: Jossey-Bass. (A phenomenological approach to the study of emotion.)

Elliott, A. and Lemert, C. (2006) *The New Individualism: The Emotional Costs of Globalization*. London and New York: Routledge. (Aiming to challenge the orthodoxy whereby globalization corrodes private life, this texts examines people's emotional experiences of coping with new individualism.)

Fish, J. S. (2005) *Defending the Durkheimian Tradition: religion, emotion and morality*. Aldershot: Ashgate. (An important contribution to the study of Durkheim and the Durkheimian tradition, this book argues that religion is an essential backdrop for understanding emotion.)

Franks, D. D. (ed.) (1985) *Symbolic Interaction*. Special issue on 'The sociology of emotions'. 8 (2). (Includes articles by Denzin, Scheff, Baldwin, Lofland, Zurcher, Wasielewski, Harris and Sandreski.)

Kemper. T. (ed.) (1990) *Research Agendas in the Sociology of Emotions*. New York: State University of New York Press. (A collection of essays by sociologists of emotion exemplifying approaches that range from positivist to social constructionist).

Scheff, T. (1994) *Microsociology: discourse, emotion, and social structure*. Chicago: University of Chicago Press. (A theory of the microfoundations of social structure based on the analysis of motivational systems, to which emotions are central.)

Scheff, T. J. (1997). *Emotions, the social bond, and human reality: Part/whole analysis*. New York: Cambridge University Press. (A synthesis of social theory, microsociology and psychology by one of the pioneers of the sociology of emotion that yields a promising methodological orientation.)

Stets, J. E. and Turner, J. H. (eds) (2006) *Handbook of the Sociology of Emotion*. Springer. (A near-comprehensive review of developments in the sociology of emotion over the last thirty years. Includes a section organised by focus on specific emotions – and much more.)

Turner, J. H. and Stets, J. E. (2005) *The Sociology of Emotions*. Cambridge: Cambridge University Press. (Reviews theoretical and empirical work in the sociology of emotion, grouped into seven basic approaches: cultural, dramaturgical, interaction ritual, symbolic interactionist, exchange, stuctural, and biological.)

Williams, S. (2001) *Emotions and Social Theory: corporeal reflections on the (ir)rational*. London: Sage. (An overview of social theoretical work on emotions with a concern to critique the reason/emotion distinction.)

Emotion, self and identity

Bosma, H. A. and Saskia Kunnen, E. (eds) (2008) *Identity and Emotion: development through self-organization*. Cambridge: Cambridge University Press. (A collection of authors taking a dynamic systems approach to self and identity as self-organizing processes rooted in emotional dynamics.)

Campbell, J. R. and Rew, A. (1999) *Identity and Affect: experiences of identity in a globalising world*. London: Pluto Press. (Based on case studies of local identities and their affective aspects in South Asia, East Africa, Melanesia and Europe.)

Crawford, J., Kippax, S., Onyx, J., Gault, U. and Benton, P. (1992) *Emotion and Gender: constructing meaning from memories*. London: Sage. (Explores the relations between emotion, memory and identity in situations of fear, anger and happiness using 'memory work' methodology.)

Fisher, A. (ed.) (2000) *Gender and Emotion: social psychological perspectives*. Cambridge: Cambridge University Press. (A collection of essays investigating the stereotype of women as the 'emotional sex', surveying a wide range of specific emotions on the basis of social psychological research.)

Letwin, O. (1987) *Ethics, Emotion and the Unity of the Self*. New York: Methuen. (A philosophical examination and critique of the role of self in romanticism.)

Lupton, D. (1998) *The Emotional Self: a sociocultural exploration*. London: Sage. (A social constructionist analysis of the relations between self and emotions that draws upon a broadly poststructuralist notion of discourse.)

Munt, S. R. (2007) *Queer Attachments: the cultural politics of shame*. London: Ashgate. (Deals with the role of shame in transformational narratives as portrayed in popular and public cultures, with a particular emphasis on LGBT identity issues.)

Nathanson, D. L. (1994) *Shame and Pride: affect, sex, and the birth of the self*. New York: Norton. (An extension and application of Tomkins' theory of affect which makes the case for the centrality of affect to the emergence and formation of self.)

Probyn, E. (2005) *Blush: Faces of shame*. Minneapolis: University of Minnesota Press. (An confrontation of Tomkins' conception of shame and Bourdieu's notion of habitus developed as a resource for rethinking 'who we are and who we want to be'.)

Schoeman, F. (ed.) (1987) *Responsibility, Character and the Emotions: new essays in moral philosophy*. (An edited volume of essays on moral philosophy which address the relationship between emotions and the responsibility individuals have for their actions and characters.)

Shields, A. S. (2002) *Speaking from the Heart: gender and the social meaning of emotion*. Cambridge: Cambridge University Press. (A study of how culturally shared beliefs about emotion are used to shape our identities as women and men.)

Tomkins, S. and Izzard, C. (eds) (1965) *Affect, Cognition and Personality*. New York: Springer. (An early collection of psychological work on the cognitive scripting of affect into personality structures.)

Emotion, space and place

Anderson, K. and Smith, S. (eds) (2001) *Transactions of the Institute of British Geographers*. Special issue on 'Emotional geographies'. 26. (A collection of essays illustrating the affective turn in geography.)

Brandstätter, H. and Eliasz, A. (eds) (2001) *Persons, Situations and Emotions: an ecological approach*. Oxford: Oxford University Press. (A collection that examines the role of temperament, personality and situation variables in everyday emotional experience in real-world settings, using time-sampling diaries.)

Bruno, G. (2002) *Atlas of Emotion*. London: Verso. (An interesting attempt to map the cultural history of the visual arts which touches upon a range of fields including geography, architecture, film and design.)

Cataldi, S. L. (1993) *Emotion, Depth and Flesh: a study of sensitive space*. Albany, NY: State University of New York. (Explores the topic of emotional depth drawing on the work of ecological psychologist J. J. Gibson and phenomenologist M. Merleau-Ponty.)

Davidson, J. (2003) *Phobic Geographies: the phenomenology and spatiality of identity*. Aldershot: Ashgate. (A geographical study of agoraphobia that expands the understanding of the relation between gender, embodiment, space and mental health.)

Davidson, J. and Bondi, L. (eds) (2004) *Gender, Place & Culture*. Special issue on 'Spatialising affect; affecting space'. 11. (Theoretical and methodological reflections on the relationship between space and affect.)

Davidson, J., Bondi, L. and Smith, M. (eds) (2007) *Emotional Geographies*. Aldershot: Ashgate. (An interdisciplinary collection gathering work by geographers and sociologists, this book explores key intersections between emotions and concepts of space and embodiment.)

Davidson, J. and Milligan, C. (eds) (2004) *Social and Cultural Geography*. Special issue on 'Emotional geographies'. 5 (4). (A collection of articles on different aspects of emotion in relation to space, place, and embodiment.)

Thrift, N. (2008) *Non-representational Theory: space/politics/affect*. London: Routledge. (A collection of Thrifts essays on which presents an approach to the politics of everyday life grounded in the notion of affect.)

Emotion and health

Anzieu, D. (1989) *The Skin Ego*. New Haven, MA: Yale University Press. (A psychoanalytic approach to embodied affect and health.)

Chiozza, L. A. (1998) *Hidden Affects in Somatic Disorders*. Madison, Connecticut: The

Psychosocial Press. (Presents an overview of the pathobiographical technique for accessing the unconscious meanings of illness as developed at the Weizsäcker Center in Buenos Aries.)

Greco, M. (1998) *Illness as a Work of Thought: a Foucaultian perspective on psychosomatics.* London: Routledge. (A genealogy of psychosomatic discourse that combines Foucaultian and Eliasian influences. Particularly relevant is the historical and theoretical focus on the inability to experience/express emotions that is labeled 'alexithymia'.)

James, V. and Gabe, J. (eds) (1997) *Health and the Sociology of Emotions.* Oxford and Malden, MA: Wiley-Blackwell. (A collection of essays exploring the potential for mutual contribution between the fields of the sociology of emotion, and the sociology of health and illness.)

Kleinman, A. and Good, B. (1985) *Culture and Depression: studies in the anthropology and cross-cultural psychiatry of affect and disorder.* Berkeley: University of California Press. (An edited collection that makes an anthropologically grounded intervention into the debate concerning the cultural relativity versus universality of depression and dysphoria.)

Kleinman, A. (1989) *The Illness Narratives: suffering, healing, and the human condition.* New York: Basic Books. (A Harvard psychiatrist and anthropologist endeavours to enhance the sensitivity to the emotional dynamics and other relations at play between doctor and patient.)

Pennebaker, J. W. (ed.) (2002) *Emotion, Disclosure and Health.* Washington, DC: American Psychological Association. (A collection of essays examining the health benefits of self-disclosure and emotional expression.)

Rousseau, G. (2004) *Nervous Acts: essays on literature, culture and sensibility.* New York: Palgrave Macmillan. (A collection of essays about the role of medical accounts of the nervous system in the rise of eighteenth century literature and sensibility.)

Scheff, T. J. (1979) *Catharsis in Healing, Ritual and Drama.* Berkeley: University of California Press. (Scheff argues that the healing power of catharsis lies in facilitating a form of distancing through which individuals can simultaneously be participants and observers.)

Spiro, H. (1998) *The Power of Hope: a doctor's perspective.* New Haven: Yale University Press. (An argument that the emotional relief obtained from hope and from a concerned focus upon patient's feelings of pain and anxiety can lessen the suffering caused by illness.)

Vingerhoets, A., Nyklíček, I. and Denollet, J. (2008) *Emotion Regulation: conceptual and clinical issues.* New York: Springer. (Addresses the health implications of coping styles and aggression, alexithymia, emotional intelligence, emotional expression and depression, emotional expression and anxiety disorders, in addition to the emotional competence in children.)

Wilce, J. M. (ed) (2003) *Social and Cultural Lives of Immune Systems.* London: Routledge. (Introduces the hypothesis that immune systems function as cultural symbols as well as material entities and hence that immunity and disease are in part socially constituted.)

Emotion in work and organizations

Ashkanazi, N. M., Hartel, C. E. J. and Zerbe, W. J. (eds) (2000) *Emotions in the Workplace: research, theory and practice.* Westport, CT: Greenwood Press. (An interdisciplinary collection exploring the factors that provoke emotions in the workplace, their effects, and how they should be managed, starting from the premise that organizations are emotional places.)

EMONET. An email list that facilitates scholarly discussion of all matters relating to the study of emotion in organizational settings. Available at: http://www.uq.edu.au/emonet/

Fineman, S. (ed.) (1993) *Emotions in Organizations*. London: Sage. (A collection of essays examining the relevance of emotions to the theory of organizations, drawing on a number of case studies.)

Fisher, C. D. and Ashkanasy, N. M. (eds) (2000) *Journal of Organizational Behavior*. Special issue on 'Emotions in organization'. 21 (2). (A collection of essays on various aspects of emotions in organizations.)

Goleman, D. (1995) *Emotional Intelligence*. New York: Bantham Books. (An authoratative summary of the state of the field of EI.)

Hochschild, A. R. (1985) *The Managed Heart: commercialization of human feeling*. Berkeley: University of California Press. (A classic, influential study of the effects of emotional labor on workers as seen in the occupations of flight attendant and bill collector.)

Hochschild, A. R. (2003) *The Commercialization of Intimate Life: notes from home and work*. Berkeley: University of California Press. (A collection of essays written by Hochschild over the span of three decades.)

Jordan, P. J. (ed.) (2006) *Journal of Management and Organization*. Special issue on 'Managing emotions and conflict in the workplace'. 12 (6). (Six articles on different aspects of the emotional dimensions of conflict at work and their management.)

Lewis, P. and Simpson, R. (eds) (2007) *Gendering Emotions in Organisations*. Basingstoke: Palgrave Macmillan. (A collection of essays exploring the connections between gender and emotion in organizations, focusing on two specific areas: emotional labour and the gendered nature of the expression of feelings at work.)

Ramírez-Ferrero, E. (2004) *Troubled Fields: men, emotions, and the crisis in American farming*. New York: Columbia University Press. (The author goes beyond the traditional focus on political and economic interpretations of the American farm crisis of the 1980s and 1990s, using gender and emotion as modes of analysis to explore the causes of suicide and other responses to the crisis among male farmers.)

Raz, A. E. (2002) *Emotions at Work: normative control, organizations, and culture in Japan and America*. New Haven: Harvard University Press. (A cross-cultural study of emotions as role requirements in the workplace.)

Emotion, economics and consumer culture

Agres, S. J., Edell, J. A. and Dubitsky, T. M. (eds.) (1990) *Emotions in Advertising: theoretical and practical explorations*. Westport, CT: Greenwood Press. (A collection exploring the relationship between emotion and advertising.)

Dittmar, H. (2007) *Consumer Culture, Identity and Wellbeing: the search for the 'good life' and the 'body perfect'*. Hove: Psychology Press. (A prominent social psychologist empirically documents some of the psychological dysphoria associated with consumer culture.)

Erevelles, S. and Granfield, M. (eds) (1998) *Journal of Business Research*. Special issue on 'The role of affect in marketing'. 42 (3). (Ten articles on different aspects of the role of affect, emotion, fantasy and memory in marketing.)

Martin, B., Anleu, R. A. and Zadoroznyj, M. (eds) *Journal of Sociology*. Special issue on 'Commercializing emotions'. 39 (4). (Includes articles on e-commerce, self-help books, sign consumption, the home, the wedding.)

O'Shaughnessy, J. and O'Shaughnessy, N. J. (2002) *The Marketing Power of Emotion*. New

York: Oxford University Press. (An analysis of the significance of emotion in marketing and consumer experience.)

Pilz, F (2007) *Emotions and Risky Choice: an experimental and theoretical study from the economic psychological perspective*. Saarbrücken: VDM Verlag (A data-grounded argument that an account of the emotions must be incorporated into any proper understanding of risky economic behaviour.)

Pixley, J. (2004) *Emotions in Finance: distrust and uncertainty in global markets*. Cambridge: Cambridge University Press. (A study of the views of experienced elites in the financial world, offering an account of the influence of emotion and speculation on the world's increasingly volatile financial sector.)

Rick, S. and Loewenstein, G. F. (2007) *The Role of Emotion in Economic Behavior*. Available at SSRN: http://ssrn.com/abstract=954862 (An article prepared for the forthcoming third edition of *The Handbook of Emotion* which reviews behavioral economic and neuro-economic research on emotional influences on risky decision making, intertemporal choice, and social preferences.)

Strasser, S., McGovern, C. and Judt, M. (eds) (1998) *Consuming Desires: consumption, culture, and the pursuit of happiness*. Cambridge: Cambridge University Press. (An edited collection exploring the relationship between subjectivity and consumer culture.)

Emotion and politics

Ahmed, S. (2004) *The Cultural Politics of Emotion*. London: Routledge. (An analysis of the role of emotions in debates on international terrorism, asylum and migration, and reconciliation and reparation, with reflections on the role of emotions in feminist and queer politics.)

Clarke, S., Hoggett, P. and Thompson, S. (eds) (2006) *Emotion, Politics and Society*. London: Palgrave Macmillan. (A psychosocial approach aiming for an integration of rationalism and emotion in an understanding of political issues such as racism, populism, protest and terror.)

Flam, H. and King, D. (eds) (2005) *Emotions and Social Movements*. London: Routledge. (An edited collection of papers on the emotional dimensions and dynamics of social movements and protest.)

Froggett, L. (2002) *Love, Hate and Welfare: psychosocial approaches to policy and practice*, Bristol: Policy Press. (An argument for a psychosocial conception of welfare practice which centres on human affectivity.)

Furedi, F. (2005) *Politics of Fear: beyond left and right*. Continuum Press. (Argues that modern politics has come to revolve around personal topics. Antagonistic to the perceived enfeeblements of 'therapy culture', it makes the case that human are more resilient and adaptive than is sometimes thought.)

Gandhi, L. (2006) *Affective Communities: anticolonial thought, fin-de-siècle radicalism, and the politics of friendship*. New Haven, MA: Harvard University Press. (A study of cross-cultural collaboration between oppressors and oppressed in late ninetenth-century empire.)

Girling, J. (2006) *Emotion and Reason in Social Change: insights from fiction*. New York: Palgrave Macmillan. (A study of the emotional aspects of globalization, neo-imperialism, modernization and other political issues through the medium of works of fiction.)

Goodwin, J. and Jasper, J. M. (2004) (ed) *Rethinking Social Movements: structure, meaning and emotion*. Totowa, NJ: Roman and Littlefield. (A volume which gathers the key players in social movement theory and strives to overcome the theoretical divide between structural and cultural approaches.)

Marcus, G. E. (2000) 'Emotions in politics'. *Annual Review of Political Science*, 3: 221–50. (A review article covering research on emotions in politics up to the year 2000).

Redlawsk, D. P. (ed.) (2006) *Feeling Politics: emotion in political information processing*. London: Palgrave Macmillan. (This volume adopts a conventional cognitive approach to the role of affect in political action and decision making.)

Satterfield, T. (2003) *Anatomy of a Conflict: identity, knowledge and emotion in old-growth forests*. Vancouver: University of British Columbia Press. (An ethnographic study of the dispute between activist loggers and environmentalists over the fate of Oregon's temperate rain forest.)

Svašek, M. (ed.) (2006) *Postsocialism: politics and emotions in central and eastern Europe*. Oxford: Berghahn. (A collection of essays on the political use of emotions and the emotional use of politics in central and eastern Europe.)

Emotions and the media

Altheide. D. L. (2002) *Creating Fear: news and the construction of crisis*. New York: Aldine de Gruyter. (Adopts a social constructionist approach and charts the growth of a fear discourse in US newspapers since the nineteen-eighties.)

Boltanski, L. (1999) *Distant Suffering: morality, media and politics*. Cambridge: Cambridge University Press. (A study examining the moral and political implications for a spectator of the distant suffering of others as presented through the media.)

Carroll, N. (1990) *The Philosophy of Horror, or Paradoxes of the Heart*. London: Routledge. (Applies insights from cognitive philosophy to the problem of how emotions are provoked in audiences by films. A consideration of the nature of the 'monstrous' in the horror film genre.)

Chouliaraki, L. (2006) *The Spectatorship of Suffering*. London: Sage. (An analysis of the codes and formats of news coverage of distant suffering, and an exploration of its political, moral and cultural effects on spectators.)

Grodal, T. (1997) *Moving Pictures: a new theory of film genres, feelings and cognition*. Oxford: Oxford University Press. (An explanation of filmic emotions based on cognitive psychology that centres on processes of identification.)

Meštrović, S. (1997) *Postemotional Society*. London: Sage. (Critique of the role of the media in generating depthless 'quasi-emotions' with no relation to action.)

Moeller, S. D. (1999) *Compassion Fatigue: how the media sell disease, famine, war and death*. London and New York: Routledge. (A series of case studies examining newspaper, newsmagazine and television coverage of international crises.)

Plantinga, C. and Smith, G. M. (1999) *Passionate Views: film, cognition and emotion*. Baltimore: John Hopkins University Press. (A collection of essays by scholars in film studies, philosophy and psychology, exploring the emotional appeal of the cinema.)

Smith, M. (1995) *Engaging Characters: fiction, emotion and the cinema*. Oxford: Clarendon Press. (A study of emotional responses to films, integrating them into a theory of engagement, or identification with, characters in cinematic and literary fictions.)

Tan, E. (1996) *Emotion and the Structure of Narrative Film: film as an emotion machine*. Mahwah, NJ: Lawrence Erlbaum. (Draws upon Nico Frijda's [see above] cognitive account of the 'laws of emotion' to explain the capacity of film to shape the affective virtual action tendencies of their audiences.)

Tester, K. (2001) *Compassion, Morality and the Media*, Buckingham: Open University Press. (Written in the tradition of European critical theory, this volume explores the 'something has to be done' response to horrific media presentations.)

Emotions and law

Bandes, S. (ed.) (1999) *The Passions of Law*. New York: New York University Press. (An anthology on the function of emotion in legal theory and practice that deals with digust, shame, remorse and the desire for revenge, as well as love, forgiveness and the passion for justice.)

Bornstein, B. H. and Wiener, R. L. (eds.) (2000) *Law and Human Behaviour*. Special issue on 'Emotion in legal judgment and decision making'. 30 (2). (An interdisciplinary collection at the interface of law and psychology dealing with the role of emotion in juridical decision making processes.)

De Haan, W. and Loader (eds) (2002) *Theoretical Criminology*. Special issue on 'The emotions of crime, punishment and social control'. 6 (3). (A special issues aiming to stimulate debate on the relationship between emotions and social regulation.)

Douzinas, C. (1998) *Law and the Emotions: prolegomena for a psychoanalytic approach to legal study*. Florence: European University Institute Press. (Aims to bring contemporary psychoanalytical notions of affect into relationship with critical legal studies.)

Duncan, M. G. (1996) *Romantic Outlaws, Beloved Prisons: the unconscious meanings of crime and punishment*. New York: New York University Press. (Adopts a psychoanalytical approach to understand the ambivalence of public feeling towards criminality.)

Hope, T. and Sparks, R. (eds) (2000) *Crime, Risk and Insecurity: law and order in political discourse and everyday life*. London: Routledge. (An analysis of the fear of crime in late modern society and how this impacts upon the lives of citizens.)

Norman, J.,Finkel, N. J. and Parrott, W. G. (2006) *Emotions and Culpability: how the law is at odds with psychology, jurors, and itself*. Washington, DC: American Psychological Association, (Argues that U.S. law should take more account of the psychology of emotion if it is to be in touch with the commonsense justice employed by jurors.)

Nussbaum, M. C. (2004) *Hiding from Humanity: disgust, shame, and the law*. Princeton, NJ: Princeton University Press. (A detailed examination of the relations between the law and disgust, shame, and conceptions of the human by a prominent US philosopher.)

Posner, E. A. (2001) *Law and the Emotions*. Chicago: University of Chicago Press. (A comprehensive survey of the different ways in which law and emotions have been brought together in academic literature.)

Solomon, R. (1995) *A Passion for Justice: emotions and the origins of the social contract*. Lanham: Rowman and Littlefield. (An argument that justice is grounded in the personal characteristic of virtue and that sensibility needs to be cultivated rather than blocked.)

Compassion, hate and terror

Anleu, S. R., Martin, B. and Zadoroznyj, M. (eds) (2004) *Journal of Sociology*. Special issue on 'Fear and loathing in the new century'. 40 (4). (Includes articles on the refugee crisis, immigration and multiculturalism, everyday incivility, terror.)

Berlant, L. (2004) *Compassion: the culture and politics of an emotion*. London and New York: Routledge. (A collection of ten essays on compassion by scholars drawing on literature, psychoanalysis and social history.)

Boltanski, L. (1999) *Distant Suffering: politics, morality and the media*. Cambridge: Cambridge University Press. (An influential study of the various ways in which spectators come to be affected by images and narratives of suffering conveyed by the media.)

Butler, J. (1994) *Excitable Speech: a politics of the performative*. London: Routledge. (A social theoretical analysis of hate speech by a prominent US philosopher.)

Cohen, S. (2001) *States of Denial: knowing about atrocities and suffering*. Cambridge: Polity. (An examination of the psychological and social forms of denial that prevent full recognition of the effects of atrocities.)

Eng, D. and Kazanjian, D. (eds) (2003) *On Loss: the politics of mourning*. Berkeley: University of California Press. (Edited collection exploring the ethical, political and identity-based dimensions of suffering from loss.)

Moeller, S. D. (1999) *Compassion Fatigue: how the media sell disease, famine, war and death*. London: Routledge. (A sustained argument about the emotional numbing that is thought to result from the oversaturation of media reports of suffering and atrocity.)

Wilkinson, I. (2005) *Suffering: a sociological introduction*. Cambridge: Polity. (An effort to inaugurate a new field of sociology devoted to the understanding and alleviation of suffering.)

Index